ENGLAND

Prehistory to the Present

Arvel B. Erickson received his Ph.D. from Western Reserve University, where he is presently Professor of History. A visiting professor at other universities, he has also spent several years in research in Britain. In addition to many articles for professional journals, Professor Erickson has written two biographies, *The Public Career of Sir James Graham* and *Edward Cardwell: Peelite*.

Martin J. Havran, who also received his Ph.D. from Western Reserve University, is Associate Professor of History at Kent State University. In 1967–68, he is Visiting Associate Professor at Northwestern University. His articles have appeared in several journals, and he is the author of *The Catholics in Caroline England*. Professors Erickson and Havran are also co-editors of *Readings in English History*.

ARVEL B. ERICKSON

MARTIN J. HAVRAN

ENGLAND

Prehistory to the Present

WITHDRAWN

FREDERICK A. PRAEGER, *Publishers*
New York · Washington

GAVILAN COLLEGE
LIBRARY

BOOKS THAT MATTER
Published in the United States of America in 1968
by Frederick A. Praeger, Inc., Publishers
111 Fourth Avenue, New York, N.Y. 10003

© 1968 by Arvel B. Erickson and Martin J. Havran

All rights reserved

Library of Congress Catalog Card Number: 68-21356

Published by arrangement with Doubleday & Co., Inc.

Printed in the United States of America

To Justin, Sharon, and David

Grateful acknowledgment is made to the following for granting permission to reprint the illustrations that appear in this book.

BLAISDELL PUBLISHING CO. Shire map of England, based on a similar one in Edward P. Cheyney, *A Short History of England* (1945). Reprinted by permission of the publisher.

METHUEN & CO. Map of the principal towns and products of England, 1746, based on a similar map in Cole & Postgate, *The British Common People 1746–1938*. By permission of Methuen & Co.

PRENTICE-HALL, INC. Map of England and France during the Hundred Years' War. From Brinton, Christopher and Wolff, *Civilization in the West*. Copyright © 1964. By permission of Prentice-Hall, Inc.

UNIVERSITY OF MICHIGAN. Genealogical table of the Houses of York and Lancaster, from A. L. Cross, *A Shorter History of England and Greater Britain*. By permission of the University of Michigan.

Contents

Illustrations

Preface

This book is designed for courses in English history and for the general reader. We have striven to reach a balance between brevity and clarity so that the account would be neither so brief as to be jejune, nor so long as to be discouraging to its readers. Experience has taught that one can more easily digest material that is presented in such a manner that facts and interpretations are not clouded by excessive discourse. It is therefore our hope that this work will provide both students and the general public with sufficient information, factual as well as interpretative, to arouse and retain their interest in the exciting saga of the British people. To keep the volume to a reasonable length and yet to relate the main threads of England's political, economic, social, religious, and intellectual progress, it has been necessary to omit some purely military history and to eliminate a substantial amount of detail. Space has also prevented any consideration of literature and the arts. The discussion of imperial and colonial affairs has been for the most part restricted to those developments that directly affected the history of England.

We owe a great debt of gratitude to the scholars of the past and present whose prodigious labors have eased our task. Those who have studied the period prior to 1688 deserve as much attention in a survey of English history as do others whose work concerns the later centuries. Hence we have tried not to give inordinate weight to recent times. Scholarship races at a bewildering pace, and no historian, regardless of his industry, can be *au courant* with every new idea and development in a field as broad and demanding as English history. Accordingly, despite our care, experts in various phases of the subject will no doubt discover sins of omission and commission in the treatment and interpretation of events that relate to their particular competence. We hope it will be remembered that our book is intended for undergraduates and the general reader, not for advanced students and specialists. Those who wish to pursue further any particular topic may consult the bibliography, where books dealing with more specialized areas are listed.

We wish to acknowledge with gratitude the generous and able assistance of Professor Marion C. Siney of Western Reserve University. We also wish to thank Mrs. Kay Scheuer, History Editor of Doubleday & Company, for her many valuable comments and suggestions, and for expediting the completion of this book.

A. B. E.

M. J. H.

ENGLAND

Prehistory to the Present

1

Celts, Romans, and Saxons

Many millenniums before the Greek geographer Pytheas swept northward to Brittany and Cornwall three centuries before Christ, the sea
rushed through a long valley of sunken chalk to form the English
Channel, which separates Britain from the Continent, and filled in
the marshland of its extended northeastern rim with the waters of the
North Sea. The wide-spreading Rhine River system was reft of its trib-
utary, the Thames, which meandered from its source in Gloucestershire
in ever-widening breadth through southern England to the sea. In the
fullness of time, four massive glaciers in turn covered most of the
Northern Hemisphere and gradually receded toward the Pole, grinding the rocks beneath them, gouging out valleys and lake beds, scraping
mountains, and depositing fertile soil. The facts of man's first appearance in Britain, whether he was already there when it became an
island or crossed over later from the Continent, are lost in the abyss
of unrecorded time. That Britain is an island is more significant than
conjecture about when man first inhabited it. The British have been
deeply affected by the sea around them. On the one hand, they were
drawn in upon themselves, with the result that they eventually formed
a governmental and social system peculiar to themselves even though
at first their Continental neighbors developed in similar ways. On the
other hand, the sea, no farther than seventy miles from any point in
Britain, lured men to trade, explore, and colonize so that their ideas
and institutions spread throughout the world.

Pytheas found Britain covered with dense forests and scrubland
teeming with wolves and boar. It was a country of enormous contrast
between the highlands in the north and west, the heavy clay soil in the
Midlands, and the fens and heaths in the south and east. The natural

geological line that extends from Exeter in Devon northeast to Durham not only delineates two markedly different landscapes; it divides what traditionally have been the populous, developed regions of the south-east from the rugged, underpeopled districts of Cornwall, Wales, and Scotland. In the latter, the "Celtic fringe," lived the tribesmen whom the Romans tried unsuccessfully to subdue; here were the areas that English kings could not conquer until the sixteenth century; and here the most individualistic and hardy of the British still cling to their traditional ways.

Although the primitive peoples of prehistoric Britain lived through-out the island, the heaviest concentrations of population were in the Midlands, Somerset and Wiltshire, the Thames Valley, and the Kentish Downs, where the porous soil, temperate climate, and open country made farming easier. The Wiltshire downland, especially the Salisbury Plain, was probably the center of earliest occupation. There stand the great megaliths of Stonehenge, and from there radiate the principal chalk and limestone ridges atop which the ancient footpaths of Britain were worn. From west to east ranges a succession of mountains and hills frequently interrupted by valleys watered by numerous rivers. In a trip from Cardigan Bay off the Welsh coast to Dover one would cross the Welsh highlands, the Cotswolds, the Chilterns, the North Downs, and the Weald. Going north from Southampton to the Scottish border the traveler would traverse the Salisbury Plain, the Cotswolds, the Midland plain, the Pennine Mountains, the Cheviot Hills, and the northern lowlands of the Solway Firth isthmus. From Perth north-ward the forboding Scottish Highlands continue to Inverness and John o'Groat's House. England's north country and much of Scotland is rocky and moorish land fit only for sheep and cattle and the hardy peo-ple who brave the heavy snow and fierce gales that sweep over the Western Islands and Scottish lake country from the Irish Sea and North Atlantic.

English rivers, many of them mere streams by North American standards, and an abundant rainfall that averages about forty inches a year for the whole country, water a land that wears green throughout the year. The Severn, Mersey, and Trent rivers carved paths through the soft chalk, limestone, and clay of the Midlands. The marshy south-ern and eastern coasts are frequently indented by streams and rivers, among them the Tyne, Humber, and Ouse. The Wash, a large bay north of East Anglia, and the Thames estuary are inviting avenues into England's heartland, which invaders have often followed. Throughout

East Anglia, the southeast, and the south to the Lizard in Cornwall, the climate is generally mild even in the rainy winter months. The snowfall averages only a few inches, and one can often pluck cabbages and Brussels sprouts from loose soil even in January.

The early inhabitants of Britain settled in the south and southeast. The various stages of culture through which they survived—the Paleolithic, Mesolithic, Neolithic, Early and Middle Bronze, and Early Iron Ages—should be sufficiently familiar not to warrant repetition. Museums of art and natural history contain ample visual evidence of the flint stones, ivory needles and combs, bronze weapons, and iron shields that were used. Much more important are the several waves of immigration to Britain during the thousand years before the Romans came, and the social, political, and religious institutions of the tribes they conquered.

The men of the Neolithic Age who migrated to Britain from western Europe after 10,000 B.C. were sufficiently advanced to spin and weave, farm, hunt, and decorate the walls of their cave homes, but they succumbed to successive waves of Celts driven west by marauding eastern tribes. These Gallic and Belgic peoples, who perhaps originally sprang from central Europe, probably first reached Britain at the beginning of the last millennium before Christ, and the last of them, the Belgae, had begun to cross the Channel at least a generation before the death of Caesar. The tall, strong, fair-skinned Celts brought with them iron tools and weapons, lived in wooden or circular stone houses, minted gold coins, traded extensively with the Continent, and mined tin in Cornwall. The Celtic tribes were quarrelsome and fierce, and some stained their bodies blue with dye made from woad and painted ghoulish figures on their torsos to terrify their enemies. They were organized into tribes, each headed by a chieftain and composed of aristocrats, free warriors, and slaves. These tribes ordinarily shunned contact with one another and often went to war, as in the case of the Catuvellauni, who, about the time of Caesar's coming, disputed the dominance of the Atrebates, the masters of southern England from Essex to Dorset. The Celts were sophisticated peoples compared with neolithic men and they had been in close contact with Continental civilization for at least three generations before the Roman conquest.

The Celts' religion merits some attention because it caused the Romans considerable trouble and therefore had to be utterly suppressed. The crafty Druid priests of Britain and Gaul served as teachers, judges, advisers, and preservers of folklore. At sacred places such as Stonehenge and the Isle of Anglesey they presided over rites dedicated to a plethora of deities whom they believed inhabited forboding fens, forests, and groves, commanded weather and the fortunes of war, and sometimes acted like prankish elves. The Druids regularly made sacrifices, sometimes of humans; fashioned fetishes of stone amulets; and attributed magical powers to mistletoe and wishing wells. Not least of all, the Druids spurred on their warriors in battle and preached against alien influences that jeopardized their enormous power.

The Druids undoubtedly warned the Belgae and their allies of the imminent coming of Roman legions under Julius Caesar, the victorious conqueror of Gaul, in 55 B.C. Since 58 B.C. he had vanquished the tribes of Europe north of the Alps from the Danube on the east to the Channel and the Pyrenees on the north and south. He first looked toward Britain in 57 B.C., angry that the Celts had regularly sent help to their compatriots in Gaul, but it is clear that he also invaded Britain to increase his fame toward the day when he hoped to rule the Empire. The British tribesmen knew of his plans because merchants had carried stories of his preparations and Caesar himself had sent representatives from Gaul to demand their surrender. In August, 55 B.C., after sending one of his lieutenants to reconnoiter the Dover coastline, Caesar sailed from Boulogne with about ten thousand troops of the Seventh and Tenth Legions in eighty transports, the cavalry to follow in eighteen ships. As he approached the chalk cliffs he saw the Kentish Britons, thousands strong, lined up in rows of infantry, cavalry, and charioteers awaiting his landing; he came ashore east of Dover at high tide, and the legionnaires had to fight for a beachhead in several feet of water. The Britons fought fiercely in hand-to-hand combat, but their lines broke in the face of superior Roman arms and valor even though the Roman cavalry, stranded on transports in the Channel after two futile efforts to cross, could not help. The Britons sued for peace and sent a few hostages, but a Channel storm wrecked many of Caesar's ships, a circumstance that, together with his lack of supplies for a long campaign, encouraged the enemy to attack again. The Romans managed to drive them back and put a part of their territory to the torch. The Britons promised Caesar tribute and hostages, but he withdrew, worried about rebellion in Gaul and the approaching autumn.

Caesar certainly intended to do more than merely teach the Britons a lesson. He hoped to learn something of their strength and military tactics and the nature of their country against the day when he could return in a massive assault aimed at the conquest of the whole island.

Accordingly, he again crossed the Channel in the early summer of 54 B.C. with nearly eight hundred vessels carrying six legions of Romans and a few thousand Gallic cavalry. They landed at approximately the same place, but this time met no resistance. Caesar made a forced night march and by morning was looking down upon the Stour Valley about two miles from present-day Canterbury, which was then merely a small fort. Celtic charioteers made a brief foray but quickly retreated into the forest. That day, however, Caesar learned that another storm had dashed his ships against the shoreline, and he hurried there to repair the damage. Encouraged by this setback, the Kentish chiefs, led by the powerful King Cassivellaunus, who controlled the country north of the Thames, drew up their forces and surprised the Roman camp near the Stour River in a lightning cavalry raid that did great damage. Caesar followed them north, crossing the Thames at Brentwood despite the sunken pointed stakes the enemy had driven into the river bed to stop him. As the Britons retreated, evacuating their villages and fortresses as they went, Caesar burned their crops and leveled their ramparts. After he successfully stormed their main fortress at Colchester, they made a truce. Why he did not go farther is not certain, but he undoubtedly had the affairs of rebellious Gaul in mind. He left Britain in late summer, never to return. His two invasions can hardly be called an unqualified success, but at least he exposed Britain to Rome and received the lavish tribute at home that he craved.

The Romans, troubled by domestic problems and able to maintain only what they had already acquired, ignored Britain for almost a century thereafter. Meanwhile the Britons created five kingdoms, three southeast of the Thames, increased their trade with Gaul, and were strengthened by at least one more wave of Belgic migrants. The concentration of population and political authority had shifted by this time from Somerset and Wiltshire to the southeast, which King Cymbeline of the Catuvellauni tribe controlled during the first forty years of the Christian era. Emperor Claudius, smarting under criticism that the Empire was at a standstill, and undoubtedly greedy for the silver, tin, and grain to be had in Britain, sent Plautius to conquer it in 43 A.D., when Cymbeline's death temporarily set his sons quarreling over the succession. Plautius made a surprise landing at Richborough, northeast of Dover, and his army of thirty thousand men, assisted by the defection of several tribes to the Romans, pushed to the Thames where Claudius joined it. King Caratacus was forced to flee toward Wales; his capital at Colchester was easily taken, and there Claudius remained two weeks, accepting the submission of many tribes and formulating plans for the conquest of the rest of Britain.

It proved easier to formulate plans than actually to achieve the conquest. Roman armies moved north into Lincolnshire and Yorkshire, northwest into the Midlands, and west to the Severn River valley, which took four years to subjugate. Thereafter a succession of Roman commanders, notably Vespasian and Agricola, carried the Roman standard into Cornwall, Wales, and the Scottish Lowlands so that by the year 85 the island, except for the extreme west and the Scottish border country, had been fairly well occupied. The campaigns had been arduous. Caratacus, who had organized tribal resistance in Wales, had to be taken to Rome in chains before his followers would submit, and, in 61 A.D., Queen Boudicca rose in revolt, taking advantage of the absence of Suetonius Paulinus (governor of Britain since 58 A.D.) in north Wales, where he and half the Roman legions under his command had gone to destroy the Druids' holy places. The cause of Boudicca's rebellion was apparently the injustice and rapacity of Roman administration. Prasutagus, king of the Iceni tribe, had made his two daughters coheirs with the Roman emperor in the hope of keeping his great wealth, but the governor seized it, which led Boudicca, Prasutagus' widow, to protest. When she was scourged in nakedness and her daughters were abused, she roused the tribes of the district to revolt, trapped and slaughtered the Roman garrisons at Colchester and St. Albans, and burned London. Suetonius finally defeated her forces at approximately the present site of St. Paul's Cathedral.

During the next hundred years Roman civilization was extended and consolidated in Britain. As Scotland could not be held against the Picts, Emperor Trajan abandoned it, and the Romans fell behind a line of defense marked by Hadrian's Wall from the mouth of the Tyne to Solway Firth. The wall, built between the years 122 and 128 of stone, mortar, sod, and clay, extended seventy-three miles, was about ten feet thick and twenty feet high, and had a trench thirty feet wide just north of it and a ditch, called the vallum, behind it. Small forts to house the garrison were built in the wall at mile intervals, and between every two forts two taller turrets served as watchtowers. The Romans occasionally ventured north, sometimes as far as Scotland, to break the strength of marauding Picts who regularly besieged the wall. Wales was practically ignored.

The Romanization of Britain took a good deal longer than was expected. Even so, from the beginning of the occupation the Britons gradually accepted Roman ways to a surprising degree. Roman market places, temples, and country houses rose on the island; the tribesmen garbed in togas strolled through colonnades speaking crude Latin, knowledge of which was a sign of social prominence. Legionnaires married local women, merchants exchanged goods produced by both peoples, and Roman and Briton mingled easily. Roman civilization flourished at key urban centers like London, York, St. Albans, Colchester, Lincoln, and Bath. In typically Roman fashion, no attempt was made to impose a rigid centralized control on the Britons, who, as far as possible, were allowed tribal government so long as they paid taxes and kept the peace. This was especially true in sparsely populated regions like Norfolk, Warwickshire, and Yorkshire, where the Britons still lived in varying levels of Stone or Bronze Age culture. Outside the municipalities and the authority of Romans living in country villas, little or no Roman government prevailed.

The Roman urbanization of primitive villages is one of the most significant developments of the occupation. Although only the four *coloniae* of Gloucester, Lincoln, Colchester, and York enjoyed virtual civil autonomy, towns such as Chester, Canterbury, and London prospered under Roman rule. London became the commercial center while York, heavily garrisoned and surrounded by broad ramparts (which were rebuilt in the thirteenth century and still stand), was the military and civil capital of the country. Its numerous temples, baths, and public buildings give ample evidence of its prominence, and it was there that the Britons first learned officially of Constantine's emperorship (306–337). At towns like Chester the community grew from a maze of merchants' booths outside the camp to a large settlement with permanent walls and shops and a heterogeneous population of Romans, Britons, and foreigners, some of whom were brought as slaves from the far corners of the Empire.

The major population and garrison centers were connected by a network of roads built by the Romans to ease communication, facilitate troop movements, and encourage trade. Some of these roads followed the natural line of chalk ridges already marked by pre-Roman footpaths and others rested on new beds of rock. Watling Street connected London, St. Albans, and Chester; and Ermine Street, now a part of the Great North Road, began at London and extended northward through Lincoln and York to the Antonine Wall, built across the Forth-Clyde isthmus about 142 A.D. The Fosse Way ran from Exeter to Lincoln, and other roads linked Colchester, Silchester, and Dover to London.

Over these straight roads trod the merchants, who probably benefited most from the Roman occupation. Foreign traders acquired great
wealth, which they loaned to aristocrats who craved the luxuries that
poured into Britain from the Continent in increasing volume until
about the middle of the second century, when native industry, which
the Romans encouraged, could compete in certain commodities. Britons
could not provide fancy pottery, fine wines, or silver jewelry, but they
were skilled in the manufacture of ornamental iron and bronze brace-
lets, pots, and ordinary wooden furniture. Abundant tin and lead made
possible a thriving pewter industry, and domestic tallow replaced foreign oil. Although the finest goods continued to trickle in, British wares
supplied most of the country's needs by the middle of the third century.
The Romans worked the lead, tin, copper, and silver mines, most of
which belonged to the state, and exported the bulk of these minerals.
Improved agricultural techniques, including iron-tipped plows, increased the yield of grain, which became an important export in the
fourth century. The population of Rome, like a ravenous beast, de-
voured most of the goods produced in Britain so that the imbalance of
trade continuously encouraged British productivity.

No one can be certain as to the origins of Christianity in Britain,
although there appeared to have been a few Christians there by about
the early third century. They lived among persons who worshiped
Persian, Egyptian, Gallic, and Roman deities, few of whom were remembered after the Anglo-Saxon acceptance of the Christian God.
British bishops could more easily increase their flocks after Constantine
extended religious toleration to Christians in the Edict of Milan (313),
which also encouraged the aristocracy to join the religion that had
formerly been popular only among the poorer urban classes. Toward
the end of the fourth century virtually every major town had Christians
who had survived the religious persecutions by Diocletian and his successors. Alban is reputed to have been the first British Christian martyr
and the place of his execution is marked by a magnificent abbey in the
city that bears his name. Ninian spread Christianity in Ireland a generation before the arrival of St. Patrick, whom several nations claim,
but who probably was enslaved by pirates at his Christian father's
home near the Bristol Channel and taken to Ireland. St. Patrick returned there as a bishop about 432 after study in Gaul and Rome and
died in 461 after a long and fruitful apostolate. Christianity spread
rapidly in Devon and Cornwall, Wales, and Ireland and was thriving
long before the last Roman left Britain.

The Roman Empire in the west showed unmistakable signs of decay at least a century before its collapse, and Britain, a remote diocese within the Province of Gaul, was bound to suffer the consequences sooner than areas closer to Rome. The debilitating forces that sapped the strength of the Empire, such as gross social inequalities that fomented widespread peasant revolts, the inroads of barbarians who broke through the Rhine-Danube frontier, and economic inflation, affected Britain as well. Beginning about 350, the island also sustained raids from three directions. The Irish Celts, some of whom had migrated to western Scotland, attacked coastal settlements in Cornwall, Wales, and Cumberland, and Hadrian's Wall was repeatedly stormed from the north by tribesmen who seized the opportunity to occupy land vacated by retreating Romans. Small parties of Saxons, Angles, and Jutes crossed the Channel as early as the end of the third century, and came more frequently and in larger numbers during the fourth until most of the southern and southeastern sections of Britain were overrun, causing the depopulation of country villas. These attacks greatly weakened Roman government and encouraged native revolts, mutiny in the army, and general disorder. Some Roman and Romanized native officers usurped military and civil command in sections of the country where the duly constituted authorities either relinquished authority or were unable to exercise it. Others engaged in plain treachery—for example Carausius, a Roman naval officer at Boulogne, who employed his fleet to augment his personal wealth and power and settled in Britain, claiming to be its governor.

The Romans tried unsuccessfully to repel the invaders and finally had to withdraw from Britain. Resistance did not collapse overnight, and some of the defenders remained even after their enemies had defeated them. Emperor Constantine strengthened Britain's defenses by appointing a Count of the Saxon Shore who built forts along the coast from Southampton to the Wash. During the fourth century, however, the barbarian peril became so serious, especially after the disastrous Roman defeat at Adrianople in 378, that several legions were recalled to Italy, thereby further weakening Britain, which by that time swarmed with Saxon raiders. The Picts, Scots, and Saxons cooperated on one occasion in 368 to invade Britain on three fronts. They besieged London, roved at will through the deserted countryside, and carried off mountains of booty. The undermanned Roman garrison abandoned Hadrian's Wall at the end of the fourth century. One of the last two legions left Britain hurriedly at the news of the Roman battle with

Alaric's Visigoths in 403 at Verona. Political confusion characterized the final years of Roman rule, during which time the remnant of its once powerful army of fifty thousand men pledged loyalty to a series of usurpers, the last of whom, Constantine, led all but a handful of Roman soldiers out of Britain about 407.

The events of the two centuries following Rome's abandonment of Britain are shrouded in legend so that it is impossible to speak authoritatively of them. The *Anglo-Saxon Chronicle,* which monks began to compile about the end of the ninth century, makes only fleeting references to the fifth and sixth centuries, and the Venerable Bede's *Ecclesiastical History* serves no better. Archaeological evidence has little to add, primarily because the Anglo-Saxons' wooden buildings decayed long ago. Aerial photography can locate the sites of many Saxon cemeteries, which contain artifacts and reveal concentration of population, but such information is scanty. Gildas, a Celtic monk born about 519, left an account of the conquest that is generalized, partly unhistorical, and inaccurate. But he does convey the Britons' sense of fear and the turmoil caused by successive waves of Saxon invaders.

Historians have been able to piece together enough information to provide a broad outline of events during these two centuries. After Emperor Honorius advised the Britons in 409 that he could give them no help against invaders, the Britons held out alone for more than half a century. The Saxons conquered southeastern Britain in fits and starts without apparent plan or determined advance from one side of the island to the other, contrary to what Gildas would have us believe. It is not accurate to say that each of the three major tribes settled in neatly parceled regions—the Jutes in Kent, the Angles in Mercia and Northumbria, and the Saxons in Sussex and Wessex. They often intermingled in colonies established beside rivers and avoided the scrub and forested country of the interior. Although many Britons fled to Wales, Strathclyde, and Cornwall, or migrated to Brittany, Ireland, and the Channel Islands, others remained at their hearths. Heavy fighting between Britons and invaders did not occur often, and in some areas they mingled easily in the same village. Temporarily, Christianity all but disappeared among the Britons, but missionaries such as Germanus, David, and Columba eventually restored it. As the Anglo-Saxons preferred the country to the town, urban life virtually ceased except at a few major centers like Winchester, York, and London, and even they lost many of their residents. Roman roads deteriorated, toppled columns lay untouched, and stripped fields went unattended. About the middle of the sixth century, despite a terrible plague that further disrupted society, most of the eastern and southern sections of Britain were carved into tiny kingdoms, each of which had a succession of monarchs whose names defy memory. These petty kingdoms were eventually reduced to twelve by conquest and internal pressures, and, by about 600, the twelve were consolidated into the seven principal kingdoms of Kent, Essex, Sussex, Wessex, East Anglia, Mercia, and Northumbria, called the Heptarchy.

The Anglo-Saxons' language, customs, and political and social institutions were superimposed upon the Celtic and Roman civilizations and left a lasting influence on England. It is generally assumed that Anglo-Saxon political and social organization was little different from that of the barbarians on the Continent, whom Tacitus described in his *Germania* in the first century A.D. Each tribe had a chief or king, some of whom assumed power because they had been military leaders during the conquest of Britain. The exact origin of kingship among the Anglo-Saxons is unclear. As certain men had been leaders in war and judges in peace, it was not unnatural that they should become monarchs, who managed to assume power permanently and pass it on to their successors. These kings were ordinarily chosen from one family by a small group of men, usually the wisest and strongest in the kingdom. Because the electors generally favored a particular family, monarchy often became hereditary, although this was not always the case. For one reason or another, kings were deposed and new families were elevated to the kingship. At the same time, the longer one family ruled, the easier it became to rule absolutely, and very often the king came to be regarded as nearly divine, which of course augmented his authority even more. But the Anglo-Saxon kings could not rule without the advice and consent of a council, the witan, which counseled them on all important matters, elected new kings and deposed others, and administered justice in both civil and criminal cases. Together with the king, the witan also promulgated laws that were usually based on common practice according to ancient customs.

The Saxons were divided basically into three classes. The aristocracy consisted of eorls (earls), who were nobles by birth, and thegns, who were lesser nobles and the personal companions of the king. Both the eorls and thegns held land from him, ruled it in his name, and were expected to provide fighting men to defend it. In earlier Saxon times, certain noblemen called ealdormen (aldermen) were given magisterial authority. Most Saxons were ceorls (freemen), who were obliged to help maintain roads, bridges, and forts, and render military service in the fyrd (militia). Whether freemen were allowed to give counsel in tribal assemblies is problematical, although they seem to have done so on occasion. Slaves existed among the Anglo-Saxons as a third class, but they were not so numerous as among the Romans. Some were descendants of Roman slaves; others became slaves after being captured in tribal warfare or as a result of debt. They had no legal rights and were regarded as mere chattels, frequently bought, sold, and transported to the Continent to serve new masters. As late as the eleventh century, possibly a sixth of Britain's population was in one way or another in bondage.

The Anglo-Saxons developed a primitive legal system based on retribution and strength that recognized the intervention of God, who punished the guilty and sustained the innocent. The tribe, clan, or family of a homicide victim carried out the sentence against the murderer according to customary practice. Every man's value was reckoned in terms of a wergeld (man money), depending on his social class and varying from district to district and from century to century, which had to be paid by the murderer. In Wessex and Mercia, for example, a freeman was worth 200 shillings in the seventh century, and a nobleman about 1200 to 2400 shillings. Sometimes, as in tenth-century Wessex, the wergeld was paid in cattle and sheep. Mortal combat frequently settled serious personal disputes, and lesser crimes carried penalties of fines.

The shires, the largest units of Anglo-Saxon local government, existed in Wessex from its earliest days and were pretty well formed throughout England by 1066. When the Wessex kings enlarged their domain by the acquisition of the subkingdoms Essex, Sussex, Kent, and Norfolk, these were also made shires. Territory conquered from the Danes in the tenth century was parceled into shires that consisted of sufficient land surrounding the fortified boroughs to support them agriculturally and militarily; these shires usually took their names from the boroughs, such as Derby, Nottingham, and Lincoln. Other shires, Northumberland and Cornwall for instance, were formed from existing Danish and Celtic kingdoms. The chief administrative officer in each shire was the ealdorman, the king's personal representative, whose duties consisted of leading the shire's fyrd in wartime, implementing the king's writs, and presiding over the shire court. Some ealdormen were in charge of several shires by the tenth century, and they seem to have been gradually replaced by stronger and more independent noblemen called earls. As an earl could not effectively govern several shires, shire reeves (sheriffs) were appointed to rule in his stead. Eventually the shire reeve replaced the earl as the king's chief deputy, judicial officer, and tax collector. The shire court, which ordinarily met twice annually, was conducted by the ealdorman (later by the shire reeve) and the bishop of the diocese, both of whom together judged secular and religious cases. The bulk of the legal business involved disputes over land, although there was no restriction on the kinds of cases that might be heard. At first the shire courts were available to all freemen and nobles, but the difficulties and expense of travel later restricted attendance largely to thegns. Testimony by those having firsthand knowledge of a crime or dispute was ordinarily the only evidence admitted, although the accused might be supported by the oaths of others who swore that he was telling the truth. To prove his innocence, he could also submit to a physical ordeal; some, for example, had to take a stone from boiling water, after which their arms were bound up. If a man's arm was healing cleanly after three days the court ruled him to be innocent because God would not permit a just man to suffer a festering wound. The shire court also served as a public assembly at which royal commands, affairs of the shire, and military plans were publicized.

The shires were subdivided into hundreds, the origin of which is obscure. The hundreds, called wapentakes in areas controlled by the Danes, are probably of Germanic origin and may have been introduced by the earliest Anglo-Saxon invaders. They were presumably established as parcels of land large enough to support units of a hundred warriors and their families (a hundred hides of land), but they soon ceased to have that meaning, for, by the tenth century, the size and number of hundreds in each shire varied considerably. The hundred later developed into a judicial district in which a moot court was held every four weeks, presided over by the reeve. All freemen, representatives from each agricultural village (tun), and the thegns of the hundred were expected to attend. All types of criminal cases were heard, but thievery was the most common offense. The conduct of trials was similar to the procedure followed in the shire courts.

The boroughs (towns) also obtained a measure of self-government in later Anglo-Saxon times. These communities, which developed within walled fortresses inhabited by soldiers, merchants, and their families, were not very large. Most boroughs, except those like Winchester and London, which prospered because of commercial or governmental prominence, were founded as military bases. All boroughs needed to regulate trade and industry. Accordingly, they acquired charters from the magnate, very often the king, who owned the land on which they were built, which entitled them to special privileges such as the right to collect their own taxes, hold assemblies, and establish public markets.

All these points considered, it should be remembered that the vast majority of the population still lived in rural villages that had no administrative authority beyond the arrangement of agricultural details like the assignment of strips of the arable land. These communities consisted of only a few crude one-story cottages of thatch and wattles containing the needs of every household—a few sticks of rough furniture, locally manufactured pots, and one or two prized possessions like iron broaches, weapons, or a statuette. Livestock, mostly hogs, cattle, and sheep, was privately owned, as was the land around the cottage that yielded vegetables and herbs. The village freemen owned the farm land, woods, pastures, and meadows communally. They generally divided the plowland into three large fields, each of which was subdivided into strips measuring about 220 by 20 yards. Most families worked a hide of land (ordinarily 120 acres) made up of widely scattered strips of good and poor land over all three fields. As they knew nothing about artificial fertilization, the villagers allowed one field at a time to lie fallow for a year or more. Agricultural tools and oxen to pull the plows belonged collectively to all the freemen, who probably sowed and reaped their crops together. Barley, oats, and wheat, along with meat, provided the staple foods, and people drank ale and—at their spring and winter festivals, which later were celebrated at Easter and Christmas—mead made from honey.

The earlier pagan Anglo-Saxons practiced a polytheistic religion that honored a hierarchy of gods who were given human form and traits. Although a few of the gods were benevolent and helpful, most were vengeful and violent, and were therefore feared. Not one pagan temple of Anglo-Saxon times has been found, but the historian Bede mentions them. The Saxons slaughtered valuable animals to placate spiteful deities who commanded the sea and wind, provided a plentiful crop, or sent famine. Like other primitive folk, the Saxons feared the elements and nature. Death struck terror in their breasts, whether it stilled the heart or froze the fields in winter. The mystery of Nature's rebirth in fertile spring gave rise to the worship of the goddess Eostre and the god Frey. Thor, the god of power, created thunderstorms; Woden, the master of battle, protected the righteous and provided a haven in after-life for fallen warriors, whose every physical desire was gratified. The widespread worship of idols is attested by place names that are adaptations of Woden and Thor, and by the fact that Christian missionaries had to allow the sacrifice of animals to them even after the Saxons were baptized.

About the end of the sixth century the twin forces of Christianity and strong monarchy began to work toward the unification of Britain. There is an important connection between the rejuvenation of Christianity and the rise of strong monarchy, as can be seen in the conversion of important kings from Ethelbert of Kent to Alfred of Wessex. Both the monarchs and the Church benefited from their relationship. The missionaries realized that the conversion of kings would likely lead to the conversion of their subjects, and that the Christian monarchs would lend their support to the acquisition and protection of Church property. The kings, on the other hand, welcomed Church support because they could rely on the clergy to preach respect for civil as well as ecclesiastical authority, and because the Church provided them with an excellent example of centralized authority applicable to the state as well. The monarchs also believed that they were not truly kings unless at their coronations priests had anointed them. Since very early times, monarchy had been surrounded by the aura of divinity—that God had destined or ordained some to be kings—and until the early seventeenth century, all English kings assumed that they governed by divine sanction. Such a conviction buttressed by Church teaching was far more advantageous to monarchs than the old religions that worshiped a plethora of pagan gods, none of whom apparently was ranged on the side of kings or had priestly disciples willing to define the sanctity of monarchy.

Following the consolidation of Britain into seven major kingdoms, first one and then another of them gained a temporary ascendancy. Kent became prominent in the early seventh century, Northumbria in the later seventh century, Mercia in the eighth, and, finally, Wessex in the ninth and tenth centuries. But England cannot be considered a politically united country until the reign of Cnut (1016–35), for, even from the seventh century, sovereignty over the southern half of England was hotly contested. Under King Ethelbert of Kent (560–616), for instance, kings continued to rule in Wessex and East Anglia even though they paid homage to him, and the Northumbrian expansion south was stoutly resisted by the Welsh and Mercians, especially during

King Penda's reign (626–655). Were it not for the Viking conquest of northeastern England in the ninth century it is doubtful that Alfred (871–899) could have unified the south.

The kingdom of Kent exercised a very short dominance under Ethelbert, who married Bertha, a Frankish Christian princess. That she was a Christian probably helped to bring missionaries from Rome, but Pope Gregory the Great allegedly had made plans twenty years earlier to convert the Britons. Tradition has it that in about 578 he questioned some young men from Britain who were being sold into slavery, and he was so taken with their intelligence that he resolved one day to make their countrymen Christians. Gregory sent Augustine and other Benedictines to Kent in 597. Ethelbert received them cordially, and within the next few years Augustine converted him and many of his subjects, brought more missionaries to England, established a monastery at Canterbury, and appointed three bishops, one each for Canterbury, Rochester, and London. Christianity temporarily waned outside Kent following the deaths of Augustine and Ethelbert, but the rise of Northumbrian dominance under King Edwin soon revitalized it.

The conversion of Northumbrians to Christianity began with the mission of Paulinus, one of Augustine's companions, who accompanied a daughter of Ethelbert to York, where she wed Edwin. He had promised to respect her religion and accept it himself if his councilors consented. Edwin's infant daughter, his councilors, and Edwin himself were baptized after his allegedly miraculous escape from two attempted assassinations. Paulinus also carried Christianity north to the Cheviot Hills and south to Lincoln, but he and all but one of his followers had to flee with the royal family when the pagan Penda of Mercia slew Edwin in battle in 632. In the meantime, however, Christian priests also proselytized fruitfully in East Anglia.

Oswald (633–641), who succeeded Edwin as king of Northumbria, quickly restored order. As he drove out the Mercians he also encouraged the spread of Celtic Christianity, which he had adopted while living in exile at Iona, an island off the west coast of Scotland where Columba, a sixth-century Irish missionary, had founded a monastery. At Oswald's accession a renowned monastic community led by the missionary monk Aidan was founded on the Holy Isle, Lindisfarne, off the Northumbrian coast. Although Penda killed Oswald in 641, the latter and his son, Oswy (641–670), firmly established Celtic Christianity throughout Northumbria and Mercia, where Penda's heir, Peada, was himself baptized in 653 following his marriage into Oswy's family.

The truce between the two families also permitted Roman Christian missionaries to return, touching off a dispute between the two Christian sects over the Church calendar of feast days, doctrine, and form of worship. During the Anglo-Saxon conquest the Celts had lost touch with Rome so that their religion developed apart from the mainstream of Christian thought. As the popes considered the Celtic Christians schismatics, means had to be found to reunite them with the parent Church.

The differences between the Roman and Celtic Christians were aired at the Synod of Whitby (Yorkshire) in 664. Representatives including Hilda, abbess of Whitby, Bishop Cedd of the East Saxons, Bishop Coleman of Lindisfarne, and King Oswy spoke for the Celtic viewpoint; Bishop Agilbert of the West Saxons, James the Deacon (one of Paulinus' companions), and Wilfrid, abbot of Ripon, for Rome. According to Bede, the principal issue involved the cycle of dates on which Easter should fall, but it is apparent even from Bede's own words that the much more significant question of Christian unity in England was debated. Wilfrid, an ambitious, energetic missionary among the South Saxons who had journeyed north into Mercia and Northumbria to build many churches and monasteries, spoke so convincingly that King Oswy agreed to accept Rome's supremacy—as Oswy put it, Christ had given the keys of heaven to Peter, not to Columba. Oswy's subjects followed him at a crucial time when Northumbria dominated most of England. But, as the events of the next seventy years were to show, it took more than a Roman evangelist's impassioned oratory to bring Christian unity in England in the face of political rivalry and an essentially unorganized ecclesiastical administration.

The difficult task of appointing an efficient hierarchy and of establishing diocesan boundaries fell to the Greek patriarch Theodore of Tarsus, the new archbishop of Canterbury, who, with the African monk Hadrian, reached England in 669. During the next three years Theodore consecrated many new bishops and deposed others unworthy of the office. At a general Church council at Hertford the functions of bishops and secular clergy were defined, and steps were taken to curb self-willed ecclesiastics like Wilfrid, who had twice been exiled from Northumbria and was now allowed to return to Ripon on condition that he give up his authority. Successive archbishops of Canterbury found the problems of supervising ecclesiastical affairs in northern England so difficult that a second archiepiscopal see was created at York in 735.

Theodore and his successors at Canterbury brought Church unity to England, but the Heptarchy still wallowed in political rivalry. Northumbrian hegemony had declined quickly following Oswy's death (670) and the Mercian military victory over his heir, Ecgfrith, in 678. Northumbria ceased to be important even though its monarchy continued, and Mercia made no further effort to control it. The warlike character of the age is illustrated by the fact that all the Northumbrian monarchs in the seventh century except Oswy had perished in battle against invading armies of Picts, Welsh, and Mercians. For about fifty years no kingdom could gain the ascendancy; then Mercia emerged supreme under Kings Ethelbald and Offa II from 716 to 796. Their reigns resulted in the control of Wessex, Kent, and Sussex, and the annexation of East Anglia, and brought about a weak political centralization in southern England. The subject kingdoms virtually ceased to exist separately even though they too continued to have a succession of short-lived kings, most of whom met violent deaths. Offa, probably the greatest Anglo-Saxon king next to Alfred, is best known for a dyke that he constructed to delineate the boundary between England and Wales and for the silver coins he minted. His importance may be inferred from the marriage of one of his daughters to a son of Charlemagne. The pope also recognized Offa's prestige by sending legates who styled him "King of the English." But Mercian suzerainty collapsed after Offa's death in 796 and passed to Wessex during the reign of Egbert (802–839), who had to face the earliest onslaughts of a more dangerous enemy in the Vikings. Over the next three quarters of a century Egbert, Ethelwulf, and Alfred led the English against these invaders, who made one of their first raids at Lindisfarne in 793.

The Vikings (also called Norsemen or Danes), who lived in Denmark, Sweden, and Norway, left their homeland in seventy-foot oar-propelled and sail-powered boats to raid and settle the coasts of Europe and the Middle East during the ninth and tenth centuries. These intrepid sailors, not unlike the Anglo-Saxons of the fourth century in political, social, and cultural development, roamed the open seas in fleets of as many as 350 ships to attack vulnerable settlements in northern Europe and the British Isles, on the eastern Baltic, in Russia, and even in Constantinople. Vikings also established communities in Iceland, Greenland, and Newfoundland. As several accounts in the *Anglo-Saxon Chronicle* show, Viking raids against Britain and Ireland began in the late eighth century. It is uncertain why they suddenly left their fiords to plunder abroad, but the barrenness of their own countries, their rapidly expanding population, and a deep love of adventure have commonly been accepted reasons. The sporadic attacks on Lindisfarne, Jarrow, and other points on the eastern coast of England during the 790s and early 800s were followed by annual piratical expeditions against the Western Isles of Scotland and the northern coast of Ireland, particularly between 800 and 850. The Vikings moved into British waters from two directions: one route took them to the Orkney Islands and then south to the Western Isles and Ireland where, by the early ninth century, they founded a kingdom centered at Dublin; the other route went from Denmark (Jutland) to the mouth of the Rhine and thence westward down the Channel to the shores of Normandy, Brittany, and western England.

The Danes concentrated their attacks on southern England beginning about 835, when the Isle of Sheppey in the Thames estuary was pillaged. Over the next thirty years they made landings all the way from Cornwall to East Anglia, attacking places such as Southampton, Winchester, and Canterbury. In their annual raids, the Vikings ordinarily came in spring and spent the summer and early autumn spreading death and destruction in an area only a few miles inland. Their favorite objects were monasteries and churches because of the treasures they held. The English had no adequate defense against these sorties because two centuries of relief from foreign invasion had left most of them militarily weak. Only Wessex was prepared to meet the Danes in pitched battles, for, since Egbert's campaigns against the Mercians earlier in the century, the West Saxons had maintained their strength. But no kingdom had a navy to pursue the enemy when they took to their boats following a raid. In addition, the Vikings generally avoided battles in the open country and when they met stiff English resistance retreated to invade at another point along the coast.

A strong Danish army came during the fall of 865 to conquer and settle Britain. It landed in East Anglia, forced the cooperation of the inhabitants, set up headquarters at Thetford, and undertook a series of campaigns that won most of northern and eastern England during the next fifteen years. They first marched north in 866 to York, which they took easily, and followed this up with an invasion south into Mercia. Since the Mercian king, Burgred, was married to a sister of Ethelred of Wessex, the Mercians allied with the West Saxons, and the coalition forced the temporary withdrawal of the Danes into East Anglia, which they ravaged heavily. The invaders finally marched on Wessex late in 870, advancing as far as Reading.

Alfred, a learned man who succeeded to the Wessex throne on Ethelred's death in 871, had already participated in wars against the Danes, and though only twenty-three years old, he was fully prepared in mind and body to fight them. He wisely arranged an early truce by promising tribute, and the Danes retired to London; the resulting five years of peace afforded Alfred time to reorganize his defenses and build a navy. In 876, the Danes, fresh from a brutal assault on Mercia, again invaded Wessex, pushing Alfred as far as Athelney in Somerset. He beat off several onslaughts from both east and west until he finally inflicted a heavy defeat on the Danish King Guthrum in 878 at Chippenham (Wiltshire). Guthrum was forced by the Treaty of Wedmore to accept Christianity and evacuate Wessex, but when other Danes migrated to England in 884 he joined forces with them. Alfred triumphed once more, however, taking London and forcing Guthrum to accept another treaty in which he agreed to retire northeast of a line that ran along the north shore of the Thames to London and thence to Chester, marking off the area afterward known as the Danelaw. The English and Danes occasionally warred thereafter, but Alfred won all the important battles.

It is a tribute to Alfred's greatness that he was a keen supporter of intellectual endeavors at a time when political and military affairs might well have taken all his energy. This English Charlemagne, himself the translator of several works from Latin into English, led the revitalization of monastic learning, brought foreign scholars to his court, and encouraged the creation of English prose. The Danes' destruction of many monastic libraries had seriously retarded the intellectual development that Christianity had stimulated in the centuries following Augustine's apostolate. In the preface to his translation of Gregory's *Pastoral Care* Alfred commented how English monks, who earlier had been eager to learn and teach, were now dependent on foreign scholars, and he also lamented that at his accession very few clergymen could understand the English versions of their prayer books or could even translate a Latin letter into the vernacular. Let as many as possible be taught to read their native tongue, Alfred admonished, and encourage only those who aspire to higher education to learn Latin. Accordingly, key books were translated into English, including Orosius' *History*, Gregory's *Dialogues*, Boethius' *Consolations of Philosophy*, Augustine's *Soliloquies*, and Bede's *Ecclesiastical History*. Alfred also put monks to work under royal patronage writing current history at several monasteries. The result was the famous *Anglo-Saxon Chron-*

icle, a cryptic account of major English events from Roman times to the year 1155. Moreover, Alfred founded a court school to which distinguished academicians came from all over the Christian world. The scholarly revival that he generated retained its momentum long after his death and was nourished by men like Dunstan, abbot of Glastonbury, one of the greatest scholars of the medieval world.

At Alfred's death in 899 England was divided into three large territories, none of which was politically united. Several Danish and Norwegian kings controlled parts of the Danelaw; Scottish and Welsh chiefs ruled the northwest and border country; and the Anglo-Saxon domain had fallen under the influence of Wessex by reason of its leadership against the Vikings and the virtual disappearance of royal families in the subject kingdoms of Kent, Sussex, and Mercia. Alfred's successors took advantage of the disunity within the Danelaw during the next half century to reconquer it piecemeal. Edward (899–924), Alfred's son, used an attack on Mercia from the north as the excuse to launch a campaign in 910 against the Danish Five Boroughs Confederation of Leicester, Derby, Lincoln, Stamford, and Nottingham. Ethelfled, Edward's sister and the wife of the Mercian king, helped against the Danes by invading from the west, and at her death in 918 Edward annexed all of Mercia and fortified its major towns. His brief campaign into Northumbria resulted in the submission of the Norwegian king and several of his Scottish and Danish allies, which allowed Edward to exercise a general control of England south of the Humber River. He set up a defensive line centered at Bakewell in the Derbyshire Peak district, but it was broken during Ethelstan's reign (924–939) by a fearsome alliance of the Scottish King Constantine, the Northumbrian King Olaf, the Strathclyde Welsh, and Irish Vikings. Somewhere along the north shore of Solway Firth, Ethelstan and his brother, Edmund, met them in the Battle of Brunanburh (937), which raged from dawn until sunset. It was a bloody battle: five kings and many earls were slain, and Constantine and Olaf fled northward. Ethelstan was succeeded by Edmund (939–946), who likewise spent most of his energy in simply withstanding the periodic incursions of Viking and Scottish kings. After Northumbria's capitulation in 954, England remained fairly peaceful until a series of invasions from Scandinavia beginning about 980 once more threatened Anglo-Saxon hegemony.

A spiritual revival that originated at the monastery of Cluny in Burgundy deeply affected England during the brief interlude of peace while Edwig (955–959) and Edgar (959–975) reigned. The monks of

Cluny, distressed by the decline of spirituality and the weakening of the Benedictine rule in the monasteries of western Europe, instituted a movement to enforce clerical celibacy, eradicate simony (the buying and selling of Church posts) and nepotism, and free the clergy from the evils of lay investiture (the bestowal of an ecclesiastical fief—and consequently religious authority—by a layman). Since the end of the eighth century, despite Alfred's good work, English monastic communities had been fraught with abuses: benefices were bought and sold; clergymen often married; secular and regular priests lived together without regard for the Benedictine rule; and those bishops who also held civil government posts sometimes lost sight of the primacy of their duty to the Church. Dunstan, by then archbishop of Canterbury and Edgar's principal adviser, led the reform in England, assisted by King Edgar and several friends from the monastery at Glastonbury. The king and Dunstan traveled throughout England, recruiting Englishmen to fill vacancies in monasteries that were controlled by foreigners, staffed with secular priests, or underpeopled, purging canons who would not follow the rule or send away their wives, and appointing trustworthy abbots and bishops. Dunstan also drew up new ecclesiastical laws for the laity to stop vices respecting marriage and moral conduct. As a result, more than fifty monastic houses were reformed or re-established and the tone of spirituality throughout the Church was deepened.

Edgar's tranquil reign, in which he achieved Danish and Saxon cooperation in civil and ecclesiastical affairs and won the support of Viking, Welsh, and Scottish vassals, ended with his death in 975 at the age of only thirty-two. He left two sons by different mothers, Edward and Ethelred, aged thirteen and seven, respectively, who obviously could not yet govern in their own right, much less cope with an age of fierce rivalry, intrigue, and tenuous allegiances. Almost immediately upon Edward's accession, struggles broke out among factions of earls probably aiming to gain control of the government through the superintendence of the young king. Some noblemen took sides in the dispute caused by Dunstan's insistence that Danes be given important clerical and political positions, and other earls hoped to break restraining monarchic ties in their shires. Edward did not reign long, however, for he was murdered in 978, probably with the connivance of his stepmother, who was ambitious for her own son, Ethelred. The latter's reign was marred from the first by the stigma of this heinous crime, but while Ethelred may be excused for his mother's transgressions, he fully merits the epithet "redeless," which means devoid of counsel, for his own failures. This corrupt, spiteful, and irresponsible monarch had a penchant for making wrong decisions, vacillated between indolence and inadequate action, and died in disgraceful exile among the Normans. He did virtually nothing to stop the Viking advance at a time when, if there had been proper leadership, the manpower and resources of England should have been more than sufficient to do so. Small wonder that the chronicler William of Malmesbury described him as "wretched," and that history has labeled him "the Unready."

As their ancestors had done two centuries earlier, the Vikings came in about 980 to raid the English coast from Devon to Northumbria. The domestic turmoil that plagued Scandinavia for more than a century was settled by the accession of Harald Bluetooth, who became the Christian king of Denmark and Norway shortly before Ethelred's reign. Some Vikings, such as the Norwegian Olaf Tryggveson, disputed Harald's authority, were forced into exile, and took to leading pirate fleets in the Baltic and North seas. The Danes pillaged and murdered in England without apparent organization until 991, when Olaf came with a large army to attack Ipswich and Maldon in Essex, where Ealdorman Byrthtnoth and his fyrd courageously met him in a horrendous battle, and died to a man after stiff resistance. The Vikings then took to their horses, ravaging and looting in Essex and Kent until Ethelred, who did nothing to stop them, agreed to pay a tribute amounting at first to £10,000. The money was raised by a general tax on land, called the Danegeld, which was frequently levied thereafter to pay more tribute. But the loot and tribute only whetted the Vikings' appetite, as for example in 994 when Olaf and Sweyn, Harald Bluetooth's renegade son, combined their forces to attack London, which successfully repelled them without any help from Ethelred. For several years beginning in 997 the Danes attacked Wales, Cornwall, and Devon by way of the Severn River, Dorset, and Kent through the Medway River. The Anglo-Saxon Chronicle for that period is replete with accounts of Viking raids, shameful English defeats, and virtually continuous plundering in East Anglia and the south. Meanwhile, Ethelred thought fit for some unknown reason to ravage a large part of Strathclyde, raised armies that never seemed to be in the right place, and continued to pay the Danegeld in staggering amounts.

Sweyn, who succeeded Harald Bluetooth as king of Denmark and Norway, undertook the systematic conquest of England in 1009 at the head of a huge professional army that had been trained at Jomsborg

Fortress in Jutland. The experienced commanders, Thorkell the Tall and his brother, Hemming, led divisions of Sweyn's forces in defeating several English militia armies and in devastating one community after another from East Anglia to Wiltshire during a three-year campaign. Sweyn already controlled all of southern England when he returned in 1013 from a brief trip to Denmark to make good his claim as king of England. He landed in Northumbria, and, as he had expected, the Danish nobles proclaimed him king. The thegns of Mercia did the same so that by the end of the year Ethelred had lost control of the country. When his last stronghold in London surrendered, he fled to Normandy, which was the homeland of his second wife, Emma, sister of Duke Richard II of Normandy.

Sweyn died suddenly in February, 1014. The Danes in England immediately swore allegiance to his son, Cnut, an inexperienced youth of eighteen who had been nominal commander in the north. When he went to Denmark to confer with his brother, Harald, new king of Denmark and Norway, a number of English earls offered to help Ethelred regain the throne on condition that he abate their grievances and govern well. In the interval, when there was no effective leadership in England, Edmund Ironside, Ethelred's son, got the support of northern Danelaw and the Five Boroughs. Accordingly, England was badly divided in the summer of 1015: Ethelred occupied the southeast, Cnut controlled Mercia and Wessex, and Edmund Ironside dominated the north. The armies of Edmund and Cnut exchanged frequent raids into each other's domains without decisive result. Ethelred and Edmund joined forces in London early in 1016, but Ethelred died soon thereafter. Finally, a large representation of earls, thegns, and bishops at Southampton proclaimed Cnut monarch. Edmund carried the fight into Wiltshire and followed the Danish army to Essex, where he was soundly beaten by Cnut and forced to accept a treaty that divided England into two kingdoms. But, at Edmund's death in November, 1016, Cnut became the undisputed master of England.

It may seem odd that Englishmen should so readily have accepted a Dane as king, but it should be remembered that Anglo-Saxons and Vikings had lived together for more than two centuries, and that, primarily because of the efforts of King Edgar and Archbishop Dunstan, representatives of both peoples had become leaders in the Church and government. Moreover, Cnut came from a Scandinavian society at least as fundamentally advanced and Christianized as England's. Though Cnut's military career had been ruthless, his reign (1016–35) was in general beneficent, considerate, and wise. Englishmen eventually realized that it was better to have a purposeful monarch who could govern effectively than to support a king like Ethelred, whose weak administration invited disorder. The character of Cnut's reign is amply shown in his decree of 1018, issued with the consent of the witan, that Danes and Englishmen should live together harmoniously in one Christian faith according to the laws promulgated by King Edgar. Most of the Danish fleet and army returned to Jutland, and although Viking commanders such as Thorkell and Eric of Norway governed the four administrative divisions of Wessex, Mercia, East Anglia, and Northumbria into which Cnut partitioned England, Englishmen were not generally excluded from the influence they previously enjoyed, especially in the Church. Before Cnut died in the full bloom of manhood he had added Norway, Denmark, and part of Sweden to his domain; he had won the esteem of his subjects by a firm but affable rule; and he had gone on a pilgrimage to Rome, where the pope and the major monarchs of Europe who had gathered for Emperor Conrad II's coronation paid Cnut deep respect. Above all, he had restored the authority and dignity of monarchy in a united England.

Cnut's two sons, Harold and Harthacnut, did not perpetuate their father's enlightened monarchy. Harold, Cnut's illegitimate son, was proclaimed king on condition that his father's second wife, Emma, Ethelred's widow, should reside at the capital, Winchester, with the witan and the royal treasure—obvious evidence of distrust. Cnut had hoped that his second son, Harthacnut, then Danish king, would govern both England and Denmark, but he was forced to remain in Scandinavia to suppress rebellion. Meanwhile, Harold strengthened his own position by exiling Emma. The struggle between the brothers over the English throne once more divided the allegiance of earls and thegns: some favored Harold, others espoused Harthacnut's succession, and still others hoped for the restoration of one of Ethelred's sons, then living in Normandy. When Alfred, the younger son of Emma and Ethelred, came to visit his mother in England shortly before her departure, Earl Godwin of Wessex, Harold's man, arrested him and his troop, killed most of them, and injured the prince so severely that he died as a result. Harthacnut became king when Harold died in 1040, but he lived for only two more years. As neither brother had heirs, Ethelred's surviving son, Edward, became king, thereby restoring the Anglo-Saxon royal line.

Edward, then in his mid-thirties, had lived for about twenty-five years in Normandy, a French-speaking duchy settled by Vikings three generations earlier. He was unsuited for the throne by both temperament and training. He had spent much more time with ascetic monks than with militant noblemen accustomed to clawing for power. His extraordinary piety and gentleness astonished his enemies, provoked his advisers, who tried unsuccessfully to persuade him to prepare England for a likely Danish invasion, and led to his canonization a century later by the pope, who entitled him the Confessor. No doubt Edward was popular, for in 1051 he abolished the tax that had been levied annually to support the fleet long after the Viking raids had ceased, and he astonished his subjects by unusual thrift, simplicity of life, and a vow of chastity that he is said to have kept even after his marriage to Earl Godwin's daughter. Edward did not dismiss Danish and English administrators in either the witan or the shires, but he understandably showed preference to Normans, on whom he lavished huge estates and clerical benefices. A welcome peace reigned for most of his rule, primarily because the two factions of nobles headed by Godwin of Wessex and Leofric of Mercia maintained an uneasy truce. In fact, the only ripple on an otherwise tranquil political sea arose in 1043 when Edward, at Godwin's insistence, robbed Queen Mother Emma's enormous treasure at Winchester and confiscated her estates. Little else worth mentioning stirred the country after that until Godwin's ambition caused a near civil war in the 1050s.

Godwin wielded enormous power. He was Edward's father-in-law and his sons Sweyn and Harold were earls in eastern Mercia and East Anglia. He had great wealth, many estates, and a formidable army. Among the three most important noblemen—Leofric of Mercia, Siward of Northumbria, and Godwin—the latter most resented the favors Edward bestowed on his Norman friends. Godwin, whose ancestry was Anglo-Danish, may have been motivated in part by patriotism, but it seems more likely that he wanted to promote the welfare of his family, even to the point of making a son Edward's successor. Godwin probably had even more influence than Edward, whose accommodating nature left him an easy prey to the ambition of clever and unscrupulous councilors. At a time when the right of hereditary succession was not firmly established, a man like Godwin could have dethroned Edward had it not been for the loyalty of Leofric and Siward to the king.

Godwin showed his hand in 1051 on the occasion of a visit to England by Count Eustace of Boulogne. Eustace's troop was at Dover, ready to embark for home, when a local man killed one of them, causing a melee in which several soldiers on both sides were slain. Edward responded to Eustace's complaint by ordering Godwin to ravage Dover, but he refused and raised an army to defy the king, although he had to surrender when Siward and Leofric hurried to Edward's defense. Godwin was exiled, but Edward pardoned him within a year and restored his and his sons' titles, offices, and land. Two other significant events occurred in the same year: Edward translated the Norman bishop, Robert of Jumièges, from the see of London to the archiepiscopacy of Canterbury; and Duke William of Normandy visited Edward, who allegedly promised him the succession to the English throne. The elevation of Robert to Canterbury in the face of Godwin's open support of the Danish Bishop Stigand of Winchester's candidacy caused rebellion. Godwin gathered a formidable fleet and army and laid siege to London. But Stigand arranged a truce in which Edward agreed to banish Robert and other Norman officials.

During the next decade Edward's position deteriorated. Godwin, Siward, and Leofric were all dead by 1057, but two of Godwin's sons, Earl Tostig of Northumbria and Earl Harold of Wessex, rose to dangerous heights of power and popularity. Tostig ruled Northumbria as if there were no king in England and was envious of Harold, who clearly sought the throne. Harold won fame in a series of campaigns against the Welsh King Llewelyn, who raided the western Midlands annually from 1055 to 1063 until Harold drove him back into the mountains, where his own men murdered him. Edward had already lived longer than any other English king since Alfred, and in advanced age he lost interest in public affairs. As he retreated into virtual monastic isolation, a number of claimants to his throne pressed their candidacy. Edward the Etheling, Edmund Ironside's son, had the strongest hereditary right even though he had lived abroad since Cnut's succession in 1016, but he died leaving a son, Edgar, who was too young to compete for the throne. Harold Hardrada of Norway, captain of a pirate fleet that roamed the Irish Sea, was likewise an aspirant because of his descent from Cnut. Finally, King Edward named Earl Harold his heir. He had no royal blood in his veins, and no king could legally dictate his successor, but the witan proclaimed Harold monarch and he was crowned January 16, 1066.

William of Normandy insisted that the throne rightly belonged to him. Although of illegitimate birth, he claimed England by right of blood, by right of Edward's promise of 1051, and by right of an oath, which Harold had taken over sacred relics following his shipwreck on Norman shores, that he would assist William to win the crown. William also had the support of the pope, who resented Stigand's usurpation of Robert of Jumièges' archiepiscopal see and sent a banner that the Conqueror carried like a crusader into England. As William marshaled his mighty army in Normandy, Harold sat uneasily on a throne that Tostig and Hardrada also meant to topple.

2

Norman and Early Angevin England, 1066–1216

Harold of Wessex has long been popular in legend as the defender of England against the foreigner. Historians, on the other hand, have often portrayed him as the villain, with William of Normandy the champion, and England as the coveted prize of the struggle over the throne in October, 1066, culminating on the bloody battlefield of Hastings, where the last Anglo-Saxon king fell dead with an arrow through his brain. The contemporary Anglo-Saxon chroniclers, William of Malmesbury, and the weavers of the Bayeux tapestry (which documents in colored worsteds the panorama of English history from the last days of Edward the Confessor to the Conquest) sensed the significance of Hastings and have added to William's fame by carefully recording his victory. But Harold showed, during the nine months that he reigned, that he was at least as good a general and as capable an administrator as William. King Edward, realizing that England seethed with internecine broils—particularly in Northumbria, where the rapacious policy of Tostig led the local magnates to overthrow him in favor of Morcar, who later came to terms with Edward—chose wisely in naming Harold his successor. At Edward's death the Northumbrians were again rebelling, the Welsh threatened the marches—the lands on the England-Wales border—and Harold Hardrada, king of Norway, plied English waters planning invasion. Under these circumstances, the witan naturally turned to Harold because he was an Englishman with a brilliant military record and proven administrative ability. William of Normandy had a better lineal claim to the throne, but the witan could not honor it except at the peril of interjecting yet another discordant element among Englishmen who were already badly divided.

But William cared little about logic. He had often faced baronial opposition aimed at depriving him of his ducal authority, and he pressed his claim. He became duke of Normandy in 1035 at the age of seven upon the death of his father, Robert I. William's youth and the fact that he was the illegitimate son of a tanner's daughter provided his uncles and cousins, themselves ambitious for the throne, with an excuse to depose him. Powerful barons, chafing under feudal vassalage, likewise gathered like vultures to rip the duchy into independent baronies dominated by newly erected castles and liveried mercenary troops. That the young duke survived at all owed much to the loyalty of several stouthearted regents, his half-brothers, Odo and Robert, and faithful advisers like William FitzOsbern. Henry I, king of France, at first also helped William against his enemies, but later joined them in an effort to steal Normandy for the Capetian royal family who were scarcely stronger, wealthier, or more prestigious than Norman, Flemish, or Breton dukes and counts. William therefore matured amid constant insurrection and became accustomed to using the sword to maintain his rights. By 1063 he had restored order in Normandy and had conquered additional territory in Flanders and Maine. At thirty-one, he was in 1066 one of the strongest noblemen in northern Europe, and he had acquired an enviable reputation as an able governor and fearless soldier.

William was hunting near Rouen when he learned that Harold had robbed him of the English throne. He first wrote to remind Harold of his solemn oath (which Harold denied having taken) allegedly made in 1064 over sacred relics, that he would assist William to obtain the succession. When Harold refused to honor his promise, William complained to the pope and began preparations for the invasion of England. He drove his smiths and shipwrights hard during the spring and summer to build a fleet of about seven hundred ships and to amass a huge store of chain mail and weapons. The manpower of Normandy alone would not be sufficient to defeat a prosperous kingdom like England, so agents went out to the neighboring countries of Flanders, Anjou, and Ponthieu, and to Norman kingdoms in Spain and southern Italy to raise an army of experienced knights who joined it on the promise of booty and land. When all was at last ready, the winds blew unfavorably, and William spent anxious weeks awaiting a change.

This delay and trouble in the north proved to be Harold Godwinson's undoing. His brother Tostig, angry about his displacement in Northumbria, attacked several settlements from the Isle of Wight to Sandwich, which forced Harold to station his fleet and army in southeastern England. But the militia could not be held in camp at harvest time, and most of it disbanded. Then Harold Hardrada, an ally of Tostig's, landed with three hundred ships at the mouth of the Tyne River, and defeated the combined forces of Morcar and Edwin of Mercia at Fulford. King Harold hurried north to meet the enemy on September 25; and at the Battle of Stamford Bridge near York, Tostig, Hardrada, and at least three-quarters of their army were slain. Godwinson was immersed in affairs of state in Yorkshire when he learned that William had landed at Pevensey in Sussex on the twenty-eighth. A forced march covering some 180 miles brought Harold to London in less than a week. There, in haste, as he wished to confront William before he could consolidate his position, Harold threw together a makeshift army composed of the remnants of his northern forces, inexperienced and poorly-equipped infantry and his thegns, who were well accustomed to wielding two-handed swords and battle-axes. On October 13 Harold pitched camp on a hill overlooking rolling country between Pevensey and Hastings, five miles from the wooden fortress William had erected. If it be true that the Saxons spent the night at a drunken feast, they were none the worse for it at nine the next morning when William's men moved over a succession of knolls into a shallow valley at the foot of Harold's line of defense.

The Battle of Hastings raged furiously until nightfall, the Normans repeatedly charging a solid wall of interlocked Saxon shields. William's assaults at first failed to budge the stalwart Saxons, who inflicted heavy losses on the Normans. Harold had the advantage until William allegedly perceived that when a charge was repulsed the enemy broke ranks to pursue retreating Normans. He twice ordered apparently feigned retreats and then sent out his cavalry to cut down the unprotected Saxon infantry. Late in the evening, with the English front line still holding despite heavy casualties, the Norman archers again shot their arrows at an angle that brought them raining down on the troops behind the shield wall. Harold fell dead, and his dispirited followers turned and fled into the forest under cover of darkness. This battle, which involved probably less than fifteen thousand men, fixed the future of England for the next three centuries under Norman and Angevin kings.

Though Harold had been killed and his army routed, William was not yet king in the eyes of most Englishmen or of the witan, which huddled in London to make Edgar king, even though there was no English army to enforce its foolish decision and no will in the country

GAVILAN COLLEGE
LIBRARY

to resist William. He remained briefly at Hastings to await the witan's capitulation. When it did not come, he marched northwestward toward London, ravaging the country in a wide swath as he went. In late December, fearing the results of a direct assault on London, he crossed the Thames at Wallingford (Berkshire) to move toward the capital from the west. The witan finally came to its senses and sent a delegation of bishops and earls to surrender the city and pay William homage. The archbishop of York crowned him king of England in Westminster Abbey on Christmas Day. He celebrated the new year the master of England, Normandy, Maine, Brittany, and Flanders. Every English monarch thereafter held some territory on the Continent until Mary Tudor surrendered Calais in 1558.

It should have come as no surprise to William that, once the shock and disorder resulting from the invasion had subsided, some of the English magnates attempted to restore Saxon control. All contemporary accounts mention William's moderation, but they also impress the reader with his capacity for terrible vengeance in the face of insurrection. William changed little for the first two years of his reign. At first he allowed most English noblemen to retain their lands and titles, except for the estates that he gave to favorites, and the earldoms of Kent and Hereford that he bestowed on his half-brother, Bishop Odo of Bayeux, and his companion, FitzOsbern. He granted London a charter that guaranteed its inhabitants the privileges they had enjoyed since the Confessor's time, but he also built the White Tower in the east end of the city as a prison, fortress, royal palace, and stark reminder of his power. Nonetheless, on returning from a trip to Normandy to fetch his Flemish wife, Matilda, he faced uprisings in Yorkshire and Cambridgeshire, and raids by Scots and Danes. He also marched on rebellious Northumbria, where he besieged York, starved its garrison into submission, and devastated the surrounding villages and fields so completely that they remained deserted and uncultivated for two centuries. He easily crushed insurrection in Chester and Exeter. The last serious rising against William erupted in the marshland of Ely, Cambridgeshire, where Hereward the Wake staunchly fought him with only a handful of men until he, like the rest, fell before the Conqueror. Except for another brief revolution in 1075 and occasional raids from Scotland, William was the undisputed master of England until his death in 1087 at the age of fifty-nine.

The primary importance of the reign of William I lies in the superimposition of Norman on Anglo-Saxon political and economic institutions. William inherited the land that formerly belonged to Harold and his earls and thegns. As was the custom in Normandy, William granted parcels of land (called fiefs) to his noblemen in accordance with the contribution they had made in the conquest or on account of filial or other close relationship. These large landholders, who received estates directly from the king, became his tenants-in-chief. They in turn subdivided their fiefs among lesser nobility in a transaction called subinfeudation. Some earls, such as FitzOsbern and Odo, got dozens of manors, the smallest units in the feudal system, but they were scattered over several counties so that no nobleman could muster military power greater than the crown's. After an initial period of grace during which William allowed the Saxons to keep their lands and titles, he abolished the Anglo-Saxon earldoms and reapportioned them among Norman earls, who exercised considerably less authority than had their predecessors. The only earls whom William allowed to govern shires in his name controlled the vulnerable frontier counties palatine of Chester, Durham, and Kent (and later, Lancashire and Shropshire). These fiefs were not bestowed free and clear; they were given as rewards and were held at the king's pleasure. William compelled not only his tenants-in-chief, but also his subtenants to swear an oath of fealty and to pay homage, which meant that, unlike feudalism on the Continent, Norman feudalism in England provided for contractual ties between the king and every holder of a fief, regardless of its size.

The Conqueror also strengthened royal authority by constructing castles at strategic points. They were ordinarily built on high ground overlooking a gorge or precipitous cliff. Some were little more than crude wooden forts; others had massive proportions with walls fifteen feet thick. (Returning crusaders, having learned something of Moslem bastions, perfected the art of castle-building in the twelfth century by adding moats, heightening ramparts, and erecting stone corner towers.) William kept the Anglo-Saxon fyrd by which, together with castle garrisons, he could crush rebellion in any district. Small wonder that he is credited with instituting England's first thoroughly centralized national government.

Feudalism involved a personal contract between the liege lord and his vassal with rights and obligations affecting both parties, whether on the level of the king and his tenants-in-chief, or of a large landholder and his subtenants. The contractual obligations varied widely from district to district and from person to person, depending on local customs and needs. In general, however, the lord granted the fief that provided the vassal's livelihood, assumed the wardship of his children at his death (his lands escheating to the lord if there were no heirs), and reared them as his own until he found the orphaned daughters suitable husbands and provided knighthoods and fiefs for the sons. In return, the vassal furnished his lord with armed and mounted soldiers, the number being individually determined on the basis of the size and profits of the fief, for no more than forty days a year. He was constrained to take an oath of fealty and pay homage annually, usually in early spring when the feudal contract was renewed. A vassal also paid such monetary "aids" as might be required to raise ransom, meet the lord's extraordinary expenses, or provide a dowry for his daughter. Moreover, the lord expected hospitality at his vassal's home. In addition, the king's tenants-in-chief attended the royal court and gave him counsel.

The Normans retained the basic structure of Anglo-Saxon village life on the manor except that the free villagers lost some of their personal liberty. Relatively few of the English lower classes continued to be freemen; most of them became villeins who, while technically not slaves, could not leave the manor, had to work a stipulated number of days (plus boon days) on the lord's land (demesne), and were usually allotted strips of land amounting to about thirty acres. They paid taxes and what might be called service charges for the use of the lord's oven, brewhouse, and mill, and were not ordinarily allowed to hunt, fish, or gather wood in his forest and stream. The status of the villein slowly declined over the next three centuries and eventually led to a great deal of economic unrest and even rebellions during which the villeins sought to destroy the manor rolls that defined their inferior status. The feudal system bound people to the land, with heavy and often arbitrary taxation, and made for much more rigorous and much greater social distinctions that left those on the bottom without economic rights. There was little that the villeins could do to better their position, for, if they left the land, there was no place for them in an overwhelmingly agricultural society.

The agricultural system remained essentially the same for centuries. Most villeins lived in manor villages, a collection of rough wattle and thatch cottages with few amenities. Virtually every manor had common and meadow land, a forest, a stream, wasteland, and arable land, the best of it reserved for the lord's use. The arable land was divided according to the time-honored system into three fields, two of which were parceled out in strips while one was allowed to lie fallow. The lord lived in a castle or manor house, which, if he were a poorer knight, might be little more than a wooden building of sufficient size to house him and his family in modest comfort. The average man today lives much better than did the richest Norman earl, who had few spices for his food, no rugs on the floors, and no glass in the windows, not to mention the biting cold of drafty halls and the pain he suffered as a result of diseases for which there were no remedies.

William brought greater dignity and power to the English crown, whose authority under the later Anglo-Saxon kings was theoretically supreme but rarely fully implemented. The Conqueror, unlike the Capetian monarchs of France, was clearly superior in social status, prestige, and jurisdiction to any Anglo-Norman baron (until 1485, "baron" is used generically to mean any feudal magnate holding his lands directly from the king). As the headstone in the feudal hierarchy, William could raise an army from among his vassals against which no opposing force could successfully stand. As the largest landowner in England, he received rent, gifts, and monetary "aids" from thousands of tenants. He collected the Danegeld at a rate three times larger than his predecessor even though the threat of Danish invasion was remote. He also enjoyed the support of the Church, which was pleased at his deposition of Stigand, the illegally-elected archbishop of Canterbury. But William occasionally quarreled with the pope, as will be seen presently, and used Church property to his own advantage by leaving ecclesiastical benefices vacant for long periods in order to keep their incomes. William was also the primary lawgiver of the land, and although he enforced the laws of Edward the Confessor, he made a few new ones that protected the royal prerogative. For instance, he set aside vast areas as royal forests, including the sixty-thousand-acre New Forest in Hampshire, and blinded poachers of royal deer. Another Norman law abolished the death penalty but substituted mutilations or fines, depending on the crime. William made a distinction between the murder of a Frenchman or an Englishman; if a Norman was slain, the community where the body was found had to pay a corporate fine unless it surrendered the culprit. This effectively stopped clandestine assassinations of government officials.

The extent to which William controlled every facet of the national government is best illustrated in the Domesday Book, the record of the Domesday survey begun in 1085 and completed the following year. Agents surveyed and assessed the entire country, village by village, and, except for certain northern counties, the work was done within a few months. Presumably the purpose of the census was to determine England's military and financial condition in preparation for a Danish invasion, but it is also likely that William wanted to know exactly how much tax the country could provide. Whatever the purpose, the survey provided the most complete contemporary record of any country in western Europe, and it is evidenced—by the very fact that the population readily answered questions involving their private affairs—that William commanded universal obedience. According to the *Anglo-Saxon Chronicle*, nothing escaped the commissioners' eyes, whether it be cottages, land, animals, or beehives. And William frequently sent in a second group of commissioners to check on the honesty and accuracy of others. They inquired into the ownership of land in three periods—in the reign of Edward the Confessor, at the Conquest, and in 1086. They learned the names of manors, the number of freemen, villeins, cotters (unfree cultivators of less than ten acres), and slaves living there, the acreage of plowland, meadows, and pastures, the number and size of fishponds, and the financial resources of every man. Thousands of these reports were consolidated into summaries for each county, all of which were then bound in two fat volumes, the second dealing solely with East Anglia.

William transformed the Anglo-Saxon witan, through a few substantive changes in its membership and functions, into the Norman great council. As membership was based on landholding directly from the king, it theoretically included at first all his tenants-in-chief—earls, barons, the two archbishops, bishops, and most abbots—possibly as many as six hundred persons. They met with the king three times annually, ordinarily at Easter in Winchester, at Whitsun (the feast of Pentecost, seventh Sunday after Easter) in London, and at Christmas in Gloucester, but the king could summon his council at any time. Such a large group was too unwieldy either to conduct the day-to-day business of government or to be in constant attendance on the monarch, who frequently moved from one to another of his many residences. William therefore came to rely on a smaller group of advisers and civil servants called the Curia Regis, the king's council or court, which included close companions, the officers of his household, a few ecclesiastics, and clerks who later became a rudimentary civil service. Under William the chief administrative officers were the chancellor, treasurer, and justiciar. The chancellor, who subsequently became the most important royal servant, was the keeper of the great seal with which all royal writs were embossed. The treasurer received and disbursed all money relating to the crown, issued and maintained the quality of coins, and guarded the royal treasury at Winchester and London. The justiciar served as viceroy or regent in the king's prolonged absences.

The early Normans made no distinction between the duties and authority of the great council and Curia Regis, for both interchangeably advised the king, helped make laws, proclaimed his successor, and consented to the collection of feudal taxes (though William and other kings sometimes acted on their own authority, especially in levying extraordinary taxes). The king's council also acted as the country's highest court of justice in both criminal and civil cases, sometimes as a court of origin and sometimes on appeals from the shire courts. The Curia Regis had, therefore, executive, legislative, and judicial functions when it sat with the king. Moreover, the great council developed by the thirteenth century into Parliament and the Curia Regis into the privy council.

The Normans made few changes in local government. It has already been noted that William reapportioned the earldoms and that the new earls lost most of their administrative and magisterial authority. The shire courts remained as before except that the sheriffs replaced the earls as the crown's local judges, tax collectors, and keepers of the peace. The laws of Edward the Confessor and royal writs were enforced except that, in addition to trial by oath and by ordeal, trial by battle was introduced. The rules of chivalry subsequently ordered these ceremonious but ferocious duels fought on horseback with lances, swords, and battle-axes. The Normans kept the hundreds and the hundred courts, but the latter gradually lost most of their functions to the shire courts. Lords ruled their manors as they pleased so long as they observed feudal obligations and royal law. Manor courts settled the innumerable quarrels and petty legal infractions to which contentious villeins were prone. Borough governments, though not yet important, were granted new charters guaranteeing local privileges for a handsome fee imposed by the crown.

William applied his talent and energy as fervently in ecclesiastical affairs as he did in governmental business. He owed much to Pope Leo IX, whose standard he had carried to Pevensey, and whose wish that the Saxon archbishop of Canterbury, Stigand, should be deposed, was honored by the election of Lanfranc, an Italian monk who had been abbot of Bec in Normandy, and who became William's chief

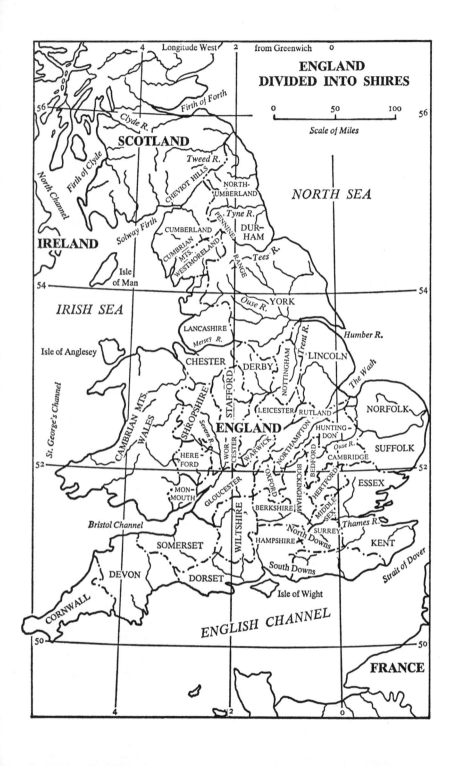

ENGLAND
DIVIDED INTO SHIRES

Longitude West from Greenwich

0   50   100
Scale of Miles

SCOTLAND

NORTH SEA

IRELAND

NORTH CHANNEL

Firth of Forth

Clyde R.

Firth of Clyde

Tweed R.

CHEVIOT HILLS

NORTH-UMBERLAND

Tyne R.

Solway Firth

CUMBERLAND

DUR-HAM

PENNINE RANGE

CUMBRIAN MTS.

WESTMORELAND

Tees R.

Isle of Man

IRISH SEA

Ouse R.

YORK

LANCASHIRE

Mersey R.

Humber R.

Isle of Anglesey

CHESTER

DERBY

NOTTINGHAM

Trent R.

LINCOLN

The Wash

St. George's Channel

CAMBRIAN MTS.

WALES

SHROPSHIRE

STAFFORD

Severn R.

ENGLAND

LEICESTER

RUTLAND

NORFOLK

HUNTING-DON

WOR-CESTER

WARWICK

NORTHAMPTON

BEDFORD

Ouse R.

CAMBRIDGE

SUFFOLK

HERE-FORD

MON-MOUTH

GLOUCESTER

OXFORD

BUCKINGHAM

HERTFORD

ESSEX

WILTSHIRE

BERKSHIRE

MIDDLE-SEX

Thames R.

SOMERSET

HAMPSHIRE

North Downs

SURREY

KENT

Strait of Dover

DEVON

DORSET

South Downs

Isle of Wight

CORNWALL

Bristol Channel

ENGLISH CHANNEL

FRANCE

adviser. William and Lanfranc continued in England the Church reform they had begun in Normandy in the spirit of the Cluniac movement, which was still gaining momentum. Leo IX and his successor,
Gregory VII (1073–85), hoped for much from William, for he had
built monasteries and had helped Lanfranc eradicate simony and enforce clerical celibacy in Normandy. William cooperated with
Gregory up to a point in order to strengthen royal authority by means
of stricter clerical supervision. Lanfranc gradually replaced all but one
of the English bishops and most of the abbots with Normans, built
huge stone cathedrals and abbeys in several provincial towns like Rochester, Exeter, Durham, and Bath, and moved episcopal seats to them.
He rebuilt or enlarged monasteries to house larger numbers of monks
and founded schools on the model of those at Bec and Caen in Normandy. He also tried to extirpate simony, which had persisted despite
Dunstan's earlier reforms. He honored the English custom of allowing
clergymen who had taken wives to keep them, but he would not ordain
married men. For the first time in over a century, Church councils
and provincial and diocesan synods were convened regularly to pub-
licize canon law and royal writs and to make rules for both clergy and
laity. The archbishop of York, who had formerly been the equal of
the archbishop of Canterbury, recognized Lanfranc's primacy. Moreover, with William's consent, Lanfranc established separate ecclesiastical courts with primary jurisdiction in cases involving "matters of the
soul," and in all crimes involving the clergy—an innovation that later
caused a serious rift between English kings and the popes. For the
time being, however, William was not disturbed that decisions rendered in the ecclesiastical courts could be appealed outside the realm
to the higher courts of the Roman Curia. The feudal system, which
made bishops and abbots the vassals of the king, and the employment
of churchmen as royal councilors because they were often the only
educated persons in the country, encouraged an intimate relationship
between Church and state.

During the eleventh and twelfth centuries the papacy began to implement the claims of papal supremacy in both temporal and spiritual
affairs that earlier popes had claimed since the late fifth-century pontificate of Gelasius. According to the Gelasian theory, also known as
the theory of the two swords, Christ had given Peter and his successors all authority, political as well as religious, and therefore secular
princes derived their temporal authority from Christ through the pope.
Thus the pope was superior to all secular princes. As William was the

undisputed master of England, it is not surprising that he should have resisted papal assertions that he was subject to the Holy See. It had been the prerogative of kings throughout western Europe to appoint bishops and abbots and to invest them with the temporal symbols of office, the appointments later being confirmed by the pope, who sent archbishops the pallium (a wool stole). This practice, known as lay investiture, was appropriate within the context of the feudal system, for diocesan boundaries occasionally coincided with the borders of a fief (though dioceses were normally much larger than fiefs), and bishops and abbots were made vassals like their secular counterparts and were bound by contractual obligations imposed by the oath of fealty. As the ecclesiastic who controlled a fief had to supply men and arms, obey his lord, and uphold his laws, conflicts of allegiance sometimes arose between his duties to the Church and to his lord. This was especially true when, for reasons of state, the king invested bishops and abbots whom he knew would be better political administrators than spiritual leaders. The welfare of the Church, particularly the interests of the papacy, suffered accordingly.

Gregory VII regarded all Christendom as his feudal domain and all secular princes as his vassals. He boldly proclaimed in 1075 that henceforth lay investiture would not be tolerated, and threatened kings and clergymen with excommunication if they permitted it. Gregory dealt high-handedly with powerful princes like the Holy Roman Emperor, who dared to nominate an archbishop against the will of the Holy See. Southern Italy, Denmark, and Hungary became papal fiefs. The same thing might have happened to England had not William and his archbishop of Canterbury stoutly resisted such an encroachment on the powers of the English monarchy. They readily acknowledged papal spiritual supremacy and encouraged the reforms that the pope advocated to improve the clergy, but they would not allow direct papal intervention in political affairs. William, in fact, took steps to ensure that the English clergy remained under his firm control: he continued to nominate and invest bishops and abbots; he permitted papal decrees and English synodal and conciliar decisions to have legal force only upon his approbation; papal legates could not enter the kingdom without his consent; and he would not allow his ecclesiastical and civil officers to be excommunicated as a means of enforcing their conformity to Rome. Gregory reluctantly acceded to William's conditions because he had his hands full with German and French monarchs. But the near rupture of Anglo-papal harmony under William sowed the seeds that later blossomed into frequent quarrels between popes and English kings.

William's enemies in England and Normandy left him little time to enjoy the just fruits of an arduous life during his later years—during which he grew uncomfortably fat and churlish despite frequent exercise in hunting the stag, which he dearly loved. He often traveled between Normandy and England, staying only long enough in each kingdom to repair the damage done to his authority and to ward off the incursions of aggressive neighbors. King Malcolm of Scotland invaded Northumberland in 1079 and had to be driven back. In the same year William's son, Robert, who had already led a rebellion against him in 1077–79, allied with Philip I of France in an attempt to seize Normandy even though Robert was then heir to the English throne and master of Flanders. William had to hurry to England in 1085 to make preparations against an expected Danish invasion, which did not materialize. During 1086, one national disaster after another weakened England and worried William. A cattle plague and heavy thunderstorms during the growing season left thousands dead from starvation, and others were struck down by a terrible pestilence. Finally, there came a war against Philip of France in which William, who had just taken and ravaged Mantes in late August, 1087, was thrown from his horse with such force that he died of injuries on September 7. Some wretched servants robbed him in death of his clothes and jewels, and his body was hastily embalmed and taken to St. Stephen's Monastery at Caen where it was stuffed into a sarcophagus too small for the corpulent corpse.

William left three sons, Robert, William, and Henry, and a daughter, Adela, who had married Count Stephen of Blois. According to the Conqueror's dying wish, the two older sons divided his domain, England for William and Normandy for Robert. Henry, still only a boy, received a huge inheritance. Neither William nor Robert deserved what their father had struggled to acquire. Robert, treacherous, weak-willed, and incompetent, ruled Normandy with such abandon that his vassals desolated the duchy in a round of petty wars that made a mockery of law. Had he not served bravely in the First Crusade, there would be nothing good to say of him. William Rufus, whose nickname was prompted by his great shock of red hair and ruddy complexion, hurried to England without bothering to await his father's impending death to grasp the throne he had long coveted. The generosity with which, at his accession, he distributed some of the royal treasure to

churches and monasteries belied his true character, which was vengeful and devoid of spirituality. The English court became a den of vice
and a haven for ignorant mercenaries. William's love of hunting was
exceeded only by his lust for wealth, which he drained from his victimized subjects to the last possible farthing.

There was no love lost between William Rufus and his vassals, who
rebelled under the leadership of the Conqueror's half-brother, Bishop
Odo of Bayeux, in the hope of substituting Robert for William. Once
the lethargic Robert was king, Odo planned to take Lanfranc's place
as archbishop and be the real power behind the throne. Half a dozen
barons stirred up insurrection in several counties and waited for a
Norman army to attack England in the southeast. But William threw
his mercenaries against the rebel army in the west, and, with the support of Lanfranc and other bishops, as well as the promise of governmental reforms in the hated forest laws and the exorbitant taxes, won
sufficient sympathy from the fyrds around London to force the surrender of rebel castles in Surrey and Kent and repulse a small invasion
force sent by Robert near Hastings. The last rebel stronghold at Rochester likewise fell to William, and Odo was exiled to Normandy.

Except for putting down another English rebellion in 1095, William
II directed most of his attention to Normandy, where misgovernment
had seriously weakened defenses and encouraged baronial anarchy.
The political situation in Normandy was further complicated by the
fact that both William and Robert claimed identical fiefs and vassals,
who frequently changed sides. On a promise of the succession to the
English throne, the youngest of the Conqueror's sons, Henry, allied
with William to invade Normandy in 1090. The invasion succeeded
initially, largely because the coastal fortresses surrendered and because
Robert refused to fight in the campaign. Henry, playing both sides
against the middle, defected to Robert's side. But Robert again took
the easiest course by making peace with William, according to which
the exiled Norman rebels of 1088, save for Bishop Odo, were pardoned,
and Henry, victim of the unexpected peace, was deprived of the wealth
and land he had inherited. Meanwhile Rufus repelled an attack by
King Malcolm of Scotland in 1091 and forced him to accept England's
titular sovereignty over southern Scotland. No sooner was Malcolm
disposed of than Rufus broke the truce with Robert and persuaded
many of his vassals to abandon him. Already in control of half of
Normandy, Rufus began preparations in 1094 for the conquest of
the other half. In order to support the war, he aroused general ani-

mosity among his barons and villeins by imposing exorbitant taxes in the form of feudal aids and the Danegeld at twice the normal rate. So unscrupulous was Rufus that he even robbed his militia of the money he had instructed them to bring to the rendezvous with which to buy food, and sent them home empty-handed. He no longer needed them to take Normandy, for Robert, who was about to depart for the Holy Land, entrusted his brother with his duchy, mortgaging it to him for 10,000 marks. But the Crusade kept Robert away longer than he had anticipated so that Rufus ruled both England and Normandy until he was killed, accidentally or treacherously, on a hunt in the New Forest in August, 1100.

At his death his youngest brother, Henry, hurried to Winchester to seize the royal treasure and secure his election and coronation at Westminster. Whether or not Henry had been a party to the supposed murder of Rufus, he proved a better king. He granted a charter of liberties promising to abolish his brother's oppressive practices, thereby substituting the velvet glove for the clenched fist, and the rule of law for arbitrary government. But he was no less avaricious, ambitious, or purposeful than William, though his calm deliberations were a welcome change from the boastful curses the court had been accustomed to hear. The reign of Henry I (1100–35) was characterized by three principal policies, two of which were a continuation of what William II had begun: he meant to rob Robert of Normandy and carry on the expansion of its borders at the expense of the Capetians; he tried to undermine papal authority over the English clergy; and he made constitutional changes that one of his successors, Henry II, greatly expanded.

William II and Henry I severely strained Anglo-papal friendship during the archiepiscopal reign of Anselm, who became primate of England in 1093, William having kept the benefice vacant since Lanfranc's death in 1089 in order to receive its income. The mild-mannered Anselm, like Lanfranc a great theologian and a former abbot of Bec, preferred scholarship to administration, and he was therefore unsuited to assume the heavy burdens of England's most important ecclesiastical post. William may well have chosen Anselm because his great learning would add a measure of dignity to an otherwise undistinguished coterie of royal servants, but it is also probably true that William expected him to be a submissive agent of royal policy.

But Anselm surprised everyone by concurring with papal claims to temporal sovereignty over secular princes. He refused to accede to William's controlling influence over the English clergy, who owed, he said, primary allegiance to the pope. Anselm, in fact, laid down a number of conditions that he expected William to observe: he should restore estates confiscated from the see of Canterbury; he should continue the ecclesiastical reforms begun by Lanfranc; he must officially uphold the legal election of Pope Urban II against the rival claims of the antipope, Clement III; and, finally, he should allow Urban to bestow the pallium on Anselm *in Rome.* William could not accept such terms without surrendering lay investiture, which was the key issue. As a result, they became bitter opponents. William saw only one course open to him: he must get Pope Urban to depose Anselm in exchange for England's support of his election. It was a shrewd plan, but it backfired. Urban sent a papal legate to England, got the king's approbation of the former's election, and then refused to allow him to bestow the pallium on Anselm. William was furious, but he could do nothing save at the risk of alienating his ecclesiastical vassals on whom he counted for money to support his Norman war. Two years later, in 1098, Anselm voluntarily went into exile to escape the pangs of continuous controversy. But he had upheld papal supremacy, and most English hierarchs were subsequently elected by the group of administrative clergy, called the chapter, attached to every cathedral and monastery. Henry I, however, often compelled bishops and abbots to accept lay investiture.

Henry I, a pious man who at least went through the formalities of being a just ruler at the outset of his reign, induced Anselm to return. The archbishop, however, upheld new papal decrees against lay investiture, would not pay Henry homage as his vassal, and refused to consecrate bishops who did so. But the pope was so anxious to reach a compromise with Henry that he arranged for him to invest bishops and abbots solely with their temporal power. That did not mean the end of royal authority over the hierarchy, however, for Henry and his successors saw to it that chapters elected bishops who were known to be sympathetic to the crown.

The return of Robert, duke of Normandy, from the Holy Land in the autumn of 1100 challenged Henry's position as king. Although Henry had already secured the succession, some English and Norman barons encouraged Robert to dispute it on the grounds of age, he being the second oldest of the Conqueror's three sons. Robert was not anxious to accommodate them, for, as we have seen, he cared little for administration or power, but the barons, who saw a better chance of having their own way under Robert than under Henry, urged him to undertake the war. Accordingly, Robert led a Norman army across the Channel and marched on London. Henry was desperate; he had almost no support and a military defeat at the hands of Robert, a good soldier, would cost him the crown. Mustering all the persuasive tact of which he was capable, Henry offered a truce and the promise of a huge indemnity. Robert had already gone through two fortunes and he foolishly agreed to Henry's terms when one battle could have made England his. With Robert gone, Henry took vengeance on his rebellious vassals and prepared to invade Normandy, his excuse being that Robert protected exiled English nobles who plotted to overthrow him. Together with the Count of Flanders and the French king, Henry attacked Normandy in 1105 from three sides, and gained an overwhelming victory, bringing baronial insurrection in the duchy to an end. Robert spent the rest of his inane life in comfortable confinement in England.

Henry, the best administrator among the Conqueror's sons, exhibited skill in constitutional and legal reform, earning himself the title of "Lion of Justice." Although he assiduously collected every farthing due him and guarded royal prerogative as carefully as his father and brother had done, he followed the letter of the law and expected his subjects to do likewise. Unlike his predecessors, he trusted his affairs to no chief minister, and perhaps partly for this reason, as well as for expediency, he insisted on greater governmental specialization and efficiency. We have already seen that the Curia Regis performed manifold tasks dealing with justice, legislation, and finance, and that certain royal officers including the chancellor, justiciar, and treasurer assumed special duties within the curia. The complexity and volume of government business had grown considerably since the Conquest and certain functions within the curia became more exacting. Henry therefore enlarged the personnel in the office of the treasurer to manage the increased royal revenue. The treasurer and his clerks facilitated the counting of money, which the sheriffs brought in twice annually, by devising a checkered cloth (or perhaps a table top painted in squares) on which were piled stacks of coins in different denominations. When the treasurer's principal assistants, the barons of the Exchequer, had determined the exact amount received, they informed the curia, which ordered the figure recorded on a long strip of parchment rolled around a pipe. Thereafter the crown's financial records were kept on the pipe rolls.

Henry made a few legal changes, the principal one being to reinstate the death penalty for certain crimes involving property, but he ordered that the law should be uniformly enforced. This proved difficult partly because the shire courts often rendered their judgments on the basis of custom, and, depending on the region of England, this might be Saxon, Danish, or Norman. Moreover, although William I and his sons followed the laws extant in the time of Edward the Confessor, they had been greatly modified by royal decrees and the creation of the feudal system, which had its own legal framework, so that some confusion arose in cases where there was no clear precedent. The shire courts permitted trial by ordeal, by oath, and by combat, and they meted out punishments such as mutilation or execution in a haphazard fashion. As the king's council, which had judicial authority, followed him around the country, and as it was difficult for a suitor to undergo the hardship of travel and expense to plead his case before the council, Henry I sent out royal commissioners who conducted the king's court at the same session at which the shire court sat. Sometimes these itinerant justices went on regular circuits through several shires. At these extraordinary sessions of the king's court law was uniformly enforced, particularly in cases which involved royal interests. As the shire court and king's court heard all major cases, the importance of the hundred and manor courts declined still further; by Henry I's death in 1135 their jurisdiction was restricted to litigation involving purely parochial matters.

A stern ruler who punished the mighty as well as the humble was perforce unpopular with the English barons who were contentious, proud, and independent men, not easily repressed or cajoled. Although they themselves often victimized their subordinates, they resented Henry I's heavy financial exactions to support the central government at the expense of baronial rights. When they rebelled, Henry suppressed them by brute force. It is no coincidence that the strongest kings were also the best soldiers.

Only two of the many children Henry I fathered were legitimate, and of these two Matilda alone survived him. No woman had ever sat on the English throne, and it was unthinkable that the feudal hierarchy, based on military service, should be headed by a woman. Henry I, naturally anxious about the succession, forced his tenants-in-chief in 1127 to take an oath promising to honor her as queen. But he should have known that heredity and an oath were insufficient guarantees. At the news of Henry's death, Stephen of Blois, his nephew and Matilda's first cousin, hurried to England, seized the royal treasure at Win-

students, whether or not they intended to become priests, took tem-
~ary vows as acolytes, lectors, exorcists, subdeacons, or deacons in the
~cess of their education. As a result, virtually every literate person
~s a clerk of some kind, and could claim "benefit of clergy," which
~titled him to trial in Church courts. There were many advantages
~ being tried in a Church court, which could impose no penalty
~rse than imprisonment or a fine for clerks, and defrocking for or-
~ned priests. Moreover, convicted clerks had the right to appeal to
~ Roman Curia. Clerks found guilty of murder got off with light
~alties whereas others convicted of an identical offense were exe-
~ted. Small wonder that Henry II resented this double standard,
~ich permitted a thief or murderer to escape a sentence that drew
~od simply because he could read a little Latin. Henry argued that a
~lty clerk should be turned over for punishment to a royal magis-
~te—the procedure followed in the shire courts before the establish-
~nt of the Church courts under William I. Becket, who had already
~noyed Henry by not allowing the archiepiscopal estates of Canter-
~ry to be taxed, stanchly resisted this innovation. He finally gave
~y, however, under pressure from Pope Alexander III, who desired
~nry's friendship. But with the Constitutions of Clarendon (1164),
~nry went farther than either the pope or Becket had expected in
~orming the jurisdiction of the ecclesiastical courts and regulating the
~hts of the clergy. The Constitutions, promulgated at a meeting held
~ Clarendon, subjected the clergy to the following rules: priests or
~rks found guilty of civil crimes in Church courts were to be sen-
~ced and punished by the king's magistrates; henceforth there would
~ no appeals to Rome from English Church courts, and priests could
~t leave England without the king's permission; he alone could ap-
~int hierarchs to vacated benefices, which reverted to the crown at
~ incumbents' deaths; and neither the pope nor an English bishop
~ld excommunicate an Englishman except by royal consent. The
~hbishop refused to accept the Constitutions and went into volun-
~y exile in France for six years.

With Becket safe from Henry's anger, which manifested itself in
~ confiscation of the lands and revenue of the see of Canterbury
~re followed six years of claims, counterclaims, and letters by th
~ iron-willed antagonists. Henry finally induced Becket's return
~70, even though he made no promise to rescind the Constitutions
~arendon or to restore the confiscated estates. As was to be expec
~ quarrel flared up anew. Becket, determined not to relinquish

chester, and won enough support from the barons to become king.

Stephen (1135–54) ushered in a period of anarchy and misgovernment. Stephen and Robert were birds of a feather, alike in piety,
affability, gentleness, and incompetence. Whatever support Stephen
originally enjoyed from the Church and his barons was a result of gifts
and privileges lavishly bestowed on them. Before long the magnates
on both sides of the Channel were building castles without royal license, enlarging their feudal armies, and sporadically pillaging neighboring fiefs without fear of reprisal or regard for the law that
Stephen's ancestors had labored so hard to enforce. Powerful earls in
Gloucester, Devon, and Norfolk besieged adjacent fortresses; the
Welsh rebelled; King David of Scotland twice invaded Northumberland and Yorkshire; and pirates lurked off the southern coast to seize
English merchantmen. Stephen reduced some rebel strongholds, particularly in the west, but he won only one unqualified victory through-
out his reign, the Battle of the Standard in 1138, which forced
Scotland to capitulate.

Two developments in 1139 transformed baronial rebellion into a
full-fledged dynastic war in which Stephen lost the valued assistance
of the Church. He had kept Henry I's chief councilors, Bishop Roger of
Salisbury, his son Roger, also a bishop, and his nephew, Bishop Nigel
of Ely, who were respectively the justiciar, chancellor, and treasurer.
They were arrogant men who took advantage of Stephen's conciliatory nature by building up tremendous power at court, arming their
castles as though they were temporal lords, and acting brusquely toward important nobles. Stephen, after a brawl in Oxford involving
Roger of Salisbury's men, stormed his and his relatives' strongholds and
manhandled the three bishops. He had every justification to do so, but
important ecclesiastics, though temporal lords as well, enjoyed immunities because of their clerical station that even the king had to respect.
The scandal angered the pope, but he would not go so far as to punish
or depose Stephen even though he had antagonized the English clergy.
Matilda and Robert, duke of Gloucester (d. 1147), an illegitimate son
of Henry I, had meanwhile returned to England to lead a civil war,
and the arrival in 1149 of Henry, Matilda's son, further complicated
the situation. Henry had a better lineal claim to the English throne
than Stephen, and he sought to make it good by commanding his mother's forces in the wars that reduced the country to desolation and
prolonged suffering. The hope Stephen had cherished that his son,
Eustace, might succeed him vanished with the latter's sudden death

in 1153, and Henry and Stephen arranged the Treaty of Wallingford, which ended the civil war, provided for the destruction of a great
many castles and the dispersal of their garrisons, and guaranteed
Henry the throne on condition that he pay Stephen homage for the
rest of his life. The heir had not long to wait; Stephen died in August,
1154, having served as an excellent example to Henry II of how not to
be king.

Theobald, archbishop of Canterbury, crowned the twenty-one-year-
old Henry II king on December 19. This square-jawed, redheaded
monarch, son of Matilda and Geoffrey of Anjou, began the line of
kings called the Angevins or Plantagenets, the latter name taken from
the sprig of a plant, known in French as the *plante-genêt,* which Geoffrey customarily wore in his helmet. Henry added England to an already extensive empire that stretched from the English Channel to
the Pyrenees and included Normandy, Anjou, Brittany, Maine, Touraine, and Aquitaine, the last of which he acquired by marrying
Eleanor, the divorced wife of Louis VII. Henry ruled his domain with
astounding vigor. For thirty-five years he was constantly on the move,
creating, destroying, and amending. His councilors and servants were
often at wits' end because he took them at a moment's notice from
one country house to another and from province to province. His restless nature and remarkable stamina sustained him in battle, in study,
and in administration. Probably no other monarch since Alfred the
Great was as well educated as Henry II, who could intelligently check
financial records with the clerks of the Exchequer and write letters
in several languages. He hated disorder and lawlessness but had an
ungovernable temper of his own, and sometimes flew into rages that
bloodied the whites of his steel-gray eyes. The short tunic he wore
to facilitate riding earned him the nickname "Curtmantle" and set a
new fashion at court. Eleanor, his wife, was also a remarkable person,
as intelligent, forthright, and energetic as Henry. Although he treated
her as basely as he did the concubines who mothered his brood of
illegitimate children, Eleanor and Henry got along for the first few
years of marriage. But she spent most of her later life plotting with
her ambitious sons against him.

Henry ruled firmly, and though not popular, his government was
so efficient and he worked so hard that his contemporaries admired
him, and not even the irresponsible reigns of the sons who succeeded
him could undo the constitutional and legal reforms he instituted.
He restored the English monarchy's authority and dignity, which had

fallen to a disgraceful low under Stephen. One afte
bellious barons surrendered their heavily fortified
castles to him. He melted the debased coins circulate
her allies and issued new silver pieces. Out of respe
father, Henry I, whom he resembled in appearance
he promulgated a charter reaffirming the laws and
promises of good government which the former ha
missed Stephen's Flemish mercenaries and most of h
appointed new ones whom he could trust. With the re
the barons behaved themselves and ordinary men coul
to the simple pleasures of labor and innocent recrea
of insurrection, hardship, and uncertainty. In this
aided by his close friend, Thomas Becket, appointed cl

Becket advanced in importance under Henry, his
panion and confidant until shortly after his appointm
of Canterbury in 1162, when, like Anselm, he becam
ful disciple and Henry's antagonist. Of Norman stoc
been a merchant and sheriff of Middlesex), Becket
mentary education in Paris and a year or so of lega
entering the service of Archbishop Theobald, who
deacon of Canterbury in 1154. Becket played a si
pressing Henry's claims to the province of Toulouse
Louis VII, and although he cared little for detail,
his duties out of friendship and loyalty to his young
nized his adviser's outstanding administrative abilities.
that, during the earlier years of his reign, Henry had
terms with Pope Adrian IV and most of the Engli
stead of offering the archiepiscopal see of Canterbur
following Theobald's death in 1162, he nominated Bec
the chapter was loath to elect a strong nationalist w
been ordained a priest. Under these circumstances, r
surprised than Henry when Becket favored the pap
specting the jurisdiction of the ecclesiastical courts in

The ecclesiastical courts of each diocese and of tl
copacies had enjoyed separate magistracy in cases cor
questions since the time of William the Conqueror.
first heard civil disputes only when they involved cler
Stephen they gradually extended their jurisdiction
clerks" in civil cases as well, that is to say, over anyor
orders. As education was then wholly in the hands of

iota of what he regarded as properly under his authority, angered Henry. Four of the latter's knights, overhearing some remark the king made about Becket, murdered the archbishop on December 29, 1170, at Canterbury Cathedral. Although Henry was not personally responsible for the "martyrdom" of Becket, canonized a saint three years later, he suffered the inevitable consequences imposed by a Christian society that would not tolerate such a heinous crime. The king did public penance at Becket's shrine, which helped to soothe his conscience and mollify public resentment, and he acquiesced in the pope's demand that criminous clerks should be tried and punished by ecclesiastical courts and could appeal sentences to Rome, but the remainder of the Constitutions of Clarendon continued in force. Henry had won a Pyrrhic victory, but the dispute with Becket tore open an old wound which neither the Church nor Henry's successors were anxious to heal.

Of all the accomplishments for which Henry II is justly renowned, none surpasses his constitutional reforms, which were inspired by the governmental changes Henry I had already wrought and which are today part of the legal system in much of Western civilization. The trouble that Henry II took to bring the clergy within the bounds of royal law should amply illustrate how passionately he wanted one legal system that would apply equally to everyone everywhere in England. William the Conqueror, as we have seen, had dispatched royal commissioners to make financial inquiries for the crown, and Henry I had appointed a few magistrates from the Curia Regis to go on circuits of several shires to preside over cases concerning royal interests. Gradually, because of their legal training or familiarity with the king's business, these royal representatives became involved in all types of litigation. Henry II, realizing that one national legal code could not be made to work by trusting its implementation solely to sheriffs, some of whom were illiterate, who often were not conversant with the law, and who could not be adequately supervised when they came to the king's court only twice annually to surrender taxes, established regular circuits traveled by royal magistrates. Beginning in 1166 with the Assize of Clarendon, and supplemented by the Assize of Northampton (1176), the magistrates were charged to hear personally cases involving forgery, murder, arson, and larceny. In addition to the eighteen circuit justices, Henry appointed five judges to sit permanently at his council to adjudicate lawsuits brought by any citizen. This court later became the Court of Common Pleas, one of the most important common-law courts.

The royal courts employed the Frankish-Norman custom of learning the truth by relying on the testimony of local residents who were impaneled under oath as a board of inquest. Itinerant justices, after all, were unfamiliar with local events and had no time to apprehend and present alleged criminals. A number of law-abiding men from the area (usually sixteen persons of the propertied class), therefore, were summoned to attend the king's court to give an account of persons suspected of having committed serious crimes. This jury of presentment, much like the grand jury that developed from it, collected facts, ascertained the probable guilt or innocence of alleged criminals, and indicted those thought to be guilty. The accused, having been presented, underwent the ordeal, usually of cold water, an ancient and primitive test that supposedly left to God the determination of guilt. Bound hand and foot, he was thrown into blessed water; if he sank, as most did, he was judged innocent because holy water would reject the sinful; but if he floated he was guilty, and he suffered appropriate punishment. In 1215 the Church put an end to this unreliable procedure by forbidding the clergy to be party to trials by ordeal, which often resulted in penalties that drew blood. Thereafter, it was customary for a petit jury of twelve men, whose decision was rendered by majority vote usually on the basis of witnesses' testimony, to determine the guilt or innocence of the accused. Although Henry II did not live to see the petit jury function, he recognized the flaws in the ordeal, which sometimes exonerated the guilty. He therefore ordered those who had passed the ordeal to leave the country within eight days on the assumption that a jury would not accuse a man of serious crime unless there was overwhelming evidence of his guilt. Moreover, those presenting jurors who concealed testimony or shielded criminals were punished.

Henry II and his successors in the thirteenth century were particularly anxious to apply the jury system in cases involving landed property, not only because it helped to clarify disputes over land better than any other means, but also because the system was a lucrative source of royal revenue. Hence jury trials came to be applied both to criminal and civil cases. Trials by jury could be had by obtaining the king's permission through one or other of several types of royal writs or assizes, the latter name being applied subsequently to the court sessions themselves. For these writs the crown charged a fee. For example, the writ of *mort d' ancestor* allowed a jury to determine exactly what property a landholder held at his death and bequeathed to his heir. Another writ, *darrein presentment*, awarded through a jury the temporary privilege of making appointments to a disputed Church living to the patron who had most recently exercised the right of presenting a candidate to the living under dispute. While many royal writs concerned cases of disputes over property, more than thirty other types entitled litigants to jury trials in other sorts of civil and criminal cases. The chancellor's office (the Chancery) eventually standardized its writs, and by the late thirteenth century trial by jury was the rule rather than the exception in the king's courts. Partly because the issuance of writs was a fruitful source of royal revenue, persons who refused a jury trial, particularly those whose guilt was so well known that the jury would surely find them culpable, were imprisoned or compelled to undergo the torture of *peine forte et dure,* in which weights were piled on the obdurate person until he either consented to a jury trial or died.

Countless verdicts by royal justices based on customary practice, and legal procedures imposed by writs, set precedents that fixed penalties for particular crimes and ordered the legal steps that defined the conduct of suits. There developed from these precedents and royal decrees, many of which went back to Saxon times, an unwritten and unsystematized body of law called the common law. The name itself indicates that Henry II's ideal of a uniform national law had been achieved. Even before his death, and some years before the constitutional changes he instituted had been fully implemented, Ranulf de Glanville (or possibly Hubert Walter) compiled a *Treatise on the Laws and Customs of England* (c. 1189), the existence of which is evidence of the keen contemporary interest in legal reform.

The fates are rarely so kind as to allow anyone, much less a king charged with the administration of the vast Angevin empire, the opportunity to concentrate on one task at a time. Henry II had to cope with Scottish, Welsh, Irish, and French affairs along with Church problems and constitutional and legal reforms. The first Plantagenet was a very busy man who could not afford to waste time in petty quarrels, and though he preferred administration to battle, he had to protect his domain against the encroachments of domestic and foreign enemies. The Scottish forces of King Malcolm were driven from the counties of Cumberland and Northumberland and Malcolm was forced to pay homage. The Welsh proved somewhat more troublesome, but they too succumbed to an English army that Henry led into the northern Welsh highlands. He also cast covetous glances toward Ireland, which Adrian

IV, the only Englishman ever to be pope, desired as a papal fief. He issued a papal bull in 1155 authorizing Henry to subjugate Ireland, but other pressing business forced the king to put off all thoughts of doing so until 1170.

The English knew practically nothing about Ireland, and had they known more, they would have cared even less. The country's Celtic and Viking inhabitants, isolated for centuries from the mainstream of western European culture, were semicivilized, fiercely independent, and contentious clansmen, some of whom had scarcely risen above a Stone Age culture. Dozens of petty chiefs and kings spent their lives in ceaseless rounds of purposeless warfare to acquire political authority that few respected and landed estates that were often not worth the trouble to conquer. The Church, originally a vibrant and progressive social and intellectual force, had fallen on evil days, and its clergy were almost as backward as their parishioners. Four principal kings ruled Ulster, Connaught, Munster, and Leinster, and vied for the high kingship of Ireland, though to achieve it meant almost nothing beyond temporary fame, the opportunity to demand tribute and, at best, tenuous authority. Clannish chiefs, averse to legal restraint, led their followers in migratory progressions over the island and warred with one another.

Henry II intervened in Ireland at the request of Dermot McMurrough, king of Leinster, whom High King Rory O'Connor had driven out in 1166. As Henry was too busy in Aquitaine to go to Ireland himself, he allowed several English and Welsh peers to help Dermot recover his throne. The Earl of Pembroke, called Strongbow, raised a thousand warriors and made for Ireland in late summer, 1170, in the hope of regaining the honor and wealth he had lost in supporting King Stephen, to please Henry whose disfavor he had incurred, and to wed Dermot's daughter and become king of Leinster if he succeeded. O'Connor's ill-equipped and unorganized army scattered before Pembroke's superior forces, and he and Dermot easily captured Dublin and Waterford. When Dermot died in 1171, Strongbow inherited his lands and title. Henry II had not expected a turn of events that would make one of his vassals the king of Ireland. Besides, Henry was anxious to quit England temporarily to escape the censure of two papal legates already on their way from Rome to investigate the murder of Becket, which had occurred a few months earlier. He therefore summoned Pembroke to Wales, forced him to surrender the captured coastal towns, and went himself to Ireland where he stayed, mostly at Dublin, from October to April, 1171–72. Although he received the homage of chester, and won enough support from the barons to become king. Stephen (1135–54) ushered in a period of anarchy and misgovernment. Stephen and Robert were birds of a feather, alike in piety, affability, gentleness, and incompetence. Whatever support Stephen originally enjoyed from the Church and his barons was a result of gifts and privileges lavishly bestowed on them. Before long the magnates on both sides of the Channel were building castles without royal license, enlarging their feudal armies, and sporadically pillaging neighboring fiefs without fear of reprisal or regard for the law that Stephen's ancestors had labored so hard to enforce. Powerful earls in Gloucester, Devon, and Norfolk besieged adjacent fortresses; the Welsh rebelled; King David of Scotland twice invaded Northumberland and Yorkshire; and pirates lurked off the southern coast to seize English merchantmen. Stephen reduced some rebel strongholds, particularly in the west, but he won only one unqualified victory throughout his reign, the Battle of the Standard in 1138, which forced Scotland to capitulate.

Two developments in 1139 transformed baronial rebellion into a full-fledged dynastic war in which Stephen lost the valued assistance of the Church. He had kept Henry I's chief councilors, Bishop Roger of Salisbury, his son Roger, also a bishop, and his nephew, Bishop Nigel of Ely, who were respectively the justiciar, chancellor, and treasurer. They were arrogant men who took advantage of Stephen's conciliatory nature by building up tremendous power at court, arming their castles as though they were temporal lords, and acting brusquely toward important nobles. Stephen, after a brawl in Oxford involving Roger of Salisbury's men, stormed his and his relatives' strongholds and manhandled the three bishops. He had every justification to do so, but important ecclesiastics, though temporal lords as well, enjoyed immunities because of their clerical station that even the king had to respect. The scandal angered the pope, but he would not go so far as to punish or depose Stephen even though he had antagonized the English clergy. Matilda and Robert, duke of Gloucester (d. 1147), an illegitimate son of Henry I, had meanwhile returned to England to lead a civil war, and the arrival in 1149 of Henry, Matilda's son, further complicated the situation. Henry had a better lineal claim to the English throne than Stephen, and he sought to make it good by commanding his mother's forces in the wars that reduced the country to desolation and prolonged suffering. The hope Stephen had cherished that his son, Eustace, might succeed him vanished with the latter's sudden death

in 1153, and Henry and Stephen arranged the Treaty of Wallingford, which ended the civil war, provided for the destruction of a great
many castles and the dispersal of their garrisons, and guaranteed
Henry the throne on condition that he pay Stephen homage for the
rest of his life. The heir had not long to wait; Stephen died in August,
1154, having served as an excellent example to Henry II of how not to
be king.

Theobald, archbishop of Canterbury, crowned the twenty-one-year-
old Henry II king on December 19. This square-jawed, redheaded
monarch, son of Matilda and Geoffrey of Anjou, began the line of
kings called the Angevins or Plantagenets, the latter name taken from
the sprig of a plant, known in French as the *plante-genêt,* which Geoffrey customarily wore in his helmet. Henry added England to an already extensive empire that stretched from the English Channel to
the Pyrenees and included Normandy, Anjou, Brittany, Maine, Touraine, and Aquitaine, the last of which he acquired by marrying
Eleanor, the divorced wife of Louis VII. Henry ruled his domain with
astounding vigor. For thirty-five years he was constantly on the move,
creating, destroying, and amending. His councilors and servants were
often at wits' end because he took them at a moment's notice from
one country house to another and from province to province. His restless nature and remarkable stamina sustained him in battle, in study,
and in administration. Probably no other monarch since Alfred the
Great was as well educated as Henry II, who could intelligently check
financial records with the clerks of the Exchequer and write letters
in several languages. He hated disorder and lawlessness but had an
ungovernable temper of his own, and sometimes flew into rages that
bloodied the whites of his steel-gray eyes. The short tunic he wore
to facilitate riding earned him the nickname "Curtmantle" and set a
new fashion at court. Eleanor, his wife, was also a remarkable person,
as intelligent, forthright, and energetic as Henry. Although he treated
her as basely as he did the concubines who mothered his brood of
illegitimate children, Eleanor and Henry got along for the first few
years of marriage. But she spent most of her later life plotting with
her ambitious sons against him.

Henry ruled firmly, and though not popular, his government was
so efficient and he worked so hard that his contemporaries admired
him, and not even the irresponsible reigns of the sons who succeeded
him could undo the constitutional and legal reforms he instituted.
He restored the English monarchy's authority and dignity, which had

fallen to a disgraceful low under Stephen. One after another the rebellious barons surrendered their heavily fortified and garrisoned
castles to him. He melted the debased coins circulated by Matilda and
her allies and issued new silver pieces. Out of respect for his grandfather, Henry I, whom he resembled in appearance and personality,
he promulgated a charter reaffirming the laws and guaranteeing the
promises of good government which the former had made. He dismissed Stephen's Flemish mercenaries and most of his councilors, and
appointed new ones whom he could trust. With the restoration of order,
the barons behaved themselves and ordinary men could once more turn
to the simple pleasures of labor and innocent recreation without fear
of insurrection, hardship, and uncertainty. In this work Henry was
aided by his close friend, Thomas Becket, appointed chancellor in 1155.

Becket advanced in importance under Henry, his inseparable companion and confidant until shortly after his appointment as archbishop
of Canterbury in 1162, when, like Anselm, he became the pope's dutiful disciple and Henry's antagonist. Of Norman stock (his father had
been a merchant and sheriff of Middlesex), Becket had only a rudimentary education in Paris and a year or so of legal training before
entering the service of Archbishop Theobald, who made him arch-
deacon of Canterbury in 1154. Becket played a significant role in
pressing Henry's claims to the province of Toulouse in 1159 against
Louis VII, and although he cared little for detail, doggedly pursued
his duties out of friendship and loyalty to his young king, who recognized his adviser's outstanding administrative abilities. Despite the fact
that, during the earlier years of his reign, Henry had been on cordial
terms with Pope Adrian IV and most of the English hierarchs, instead of offering the archiepiscopal see of Canterbury to one of them
following Theobald's death in 1162, he nominated Becket, even though
the chapter was loath to elect a strong nationalist who had not even
been ordained a priest. Under these circumstances, no one was more
surprised than Henry when Becket favored the papacy's position respecting the jurisdiction of the ecclesiastical courts in England.

The ecclesiastical courts of each diocese and of the two archiepis-
copacies had enjoyed separate magistracy in cases concerning religious
questions since the time of William the Conqueror. These courts at
first heard civil disputes only when they involved clergymen, but under
Stephen they gradually extended their jurisdiction over "criminous
clerks" in civil cases as well, that is to say, over anyone holding minor
orders. As education was then wholly in the hands of the clergy, nearly

all students, whether or not they intended to become priests, took temporary vows as acolytes, lectors, exorcists, subdeacons, or deacons in the process of their education. As a result, virtually every literate person was a clerk of some kind, and could claim "benefit of clergy," which entitled him to trial in Church courts. There were many advantages to being tried in a Church court, which could impose no penalty worse than imprisonment or a fine for clerks, and defrocking for ordained priests. Moreover, convicted clerks had the right to appeal to the Roman Curia. Clerks found guilty of murder got off with light penalties whereas others convicted of an identical offense were executed. Small wonder that Henry II resented this double standard, which permitted a thief or murderer to escape a sentence that drew blood simply because he could read a little Latin. Henry argued that a guilty clerk should be turned over for punishment to a royal magistrate—the procedure followed in the shire courts before the establishment of the Church courts under William I. Becket, who had already annoyed Henry by not allowing the archiepiscopal estates of Canterbury to be taxed, stanchly resisted this innovation. He finally gave way, however, under pressure from Pope Alexander III, who desired Henry's friendship. But with the Constitutions of Clarendon (1164), Henry went farther than either the pope or Becket had expected in reforming the jurisdiction of the ecclesiastical courts and regulating the rights of the clergy. The Constitutions, promulgated at a meeting held at Clarendon, subjected the clergy to the following rules: priests or clerks found guilty of civil crimes in Church courts were to be sentenced and punished by the king's magistrates; henceforth there would be no appeals to Rome from English Church courts, and priests could not leave England without the king's permission; he alone could appoint hierarchs to vacated benefices, which reverted to the crown at the incumbents' deaths; and neither the pope nor an English bishop could excommunicate an Englishman except by royal consent. The archbishop refused to accept the Constitutions and went into voluntary exile in France for six years.

With Becket safe from Henry's anger, which manifested itself in the confiscation of the lands and revenue of the see of Canterbury, there followed six years of claims, counterclaims, and letters by the two iron-willed antagonists. Henry finally induced Becket's return in 1170, even though he made no promise to rescind the Constitutions of Clarendon or to restore the confiscated estates. As was to be expected, the quarrel flared up anew. Becket, determined not to relinquish an iota of what he regarded as properly under his authority, angered Henry. Four of the latter's knights, overhearing some remark the king made about Becket, murdered the archbishop on December 29, 1170, at Canterbury Cathedral. Although Henry was not personally responsible for the "martyrdom" of Becket, canonized a saint three years later, he suffered the inevitable consequences imposed by a Christian society that would not tolerate such a heinous crime. The king did public penance at Becket's shrine, which helped to soothe his conscience and mollify public resentment, and he acquiesced in the pope's demand that criminous clerks should be tried and punished by ecclesiastical courts and could appeal sentences to Rome, but the remainder of the Constitutions of Clarendon continued in force. Henry had won a Pyrrhic victory, but the dispute with Becket tore open an old wound which neither the Church nor Henry's successors were anxious to heal.

Of all the accomplishments for which Henry II is justly renowned, none surpasses his constitutional reforms, which were inspired by the governmental changes Henry I had already wrought and which are today part of the legal system in much of Western civilization. The trouble that Henry II took to bring the clergy within the bounds of royal law should amply illustrate how passionately he wanted one legal system that would apply equally to everyone everywhere in England. William the Conqueror, as we have seen, had dispatched royal commissioners to make financial inquiries for the crown, and Henry I had appointed a few magistrates from the Curia Regis to go on circuits of several shires to preside over cases concerning royal interests. Gradually, because of their legal training or familiarity with the king's business, these royal representatives became involved in all types of litigation. Henry II, realizing that one national legal code could not be made to work by trusting its implementation solely to sheriffs, some of whom were illiterate, who often were not conversant with the law, and who could not be adequately supervised when they came to the king's court only twice annually to surrender taxes, established regular circuits traveled by royal magistrates. Beginning in 1166 with the Assize of Clarendon, and supplemented by the Assize of Northampton (1176), the magistrates were charged to hear personally cases involving forgery, murder, arson, and larceny. In addition to the eighteen circuit justices, Henry appointed five judges to sit permanently at his council to adjudicate lawsuits brought by any citizen. This court later became the Court of Common Pleas, one of the most important common-law courts.

The royal courts employed the Frankish-Norman custom of learning the truth by relying on the testimony of local residents who were impaneled under oath as a board of inquest. Itinerant justices, after all, were unfamiliar with local events and had no time to apprehend and present alleged criminals. A number of law-abiding men from the area (usually sixteen persons of the propertied class), therefore, were summoned to attend the king's court to give an account of persons suspected of having committed serious crimes. This jury of presentment, much like the grand jury that developed from it, collected facts, ascertained the probable guilt or innocence of alleged criminals, and indicted those thought to be guilty. The accused, having been presented, underwent the ordeal, usually of cold water, an ancient and primitive test that supposedly left to God the determination of guilt. Bound hand and foot, he was thrown into blessed water; if he sank, as most did, he was judged innocent because holy water would reject the sinful; but if he floated he was guilty, and he suffered appropriate punishment. In 1215 the Church put an end to this unreliable procedure by forbidding the clergy to be party to trials by ordeal, which often resulted in penalties that drew blood. Thereafter, it was customary for a petit jury of twelve men, whose decision was rendered by majority vote usually on the basis of witnesses' testimony, to determine the guilt or innocence of the accused. Although Henry II did not live to see the petit jury function, he recognized the flaws in the ordeal, which sometimes exonerated the guilty. He therefore ordered those who had passed the ordeal to leave the country within eight days on the assumption that a jury would not accuse a man of serious crime unless there was overwhelming evidence of his guilt. Moreover, those presenting jurors who concealed testimony or shielded criminals were punished.

Henry II and his successors in the thirteenth century were particularly anxious to apply the jury system in cases involving landed property, not only because it helped to clarify disputes over land better than any other means, but also because the system was a lucrative source of royal revenue. Hence jury trials came to be applied both to criminal and civil cases. Trials by jury could be had by obtaining the king's permission through one or other of several types of royal writs or assizes, the latter name being applied subsequently to the court sessions themselves. For these writs the crown charged a fee. For example, the writ of *mort d' ancestor* allowed a jury to determine exactly what property a landholder held at his death and bequeathed to his heir. Another writ, *darrein presentment*, awarded through a jury the temporary privilege of making appointments to a disputed Church living to the patron who had most recently exercised the right of presenting a candidate to the living under dispute. While many royal writs concerned cases of disputes over property, more than thirty other types entitled litigants to jury trials in other sorts of civil and criminal cases. The chancellor's office (the Chancery) eventually standardized its writs, and by the late thirteenth century trial by jury was the rule rather than the exception in the king's courts. Partly because the issuance of writs was a fruitful source of royal revenue, persons who refused a jury trial, particularly those whose guilt was so well known that the jury would surely find them culpable, were imprisoned or compelled to undergo the torture of *peine forte et dure,* in which weights were piled on the obdurate person until he either consented to a jury trial or died.

Countless verdicts by royal justices based on customary practice, and legal procedures imposed by writs, set precedents that fixed penalties for particular crimes and ordered the legal steps that defined the conduct of suits. There developed from these precedents and royal decrees, many of which went back to Saxon times, an unwritten and unsystematized body of law called the common law. The name itself indicates that Henry II's ideal of a uniform national law had been achieved. Even before his death, and some years before the constitutional changes he instituted had been fully implemented, Ranulf de Glanville (or possibly Hubert Walter) compiled a *Treatise on the Laws and Customs of England* (c. 1189), the existence of which is evidence of the keen contemporary interest in legal reform.

The fates are rarely so kind as to allow anyone, much less a king charged with the administration of the vast Angevin empire, the opportunity to concentrate on one task at a time. Henry II had to cope with Scottish, Welsh, Irish, and French affairs along with Church problems and constitutional and legal reforms. The first Plantagenet was a very busy man who could not afford to waste time in petty quarrels, and though he preferred administration to battle, he had to protect his domain against the encroachments of domestic and foreign enemies. The Scottish forces of King Malcolm were driven from the counties of Cumberland and Northumberland and Malcolm was forced to pay homage. The Welsh proved somewhat more troublesome, but they too succumbed to an English army that Henry led into the northern Welsh highlands. He also cast covetous glances toward Ireland, which Adrian

IV, the only Englishman ever to be pope, desired as a papal fief. He issued a papal bull in 1155 authorizing Henry to subjugate Ireland, but other pressing business forced the king to put off all thoughts of doing so until 1170.

The English knew practically nothing about Ireland, and had they known more, they would have cared even less. The country's Celtic and Viking inhabitants, isolated for centuries from the mainstream of western European culture, were semicivilized, fiercely independent, and contentious clansmen, some of whom had scarcely risen above a Stone Age culture. Dozens of petty chiefs and kings spent their lives in ceaseless rounds of purposeless warfare to acquire political authority that few respected and landed estates that were often not worth the trouble to conquer. The Church, originally a vibrant and progressive social and intellectual force, had fallen on evil days, and its clergy were almost as backward as their parishioners. Four principal kings ruled Ulster, Connaught, Munster, and Leinster, and vied for the high kingship of Ireland, though to achieve it meant almost nothing beyond temporary fame, the opportunity to demand tribute and, at best, tenuous authority. Clannish chiefs, averse to legal restraint, led their followers in migratory progressions over the island and warred with one another.

Henry II intervened in Ireland at the request of Dermot McMurrough, king of Leinster, whom High King Rory O'Connor had driven out in 1166. As Henry was too busy in Aquitaine to go to Ireland himself, he allowed several English and Welsh peers to help Dermot recover his throne. The Earl of Pembroke, called Strongbow, raised a thousand warriors and made for Ireland in late summer, 1170, in the hope of regaining the honor and wealth he had lost in supporting King Stephen, to please Henry whose disfavor he had incurred, and to wed Dermot's daughter and become king of Leinster if he succeeded. O'Connor's ill-equipped and unorganized army scattered before Pembroke's superior forces, and he and Dermot easily captured Dublin and Waterford. When Dermot died in 1171, Strongbow inherited his lands and title. Henry II had not expected a turn of events that would make one of his vassals the king of Ireland. Besides, Henry was anxious to quit England temporarily to escape the censure of two papal legates already on their way from Rome to investigate the murder of Becket, which had occurred a few months earlier. He therefore summoned Pembroke to Wales, forced him to surrender the captured coastal towns, and went himself to Ireland where he stayed, mostly at Dublin, from October to April, 1171–72. Although he received the homage of numerous Irish clerical and secular vassals and began a governmental reform, he left before completing it or conquering the country that lay behind the coastal towns. However he did "plant" a colony of Bristol merchants in Dublin, a policy that several English monarchs followed until the middle of the seventeenth century in order to control the Pale, an area subject to English law. The justiciar, Hugh de Lacy, whom Henry left to govern it, could hardly maintain order, and before long effective English sovereignty virtually collapsed. The last of Henry's expeditions to Ireland, undertaken by his son, John, in 1185, failed miserably. Save for the introduction of Norman feudalism in a small part of Ireland, the Henrician dominion there achieved no lasting results.

The efforts of the Capetian kings Louis VII (1137-80) and Philip Augustus (1180-1223) to consolidate their monarchical authority and enlarge their territory at the expense of the Angevin empire caused Henry II a great deal of trouble. Moreover, the rebellious alliances between Henry's sons, anarchistic barons, and the French crown kept him away from England for several years at a time. He cared little for his family, but took the trouble to make advantageous marriages for his daughters and to bestow huge portions of his empire on his treacherous sons in order to strengthen England's position on the Continent. The daughters, Eleanor, Matilda, and Joan, married the king of Castile, the king of Sicily, and the Duke of Bavaria respectively, thereby allying these states with England against France. As for his sons, Richard received Aquitaine, Henry was crowned king of England in 1170 (his authority to become effective at his father's death), and John eventually got Ireland; Geoffrey inherited the duchy of Brittany by marrying the duke's daughter. Henry's sons ought to have appreciated his beneficence, but none of them was willing to await his death in order to acquire full control over the territories that he asked them to govern under his will and in his name. Louis VII naturally took advantage of their ambition to sow the seeds of family quarrels by which he hoped to divide and someday rule their father's Continental possessions.

Louis VII and Eleanor of Aquitaine inspired and assisted her sons, Henry, Geoffrey, and Richard, in the rebellion of 1173-74, which erupted against Henry II on both sides of the Channel. Louis urged young Henry, already twice crowned English king (the second time in 1172), to depose his father, and with the help of his two brothers and a number of Angevin barons, who chafed under Henry's control, insurrections broke out in England, Normandy, and Poitou. Simultaneously the Scots and an army led by Earl Robert of Leicester invaded in the north and southeast. Henry II could hardly have suppressed such widespread rebellion without the support of the Church and his principal vassals, who remained loyal, and the fact that the opposition was utterly disorganized. He darted back and forth across the Channel and from province to province at the head of armies that besieged rebel strongholds and ravaged their dependencies. When one after another of the castles fell, the rest simply surrendered and even Louis VII quit the war. Henry had sustained his authority, his sons had failed miserably to unseat him, and Eleanor, captured while trying to escape to France, was kept in confinement for the next fifteen years. Henry had every reason to punish his brood of vipers and deprive them of their possessions, but he wisely pardoned them in order to discourage further rebellion.

In these wars against his sons and the French, Henry employed foreign mercenaries. He paid them with money raised by a tax called scutage (shield money), which he first imposed on his vassals in 1159. He accepted scutage (originally set at two marks, a mark being 13s. 4d.) in lieu of the feudal obligation of military service. Henry also promulgated the Assize of Arms, which restored the old Anglo-Saxon militia. An army composed of militia and mercenaries freed him from the baronial levies on whom earlier monarchs had depended for support. These two measures strengthened the monarchy by releasing it from the necessity of making bargains with grasping barons who sought to undermine royal authority.

Philip Augustus, a shrewder diplomat and a more unscrupulous aggrandizer than his father, Louis VII, continued the policy of fostering family disloyalty among the Plantagenets. Prince Henry and Richard quarreled over Anjou and Normandy in 1181 and Henry II reluctantly threw his troops against Richard's in Aquitaine in 1183 because he, Richard, would not pay homage to his older brother, Henry. Geoffrey and Richard deepened the rift within the family by joining against their father in the same year. Meanwhile Prince Henry died, but Richard, on whom Henry II then wanted to bestow the English crown, would not surrender Aquitaine to John in exchange for England. When Geoffrey and John failed to vanquish Richard in 1184 on the battlefields of Poitou, the old king gave in and consigned Ireland to John, but the Irish drove him out in 1185. Finally, in 1186, Philip Augustus, acting on the flimsy pretext that Henry had unnecessarily delayed the promised marriage of Philip's sister, Alais, to Richard (who repeatedly refused to marry her), and that the English king would not settle amicably several minor disputes over the Normandy border, plotted with Richard to depose Henry II. Richard swore fealty to Philip and the two harassed the old king's army at Le Mans, driving him back to Chinon, where he died on July 6, 1189, bitterly denouncing his sons and his miserable fate.

The succeeding reign of Richard I, Coeur de Lion (1189–99), need not detain us long. He spent most of it in Europe and the Holy Land fighting Philip Augustus, and leading the Third Crusade. The principal events of Richard's life have only a passing relevance to English history, though the fact that he stayed in England for only five months of his ten-year reign should lead one to the correct conclusion that the country suffered in consequence of his prolonged absence. A tall, gangling man with reddish-blond hair and pompous bearing, Richard lacked compassion and practical wisdom, but he repeatedly proved his boundless courage on the battlefield and his chivalric honesty. Contemporary accounts uniformly praise his reliability, for he never gave a promise, it was said, that he did not keep. He had a passion for music and poetry, as had many Provençals of the twelfth century— admittedly unusual tastes for a ruthless militarist. He thought little about and cared less for public welfare, and his English subjects were unimportant to him save as a source of men and money with which to carry on his campaigns. Accordingly, he continued to collect Henry's tax on movable property (at the rate of a penny in the pound) and the so-called Saladin Tithe, first imposed in 1166 and 1188 respectively, to support Angevin crusaders.

Richard left England for Normandy in December, 1189, on the first leg of a two-year journey by way of Marseilles, Sicily, and Cyprus to Palestine where, with Philip Augustus and other princes, he hoped to recapture the kingdom of Jerusalem, which had fallen to the Turks in 1187 after nearly a century under Christian control. Repeated delays lengthened his pilgrimage: he could not secure naval transportation at Marseilles; a revolution by Tancred (crowned king of Sicily in 1190) against his aunt, Constance, the widowed duchess of Sicily, forced Richard to besiege Messina and restore order; and he spent part of the spring of 1191 overthrowing the tyrannical government of the Greek, Isaac Comnenus, in Cyprus. Richard finally arrived before the walls of Acre in June, 1191, and under his command the crusaders forced the city to surrender within a month. But try as he

might, he could not take Jerusalem from Saladin, one of the mighti-
est soldiers of world history. Eventually, in the fall of 1192, the two
warriors, who admired each other and exchanged medicines when they
were ill, concluded a truce whereby Jerusalem would remain under
Saracen control, but pilgrims would be admitted to the holy places
associated with Christ. Meanwhile, Philip, pleading ill health, left for
France where he conspired unceasingly to undermine the Angevins.
John, Richard's only surviving brother, proved no less scheming. He
overthrew the regency of Bishop William Longchamp of Ely, an able
but brutal and mercenary administrator whom the English barons drove
into exile in 1191. Richard left Palestine in October, 1192, and made
his way to the Istrian coast, and from there to Vienna, hoping to reach
England by a circuitous route around France. But Duke Leopold of
Austria, with whom he had quarreled in the Holy Land, took him prisoner and turned him over to Emperor Henry VI, who demanded a
huge ransom as the price of his freedom. Philip and John tried
their best to dissuade Hubert Walter, justiciar in England, from
paying it, but he did so nevertheless. Henry VI released Richard in
February, 1194. Meanwhile, John, anxious to secure French help in
making good his claim to the English throne, surrendered Normandy
and Touraine to Philip.

Richard returned to England for only two months, during which
time he set the kingdom on the straight and narrow road of legality
and punished the barons who had helped John. He then hurried to
Normandy to deal with Philip Augustus. Richard never returned to
England. He left it under the regency of Hubert Walter, a half-
educated but skillful financier whom Richard also made archbishop
of Canterbury even though he had not a single virtue to commend
him for the post. Richard knew, however, that he could count on Walter
to follow directions and raise huge sums by taxation from the already
victimized merchants and landowners. Walter exhausted his imagination in contriving new ways to mulct money from the outraged citizenry: he struck a new royal seal and repudiated grants issued under
the old one; he collected scutage from knights who refused to serve
abroad; he taxed arable land at the rate of five shillings for each plow;
and he sold state and ecclesiastical offices for outrageous sums. The
chapter monks of Canterbury, angry at these excesses, induced Pope
Innocent III to force Walter out of the regency, though he managed to
keep the archbishopric. Richard meanwhile spent five futile years fighting Philip. Hearing about an alleged fortune in gold discovered by a

farmer near Chalus in Limousin, he besieged the fortress. During the battle he was wounded by an arrow and, with characteristic stubbornness, refused to have it tended, with the result that he died of gangrene on April 6, 1199.

Richard's unexpected death left the succession to the vast Angevin empire temporarily uncertain. Feudal custom and the rule of primogeniture dictated that the new sovereign should be Arthur, Richard's nephew, but most Anglo-Norman barons, including Archbishop Walter, favored John, whom Richard himself had designated his heir. With the support of Philip Augustus, to whom John gave part of Normandy, he succeeded in gaining the throne, and Arthur retired to the French court. Philip eased Anglo-French rivalry by accepting Arthur's homage for Anjou and Maine, and Eleanor's for Aquitaine, but this cozy arrangement had no chance of permanence. Philip watched and waited for the opportunity to renew his aggression against the Angevins. For four years following the disruption of the truce of 1202, Philip and John fought a series of wars north of the Loire River that resulted in the French conquest of all England's Continental territories except Poitou and Gascony.

John had broken the truce and invited Philip's censure by indiscreetly putting aside his wife after ten years of marriage to wed a twelve-year-old girl already betrothed to one of Philip's Poitevin vassals, Hugh the Brown. Betrothal in those days was as sacred a contract as marriage itself, so that John committed a serious breach of feudal law, despite the fact that the annulment of his first marriage was canonically legal on grounds of consanguinity. The furious Hugh quite properly appealed for redress of his grievance to his suzerain, Philip, who summoned John to appear before a Parisian court to answer the charge. John's refusal left Philip no recourse but to declare him contumacious and his fiefs forfeit to Philip, who no doubt welcomed the chance to clothe his sinister plans in the cloak of moral righteousness.

The war went badly for John, who did almost nothing effectively to oppose Philip. In addition, he became involved in a scandal in connection with the mysterious murder of young Arthur. Normandy, the most brilliant jewel in the Angevin crown, fell to Philip in 1204; Maine, Anjou, and Touraine succumbed to Capetian armies in 1205 and 1206; and Aquitaine fell under French control. But the irony of John's ignominious defeat is that the loss of most of his Continental possessions indirectly advanced English national feeling. The Angevin barons not only enjoyed relief from the heavy taxes that several monarchs had imposed to support Continental wars, but they were also forced to decide whether they would henceforth honor the French or English king as their feudal lord. The growth of English nationalism, which has justifiably been described as one of the results of the Hundred Years' War (1337–1453), therefore actually began as early as the reign of King John.

John suffered as crushing a defeat at the hands of the Church over the disputed election of a new archbishop of Canterbury in 1205 as he did in the French wars. Custom dictated that the cathedral chapter at Canterbury should elect the primate of the Church in England, but the king commonly suggested an appropriate candidate. John induced a majority of the canons at Christchurch Cathedral to elect his friend John de Gray, bishop of Norwich, only to learn later that a small group of younger monks had already secretly elected another candidate and had sent him with a delegation to Rome to secure the pallium from Innocent III. This brilliant lawyer-politician and theologian who had mounted Peter's throne at the age of thirty-seven and who, like Gregory VII, espoused the widest claims of papal supremacy, grasped the opportunity to depose both claimants in favor of Stephen Langton, an English cardinal of great learning and sterling character whom he could trust to protect papal interests. John was furious, and his refusal to allow Langton to re-enter England resulted in an interdict being laid upon the whole country. The papacy frequently used this means to induce conformity by important persons who could easily override lesser penalties. An interdict, which suspended the administration of certain sacraments, forbade burial in consecrated ground, permitted marriages only outside churches, and silenced the bells, naturally aroused the fear and anger of Christians, who brought tremendous pressure to bear upon John to conform for the sake of their souls. John responded, with expected contumacy, by confiscating the episcopal estates of the English hierarchy and the incomes of all clergymen in excess of the amount they needed to sustain themselves. Innocent promptly excommunicated him, which meant that he was denied the sacraments, that he was deposed as king in the eyes of the Church (and therefore of all Christians), and that his subjects no longer owed him obedience. Had he had the sympathy and support of his countrymen, the excommunication would have been virtually meaningless, but his rapacious and selfish disregard for their welfare and his shameful defeat by Philip had left him without public support. Under the circumstances, John realized that he had either to give in to the pope or to face immediate rebellion at home. He therefore approved Langton's election, knelt before a papal legate in homage for England and Ireland, which became papal fiefs, and promised to pay Innocent and his successors a large annual subsidy. Innocent consequently lifted the interdict in 1214, but John's sudden humility could not undo overnight the misdeeds of a lifetime. Some recent historians have attempted to whiten his character, and to some degree this is justifiable, but his contemporaries knew what sort of man he was and rebelled against him.

John's transgressions were numerous. Although they were probably no worse than those of some of his predecessors, he had a disgusting way of flaunting them before his subjects. Suffice it to say that his victimization of churchmen, barons, merchants, and burghers in matters of finance, law, and personal rights provoked the rebellion that plagued him from 1213 until his death in 1216, and resulted in the greatly misunderstood document called the Magna Carta. The barons had long held that they had certain rights under the feudal contract beginning in the time of William I (although, along with William II and Henry I, he frequently violated them). Accordingly, in 1100, they extracted from Henry I the famous Charter of Liberties, in which he promised, probably with tongue-in-cheek, to abjure absolutism to the advantage of justice and legality, to permit the barons to fight private wars, not to tax them excessively, and to accept their advice in all important matters of state. The barons expected Henry I and his successors to keep these promises, but few of them did, one reason why barons and monarchs had so often resorted to arms.

Consequently, when King John likewise repeatedly violated what the barons believed were their traditional rights, they revolted. The revolt germinated at a meeting in St. Albans, where they decided to demand the restoration of good, just, and legal government through the abatement of their grievances and John's confirmation of Henry I's Charter of Liberties. At subsequent meetings, the barons strengthened their resolve against John and furthered their plans to gather an army with which to force him to honor their demands. The most important of these sessions took place at Bury St. Edmund's, where the conspirators swore to make war on John unless he granted a new charter. He hedged, asking for time to consider the demands, despite the fact that he had just returned from France, smarting from defeat. On his refusal to entertain baronial demands made at Northampton in 1215, the barons decided to resort to force. Their army marched on London, which welcomed them with open arms, a sure sign to John that he would have to come to terms.

John met a small group of barons, clergymen, and merchants led by Robert FitzWalter in June 1215 in a meadow called Runnymede on the south bank of the Thames about twenty miles southwest of London. He faced a difficult situation, not only because the barons meant to have their way, by force if necessary, but also because he could not bargain from a position of strength based on good government and success in war. But it is wrong to surmise that he was a cowering slave to blameless barons who represented even the majority of their feudal equals, much less of Englishmen in general. The Magna Carta (the Great Charter), so named to distinguish it from a contemporary forest charter, and its subsequent confirmation more than thirty times, was neither the first document of human liberty in English history nor the source of constitutional monarchy. It was a feudal document involving the temporary redress of monarchic abuses against barons, clergymen, merchants, freemen, and others. It says not one word about the mass of Englishmen. Contemporaries themselves did not take the document too seriously, for some barons left Runnymede before John had sealed it, and both he and the barons repeatedly violated its clauses. The Charter was also frequently amended.

Sixty-three clauses of the document defined and clarified such questions as the rights of tenants-in-chief and widows, marriage and wardship, property, the privileges of the clergy, legal procedure in the king's courts, the liberties of towns and mercantile enterprise, forest laws, and so forth. Three clauses must be singled out here because of their implications in later English legal and constitutional history. Clause 39 stated that no freeman should be arrested, imprisoned, deprived of property, or outlawed without due process of law and according to the judgment of his peers (equals). Members of Parliament, common-law lawyers, and scholars until quite recently had argued that in this clause was rooted the right of trial by jury and freedom from arbitrary arrest through habeas corpus, but they were wrong, for neither John nor the barons had anything of the sort in mind in 1215. Indeed, the right of habeas corpus (which required that one accused of a crime had either to be formally charged with it or be released from prison) was not defined as law until 1679, and for some years afterward was not widely employed. Clause 61 established a committee of twenty-five barons, who were to see that the Charter was honored by hearing complaints of its violation by the king or his advisers and agents. If the king did not remedy such transgressions within forty days of their being reported, the barons could confiscate his castles and estates. He thereby technically became subject to baronial supervision in the execution of his duties. Inasmuch as neither John nor his successors intended to reign without actually governing personally, this clause proved unworkable, for, since it legalized insurrection against the king, it subverted the preservation of law and order, the very things that the Magna Carta was partly intended to secure. Moreover, although it is understandable that the barons, who had often been the victims of the king's broken promises, wished to ensure that his honesty should be guaranteed by more than the royal word alone, there was no guarantee, considering the past behavior of many barons, that a supervisory body of their number would rule justly and legally. Indeed, as the following pages will show, their own transgressions against the law of the land and the national interest were often more serious than the king's. Clause 12 prohibited the king from collecting feudal monetary dues above a certain sum, except for three specific "aids," without the consent of the great council. Parliamentary apologists later erroneously cited this provision to challenge the crown's right to levy any tax without the consent of Parliament.

John spent the last year of his reign trying to extricate himself from the obligations imposed by the Charter and fighting Philip Augustus of France. John's mercenaries ravaged baronial estates with such ferocity that the English magnates appealed in desperation to England's archenemy, Philip, to send his son, Louis, to help them. Louis led an army of 1200 knights across the Channel, landed at Stonor, and marched virtually unopposed to London, taking Canterbury and Rochester on the way. When he took Winchester in June, the French knights and English barons controlled most of the south and southeast, although John recovered much ground during July and early August because his English enemies began to have second thoughts about supporting a foreign army on English soil. On October 19, 1216, in the midst of this turmoil, John suddenly died, leaving the throne to Henry III, his nine-year-old son.

3

The Later Angevins, 1216–1399

Henry III began a reign of fifty-six years in 1216. He has been accused of incompetence, of being a spineless dilettante, of overtaxing his subjects, of breaking promises, of servility to the Church, and of nepotism. To some degree, he was guilty of all these charges, but he was not the blackhearted man that his enemies made him out to be. Henry appreciated and bountifully subsidized the visual arts, especially Gothic cathedrals. He was gentle, kind, and peaceful at a time when many brutal barons wasted their lives in petty feuds and futile wars. He encouraged the work of the recently founded orders of friars, the Franciscans and Dominicans, who aided the downtrodden and taught in the new universities at Oxford and Cambridge, and he lived a wholesome married life with Eleanor of Provence and reared Prince Edward, who became one of England's greatest kings. With all his faults, Henry glimpsed the dignity of monarchy and, largely because of his influence, Englishmen took giant cultural strides during his reign.

King John entrusted Henry III and the country to three guardians. William Marshal, though over eighty, headed the regency, which also included Justiciar Hubert de Burgh and Bishop Peter des Roches of Winchester, tutor to the king. Marshal and de Burgh accomplished much in a short time. They reconfirmed the Charter and promised that Henry would honor it when he came of age in 1227. This concession to the opposition barons, then supporting Prince Louis's mercenaries in occupation of southern England, weakened the French drive to control the country. Marshal also captured the rebel stronghold at Lincoln while de Burgh defeated the French in a naval engagement off Dover. These defeats forced Louis to sue for peace at

Kingston (1217); he agreed to withdraw from England on receipt of an indemnity and the promise of pardons for his English allies.

Marshal's death in 1219 resulted in a new power structure at court consisting of de Burgh, des Roches, and Pandulf, the papal legate whom Marshal designated as the king's guardian. But Pandulf acted high-handedly with des Roches and the others, and relations were strained until his resignation as legate in 1221. De Burgh replaced Pandulf (d. 1226) as the strongest regent in the government until 1232 despite the rivalry of des Roches, whom Henry favored. Thereafter Henry purposely filled the Curia Regis with second-raters.

The barons, whom Marshal had cleverly mollified, resented the policies of de Burgh and des Roches. De Burgh dismissed many of them from lucrative local offices, forced them to relinquish command of royalist strongholds, and efficiently suppressed baronial feuds and insurrections. Several revolts, the most important of which were led by Richard Marshal and Archbishop Edmund Rich of Canterbury, weakened the crown's authority. The barons also disliked des Roches because he filled state and Church posts with friends and relatives from France. Opposition to Henry III therefore stemmed originally from the failure of his regents to keep the promises made in the confirmation of the Great Charter and from the nationalistic opposition to foreigners.

The dismissal of de Burgh and des Roches did not stop the agitation. One source of discontent stemmed from the marriage of Henry and Eleanor in 1236. Provençals and Savoyards followed her to England to grab the rich posts vacated by des Roches's friends. The barons particularly hated Eleanor's four uncles, who regarded their lucrative English sinecures as steppingstones to greater wealth and power. Henry, weak-willed, malleable, and disarmingly accommodating, fell under their influence to such an extent that England became virtually a French dependency for ten years. This coterie of opportunists, who drained the financial resources of the crown, was followed in 1246 by the four sons and their friends of the second marriage of Isabelle of Angoulême, Henry III's mother, to Hugh de Lusignan. Administrative pressure exerted by the French king upon his Poitevin vassals induced some of them to seek their fortunes under the protection of their English half-brother, who lavished titles, high offices, and grants of royal land on them despite heavy expenses incurred during his wars in Brittany, imprudent gifts to finance the building of cathedrals, and heavy papal taxes.

Henry III paid dearly for the dubious privilege of being the pope's vassal. A succession of papal legates collected revenue in England for the Holy See more thoroughly than the most adroit sheriff did for the king. Gregory IX levied the first successful tax on the English clergy in order to support the war between the Papal States and the kingdom of Sicily ruled by the Hohenstaufen Emperor Frederick II. Henry not only allowed the papal tax to be collected, he also permitted Gregory to appoint three hundred Italians to English ecclesiastical benefices that many of them neither administered nor even visited. Their revenue went to the pope. Papal taxes and clerical interference in government increased during the residence in England of the legate Cardinal Otho (1237–41), who collected a fifth of the Church's annual income.

Henry's wanton disregard for the welfare of the English Church in the face of strong English opposition to foreign dominance led to rebellion. Spontaneous riots in the 1230s against alien clergymen, French as well as Italian, culminated in a personal attack upon Otho, who barely escaped the murderous designs of Oxford students by hiding in a tall church tower. Two English hierarchs, Archbishop Rich and Bishop Robert Grosseteste of Lincoln, tried to dissuade Henry and his advisers from continuing the payment of excessive papal taxes. The saintly primate once threatened the king with excommunication, which brought him temporarily to his senses, but Rich eventually retired to the Continent to escape the vicissitudes of public wrangling. Grosseteste, as learned in classics and theology as his friend Roger Bacon, rose from the villein class through a succession of minor ecclesiastical preferments to the bishopric of Lincoln. His sweeping Church reforms drew the attention and support of other clergymen who looked to him for leadership. But he disappointed them because he would not challenge papal supremacy in temporal affairs. Grosseteste occasionally criticized the government's abuses and refused to confirm several papal nominations to benefices in his diocese, but he offered little more than token resistance to the collection of papal subsidies even though he personally disapproved of them.

The extent to which Henry III sacrificed English interests to help the pope is best illustrated in the Sicilian complication. In 1257 the pope declared the dethronement of the king of Sicily, and then offered the crown to Edmund, Henry's second son. Acceptance would necessitate a war in Sicily (the pope called it a crusade) to drive out the former king. Henry agreed to this and to the payment of £90,000 to defray the expenses of the war. This arrangement followed on the heels of a regular papal tax and a special tithe that Henry allowed the pope to collect in 1252 for financing another Crusade. Henry had consulted neither the clergy nor the great council in these matters with the result that, when he asked for the first payment of the £90,000, a storm of protest arose.

A king with military victories, territorial conquests, or constitutional reforms to his credit might have been allowed the luxury of occasional errors of judgment and still have retained popular support. But Henry III had made one blunder after another, thus driving many of the English clergy and barons into open opposition. The waves of aliens who assumed high, lucrative places, the Italian absentee clergymen who drew English money to the papacy, and the heavy expense of papal taxation and wars against France and Wales, which resulted in the loss of Angevin territory and honor, heaped disgrace on him. The enormous financial burden that the new sum promised to the pope, several times greater than the crown's annual revenue, placed on the country, forced Henry to take heavy loans at high interest rates from Italian moneylenders, to increase the fees charged by government agencies, and even to sell the royal plate and jewels.

The opposition barons, headed by Simon de Montfort, rejected Henry's plea for money in 1258 and compelled him, under threat of force, to accept the Provisions of Oxford, which substituted baronial oligarchy for royal absolutism. The Magna Carta, which the barons used as an anchor for their arguments against the crown's transgressions, unfortunately left no recourse but force to remedy misgovernment. The Provisions vested control of the government in a committee of fifteen nobles and clergymen, half nominated by the crown, to whom Henry was responsible and without whom he could not act. The Provisions also required the dismissal of foreigners from public office in Church and state and a review of office holders in local government, particularly sheriffs, many of whom were subsequently discharged. Henry was obliged additionally to call Parliaments at least three times annually for consultation with the fifteen overseers.

But the barons governed no better than Henry and brought no greater unity in England. Power naturally gravitated to the clique controlling affairs, to the distress of other nobles, who resented their privileged places. Meanwhile Henry, anxious to evade the obligations imposed on him, secured papal approval to reject the oath he had made in 1261 to keep them, dismissed councilors appointed by the overseers, and persuaded some opposition nobles to defect to the crown. Prince

Edward, Henry's son, disregarding the rights of the recently nominated local officials, replaced them with royalist sympathizers. De Montfort, patient and accommodating though he was, lost hope of mediating the differences between the barons and the king, raised an army made up largely of inexperienced militia, and marched on the king at Lewes in Sussex. On May 14, 1264, de Montfort, taking advantage of the enemy's tactical blunders, inflicted a heavy defeat on Henry III and Prince Edward, who were both captured.

De Montfort had Henry at his mercy but he failed to press his advantage. His truce with the king simply restated many of the Provisions of Oxford, which Henry again swore to uphold. But the royal oath, so often violated, was an insufficient guarantee of baronial security against authoritarian government. Therefore de Montfort sought the support of an assembly more widely representative of England's classes than any theretofore convened. Two burghers from certain towns and two knights from every county joined the representatives of the clergy and barons in 1265 to give their consent to his governmental reforms. This Parliament, often considered the archetype of all subsequent Parliaments, is important primarily because it embodied the principles of representation and consent that, together with the long-standing right of the great council to authorize certain types of taxation, which Parliament eventually assumed, set the *modus operandi* under which Parliaments were to function for hundreds of years. But de Montfort's Parliament failed to force the king to abide by the reforms largely because Henry considered the assembly, since it had not been summoned by royal order, to be unlawful. Hence, civil war erupted again, and de Montfort died in the Battle of Evesham in 1266 at the hands of Prince Edward, who became king in 1272.

The dismal record of thirteenth-century politics is partly balanced by the cultural renascence that affected English language and literature, architecture, and education. English scholarship had waned for at least a century after 1066 while Frenchmen and Italians forged ahead. The foremost scholars, churchmen, and master builders of the twelfth and thirteenth centuries were Continentals, so that the inspiration for the rejuvenated English intellectual life had its source largely in France from which came French-speaking Norman and Angevin kings and their advisers. The intimate connection between England and her Continental possessions, the marriages between English and Continental royal families, and the increased trans-Channel trade all helped to transport ideas, modes, and styles to the island.

Scholars and professionals in the Church, universities, law, government, and diplomacy spoke and wrote Latin during the twelfth and thirteenth centuries (in some occupations, well into the seventeenth). But the vernacular languages, particularly French and Italian, were becoming widely known among courtiers and intellectuals largely because of the many Norman kingdoms in Europe and because of the commercial importance of Italian city-states like Venice. Moreover, Anglo-Norman and French crusaders had carried the French language throughout southern Europe and the Near East with the result that, like Latin, it was becoming a universal tongue. Edward the Confessor first introduced French language and culture into England, and his Norman and Angevin successors also spoke French. But it never became widely known among ordinary Englishmen, who spoke at first several dialects of the German-rooted Old English which later evolved into the Middle English that was used in some of the earlier English prose and poetry. By the thirteenth century, Middle English was more commonly understood than French. Henry III, for instance, ordered that English be spoken in all law courts and, despite regulations requiring university students to use Latin exclusively, they frequently reverted to English. It became the customary language of all classes by the middle of the fourteenth century.

The origin and growth of Oxford and Cambridge Universities manifest the twelfth and thirteenth centuries' intense interest in education as well as the demand for trained people to fill administrative and professional posts in the Church, government, and business. The education of laymen became especially important in view of the prolonged Anglo-papal quarrel that alienated many of the clergy. Chantry and monastic schools had long taught sons of prominent families, often for the priesthood, but they could not cope with the hundreds of students who sought further education. Their numbers led to a greater need of faculty, and early university degrees automatically licensed their recipients to teach anywhere in Christendom—a task made easier because of the general use of Latin among scholars.

Although an academy for theological and philosophical studies existed at Oxford in the early twelfth century, the establishment of the university is usually ascribed to the arrival of English professors and students from Paris in 1167 as a result of Henry II's decree forbidding clerks (those holding minor orders) to leave England without license or to remain abroad if they received income from home. Cambridge University also allegedly sprang from students' migration. When some

Oxford students were arrested and executed in 1209 following the violent death of a townswoman, a large number of students protested, lectures were suspended, and many scholars moved to Cambridge. Such town and gown fights were not uncommon: students customarily carried knives for protection and often complained about exorbitant prices for food and lodging, while the community was equally bitter about their drunkenness and riotousness.

Students at first lived in halls apart from the college buildings, which were reserved for graduate students and fellows. Later, in the thirteenth century, royal, clerical, and lay benefactors began to endow the residential colleges that became the basis for the collegiate system that still prevails. Students, who often matriculated at the age of fourteen or fifteen, lived in these colleges, the earliest of which were University, Merton, and Balliol at Oxford and Peterhouse at Cambridge. The colleges were separately administered but they conformed to some general university regulations, particularly in matters of personal conduct and requirements for degrees. Lecturers at first earned their livelihood directly from students' fees and taught in rented quarters. Textbooks, handwritten and bound in leather and iron, were too expensive for many to buy. The lecturer therefore read the text aloud and commented on it, and the students made copious notes, from whence derived the timeworn functions of lecturing and note-taking. Lectures normally began at five or six in the morning, with afternoons given over to discussion and private study. The college curriculum in the thirteenth and fourteenth centuries seems narrow, and the years spent in residence unduly long—seven for a Master's degree and as many as fifteen for a Doctor of Divinity. Philosophy (particularly Aristotle's works), theology, and rhetoric dominated the curriculum in Arts. Science was virtually ignored. Students of law attended one of the four Inns of Court in London where, after an apprenticeship of as many as ten to fifteen years under sergeants-at-law, they entered the privileged guild of lawyers, whose services were increasingly in demand. Medicine benefited as knowledge about drugs and surgical techniques was gained from the Moslems, but many physicians were still little more than druggists, and their exotic remedies composed of repulsive ingredients often did patients more harm than good.

The Franciscans and Dominicans undoubtedly did more for unfortunate and unlettered Englishmen than did physicians. The regular Orders ordinarily lived sheltered lives in monasteries, and though they often performed charitable or educational works for their neighbors, they existed primarily for the welfare of their own households. But the mendicant Order of Friars Minor, founded by Saint Francis of Assisi, and the Order of Preachers, organized by Saint Dominic in the early thirteenth century, were different. These friars also lived by strict rules, but they mingled with society to caution the wayward and to succor the ignorant, the sick, and the poor. Christians who had lost respect for mundane priests marveled at the unselfish social, medical, and tutorial work of ragged and barefooted Franciscans and demonstrated their appreciation with bountiful gifts. The Friars Minor could then afford to build larger priories and chapels, which caused some to wonder at the sincerity of their vows of absolute poverty; but though the Order prospered corporatively, it never lost sight of its primary duty to serve the needy in mind and body. The Dominicans, and to some extent the Franciscans also, became renowned scholars. Their august company included William of Ockham, Duns Scotus, and Roger Bacon, and Robert Grosseteste taught Franciscan novices at Oxford. Kings sometimes sought the friars' advice and occasionally employed them as mediators. Above all, the Franciscans and Dominicans rekindled the zeal of complacent Christians by preaching, teaching, and good example.

Since the early twelfth century, towns had become increasingly important in trade and industry. Towns like York, Canterbury, and London, which lost population and business for a few generations after the Norman Conquest, were revived by the increased volume of commerce between England and its Angevin dominions, and the impetus afforded by the several Crusades. As most Englishmen still lived on manors, towns were not large by modern standards. London remained the great metropolis, with between 30,000 and 40,000 inhabitants, followed by York, Norwich, and Bristol with 10,000 to 20,000 each. More than 150 others, principally Newcastle, Lincoln, Coventry, Southampton, Exeter, and the Cinque Ports (Hastings, Romney, Hythe, Dover, and Sandwich) in Sussex and Kent had less than 10,000 inhabitants each.

Most towns in the thirteenth and fourteenth centuries had similar administrations and enjoyed special privileges of government and commerce by reason of royal charters, which they purchased and continued to hold by making periodic monetary gifts or paying taxes to the crown. Richard I sold dozens of charters. Although their terms varied widely, in general they conveyed the right to levy local taxes, pay a fixed annual subsidy to the king, regulate commerce in town courts conducted by the mayors or local magistrates, and hold markets and fairs. London's charter of liberties, renewed by virtually every king since Henry I, allowed its citizens to hold courts, manage traffic and trade, and collect taxes. The Cinque Ports enjoyed similar rights in return for providing the king's navy with ships in wartime. The administrative authority in most towns was vested in a mayor elected by the burghers (usually taxpayers and property owners) and a few councilors who, with the burghers' approval, made bylaws. Gradually, however, the mayor and council began to act without the burghers' approbation and came to be appointed to their positions by a small group of magnates in the town, ordinarily the wealthiest property owners. Most persons in the towns were connected one way or another with trade or manufacture; they included merchants, small tradesmen, artisans, and clergy. Except for the apprentices and perhaps some journeymen, few in the towns were as poor as the rural laborers.

Towns held weekly or fortnightly markets, often in the square before the cathedral or principal church, at which only approved merchants could deal, which meant that businessmen from the Continent or even from neighboring towns were generally excluded. Annual fairs played an important role in the economic and social life of many towns; the most famous were those held at Stourbridge, St. Ives, Boston, and Winchester. Exotic foreign products as well as the finest local handicrafts were exhibited for sale. Among the most unusual aspects of fairs were the courts of pie powder (a perversion of the French *pied poudre,* meaning dusty feet) at which merchant judges dealt summarily with various types of dishonesty by merchants on the move who had no time to await a decision in the regular courts. Very often these cases arose over the quality of goods or a violation of the just price that was fixed for every commodity, regardless of its shortage or abundance or the state of the economy, on the basis of the cost of raw materials and a reasonable profit. The guilds played a major role in fixing these just prices.

While the origins of the guilds cannot be pinpointed (for associations of merchants and artisans are to be found even in classical times), the merchant guilds were operating from the earliest days of most later medieval towns whose charters specifically mention them. Composed of merchants and merchant-artisans, they regulated trade and industry, provided social functions and services, and helped govern local affairs. The merchant guilds, older than the craft guilds that frequently sprang from them, included masters from the several types of business in the town, and protected their membership's local monopoly by rigidly excluding outsiders so that every retailer could enjoy a share of the market and no one secure an unfair advantage. The guild corporation fixed prices and ensured the quality of products as well. Guildsmen paid dues, enjoyed frequent banquets and morality or mystery plays, provided proper burials, and assisted widows, the poor, the sick, and orphans. They often were responsible for the establishment of grammar schools in the early Renaissance period and at least generally provided their members' sons with a rudimentary education. Their wealth and influence can be inferred from the large and elaborately decorated guildhalls, one of the best examples of which, built in the thirteenth century, still stands in York.

The craft guilds, most of which were founded in the thirteenth century as offshoots of the merchant guilds, performed similar functions for artisans and artisan-merchants who sold their goods directly to the consumer. Virtually every craft had its guild, and some general industries such as wool and leather often had several guilds operating within them, for the division of labor among craftsmen was carefully controlled. Each guild had masters, journeymen, and apprentices. Master craftsmen usually owned—and lived over—their own shops, and employed journeymen, who frequently served several masters in order to gain experience and money against the day when, by passing exacting practical examinations, they themselves could become masters. Apprentices worked for room and board (and sometimes had to pay their own expenses) for an average of seven years to learn trades under the instruction of masters who were obliged to (but did not always) treat them as adopted sons. The master guildsmen constituted a monied upper class that often controlled town governments. Such "guild towns," and others too, became lively business centers and, by the fourteenth century, rivaled the prosperity of Italian city-states.

There had been little change in country life over the three or four centuries since the Norman Conquest. Most Englishmen still lived in small manorial villages, followed the time-honored system of farming two fields while letting the third lie fallow, planted the same crops, and reaped them with the same crude tools. The social structure, divided essentially into three classes composed of the manorial lords, the free tenants, and the serfs, who made up by far the largest proportion of the rural population, had likewise changed little since Anglo-Saxon times. The lords, of varying degrees of wealth, owned the land on which the villages stood and the surrounding countryside, extracted rents and services from their tenants, and administered justice in petty matters relating to the manor. The free tenants or freemen held land, usually through leases that defined the amount of rents, fees, and services owed to the lord. Their heirs could inherit these holdings upon the payment of a fee to the lord, and freemen could, with the lord's permission, sell their leaseholds. They had the further advantage of being able to leave the manor at will and to appeal above the manor courts to the royal courts. Most of the serfs were villeins (customarily allowed to farm strips of land amounting to thirty acres), but the status and rights of villeins varied from place to place. Like their lesser brethren the cotters (who had less land to work and performed more services for the lord), the villeins were tied to the land and therefore could not legally leave without the lord's consent. If their lord was a hard man, as many were, their lot might be oppressive and their obligations heavy. On the other hand, villeins were technically protected against physical harm by their contractual arrangements with their lord and by the king's courts. Naturally many resented their servile status, and particularly the fees demanded in money and in kind, but they could do little short of escaping to the towns, which meant risking severe penalties and unemployment, until the middle of the fourteenth century, when the coming of the plague (described later) and the consequent death of a large number of manorial workers provided the opportunity for those who survived to insist on an improvement in their status.

These years also witnessed a considerable increase in overseas trade, and the crown sometimes extended commercial privileges to foreigners in order to encourage it. Until the end of the fifteenth century, foreign merchants from Baltic and western European ports dominated the English export trade. The Hanseatic League, a commercial association of north European towns led by Lübeck and Cologne, cooperated in a kind of late medieval common market to dominate trade in the North and Baltic seas until political and economic nationalism and a change in the spawning grounds of herring put it out of business. The League had several outposts, one of which was a fortified trading station on the Thames in London called the Steelyard. Henry II granted the Hanse a charter which his successors renewed despite the complaints of English merchants, particularly the internationally oriented Merchants of the Staple, who resented its privileged status. These merchants, organized during the reign of Edward I (d. 1307), established a permanent trading center at Antwerp in Flanders, where they conducted a lively market chiefly in wool and hides. As they enjoyed special export and import privileges between England and the Continent, they handled not only the trade of their own members, but also the bulk of goods exported by other English merchants, who did not necessarily have to belong to the organization to enjoy lower rates of duty.

The English monarchs also favored Jewish moneylenders, who, though hated and often basely treated by their countrymen, loaned money at scandalous interest rates of from 10 to 80 per cent, depending on the risk. Unlike Christians, they could ignore the Church's laws against usury, but they were frequently overtaxed and cheated. Public hostility against the Jews ran so hot that Edward I expelled more than sixteen thousand of them in 1290 and confiscated their wealth. He found a substitute for them in the Italian bankers of London's Lombard Street, which is still the heart of banking in England. Thereafter the Jews found no hospitality in England until Oliver Cromwell permitted a small colony to settle in London in the 1650s.

Edward I succeeded to the throne on Henry III's death in 1272 even though he was on a Crusade and did not return for two years. Edward's undisputed succession augured well for a reign of the utmost significance. He frequently summoned Parliaments broadly representative of the upper classes, which were allowed to exercise the power of taxation and enact statutes to suppress violence, regulate land tenure, harness the political authority of the Church, and impose English law in Wales. Edward invaded Scotland and fought against Philip the Fair of France in a war that prefaced the decisive confrontation between England and France in the Hundred Years' War and precipitated a quarrel with Pope Boniface VIII over clerical taxation. Like William the Conqueror and Henry II, Edward restored the crown's authority, which had fallen to its nadir under Henry III. Justly honored with nicknames such as Hammer of the Scots and the English Justinian, this six-foot-three-inch and energetic king had a passion for law and order, exercised temperate judgment, and proved his statesmanship. Edward "Longshanks" was probably the most characteristically English king since 1066, and nationalism thrived under his leadership.

The subjugation of Wales occupied his primary attention early in the reign. Behind the natural barrier of jagged mountains which sustained their flocks of sheep and discouraged invaders, that rugged nation of semi-nomadic, fiercely independent, Celtic people, whom the English considered barbarians, had doggedly resisted foreign interference for centuries. Various Welsh kings had been forced to pay homage to Anglo-Normans such as the dukes of Pembroke, who built castles in the marches and carved out enclaves of English culture imposed by martial law, but the Welsh consistently rebelled either alone or in league with the English king's enemies. Despite frequent association with Anglo-Normans in war, trade, and marriage, the Welsh feared the obliteration of their legal and social systems. Unlike his predecessors since William Rufus, Edward I had no intention of excusing the Welsh princes for rebellion simply because they swore oaths of fealty which they blithely renounced at the first opportunity. Welsh nationalism had actually been increasing during the early thirteenth century under Llywelyn the Great (d. 1240), David (d. 1246), and Llywelyn ap Gruffydd (d. 1282), who had the allegiance of Welsh lords in areas beyond their domain of North Wales (essentially Anglesey and Caernarvon) and emulated English governmental forms in convening baronial assemblies and councils. Edward, as earl of Chester, the county immediately adjacent on the east to North Wales, had watched the second Llywelyn's power mount, and realized that, to implement his grand design of bringing all Britain under the Angevin standard, he must subjugate Wales.

When Llywelyn refused to pay the English king the homage due him, Edward invaded Wales and forced Llywelyn to surrender. Edward treated him generously, allowing him to continue as Prince of Wales on condition that he pay homage and an annual tribute, but the king also dispatched English legal officers to introduce the English administrative system in Wales. This so angered Welsh noblemen that many rose in 1282 in support of David, Llywelyn's restless brother, to expel the hated foreigners. An English army quickly suppressed the rebels, killed Llywelyn in battle, and hunted down David, who was hanged, drawn, and quartered. Parliament then passed the Statute of Rhuddlan (1284), which established five counties (three in North Wales plus Carmarthen and Cardigan) where English law was directly enforced and placed the remainder of Wales under the administration of Marcher Lords in the east and south. These noblemen enjoyed a privileged relationship with the crown, which in turn permitted Welsh subjects to retain many of their legal and social customs. Edward bestowed the title Prince of Wales on his son, Edward, born at Caernarvon Castle in 1284, and since then every first-born male of the royal family has held the title. To maintain order, Edward I also built a chain of forts at strategic points within the five counties. Thereafter

Wales remained generally peaceful until 1536 when Henry VIII united it politically with England.

In Scotland, too, Edward I confronted problems of latent nationalism that forced him to invade, thereby putting an end to the cordial relations the two nations had previously enjoyed. Scotland, geographically checkered by scraggy cliffs and mountains, could barely sustain a hardy population of less than half a million persons of Scots, Pict, Viking, Saxon, and Anglo-Norman ancestry. North of Sterling, gateway to the Highlands, only small villages surrounding rude castles broke the line of enchanting glens dominated by clannish chiefs, who resisted the forces that were drawing the lowland population together, absorbing English social and political institutions, and encouraging trade in the commercial vortex of nation-states washed by the North Sea. The borderlanders who, since Roman times, had spilled their blood on both banks of the Tweed River to plunder and seize land could peacefully sow their seed and tend flocks after William the Lion (d. 1214) and King John settled their differences over frontier fortresses in the treaty of 1212. Alexander II (d. 1249) and Alexander III (d. 1286) had married respectively the sister (Joan) and the daughter (Margaret) of Henry III, thereby harmonizing the interests of the Scottish and English royal families. Many Scottish noblemen held fiefs under English monarchs, fought at their sides against Welsh, English, and French enemies, and served on their councils. Both Alexanders, having paid Edward I homage as their feudal suzerain, were allowed to govern according to Scottish law and custom with no more than token interference from the south.

But trouble fermented as a consequence of the death of Alexander III. As he left no direct heir, Scottish barons immediately recognized his granddaughter, Margaret (the Maid of Norway), only three years old and living in Scandinavia. The regency council appointed to administer the country during her minority arranged a promise of marriage between her and Edward I's son, but she died in 1290. A half-dozen contenders, most of them, like Robert Bruce and John Balliol, descendants of William the Lion's brother David, announced their candidacy for the throne, and Edward I was finally asked to settle the dispute. After tedious genealogical research, he chose Balliol to be king because he had the best lineal claim. But Edward also seized the chance to implement his contention that he was overlord of Scotland by appointing a corps of avaricious English administrators whose arbitrary acts alienated the Scots. When Balliol, weary of being a puppet king, signed a treaty with Philip IV of France, then quarreling with Edward over Gascony, and promised to invade England if it should attack France, Edward deposed Balliol and demanded fealty from every Scottish landowner. At this the clansmen rebelled under William Wallace, a brutal knight whose fame in Scottish folklore cannot gloss over his barbarous acts. Edward marched on the rebels in 1298, took Edinburgh and the northeast, and routed Wallace. But although the Hammer of the Scots forced the submission of many Scottish noblemen, he never again enjoyed peace in the northern kingdom, and his two successors were constantly plagued by Scottish insurrection.

An Anglo-French war had meanwhile erupted in 1293. It was rooted in commercial rivalry over the wine and wool trade in Gascony and Flanders and in the anachronistic feudal relationship that obliged Edward I to pay homage to Philip IV for Aquitaine, the vestige of Henry II's grand Angevin empire. Gascony still belonged to England, while Flanders had a favored commercial link with England, and the French meant to acquire both territories. Philip (1285–1314) saw that he could complete the work of governmental centralization and political unification pursued by his Capetian ancestors only by driving Edward from Aquitaine. But he dutifully did homage for it and avoided the risk of war until a fight in the Channel between English and French merchantmen gave Philip the excuse he sought to implement his plans. The Count of Flanders, though Philip's vassal, sided with Edward to protect the connection with England in the vitally important wool trade. But Philip and Edward were too busy with other problems to pay much mind to their war. Edward's campaign in northern France came to naught, and in 1303 they made peace according to the principle of *status quo ante bellum*. Although this war served to test the strength of the antagonists' forces in preparation for the larger confrontation that followed, it also is related to two other important developments: an Anglo-papal quarrel over clerical taxation and the increasing exercise of power by Parliament.

One need not be reminded today that war is costly. Edward I, simultaneously fighting the Welsh, Scots, and French, had exhausted his traditional sources of revenue. The Church in England meanwhile had continued to amass enormous wealth, and though it had often paid feudal dues and small taxes and made monetary gifts, it had never been heavily assessed; indeed, it contributed very little in return for the support and protection it enjoyed. Edward realized that, as Church property was held corporatively, it could never be alienated or partitioned as could family holdings. Moreover, laymen, seeking to escape the payment of fees and taxes on their land, often consigned title to it to the Church on condition that it guarantee the actual owner a part of the income. Edward curtailed this practice and regulated the Church's accumulation of property through the Statute of Mortmain (1279), which stipulated that alienations of property could be made only by royal license. He also interfered in the jurisdiction of the ecclesiastical courts, so that he had already strained the patience of the clergy before he levied high taxes on them in the early 1290s. They complained to the pope, Boniface VIII (d. 1303), who, in the bull *Clericis Laicos* (1296), forbade secular princes to demand and clergymen to pay extraordinary assessments without papal approval. Edward responded by outlawing the clergy, which meant that they lost royal protection and could not have recourse to the law courts. This not only brought most priests to their senses and induced their payment of taxes and fines, it also forced Boniface to moderate his attitude in the bull *Etsi de Statu* (1297), which authorized collection of extraordinary taxes from the clergy in cases of clear emergency. Edward naturally took advantage of the "emergency" through the remainder of Boniface's pontificate; and his successor, a worldly and pragmatic Frenchman named Clement V, gave Edward virtually a free hand to tax the clergy as he pleased.

Edward I generally enjoyed the support of important baronial and mercantile families whether in raising armies to fight Scotland and France or in quarreling with Boniface VIII. This was not an accident. Henry III had had to face repeated criticism and rebellion by barons caught up in the spirit of Magna Carta and the Provisions of Oxford Ordinances. Nor was Edward I free from harsh criticism, for the opposition barons forced him to reconfirm the Great Charter and to accept in 1297 the Confirmation of the Charters in which he promised to levy taxes only with the consent of "all the realm," which meant, of course, the privileged. Edward virtually disarmed criticism, however, by seeking advice in matters of trade, war, and taxation of assemblies of clergy, barons, knights, and merchants in Parliament, which had been convened on a more or less regular basis since de Montfort had summoned it in 1265. It should not be concluded from this, however, that every district sent representatives. While the shires, many towns, and bishoprics and monasteries had spokesmen at most Parliaments, the king sometimes called representatives of only two or three groups or the barons alone, and ignored the others, while some were occasionally invited merely as observers. Edward, like his predecessor and successors for centuries, was not obliged to convene Parliament regularly, and kings in the fourteenth century sometimes levied taxes without its consent. But, as he needed money, and as the burghers and knights could be troublesome and contentious, he wisely asked their advice. Therefore, the crown's gradually growing dependence on Parliament for money inevitably resulted in the increase of its authority and prestige. Subsequent discussions of the relations between Parliament and crown will demonstrate how significant the power of fiscal control became.

Members of Parliament did not truly represent all classes and districts until the late nineteenth century. Even so, practical wisdom dictated to Edward and his successors that Parliament should be broadly representative of the four most important classes—the clerical hierarchy, the barons, the knights, and the burghers—that is to say, the ruling classes of Church and state who had the money the crown needed. The clerical hierarchy and the nobles had traditionally sat together and continued to do so even after the knights and burghers were invited to join them. The burghers were at first regarded as intruders, but the social revolution of the later fourteenth century, caused principally by the decline of feudalism, the Black Death, and the crown's dependence on the merchants in finance and war, narrowed the gulf between the aristocracy and the burghers and knights. By the 1330s, the nobles and high clergy still sat together in the House of Lords, but the lesser clergy, knights, and burghers were accorded virtual equality in the House of Commons. This is the origin of bicameral legislatures in western Europe. It must also be mentioned that the clergy often discussed royal policy on religious matters (those that did not pertain to doctrine or dogma) in assemblies called Convocations. Therefore, by the 1400s, the three most important vehicles of modern English national government—king in council, king in Parliament, and king in Convocation—had been developed.

Edward I trod in the footsteps of his illustrious predecessors, Henry I and Henry II, in forwarding constitutional reform. Kings had long been regarded as the principal source of law, promulgated in decrees and ordinances, very often in consultation with the great council and baronial assemblies, though, with relatively few exceptions, kings had not been accountable to their councilors or to the barons. Statutes were new and different in that they were based on Parliamentary approbation. Parliament passed a bill, which when assented to by the king, became law. The king therefore became a partner with Parliament in framing statutes which, because they had popular approval, carried more weight than royal decrees and the common law, and superseded any contradictory laws previously established by the latter two methods. All subsequent legislative Acts of Parliament (and a few during Henry III's reign, which later generations made into statutes) became the statutes of the realm. Of course, the common law remained and was expanded along with royal decrees. Itinerant justices enforced all three types of law in the assize courts.

Edward's intense interest in the state of the country prompted him in 1274 to order a national inquiry to determine the effectiveness of local government and to learn of unlawful acts against royal authority. The inquiry revealed that certain barons still held local courts without royal license. Accordingly, by the Statute of Gloucester (1278), royal commissioners demanded of offending barons by what authority—quo warranto—they held courts, and barons who could not prove by royal charter or other means that they had this privilege had to surrender it. Edward thereby struck a mighty blow against feudalism.

He also prevented landholders from evading their feudal obligations. The second Statute of Westminster (1285) introduced the principle of entail. The clause "concerning conditional gifts" is especially important. Theretofore tenants and their heirs could dispose of fiefs as they pleased. Westminster II required the transmission of land by a deceased tenant-vassal to his eldest son (primogeniture); if there were no direct heir, the land escheated to the feudal lord who, in many cases, was the king himself. The third Statute of Westminster (1290), called *Quia Emptores*, curtailed subinfeudation and made purchasers of estates the direct feudal tenants of the king. Tenants had frequently bestowed land on subtenants who became their vassals, which meant that a part of the land originally held by the tenant's own overlord ceased to bring him income by way of fees, reliefs, and wardships. Westminster III therefore stipulated that a tenant who subinfeudated his fief lost the income from the alienated portion, which reverted to the overlord. The net result of these two laws was an increase of royal authority at the expense of the barons. As more of them became direct tenants of the king, he found it easier to control them.

The national militia and local law enforcement were reorganized by the Statute of Winchester (1285). It obliged every citizen to help catch criminals through the hue and cry in each parish and to clear the underbrush for two hundred feet on each side of main roads to rid the countryside of marauders. Walled towns were to close their gates during the night and post guards, and strangers were not allowed to stay the night unless someone assumed responsibility for them. Each man had to keep weapons and armor in good condition and have them inspected twice annually by two constables in each of the hundreds. These constables eventually assumed additional duties of local law enforcement, presented criminals at the assizes, and generally assisted county sheriffs. Edward also required those whose land yielded an annual income of at least twenty pounds to serve as knights in wartime, even if they had never been formally knighted and were not his tenants-in-chief. He never intended, of course, to use them as soldiers; Edward devised this "distraint of knighthood" primarily for fiscal purposes. His fighting army was composed of militia and mercenaries.

The increasing importance of commerce is evidenced in the Statute of Merchants (also called Acton Burnell, 1283) and in the *Carta Mercatoria* (1302), which benefited English and foreign merchants. Acton Burnell assisted merchant creditors to collect their debts even if the debtor's personal and real property had to be sold to satisfy them. Debtors frequently went to prison, and for the following five hundred years, English law inflicted the irrational punishment of imprisonment upon debtors until they paid up, even though it should have been obvious that a prisoner rarely had the chance to raise the money to gain freedom. The Court of Exchequer entertained countless suits brought by merchants and others to compel the payment of private debts. Foreign merchants, in return for payments of customs duties, which later came to be called tunnage and poundage, got the right to trade under the protection of English law. English traders resented this intrusion, but Edward I valued aliens' money more than he heeded the complaints of Englishmen.

It is disappointing to turn from the fruitful years of Edward I to the reign of his urbane, handsome, irresolute, and politically naïve son, the second Edward (1307–27). For twenty years Englishmen were forced to endure government by corrupt royal favorites like Piers Gaveston and the two Despensers, who pursued their selfish private aims. Other barons of equally low principles took advantage of misgovernment by King Edward to harness him with restraining ordinances. Like Henry III, he overtaxed his subjects, fell victim to bad advice and lost decisive battles.

The Gascon Piers Gaveston had been Edward's close friend since childhood, and they shared a love of tournaments and hunting. Edward I had banished Gaveston, but he returned full of bluster and offense to insult barons and to fill Edward II's and his own coffers with their taxes. He survived two additional periods of exile only to be murdered in 1312. It must be said in fairness to Edward II and Gaveston that trouble was caused not only by the barons' hatred of the royal favorite and by gross misgovernment, but also by the opposition barons, who took the opportunity to win back some of the power that Edward I had taken from them. Baronial indignation rose to a head in 1310–11 when a committee of twenty-one lay and ecclesiastical peers, called the Lords Ordainers, compelled Edward to accept ordinances that curtailed his authority and brought governmental reforms. The king thereafter could not act without the Ordainers' approval, and royal finances were overhauled to suit their wishes. But the Ordainers failed in practical politics for the same reason that their thirteenth-century counterparts had failed: they quarreled among themselves and ignored the welfare of the country. Their leaders, Guy of Warwick and Thomas of Lancaster, were defeated by Edward in 1322, and Warwick was executed as a traitor. Two other leeches, Hugh Despenser and his son, then began to suck from England's arteries. They may have administered with greater ability than Gaveston and the Ordainers, but they outdid the latter in feathering their own nests with rich estates stolen from important nobles.

Meanwhile another war with Scotland had begun. Edward I had died in 1307 while on a Scottish expedition and his successors carried on without lasting success. Trouble at home, as we have just seen, hampered Edward II's efforts in Scotland where the rebels besieged numerous English strongholds until in 1314 the last one at Sterling Castle was endangered. Edward's enormous army of thirty thousand men met the forces of Robert Bruce, grandson of the previously mentioned Bruce and king since 1306, at Bannockburn. There the flower of English knighthood perished in a disastrous rout that sent Edward fleeing south for his life. An Anglo-Scottish truce in 1323 settled their differences for the rest of their reigns to 1327–28. Thereafter Edward Balliol deposed Bruce's heir, David, who had returned after long exile to regain the throne. In the midst of this civil war the Scots invaded England in 1346 in support of their allies, the French, with whom the English were already involved in the first phase of the Hundred Years' War. Although the English decisively vanquished the Scots at Neville's Cross, the victory was anticlimactic because Scotland had really been

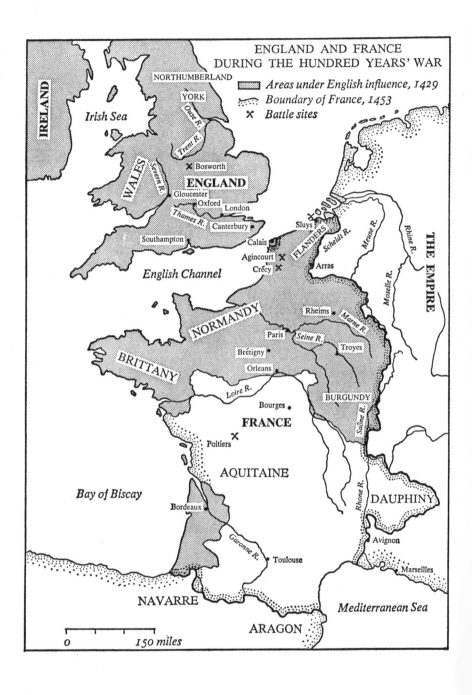

ENGLAND AND FRANCE
DURING THE HUNDRED YEARS' WAR

▨ *Areas under English influence, 1429*
⟋⟍ *Boundary of France, 1453*
✕ *Battle sites*

IRELAND

Irish Sea

NORTHUMBERLAND

YORK

Ouse R.

Trent R.

WALES

Severn R.

✕ Bosworth

ENGLAND

Gloucester
● Oxford
London

Thames R.
Canterbury ●

Southampton ●

Calais

Agincourt ✕
Crécy ✕

English Channel

Sluys

FLANDERS

Scheldt R.

Meuse R.

Rhine R.

THE EMPIRE

Arras ●

NORMANDY

BRITTANY

Rheims ●

Paris

Seine R.

Marne R.

Brétigny ●

Troyes ●

Orleans ●

Loire R.

BURGUNDY

Bourges ●

Moselle R.

FRANCE

✕
Poitiers ●

AQUITAINE

Saône R.

Bay of Biscay

Bordeaux ●

Garonne R.

Toulouse ●

DAUPHINY

Rhône R.

Avignon ●

Marseilles ●

NAVARRE

ARAGON

Mediterranean Sea

0   150 miles

independent since Bannockburn. It became a rule of thumb thereafter that, when England and France warred, the Scots attacked England.

While these events were taking place, the French again invaded Gascony. Edward II sent his wife Isabelle to France to convince her brother, the king, to withdraw his army, but she fell instead into an adulterous relationship with Roger Mortimer. Mortimer, an enemy of the Despensers, returned with her in 1326 at the head of an army that hunted down and destroyed the two favorites and captured Edward, who naïvely continued to write pathetic love letters to Isabelle. Mortimer convened a Parliament, and, under its authority, deposed Edward in favor of his fourteen-year-old son, Edward III. Weeping and cringing, Edward II was shuttled from castle to castle until Mortimer had him brutally murdered. If Edward II's fate was tragic, at least it proved that the power of Parliament had grown, and that henceforth it would take more than a casual share in shaping the destiny of England.

The "she-wolf of France" and her murderous partner headed a regency that governed during the minority of Edward III. He put up with them for only three years. In 1330, Mortimer was condemned by Parliament and executed. Isabelle received more compassion than she deserved: Edward confined her to Castle Riding in Norfolk, where she spent the rest of her days in nun's garb atoning for treason. Edward enjoyed phenomenal success for fifty years (he died in 1377) despite the strain of many military campaigns, scrambling for money to pay for them, and the revolutionary social, economic, and religious consequences of the plague of 1348–49. He was extraordinarily energetic, courageous in battle, a patron of the arts, and reasonable with Parliament, on which he depended for money and which expected concessions in return for it. Social forces were churning and boiled over in the Peasants' Revolt of 1381. But Edward escaped serious domestic turmoil and led his gallant knights and longbowmen like a modern King Arthur to the long-awaited victory over France. Although Edward emulated his grandfather in hammering the Scots—at the battles of Dupplin Moor and Halidon Hill in 1332–33—he is best remembered for his victories during the first period of the Hundred Years' War.

The causes of the Hundred Years' War go back to the battlefield of Hastings, when a vassal of the French king became English monarch. From that moment England fought to retain its Continental possessions, which the Capetian sovereigns repeatedly attacked until Edward II died in possession of only Gascony and Ponthieu. The tidal wave of French nationalism that began in the late twelfth century rolled over Angevin land with only brief interruptions. As the French monarchs fitted the parts of the country together like the pieces of a giant jigsaw puzzle, the first and second Edwards unsuccessfully pursued the dream of recreating Henry II's empire, and Edward III, with the country staunchly behind him, took the first step toward it. Charles IV died in 1328, and the direct male line died with him. Edward III took advantage of this succession crisis to claim the French throne through his mother, Isabelle, Charles's sister. But the French refused to honor the right of hereditary succession through a woman and crowned Philip of Valois (Philip IV's nephew) as King Philip VI (d. 1350). France also interfered in the Flemish wool trade, which England prized above all other commercial connections. Count Louis of Flanders favored the French, to the distress of Flemish burghers who, led by the wealthy Ghent merchant Jacob van Artevelde, organized a hostile federation when Philip VI suspended Anglo-Flemish trade. Minor disputes, such as occasional conflicts in the Channel between their merchantmen and the nominal Franco-Scottish alliance, which did not really help either signatory, also provoked Anglo-French animosity.

Philip VI instigated the war in 1337 by declaring forfeit to him the English fiefs of Gascony and Ponthieu on the grounds that Edward III, even though he had taken an oath of fealty as Philip's vassal, had refused to pay him homage. Edward had hoped to avert a French war while he was busy fighting the Scots, but he nevertheless hurried to make allies in case war should come. He befriended the German King Lewis of Bavaria (his brother-in-law), the Count of Hainault (his father-in-law, whose lands bordered Flanders on the southeast), the burghers of Brabant (Flanders' commercial rivals), and other princes in the lower Rhineland. Although France stood virtually alone against this alliance, one might well have thought the odds in its favor: it had many times Britain's population and the sympathy and support of the French-dominated papacy, centered at Avignon since 1307. Edward III, on the other hand, had the popular support of his countrymen, superior weapons in the longbow and gunpowder, and, as soon became apparent, naval supremacy in the Channel.

The Hundred Years' War may be divided into three periods. England dominated the first from 1337 to 1360 because of its victories at Sluys (1340) and Crécy (1346), the aggressiveness of Edward III and his son, the Black Prince, and the unpreparedness of France, which unwisely relied on essentially feudal personnel, tactics, and weapons.

The second phase, 1369–86, though inconclusive for either side, saw the rejuvenation of French nationalism and the reorganization of French forces under Charles V (1364–80). England at first dominated the third period, 1415–53, because of the overwhelming victory of Henry V (1413–22) at Agincourt (1415) and the conquest of Normandy. But Joan of Arc turned French defeat into victory by stabilizing the monarchy under Charles VII (d. 1461). Periods of armed neutrality often interrupted the war which, by the middle 1430s, had been all but won by France even though sporadic fighting continued for twenty years thereafter.

Brevity will be best served by a summary of the major achievements and failures of both antagonists. The naval victory at Sluys not only protected the Anglo-Flemish wool trade, it also made England mistress of the Channel and enabled Edward III and his successors to invade France without fear of reprisal on Britain. Edward concentrated his attack on Normandy, which he hoped to cut off with the help of his Flemish allies. The armies of Edward and Philip VI clashed at the Battle of Crécy, a small village near the mouth of the Somme River. On August 26, 1346, Edward's 10,000 men, including about 7,000 infantry bearing longbows, encountered a larger French army of mounted knights and Genoese crossbowmen. The French had the better position, but the afternoon sun shone full in their faces and English archers shot their arrows with such deadly accuracy that at day's end 15,000 French armored knights lay dead. The longbow, adopted from the Welsh about 1250, and gunpowder to fire cannons, which frightened cavalry horses, had revolutionized warfare and dealt a fatal blow to feudal military tactics.

Immediately after Edward III had taken Calais, the Black Death arrived to decimate the ranks of civilians and soldiers alike on both sides of the Channel. This devastating plague resulted in the death of between a third and a half of England's population. Asiatic black rats infested with plague-ridden parasites crawled deep in the holds of ships that carried goods between Middle Eastern and western European ports. Beginning in 1346, the contagion, which caused high fever, violent vomiting, running sores that hardened into carbuncles, and black nodules on the body, spread from India to the Atlantic like atomic fallout, destroying everything it touched. It reached England within two years, and spread rapidly from Dorset ports eastward to London and the southeast, and northward to Scotland. The fortunate, like Boccaccio's storytellers, left crowded towns strewn with garbage and filth, which multiplied the vermin. Their mortal enemies, pigs, cats, and dogs—the sanitary department in medieval towns—could have helped had not the authorities slaughtered them, thinking that they spread the disease. Not enough men were spared in some communities to bury the dead in common graves purified with lime; clergymen who tended the dying themselves succumbed, and the intimate association of monks naturally depopulated the monasteries, in some cases to the last man. Fields of grain rotted for want of harvesters; livestock perished of starvation; prices and wages zoomed to unprecedented heights. The worst of the plague was over by the early winter, 1349, but its effects were felt for more than a hundred years. It returned periodically until the late eighteenth century.

Englishmen necessarily neglected the French war in the face of this national catastrophe, whose consequences demanded immediate remedies. The law of supply and demand created a laborers' market. Landlords lost many tenants, and villeins on manors bargained successfully for relief from feudal dues or left to seek their fortunes in towns. Some rose from serfdom to tenant status; others became freemen on their own plots. Agricultural workers demanded and often got higher wages, and prices rose. The Statute of Laborers (1351), which fixed wages and prices of essentials at rates customarily paid in 1347 and fined employers and workers for paying and taking higher wages, failed to stabilize the wage spiral. Even though some were punished for breaking this law, landlords nevertheless paid whatever laborers demanded, rather than lose their crops and herds. Merchants and craftsmen were also affected, but to a lesser degree. Wage and price regulations could not be enforced adequately, and the lower classes continued to take advantage of their altered situation until the Peasants' Revolt set them back thirty years later. The Church also suffered. Some monasteries never again achieved a full complement of inmates and their role as centers of intellectual life was seriously impaired. Mere boys, without spiritual vocation or much formal education, were ordained as priests, and unworthy ecclesiastics rose to high administrative posts. Lastly, the scarcity of money weakened the king's bargaining power with Parliament, which consequently grew in power and prestige.

The war was resumed in 1355 with Edward III and the Black Prince making two expeditions to France against the new French king, John II (d. 1364). Edward's short campaign around Calais accomplished only the usual destruction and pillage. But the Black Prince, then twenty-five, achieved more. He landed with 10,000 men at Bordeaux and pushed northward through Gascony to Poitiers (1356), where the French army, possibly six times larger, attacked the English who took positions behind ramparts and ditches among grapevines and hedges. The 4,000 longbowmen reaped a terrible harvest of French knights that day, and King John was taken a prisoner to England. In the next three years English armies roamed almost at will in the vicinity of Paris and in northwestern Burgundy with the result that the French made peace at Brétigny (1360), agreeing to ransom John and recognize English sovereignty south of the Loire River. Edward promised not to press his claim to the French throne.

Edward III's last years do not compare favorably with his earlier successes. After the resumption of war in 1369, English armies invaded northern France almost annually without significant result. French resistance increased because of the military reforms made by King Charles V (d. 1380), who also restored the supremacy of the crown by an accommodation with the upper classes after the abortive but bloody revolt of the peasant-dominated *Jacquerie*. The new and powerful French army, avoiding direct battles with the English invaders, gradually wore them down and recovered most of the territory France had lost in the first period. Moreover, the English war effort suffered because of domestic factionalism. As Edward was very old and no longer able to keep a close watch on the government, his younger son, John of Gaunt, plotted to snatch the throne from Edward's rightful heir Richard, the eleven-year-old child of the Black Prince, who had died in 1376. Alice Perrers, a greedy courtesan whom Edward favored after Queen Philippa's death in 1369, also exerted an evil influence at court. Only the direct intervention of the so-called Good Parliament prevented a dispute over the succession. It declared forthrightly in favor of Richard II (1377–99), and also, because governmental corruption had become so widespread, was able to impeach royal advisers and make reforms. This set a precedent that Parliaments used as a weapon against royal absolutism well into the seventeenth century.

Richard II was only a boy, requiring a council of regency until he came of age in 1389. His uncle, John of Gaunt, duke of Lancaster (d. 1399), dominated the council. Although his French campaigns proved him an incompetent soldier, the duke showed considerable administrative ability in manipulating the barons in Parliament and in forming a Lancastrian opposition to royal favorites like Robert de Vere and Michael de la Pole, whom Parliament impeached in 1388 for gross misgovernment. Parliament's interference irked Richard, but it forced him to cooperate when, in the same year, the Lords Appellant, a small but powerful and wealthy group of barons interrelated by marriage, charged five of his councilors with treason and forced their dismissal.

The reader may have noticed that the events of the last half of the fourteenth century border on the revolutionary. Restless peasants demanded concessions from landowners, who grudgingly granted them. Parliament quarreled with kings over foreign policy, royal authority, excessive taxation, and its rights. Barons pursued selfish aims first by criticizing and then by restraining the king and his councilors, even though the baronial oligarchy did no better than the monarchs. The old order in the Church gasped beneath the weight of general complaint over papal taxation, the incursion of spirited mendicant friars, and the Black Death decimation of the numbers and quality of the priesthood. Society tends to be complacent, but it periodically takes stock of existing institutions and recognizes the urgent need for change. So it was that Englishmen became dissatisfied with their economic, religious, and social institutions and, like impatient adolescents, threw off the shackles of tradition to reorder their lives according to untried principles. The Peasants' Revolt, antipapal and anticlerical legislation, and the social criticism of Chaucer and William Langland, were all symptoms of changes that were transforming England into an adult nation. Most of the causes of the Peasants' Revolt have been suggested already in terms of the results of the Black Death and the unprincipled administration of John of Gaunt, who wasted the country's money when it was urgently needed to finance the wars with France and Scotland. Edward III had devised various means to reduce the rapidly mounting military expenses. These included a greater reliance on Parliament for "tenths" and "fifteenths," that is to say, a tax of one-tenth or one-fifteenth of one's movable property and income, and tunnage and poundage, which was a tax on each ton of wine and on every pound sterling's worth of other goods imported into England. This income, together with the crown's traditional sources of revenue from land, fees, fines, and services, did not satisfy John of Gaunt's extravagant needs, so he imposed a poll tax of roughly a week's wages on every person over fifteen years of age. In the following two years (1379–80) everyone, rich and poor alike, had to pay taxes at a rate fixed by the government, generally based on their ability to pay. These taxes might not have been so obnoxious but for the other grievances of serfs, whose landlords imposed fees and services and tried to ignore demands for better wages and an improved status. Worst of all, the poll tax was ruthlessly collected; Wat Tyler of Kent killed a tax collector who had insulted his daughter.

The Peasants' Revolt, led by Tyler and John Ball, an itinerant priest, exploded in Essex and Kent with terrible force, and spread over much of East Anglia and southeastern England. Thousands of irate peasants followed Tyler and Ball to London, burning manor houses, destroying manor rolls, and murdering some landlords and lawyers. Other insurgents from East Anglia, Cambridgeshire, and Hereford also tramped to London, where they converged at Blackheath just outside the city, sallying forth daily for three weeks of destruction. Richard II and most of his councilors, including John of Gaunt whose magnificent house went up in flames along with hundreds of other residences and public buildings, watched apprehensively from behind the thick walls of the Tower around which the mob milled. At Richard's request, Tyler and the others, professing loyalty to the king, made known their demands: the abolition of villeinage, social equality, reduction of land rents, free trade, division of Church estates among peasants, and a general pardon for all rebels. Richard and a committee of the rebels discussed these terms in an open field, and they were unconditionally accepted. But during the course of the negotiations, one of the Lord Mayor's men killed Tyler when the crowd pressed too closely on the king, who immediately rode into it demanding allegiance. The demoralized peasants dispersed, some of them following Richard into London. Meanwhile other riots had run their course in several counties around London.

Although Richard himself hoped that the rebels would go home peaceably and that no reprisals would be taken against them, his councilors and Parliament would not permit such leniency. At their prodding he revoked his promises and allowed the prosecution of the major rebels in trials that lasted throughout the summer of 1381. John Ball and many others were executed, but most of their followers were acquitted. The immediate results of the rebellion were disappointing; none of the grievances were abated. But in the following century, because of the gradual amelioration of the peasants' status that had begun long before the uprising itself, some of the old restrictions were abolished, and villeinage had almost disappeared by the early sixteenth century.

The extension of royal authority since the Norman Conquest usually coincided with the diminution of papal and clerical power in temporal affairs. Concern over the increasing wealth of the Church, papal taxes, foreign absentee clerics holding English benefices, and other ecclesiastical disputes strained Anglo-papal amity and increased anticlericalism. The theory of papal supremacy put into practice by forceful pontiffs like Gregory VII and Innocent III had few apologists in England during the fourteenth century partly because of a national sentiment which militated against the subordination of the state to an international organization, and partly because of the decline in the quality of the popes themselves. The fact that Edward I and Philip IV had triumphed over Boniface VIII in the matter of clerical taxation illustrates the fading prestige of the Holy See as a temporal force. It sank deeper during the so-called Babylonian captivity of the Church, when French popes resided at Avignon in southern France and refused to return to Rome until 1378. Englishmen naturally suspected the intentions and demands of the Gallic-dominated papacy and college of cardinals at a time when England and France were enemies in the Hundred Years' War. The quality and spirituality of the English clergy had also declined. Although the heavy mortality among the clergy occasioned by the Black Death had much to do with this, it had begun long before the plague. Otherwise, the mendicant friars would not have had such an impact in the thirteenth century.

Parliament spearheaded the movement to sever the temporal ties between England and the papacy. In 1333 it refused to pay any longer the annual tax of one thousand marks that kings had sent to the Holy See since England became a papal fief in 1213. Another grievance involved the pontiff's long-standing practice of appointing foreigners to English benefices. These provisors of benefices, the name given to papal grantees, frequently neither fulfilled their administrative duties nor understood English, and gave part or all of their incomes to the pope, resulting in a serious drain of money from England to the papacy which, resident during these years at Avignon, generally supported England's enemy. The English believed the right to fill benefices should rest in the previous incumbent, the king, the cathedral chapter, and the lords of manors, whomever held the property connected with the benefice. Edward III therefore first refused to allow papal provisors to enter England and then had Parliament enact the first Statute of Provisors (1351), which fined them and held them prisoners until they surrendered their benefices. They were also forbidden to appeal to the papal Curia. This Statute and another in 1390 had less than the desired effect, because they were loosely enforced, and as appeals continued to be made to Rome from English courts, in 1353, through the Statute of Praemunire, Parliament made all appeals to any foreign court illegal. Later revisions of this law in 1365 and 1393 specifically mentioned the curia and prescribed heavy fines for appellants to it. Edward III and Richard II tried mightily to enforce these statutes, but the pope continued to insist on his right to approbate beneficed bishops, who required it in order to exercise their authority.

Royal efforts struck only at Church administration, but John Wycliffe (d. 1384), an Oxford theologian and priest of Lutterworth, attacked Church dogma as well. He denied transubstantiation, the power of a priest at Mass to change the substance of bread and wine into the substance of Christ's body and blood (the outward appearance, or accidents, remaining unchanged). Wycliffe also questioned the necessity of intermediaries (priests) between God and man, the efficacy of pilgrimages, good works, sacramentals, and papal supremacy. In order that ordinary literate men might read the Scriptures in English, he encouraged the translation of the Bible from the Latin Vulgate of St. Jerome. Such views clearly branded Wycliffe a heretic. But his enormous popularity (due to the strong antipapal and anticlerical feeling in the country), and his protection by John of Gaunt, saved him from the fires of Smithfield (London site of executions). He died a natural death in 1384.

His followers were called Lollards, which in the usage of that day meant variously psalm singers, babblers, or poor preachers. Dressed only in red sackcloth and carrying staffs, they traveled from village to village over the length and breadth of England preaching his doctrines. That they had much influence over the common people is explained primarily by their advocacy of social and economic reforms such as the abolition of class distinctions. The Lollards therefore had a hand in stirring peasants to revolt in 1381. Wycliffe's teachings lived on long after his death; students carried his ideas to Bohemia, where John Huss espoused them, and the Council of Constance ordered Wycliffe's remains exhumed and burned ceremoniously in 1415.

For several years after the Peasants' Revolt, as a thirty-year peace with France had been arranged, Richard II ruled without friction. But self-restraint was not one of his virtues, as he demonstrated during the last three years of his reign in a round of senseless reprisals against landowners, judges, the Lords Appellant, members of Parliament, and others. He ignored legal restraints, imprisoned hundreds without benefit of trial, and overtaxed his subjects. Most significantly, Richard drove John of Gaunt's son, Henry Bolingbroke, into exile and confiscated his estates. Bolingbroke did not need to stir the country to revolt;

Richard's tyranny had already seen to that. Accordingly, in the summer of 1399, while Richard was in Ireland suppressing rebellion, Bolingbroke landed in Yorkshire, easily raised an army, and demanded the restoration of his confiscated estates and governmental reform. Richard hastily returned to find the country up in arms against him. After several months of futile bargaining, he formally abdicated in the presence of Parliament, which made Bolingbroke King Henry IV, the first of the Lancastrian dynasty.

4

Lancastrians and Yorkists, 1399–1485

Henry Bolingbroke deposed the unpopular Richard II to become Henry IV (1399–1413). He owed his succession to the assistance of powerful friends such as the Percys of Northumberland, the approbation of Parliament, which expected him to follow its advice, and his indirect claim to the throne through his father, John of Gaunt, fourth son of Edward III. But Richard II, whom Henry IV imprisoned in Pontefract Castle (Yorkshire), still lived, and his rightful heir, the infant Edmund Mortimer (d. 1424), earl of March, a direct descendant of Lionel, duke of Clarence, third son of Edward III, had a better claim to the throne and a strong baronial following led by his uncle Sir Edmund. Two contenders with better lineal claims than Henry were bound to be dangerous enemies. Parliament, though primarily responsible for Henry's succession, trusted him no more than it had trusted Richard. It doled out money in paltry sums, quarreled with him over the crown's financial needs, and sided with the council, whose instructions Henry had promised to heed. Therefore, without adequate funds or a strong military force, and without the full cooperation of Parliament, the council, and many of the barons, Henry was hamstrung from the outset of his reign.

Plots in favor of Richard II and Edmund Mortimer sprang up immediately. Despite the generosity Henry had shown Richard's councilors and bishops, a few of them planned late in 1399 to assassinate him and his four sons at Windsor Castle. Henry learned of their plans at the last moment and had them executed or imprisoned. Harried and desolate, Richard II died shortly afterward, possibly of starvation, but many suspected that Henry had had a hand in it. He publicly displayed Richard's corpse in St. Paul's Cathedral in order to squelch rumors that he still lived, but this only added credence to the rumors of Henry's complicity in regicide. Owen Glendower of North Wales, related by marriage to the Mortimers and an old friend of Richard, took advantage of a personal quarrel with one of the Marcher lords to rouse Welshmen to rebellion in support of the Plantagenet cause and Welsh independence. This insurrection alone would have caused Henry little trouble, but it coincided with a Scottish invasion of Northumberland and French attacks on English coastal shipping in the Channel, which cut deeply into Henry's profits in the Flemish trade when he desperately needed money. Henry marched on Edinburgh, but he could not defeat the Scots until the Percys' men joined him in 1402 at the victorious Battle of Homildon Hill. Meanwhile repeated attacks against Glendower's elusive Welsh mountaineers all failed. He became a Welsh hero, and Englishmen, severely hampered by inclement weather whenever they moved into the Cambrian Mountains to attack, thought him to be a warlock capable of black magic.

Henry's star was further dimmed when Sir Edmund Mortimer and the three Percys joined Glendower. Henry had rewarded the Percys magnanimously for their help against Richard II: Henry Percy, earl of Northumberland, became marshal of England; Thomas Percy, earl of Worcester, controlled the west Welsh march; and Sir Henry Percy, known as "Hotspur" because of his uncontrollable temper and eagerness for battle, governed the east march and was justiciar of North Wales. They nevertheless expected additional rewards for having helped Henry against the Scots. The king had further alienated Sir Henry by refusing to pay ransom for one of his kinsmen whom Glendower had captured. As a consequence, the Percys, Glendower, and the Scottish Earl of Douglas united in an alliance that would have been disastrous for Henry had he not intercepted Hotspur and Douglas when they moved south to effect a union with Glendower's army. The resultant Battle of Shrewsbury (1403) in Shropshire could have gone either way, but at day's end Hotspur lay dead, Douglas was a prisoner, and the rebels were in flight. For the next two years the French continued depredations against the Gascony border and English merchantmen, and Henry fruitlessly pursued Glendower. Parliament bickered over subsidies, finally granting Henry less than he could have reasonably expected, and his popularity waned.

Criticized for his inability to counter French and Welsh aggression or to enforce English authority in Scotland, Henry and his oldest son, Prince Hal, faced another challenge from the Percys and their allies in the northern insurrection of 1405. They charged Henry with ineptitude against foreign and domestic enemies and with having usurped the crown. Following the king's denunciation of the Percys as outright traitors, Henry Percy summoned his Yorkshire levies in order to protect his authority there. The king besieged and captured their northern castles, but the cowardly Percy escaped to Scotland, leaving his men to die on the battlefield or the gibbet. Henry had successfully suppressed several rebellions against heavy odds; after 1406 he faced no more major threats to his throne. Glendower fought on until 1415, but Henry Percy perished in battle in 1408, and the capture of the heir to the Scottish throne (later James I) in 1406 forced the Scots to keep the peace.

Even so, the remaining nine years of Henry's rule brought him little comfort. Parliament frequently foiled his plans and humbled him by refusing to authorize sorely needed taxes. Three factions in the council struggled to gain control of affairs or interfered with royal policy: the first was led by Archbishop Thomas Arundel of Canterbury (d. 1414); the second by John Beaufort (duke of Somerset, d. 1444) and Henry Beaufort (bishop of Winchester, d. 1447), both sons of John of Gaunt and Henry IV's half-brothers; and the last by Prince Hal. Prince Hal even sent English troops to France in 1411 without the king's permission to complicate the quarrel then raging between the Orleanists and Burgundians, and openly avowed his impatience to assume the English throne. Henry IV managed to restrain his contentious councilors despite a painful disease that partly crippled him in 1407 and eventually caused his death.

Henry IV was in addition uneasy about the Lollards, who gathered in London in 1401 to pressure Parliament into enacting social and economic reforms. The Lollards constituted no crucial threat to the crown, but their complicity in the Peasants' Revolt of 1381 forever branded them as dangerous malcontents, and Henry, surrounded as he was by insurgents and rivals, was apprehensive lest a lenient policy toward them might alienate the clergy and lose for him the valued support of the Church. Archbishop Arundel strongly urged Henry to persecute the Lollards, and the persecution began when Convocation found William Sawtre, a Lollard priest who had questioned transubstantiation and denied the efficacy of venerating relics, guilty of heresy and the secular authorities burned him at the stake at Smithfield in the outskirts of London before a large crowd. Shortly thereafter Parliament passed the statute De Heretico Comburendo (1401), which authorized bishops to fine and imprison convicted heretics for minor heresy and to recommend to the secular arm the burning of contumacious and relapsed heretics. Only one other Lollard was burned during the reign of Henry IV, but the severity of the punishment for heresy was so awesome that casual Lollards eschewed their views. In the short reign of Henry V, Sir John Oldcastle, the foremost Lollard, conspired to overthrow the government and destroy the monasteries around London. But Henry V discovered his plans, put his followers to the sword, and burned him and several of his lieutenants at the stake on the double charge of treason and heresy. The practice of burning heretics continued until the early seventeenth century, most of them suffering during the reigns of Mary and Elizabeth Tudor (1553–1603).

Henry V (1413–22) ruled in a decade of relative domestic tranquillity, growing prosperity, and military victory over France. His father had weathered several rebellions, thereby greatly easing Henry V's administration and securing the Lancastrians' place on the throne. Henry V had led a boisterous youth, during which he spent more time carousing with drunken companions, cavorting with women, and fighting rebels than he had in study at Queen's College, Oxford, or in government business. But the responsibilities of high office sobered him virtually overnight, and he became a judicious, politically astute, and energetic monarch. The Beaufort brothers, whom he had befriended toward the close of his father's reign, assumed important conciliar posts and, as a sign of leniency aimed at winning popular support, Henry V welcomed back his father's enemies to royal favor. He also exhumed and displayed the gruesome remains of Richard II to stop once and for all the persistent rumors that the old king still lived, and the decomposed corpse was respectfully reinterred in Westminster Abbey. Parliament voted ample supplies, ceased to quibble over its grievances and rights, and joined in the whirl of excitement that followed Henry's revival of Edward III's claim to the French throne and preparations for the invasion of Normandy. It may not have occurred to many that England's involvement in foreign war would take men's minds off troublesome domestic issues and help to restore national unity.

France was utterly unprepared for war. Its monarch, Charles VI (1380–1422), at first fell under the influence of the Duke of Burgundy (his uncle) and later suffered frequent fits of insanity that permitted the opposing factions of Burgundians and Orleanists (or Armagnacs) to implement their plans to gain control of the country. At Henry V's accession these factions were at one another's throats in a bloody civil war that resulted in an Orleanist oligarchy and the expulsion of the Burgundians. Although Henry had sent a small force to assist the Orleanists in 1411, three years later it was to his advantage to join the Burgundians, who also declared war on the French king.

After exhaustive military preparations at Southampton, and a short delay occasioned by the need to suppress another plot in favor of Edmund Mortimer, Henry V crossed the Channel and landed his army at Harfleur in Normandy. He successfully besieged several towns on route to Calais, which he intended to make a base of operations for the Normandy campaign. About halfway between Crécy and Calais, the advance of the French army forced Henry to fight the Battle of Agincourt (1415), even though his army was exhausted from heavy fighting and ridden by disease. The struggle of October 25 raged over rolling country made muddy by a heavy downpour the previous night. The English were outnumbered at least six to one, but the armored French knights could not move speedily in the mud and were stopped short by the pointed stakes that had been driven into the ground to break the charge. The French who escaped the deadly shower of arrows were crushed by their stumbling steeds or had their throats cut by the swift English infantry. French casualties exceeded the English by several thousand.

The triumphant Henry left immediately for England and did not return to Normandy until 1417, by which time the Burgundians were pushing relentlessly from the southeast toward Paris. The French cause was doomed: its army had insufficient strength to wage a two-front war; the economy had virtually collapsed; and factionalism badly divided the government. Henry therefore had little trouble capturing the major fortresses in Normandy and Champagne, and the Burgundians occupied Paris and made Charles VI their prisoner. Hopelessly defeated, the French signed the Treaty of Troyes (1420) according to which they paid a large indemnity, agreed to a marriage between Charles VI's daughter, Catherine, and Henry, and promised him the French throne on the death of the king. While English and Burgundian soldiers continued the fight against the dauphin Charles, the rightful heir to the French throne, Henry returned with his bride to England, where he stayed during the winter of 1420–21. The success of French arms forced him to hurry back in the following summer, accompanied by his newborn son. But Henry, only thirty-five years old, died of exhaustion and dysentery in 1422 and Charles VI followed him to the grave shortly afterward. The crowns of both countries therefore devolved upon a nine-month-old boy, Henry VI (1422–61), whose two uncles, dukes Humphrey of Gloucester and John of Bedford, became respectively the regents of England and France.

The sudden death of Henry V and the long minority of his son complicated the affairs of both countries. Henry VI technically ruled France under the regency of Bedford (d. 1435), an able, unselfish, and devoted administrator, soldier, and member of the royal family who resided at Rouen. He governed Normandy, Maine, and Champagne and preserved the alliance with the Burgundians despite their anger over his brother Humphrey's illicit marriage to Jacqueline of Hainault, whose first husband, a Burgundian, was still living. The dauphin pressed his claim to the French throne following Charles VI's death, repudiated the Treaty of Troyes, and took control of France south of the Loire except for the greatly reduced English county of Gascony. Although Henry V had declared in his will that Duke Humphrey (1391–1447), the youngest son of Henry IV and an uncle of Henry VI, should be regent of England during the king's minority, neither Parliament nor the supporters of his principal rival on the council, Bishop (later Cardinal) Henry Beaufort of Winchester, would permit this licentious and contentious opportunist to exploit the country for personal gain or complicate relations with France. Humphrey was the formal head of the government, but his enemies on the council managed to usurp most of the powers he claimed by virtue of his being regent. He nevertheless caused a great deal of trouble by trying unsuccessfully to kidnap the young king, plotting to overthrow Bishop Beaufort, and virtually destroying his country's unity in the war effort. He even tried to seize his wife's lands in Hainault and contrived to undermine the council's plans, but nonetheless he managed to outlive his opponents and spent the last few years of his life amassing books and manuscripts that later became an important part of the Bodleian Library at Oxford. In 1447 a majority of the councilors, seeking peace with France against his wishes, had him arrested, but he died before they could remove him from office.

Englishmen hailed Henry V's victories as glorious achievements heralding the birth of a new English Continental empire, but all he had achieved was doomed to crumble within a few decades. Bedford did what he could to carry on the war effectively despite factionalism at home and renewed French counterattacks. He won a smashing victory over a Franco-Scottish army in 1424 at Verneuil in Normandy and followed with an attack along the entire Loire River line. The culmination of this campaign was the siege of the great fortress city of Orléans, about seventy miles southwest of Paris. English arrows, cannon balls, and rams battered its walls, and courageous soldiers sallied forth daily from temporary wooden forts surrounding the city for six months during the winter of 1428–29. Orléans's beleaguered garrison was starving and at the point of surrender when a seventeen-year-old peasant named Joan of Arc left Domremy in eastern France to tell the dauphin at Chinon that Saints Michael, Catherine, and Margaret had commanded her in God's name to save the country. Clad in armor, astride a charger, and exuding faith and courage, she led an inspired army to relieve the siege of Orléans, crown the dauphin as King Charles VII at Rheims, and drive the hated English from French soil. She achieved within the year virtually all that she had prophesied, but the Burgundians captured her near Paris and sold her to the English. They treated the "Maid of Orléans" shamefully, convicted her of heresy and, in May, 1431, burned her at the stake in a slow, agonizing fire. The ungrateful Charles VII did not lift a finger to save her.

The flames that consumed her body rekindled the embers of French nationalism. Burgundy sued for peace with France at Arras, Bedford died in 1435, and the English war effort tottered at the brink of collapse. The lack of money and of a competent commander of Bedford's caliber, as well as factionalism in the council, were the principal causes of English governmental weakness. As the sources of royal revenue had been strained, Parliament authorized a graduated tax on real estate and borrowed heavily, and in doing so, became more dependent on barons and merchants, who expected favors in return for their money. With the war going badly, most of the councilors agreed with the Beauforts that England should sue for peace at once, but Duke Humphrey intervened to prolong the useless war. Richard, duke of York, replaced Bedford as field commander, but inexperience and complacency led to his recall. Richard Beauchamp, earl of Warwick, old and unimaginative, did no better. Finally, English troops reeled back in Normandy under the disgracefully incompetent leadership of the Earl of Somerset, whose reputation was saved by a timely Anglo-French truce from 1445 to 1449. England ceded Maine to France in return for a marriage between Henry VI and Margaret of Anjou, niece of Charles VII, but even so, with England clearly on the run, Charles could not resist for long the resumption of the war that would finally drive the English from France. William de la Pole, duke of Suffolk, who had arranged the truce of 1445 and the king's unpopular marriage, led the English army four years later when the war was renewed, but he failed to win a victory and was impeached by Parliament and murdered on the Channel in 1450 as the scapegoat for English military disgrace. The Hundred Years' War terminated in 1453, only the city of Calais remaining in English hands as a painful reminder of the once mighty Angevin empire.

England's lengthy involvement in Continental affairs to preserve an empire that became an anachronism with the decline of political feudalism was a constant source of irritation. While English merchants had made a great deal of money trading with the Angevin provinces, they were forced to pay back a large part of it in taxes to support the tremendous cost of equipping and maintaining armies abroad. Courtiers from Angevin lands enjoyed royal favors, important government posts, and rich sinecures in place of Englishmen, who understandably resented them and often rebelled. English kings had frequently become embroiled in Continental problems that had no direct bearing upon domestic welfare, and that were sometimes associated with Scottish and Welsh rebellions against which insufficient force was brought rather than weaken English arms on the Continent. Englishmen undoubtedly benefited culturally by their relationship with Angevin provinces; on the other hand, Cambridge and Oxford Universities would probably have been founded, Gothic churches would have been built, and French literature would have inspired English litterateurs and minstrels without it. Manifold domestic problems required careful attention during the fourteenth and fifteenth centuries, and the loss of the Hundred Years' War not only brought them to a head in the Wars of the Roses, but also at last permitted the government to concentrate on them without reference to Continental questions. It may have been no coincidence that the rebels led by Jack Cade, sparked by widespread dissatisfaction with the Lancastrians' conduct of the war, supported the Yorkists and helped to provoke the Wars of the Roses. These civil wars decided not only whether Lancastrians or Yorkists would reign, and whether baronial cliques should be tolerated, but essentially whether England would support a royal family that could restore peace and prosperity to a people who had tasted them for only brief interludes in a tumultuous age of insurrection, factionalism, and disorder that lasted the better part of three centuries. While Henry VI's generation regarded England's loss of the French war as a national disaster, ours realizes that it was the best thing that could have happened.

THE HOUSES OF YORK AND LANCASTER

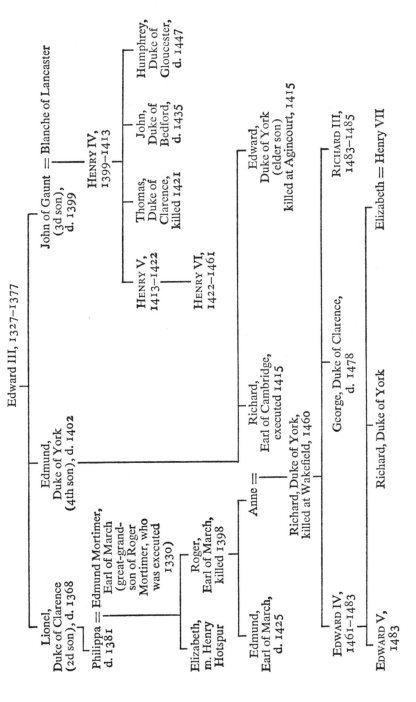

The ugly character of English politics toward the close of the French war aroused popular indignation. Misgovernment was not entirely the king's fault, although his obvious lack of political sagacity and weakness of mind certainly encouraged dissension in the council between the rival royal families of York and Lancaster. He was kindly, generous, pious, and dutiful when he ought to have been forceful, decisive, and even ruthless. His councilors were ambitious men who, for the most part, sought their own advancement over England's welfare, strained to placate important magnates whose liveried soldiers added strength to their threats, and solicited the king's favor only for the sake of propriety. As the older advisers died, others scrambled for their lofty places. The two great antagonists earlier in the fifteenth century, Cardinal Beaufort and Humphrey of Gloucester, had both died in 1447, the latter while in prison under taint of treason. Their demise and the murder of the Duke of Suffolk in 1450 opened the road to Richard, duke of York (d. 1460), Humphrey's successor as leader of the Yorkists, and Edmund Beaufort, duke of Somerset (d. 1471), who was loyal to Henry VI and the Lancastrians. As they were the respective male heirs of the royal houses of York and Lancaster, through Edmund of York and John of Gaunt, sons of Edward III (see the genealogical table, p. 103), they carried on the rivalry that had begun when Henry IV deposed the Yorkist Richard II in 1399. Richard of York knew that he had a chance for the throne so long as Henry VI was childless, which was the case until 1453, but for many years he said nothing of it and seemingly directed his opposition against Somerset, when all the while he was biding his time against the day when he could depose the Lancastrian king. Against him there stood not only Somerset and his relatives, but also Queen Margaret of Anjou, a resolute, temperamentally explosive, shrewd, and devoted wife, who did much to protect her weak-willed and feeble-minded husband's throne. Richard finally made his move in 1452, when, threatening to war against Henry VI, who by that time had slipped into insanity, he forced the Lancastrians to accept him as regent. From this crisis developed the Wars of the Roses.

The rivalry between the Lancastrians and Yorkists at the top of the social scale was matched by rebellion among the masses. An outburst of indignation over governmental blundering, centered in Kent and Sussex in June and July, 1450, was led by Jack Cade, whose origin and intent are still shrouded in mystery. Whether he was from Ireland or Kent, and whether he had been a soldier, physician, or simply an adventurer does not really matter. He claimed to be a Mortimer, a descendant of Edmund Mortimer, earl of March, whom Henry IV had bested in the contest for the crown in 1399. Some believed that Cade intended to boost the candidacy of his alleged cousin, Richard of York; others ascribed the cause of his rebellion to demands for political reform. Whatever his actual intentions, he led a disciplined and well-equipped army into London where he professed loyalty to the king and issued proclamations that denounced certain councilors as being responsible for the English defeat at the Battle of Formigny, governmental rapacity, excessive taxation, and irregularities in the elections of members to Parliament. Unlike Wat Tyler, Cade said virtually nothing about social reform. He managed at first to restrain his men, but they later got out of hand, rioting and looting in London for three days in early July. They also executed several dignitaries, including the treasurer, Lord Saye, without trials. The authorities offered no resistance so long as the rebels respected law and order, but when they broke it, the local militia drove them from their camp on the outskirts of the city. Henry VI, under pressure from the council, revoked his promise of a general pardon, and Cade and many of his followers paid for treason with their lives.

Cade's Rebellion had no more than a passing influence in a century characterized by turbulent politics and rapidly changing political allegiances. Nevertheless, it does serve conveniently to introduce the generation from 1455 to 1485 who fought the misnamed Wars of the Roses. Shakespeare perpetuated in *Henry VI* (Act II, scene iv) the apocryphal tale of a confrontation between the Lancastrian Duke of Somerset and Richard of York in London's Temple Garden, where the deep enmity between the rival royal families was supposedly symbolized by their picking of red and white roses. The white rose was indeed a Yorkist emblem, but the red rose, which sculptors carved in wood and stone on virtually every important sixteenth-century building, became associated with the Tudors (who fought for the Lancastrians) after they came into power. The civil wars that erupted at St. Albans in 1455 concerned mainly the aristocratic supporters of the two houses, and were neither continuous nor particularly severe. Only a few major battles were fought, and long periods of truce or idleness were occasionally broken by skirmishes, mostly in the Midlands and the northeast. It has indeed generally been assumed that the dislocation caused to ordinary citizens by the Wars of the Roses was no worse than that of other baronial squabbles of the fourteenth and fifteenth centuries. To a certain extent this is probably true. War was still a gentleman's "sport" conducted according to strict rules, and a distinction was made between belligerents and civilians. On the other hand, a nation of less than two million people could hardly have not been affected, at least indirectly, by mounted mercenaries riding destructively over wheat fields, breaking down hedges, pillaging the countryside, and besieging estates. Other than the powerful barons who supported either the Lancastrians or the Yorkists, there were nobles who fought private feuds with neighboring nobles for spoils and power. The French war had afforded them ample opportunity for plunder and adventure abroad; after 1453 they plundered each other at home.

The fact that the Lancastrian-Yorkist struggle for the throne could have exploded into warfare owed much to the widespread system of livery and maintenance. Noblemen had long regarded the art of war as an honorable vocation, but in the old feudal system it was usually undertaken as a duty against the enemies of the crown. It had become apparent during the thirteenth century, however, that the crown could no longer depend on the loyalty of baronial levies; accordingly, militia and mercenaries were substituted for them. But the Hundred Years' War put such a strain on the human and financial resources of the crown that it commissioned rich noblemen to muster, outfit, and sustain private regiments for the king's army at their own expense. Great men such as the Percys, Beauforts, and Staffords therefore enlisted soldiers whom they dressed in the family's colors and maintained in return for their services on the battlefield. When the French war had ended, these noblemen retained their private armies as household guards to settle feuds with neighbors or to support the Lancastrians or Yorkists.

Richard of York kept the peace so long as there was a chance of his succession to the throne at Henry VI's death. Two events intervened in 1453–54 to thwart his plans: Margaret of Anjou gave birth to a son who would perpetuate the Lancastrian dynasty and Henry VI regained his senses after sixteen months of imbecility, during which time Richard had used his power as regent to consolidate his strength. Henry at once dismissed Richard from the council and restored to power the Duke of Somerset, whom Richard had imprisoned. This so provoked Richard, who had governed exceedingly well and had restored some semblance of law in the kingdom, that he marched at the head of a three-thousand-man army from Yorkshire toward London. Somerset's forces simultaneously moved north toward Leicester. The armies clashed in the streets of St. Albans in May, 1455. This battle, which formally opened the Wars of the Roses, lasted less than an hour, and though Somerset was killed, casualties on both sides were light. No retributions followed, primarily because Richard had captured the king and had the support of Richard Neville, earl of Warwick, England's most powerful baron, who commanded an army of almost eight thousand men stationed at Calais. While private family feuds occupied nobles such as the Earl of Devon in the west, Richard of York's victory at St. Albans permitted a Yorkist hegemony in London for almost a year. But in 1456 Margaret of Anjou took the initiative by moving the court to Coventry and reconstituting the government in the hands of Lancastrian sympathizers. The docile king meanwhile tried vainly to arrange a truce with the Yorkists between frequent lapses of mind. Parliament remained idle; large sections of the country fell into virtual anarchy because of corrupt judges and juries who refused to enforce the law against barons who intimidated them; and Margaret sought supporters against the day when she could strike a decisive blow against Richard of York. Her forces resumed the war in 1459, but the Yorkists triumphed in several battles the following year, the two principal ones being at Bloreheath (Staffordshire) and Northampton. Although the queen and Prince Edward managed to escape to Scotland, Richard took Henry prisoner and demanded his abdication. Henry, in a rare exhibition of courage, refused, and Richard finally agreed to allow him to reign on condition that the throne should pass at his death to Richard and his heirs.

Richard had at last achieved the goal that his family had pursued since the revolution of 1399, but he did not survive to enjoy his triumph. Lancastrians such as the young Duke of Somerset and the Earl of Northumberland, seeing that Richard had already usurped power as protector of England ruling in the name of an inept and insane king who sacrificed everything for the sake of tranquillity in his old age, sulked over the prospect of losing wealth and position at Henry's death. Richard did not help to soothe their apprehensions. He took possession of enormously rich Welsh estates and marched north to secure his Yorkshire lands against Lancastrian encroachments. While in residence at Sandal Castle, Richard was attacked by Somerset and Northumberland under prodding from the queen, who was not as willing as Henry to set aside her son's right to the throne and who taunted Richard daily to come out and fight. He foolishly succumbed to her gibes and lost the Battle of Wakefield (1460) and his life. Margaret mocked him even in death by putting a paper crown on his severed head, which she perched atop the highest pole at York.

The earls of Warwick and March, Richard's friend and son respectively, took up the disgraced Yorkist standard and inflicted terrible vengeance upon the Lancastrians. While Edward of York managed to rout a makeshift army of Welsh, Irish, and French allies of Henry at Mortimer's Cross, Warwick brought over his large army from Calais to London, where Edward joined him early in 1461. Queen Margaret's forces, hoping to occupy the capital and regain popular support for Henry, got only as far as St. Albans before she learned that the London militia, the principal councilors, and the peers of the region, eager for the return of a strong and stable monarchy, had recognized the succession of Richard of York's son as King Edward IV. Her men also lost the second Battle of St. Albans.

Warwick had made Edward king in name, but he had to prove that he was also king in fact. Edward and Warwick therefore led their forces in hot pursuit of Margaret's regiments, which hurried into Yorkshire. At Towton (March, 1461), in a heavy snowstorm, the armies met in the bloodiest battle of the war. Although outnumbered, Warwick's forces inflicted a terrible slaughter upon thousands of Lancastrians; the fresh snow was red with the blood of corpses, which littered the ground for ten miles around the center of battle. Margaret, Prince Edward (1453–71), and Henry VI escaped to Scotland, where King James III offered them asylum because of a previous treaty in which Margaret had agreed to give up Berwick in return for a marriage between James's daughter and Edward, which never materialized. Two months later Edward of York was formally crowned king of England.

Edward IV (1461–83), just nineteen years old, had many endearing qualities, and most Englishmen were glad to be rid of Henry VI, whose impotent administration had led to factionalism, anarchy, and the perversion of justice. The Yorkists, though bemoaning the death of Richard of York, willingly accepted the leadership of Edward IV, for his boyish, handsome face, charming personality, and generous nature were coupled with political acumen and good business sense. He also worked hard, took criticism, and was loyal to honorable friends. But his proclivity for satisfying his sexual desires at the expense of the virtue of merchants' and barons' wives and the not too modest harem of concubines that he kept at court ruined his reputation as a just man and, according to his contemporaries, helped to undermine his robust constitution.

With Warwick's valuable help, Edward wasted no time implementing his policies. The Lancastrian officeholders, down to the lower officers in the Exchequer, were the first to suffer the effects of the king's administrative appointments in what may have been England's first general application of the spoils system. Some Lancastrian nobles lost their heads; others lost only their estates. Edward thereby began a movement to restore law and order at the expense of baronial power that historians have often attributed unjustifiably to Henry VII. The courts once more punished criminals without fear of reprisals, and local law-enforcement officers regained confidence that their actions had the full support of the crown. Finance likewise received Edward's attention. Although he was liberal in doling out land and money to those who had helped him in the war, he also knew the value of a penny, as is evident in his attempts to root out financial corruption, increase royal revenue, and encourage the revitalization of the wool trade, which augmented income through foreign commerce and customs duties.

As a result of these policies, Edward managed by 1464 to win popular favor and secure the Yorkist succession despite the continuous danger of Lancastrian raids from Scotland and Wales and the imminence of a Lancastrian alliance with Louis XI of France. Margaret of Anjou made several trips to France in order to arrange a marriage between the Lancastrian Prince Edward and a Valois princess and the surrender of Calais to Louis in exchange for his military and financial aid in the restoration of Henry VI. Warwick attempted to counter this plan by offering Edward IV's hand to Louis's sister-in-law, and his negotiations were about to bear fruit when Edward secretly married Elizabeth Woodville, daughter of Earl Rivers. She was older than Edward and a widow, and she had an illustrious pedigree, but, regardless of Edward's infatuation for her, she was a member of a family with strong Lancastrian connections. As this marriage destroyed Warwick's plans to prevent a pernicious Franco-Lancastrian military alliance, he and Edward were thereafter at loggerheads.

By 1464 the Lancastrians, whose principal strength lay in the northern counties of Northumberland, Lancashire, and Cheshire, had sufficiently recovered from their costly defeat at Towton to renew the war. But they could do no more than field small armies, which Warwick overwhelmed at Hedgely Moor and Hexham (1464). The next year, Henry VI, whom James III had expelled from Scotland after signing a treaty with Edward IV, was captured and imprisoned in the Tower, where he remained for five years. Meanwhile the Yorkists became involved in an internal struggle for power. Warwick deeply resented Edward's marriage to Elizabeth Woodville and the favors he showered on her and her family. His resentment deepened when Edward refused to be the puppet Warwick expected him to be and befriended the Duke of Burgundy, the rival of Louis XI with whom Warwick was still attempting to reach an accommodation against the Lancastrians. Having lost Edward's favor, Warwick plotted his overthrow in 1468–69, forced him into exile on the Continent, and restored Henry VI to the throne, an unusual Lancastrian-Yorkist alliance that was strengthened by the Lancastrian Edward's marriage to Warwick's second daughter. The insanity and unpopularity of the old king notwithstanding, Warwick had his own way for about a year in 1470–71. But he did not realize that Edward IV had built a strong following among Yorkist barons and merchants, who respected the young king's aggressive efforts to restore orderly government and a sound financial policy. Edward, with men and arms furnished by the Duke of Burgundy, took advantage of his popularity in an invasion of southeastern England, which resulted in the occupation of London, Warwick's flight north, and Henry VI's reincarceration. Events thereafter moved rapidly toward a crisis. Within a few months Edward once more sat on the throne. He met Warwick at the Battle of Barnet (1471), where the Kingmaker-turned-traitor was slain. Three weeks later Edward attacked the army of Margaret of Anjou and Prince Edward at Tewkesbury. Prince Edward was killed, Margaret lived for another eleven years in comfortable retirement in France, and Henry died mysteriously in the Tower, probably murdered at the order of Edward IV. Lancastrian opposition had been broken for the time being and Yorkist intrigue had been stifled. The remaining years of Edward's reign, with the exception of a foolish invasion of France and the Duke of Clarence's rebellion in 1478, was a period of unaccustomed commercial prosperity and domestic tranquillity.

Edward's invasion of France in July, 1475, a needless act of retribution against Louis XI, who had helped Warwick five years earlier, brought unexpected results. Under pressure from the crown, Parliament liberally financed the large army that Edward landed at Calais, even though Englishmen rightly saw no logic in making war simply to assuage the king's personal grievance against Louis or to assist the latter's archenemy, Charles the Bold of Burgundy. Edward expected Charles's help, but trouble on Burgundy's eastern border with Emperor Maximilian forced Charles to concentrate his forces there. Accordingly, without fighting even one battle, Edward and Louis came to an agreement by which Edward received seventy-five thousand crowns and the promise of an annual pension for seven years in return for his withdrawal and a marriage between one of his daughters and the French dauphin. Shortly before his death Edward also made a peace with Scotland that permitted him to reoccupy Berwick, which Margaret of Anjou had surrendered to James III in return for aid against the Yorkists.

At home Edward had to contend with the treacherous ambition of his younger brother, George, duke of Clarence (1449–78), who in 1469, against the king's express opposition, had married Isabella Neville, Warwick's daughter and heiress to a portion of the huge Neville estates. For a time, before he had sided with the Lancastrians, Warwick secretly planned to make Clarence king in place of Edward IV. This plan was soon abandoned but the resultant fraternal discord threw Clarence on Warwick's side in the Battle of Barnet. Although Warwick died there, Clarence lived on to press his claim against Edward IV until the latter lost patience and persuaded Parliament to bring a bill of attainder against Clarence on a trumped-up charge of treason. While awaiting execution in the Tower, Clarence died, purportedly drowned in a barrel of wine, probably with the king's approval.

Edward IV had burned the candle at both ends in a fast and furious life of wanton pleasure and hard work which caught up with him suddenly in 1483, when he died at forty-one, leaving the throne to his twelve-year-old son, Edward V. Clarence's death had freed the government from intrigue, and the Wars of the Roses had broken down from sheer *ennui* and the want of Lancastrian leaders. There was no good reason to suspect that Queen Mother Elizabeth (Woodville) and her brother-in-law, Richard of Gloucester, could not rule jointly as regents during the king's minority. Even though Elizabeth and her family were unpopular, she could be tolerated for a few years, and Richard, save for his grasping after a part of the Neville lands, which Edward IV had eventually given him following Warwick's death, had not shown cause why he should not be trusted. Yet Elizabeth was weak, and Richard was unwilling to await his turn on the throne after the reigns of Edward V and his brother, Richard of York, which would probably be long. Gloucester therefore began a purge of Elizabeth's family and supporters, seized the young king, and made himself protector. Success emboldened him. He charged in Parliament that, as Edward IV had married a commoner, and as the marriage was illegal, his sons should not succeed him. With the approbation of Parliament, which Richard packed with his friends, he put Edward V and his brother in the Tower, usurped the throne by a specious argument based on hereditary succession, and shortly thereafter both boys were found dead, the victims of treachery that has commonly been attributed to Richard III, who had come to power in the third "palace revolution" of the century.

Richard's guilt, character, and appearance have since been the subject of interminable discussion. Many of his countrymen, particularly in the strongly Yorkist counties in the north, seem to have supported Richard III's accession. There was much less evidence then of his complicity in the murder of his wife and nephews than there is today. There is little doubt that he was brutal, vengeful, and ambitious, and that he destroyed the opposition by wholesale executions, including that of his former friend, the Duke of Buckingham. But such personality traits and acts of brutality were common among fourteenth- and fifteenth-century kings. We can dismiss Shakespeare's description of Richard, for it was based on the prejudiced accounts of Tudor historians, who were interested primarily in justifying their patron's succession in 1485. Portraits of Richard III are said to depict a man of deceit and unscrupulous ambition, but that is reading a great deal of conjecture into a painting. He may simply have looked strained and provoked in the same way that Abraham Lincoln did in sitting for portraits that bored and tired him. Posterity, in short, has tended to view Richard as some sort of fifteenth-century Frankenstein, whose crippled body (if indeed it was deformed) symbolized his pernicious soul, but again this view may be the result of Tudor propaganda against lingering pro-Richard sentiment. In the end, apart from the craving for the whole truth, does it really matter whether he was hunchbacked, limping, or withered in one arm? Or is it of much consequence whether he or another (Henry Tudor?) murdered Edward IV's sons? It does matter, however, that most of his supporters abandoned him (Yorkists fought against him in the rebellion of 1484), and that opposition was centered in the person of Henry Tudor.

The short reign of Richard III ended on Bosworth Field (Leicestershire) in August, 1485, at the hands of Henry Tudor, duke of Richmond, the scion of a Welsh family distantly related to the Lancastrian royal house through the marriage of his great-grandfather, Owen Tudor, to Henry V's widow on one side, and through his mother, Margaret Beaufort, descended from Edward III, on the other. Henry had long fought for the red rose, but the Yorkist triumph in 1471 forced him into exile in France where he awaited the chance to lead the Lancastrians against Richard, whose treacherous rule invited Henry's intervention. With French money and arms, Henry sailed from Harfleur to Milford Haven in his ancient homeland, where his countrymen flocked to his banner as he moved northeast toward Shrewsbury. Richard hurried southwest to meet what he first believed was merely another rebellion. The two armies clashed at sunrise on the twenty-second. Although Richard's forces were more numerous, they had no stomach for blood and thousands defected to Henry. The king, unhorsed, was cut down. Tradition has it that his crown fell upon a bush from which a Lancastrian nobleman took it and placed it on Henry's head.

The death of Richard III terminated the wasteful and dreary Wars of the Roses. Many fathers and sons of royal and noble families had perished in battle and on the scaffold. Edward IV had since 1471 improved business, curtailed livery and maintenance, rehabilitated justice, and restored virile monarchic government, but such reforms did nothing to wither the roots of England's troubles in the fourteenth and fifteenth centuries. The poetry of Langland and Chaucer, the rebellions of Tyler and Cade, and the constantly shifting political scene should have been warning enough that there were major problems whose presence betrayed a creeping malignancy that was surreptitiously draining the nation's moral strength. A substantial change had been occurring in the attitude of the upper classes in the century from 1350 to 1450 from an emphasis on spirituality to an emphasis on materialism. There were, to be sure, still pious, dutiful, and honest men, but an increasing number of barons, merchants, and churchmen paid less attention to or abandoned the old medieval precepts that cautioned against a commitment to the fickleness of life and its pleasures and turned to pursue such worldly aims as comfort, wealth, and power. Englishmen shared these ideas with people throughout western Europe. Although the mundane principles of Renaissance thought (which accompanied its salutary effects) had not yet fully influenced England, pragmatism was germinating in the minds of fifteenth-century Englishmen as it was in the minds of Italians. Such ideas led to family feuds and governmental instability alike in England and the Italian city-states, and to the decline in the leadership, strength, and tone of the Church.

The Church in England underwent a gradual decline during the fifteenth century. On the surface, it appeared as prosperous and influential as ever: the hierarchy endowed residential colleges at Oxford and Cambridge; parishioners still paid tithes and other ecclesiastical taxes; and parochial churches were built or refurbished in large numbers.

On the other hand, monks and friars often ignored their vows of poverty, and parish priests, rarely of rich families, sought wealth and comfort at the expense of their spiritual duties. These problems were not confined to the fifteenth century, but the great reform movements within the Church from the eleventh to the fourteenth centuries had managed temporarily to rejuvenate the spirituality and zeal of the clergy. Similar reforms instituted in the fifteenth century were much less successful. Some wealthy Englishmen, avaricious and indifferent toward religion, sensed the same traits among many clergymen and consequently made fewer grants to worthy religious foundations.

The Church lost prestige and strength largely because it remained rigid and inflexible in an age of change. The harassment of Bishop Reginald Pecock of Chichester, who suggested a fresh approach to old doctrines, is a case in point. Despite the persecutions since the revolt of 1381, the Lollards still taught heresy and were occasionally burned at the stake for it in the fifteenth century. Pecock, a brilliant Welsh scholar and devoted son of the Church, attacked the Lollards in a book, *The Repressor of Overmuch Blaming of the Clergy,* which brought him unjustifiably in 1457 before an ecclesiastical court on a charge of heresy. He argued that the Lollards based their beliefs solely on the Scriptures, and that they were wrong to do so. Pecock held that reason as well as the Scriptures dictated the truth and wisdom of tenets. He therefore said that papal supremacy, good works, beneficed clergy, and monasticism—which the Lollards opposed—were logical, not simply because the Church or Scriptures supported them, but because they were consistent with reason. He pointed out, for instance, that the dogmas enunciated in the Apostles' Creed were true, regardless of the fact that the Apostles had not composed it. Many today would agree with Pecock, but his contemporaries grossly misinterpreted his arguments in favor of a broadly based religion and threatened to burn him at the stake. He recanted, saw his books burned, resigned his episcopal seat, and spent the remainder of his life in monastic seclusion.

While Englishmen may have lacked zeal in religion during the fifteenth century, they lacked none in promoting domestic industry and foreign trade. The depression of the later fourteenth century, caused principally by the effects of the Black Death and the interference with Continental trade by the Hundred Years' War, gradually gave way to steady economic growth, which culminated in the modest prosperity of Edward IV's reign. The Wars of the Roses did not materially affect business. Englishmen had long exported raw wool to Flanders where it was washed, carded, dyed, and woven into finished cloth. The Merchant Staplers, operating through the staple town of Calais, continued to ship fleeces abroad, but the volume of their trade decreased because of competition from the Merchant Adventurers, chartered by the crown in 1404, who, by Richard III's reign, controlled about 75 per cent of English trade. This loosely-knit commercial federation, with associates in several major towns like York, London, and Bristol, monopolized overseas commerce in unfinished broadcloths, lead, tin, hides, dairy products, and other commodities with Flanders, southern France, and the western Mediterranean. Hundreds of their ships left the ports of London, Southampton, Hull, and particularly Bristol to establish trade connections with Antwerp, Bruges, Bordeaux, Naples, and Venice. The Adventurers also broke into the Icelandic, Scandinavian, and Baltic markets during the later fifteenth century, competing with the Hanseatic League. In fact, the Adventurers played a significant role in the early sixteenth century in destroying this economic alliance of more than sixty northern European towns. For the time being, however, the Hanse continued to import grain, pitch, tar, timber, and furs into England through its station at the Steelyard in London. Similarly, merchants from northern Italian city-states like Genoa, Florence, and Venice established bases in Southampton and elsewhere in order to import coveted luxury goods, such as sugar, spices, and cotton.

The fervid activity of the Merchant Adventurers resulted in the widespread manufacture of unfinished and undyed broadcloths, which became England's principal export by the end of the fifteenth century. Mills for washing and carding wool sprang up throughout England, but especially in areas watered by rushing streams, which turned wooden machinery and were suitable for washing wool. Eventually the production of broadcloth centered in East Anglia, the West Riding of Yorkshire, the western counties of Gloucestershire, Somerset, and Wiltshire, and, to a lesser extent, in Oxfordshire and Leicestershire. The major industry in many villages and towns in the Cotswolds and the Stroud Valley was cloth weaving, and Stroudwater in Gloucestershire and Worsted in Norfolk became world-famous as cloth centers. Families of weavers, working in the domestic or putting-out system, manufactured cloth on commission from entrepreneurs who sold it to drapers in key commercial centers. The Merchant Adventurers purchased the drapers' broadcloths and transported them throughout western Europe.

The heavy demand for wool to meet the needs of a rapidly expanding foreign market naturally encouraged sheep farming. Furthermore,

England's growing population required more food. The acreage given over to plowland and sheep grazing therefore increased substantially. As there was still plenty of land for everyone, few paid much attention to the enclosure of arable land to sustain larger flocks of sheep. Enclosure, which became a serious problem from the early sixteenth to the later eighteenth centuries, will be discussed in the following chapters.

The vast majority of Englishmen still lived on the land and derived their livelihood from it. They found no reason to change the system of open-field farming with limited crop rotation practiced since Anglo-Saxon times. There were changes, however, in social structure. The country gentry, of varying prosperity depending on the amount of land they owned, were becoming more important corporatively in local government and in prestige. Many of them managed to increase and consolidate their estates during the fifteenth century, mostly at the expense of extinct baronial families. The barons' involvement in the vicissitudes of national politics also often affected landholding; some baronial estates were partitioned or alienated, and the gentry benefited. The social status and economic welfare of the gentry and yeoman class improved during the century and a half from the end of the Wars of the Roses to the outbreak of the Puritan Revolution in 1642. There were also fewer villeins; since the Black Death many had advanced to the status of freeholders and copyholders. Although not all freeholders owned the land they tilled, they could will or sell the right to farm on it at their pleasure. Other tenants were copyholders, the name derived from their having a copy of the lease stipulating annual rents and other contractual obligations to their landlord which they or their predecessors had obtained from the inscription on the manorial rolls. At the bottom of the social scale were thousands of landless agricultural laborers who received hourly or weekly wages. Some of them had the same employer all year; others were migrant workers. During hard times the latter sometimes sought employment in towns where they became a serious problem for local officials, who could not use them in an industrial community requiring trade skills regulated by the craft guilds. But, on the whole, English society during the fifteenth century was amply nourished and busy.

The fifteenth century was an age of increased educational opportunity as well as mounting prosperity for the upper classes. Wealth brought leisure and leisure begot learning, so that an increasing number of persons could read and write well enough to carry on business and enjoy books. Affluent bishops, nobles, and merchants collected small libraries, which they often willed to colleges. The most significant additions to Oxford's library (called the Bodleian Library after the sixteenth century) were made by Duke Humphrey of Gloucester, who gave about 120 books and 300 manuscripts on theology, history, and literature, including the works of Boccaccio and Dante. Humphrey was also a patron of musicians and endowed professorships. The growing number of grammar and chantry schools (the latter attached to cathedrals) helped to educate the sons of guildsmen, who often founded and supported these schools. Henry VI took great interest in education. In 1440 he established Eton College (later a "public" school), across the Thames from Windsor, requiring it to take in scholarship boys from poorer families. Winchester, another famous "public" school that still exists, was established in 1394 by Bishop William Wykeham. His beneficence was not unusual, for several hierarchs donated fortunes to build residential colleges at Oxford and Cambridge. Four colleges (King's, Queen's, St. Catharine's, and Jesus) were founded at Cambridge, and three (Lincoln, All Souls, and Magdalen) at Oxford during the fifteenth century, each of them housing between forty and seventy scholars. Other colleges expanded their buildings, grounds, and libraries.

The new availability of books gave tremendous impetus to education. William Caxton, a Kentish printer who learned his trade in Flanders, set up a press in Westminster and in 1475 produced what is thought to be England's first printed book, probably *Le recueil des histoires de Troyes*. During the next sixteen years (he died about 1491), he printed almost a hundred books, many of which he translated and edited. He published old books on ancient and medieval history as well as newer works by popular authors such as Gower and Chaucer. The flood of books, pamphlets, and broadsides began before he died, and it is not altogether surprising that Renaissance ideas and modes took hold in England during Caxton's later life and played a mighty role in changing his countrymen's concepts in nearly every sphere of human endeavor during the early sixteenth century.

Among the authors contemporary with Caxton was Sir John Fortescue (d. 1476), chief justice of the Court of King's Bench, whose principal book, known as the *Governance of England* (which was not printed until 1714), exposed the weaknesses of contemporary national government and proposed reforms that the Tudors implemented during the following century. As a staunch Lancastrian, he also wrote a primer—*De Laudibus Legum Angliae*—for Henry VI's son, Edward, killed at Tewkesbury. After ten years in exile, Sir John served Edward IV for five years as judge and councilor. In the *Governance* he rejoiced that Englishmen lived freer and more prosperous lives than the French, who labored under grinding royal absolutism, but he was nevertheless distressed that England had so often fallen victim to selfish nobles who betrayed public trust. He therefore advocated a system of government headed by a strong monarch who ruled lawfully (he considered him subject to statute law) and without taint of absolutism for the common good of all his subjects so that their personal property and liberties would be safe from the whims of self-seeking private interests. Fortescue's experience over a long life in the reign of Henry VI taught him the pitfalls of government under a weak monarch dominated by cliques. If monarchy was to fulfill its duty to rule for the common good, he believed, it must never be dependent on the support of factions or be reduced to begging for money from a hostile Parliament controlled by them. Although he considered Parliament subordinate to the king, he recognized its value as the partner of the monarch in making laws that in themselves were a deterrent to royal absolutism. If, in the end, the existing government proved unable to initiate necessary reforms, revolution was the only alternative, as the events of the fifteenth century proved. By way of reform, Fortescue recommended that privy councilors and other high officials hold office on the basis of talent, not social status achieved by birth or favoritism.

One would like to think that Fortescue's sharp eyes perceived not only England's faults in government since 1399, but also its achievements. On the basis of hindsight as well as of his legal knowledge, he must have realized that Parliament had consistently increased its power and prestige. That it could make and depose kings, as it had with Richard II, Henry IV, and Edward IV, and could authorize the collection of most forms of taxation greatly augmented its position vis-à-vis the crown. Before factions of Lancastrians and Yorkists began to manipulate the House of Commons to suit their ends after the outbreak of the Wars of the Roses, it had won several basic privileges. In 1376, for instance, the Commons first impeached royal ministers, and thereby held the king responsible for the policies they carried out. In 1406, Commons demanded that the king account for the money he spent, and sometimes refused to grant further subsidies unless he did so. In the following year Commons began to authorize all monetary grants to the crown. It also made a distinction between money spent for the crown and money spent for the state, and the latter could not be used

for the king's private welfare. Although it is true that all these privileges, except authorization of taxes, were not always enforced by the
Commons from about 1460 to the early seventeenth century, because of
the strength of monarchs from Edward IV through Elizabeth I, the
precedents served to restrain the divine-right kings, James I and
Charles I (1603–49), when the Commons determined to re-establish its
ancient privileges. How the Tudors managed to put Fortescue's theory
on strong monarchy in tune with the interests of Parliament, the law,
and the public good is, to a large extent, the subject of the next two
chapters.

5

The Early Tudors, 1485–1558

The heavy hand that struck down Richard III on Bosworth Field opened the road to London for a new monarch and a new family. Henry VII brought to the throne more wisdom than pride, more power than mercy, more suspicion than trust. His portraits show the piercing eyes, the haggard, almost emaciated face, the tight, thin lips which seem to bespeak that ambition and reserved, unromantic character that fortune had forged in exile and on the battlefield against the Yorkists. If history has not adequately illuminated his contribution as the founder of much that his son and grandchildren built upon, it is perhaps because Richard III and Henry VIII were more colorful. But it was Henry VII who snatched the throne, made it secure against enemies, and provided the financial and governmental stability of which Henry VIII and Elizabeth I took advantage, and for which they got most of the credit. The first Tudor expanded the economy, created a mercantile fleet and enlarged the small Royal Navy, harnessed anarchy, made advantageous alliances with strong European states, and formulated a successful Irish policy.

Military victory alone could not sustain his claim to the throne, for others, such as the descendants of the Duke of Clarence, third son of Edward III, had more royal blood in their veins, and Parliaments and councils had previously made and deposed monarchs for less reason. Henry had first, therefore, to secure his own place as king. He summoned Parliament in November, 1485, and won its recognition by an Act of Succession, and he married Elizabeth, the daughter of the Yorkist Edward IV, thereby grafting the stems of the white and red roses. And while papal approbation meant less in 1485 than a century earlier, Henry gladly accepted it too. But he recognized that whatever legal claim he had to the throne would crumble without support from the upper classes of town and country, who wanted stable government, state support toward increased markets, and relief from patronizing factional ties. Mostly men of promise, not privilege, gathered round him, including Sir Richard Guildford, Bishop John Morton of Ely, Sir Reginald Bray, and Bishop Richard Fox of Winchester.

The deposed Yorkists, who had considerable support in the country, almost immediately provoked opposition to Henry, for in that gullible age men knew even less about the fate of Edward IV's sons than we do. Two impostors, Lambert Simnel and Perkin Warbeck, were put forward, claiming to be the Earl of Warwick, Richard III's nephew, and Richard, duke of York. Richard Symonds, an Oxford clergyman and Yorkist sympathizer, transformed his pupil, Simnel, almost overnight into a Yorkist pretender, acquired the support of Edward IV's sister, Margaret, duchess of Burgundy (to whose court Yorkist exiles had flocked), and took his protégé to Ireland where the English Lords Lincoln and Lovell and several powerful native peers bolstered his flagging courage for an English invasion. The eight-thousand-man army that Margaret raised suffered defeat at Stoke in 1487, and Henry contemptuously assigned Simnel to labor in the royal kitchen, and Symonds to a dungeon. The plot surrounding the handsome Perkin Warbeck, an unlettered Flemish apprentice, won the support of most of Henry's enemies, including James IV of Scotland, Irish malcontents like the Earl of Kildare, Maximilian of Germany and, of course, Margaret. Charles VIII of France also helped Warbeck by allowing him refuge at Calais, but the Anglo-French Treaty of Étaples in 1492 obliged him to forsake Yorkist pretenders, and Warbeck left for Burgundy. By 1495 most of his supporters had abandoned him for reasons of Continental politics revolving principally around the success of Charles VIII in northern Italy, and the peace that Maximilian made with Henry to keep him from allying England with France. Scotland invaded northern England the following year, but James was easily driven back only a few months before Cornishmen rebelled against royal taxation and Warbeck landed from Ireland in Cornwall. Henry suppressed all three rebellions with characteristic thoroughness so that by 1500 the Tudor family had secured its place on the throne.

Henry also negotiated treaties that raised the international prestige of England. Spain, under Ferdinand of Aragon and Isabella of Castile, was in the last stages of governmental centralization and unification.

The joint monarchs had been waging war against the Moors of Granada for almost a decade, and they now coveted the French-controlled provinces of Cerdagne and Roussillon on the Pyrenees border. But Spain alone could not defeat France. The Anglo-Spanish Treaty of Medina del Campo committed Henry to help Spain by invading France from the north. Spain for its part agreed to a marriage between Catherine of Aragon and Arthur, Henry's older son. Henry had only just sent troops to Brittany to help repel a French invasion, and to Burgundy to throw off French and Flemish encroachments, when Charles VIII resolved to concentrate his drive against the Hapsburg dominions in northern Italy. As he could not effectively wage a two-front war against both England and the Empire, he concluded peace with Henry at Étaples. Henry withdrew gracefully, enriched by a huge French indemnity of £18,000 and an alliance with Spain.

With the Scots and Irish, Henry enjoyed equal success. He temporarily resolved the threat of Scottish invasion by a marriage in 1503 between his daughter Margaret and James IV, king since 1488. Ireland proved more troublesome if for no other reason than that it had been virtually ignored since Richard II invaded it in 1399. What Anglo-Irish there were left in the Pale supported the Yorkist claim, and both pretenders had found considerable help there. Moreover, the native earls of Kildare constantly thwarted English authority. In order to re-establish effective control over the Pale, Henry dispatched a new lord deputy, Sir Edward Poynings, whose statutory reforms of 1494 settled Irish affairs until the devastating revisions Oliver Cromwell made in 1649. The Irish feudal barons could no longer have private levies, pillage and plunder the countryside, employ clannish battle cries, or make laws in their own Parliament without royal consent. Henceforth, all English laws were binding on the Irish, and their Parliament could not sit except by the deputy's permission. Yorkist sympathizers went to prison or to the gallows, the Earl of Kildare among them.

The factional selfishness of English nobles proved no less a problem for Henry at the outset of his reign. For too long, recalcitrant cliques had manipulated monarchs to suit private aims, abused or altogether ignored the law, sent their liveried armies against the king or one another, and ravaged the countryside. The Wars of the Roses permitted all manner of abuses—mercenary armies pillaged, sheriffs and juries accepted bribes, Parliament bickered over rival claims of the nobility, and weak monarchs like Henry VI were rendered virtually helpless.

But the Hundred Years' War and the struggle between the Lancastrians and Yorkists, as well as natural attrition, had somewhat reduced the ranks of the aristocracy. Moreover, Edward IV had already begun the task of suppressing them. Nevertheless, when Henry VII assumed the throne, the nation had forsaken the precepts of Magna Carta, the common law, and the prerogatives of the sovereign monarchy. While the nobility corporatively had lost ground, individually they still sometimes pitted themselves against the royal will.

Henry quickly made it clear that no nobleman could stand against him. Few of the feudal aristocracy found a place at the council table and they were not allowed to exercise independent judgment beyond the bounds of law. Henry obliged them under oath to eschew livery and maintenance, and gradually private armies dispersed. A number of Acts restored the jury system, and law throughout the land once more was commonly enforced. Henry also formalized the Court of Star Chamber against powerful felons whose social status or local influence had disarmed cowering constables and sheriffs. The privy council had long functioned as a court in cases not involving treason, felony, or confiscation of property. The Act of 1487 simply gave legal recognition to a panel of councilors consisting of a bishop, a temporal councilor, any two of Chancellor, treasurer, and Lord Keeper of the Privy Seal, plus the chief justices of Common Pleas and King's Bench. This Court of Star Chamber (it met in a chamber of the royal palace decorated with stars) privately questioned persons suspected of "murders, robberies, perjuries, and unsureties of all men living, and losses of their land and goods. . . ." The Court was particularly interested in enforcing the common law, but it was often swayed to protect the king's welfare. Both the extent of its influence and the severity of its sentences have been grossly exaggerated, and far from having under the Tudors the reputation as the crown's great weapon against the liberties of Englishmen that is associated with its later development, the sixteenth-century Court served both the law and royal welfare.

In addition to insisting that his subjects follow the king's law, Henry tried to enrich the crown, realizing that the weakness of some of his predecessors had been due to their relative poverty. As king, he had several traditional sources of revenue, such as benevolences and feudal dues (escheat, aids, and wardship), not to mention the fines levied for violations of livery and maintenance; in 1485 Commons voted him tunnage and poundage for life. But these sources brought in an insufficient revenue to suit Henry, and he therefore did what he could to tap other sources. For example, he gave his son and daughter in marriage to Spain and Scotland in return for substantial dowries, and took more money as the price of peace with France in 1492. He also recovered for the crown most of the lands it had lost during the Wars of the Roses and made no bones about taking away his enemies' estates, thereby augmenting revenue from rents.

Henry likewise encouraged the expansion of foreign trade in order to acquire money. Generally speaking, new laws were passed to protect domestic industry by raising customs duties on competitive goods (a new book of rates was written in 1507), prohibit the drain of bullion to the Continent, and enlarge substantially both the merchant and royal fleets. The staple of English foreign commerce was wool, which had been exported in ever-growing volume for centuries, and Henry did what he could to raise productivity by increasing the market for wool as well as for the textiles that were manufactured principally in East Anglia. Prior to Henry's reign, English commerce had suffered from the depredation of pirates (which continued intermittently until the mid-seventeenth century) in the narrow seas and from the monopolistic regulations of international organizations like the Hanse. Moreover, English trade was hampered by growing competition from the emerging nation-states ringing the Atlantic's eastern edge. Above all, the English government had been harried by the demands of the French war and internal disorder during the fifteenth century, and had not given much encouragement or protection to English merchants. Henry tried to remedy these inadequacies. In addition to providing warships to guard the Channel, he had Parliament pass the Navigation Act of 1485, whereby wines and other commodities from Gascony could be imported only in English ships manned by English sailors, thereby stimulating shipbuilding and employment. The Hanseatic stations in the Steelyard (London) and elsewhere in England and the depots of Italian and other foreign merchants were either eased out or made less profitable by higher import duties. To gain some badly needed imports that did not compete with domestic output, Henry extended trading rights to Dutch, German, Danish, Polish, and Italian merchants. One of these commercial arrangements was the *Intercursus Magnus,* signed in 1496 with the Flemish, Germans, and French in the Low Countries, by which they agreed to freer trade in certain items based on lower customs duties. Although the rising curve of English commercial enterprise leveled off about 1506, when the treaties with Denmark and Riga failed, business generally remained good. The resulting growth in trade and the profits realized in the slowly expanding domestic market augmented the royal treasury to an unprecedented size, amounting to about £100,000 by 1509. It is no coincidence that in 1497 Bristol merchants could well afford to send the Genoese navigator, John Cabot, with five ships across the Atlantic to explore the southern shore of Labrador, even if the frugal king rewarded him with a pension of only ten pounds for claiming all North America for England.

Along with this expansion of foreign commerce there went some growth in domestic industry, although its momentum did not quicken markedly until the later sixteenth century. Most of England's industry was related to the production and processing of raw wool and undyed woolen broadcloths, which accounted for about 80 per cent of English exports during the century. The manufacture of broadcloths, principally in the southwestern counties and in East Anglia, where drapers purchased raw wool and apportioned it out to various householders for weaving in what has been called the domestic system, became very important during the reigns of the first two Tudors. When the cloth had been woven, the drapers generally shipped it to London and other ports from which the Merchant Adventurers carried it to Antwerp for distribution throughout the Continent. Mining was also increasing. The tin industry, centered in Cornwall and Devon, supplied most of the European tin market as well as the pewter manufacturers of London. Next to tin, lead drawn from shallow mines in Somerset, Derbyshire, and Yorkshire became England's greatest mineral resource, and was commonly used to roof important buildings. Coal, extracted primarily around Newcastle, was still a small industry, and was used to some extent for domestic heating, in the iron-smelting shops (although wood was still the main source for domestic and industrial fuel, which accounts for the location of most ironworks in forests), and in the cutlery works in the Midlands. Many other goods necessary to everyday life were still produced, of course, by the several guilds.

The guilds were declining during the early sixteenth century. There were several reasons for this. They were essentially local organizations with restrictive regulations and monopolistic aims that were inconsistent with the increasingly national and international character of trade and commerce. Furthermore the guild system was weakened by the growth of the domestic, or putting-out system, as capitalistic entrepreneurs, who supplied rural craftsmen with raw materials and purchased their products for resale, operated outside the purview of the old merchant guilds. Many guildsmen also objected to paying fees for membership and the fact that their organizations had traditionally been closed corporations dominated by the master craftsmen. By the late fifteenth century, the masters, worried about their share of profits should their ranks multiply, began to make examinations so exacting that journeymen had great difficulty passing them. Seeing this, many journeymen moved out of the towns, where the guilds had jurisdiction, into the suburbs or country, where they did not, and engaged in their crafts without restriction, often managing to undersell the masters. As a consequence, some masters themselves abandoned their guilds and became entrepreneurs. Finally, Parliament enacted laws (1504) regulating the guilds' right to govern their own affairs, thereby subjugating their parochial interests to the national welfare.

The government had less success combating the spread of the enclosure movement, which had been going on here and there on a small scale for centuries, but which increased sharply in the later fifteenth century. Enclosure is related to the decline of the feudal system as well as to the expansion of the wool industry. As the debilitating effects of the Wars of the Roses and the strengthening of the central government after 1485 helped to kill feudalism, so too did the changing character of English economic activity gradually destroy the basis of manorialism. Since the Conquest, the rural landed classes had relied on their estates for income and on their tenants for soldiers. By the reign of Henry VII, however, the demand for wool to feed the expanding textile manufactures interested landowners and wealthier tenant farmers in sheep, which returned a greater profit than farming land or rental income, and private armies were no longer permitted. Landowners therefore began to view their estates in terms of capital investment from which there should be derived the greatest possible profit, rather than as simply a means of livelihood for the landowner and his tenants. As a result, many landowners enclosed with hedges their former farm lands as sheep runs, and often confiscated the common lands on which their tenants had customarily grazed their livestock. Enclosure had several consequences, most importantly depopulation, the decay of manorial villages, a reduction in Church revenue due to the loss of tithes, and unemployment among dispossessed smaller tenants, who lost their leases, often could find no other farms to rent, and were unable to obtain work in a restricted labor market. Complaints poured in to the council and Parliament about enclosure, but little could be done to curtail it. What legislation Parliament did pass to aid dispossessed farmers amounted to feeble efforts, partly because the Lords and Commoners themselves or their wealthy friends converted much of their land to sheep farming. Moreover, commissioners sent to enforce the enclosure Acts met strong opposition from landlords, and suits brought by former tenants against them rarely succeeded, partly because there were loopholes in the law. Although there are no reliable figures to indicate the number of persons affected by enclosure, one can form an impression by remembering that in the sixteenth century the movement was largely restricted to the Midlands, and that probably no more than 10 per cent of the land in that region had been enclosed by 1603. On the other hand, virtually every rebellion and riot in the first half of the century was related in one way or another to agrarian discontent, and between 20,000 and 25,000 peasants were involved in the Pilgrimage of Grace and Kett's Rebellion (both discussed later).

The winds that blew merchant ships across to the Continent also carried English students to Italy in search of the new learning that for almost two centuries had preoccupied Renaissance scholars. They returned home imbued with humanistic ideas, and reverence for classical languages and antiquity, individualism, the fine arts, and a sense of urgency for progress. Because of their lectures and writings, the long winter of intellectual apathy that had characterized much of the fifteenth century gave way to the lush fertility of the English Renaissance, particularly at Oxford and Cambridge. Duke Humphrey of Gloucester, Chaucer before him, and other Englishmen since the thirteenth century had shown interest in Renaissance ideas, but England had not achieved a sufficient cultural awareness in their day to nurture the seed of their minds. But during Henry VII's reign it became increasingly important for influential families to educate their sons in grammar schools and universities, and in the Inns of Court at London, and men were alive to the demands of secular governments that required trained laymen familiar with the newest ideas.

Most of the English humanists (the earlier of them under Henry VII and Henry VIII were called the Oxford Reformers) traveled and studied in Italy and returned to fill university and Church posts. William Grocyn went from Oxford to Rome, Padua, and Florence to study Greek, which he introduced into the English university curriculum on a formal basis. Thomas Linacre, first a student of medicine, later studied Greek, which he used to translate Galen's works, and in 1518 founded the Royal College of Physicians. John Colet, likewise Italian-educated, lectured on Paul's Epistles and taught Biblical literature while dean of St. Paul's in London. Their work drew the attention of Europe's greatest humanist, Erasmus of Rotterdam, who journeyed to England three times to lecture at Oxford and Cambridge, residing for a time with Colet and Thomas More, who later became Henry VIII's Chancellor. At Cambridge, though somewhat later, the Renaissance spirit took hold of John Cheke, Roger Ascham, Miles Coverdale and others, who became as concerned about Continental religious ideas as they had been about classical languages, so that Protestantism spawned there.

The last few years of Henry VII's reign do not compare favorably with the earlier years. The Queen Mother, Arthur, Bray, and Morton had all died by 1503. Most of Henry's accomplishments at home and abroad had already been achieved. He had grown prematurely old, aloof, and caustic, strained no doubt by an energetic and troublesome life. But few persons alive in 1509 who remembered England in 1485 would have denied the substantial changes he had wrought, and passed on to his son.

The great hulk of flesh ridden with gout and syphilis that Henry VIII became in later life is scarcely the image that this most formidable monarch merits. When he ascended the throne, he was in mind, body, and personality all that Englishmen could have desired. Henry stood about six feet, was heavy-boned and muscular, and became adept at the chase, in athletics, and in scholarship. Plato might well have smiled down on this ideal governor, the master of languages, scientific and theological studies, and administrative skills. He could compose poetry and play the lute as well as he could wear colorful costumes on the stage; he laughed and frolicked through half the night with the gayest and most gregarious courtiers in England. Far from a profligate, he was a forceful, shrewd, and accomplished Renaissance man, the idol of his subjects. Whether jousting in a tournament or holding stern audience with foreign emissaries, he always commanded respect, and often fear. Most of his advisers were little more than lackeys bowing before the royal will, and if some like Thomas Wolsey, William Warham, or Thomas Cromwell took advantage of his favor to push their own policies, one way or another Henry always had his way. Few who crossed him lived long to gloat.

In the first half of his reign, Henry devoted much of his time to foreign affairs. The states of western Europe (except for the Empire, where the hopes of political centralization under the Hohenstaufens and Hapsburgs had gradually faded before the particularism of over three hundred German states) had consolidated their governments and looked beyond their boundaries at weaker neighbors. France, Spain, and the Hapsburg dominions had been at war over territorial aggrandizement since 1494. The city-states of northern Italy, fraught with internecine wars waged by rival dynastic factions, became the pawn in the Valois-Hapsburg rivalry (especially during the reigns of Charles V and Francis I), of which both England and Spain took advantage at the expense of the Holy Roman emperor. The ambitions of such states shaped European diplomacy, and Henry VIII could not afford to ignore them.

The chief architect of his foreign policy was Thomas Wolsey, a clever and ambitious adviser who sprang from an industrious Ipswich family into the High Chancellorship, and who later became papal legate in England and a cardinal, rich enough to build the magnificent Hampton Court Palace. While Henry pursued his pleasures, Wolsey worked and planned. He filled Henry's mind with ideas about becoming emperor, and he made no secret about his own quest of Peter's chair. All things were possible if he manipulated European politics to England's best advantage. No state or alliance should be allowed to jeopardize the Continental power structure, and England should join any combination of states that might avert Valois or Hapsburg supremacy.

This policy of balance of power involved England in a French war, when it was endangered in 1511. The League of Cambrai, made up of the Empire, Spain, the Papal States, and France, had combined to attack Venice in 1509. But France gained too much and the others grew jealous so that Spain, Venice, and the Papal States invited England to join the Holy League against France. The privy council opposed Henry's involvement in affairs having little to do with England's interest, but he acquiesced to the entreaties of his father-in-law, Ferdinand, and Wolsey grabbed the chance to implement his new policy. Besides, a French war would provide Henry with an opportunity to emulate the military exploits of Henry V, the chance to strike a blow against England's archenemy, France, and an occasion to prove his devotion to the Church. Accordingly, Henry sent an army to southern France—but it returned home after several months of inactivity. Ferdinand in the meantime had captured Navarre, and the French had lost control of Venice. Faced with disgrace, Henry himself led an army into Artois in 1513 and crushed the French at Guinegate in the Battle of the Spurs. The Scots, who for two centuries had taken advantage of Anglo-French war to invade England, crossed the Tweed only to meet crushing defeat at the hands of the old Lord Treasurer Thomas Howard, earl of Surrey, on Flodden Field, a battle that cost James IV his life and earned Howard the dukedom of Norfolk. The following year Henry made peace with Louis XII.

Within three years, new monarchs ascended the thrones of Spain, France, and the Empire, but the old animosities continued unchanged. Francis I replaced Louis XII in France in 1515, and Charles V assumed the Spanish throne in 1516 and the emperorship in 1519 upon the deaths of Ferdinand and Maximilian, thereby combining the power of both dynastic states, which France could ill afford to ignore. Francis, eager to regain honor, threw his army against the Venetians in 1515 and sent the dauphin, Albany, into Scotland to arrange another Scots invasion of England. Henry responded to this affront by helping the aging Maximilian with money, partly because he was jealous of the bustling, bragging, and athletic French king. But the privy council restrained his inclination to plunge England into another French war, and a temporary Anglo-French accord in 1518 brought Henry an indemnity. The next year Charles and Henry exchanged visits in England and Flanders, and in 1520 Henry tried to impress Francis by an ostentatious display of pomp and circumstance on the Field of the Cloth of Gold on the French coast, but he would never admit that Francis had honestly thrown him in a wrestling match there.

Francis and Charles had obviously been soliciting Henry's favor in the impending confrontation between them. France and the Empire went to war in 1521 as expected. England sided with Charles V for several reasons: Charles was the nephew of Catherine of Aragon, English queen; he led the attack against the heresy of Martin Luther (Henry lent him literary support in a book against Luther); and perhaps most importantly, Francis was too arrogant a contender for the role of Europe's most accomplished ruler to suit Henry. Wolsey favored the Anglo-German alliance because he hoped Charles V would support his candidacy for the papacy, but Leo X and Adrian VI died in 1521 and 1523 without the emperor's lifting a finger to help the English cardinal. The several waves of troops that Henry sent into France accomplished nothing, and Charles V achieved his objective against Francis by defeating him at the Battle of Pavia in 1525, rendering the English alliance meaningless for the future. Nevertheless, Wolsey, still bent on making England a crucial power in Continental politics, made peace with France through a marriage treaty in 1527 and offered Francis further help after the unpaid, rebellious mercenaries of Charles V sacked Rome the same year. But France did not accept it and made peace with the Empire in 1529. Wolsey had clearly failed to effect a balance of power, and to support England's wars he had drained the last penny in taxes and "amicable" loans that the country would tolerate. If anything, Henry had been hurt in reputation both abroad and at home by Wolsey's bad advice, a state of affairs that was made the more intolerable to Henry by his failure to secure a divorce.

Henry had married Catherine of Aragon in June, 1509. This union ordinarily would have been impossible because she had been the wife of his brother, Arthur, who died in 1502, a few months after the wedding. But the Spanish alliance was important to Henry VII, and so, too, was the handsome dowry that went with it. He therefore asked Rome for a dispensation that would permit his second son to wed his sister-in-law despite the ecclesiastical law of affinity. Catherine swore that her first marriage had never been consummated, and Pope Julius II, more soldier and diplomat than moral theologian, saw no reason to thwart the request of a possible ally. For about eighteen years Henry and Catherine apparently lived wholesomely together, and if he frequently committed adultery, she faithfully provided six children, all of whom except Mary died at or shortly after birth. Quite unexpectedly, in 1527, Henry announced that he wished to dissolve the marriage. A series of negotiations between Henry and Pope Clement VII ensued, culminating in 1534 in the Act of Supremacy.

The divorce, the king's so-called "great matter," was only the proximate cause of the English Reformation, if indeed it should be admitted at all that any substantial reformation took place during the reign of Henry VIII. It has already been seen that animosity to the Church had flared up numerous times since the Conquest over several issues, including the authority of the archbishops of Canterbury, the jurisdiction of ecclesiastical courts, the taxation of the clergy, and the Lollard movement. Chaucer, Langland, Erasmus, and Colet, among others, had criticized the Church for the materialism which, they said, had corrupted the pristine spirituality of apostolic Christian times. Even before Martin Luther had cracked the foundation of traditional Christianity by his theological views, Englishmen had questioned some of its dogmas and practices. Elizabeth Sampson and William Sweeting, for instance, died in the 1510s in the fires of Smithfield for doubting transubstantiation, and anticlericalism grew strong in London. Richard

Hunne, a merchant tailor, was imprisoned in the Tower for condemning a priest who took from him an unreasonable mortuary fee. In 1514 Hunne was found hanged and a jury judged the deed to be murder committed by the bishop of London's officers. Bishops in Convocation accused Hunne of heresy, as they had allegedly found an unauthorized Bible in his rooms, and burned his exhumed body. But Commons passed an act restoring his property to his heirs, and considered a bill to deprive those holding minor orders of the right to be tried in ecclesiastical courts, which speaks for the feelings of some important persons toward the Church. Continental Protestant ideas filtered into England in the 1520s and won supporters among university dons and clergymen, especially at Cambridge. Robert Barnes, prior of the Austin Canons there, preached against clerical abuses and stood trial for heresy in London in 1525. Henry VIII himself entered the arena of religious disputation by penning a book, *Defense of the Seven Sacraments* (1521), against Lutheranism, for which Pope Leo X rewarded him with the title Defender of the Faith.

Because he said his conscience troubled him, Henry contended that his marriage should be annulled, or that he should at least be permitted to take a second wife. His marriage to Catherine had provided no son, and he reminded Clement VII of a sentence in the Book of Leviticus (20:21): "He that marrieth his brother's wife, doth an unlawful thing; he hath uncovered his brother's nakedness: they shall be without children." Henry believed, or said he believed, that his having no son (in an age of unsettled politics that demanded a king to carry on the Tudor family's rule) was a sign of divine displeasure over an adulterous union. If Henry's conscience did trouble him, such rumblings came very late. It may have been that, since Catherine was then beyond childbearing years, he wished to take a new wife to provide him with a male heir. He had indeed already chosen Anne Boleyn, a niece of the old Tudor councilor Norfolk, despite her lack of scruples and plain appearance.

Henry, who had proved his devotion to the Church as an ally of the pope, and who was unaccustomed to being contradicted, fully expected Clement VII to nullify the marriage, although it would mean the reversal of a previous papal decision. Cardinal Wolsey lent his support to obtain the divorce or annulment, or to allow bigamy, whichever the pope might suggest. So certain was Wolsey that Clement would cooperate that, while the request for action was under consideration at Rome, he convened a court, set lawyers preparing the case, and held preliminary hearings, only to learn in the end that Clement would not permit an English court to decide the matter. Wolsey then dispatched Dr. William Knight to Rome to plead the king's cause personally. But Knight arrived at a critical time, for Clement had fallen under the control of Charles V, whose renegade army had just sacked Rome in four days of wild, bloody conquest, and the pontiff, normally inclined to indecision, was further unwilling to insult his captor's aunt, Catherine. Over the next two years Clement remained vacillating, irresolute, and frightened, hoping that some expedient such as Henry's change of heart or Catherine's entry into a nunnery might end his tortuous quandary. Finally, in 1529, he sent a special legate, Lorenzo Cardinal Campeggio, to England to hear the suit. The trip could have been made comfortably in four to six weeks, but Campeggio took much longer. Nor was it coincidence that he hesitated as long as the king's patience would bear before convening the court in May, 1529, at Blackfriars. Wolsey and Campeggio summoned many witnesses, among them Catherine, who defended her marriage courageously despite her husband's obvious scorn. The proceedings dragged on intermittently into July when Campeggio adjourned them, never to be resumed. He returned to Italy in the fall, and Clement VII later gave Henry notice that the appeal would have to be made in Rome.

Henry replaced key royal councilors at this juncture. Wolsey, whose fat, comfortable body had withered to half its former size in worry over the failure of his foreign and domestic policies, both of which came crashing down about his head in 1529, bore the brunt of Henry's wrath. The fact that this wealthy, arrogant, and powerful royal servant had antagonized noblemen, parliamentarians, and common folk alike without a moment's concern made it easier for Henry to strip him of all his palaces and honors. Broken in body and in spirit, Wolsey retired into the north, where he honestly tried as archbishop of York to reform the administration of the Church, only to be summoned within the year to stand trial in London for his "crimes." En route south he stopped at Leicester Abbey, where his unexpected death robbed the executioner of his fee. Henry then turned to Thomas Cromwell, son of a blacksmith, who had widened his experience by extensive Continental travel, and who by 1529 had already crept into considerable power on Wolsey's coattails. Such an ambitious man, accustomed to trimming his sail to the wind, could be useful to a king determined to prevail against the awesome authority of the Church. Thomas Cranmer (1489-1556), who had spent most of his adult life as an unobtrusive and amiable fellow in theology at Jesus College, Cambridge, and who, despite his priestly vows, had married a German Lutheran woman with whom he shared essentially Protestant views, became archbishop of Canterbury at Warham's death in 1533. Sir Thomas More (1478–1535), a brilliant lawyer and scholar, although temperamentally and spiritually at odds with Henry VIII, became his Chancellor.

When Henry convened Parliament in 1529 he had the country's support against the pope. Accordingly, this "Reformation Parliament" followed his directions in passing statutes that, by depriving some English clergymen and the pope of income, were designed to force Clement's cooperation. In 1529–30, for instance, Parliament fixed the fees priests could charge for burials and probate of wills, and forbade pluralities except where parishes were too small to support their own clergy. Clement in turn issued a bull in January, 1531, which forbade Henry to marry under pain of excommunication, the approbation of law courts or universities notwithstanding, an obvious retort to the favorable verdicts on the divorce question that several English and Continental universities had rendered. In its second session, which opened in January, 1532, Parliament passed the Supplication against the Ordinaries. This threatened to deprive Convocation (the bishops in conference about Church government) of its right to amend ecclesiastical laws, which frightened them as much as had Henry's charge that all the clergy, by recognizing Wolsey's legatine jurisdiction, had violated the Statute of Praemunire (1353; revised 1393), which had forbidden procuring bulls from Rome. But by that time the clergy were so docile that in May, 1532, most of them accepted the Submission of the Clergy, a document that denied their right to enact without royal permission any new Church laws, and allowed a review by the crown of all existing ecclesiastical ordinances. Finally, Parliament passed the Conditional Restraint of Annates Act, by which Henry could at any time stop the payment by bishops of annates (the first year's revenue from a bishopric) to the papacy.

Because Clement would still not allow the divorce, Henry took matters into his own hands. Cranmer held a special ecclesiastical court session in May, 1533, and on his private authority as archbishop granted Henry the divorce, even though by that time Henry and Anne had already married (January, 1533), making a mockery of Cranmer's favorable verdict. Paul III, successor to Clement, hearing of the illicit marriage, issued a bull of excommunication against Henry, to become effective in September, 1533, if by that time he had not repented. Appeals to Paul from Francis I and others temporarily delayed final action, but in March, 1534, another papal decree declared the marriage between Henry and Catherine valid, excommunicated Henry, and absolved his subjects from their duty of obedience. Meanwhile, Parliament stopped all English revenue to Rome, confirmed the right of ecclesiastical appointments to Henry, and passed the Act of Supremacy.

With this Act Parliament severed the connection between England and the papacy and instituted a state Church governed by the king and his bishops in Convocation. By this statute the king was declared the only supreme head of the Church in England, and the Treasons Act made it high treason for anyone to deny it. Not long thereafter Parliament passed an Act of Succession, which deprived Mary of her right to the throne and made Elizabeth, just born to Anne Boleyn, the heir. It is surprising that more persons did not raise their voices against the schism, particularly among the clergy. Among those who did, however, were Thomas More and Bishop John Fisher of Rochester, who refused to take the oath of supremacy and paid with their lives. The general acceptance of the Anglo-papal split may have been due partly to the care that Henry had taken to prepare the way with the Submission of the Clergy, and partly to his instant revelation that there would be no substantive changes in dogma or ritual. Before long, however, he allowed some reformation, as, for example, in the first and second Confessions of Faith in 1536-37. In the first Confession, Convocation drew up the Ten Articles, effecting a compromise between Catholic and Protestant theory in that only baptism, the Eucharist, and penance were admitted to be true sacraments. The second Confession made more specific doctrinal definition, and finally, the Six Articles of 1539, wherein auricular confession, clerical celibacy, transubstantiation, and other traditional tenets were affirmed, fixed doctrine for the remainder of the reign.

Henry also ordered an inquiry into the state of the monasteries and convents in England, and later in Ireland, which resulted in their dissolution by 1539. According to the text of the Act of 1536, which suppressed the lesser houses, they were to be dissolved because their inmates were living slothful, sinful, and carnal lives. However, considering Anglo-papal relations during the divorce question, the king's subordination of the clergy, and the final break with Rome in 1534, it would be hard to believe that Henry did not have money on his mind among all other considerations. He had nationalized the Church in England by becoming its supreme head, and the next logical step was the nationalization of Church property, though for him to have confiscated it outright with no moral pretext for justification would have been completely out of character. Cromwell and his investigators did find some evidence of evil in a few monasteries and convents, and others were undoubtedly not living up to the ideals of their orders, but, generally speaking, the inquisitors considered many of the houses worthy of perpetuation. Nevertheless, by Parliamentary mandate, the smaller monasteries and convents (with twelve or fewer inmates and an annual income of less than £200) were dissolved and their holdings confiscated in 1536, while the larger establishments suffered the same fate in 1539.

The effects of the dissolution were considerable. First of all, between 7000 and 8000 clergymen were displaced by 1540, about 1500 by the suppression of the lesser houses and the rest in the second suppression. The 1536 Act made provision for the evicted inmates: superiors were to be paid annually an amount of money commensurate with their former positions, with special favor shown to those superiors who handed over all the property of their houses as it had been at the inquisition: ordinary monks and nuns were given the choice of living as secular clergy and religious or of moving into one of the larger, as yet undissolved, monasteries and convents. How many actually did so cannot be accurately stated, but it is certain that a good many survived on the charity of benefactors or wandered aimlessly about without a permanent home or fixed station. Others abandoned the religious life altogether. Similar fates befell the evicted priests and nuns from the larger establishments, though, with the exception of a very few houses that the government allowed to remain in operation, there was no monastic refuge to which they could go. Abbots and prioresses usually got government pensions or filled other ecclesiastical posts, while most of the rank-and-file monks and nuns, unless they gave up religious life, were given meager allowances. As for the property itself, the richly gilded plate and jewels and other valuable movable items filled the king's treasury, and many of the buildings were razed after building materials such as lead, tin, and timber were salvaged and sold. A few of the monasteries were purchased by private parties for conversion into halls, businesses, and the like. Although a part of the monastic lands was sold before 1540, much of it was retained by the crown for the annual revenue it brought. After 1540, and especially until 1545, the crown either sold or gave away most of it, to the value of nearly £800,000. More than 1500 buyers and grantees therefore built their estates and established their family titles on the ruins of the monasteries. Not unexpectedly, they became the staunchest supporters of the Tudor dynasty and the English Reformation that it had brought about. There does not seem to have been much discomfiture worked upon the tenants who lived on the monastic properties. Although some were dispossessed and others had their rents and fees raised by the new landlords, for the most part they were probably not greatly affected by the change-over.

But the near economic revolution created by the transfer of so much capital in money, goods, and land was bound to have repercussions, which erupted, particularly in Lincolnshire and Yorkshire, in the Pilgrimage of Grace in 1536. Religious causes played a secondary role in provoking the uprisings led by Robert Aske, for the peasants, gentrymen, yeomen, and priests who marched with banners aloft behind him had grievances over the enclosure movement, the inflationary economy that pushed up rents and prices, the policies of Cromwell and Cranmer, the break with Rome, and high taxes. They were also afraid that the dissolution of the monasteries would be followed by a general confiscation of all Church property, and that taxes would be increased again. While they were careful to profess their loyalty to the king, they also demanded the restitution of the monasteries and the dismissal of the crown's "wicked" councilors, particularly Cranmer and Cromwell, whom they blamed for all their troubles. The rebellion worried the government for several months, but it was so unorganized that it was never a serious threat to the established order. Henry nevertheless sent troops led by the Duke of Suffolk to strike the rebels down mercilessly. Far from saving the monasteries or abating their grievances, the petitioners had only incurred the king's wrath, and he put to death the leaders as well as some of their humble followers.

In the same year he ordered the execution of his wife, Anne, whom he accused of adultery. She had provided no male heir, probably a greater sin in Henry's eyes. He took a third spouse in Jane Seymour. She died in 1537, shortly after giving birth to the long-awaited son, Edward. Within three years Henry married Anne of Cleves for the sake of an alliance arranged by Cromwell. The latter had outlived his usefulness by 1540, for Henry wanted neither treaty nor wife, so for these "indiscretions," together with the charge that he harbored Lutheran ideas, Cromwell went the way of other Tudor councilors up Tower Hill to greet the executioner. Anne was honorably dismissed. Henry took two more wives after her, Catherine Howard and Catherine Parr, the last of whom survived him.

Much has been made of the revolutionary character of the reign of Henry VIII. He made important administrative changes, but one may ponder whether his reign marks the division between medieval and modern England, as some recent historians have suggested. The long-established forms of local and national government remained unchanged for the most part, although Henry did create the Council of the North after the Pilgrimage of Grace to control affairs in that remote, underpeopled, and often rebellious region. He also set up new courts to handle certain tasks separately from the privy council and Household offices. Among these was the Court of Augmentations, which superintended cases involving revenue from monastic land and property after 1536. Henry also formally instituted the Court of Wards and Liveries in 1541 to raise revenue at the expense of heirs to royal tenants-in-chief and orphaned girls of noble birth, whose property provided the crown with income until it found them husbands, and from the sale of knighthoods and coats of arms. This court helped pay the heavy expenses incurred by all the Tudors, but as an instrument of royal prerogative it became much more burdensome under the early Stuarts, and it was abolished by 1641. In 1536 Wales was united governmentally with England, five new shires being added to the existing seven, all of which sent representatives thereafter to sit in Parliament. At times Henry acted ruthlessly, executing, fining, and imprisoning thousands of his subjects over a long reign of thirty-eight years, particularly in his later years when he grew crusty and ill. Yet, he would have been little different from his predecessors in this regard were it not that he almost always functioned within the law, using the courts and Parliament as battering rams to break opposition. The Henrician genius for government lies in cooperation with Parliament, sensitivity to popular opinion, and expediency in the face of dangerous crises. All did not always go well for Henry, but he found scapegoats such as Wolsey and Cromwell when royal policies rankled the country or ran counter to particular interests. In the end, therefore, Henry was as popular as he had been at his accession, even though most Englishmen were no better off because of him.

When Henry VIII died in 1547, he left a boy of nine and a council of sixteen men, some Catholics and some reformers, as regents to govern according to his will. He had hoped that no one person or either religious faction would gain control until Edward VI was able to rule by himself. But Jane Seymour's brother Edward, later duke of Somerset, persuaded his royal nephew to make him lord protector and to appoint a new, larger council more inclined to Calvinism. Edward Seymour had risen fast in royal circles since his sister's marriage to Henry VIII, and he had shared in the spoils of monastic dissolution so abundantly that he could afford to build the magnificent Somerset House. Most of his popularity and power was generated by his victories in the Scots war that Henry began in 1542 to crush James V, recently married to the French Mary of Guise. Scotland had allied with France, and James harbored English refugees and refused to dissolve the monasteries, undoubtedly because of the advice of his chief counselor, the pro-papal Cardinal Beaton. The border raids going on since 1540 brought war that ended in Scottish defeat at Solway Moss. The Peace of Greenwich, which resulted in Beaton's imprisonment and a promised marriage between the five-year-old Edward and Mary, the infant daughter of the then dead James V, could not last. When a French force invaded Scotland at St. Andrews, Somerset led an English army across the border in 1547 and won the decisive Battle of Pinkie. But the following year France again gained control of Scotland, a suzerainty that began with the betrothal of Mary to the French dauphin and ended with the return of John Knox from Geneva in 1559.

Somerset also faced serious internal problems. Thomas Seymour, his brother, became a source of constant embarrassment. This handsome, ambitious, and profligate admiral of the fleet attempted to enhance his influence by marrying too hastily Catherine Parr, widow of Henry VIII. His intrigues grew more serious as he bargained profitably with pirates in the Channel and tried to talk the impressionable young king into marrying Lady Jane Grey, whose progeny Seymour wanted to use to organize a new power structure at court. Despite all the protector's patience and good advice, in the end Seymour paid for his indiscretions by execution in March, 1549. Additionally, Somerset was opposed by political rivals led by John Dudley, earl of Warwick, later duke of Northumberland, who for their own purposes strove as mightily as fifteenth-century barons to block the protector's efforts to ameliorate the economic problems of the country. Although popular grievances against his government were none of Somerset's doing, but the result of Henrician times, Northumberland used them to bring on the protector's downfall in 1549.

Popular discontent with Somerset mounted despite the fact that, more than Henry, he believed in Parliamentary processes and a reform program to remedy social and economic distress. Henry VIII had tried to cope with widespread poverty, caused by poor harvests, famine, high prices, and enclosure. An Act of 1536, for instance, enjoined every parish to collect a voluntary fund to sustain the growing ranks of the unemployed and hungry. But this measure, which partly compensated for the slackening of relief work formerly carried on by monasteries that Henry was even then suppressing, could not solve problems that had much deeper roots in the changing English economy. As we have already seen, enclosure had become a serious matter. Despite numerous laws passed since 1489 to prevent arable land from being converted into pasturage, to preserve manorial villages, and to limit the number of sheep (as in the Act of 1534) each man might own to two thousand, enclosure continued, not only because these laws were not enforced, but also because the laws themselves were not foolproof. Wolsey had recognized the evil of widespread enclosure, but he had been unable to stop it, and neither could Somerset, even by imposing a stiff sheep tax.

The plight of the poor was made worse by inflation and debasement of coins. The causes for the rise in prices that began during the reign of Henry VII and continued throughout the century are complex. Broadly speaking, the increase in population without a significant increase in the food supply combined to push up food prices, which also tended to elevate prices for other goods, while the abundance of labor depressed wages. The influx of gold from mines in Mexico and Peru that poured over Europe through the Hapsburg dominions also inflated England's economy. In 1544, Henry VIII had begun to debase gold and silver coins by mixing in alloys and by reducing the carat value of the gold itself, and this systematic debasement continued during Edward VI's reign so that, while the crown was enriched by the precious metals saved in the minting of debased coins, their subjects paid the price. Hence, while wages either remained the same or were lowered, prices rose in both town and country, and there was a decline in the real purchasing value of wages due to the cheaper currency. Farm rents rocketed to as much as ten or fifteen times what they had been at the beginning of the century. Neither Somerset nor Northumberland, or Elizabeth's full restoration of bullion in coins, could halt the price spiral that continued until the outbreak of the Puritan Revolution in the 1640s.

The riots that broke out sporadically because of inflation, enclosure, debasement of currency, and the moderate Protestant reform that Somerset allowed, erupted in 1549 into open, organized revolt in the southwest, and later in the eastern county of Norfolk under Robert Kett, a prosperous tradesman. He managed at first to keep some twenty thousand peasants under control with the help of sympathetic clergymen, who advised moderation, even though some had themselves been turned out of monasteries. Kett prepared a petition asking for restraint of enclosure, reduction of rents, and other reforms, but it went unpresented when the peasants exploded in a fury of pillage, maltreatment and murder of landlords, destruction of hedgerows, and general lawlessness. Somerset offered Kett a truce, but he refused. The protector, though sympathetic toward the rebels, who had genuine grievances, finally had no choice but to call on Warwick to lead an army to Norwich, where he slaughtered or captured most of them in a bitter one-sided battle. Kett and nearly fifty others were later hanged.

In the west country of Cornwall, Devon, and Gloucestershire simple folk, clinging to religious tradition, had also revolted against the Protestant reforms implemented by Cranmer. After the reconstruction of the council of regency, Continental Protestant ideas took hold in place of Henrician reformed Catholicism. England became a haven for Protestants from many states within the Empire, and many got university or clerical posts. Somerset almost immediately had Parliament repeal the Treasons Act, the Six Articles, and Acts against the Lollards, and pass statutes allowing priests to marry; it also abolished the use of Latin in public worship. Convocation ordered Communion to be distributed in both kinds, and a royal injunction forbade statuary and other decorative art in churches. Mobs loosed their fury against Catholic churches in a round of iconoclasm that destroyed overnight the magnificent stained glass, frescoes, and sculpture accumulated over centuries. The endowments given by deceased benefactors for education and for Masses in major churches were confiscated in the Chantries Act of 1547, most of the money going to the crown. Finally in 1549, Parliament passed the Act of Uniformity, which required outward religious conformity but not doctrinal subscription to a state religion that was a compromise between Catholicism and Protestantism, essentially what Somerset and Cranmer themselves upheld privately. The Act retained many of the Catholic forms, including the Real Presence view of Communion, vestments, and sacramentals, while the liturgy became more Protestant. Cranmer and an ecclesiastical commission drew up the Book of Common Prayer, which defined religious services, but this beautifully composed book contained passages from the Catholic Missal and Breviary as well as from Lutheran and Calvinist sources, and therefore pleased the extremists of neither side. The fact that more than half the bishops, including Gardiner and Bonner, went to prison rather than subscribe to it, proves that it had less than general acceptance among churchmen.

Somerset, though well-meaning and industrious, had displeased all the elements of English society. Neither Protestants nor Catholics fully upheld his religious compromise; merchants, landowners, and peasants found fault with his economic and social policies; and the political faction led by the Earl of Warwick (later the Duke of Northumberland) threatened his administration throughout. In 1549 the privy council turned against Somerset to support Warwick. When Somerset fled to Windsor Castle, the council ordered his arrest and imprisonment in the Tower. (Three years later Northumberland had him beheaded on a charge of consorting with Catholics to overthrow the government.)

His authority passed to Warwick. Tall, charming, talented, and opportunistic, Warwick had risen steadily with the help of a judicious marriage to the daughter of his guardian, Richard Guildford, and by cultivating advantageous connections at court. These assets overcame the disgrace of his father, Edmund Dudley, one of Henry VII's principal officers, who had allegedly victimized hundreds of persons by imposing unusually harsh fines for minor transgressions to raise revenue, for which Henry VIII sent him to the block in 1510, when Warwick was but nine years old. His rise to supreme power in 1549 lent strength to the extreme Protestant faction in the council of regents, who, though probably sincere in their Protestantism, nevertheless plundered their enemies for almost four years. Although Northumberland made some effort to stem economic distress in the country and promote trade, he also feathered his own nest financially and had Edward VI bestow knighthoods and peerages on unworthy supporters. Northumberland also compromised national honor by surrendering Boulogne to the French at the conclusion of war in 1550.

He was energetic in carrying the nation further along the road to Protestantism. Cranmer once more took the lead. Several bishops stayed in prison and others joined them; their sees were given to reliable reformed clergy. A new Ordinal (a form of prayers outlining ceremonies for conferring holy orders) was introduced by which the minor orders of subdeacon, acolyte, exorcist, and lector were abolished. A Catechism and Book of Homilies (a collection of sermons explaining sacred Scripture) embodied entirely Protestant tenets. Stone altars used in Mass were smashed and replaced by wooden Communion tables situated in the middle of churches. A new edition of the Book of Common Prayer published in 1552 omitted any reference to the Real Presence in Communion and made it merely a commemorative service. Moreover, many clergymen refused to wear vestments such as the surplice and cope. In place of the Six Articles of 1539, Cranmer imposed the Forty-two Articles, Lutheran in tone. He retained only the sacraments of baptism and Communion, and salvation by faith alone and the denial of free will became major doctrines of the reformed English Church. A second Edwardian Act of Uniformity required weekly attendance at services conducted according to the prayer book on pain of excommunication for a first offense, and fine and imprisonment for second and third violations. Such sweeping reforms naturally turned moderates against Northumberland. Even Bishop Hugh Latimer preached against him before the king, saying that he had never seen such callous disregard for the common people. Others became alarmed at Northumberland's greed for plunder, which he exhibited, for example, in confiscating or giving away to friends charitable foundations and all but eighteen Church schools; the remaining few were turned into grammar schools named after King Edward.

As the young monarch grew weaker from consumption, and popular opposition to Northumberland mounted, he began to worry about the future. He knew that the Henrician Act of Succession provided for the accession of Mary upon Edward's death and after her, Elizabeth; and he also realized that neither Mary nor Elizabeth could be manipulated. Edward himself was ready to set aside Mary's right to the throne in favor of Elizabeth, but Northumberland rejected that plan. He decided instead to make Lady Jane Grey, wife of his fourth son, Guilford, and the grandniece of Henry VIII, the queen, and Edward recorded this as his intent in his will. Four days after his death on July 6, 1553, the consent of the council and the principal judges having already been given under duress, Northumberland proclaimed Lady Jane the monarch. But she reigned for only ten days. This naïve, unwilling tool of Northumberland's ambition simply would not do for lawful Englishmen. Men of the eastern counties rushed to support Mary against the usurper Northumberland, who led a largely mercenary army of ten thousand out of London to attack them. The ominous silence of even the city's staunch Protestants on his departure foretold the outcome. Levies were raised for Mary in most counties;

the council abandoned Northumberland; the fleet rebelled; and even
Lady Jane's father declared for Mary. Finally, Northumberland himself
acknowledged her right to the throne and begged for mercy. She sent
him to the block together with three accomplices even as he professed a
sudden conversion to Catholicism. And for the hapless Lady Jane
there remained only disillusionment in a Tower dungeon.

Londoners who had seen Mary Tudor as a child may well have
been shocked at her appearance in the procession that entered the city
in August, 1553. Years of anguish and ill health, brought on perhaps
by her father's casting off Catherine without a spark of compassion
and having Mary declared a bastard, had withered her frail, short
body and drawn her face. Weaker women would have succumbed to
the harrowing pressure that Henry VIII, Somerset, and Northumberland had brought to try to force her religious conformity. In long retirement Mary became introspective, brooding, and fanatical about
religion. She regarded her accession as a divine mandate to reverse
Protestantism by making her Church once more supreme in the land.
This hope had sustained her over long years of quiet study, and even
though she had many of her father's tenacious qualities, she lacked the
essential virtue of moderation. Precisely because the mainstream of
English life had bypassed her for more than twenty years, she knew
too little about current politics or the fundamental changes that had
altered society in the interim. Her values and attitudes were those of
the country as she had known them at her mother's knee—Catholic,
pro-Spanish, stable—not as they existed in 1553. Probably about half
the nation still clung to the old religion, but the other half largely
controlled the land, the wealth, and the political power structure.
Mary's reign was therefore essentially a troublesome interlude in the
march from Henrician reformed Catholicism to Elizabethan Anglicanism—a march that laws, royal injunctions, or persecution could not
stop, as Mary should have realized.

The legal and practical restoration of Catholicism occurred during
the first two years of the reign. Mary released the imprisoned Catholic
bishops and restored them to their sees. Latimer, Bishop Nicholas Ridley, and other reformed hierarchs took their turn in the Tower. Bishop
Stephen Gardiner of Winchester became Lord Chancellor, and Henrician and Edwardian councilors such as Shrewsbury, Arundel, and
Russell served Mary as well. Reginald Cardinal Pole, who had strongly
criticized Henry VIII during the 1530s, returned from Rome late in
1554 as papal legate, and became archbishop of Canterbury after Cran-

mer's execution in 1556. The Protestant immigrants who had found comfortable posts in the pulpits and universities, along with some of their English Protestant friends, totaling nearly eight hundred persons, took advantage of the government's invitation to leave the country. About a quarter of the ordinary clergy lost their benefices, but the rest went along with the Marian reformation as they had done under Henry and Edward, which seems to indicate that expediency, fear of the royal will, and the law carried more weight with them than convictions of conscience. Pockets of Protestantism persisted in England, particularly in London, the southwest, and Oxford and Cambridge. Parliament met in three sessions during 1553 and 1554 and, after some opposition by the Protestant members, passed several acts relating to religion and the succession. It became treason to speak of anyone's having a better claim to the throne than Mary, or to pray that God should shorten her days. The familiar forms of Catholic worship were restored, and the Mass once more became the core of the service despite occasional riots against it. As Parliament at this time would surely have resisted any attempt by Mary to reunite England and Rome out of fear that the confiscated and redistributed monastic lands might be restored to the Church in consequence (many in Parliament held former monastic property), she said nothing of the pope to Parliament and made no effort to restore the lands. Consequently, up to this point, despite the religious reformation, in general the country still supported her.

But a storm of protest arose when Mary announced in October, 1553, that she intended to marry Philip, heir to the huge Hapsburg dominions. From her point of view no more natural union could be conceived, for Philip was already showing signs of becoming the champion of Catholic imperialism on the Continent. An Anglo-Spanish alliance would lend support to Mary's hope that one day she might re-subject England to papal sovereignty (which she carefully avoided mentioning to Parliament) and to Philip's design to suppress Protestantism everywhere in Europe. Nevertheless, popular indignation over her impending marriage caused uprisings and a rebellion and greatly weakened her popularity. Risings in the west under Sir Peter Carew and in the Midlands under the Duke of Suffolk were quickly suppressed. But, in January, 1554, Kentishmen led by Sir Thomas Wyatt, who were excited by rumors of a Spanish invasion, caused grave concern. With the insurgents marching on Southwark, Mary spoke to a crowd at the London Guildhall in a typically Tudor burst of charm, courage, and wisdom. She promised she would not go through with the marriage if it endangered English national interest, and Londoners closed ranks behind her. Unable to cross the Thames at Southwark, Wyatt went to Kingston and moved toward the city from the west. Royal forces diverted a part of his troops at the present site of Hyde Park, and those who got through fought in vain along the walls. Wyatt himself was taken at Temple Bar and imprisoned in the Tower. He and his lieutenants went to the block along with Lady Jane Grey, her father, her uncle, and her husband in the retribution that followed. Mary also tried to implicate Princess Elizabeth, whom she imprisoned, but Parliament and the privy council intervened to save her. The severed heads of the insurgents perched atop the city's gates were a stark reminder of Tudor justice.

Mary misunderstood the support of her countrymen against Wyatt, for although she had many suitors whom Parliament and her council would have welcomed as the royal consort, her marriage to Philip in July, 1554, displeased virtually everyone if for no other reason than that their progeny would assume the English throne at a time when nationalistic Englishmen would not tolerate a Hapsburg ruler. For this reason Parliament agreed to the terms of the marriage in the preceding April only on condition that neither Philip nor his heir should become monarch of England on Mary's death. After their wedding Philip spent only a few months in England, in 1555 and 1557, and they had no children, although Mary at one point falsely announced she was pregnant.

She also set out to reunite England and Rome and to crush Protestantism in a round of persecution soon after the re-enactment of the heresy laws and the repeal of all antipapal legislation since Henry VIII's time. Shortly after Pole's return to England as papal legate, he solemnly absolved the English nation for its break with Rome and declared before the assembled Parliament the reunification of Englishmen with the Roman Catholic Church. Parliament did not object because, as part of the bargain, Pole made it known that the disposition of the monastic lands would not be disturbed. Such leniency did not continue for long. At first, during the spring and summer of 1554, only a few Protestants were put into the pillory or burned at the stake. Among the first victims was John Rogers, who perished courageously before a cheering crowd while his wife and ten children looked on in horror. During 1555, 1556, and 1557, nearly three hundred more were burned for heresy, including Bishops Hooper, Saunders, Ridley, and

Ferrar. Cranmer, having recanted six times only to reaffirm his Protestantism in the end, likewise was burned. While many more important Protestant leaders were not put to death because their executions might have led to rebellion and thus endangered the crown, a large number of humble folk—weavers, farmers, young boys, and common clergymen—suffered horrible deaths, principally in the eastern counties where Protestantism was strong. These executions turned even moderates away from Mary; and far from eradicating the opposition, she strengthened it by making martyrs of political and religious rivals as well as persons she had never met or who could have done her no harm.

Mary also disappointed her countrymen in a brief escapade in Continental politics. Her husband Philip had enjoyed the strong support of Julius III in beginning the Catholic Counter Reformation, but in 1555 the fierce, aged Italian inquisitor, Giovanni Caraffa, became Pope Paul IV. He immediately broke with Philip because Spain controlled Caraffa's native state of Naples. This split resulted in a new political alignment in 1557 in which France and the Papal States opposed Spain, Tuscany, Venice, and Savoy. Philip got Mary to help him despite strong opposition from Parliament and the privy council and the irony of a staunchly Catholic queen fighting the pope. The Anglo-Spanish military alliance, which violated her promise to Parliament made in connection with the marriage treaty, aroused general popular indignation. Mary sent an army to France in January, 1558, but it failed to prevent the loss of Calais, the last English stronghold on the Continent. Ten months later Mary died, brokenhearted, probably demented, forsaken by most of her subjects, and estranged from her thoughtless husband. She had failed to achieve any of her major goals, for she suspected with good reason that Elizabeth would reverse her temporary containment of Protestantism.

It is easier to condemn Mary or to prefix the epithet "bloody" to her name than to have compassion for her. Her unquestionable cruelty toward Protestants cannot wholly be excused, even though it sprang from sincere religious convictions. But it is unfair to single her out as a bigot simply because she put dissenters to death, for on these grounds historians would also have to stigmatize Henry VIII, Edward VI, and Elizabeth. The truth is that no religious sect or monarch had a corner on the market of intolerance in the sixteenth century.

6

The Reign of Elizabeth, 1558–1603

Elizabeth became queen in November, 1558, at the age of twenty-five, and reigned for forty-five years at a time when the several roads traveled by her ancestors merged into a broad highway that led to the heights of nationalism, cultural maturity, and international pre-eminence. In appearance, personality, and talents Elizabeth symbolized what England became largely because of her. She stood tall and graceful, her red hair accentuating the alabaster complexion that her ladies-in-waiting coveted. She wore hundreds of bejeweled, colorful gowns that would have shamed a peacock and strutted about with determination and vanity reminiscent of her father. Her manly voice could gently acknowledge the flattery of the courtiers who knew the way to her heart, or bellow with an anger that frightened even stalwart transgressors. She knew the value of a penny, the comfort of good advice, and the virtue in sensible compromise. She astonished foreigners by speaking to them in their native tongue and she won the hearts of her subjects whether by galloping fearlessly after a deer or by breathing the English spirit with virtually every word. She acted like a man, but knew how to use womanly wiles. Above all, she understood human nature, the aspirations of her countrymen, and the way to be truly a queen. The very fact that she survived to become monarch despite the many dangers of her youth is testimony to her practical wisdom.

At first she tread softly. Danger surrounded her on every side. At her accession the country was suffering from the ravages of the plague, from financial instability made worse by debased coinage, spiraling prices, and weak trade connections, and from religious contention. England was still at war with France and Scotland, and Spain was an unwanted ally. Scotland and France were conspiring against England in an alliance cemented by the marriage of Mary Stuart and Francis II. This claimant to the English throne had Tudor blood in her veins, which made some Catholics, and the papacy, believe that she might do as a substitute for Elizabeth. Scotland was in the early throes of religious, political, and economic upheaval precipitated by Calvinist nobility in rebellion against the regency of the French Catholic Mary of Guise, widow of James V (d. 1560).

But these formidable problems were not insurmountable for an intelligent queen, who surrounded herself with equally intelligent and industrious councilors. These Elizabethan administrators were moderate men with strong Protestant convictions, university educations, and an unshakable devotion to the monarchy. William Cecil (1520–98, later Lord Burghley), principal secretary and lord treasurer, sprang from a family of Lincolnshire gentry who had served the crown in minor capacities since Henry VII's time. After a few terms at Cambridge he entered Parliament, then served as private secretary to Protector Somerset, and finally as a secretary of state under Northumberland before Mary's accession forced him into exile. A staunch Protestant with a reputation for administrative ability, he was a natural choice as Elizabeth's principal adviser, and one she never regretted. Sir Francis Walsingham (?1530–90) became principal secretary for foreign affairs and head of the secret service. A dour Puritan, he had easily made the transition from student to member of Parliament in his early twenties and was brought to the queen's attention by Cecil. Walsingham had great talent for acquiring "intelligence" at home and abroad, particularly relating to the Catholics' activity, and his religious views made him popular with Parliament and a useful liaison between it and the queen. Archbishop Matthew Parker (1502–75), who succeeded Pole in the see of Canterbury, and who reverted largely to the religious policies of Cranmer, had imbibed a measure of Puritan thought while at Cambridge, but he preferred moderation in religion, and was therefore distressed when later he had to combat the Puritan fundamentalists, who sought to overturn the religious settlement of 1559. These three advisers probably made more impact on governmental policy under Elizabeth than her other ministers, but she never permitted them to be as influential as Wolsey had been with Henry VIII. They and other advisers like Sir Nicholas Bacon and Archbishop John Whitgift counteracted the rash temper of court favorites such as Leicester and Essex, playboys who had caught the queen's fancy. Elizabeth infrequently attended council meetings or publicly debated her policies—

she preferred to dazzle her subjects by journeys to and from her many country houses—but in the privacy of her chambers she bluntly told her advisers what she wanted.

Elizabeth's most pressing problem in 1558 was religion. She approached it not from the standpoint of a fervent believer, but as a political question. She had no deep commitment to either Protestantism or Catholicism. If there had been deists in her day, she might have professed an association with them, since she acknowledged the existence of a supreme deity without admitting that man was much affected by such a force. In a kind of practical, earthy way she found a spark of comfort in religion, but she was devoid of deep spirituality or faith. She simply thought that wars, disputations, and the disruption of public order bred by religion were irrational. She had complied with the existing forms of religion since childhood, first as a reformed Catholic under Henry VIII, then as a Protestant under Edward VI, and finally as a reluctant attender at Mass under Mary. Not knowing what brand of religion she would authorize, Catholics and Protestants alike cheered her entry into London at her accession, and foreign ambassadors scratched their heads at her refusal to bare her mind about it. But careful observers might have noticed in her first year the freedom allowed Protestants, the removal of Catholic bishops from office, and her absence from Mass. Logic may have suggested that she hated the alliance with Philip II, champion of the old religion, which could not very well be broken except at the price of abandoning Catholicism.

Such suspicions of Elizabeth's preference for a Protestant Church were justified in the late fall of 1559, when Parliament passed two statutes, the Act of Supremacy and the Act of Uniformity, by which it established an English national Church headed by Elizabeth, who required only outward conformity to it—or so it seemed. She became supreme governor of the Church of England, a less objectionable title for Catholics than supreme head. They nevertheless could not in good conscience take the oath of supremacy, which required renunciation of papal spiritual sovereignty. Some Catholics also questioned Elizabeth's right to the throne on the grounds that the adulterous marriage of her parents made her illegitimate and therefore ineligible. Nor could the Puritans acknowledge her governorship contrary to their convictions that Christ alone was head of the Church. The Act of Uniformity prescribed for general use the revised Book of Common Prayer of 1552, and it imposed penalties of fines and imprisonment upon clergymen who altogether refused to use it or who ignored some of its forms.

Elizabeth had hoped to satisfy all Englishmen by making the new religion as latitudinarian as possible, and the majority of the clergy and their parishioners did accept the official changes. In fact, for the first ten or eleven years of the reign only a few minor incidents marred the success of the Elizabethan Settlement, which took more definite shape in the Thirty-nine Articles of 1563. The widespread popular submission to the royal will was somewhat deceiving, however, because all but one of the surviving Marian bishops had been deprived of their sees, and about 1000 of the 8400 lower clergy had lost their benefices. The shock had not yet worn off for thousands of Catholics, particularly in the remote northern and western regions of the country, and it took time for them to re-form their ranks into a hard core of resistance. Puritanism for the time being gave little cause for alarm because it had barely gotten off the ground as a broad movement to expunge Catholic forms from the Established Church. As the impact of the religious compromise began to sink in, Catholic and Puritan resistance mounted so that by the middle of her reign Elizabeth encountered the serious opposition over religion that she had hoped to avoid. Even the pope temporized at first, waiting to see the direction Elizabethan reforms would take, even though canon law decreed the excommunication of an heretical monarch. Philip II may have helped to delay action from Rome, not only because he hoped to marry Elizabeth, but also because he hoped she might be induced to send representatives to the Council of Trent. But she refused both offers.

In the closely related field of foreign affairs, her first order of business was the termination of war with France. Accordingly, as part of the Treaty of Cateau-Cambrésis (1559), which involved principally the disposition of northern Italy between the Empire and France, Elizabeth agreed to allow Calais to remain in French hands for eight years, after which time it should be returned to England or be paid for by France. On this treaty hung the fate of Scotland also. Mary of Guise, mother of Mary Stuart, ruled Scotland as regent with the help of French troops. So long as the Scottish-French alliance lasted, there was always a chance that France would help Mary Stuart wrest the throne from Elizabeth. But revolt broke out against Mary of Guise and rapidly spread, and within a year she died. The time was ripe for English intervention in Scotland.

The Scottish revolt had begun in 1557 with the formation of an association of Calvinists called the Lords of the Congregation, sworn to defend their faith and drive out the foreigners. They made little headway until the return of John Knox in 1559 from exile in Geneva, where he had learned his religion at the feet of John Calvin. Like Calvin, this stern archangel of Presbyterianism had no respect for painted women like Mary of Guise. Inspired by his infectious zeal, the Congregation refused to obey the regent's order that they give up their plan to have bishops and parish clergy elected by the faithful, and they rose against her instead. A large number of their followers, who had gathered at Perth and later swept through most of the eastern Lowlands, destroyed images, sacked monasteries, and forced the Edwardian prayer book upon Catholic congregations. From the first the Presbyterians had been in touch with Elizabeth, who first sent money and an English fleet to intercept a French invasion force; early in 1560 she dispatched an army which, with the Scots' help, took Leith and Edinburgh. In June, England, Scotland, and France signed the Treaty of Edinburgh, which caused the French to withdraw from Scotland and the government to be put under the authority of a council of the Lords of the Congregation. Mary Stuart and her husband Francis II also tacitly acknowledged Elizabeth's right to rule by removing the Tudor rose from their coat of arms. But whatever comfort Elizabeth got from the thought of having a sympathetic Protestant government in Scotland was short-lived. Francis II died in 1560 leaving Mary Stuart an unwelcome widow in a kingdom ruled by her brother-in-law, Charles IX. She therefore returned to Scotland to take her place on the throne despite the opposition of the Presbyterian Lords and many of the lowland populace, who greeted her arrival at Leith in silence. Shortly thereafter Elizabeth again went to war with France to help the Huguenots. She may have assisted them for the sake of Protestantism; but it is more likely that she hoped thereby to regain Calais and Dieppe at the price of a few arms and a small English garrison. But the garrison was surrounded and captured, and although the Queen Mother, Catherine de Médici, agreed to allow the Huguenots limited religious freedom, the English had to withdraw. By 1565 affairs in neither Scotland nor France were going well for Elizabeth.

Mary Stuart sat on a throne full of thorns. She was beautiful, bright, temperate in religion, gay, but lacking in judgment. Her antagonist, Knox, was glum, parsimonious, dour, and utterly devoted to the Calvinist creed. Their personalities, religion, and purpose in life inevitably clashed. Mary appointed a few Calvinist peers to her council and at first showed no intention of forcing Catholicism on their coreligionists, but Knox nevertheless distrusted her because he believed that at heart she was putting up with religious compromise only until she had gained sufficient strength in the country to reinstitute Catholicism. She certainly knew his opinion about female rulers if she had read his vitriolic *First Blast of the Trumpet against the Monstrous Regiment of Women,* meaning Mary Tudor, Catherine de Médici, and Elizabeth. Knox felt that neither God nor nature meant women to govern. Such "monsters" ought to be deposed and executed. Mary should have moved with caution. But she made three mistakes that led to her deposition in 1567; she asked Elizabeth to designate her as heir to the English throne; she married Henry Stuart, Lord Darnley; and she apparently conspired with Bothwell to murder Darnley.

Elizabeth could hardly have agreed to recognize Mary as her successor. To do so would have put in question her own right to the throne, angered her Protestant subjects, left her vulnerable to Catholic plots, and given support to Philip II, who was even then urging Mary to begin the persecution of Presbyterians and to depose Elizabeth. Mary's marriage to Darnley is related to her quest of the English throne. At a time when Elizabeth repeatedly rejected her councilors' suggestion that she marry so as to secure the Tudor succession, she was dismayed to learn that Mary, her rival, had taken a handsome husband. Darnley, son of the Earl of Lennox, was an irascible, vain, vicious drunkard who held large estates in England. Moreover, he was more English than Scottish, being the grandson of Margaret Tudor by her second marriage to the Earl of Angus. Darnley's mother, Margaret Douglas, was a strong proponent of the old religion. The Darnley marriage, which resulted in the birth in 1566 of a son—the future James VI—strengthened the latter's lineal claim to the English throne and united the Scottish royal house with a powerful English Catholic family. Under these circumstances it is no wonder that the marriage worried Elizabeth and provoked the Scots Presbyterians. At the first mention of it in 1564 a small number of Calvinist peers in the council and the Lords of the Congregation, principally Murray, Argyle, and Hamilton, staged a rebellion; but when Mary managed to hold the allegiance of other equally important Protestants, the insurgents fled to England.

During the next two years Mary lost her hold in Scotland because of utter foolishness. Within a few months of her marriage, she found Darnley to be an insolent rogue, and she refused to allow him to exercise constitutional authority as joint sovereign. Instead, she turned for advice and help to her Italian Catholic secretary, David Rizzio, whom Darnley murdered in a fit of rage in March, 1566, virtually before her eyes. In addition, Darnley, Lord Ruthven, Lord Lindsay, and others had actually planned to overthrow the government in order to save themselves from outright exclusion from power in a political reorganization that Mary was then contemplating. Discovered, the conspirators fled south, Darnley alone remaining because Mary thought she still might need him to make good her claim to the English throne.

One of her staunchest supporters in suppressing the coup had been the unprincipled rake James Hepburn, earl of Bothwell (1536–78), who, though barely thirty, had already become one of the most hated men in the country. Strong adjectives like licentious, corrupt, vicious, and vainglorious do not begin to characterize this Protestant courtier, who had deserted the faction of his coreligionists in favor of Mary of Guise's French faction in order to retain favor at court. After working his wiles on the Queen of Scots, he convinced her that Darnley was no longer needed, and, together with a few other councilors, conspired to murder him, a plan of which Mary herself could hardly have been ignorant. In February, 1567, Darnley was strangled to death and his house at Kirk-o'-Field outside Edinburgh was blown up. Three months later Mary married Bothwell, who had just divorced his wife.

Meanwhile Mary had been corresponding with the Guise family in France and with the pope about steps by which she could restore Catholicism. She had not approved the Parliamentary sanction of free worship for the Presbyterians insisted on by the Lords of the Congregation in 1560, and she intended to appoint Catholic councilors in place of Calvinists in preparation for a general suppression of dissenters. Her marriage to Bothwell, however, caused such public scandal that the churchmen, clansmen, and ordinary folk of the Protestant eastern Lowlands rose spontaneously to depose her. Bothwell escaped to the Continent, and Mary abdicated in favor of her infant son, James VI, under the regency of her brother, the Earl of Moray. He confined her in Latham Castle near Lock Leven, from which she escaped about a year later to England.

Mary requested and received Elizabeth's protection. What else could Elizabeth logically have done? She could not admit the legality of deposing a duly constituted monarch by surrendering her cousin to the Scots rebels. Nor could she allow Mary to go to France or Spain where she might conspire with the Guises, Philip II, or the pope to restore Catholicism in England. If Mary's presence gave encouragement to the Catholics, who hoped to make her queen, and proved an embarrassment, at least Elizabeth could keep an eye on her at Bolton Castle in Yorkshire, where she stayed for most of the time until her death in 1587.

Elizabeth had not long to wait upon conspiracy in support of Mary. Several earls in Northumberland, Westmoreland, and Yorkshire, in touch with the Spanish embassy in London, plotted in 1569 to arrange a marriage between Mary and Thomas Howard, duke of Norfolk, a Protestant leader of the English nobility, and, helped by Spanish soldiers from the Netherlands and papal money, to force Elizabeth's abdication in favor of Mary. Here is another instance of the close and complicated relationship between the religious question and national feeling under Edward VI, Mary Tudor, and Elizabeth that is hard to explain. Many of the insurgents joined this northern rising for religious reasons, as is evidenced by their destruction of Protestant prayer books and Communion tables and their attendance at Mass in Durham Cathedral; others, such as the older Protestant peer Henry Fitzalan, earl of Arundel (d. 1580), had no desire to harm Elizabeth or restore Catholicism, but joined the Catholics in order to oust Cecil, who had ignored them in the governmental change-over, and who they believed was responsible for an economic depression in the north country due to strained relations with Spain and France that might also lead to war. Many Englishmen under the later Tudors seem to have had difficulty deciding whether they hated Catholicism or Spain more, as was the case in 1569. Indeed, the charge that Catholics conspired unpatriotically with foreign powers for the overthrow of the government often weighed more heavily with Protestants than Catholic refusal to conform to the Established Church.

The northern rebellion failed. The Spanish troops never came and the insurgents were trapped and easily vanquished. Consequently Mary was not freed from imprisonment, and the traitors, rounded up in a careful search, were put to death. Norfolk deserted them in time to escape punishment. The failure of the rebellion also decided Pope Pius V to throw the whole weight of the Catholic Church against Elizabeth. The Counter Reformation seemed to be making progress on all fronts, for the Huguenots were losing in France and Philip II was making headway against the Calvinist rebels in the Netherlands. The Council of Trent, which had ended in 1565, had debated the possibility of Elizabeth's excommunication and a papal bull to that effect had been composed in February, 1569, to be published when evidence of English Catholic opposition to Elizabeth was clearly shown. Accordingly, Elizabeth was declared a heretic and excommunicated in 1570; her Catholic subjects were released from their duty of obedience, which resolved their quandary over the moral implications of rebelling against a legitimate monarch. Roberto di Ridolfi, an Italian banker residing in London, who secretly served as a papal spy, acted quickly on the heels of the excommunication. He went to Rome and Madrid to lay before Pius V and Philip II a plan to oust Elizabeth that was almost identical with the arrangements of the northern earls. Norfolk had no sooner been released from the Tower than he renewed correspondence with Mary, consenting once more to marry her and to depose Elizabeth with the help of six thousand troops supplied by the Duke of Alva. But Philip hesitated for fear that Elizabeth might make an alliance with France against him, and the conspirators' plans were found out by Walsingham and Cecil, who simply waited until they had tipped their hand. In due course Norfolk, Northumberland, and others were arrested and executed.

The result of the excommunication of Elizabeth and the northern rebellion was a series of penal laws enacted by Parliament to crush the Catholics. Although the Act of Uniformity (1559) had enjoined all Englishmen to practice the same form of religion, and another Act of 1563, which imposed the penalties of *praemunire* (i.e. outlawry; for a third offense, death) against minor governmental officials and university graduates who refused to take the oath of supremacy, sought to strengthen religious conformity, the laws after 1570 penalized dissenters for specific violations. In general, these statutes imposed penalties ranging from fines of twelve pence for each absence from Anglican services on Sundays and holy days to the horrendous punishment of hanging, drawing, and quartering for missionary priests who said Mass and distributed the sacraments. The resulting Catholic emigration to the Continent, though never large, proved very troublesome to Elizabeth, for although most of the emigrés went to the Low Countries, Spain, or Italy to live as best they could on Spanish or papal pensions, on pay for service in Hapsburg regiments, or on their own meager resources from trade or unsequestered estates back home, others studied for the priesthood in several Jesuit seminaries in the Spanish Netherlands, France, and below the Pyrenees. The Jesuit house founded in 1568 by William (later Cardinal) Allen at Douai and the seminary at Valladolid (Spain) alone trained hundreds of English priests, many of whom followed the Jesuits Robert Persons and Ed-

mund Campion back across the Channel after 1580 to bolster the flagging faith of their frightened and disillusioned coreligionists. But although these missionaries spent their lives moving clandestinely
between Catholics' country houses equipped with hiding places, and
often suffered martyrdom or torture, they failed to arrest the attrition
of Catholic ranks in the face of the financial, social, and political
disabilities resulting from the penal laws.

Parliament made the penal laws progressively more severe. Three
statutes in 1571 prescribed fines, and in some cases death, for persons
who upheld the pope's supreme authority, attempted to reconcile anyone to Catholicism, introduced religious emblems such as crucifixes,
religious pictures, or beads, or left the country without a license to
travel. Other penal laws in 1581 and 1585 ordered fines of from 100
to 200 marks and a year's imprisonment for those caught attending
Mass, and imposed a ruinous penalty of twenty pounds on recusants
(anyone who refused to conform to the Church of England) who
failed to attend Anglican service at least monthly; priests who remained
in England despite a proclamation ordering their departure were to
be ripped open and dismembered by the public executioner. Elizabeth
had obviously forgotten her promise at her accession not to "open
windows into men's souls" and sought to eradicate Catholicism in the
country, though, but for her influence, Parliament probably would
have written even stricter laws. As it was, a large number of Catholics
succumbed to such pressure, at least to the extent of conforming as
"church papists" to what the law required, to save their money, their
positions, or their social respectability; others, even among the justices
of the peace, sheriffs, and constabulary, practiced the old religion
privately. Catholicism therefore did survive.

Elizabeth meant some of the penal laws to apply to Puritans as well
as to Catholics. In the strictest sense, Puritanism was opposed to the
alleged perversion of the primitive Church through Catholic forms
adopted in the Act of Uniformity and the Thirty-nine Articles. Puritans hoped to root out these forms and to substitute Calvinism in doctrine and ecclesiastical polity. During the 1520s and 1530s a small
circle of Cambridge scholars had begun to discuss Continental Protestant ideas. These "Germans," as their contemporaries named them,
prepared the ground in which the seeds of Calvinist thought took root.
Even during the reign of Edward VI there were some Puritan-minded
clergy such as Bishop John Hooper, who complained about the retention of "popish" ceremonies and refused to wear the scarlet cope

required of his office. The virtual freedom of worship permitted Protestants during Northumberland's administration not only encouraged iconoclasm against Catholic churches; it also inadvertently encouraged in university halls, pulpits, and pubs discussions about religion that required a knowledge of the Scriptures, newly published in several English editions from the translations of Miles Coverdale and John Rogers. At Mary's accession many Protestants had gone to centers of Continental Protestantism such as Middelburg, Strasbourg, and Geneva, where they broadened their knowledge of reformed religions. They returned in 1559 with the hope that Elizabeth would make sweeping reforms based on Calvin's system and became annoyed and frustrated at her refusal to allow dissent or to consider change. Their opposition to the Elizabethan Settlement was intensified by the Erastianism of the Anglican Church—the system of government under which the Church was subordinate to the state.

Although the Puritans disagreed over doctrine, they did share some common beliefs. They stressed the Bible as the only source of faith and morals. They read it avidly, interpreted it individually, and inevitably quarreled over what form of religion it prescribed. They insisted that one's actions should in every way exhibit a profound devotion to Christ and to duty. They caustically censured what they termed "superstitious" symbols of Catholicism retained by Anglicanism, including statuary, stained-glass windows, sacerdotal vestments, the use of holy water and beads, and stone altars placed in the east end of churches. They disliked the regimen of formal religious services authorized in the Book of Common Prayer and the privileged position of the clergy, preferring extemporary prayer and preaching by ministers who did not claim to be intermediaries between Christ and the faithful. Elizabethan Puritans also decried ostentatious dress, hair styles, ceremonies, and music, although their progeny in Caroline England made more of an issue over these things. Most Puritans also subscribed to Sabbatarianism—that the Sabbath (most often Sunday, but for a few, Saturday) ought to be a day of rest and worship free from any form of recreation, travel, or work.

By the middle of Elizabeth's reign, the Puritans had split into three broad categories according to their views on Church government. By far the largest number remained within the Establishment, accepting the episcopal system but working for a greater voice for the laity in decisions respecting questions of form and faith. These moderates generally controlled the movement until about the outbreak of the Puritan Revolution in the 1640s. Other Puritans, at first led by Thomas Cartwright, advocated a Presbyterian system of ecclesiastical polity in which authority would be vested in several levels of jurisdiction from the kirk session at the bottom, through the presbytery and provincial synod, to the General Assembly at the top. Cartwright, Lady Margaret Professor of Theology at Cambridge in 1569–70, proposed such a system, and it later got widespread publicity in the *Book of Discipline,* commonly attributed to Walter Travers. Against this treatise Bishop Richard Hooker wrote his famous *On the Laws of Ecclesiastical Polity,* the classic statement of Episcopalianism. A third broad division of Puritans was the Separatists, known originally as Brownists and later as Independents, who worshiped apart from Anglican services in individual congregations or conventicles. One of the earliest Separatist leaders, Robert Browne, an irascible and undisciplined preacher, wrote several pamphlets in which he insisted on the complete autonomy of every parish, subject only to the will of Christ. They formed the first Congregationalist community at Norwich in 1581 and another at Scrooby shortly thereafter. Such Puritans advocated democracy at the parish level, but actually many of these congregations became subject to the dictates of their elected ministers, including Browne, who lost several benefices for that reason. The Congregationalists had only a handful of followers in Elizabethan England, but they grew stronger in the seventeenth century when some emigrated to Holland and America, and others fragmented into a multitude of left-wing Puritan sects such as the Family of Love, the Ranters, the Seekers, and the Levelers, whom even the Independent Oliver Cromwell would not tolerate.

Unlike some Catholics who left England to escape the penal laws, most Puritans staunchly stood their ground to do battle with the Establishment, although at worst most of them paid fines, endured short-term imprisonments, or lost their benefices. Only a few Puritans were executed because of their beliefs during Elizabeth's reign. But Puritan nonconformity became so widespread that Convocation was forced to listen to their spokesmen about reforms in 1563, and managed to defeat their adoption by only one vote. Finally, in 1566, Archbishop Parker laid down strict rules regulating clerical dress and the nature of religious services by which he hoped to settle the Vestiarian Controversy that first appeared among about three hundred dons and students in St. John's and Trinity Colleges, Cambridge, and finally spread to the clergy in London, East Anglia, and the southeast counties. When the Puritan clergy not only refused to conform, but even established their own Presbyterian congregations at Wandsworth in 1572 and elsewhere, the Anglican hierarchy subjected them to suspension and imprisonment. The Puritans responded in an *Admonition* addressed to Parliament, in which they set forth their ritualistic demands. Puritan persecution mounted after John Whitgift became archbishop of Canterbury in 1583. He employed to good advantage the recently created Court of High Commission, which punished Puritans for nonconformity. Elizabeth met their challenge to introduce through Parliament a new prayer book in 1584 by directing Whitgift to take the sternest measures with them. Accordingly, hundreds of Puritans lost their benefices, dozens went to prison, and at least six were executed on charges of treason.

One of the Puritans' chief weapons against the Elizabethan Church was pamphleteering, which created a mountain of printed pages in the 1580s. Much Puritan literature was reasoned, calm, and moderate in tone, but sometimes it was libelous, vituperative, and even treasonous. The Martin Marprelate Tracts (1588–89) are good examples. They were probably a protest against a Star Chamber order of June, 1586, that all presses should be controlled (i.e. censored) by the Stationers' Company, and that no presses be set up outside London except one each in Oxford and Cambridge. No book could be published until approved by Bishop Whitgift or his censors. The seven Marprelate tracts, a pseudonym for several Midlands authors, including probably Job Throckmorton, were printed in Northamptonshire, Worcestershire, and Lancashire. In general, they concentrated on the evils of episcopacy in rich satirical prose that enraged the opposition, who replied in more moderate but less convincing pamphlets. The Puritan threat caused Parliament to pass the Conventicle Act (1593) whereby all persons over sixteen years of age had to attend Anglican services on pain of imprisonment—an obvious effort to arrest the establishment of nonconformist congregations. But the repression of Puritans had only a fleeting effect, for even though they lost some ground in the 1590s as an organized movement for Church reform, their spokesmen in Parliament, in business, and in the learned professions were girding their loins against the day when royal displeasure would not be enough to make them conform.

Calvinism and Catholicism troubled Elizabeth abroad as well as at home. In the 1570s and 1580s, western Europe was rent with revolution that involved an interplay of Spanish, French, and Dutch affairs. The French religious wars, which began in 1562, continued between the Huguenots and the Catholics on the one hand, and among the three rival families of Valois, Bourbon, and Guise on the other. Mary, Queen of Scots, naturally favored the Guises as she was a daughter of that royal family and hoped to have its help in England and Scotland. Elizabeth surreptitiously sent arms, money, and a few troops in support of the Huguenots in order to avert a combination of French and Spanish power against her in the event that French domestic affairs should be settled. In furtherance of the same end, she encouraged talk of a possible marriage between herself and the Duke of Anjou, a brother of King Charles IX, even though she knew their differences over religion would preclude such a match. The longer the Valois entertained the prospect of an English marriage alliance, the greater was the probability that France would not assist Spain against England or the Netherlands. The massacre of several thousand Huguenots in Paris on St. Bartholomew's Day, 1572, by Catherine de Médici's forces, almost wrecked Elizabeth's plans, for many Englishmen demanded a rupture of Anglo-French relations. Elizabeth realized, however, that good or bad, the Queen Mother of France held the balance of power in her hands, and did not alter her foreign policy. Her policy toward the Dutch rebels was dictated by similar considerations. She intervened to help the Calvinist Dutch as much as was needed to keep their revolt against Spain from failing, to sap Spain's strength so that an invasion of England would be out of the question. England's international posture worsened in 1576 when Don John of Austria became governor of the Netherlands, for it was commonly known that he was encouraging Philip II to attack England. Elizabeth immediately sent £20,000 and promised £100,000 more to the Dutch, who thereby grew strong enough to unite several northern provinces in the League of Arras, which evolved by 1581 into the United Provinces. This new nation could not secure the recognition of either France or England, but Elizabeth decided that she must immediately help it to recover from the crushing military defeats that the next governor, the Duke of Parma, inflicted in 1585. Accordingly, the incompetent and petulant Earl of Leicester led eight thousand men into Flanders, but the troops fought only one battle (Zutphen), and that was such a disastrous defeat that they were forced to return to England late in 1587.

Luckily for Elizabeth, Philip II's efforts to restore Catholicism in England were as unsuccessful as his intervention in French and Dutch affairs had been. He tried at first to embroil Elizabeth in Ireland, where the lord lieutenant, Henry Sidney, could not suppress a series of bloody feuds between the Anglo-Irish and the native clansmen in the Pale. The wars continued during the 1560s and 1570s, first under the Irish Earl of Desmond and later under James Fitzmaurice, who asked for Spanish assistance. Philip sent troops to county Kerry, but Sidney butchered them to the last man in 1580. In the same year the first Jesuits entered England determined to undermine Anglicanism. However, only a few, together with a handful of Catholic laymen, took part in the abortive plots of the 1580s. Each of the conspiracies had basically similar aims—the assassination of Elizabeth was to be followed by a Spanish invasion that would free the Queen of Scots and make her monarch. Several plotters who were arrested, tortured, and executed in the early 1580s confessed that they had taken Spanish gold to kill Elizabeth, which was enough evidence to expel the Spanish ambassador and close the embassy in 1583. The next year a Jesuit sympathizer murdered the Dutch Calvinist leader William the Silent, a deed that caused many Englishmen to associate all Catholics with Spanish intrigue when actually the vast majority of English Catholics had no idea of what a few of their coreligionists were planning. The last plot, the brainchild of Anthony Babington, a Catholic convert from Derbyshire and a page to Mary Stuart, was discovered by Walsingham's agents before it could be carried out. Some of Mary's letters captured by the government proved her knowledge of and acquiescence in Babington's plans. Both Houses of Parliament clamored for her execution as did the general public, but Elizabeth hesitated for some months before signing the death warrant. Finally, at Fotheringay Castle, Northamptonshire, in February, 1587, the career of the glamorous Queen of Scots came to an ignominious and desolate end. Even her own son, James VI, did not try to save her life!

The spirit of adventure and sense of nationalism that drove Englishmen to join Huguenot and Dutch regiments in France and the Netherlands also carried strong seamen out of Devon ports to plunder Spanish ships in both the Old and New World, thereby opening up another front of attack upon the already harassed Hapsburg empire. For many years the Merchant Adventurers had traded in raw wool and partly finished cloth with the Netherlands. It is no exaggeration to say that the welfare of much of the English economy had rested on the volume of the Flemish trade since the fourteenth century, so that even though the Adventurers and other trading companies greatly expanded the scope of their mercantile enterprises during Elizabeth's reign, any interference with the Antwerp market could have serious economic results. It was therefore natural for Englishmen to become alarmed when in 1568 Philip II ordered the suspension of trade between England and the Netherlands. John Hawkins, a relative of the William Hawkins who skirted African and American coasts toward the close of Henry VIII's reign, made three trips to South America and the West Indies between 1562 and 1567 to trade in slaves carried from Africa. On his last expedition, Hawkins was attacked by the Viceroy of Mexico at San Juan de Ulúa, where he lost a ship and some of his crew. Wealthy businessmen-courtiers, who had invested heavily in the expedition, complained bitterly to Elizabeth about their losses; yet she kept her temper and the peace. This nevertheless stirred Anglo-Spanish passions, which were further heightened when Elizabeth seized a Spanish ship laden with treasure that had had to put into an English port during a storm while on route between Genoa and the Netherlands. In retaliation, Philip ordered the confiscation of the Merchant Adventurers' goods at Antwerp and stopped trade between it and England. This almost led to war, forced the removal of the Adventurers from Antwerp to Hamburg in Germany, and caused heavy trade losses, particularly among the sheep farmers in northern England.

These incidents help to explain why Elizabeth assisted the Dutch rebels and why English seamen roamed the Atlantic to break the Hapsburg commercial monopoly in world trade. Devon sailors, long accustomed to privateering against alien ships in the Channel, led the way. Elizabeth feigned ignorance when asked by Spanish ambassadors about the exploits of her seamen, but she knew very well what they were doing, was extremely pleased at the wealth they brought home, and even financed further expeditions.

Sir Francis Drake made forays in the 1570s into the Hapsburgs' New World domain. His primary goal, which set a pattern for later Elizabethan and Jacobean captains, became the Spanish treasure fleets that annually transported bullion from Peru and Mexico to Spain. Spain's economy was utterly dependent upon the arrival of this fleet each spring, for without it neither its armies nor its coterie of public servants and greedy courtiers could be paid. Drake left England in 1577 in command of five ships outfitted with money provided by Elizabeth and many of her councilors. Despite mutiny on the high seas and the loss of four ships, Drake piloted the *Golden Hind* across the Atlantic, through the Strait of Magellan, and into the Pacific Ocean, where, along the west coast of South America, he took a huge Spanish

treasure ship. He moved north along the California coast, possibly as
far north as the Strait of Juan de Fuca, and then bravely pushed out
into the vast reaches of an ocean that only Ferdinand Magellan in
1519–20 had dared to cross. After months of sailing, Drake passed
through the Indian Ocean and around the Cape of Good Hope, and
from there to Plymouth by September, 1580. He had circumnavigated
the globe, but assuredly his stockholders were more interested in the
gold, silver, and fragrant spices he brought, and in the blow he had
struck against Spain. He also plundered on the Spanish Main in 1585,
and in 1587 dared to enter Cadiz harbor, despite the massive guns
that guarded it, to sink ships and destroy supplies being gathered for
the Armada. He roamed Spanish waters off Cape St. Vincent, Lisbon,
and the Azores without any significant opposition before returning
home with the certain conviction that the gargantuan fleet Philip II
had been preparing for a grand assault on England was not so fearsome after all.

Wherever Philip turned, the specter of Elizabethan power rose to
haunt him. Elizabeth crushed Catholic plots through which he hoped
to depose her in favor of the Queen of Scots; she aided Dutch rebels
and gave help to French Huguenots. Her seamen plundered on the
Spanish Main and even attacked Iberia itself; and she hurt the Hapsburg economy throughout Europe by breaking its monopoly despite
the closing of the Netherlands' ports. Not least of all, to the frustration of Parliament, which repeatedly urged Elizabeth to marry in order
to provide a Tudor heir and guarantee the Protestant succession, she
preferred to dangle the wedding ring before eager suitors like Archduke Charles of Austria, Eric of Sweden, and the French Duke of
Anjou. Elizabeth used the possibility of her marriage as an instrument
of diplomacy, particularly when France or Spain threatened to upset
the balance of power. Her availability as a bride was also useful in
keeping at least one strong ally on the Continent or to confuse and
control diplomats pressing her to become actively involved in European
politics. In the end, of course, she married neither an Englishman nor
any one else, and died a spinster.

Out of frustration and anger, Philip renewed preparations for a
grand assault on England to achieve by war what he had hoped all
along to accomplish by diplomacy and intrigue. If successful, he would
be king of England and could restore Catholicism there. The "invin-
cible" Armada was to be the crowning glory of his lifelong devotion
to the cause of the Catholic Church. Soon all the ports of Spain and

Portugal bristled with activity to outfit a gigantic fleet of 130 ships in six squadrons carrying 2500 cannon, 8000 sailors, and 20,000 soldiers, in addition to an army of 30,000 men from Flanders commanded by the Duke of Parma.

The Armada was sighted off Plymouth on July 20, 1588, stretching seven miles across the sea and making its way slowly up the Channel. News of its approach had reached England some days before, and at the sight of it warning fires were lighted along the coast. Sixteen thousand men under the Earl of Leicester waited at the fort in Tilbury to guard London, while Lord Howard of Effingham, Drake, Martin Frobisher, Hawkins, and others commanded a lighter fleet of about 190 vessels manned by nine thousand seamen, who knew their fickle mistress, the narrow seas, better than the enemy commander, Medina Sidonia. They sailed round the great Spanish galleons and fired on them at will for six days, causing so much damage that the Spaniards made for Calais to take refuge, make repairs, and re-form ranks. On the night of July 28, while the galleons rode at anchor, the English sent fire ships at them. The utterly disorganized Spaniards hurriedly sailed north into deeper waters. Here the English vessels poured death and destruction on the vulnerable enemy, who lost sixteen ships and several thousand men in a matter of hours. As the remainder of the once grand fleet pushed into the North Sea, the wind quickened into a raging gale that dashed ship after ship against the rocky coast of England. Sailors who managed to reach shore ran the risk of being killed by the hostile English farmers. By the time the crippling storm had finally subsided, the remaining Spanish ships were sailing round Scotland and Ireland. Only fifty-three vessels, carrying about a third of the original army, returned safely to home ports; and many of the men were dying from hunger, wounds, and the pestilence that had broken out en route.

It has often been remarked that the beginning of Spain's decline was associated with the defeat of the Armada, but it must be remembered that Spain remained a great power for some time and that the connection between anti-Spanish and anti-Catholic thinking persisted in the minds of Englishmen well into the seventeenth century. The war dragged on far beyond the point of necessity or prudence until James I brought it to an end in 1604. In the intervening years, Englishmen raided Spanish and West Indian ports. Although Drake's voyage to Spain in 1589 aroused Elizabeth's anger because it failed to achieve the glorious results she had come to expect of him, and another expedition to the West Indies in 1595 commanded by Drake and Hawkins, which cost them their lives, also ended in dismal failure, Spain did no better. The Earl of Essex and Sir Walter Raleigh caused the destruction of more than forty ships and a great quantity of supplies at Cadiz in 1596, and they took enough plunder to make Essex a national hero even though Elizabeth suspected that her new-found lover was not a good admiral. All the Spanish could do in rebuttal was to send raiding parties against the Cornish coast and harass an occasional English ship off the Azores. Meanwhile, Elizabeth continued to aid with men and money the Dutch rebels and Henry IV, the Bourbon king of France, who had won by default the War of the Three Henrys in 1589. It obviously did not matter that he turned Catholic four years later.

Philip II, sick, harried, and depressed by the awful realization that all the prodigious labor of his long reign was coming to naught, had one last trick to play against Elizabeth in Ireland before he died. The suppression of Irish revolt in the 1570s and 1580s had not altered the shocking tyranny and unmitigated anarchy that had characterized that primitive land throughout the Tudor period. A government by and for Englishmen distressed the clan leaders such as the O'Neills and the O'Donnells. Even within the Pale the Anglo-Irish Anglican aristocrats, a hybrid group of malcontents, abused the native Irish Catholics who still lived largely in a Stone Age culture. Out of plain *ennui* these miserable, illiterate, virtual savages frequently found relief from the drudgery of crude farming in rounds of plundering and lawlessness. Revolt led by Hugh O'Neill of Ulster (the earl of Tyrone) broke out in 1595 and spread into Connaught. Philip promised Spanish troops, but they arrived in 1601, too late to be of much help. By 1598 the rebellion was making significant gains and Elizabeth sent her favorite, the vain, brash Essex to restore order. He led an army of about thirteen thousand men into Ireland, and without ever meeting O'Neill in a pitched battle, which Elizabeth had expected him to do, made a truce that angered her. Then, disobeying her order not to leave Ireland, he returned home to explain what he had done. He tried the usual flattery, but she summarily replaced him with Lord Mountjoy. The latter had some initial success in routing the rebels, but he suffered defeat at Spanish hands at Kinsale in 1601. The Spaniards withdrew within the year, however, allowing the restoration of English authority in the Pale.

Meanwhile Essex languished in disgrace. Elizabeth first bypassed him in a number of important administrative changes at court and later utterly ignored him despite his enormous popularity as a national hero. His stepfather, Leicester, and his friend Walsingham, both members of the so-called war party, had died in 1588 and 1590 respectively, and the old, trusted adviser, Burghley, and his hunchbacked son, Robert Cecil, who became principal secretary in 1596, would have nothing to do with him. After about eight months' banishment from court, Essex was brought to trial on a charge of malfeasance in office while commandant in Ireland. He was found guilty, ordered never to appear at court, and was completely degraded by the loss of his monopolies, offices, and honors. Elizabeth seems still to have felt deep affection for Essex, but his popularity was so dangerous that she learned to forget the pleasure of his frequent public demonstrations of contrived love. When she would not respond to his saccharine letters or grant him a private audience, he proved by his actions that he cared more for power and privilege than he did for the queen. With the Earl of Southampton, Lord Mountjoy, and others, he engaged in a round of correspondence that blossomed into a plot to depose Elizabeth and oust Burghley and Raleigh. The privy council early suspected Essex of some nefarious design and summoned him to their presence; but he remained at Essex House where, throughout the winter of 1600–1, a large number of unusual visitors gathered. On February 8 Essex led a makeshift force of about three hundred followers to London, where by reason of his popularity he hoped to win the city's support. But Londoners recognized a traitor and would not help him. Amid skirmishes between the rebels and a hastily summoned militia commanded by, of all people, the Bishop of London, Essex escaped to his own estate. There Elizabeth had him arrested, imprisoned in the Tower, and tried for treason. On February 25 he was beheaded.

Sixteenth-century Englishmen were the first of their nation to become generally aware of the vast world around them. Although they were more concerned about parochial or provincial affairs than with national or international developments (only a few members of Parliament in the sixteenth or seventeenth centuries spoke of foreign or national problems without reference to the narrow interests of their own counties), England's involvement in Continental politics, world trade, and exploration with the publicity given it by Richard Hakluyt's *Voyages,* wrenched Elizabethans from the confines of their tight little island. Anglo-Spanish rivalry on several fronts not only resulted in English naval supremacy; it also broke the commercial monopoly of the Hapsburgs on both sides of the Atlantic Ocean. Great cities such as London, with a population of about 100,000, Bristol, and Norwich hummed with energy quickened by the huge profits to be made by men with capital and a spirit of adventure. The search for Cathay, which Cabot began, was renewed under Edward VI by Hugh Willoughby and Richard Chancellor, who sailed into the Arctic to Russia. Later trips were made by Gilbert to the Carolinas, John Hawkins to the West Indies, and others to Newfoundland, Labrador, and the west coast of Africa. The businessmen who financed these ventures expected its commanders to carry home precious commodities that would bring a fortune in trade. The cautious investment of money in Henry VII's day swelled into huge enterprises supported by hundreds of stockholders. There was greater chance of success and less personal financial risk when many investors jointly participated, and precisely for that reason a number of joint-stock companies sprang up in Elizabethan England.

The idea certainly was not new, for merchants had long banded together for larger investment to win greater profits. Under monopolies to trade in specified commodities, for which privileged merchants paid Elizabeth handsomely, English commerce and industry thrived. Chancellor's momentous trip by sea to Archangel, and from there to the court of Ivan IV at Moscow, opened trade in the late 1550s between Russia and England by the Russia Company, also called the Muscovy Company, principally in tallow, masts, furs, and whale oil. Shortly thereafter, another combine of merchants gained a royal charter as the Eastland Company to trade throughout the Baltic seaports in the same products. The Levant Company, originally limited to Turkish trade, extended its influence through the Middle East after 1581, importing rich silks, cottons, dyes, and medicines to grace and comfort Elizabethans in their magnificent country houses built in the handsome capital H plan; it also exported dyed and partly finished cloth processed in the wool country of Somerset and Wiltshire and of East Anglia. The search for new markets carried adventurers around the Cape of Good Hope to Ceylon and Indo-China in the 1590s, leading to the formation in 1600 of the East India Company, which was to build the foundation of an eastern empire in competition with the Dutch and French over the next century and a half. And from Morocco, Guinea, and the Ivory Coast captains obtained slaves, ivory, and pepper for the Africa Company. To many of the capitals and ports of countries and regions where English goods found their way, the mercantile companies sent agents; and sometimes Elizabeth supported consuls, observers, and even full-fledged ambassadors so that the commercial and diplomatic ties between London and virtually every major city throughout Europe and the Middle East were well established by the opening of the seventeenth century.

Domestic trade and industry grew apace with international commerce. The first "industrial revolution" developed in England during the last half of the sixteenth century largely because Burghley and Elizabeth became vitally concerned with the expansion of mining, shipbuilding, ammunition and ordnance production, and ordinary consumer wares. Although at least four-fifths of all domestic industry was given over to wool, which was related to textile manufacturing and the enclosure movement, on the banks of the river systems of the Severn, Humber, and Tyne crude foundries processed iron drawn from shallow mines usually less than a hundred feet deep. Ships loaded with coal regularly plied between Newcastle and London, and lead from Derbyshire had long been used to cover roofs of churches and other public buildings. Salt pans multiplied first around Berwick, and later in Gloucestershire soap-boiling became very common. More specialized industries, such as cannon foundries and saltpeter works, benefited from the immigration of more than thirty thousand skilled tradesmen from the Netherlands and France, who went to England to escape religious persecution. Inventions were few and mechanical devices to ease labor were even fewer, although hundreds of monopolies and patents were granted by the Tudors for new techniques or for control of trade in particular commodities such as soap and glass.

The growth of industries requiring skilled craftsmen, the continued decline of the guilds, and the effects of the enclosure movement together created a serious unemployment problem in Elizabeth's reign. She made money sound again by restoring it to face value, thereby reversing the debasement begun by Henry VIII and continued by Edward VI; but she could not stem the mounting inflation in prices, which worked a terrible hardship on the thousands of Englishmen who lived on marginal incomes from fixed wages. If Henrician and Edwardian reforms were designed primarily to offset temporarily what they believed was an essentially personal problem, the Elizabethan poor laws aimed to strike at poverty and unemployment on the principle that the state should assume at least part of the responsibility of caring for persons who, through no fault of their own, could not care for themselves. By the Statute of Apprentices (1563) Elizabeth ordered justices of the peace, who were becoming the work horses of Tudor local government, to regulate annually the conditions of labor and wages in their districts. Sturdy beggars, that is to say, unskilled workers who would not take jobs even though they were available, were obliged to accept employment for at least a year's time whenever it was offered. Craftsmen had to serve an apprenticeship of at least seven years so that the quality of products manufactured by the livery companies remained high, while at the same time a system of forced training kept young boys from swelling the ranks of the able-bodied unemployed. But there were many others who, by reason of age, infirmity, or lack of training, languished in penury. The dissolution of the monasteries and the disestablishment of the Catholic Church cut off the charitable aid which it previously dispensed to the needy. A number of statutes attempted to compensate for this. For instance, in 1563, it became compulsory to contribute to the poor at a rate fixed by the churchwardens according to the needs of every parish. This helped somewhat, but it also brought out the worst in mankind by leading local men to force out of a parish all the poor, aged, or infirm who had not been born there. Justices of the peace were given in 1572 the additional duty of setting up and administering workhouses for the healthy but unemployed poor. Then, in 1601, Parliament passed an inclusive poor law that embodied many of the reforms already instituted. In addition to those previously mentioned, the aged and infirm were set to work at simple tasks in homes to be erected for them in parishes where they were needed; orphaned and otherwise unprovided-for children had to be apprenticed; and vagabondage and begging were made crimes punishable by fine, flogging, or imprisonment. This system of state-supported social welfare did not solve all of society's problems, to be sure, but it did establish a positive program to combat the evils in a rapidly expanding economy.

Beyond question, Elizabeth was as successful a monarch as England had seen. The great issues of her day—religion, foreign affairs, exploration and trade, and economic problems—could well have left another monarch with far less popularity then and considerably less reputation now. There had been sovereigns as ambitious, as shrewd, and as celebrated as Elizabeth, but only rarely have there been rulers whose aims and policies coincided as closely with those of their subjects. That is the clue to her greatness and strength. Her happy choice of ministers, notably Burghley and Walsingham, undoubtedly helped, as did the crisis that developed because of the Hapsburg threat to national security that brought out the best in Englishmen. That is not to say that there was unanimity of opinion in England. Parliament frequently quarreled with Elizabeth over religion, over intervention in Continental affairs, over her proposed marriages and flirtations, and over privileges like free speech in Parliament; but none of these issues provoked a constitutional impasse or a dangerous confrontation of power between Parliament and the monarch, as they repeatedly did under the early Stuarts in the next century. Circumstances in the two periods may have been different, but the principles involved were basically the same. Many have criticized the early Stuarts for ignoring Parliament, but Elizabeth convened it in only thirteen sessions totaling 140 weeks during a reign of forty-five years. She generally summoned Parliament only when she needed money or its approbation upon some controversial issue that might arouse national opposition, and she scolded and prorogued it whenever it became refractory, or pinched her pride or regal rights. Certainly she treated Sir Peter Wentworth, a Puritan champion of free speech, as basely in 1593 as Charles I dealt with Sir John Eliot, another champion of free speech, in 1629. Both were arrested, both were imprisoned for years in the Tower, and both were allowed to die there without even a show of royal compassion.

Elizabeth was often in great need of money during a reign of heavy expenses and rising prices. We have already seen that Henry VII did rather well financially by promoting trade, confiscating Yorkist estates, winning Parliamentary subsidies, and extracting benevolences (forced contributions to the crown that were considered loans but that were rarely repaid). Henry VIII, although burdened by heavy expenses in connection with war, reaped a plentiful harvest by debasing the coinage and confiscating monastic property, most of which he later sold at a profit. But most of these lucrative sources of revenue were not available to Elizabeth so that, despite the careful fiscal policies of Treasurer Burghley, the payment of niggardly salaries to government officers (who supplemented them through fees and gratuities), the exploits of her seamen against Spanish treasure ships, freedom during the first half of her reign from military expenses, and Parliament's generosity in authorizing subsidies, the crown only just managed to struggle along on about £400,000 to £500,000 annually, and often went into debt. Elizabeth's principal regular sources of revenue were proceeds from customs and crown lands, which together returned about £150,000 a year. As she disliked asking for benevolences, which were unpopular, and resorted to forced loans and ship money (both discussed in the next chapter) only in times of dire need, she frequently had to sell crown lands, monopolies, government offices, and wardships in order to make up the difference between her revenues and expenses. Although Burghley had managed to amass a modest surplus prior to the outbreak of the Spanish war and England's costly support of Continental Protestants, afterward the crown was perpetually in debt.

Finally, one must ponder why Elizabeth was so popular. A number of circumstances worked in her favor. It is frequently overlooked that she died before Parliament had reached the stage of development where it wished to be a true partner with monarchy in government, although under the Tudors since Henry VIII it had frequently been led to believe that it was needed to give advice and consent about royal policies. Under Elizabeth Parliament was neither fully ready nor fully allowed to assert its role as counselor and judge. The reliance on Parliamentary approbation from Henry VIII to Elizabeth gave it greater prestige, but although it was a short step from being an adviser to being a maker of policy, Parliament did not take it. The Elizabethan system of Parliamentary management would not permit Parliament to take it. Elizabethan councilors sat in the Commons and in the Lords, served on and sometimes chaired important committees where bills were discussed, and thereby promoted or killed matters as the queen directed. Controversial public issues did get to the floor of both Houses, but usually they were not permitted to go far enough to arouse strong opposition. Elizabeth also benefited from the status of the Speaker. Commons nominated him, but he remained the servant of the crown until about 1640, and was expected to forward the crown's interests. Since the Speaker directed the order of business, recognized members who wished to speak, and authorized, delayed, or altogether stopped a vote on any bill, he wielded great power. Elizabeth saw to it that he knew her wishes. The manipulation of business in the Commons by the Speaker continued well into the seventeenth century, although toward the end of Elizabeth's reign, Commons employed a device to lessen his authority (and hence the crown's) in Parliament, which was more widely used against the Stuarts: Commons met in the committee of the whole, that is to say, the whole House constituted itself a committee so that Parliamentary rules and the Speaker were set aside. The members could then speak their minds openly without fear of reprisal or interference from the chair. Lastly, the great bloc of opposition to royal prerogative under the early Stuarts, whom we are to discuss next, was led by the Puritans, who had insufficient strength in Elizabethan times in or out of Parliament to be to the crown the trouble they later became. James I therefore inherited the constitutional and financial problems with Parliament that Elizabeth fortuitously missed.

7

The Early Stuarts, 1603–1660

At Elizabeth's death in March, 1603, a courier rode hurriedly north to
Edinburgh to apprise her designated heir, James VI of Scotland, that
he had succeeded to the English throne. To James the news came as
no surprise: he had the best lineal claim and had corresponded with
Elizabeth, his cousin, about the succession. The transfer of authority
from Tudors to Stuarts was achieved peacefully, evidence of how much
the Tudors' brilliant and popular administration had stabilized and
strengthened the monarchy. Many Englishmen craned their necks to
catch a glimpse of their new Solomon as he made a stately progress
toward London, stopping frequently to chat with local notables, ordering criminals to be punished, accepting for consideration the Puritans'
Millenary Petition for Church reform, and creating more knights in
three weeks than Elizabeth had in forty-five years.

James I, son of the Queen of Scots and grandson of Margaret,
Henry VII's daughter, had already reigned in Scotland for thirty-seven
years with considerable skill and greater understanding of his countrymen than he ever showed for his new English subjects. He had spent
his youth in rigorous study during which his tutors instilled in him as
much Calvinist theology as Latin and Greek or rhetoric and history.
He was not permitted to waste time in silly games or idle conversation,
with the result that he became a serious, learned, and pedantic prince,
who craved close friendships and enjoyed the company of gregarious
courtiers and ecclesiastics with whom he could discuss statecraft and
theology. James had been reared a Presbyterian, but he was never particularly fond of this religion with its rigid doctrines of predestination
and abstemious personal conduct. He had had occasional trouble with
Scots Catholics, but, as far as his position and the attitudes of the age

would allow, he was quite tolerant of them. As the religious, political, and social milieu in Scotland had impaired or even occasionally prevented the exercise of firm monarchic authority over independent Highland clansmen and Presbyterian lairds and divines, James was anxious to rule a kingdom where the practical application of the divine-right theory of kingship had not yet been seriously challenged. But, although the king headed both Church and state in England, there were customary and legal restraints on the exercise of royal authority that James did not understand at first and later refused to accept. Temporarily, however, he basked in the generous acceptance of his subjects, who welcomed him with hopes of political order, religious tranquillity, and economic prosperity.

James intended to provide such leadership, but the method by which he did so became repugnant to several important segments of English society, especially the common-law lawyers, merchants, and members of Parliament, some of whom were Puritans. It is a gross oversimplification to ascribe James's later unpopularity solely to his pride, pettiness, contentiousness, and stubbornness, for Elizabeth retained the admiration and respect of her subjects despite similar weaknesses of character. She was as authoritarian and cavalier as James in her relationships with Parliament and the privy councilors, yet she did not ignore their views or refuse their help. Whether James had too much of the Calvinist rigor in him, or too little political acumen, or whether he feared Parliament intended to fetter him, he made a point of defining and practicing a political philosophy that he himself summarized—God makes the king and the king makes the law. This theory of the divine right of kings was based on the assumption that the king, divinely ordained by God to rule, was not dependent on or responsible to any earthly power. This concept was certainly not new, for, since early Anglo-Saxon times (see Chapter 1), the monarchs of England had been believed to be hedged by divinity, and the Church had encouraged the belief by anointing monarchs during coronation ceremonies. Moreover, since the fifth century, the popes had argued that all authority passed from God to them, and thence through the popes to the secular princes. As Henry VIII had replaced the pope as head of the Church in England, authority supposedly passed from God directly to Henry and his successors. Elizabeth also believed that God had destined her to rule, but she had the wisdom not to make an issue of it, thereby avoiding the inference that Parliament and all others were absolutely subject to her fiat. James certainly could not have been ignorant of the growing power and prestige of Parliament, and it was impolitic of him to insist that it had no right to initiate debate about foreign policy or to help regulate Church affairs. To be sure, Elizabeth had insisted on the same thing, but for Elizabeth to do so was one thing; for James it was another. James further believed that hereditary monarchy was unalienable, subject to neither usurpation nor rebellion. Resistance to the royal will, since it was founded on divine sanction, was mortally sinful so that even an incompetent or irresponsible monarch merited at least the passive obedience of his subjects. This political philosophy was held by most Englishmen, not by James alone, but it was to cause him no end of difficulty because he was not wise enough to "manage" it or to stop talking about it, particularly with the Puritans.

The structure of divine-right monarchy was underpinned by the Church of England, ruled by the king as governor with the advice of Convocation, the assembly of Church prelates headed by the archbishop of Canterbury. As a firm advocate of Erastianism, the supremacy of state over Church, and as one who had had disputes over religion with both Presbyterians and Catholics in Scotland, James openly rejected the Puritan view that laymen should have a voice in Church government. The Puritans, most of whom were members of the Established Church, believed that it should be purged of its Catholic practices and doctrines. For this reason, and encouraged by James's sympathy for reforms proposed by Puritan spokesmen while he was still only Scottish king, they presented him with a petition, signed by about eight hundred members of the clergy, asking that they might be allowed to preach without wearing the surplice, to solemnize marriage without using a ring, to baptize without making the sign of the cross, and other privileges. He promised to consider this Millenary Petition and, in due course, convened a conference at the royal palace of Hampton Court in January, 1604. There James heard the Puritan Dr. Reynolds propose that bishops should consult with ministers and laymen before making decisions relating to ecclesiastical polity and the liturgy, listened intently as Archbishop Richard Bancroft spoke in rebuttal, and entered the discussion himself, for he dearly loved theological disputation. But he was predisposed against the Puritans and flew into a rage when he erroneously concluded that they meant to do away with bishops. James shouted that he would have but "one doctrine and one discipline, one religion in substance and in ceremony," for any danger to the episcopacy also endangered his own security. Accordingly, he assumed that the Puritans aimed at establishing a "Scotch presbytery," which "agreeth as well with monarchy as God with the Devil." Furious at the Puritans, he threatened that he would "make them conform themselves, or else will harry them out of the land." Having vented his spleen and paraded his knowledge, James may have felt smug in his apparent victory, but the Puritans left the conference determined never to bow to his demands or cower at his threats.

The conference prompted immediate action by James. He imprisoned the petitioners and deprived hundreds of Puritan clergymen of their benefices, thereby leading many of them to convene irregular Church meetings (conventicles), preach without license, take refuge in remote rural areas, or go abroad to Holland. Meanwhile Convocation authorized the promulgation of the Canons of 1604, a set of ecclesiastical laws that reiterated and redefined existing Anglican doctrines and practices. James also appointed a committee of fifty-four scholars to translate anew the Bible, which was issued in 1611 and became the Authorized Version that served most of the English-speaking Protestant world until the publication of the Revised Standard Version.

James likewise alienated his Roman Catholic subjects, numbering perhaps a sixth of the population in 1603. Although since the Act of Uniformity of 1559 the penal laws had made it illegal for anyone to practice Catholicism, these laws were never enforced with severity under Elizabeth: a relatively small proportion of recusants paid the heavy twenty-pound monthly fines, went to prison, or were executed as the laws prescribed. Nonetheless, the penal laws had broken Catholic resistance to Anglicanism, the work of the Jesuit missionaries since 1580 notwithstanding. Catholics understandably welcomed the demise of Elizabeth and looked hopefully to James's rule, for, in his actions toward the Scottish Catholics as well as the promises of leniency he made to English Catholics before 1603, he appeared anxious to compromise with Rome.

James tried to be lenient with the Catholics for the first year and a half of his reign despite the opposition of bishops, councilors, and Parliament. He also took in stride the Cobham and Bye plots, which involved Catholics and threatened his life and his throne. But the Gunpowder Plot, uncovered by the Treasurer, Salisbury, late in 1605, so angered Parliament that leniency was no longer possible. Without the knowledge of the vast majority of Catholics, who were loyal to

James, thirteen Catholic malcontents led by Robert Catesby and Francis Tresham set a Yorkshire bumpkin named Guy Fawkes to work placing barrels of gunpowder and scrap iron underneath Westminster Hall at the end of a tunnel extending from a house across the road which the conspirators had rented. They intended to explode the powder on November 5, the day of Parliament's opening when all its members, the privy councilors and judges, and the king and his family would be present. The scheme might have succeeded but for Tresham's concern for the safety of a kinsman in the House of Lords. The suggestive note that Tresham wrote to him led to the discovery of the cache of explosives, the arrest of Fawkes and several collaborators (as well as other Catholics, who were innocent), and their ultimate execution.

James cautioned moderation because he realized that his Catholic subjects were generally loyal, but Parliament would not listen. It passed two statutes in 1606 that ordered additional penalties and restrictions on Catholics and obliged each of them to whom the question was put to take an oath of allegiance denying papal supremacy. Excluding those put to death for complicity in the 1605 plot, seventeen Catholic clergymen and six laymen were executed because of religion during James's reign. James himself, though at first commendably philosophical about the threat to his life, grew increasingly apprehensive about his safety and took to wearing ridiculous quilted clothes and sleeping surrounded by bodyguards for fear that a Catholic desperado might assassinate him. Although such fear proved to be groundless, Parliament was sincerely worried about the threat to the security of the royal family, Anglicanism, and the country posed by Catholics at home and abroad. As we shall see presently, James's pro-Spanish foreign policy, connected as it was to the religious issue in the Thirty Years' War, greatly augmented Parliament's fear of the Catholics' intentions.

James got along no better with Parliament than he did with the Puritans and Catholics. Trouble arose primarily over the antithetical attitudes of the crown and Commons in the areas of royal prerogative and finance. James should have appreciated how avidly Parliament had disputed with Elizabeth, and that she had averted serious trouble by paying it the respect its position and authority demanded. But he made peace with Spain in 1604; he was a foreigner who lacked popular support; and he did not fully comprehend that the sensitivity of Parliament was based on more than three centuries of struggle with his predecessors. Nor did he recognize that only Parliament could make and abrogate statutes or that he needed its approval to raise noncustomary taxes. As no king could hope for long to sustain government solely on his customary revenue, Parliamentary authorization of subsidies was absolutely necessary. Parliament, keenly aware of its fiscal power, used it as a means of inducing the king to come to its way of thinking on foreign policy, economic affairs, and religion.

James convened Parliament only twice during the first half of his reign—in 1604–11 and 1614. His attempt in 1604 to interfere in the disputed election of one of its members raised an issue of Parliamentary privilege. It was established in the case of *Goodwin* v. *Fortescue* that the Commons alone could determine the validity of elections and seat its members. Shirley's case shortly thereafter confirmed the customary freedom of members of Parliament from arrest except for felony and treason. The 1604 Parliament also criticized the crown's officers for the abuse of purveyance, wardship, and impositions. Commons admitted the king's right to buy commodities from local merchants at less than the market price during progresses between his residences, but it was incensed that some merchants were forced to take unreasonably low prices or see their perishable goods spoil for want of purchase by the king's purveyors who had ordered them. The members of Parliament also felt that James had abused his ancient feudal privilege of wardship, which brought the crown about £20,000 annually. There was no question that James had the legal right to take over the lands of his tenants-in-chief who were minors, and keep the profits until they came of age. Indeed, to prevent the king from exercising his right of wardship after they died, fathers often made provision in their wills for money with which their wives could purchase the wardships of their sons from the crown and thereby retain the income from their lands. The Bate case (1607) tested the king's right to levy impositions on certain types of goods, an issue that Parliament had already raised in 1604. The merchant Bate had refused to pay an import duty on currants on the grounds that impositions could be levied only when Parliament authorized them and only when this privilege was exercised by the crown solely to regulate trade, neither of which, Bate's lawyer said, was the case. The barons of the Exchequer Court ruled, however, in favor of the crown, pointing out that the king was sovereign in foreign affairs, of which foreign trade was a part, and that he had the right to levy any tax necessary to maintain an adequate revenue. As this verdict challenged Parliament's customary right to authorize nonfeudal taxes, it is not surprising that it stood firmly opposed to the crown's fiscal policy and thereafter doled out money sparingly.

The Commons clarified its position in the "Apology" (1604), in which it defined unequivocally its right to hold free elections, enjoy freedom of speech and freedom from arrest during Parliamentary sessions, and debate public issues. Its privileges and liberties, Commons asserted, "are our right and due inheritance, no less than our very land and goods . . . [and] cannot be withheld from us, denied, or impaired," and that their request to the king for the continuance of such privileges "is an act only of manners, and doth weaken our right no more than our suing to the King for our lands by petition. . . ." Although these words did not impress James, he found subsequently by hard experience that Commons meant what it said. It amply proved as much in 1606 in its opposition to his plan to unite the kingdoms of Scotland and England, and to accord Scotsmen the privileges of English citizenship. Parliament rejected both suggestions: Scotland, a traditional enemy, was as foreign to Englishmen as Portugal; Parliament resented the favors that James showered on Scots friends, and it saw no wisdom in admitting a poor and backward people to a share in England's economic prosperity. When Parliament would not budge from its position, James took the issue to court in Colvin's case, by which Scotsmen born since 1603 were ruled to be natural-born English subjects. But it was not until 1707 that the two kingdoms were united under a single government.

Such disputes with Parliament annoyed James, and he would have preferred never again to call it if he had had sufficient money to meet his expenses. Under the circumstances, Parliament could not help being suspicious of the king's motives, especially when, after receiving the favorable verdict in the Bate case, he ordered Salisbury (Cecil) to issue a modified book of customs rates so arranged as to raise royal revenue without additionally regulating trade. Parliament criticized these taxes on a wider range of goods that did not require its approval, but when it denounced Salisbury, the king lectured it for its presumption in discussing a matter of royal prerogative. Salisbury, James's hunchbacked chief minister whom he called his "little beagle," then conceived a scheme known as the Great Contract of 1610, which might satisfy Parliament's grievances on fiscal policy and at the same time assure the king a sufficient income. He proposed that, in exchange for the crown's surrendering certain customary revenues and abandoning the unpopular practices of purveyance and wardship, Parliament should guarantee the king £200,000 annually. Although Parliament initially liked the suggestion, James's cavalier indifference to its grievances and his demand for larger sums led it to reject the Great Contract and retain its bargaining power.

James did not call another Parliament until 1614, when the "Addled Parliament" sat for only a few weeks without positive result. The two parties were unable to reach an understanding because (1) Parliament suspected, probably correctly, that James had tried to manipulate elections through local agents called "undertakers"; (2) both sides were too suspicious of each other to initiate compromise to break the deadlock over subsidies; and (3) Parliament, wary of James's intention to avoid calling another Parliament, brought up old grievances over impositions and monopolies and refused to consider subsidies until the grievances had been corrected. The issue of monopolies deserves a word of explanation because they were a constant source of friction. The Tudors had allowed courtiers and friends to hold monopolies in the manufacture of certain commodities, processes, or devices, or in the importation of some types of goods. Monopolies, for which the grantee paid the crown handsomely, were ordinarily associated with patents and trade regulation. But James greatly increased the number of monopolies, granting them to favorites in order to raise revenue. Monopolies were bestowed for such privileges as licensing alehouses and inns, importing gold and silver thread and wine, and mining and manufacture. The crown and its grantees gained financially, but the consumer often suffered from higher prices and a scarcity of goods, which also declined in quality. Monopolies covered so many goods and services that they became a national scandal, and in 1624 Parliament forbade grants of monopoly to individuals.

James ruled without Parliament from 1614 to 1621, relying on the advice of favorites including Robert Carr, Viscount Rochester (later earl of Somerset), several members of the Howard family, and George Villiers, earl (later duke) of Buckingham. Carr replaced Salisbury, who died in 1612. The former had illicitly married Frances Howard while her husband was abroad, but James saw to it that his Scots councilor and his bigamous new wife were protected even though one of her antagonists, Sir Thomas Overbury, was murdered, allegedly to avoid a public scandal. Three of the Howards, of whom Thomas, earl of Suffolk, was the most important, held high posts in the government and used their offices to augment their wealth and power. Such councilors quickly aroused the opposition of their countrymen by insisting that men of means pay "benevolences" to James, that is, "gifts" of money in amounts commensurate with their station and income. It was obvious that James expected payment from everyone solicited, and sheriffs and magistrates prosecuted some who refused to contribute. The outcry against Somerset became so loud that James dismissed him in 1616 and turned his attention to a young, handsome unknown named Villiers. It has frequently been suggested that James's favoritism toward him was something less than wholesome, even immoral, but the point is not important. Villiers advanced so rapidly in power, wealth, and influence that for the rest of James's reign, and the first three years of Charles's, he actually controlled the policies of the crown. Nothing escaped Buckingham's eyes; no one got preferment without his leave; and few dared to cross him. At one time or another, he held virtually every lucrative and prestigious office that the king could bestow.

During the same interval between Parliaments there flared up the rivalry between Sir Edward Coke, chief justice of Common Pleas, and Sir Francis Bacon, attorney-general (later Chancellor). Their enmity had begun in the 1590s when both were vying for the attorney-generalship and the hand of a rich widow, Lady Elizabeth Hatton. Coke had won both. Of greater consequence was their quarrel over the prerogatives of the crown in relationship to the common law. Refusing to be merely a "lion under the throne," Coke antagonized James by rejecting his assertion that prerogative courts such as High Commission and King's Bench had unlimited jurisdiction, and rebuked him for attempting to influence the common-law judges on cases that were pending. Coke held that the common law restricted the crown's authority and that the common-law courts should guard personal and Parliamentary liberties and arbitrate disputes between Parliament and the crown, while remaining free of pressure from either party. He expressed his views forthrightly in disputes over two cases in 1615–16, both of which the king won. A Somerset clergyman named Edmond Peacham, already convicted and defrocked in High Commission for libel, was charged with treason for having allegedly written a seditious sermon predicting James's death, even though the sermon was neither delivered nor published. James, anxious that Peacham should be punished, but fearing that Coke would influence the judges against the wishes of the crown, ordered Bacon to confer with them individually while the case was still pending. Coke balked, knowing that James meant to pressure the judges into a decision favorable to the king, hence making a mockery of judicial impartiality. He also challenged the idea that the king was above the law in the case of commendams. This case involved the practice of keeping open a benefice that fell vacant and allowing a clergyman already beneficed to draw income from it—in effect, veiled pluralism. James had bestowed a benefice *in commendams* on a favorite, Bishop Richard Neile of Lichfield, a High-churchman whom the Puritans had repeatedly criticized, even though the living had been promised to another. In the resulting suit, James ordered Bacon to instruct Coke and his colleagues on the bench to defer a verdict until the king spoke to them about it. Coke again raised the issue of judicial impartiality and, unlike the other magistrates, was unmoved and unimpressed when James lectured them on their duty. As a result, James dismissed Coke as chief justice of King's Bench, a post to which he had been appointed in 1613 by way of putting him in a position where he would have to defend the king's interests. Coke did his duty, but he persistently upheld the precepts of the common law and eventually supported Parliament against the crown in the 1620s.

Bacon fell from power in 1621. Parliament, perhaps unjustly, impeached him for allegedly accepting a bribe to reverse a verdict in a lower court over a property suit. Although Bacon's guilt is still a matter of interpretation, the issue on which the impeachment was based served as well as any other for Parliament to vent its anger over monopolies, economic problems, royal favorites, and foreign policy. Like many other Tudor and Stuart administrators, Bacon bore the brunt of public displeasure actually aimed at the crown. As direct criticism of the monarch then bordered on treason, it was centered on the ministers who carried out his policies.

Judging by James's actions at Hampton Court, in Parliament, and with the judges, one might reasonably assume that he was both contentious and belligerent. It is true that he sometimes scolded advisers, lectured the Commons, and pompously paraded his knowledge, but at heart he actually abhorred conflict, disliked soldiering and war, and harbored the idealistic hope of universal peace. Of all his titles and epithets, he enjoyed most being called a peacemaker. Such an attitude in a monarch, who also insisted that he alone should formulate and direct foreign policy, helps us to understand the seemingly irrational and inconsistent policies vis-à-vis Spain and France that James pursued. Parliament became frustrated with the king, who, while claiming to be a champion of Protestantism, simultaneously courted the friendship of Spain, the strongest Catholic Continental power.

England and Spain made peace in 1604, terminating a war that had dragged on needlessly for about fifteen years after the decisive defeat of the Armada. James acted wisely but against the opposition of merchants, who were profiting handsomely from an illicit trade with the Indies, and of fervent Protestants, who felt that England should continue to fight Spain for the sake of the Calvinist Dutch, still engaged in their war for independence. Philip III was eager to put down the costly burden of being the champion of Catholicism that his predecessor had shouldered. The 1604 treaty provided for perpetual amity, mutual trade privileges, and religious freedom for each nation's merchants in the other's lands. But Spain frequently violated the treaty: merchants' claims against Spanish privateers were often ignored by the Council of State; Protestant residents in Spain were harassed; and diplomatic relations were strained to the breaking point for the rest of James's reign. Nor did James fulfill all his obligations. He interfered with Spanish merchants in England, denied Spaniards freedom of worship in their embassy, and in 1609 joined several Protestant states in a defensive alliance against Spain. Moreover, in 1613, James's daughter, Elizabeth, married the alliance's Calvinist leader, Elector Frederick V of the Rhenish Palatinate.

There arrived in England in the same year the brilliant, gracious, and shrewd Spanish ambassador, Count Gondomar, who befriended James and almost singlehandedly shaped the course of Anglo-Spanish relations for the next ten years. As mounting nationalistic and religious tensions on the Continent were inexorably leading to the Thirty Years' War, Gondomar worked toward a marriage alliance with England, which he hoped would ensure its neutrality. He believed that an Anglo-French alliance must be averted at all cost, for it would be inimical to Spain's ambitions in Europe and its security at home. He also felt that an Anglo-Spanish accord, if handled circumspectly, might lead to an ameliorization of the plight of the English Catholics and even eventually to the conversion of the English to Catholicism. Because he was sincere in his objectives, Gondomar worked partly at cross-purposes with his sovereign and Chief Minister Count Olivares, who gave the appearance of being genuinely interested in a marriage treaty without ever intending to go through with it. For his part, James hoped that a marriage treaty with Spain might result in a lessening of Continental tensions and thereby prevent the outbreak of war. The Puritans were horrified at the proposal, but James's wife, Anne, and a number of pro-Spanish councilors led by Henry Howard, earl of North-ampton, encouraged James to make the treaty.

The expected outbreak of war came in 1618, and over the next thirty years virtually every state in western Europe became involved in it. England had in no sense caused the war, and would not have entered it had not Frederick, James's son-in-law, lost his electoral throne and the kingship of Bohemia. Parliament called for war against Spain to restore Frederick, but James hoped to achieve the withdrawal of Spanish troops from the Palatinate by diplomacy through a marriage between Charles, Prince of Wales, and the Spanish Infanta. Accord-ingly, James instructed Sir John Digby and Francis Cottington, resi-dents at Madrid, to renew negotiations leading to the treaty that had been intermittently discussed since 1611. Because Philip III had no intention of sacrificing his political ambitions to relieve James's anxiety over Frederick, the tedious negotiations had no chance of success. They served ultimately only to antagonize English Protestants, particularly the Puritans in Parliament, for James appeared willing to surrender anything to enhance his family interests.

For the sake of his children, James carried his policy of peace at any price to ridiculous limits. Raleigh, still in the Tower, suggested that he be released to lead an expedition to dig for gold in the Orinoco Valley in Spanish South America. James urgently needed gold and was eager for Raleigh to go. Therefore, over Gondomar's protests, he re-leased Raleigh on condition that he avoid conflict with the Spaniards and that he bring back gold. But Raleigh was unable to resist fighting Spaniards, lost many men, and came home empty-handed. To placate Gondomar and preserve Spanish friendship, James had him executed on a specious treason charge dating back to 1604. Furthermore, a draft treaty proposed by Olivares contained provisions to ameliorate the lot of English Catholics and to guarantee the religious freedom of the In-fanta and .her courtiers. James at first balked, then temporized, and finally half agreed to accept these terms even though only Parliament could legally rescind the penal laws. Anti-Catholic and anti-Spanish sermons, pamphlets, and demonstrations notwithstanding, James fool-ishly pursued a pro-Spanish policy.

Parliament convened in 1621 amid popular outcry against a hu-miliating and pernicious compromise with Spain. To this grievance Parliament added others: hard times had fallen on the country since 1619; royal favorites ignored the public interest; Catholics went un-prosecuted; and the courts upheld the crown's interests at the expense of justice. Although it was an inappropriate time to call Parliament, James desperately needed a grant of subsidies, but he antagonized the Commons in an opening speech, forbidding it to meddle in affairs touching the royal prerogative—which in his view included religion, finance, and foreign policy. Parliament manifested its displeasure by authorizing only two subsidies, the bare minimum, and proceeded to a discussion of its grievances. It also fully investigated the hated monopolies, criticized Buckingham, impeached Bacon, and sent James a formal protest against his domestic and foreign policies. He answered this Great Protestation by dissolving Parliament and tearing contemptuously from the *Commons Journal* the pages recording the Protestation.

Anglo-Spanish treaty negotiations collapsed shortly thereafter. Buckingham resolved, early in 1623, to journey with Charles incognito to Madrid, woo the Infanta personally, and achieve in a few weeks what neither Digby nor Cottington had been able to accomplish in ten years of diplomacy. James, weeping and moaning that he would never again see his "sweet boys," let them go. Digby's displeasure at their unexpected arrival led later to his disgraceful dismissal and impeachment, but the Spanish, though at first shocked, rubbed their hands gleefully over having the heir to the English throne in their web. After six fruitless months of negotiations during which Olivares threw up every conceivable obstacle to the marriage, and Charles suddenly realized that he did not love the woman he was scarcely permitted to speak with, the two vagabonds left for home. Their landing at Portsmouth set off a spontaneous demonstration of public rejoicing that Charles had returned without a treaty or a bride and that England had not surrendered to Spanish terms. Buckingham demanded an immediate declaration of war, not just because there appeared to be no other way to drive the Spanish from the Palatinate, but because he felt Olivares had insulted him in Madrid.

The bonfires, bell-ringing, and festivities associated with Charles's return should have been ample evidence to James that the country would not tolerate an alliance with a Catholic power. But while Parliament, having declared war on Spain, was helping Buckingham prepare for it, James opened negotiations with France for a marriage between Charles and Henrietta Maria, sister of King Louis XIII. Despite general opposition to the marriage treaty, which promised Henrietta and her attendants extraordinary privileges to practice their Catholic faith and the suspension of the penal laws against English Catholics, it went through as planned in December, 1624. The new Catholic queen and her court of three hundred persons journeyed to England four months later, but James did not live to see her. Prematurely old, and troubled by debilitating diseases, he died on March 27, 1625.

The throne passed to his son, Charles I, who shared James's political convictions, dislike of Parliaments, and penchant for unpopular favorites. Born near Edinburgh in 1600, Charles was brought to England by James when only three years of age. James had naturally expected his older and most favored son, Henry, to succeed him, and therefore had virtually ignored Charles until the former's death in 1612. Although intelligent, capable, and cultivated in the sense that he knew and appreciated the arts, particularly painting and sculpture, Charles lacked social poise, vacillated between sternness and timidity, and felt uncomfortable in public because of a stutter. He had, like James, a frail body; and he enjoyed hunting the stag, not only for sport's sake, but also to drain its blood as a palliative for spindlelegs, the result of rickets in early childhood. At first Charles intensely disliked Buckingham, perhaps because of competition for James's attention, but he later became the duke's inseparable friend, making virtually no important decision without his approval. When Henrietta and Buckingham quarreled, Charles sided with his friend until his murder in 1628 finally rid the queen of her insufferable antagonist. Thereafter Henrietta exerted great influence, particularly in religious matters. Several new councilors rose to prominence during the late 1620s and 1630s, notably Treasurer Richard Weston (earl of Portland), Archbishop William Laud, Chancellor of the Exchequer Francis Cottington, Secretary Francis Windebank, and Lord Lieutenant of Ireland Thomas Wentworth (Lord Strafford).

Charles was a sincere Anglican with High-Church principles (Arminianism), but he felt no hatred for Catholics or others who believed in Christ, the Decalogue, and the Apostles' Creed so long as they remained loyal. He disliked persecution and probably would have suspended the penal laws had not the public, led by the Puritans, demanded their enforcement. The Puritans mistook Charles's latitudinarianism for compromise with papists and suspected with good reason that he was inadvertently enhancing Catholicism. The major problems Charles faced were largely attributable to his lack of political acumen, inability to compromise, reliance on advice by unpopular councilors, and to unparliamentary taxation.

Charles inherited an empty treasury and a hostile Parliament. His traditional sources of revenue were insufficient even to pay the ordinary expenses of the court, much less to wage successful war against Spain. The war went badly from the start, for although the English and Spanish engaged in no decisive battle, England lost ground because of bungling by inept commanders like Buckingham. While the duke busied himself outfitting a fleet and hiring mercenaries, Charles concluded a foolish treaty with the Dutch, promising them money and an army made up of the remnants of a corps led by Count Mansfeld, which had been virtually wiped out by disease on the Isle of Walcheren. Charles also promised £30,000 to Denmark and other north German princes if they would stay in the war against Spain, even though he lacked funds to meet this obligation. Buckingham sent six ships to France for Richelieu's use against Spain, but their guns battered the Protestant Huguenots instead. Finally, in summer and autumn, 1625, Buckingham crammed ten thousand men into a fleet of unseaworthy ships and sent them to attack Cadiz Harbor. The army landed in October but failed to capture the fort or bombard the town as planned, and returned to England. The fleet also failed to intercept the Mexican treasure ships on route to Spain; hundreds of Englishmen died on the way home; and the rotting hulks and diseased men straggled into several ports in southwest England. The vice-admiral of Devon, Sir John Eliot, a Parliamentary leader, was horrified at the sight of the men dying in the streets of his home town, Plymouth.

England and France went to war in 1627 because Charles refused to abide by the terms of the marriage treaty, because Richelieu was angry over Buckingham's expeditions to relieve the besieged Huguenot garrisons at La Rochelle and the Île de Ré, and because French privateers were attacking English shipping in the Channel. Parliament blamed Buckingham for the costly blunders at Cadiz and La Rochelle, and criticized the unrestrained activities of Henrietta's Catholic attendants residing at St. James' and Somerset House in London. Not content with rights given her by treaty, Henrietta invited criticism by allowing Catholics to hear Mass in her chapels, sent her Capuchin monks to minister to her coreligionists throughout the city, and went out of her way to insult Parliament, Buckingham, and even Charles. She made no effort to fit into an English way of life and was utterly contemptuous of her new subjects and their Protestant religion. All the while she complained to her brother of how shamefully she was treated, acted like a spoiled child, and paid more attention to the advice of her French matrons than to her husband. Much to Parliament's pleasure, Charles finally lost patience and sent most of her ladies-in-waiting, servants, and Capuchins packing off to France with only a day's notice.

These things, of course, provided fodder for the Commons. It had labored hard during James's reign to assert its alleged right to help the crown govern England, although James had consistently refused to accept its offer of governmental partnership. The Commons was therefore wary of Charles's intentions and immediately tested his mettle. It was fortunate in having brilliant leaders in men like Sir Edward Coke, Sir John Eliot, and John Pym, who were particularly concerned with protecting "true religion" against Arminianism and Catholicism, the violation of personal liberty by Buckingham and other councilors, and the war effort against Spain. The Commons differed with Charles and Buckingham over the conduct of the war, but it nevertheless showed its willingness to cooperate up to a point by granting subsidies in an amount sufficient to meet immediate needs. Before it would grant more money, however, it expected the crown to account for the expenditure of earlier subsidies, thereby challenging the crown's right to determine unilaterally England's foreign and domestic policies. Buckingham swallowed his pride long enough to make an impassioned personal appeal to the Commons for money, but it responded by again criticizing him. It even refused to grant Charles tunnage and poundage for more than a year at a time despite the fact that, from time immemorial, kings had always been granted that privilege for life. Piqued at the Commons' criticism of Buckingham and its refusal to authorize more subsidies, Charles dissolved Parliament in August, 1625.

He did so to save Buckingham from almost certain impeachment, but monetary needs were so pressing that he soon had to call it again, with essentially the same results. The old arguments against the duke, made this time by Eliot, echoed in St. Stephen's Chapel along with complaints about freedom of religion for Catholics, Digby's trial in the House of Lords (which believed Buckingham's lies that Digby caused the failure of the Spanish match in 1623), and the growing crisis with France. When the Commons refused to authorize the subsidies Charles demanded, he again dissolved Parliament and imposed tunnage and poundage and a forced loan without its consent. The forced loan was the crown's most serious unparliamentary taxation to that point, and it was employed many times with disastrous consequences. Many refused to pay the "loan" on the grounds that Parliament had not authorized it. Among them were five knights who, as a result, were tried in King's Bench and sentenced to prison. Although Charles soon released them, the court's decision implied he had a legal right to collect the loan and imprison delinquents.

Charles called his third Parliament in March, 1628, in the midst of this opposition to the loan and to arbitrary arrests. Many of his old antagonists were returned to the Commons despite Charles's attempt to control the elections. They eagerly resumed debates covering the full range of their grievances over religion, Buckingham, unparliamentary taxation, and the management of the Spanish and French wars. There are no more significant events in the constitutional history of England than those that took place in the year before Charles contemptuously dissolved Parliament in March, 1629. Parliament genuinely believed that the king, because he had not prosecuted to the limit of the law Catholics who it asserted plotted the overthrow of the kingdom and the restoration of popery, had undermined the foundation of the English Church, which needed drastic reformation along fundamentalist lines to extirpate Catholic and Arminian encroachments upon doctrine and the liturgy. The Commons also decried the imprisonment of alleged criminals without benefit of bail, formal accusation, or right of *habeas corpus*. Buckingham's insidious influence, in maladministration as well as in the forced loan and monopolies, once more commanded Parliament's closest attention. The leadership was again assumed by Eliot of Devon, who denounced Charles's foreign and domestic policies and laid the burden of the nation's calamities squarely on the shoulders of Buckingham.

The famous Petition of Right resulted from these debates in the summer of 1628. In it Parliament enunciated four grievances and asked the king to remedy them, sweetening its petition with promise of enough money to pay for the war if he answered favorably. Although there was not an angry word in the petition, Charles nevertheless returned an evasive reply; then, finding that he could get money no other way, he finally accepted. The petition stipulated that troops should not be billeted in private homes without the consent of the householders; no taxes should be levied without Parliament's approval; conviction of civilians under martial law in times of peace was illegal; and that no one should be imprisoned except on a formal and justifiable charge. The acceptance of the petition by Charles was a great victory for Parliament, as it had thereby secured his tacit admission that divine-right monarchy was subject to the restraint of law.

But the king unfortunately did not grasp the full significance of the petition, for he had no sooner prorogued Parliament than he asserted that he was accountable to God alone. During the recess, on August 23, a disgruntled officer murdered Buckingham, whose body was carried from Portsmouth to London amid cheers for the assassin, John Felton, and silence for the fallen duke. Grief-stricken at the loss of his friend, Charles had him buried in Westminster Abbey late in the day to frustrate rumored plans to desecrate the corpse. Then, determined as ever to have his way, he reconvened the unashamedly joyful Parliament in January, 1629. The Commons immediately attacked his right to collect tunnage and poundage, demanded religious reform, condemned the pardons he had granted for the release of clergymen against whom the Commons had brought charges of Arminianism, and drafted a statement of grievances. These were hurriedly drawn up in three resolutions that the Commons passed while the Speaker was forcibly held in his chair and the king's guards were pounding on the locked doors of its chamber. Two concerned tunnage and poundage; the third declared that anyone seeking to advance Arminianism or Catholicism was guilty of a capital crime against the kingdom. The Commons, refusing to accept the king's order of dissolution, adjourned on March 2. It did not meet again until 1640.

During these years of dispute with the Commons, Charles did not encounter nearly so much opposition in the House of Lords, which numbered about 150 in 1642. Whereas the antagonists of the crown, mostly Puritans and common-law lawyers, commanded a comfortable majority in the Commons in 1625–29 (and again in 1640–42), the peers who generally opposed the crown's policies were in the minority —probably about thirty members, or about a third of those in regular attendance. One should not conclude from this, however, that the Lords sided entirely with the crown against the Commons. Aside from the solid block of ecclesiastical peers, who did indeed support the crown on practically every issue, the Lords tried to steer a middle course. Since the advent of the Tudors, the role of the peers had been to act as mediators and judges, that is to say, to make certain that neither crown nor Commons did injustice to the basic constitutional principles of the realm by encroaching upon the powers of the other. The Lords held to this position until the explosive session of 1629, and again in 1640–42, when it became clear that the Commons meant to limit monarchic authority. (Most of the peers were to side with the king in the civil war, with only a small number aligning themselves with the Parliamentarians. Not unexpectedly, therefore, when Cromwell destroyed the monarchy, he also destroyed the House of Lords in 1649.)

Following the stormy session of 1629, Charles had decided never again to summon Parliament. For the next eleven years he ruled the country with the help of very able councilors in a manner that pro-Parliament historians have considered tyrannical. It is easy to surmise from a superficial glance at the period of his personal government that Charles abused his subjects and overstepped his regal authority. But it should be recalled that monarchic government without benefit of Parliament, though undoubtedly politically unwise, was by no means unconstitutional or unusual. Earlier monarchs, most recently Henry VII and Elizabeth, had ruled for long periods without calling Parliament. It is also certain, however, that few monarchs had ruled without Parliament in such crucial times as Charles now faced. Fortunately for him, peace with France and Spain was concluded in 1629 and 1630, thereby greatly reducing his expenses, although he still needed between £500,000 and £600,000 annually to operate in the black. Since Parliament did not sit between 1629 and 1640 when the crown's traditional sources of revenue were insufficient to meet all its expenses, Charles and his councilors were forced to devise technically legal but anachronistic and unpopular means of getting money. They also used the courts to justify such taxes and fines and to punish delinquents. But the Scottish rebellion and subsequent invasion of England finally left Charles no alternative but to summon Parliament in 1640, by which time it was eager to attack not only the crown's fiscal policy, but also the whole structure of absolute monarchy. It was this quarrel that resulted in the Civil War in 1642.

The crown's fiscal policy in the 1630s was devised and implemented largely by Richard Weston (Lord Portland) and Francis Lord Cottington, who were such close friends that Archbishop Laud sarcastically nicknamed them Lady Mora and her maid. As they had Catholic connections and generally favored a pro-Spanish foreign policy and no basic change in administrative machinery, they were frequently at odds with Laud, who replaced the moderate Puritan archbishop, George Abbot, in 1633, and with Thomas Wentworth, president of the Council of the North and lord deputy of Ireland. Laud and Cottington continually locked horns on the privy council. These rivalries, the result of personality clashes, office-seeking, religious and political differences, and disputes over foreign policy, weakened the king's government and prevented the council from devising anything better than a willy-nilly domestic program that virtually collapsed at the first sign of serious trouble in 1640. The rivalry between the Laud and Cottington factions was so strong that virtually the only issue they unanimously agreed upon was the urgent necessity to maintain the superstructure of royal absolutism against encroachments by the so-called "country party."

It is very difficult to define exactly the nature and composition of this "country party" in the 1630s. It certainly bore no resemblance to a party in the modern sense: it had no definite aims beyond the reduction of absolute monarchic power and some reform in religion; it had no national organization; and it had no nationally recognized leadership until 1642. Generally speaking, it consisted of all those who, for one reason or another—and grievances were variously religious, political, economic, or social—opposed the absolute monarchy of Charles I and his policies. Opposition to the crown had deep roots in English history, but it seemed to take on clearer form during the last half of Elizabeth's reign and grew steadily stronger under the first two Stuarts because of their unpopular domestic and foreign policies. The crown's opponents were very often, but not always, Puritans. As more Puritans were elected to Parliament in the early seventeenth century, opposition became more pronounced and vocal. The "country party" therefore benefited from the informal leadership of Puritan spokesmen like John Pym, John Hampden, and others who pinpointed the country's grievances in both Houses of Parliament, but most often in the Commons. The members of Parliament were in turn supported obliquely by those outside Parliament who had themselves been the victims of Stuart absolutism or were part of a group that had been affected by it. Among these persons might be mentioned landowners, who had been subjected to distraint of knighthood fines, ship money, and deforestation penalties (discussed below); the municipal and guild authorities of London, who disliked the crown's pressures of one sort or another; clergymen sympathetic to Puritan ideals; lawyers resentful of the crown's abuse of the common law and recourse to packed courts that justified its practices; businessmen who disliked monopolies and other types of restraint on trade; and pamphleteers like William Prynne. These segments of the population coalesced behind Parliament at the outbreak of the Civil War in 1642 just as other segments loyal to the king became Royalists.

In the early 1630s Portland and Cottington strained their imaginations to devise ways of raising money for the crown. They economized as much as possible, sold offices in the national and local government, granted monopolies in return for handsome fees and part of the profits to manufacturers of soap, salt, beer, and other products, increased the income from wardships to about twice what they had been under Elizabeth and James, and collected tunnage and poundage without the consent of Parliament. Through distraint of knighthood fines, based on a law dating back to Edward I by which persons with annual incomes of at least forty pounds were required to become knights or at least pay the heavy charges associated with ennoblement, Portland and Cottington collected about £125,000 in 1630 alone. They also revived Norman laws forbidding deforestation, not only in royal forests such as Sherwood and Dean, but in formerly heavily forested sections that had since become densely populated (virtually all of Essex County, for instance), and fined delinquents outrageous sums. One nobleman was fined £20,000 even though his lands had not been considered part of a royal forest for four centuries. Others were penalized for enclosing land contrary to outmoded laws of the previous two centuries. Cottington assiduously collected fees and rents for wardship to the distress of orphaned heirs and widows and commandeered a populated section of Surrey to enclose Richmond Park for the king. He kept the barons of the Exchequer busy prosecuting those in arrears and compounded (a financial settlement) with Catholic recusants, two-thirds of whose lands went to the crown. Cottington also managed to borrow large sums from friends of the court.

Such taxes resulted in widespread complaints. But when Charles overstepped the bounds of prudence in imposing ship money, he had to face more active opposition. The crown had customarily expected ports and littoral counties to provide ships in times of imminent danger or actual war. Sometimes the crown collected taxes to provide funds for the fleet. While it is true that, at the time of the first writs authorizing the collection of ship money in the 1630s, the privy council was mildly worried about the growth of French and Dutch naval strength, the shoddy condition of the English fleet, and the attacks of pirates on merchant shipping, few agreed with Charles that these constituted any real danger to England. Nevertheless they grudgingly paid. But when the king subsequently imposed a larger ship money tax throughout England, sheriffs and justices of the peace, whose duty it was to collect the tax, encountered stiff opposition—an opposition based primarily on the frequency of its imposition rather than on its doubtful legality. Rich gentlemen like John Hampden and Lord Saye and Sele refused to pay, and others were emboldened to do likewise. Only about 20 per cent of the total assessment was collected, and further levies in the later 1630s also failed.

The issue of ship money ultimately went to the courts, first by order of Charles, who got a favorable opinion on its legality in King's Bench in 1635, and then in the test case brought by Hampden in 1637. He purposely refused to pay in order to challenge the legality of ship money on behalf of the Puritans, among whom he was a leader. The case involved more than ship money alone; it challenged the royal prerogative and unparliamentary taxation. Hampden's lawyers argued in the Court of Exchequer that the essence of the case was not whether the crown could legally levy ship money in inland shires, but whether it could impose *any* tax without the consent of Parliament. Furthermore, they said, if the kingdom was in danger of invasion, as the king alleged, all he needed to do was to convene Parliament and ask for the required subsidies. Conversely, the crown's lawyers held that in the event of national emergency, which only the king could rightly determine, there was no time to hold elections to Parliament, for at least forty days were required between the issuance of writs for elections and its convening. In the interval, they said, the kingdom might be lost. Under these circumstances, therefore, the king was justified in taking whatever action he saw fit. Although the judges ruled seven to five in favor of the crown, it had won a Pyrrhic victory, for Hampden and his Puritan friends left the courtroom more convinced than ever that they could no longer rely on due legal process to preserve their liberties.

Taxation was not the only issue that steeled the Puritan-dominated "country party" against the crown. Several councilors—Portland, Cottington, Windebank, and Sir Kenelm Digby (whose father had been executed for complicity in the Gunpowder Plot) among them—had Catholic family connections, Catholic friends, or Catholic leanings, and Puritans believed that Windebank and Cottington were sympathetic to a reunion of the English and Roman Churches. The Puritans were also shocked that three priests, Leander Jones, Gregorio Panzani, and George Conn, the last two papal representatives, befriended privy councilors, enjoyed the court's hospitality, and bolstered the faith of their coreligionists. The Puritans did not realize that there was no actual sympathy for a reunion with Rome among councilors, and that Charles's friendship with Conn was founded on their mutual love of art and intelligent conversation. Moreover, they knew that Jones and Panzani were charged by the pope to effect a reconciliation between the regular and secular clergy, who had been at loggerheads over ecclesiastical administration since late in James's reign. Henrietta did not help matters. She boasted about the Protestant ladies whom her priests converted to Catholicism. The Puritans also criticized the government for failing to prosecute Catholics. Charles had endeavored to do so by royal proclamations, but as local officials were often apathetic, or in sympathy with the Catholics, or even actual believers, few were hailed before the courts. Catholics in some areas did endure great financial and personal hardships; others practiced their faith without much interference. Few paid the twenty-pound monthly fines, went to prison, or were executed. Only three Catholics—two priests and a layman—were put to death for their religion between 1625 and 1640. Certainly many more would have suffered disabilities if Archbishop Laud and many of his episcopal associates had had their way.

Laud had a brilliant career as a student, privy councilor, and prelate. His rise to prominence under Charles I is attributable to his extraordinary capacity for hard work, administrative skill, devotion to the precepts of divine-right monarchy, and firm Arminianism. The son of a Berkshire clothier, he advanced from the presidency of St. John's at Oxford to the bishopric of London and finally to the archiepiscopacy of Canterbury. He strove unsuccessfully to reform Church administration without regard to class or privilege—a policy called "Thorough" after the usage of Wentworth. Laud attacked both Catholics and Puritans forcefully and fearlessly, undertook a careful ecclesiastical visitation of his archdiocese to enforce uniformity in form and faith, and restored the beauty of dilapidated churches and decorous conduct in them by driving out the tradesmen, gossips, and vagrants who sacrilegiously misused Communion tables. The Puritans accused Laud of being preoccupied with external ceremony rather than with fundamental spiritual values, and construed his Arminianism as sympathy for Catholicism when, in fact, he probably would have preferred to die than to compromise with it. His correspondence and diary are full of references to the intrusion of Romanism and many of the privy council's proclamations against recusancy can be traced to his influence.

Laud's sincere efforts to uphold Arminianism incurred the undying enmity of the Puritans. He deposed many of their clergy, demanded their strict conformity to the prayer book, and suppressed and punished in Star Chamber Puritan pamphleteers like William Prynne and Henry Burton, who poured so much invective on High-Church Anglicanism that Laud imposed a strict censorship on the press. He branded, imprisoned, and pilloried heretical publishers and burned their books.

As a result of religious persecution, economic depression, and political absolutism, more than thirty thousand Englishmen, by no means all Puritans, emigrated to the New World by the 1640s. Others formed Separatist or Catholic islands of heresy in northern and eastern England, or refused to conform despite heavy penalties.

The attempt to enforce religious uniformity in Scotland in 1637 erupted into a rebellion that caused an English crisis culminating in the collapse of Charles's personal government. With Laud he visited Scotland in 1633 to be crowned in St. Giles' Cathedral, Edinburgh. In the next year, without consulting the Presbyterian General Assembly, he instructed the Scottish bishops to draft a new prayer book. King James had introduced the Anglican episcopal system in Scotland and made other fainthearted attempts to bring Presbyterianism within its jurisdiction, but Presbyterians had been free to practice their religion since the days of John Knox. Their strength had grown while Anglicanism steadily lost ground. The introduction of the new liturgy in July, 1637, at Edinburgh touched off a riot that ultimately led to the adoption of a Covenant by which Presbyterians swore to resist the alien Church reforms. The Assembly repudiated bishops, and military preparations began on both sides of the Tweed.

Charles's decision to force the Anglican liturgy on the Covenanters caused the two Bishops' Wars. There was virtually no money in the English Treasury to pay for an army and little will in the country to support the king. As loyal peers dug deep into their pockets to support the militia, which mustered in the north under the command of two incompetents, the cowardly Earl of Holland and the aged Earl of Arundel, London refused to pay its share of the forced loan and Henrietta organized a Catholic subscription that raised about £14,000. Meanwhile Alexander Leslie, an experienced soldier, gathered an army of eight thousand Scots. The inevitable occurred: Leslie repulsed a weak drive by Howard's cavalry without firing a shot, and Charles accepted a truce at Berwick. Wentworth, who was then recalled from Ireland to accept the earldom of Strafford and nominal leadership of the council, convinced Charles that Parliament must be summoned. The Short Parliament, which sat only about three weeks, met in April, 1640. It refused to grant the subsidies Charles desperately needed, and spoke of numerous grievances accumulated over the past eleven years. As neither king nor Parliament was anxious to compromise—Charles refused to give up ship money and Parliament had already opened negotiations with the Scots—nothing was achieved.

The dissolution of the Short Parliament further weakened Charles's position. Almost beside themselves with worry, the privy councilors searched for ways to meet the crown's expenses: Charles seized the bullion in the Tower and Cottington practically forced the East India Company to sell thousands of bags of pepper to the crown on consignment, and then sold it at a heavy loss. At this point the Scots invaded northern England and occupied the counties of Northumberland and Durham. Having no alternative, the English commissioners made peace with the Scots at Ripon, confirming their occupation of the two counties at a cost to England of £850 a day. This added financial burden forced Charles to summon Parliament again. As the members made for London in October, 1640, charges of Catholic intrigue that had supposedly led to English defeat filled the air; rioters roamed the streets of London excoriating privy councilors; Puritan authors poured out polemics against the government; and Parliamentary leaders polished their cudgels for the battle against absolute monarchy.

The Long Parliament, which sat intermittently for the next twenty years, convened on November 3, 1640. Many of those who had sat in the Parliaments of 1625–29 were returned to the Commons. Although the gentry was well represented, the number of lawyers and merchants in the lower House, many of them Puritans of one sort or another, was larger than in 1629, and there were a few more English Presbyterians, whose ranks gradually increased over the next few years. The City of London, the center of Puritanism in England, had some members of Parliament who generally worked with the iconoclasts led by John Pym, but most of the aldermen did not throw in their lot with him primarily because they were the beneficiaries of Stuart patronage in lucrative magisterial or state offices, and because the city and the crown had close financial ties. But except for a few outspoken bishops and some moderates like Edward Hyde, Charles had no spokesmen in Parliament capable of coping effectively with the likes of Pym, Hampden, Cromwell, or Sir Henry Vane. As Eliot had perished in the Tower after a long imprisonment, Pym assumed control of the "country party" in the Commons. This remarkably able man from Somersetshire, a brilliant orator and superb political manager, engineered a governmental reorganization that abolished the hated prerogative courts, reformed the Established Church, drove some privy councilors into exile, imprisoned others, executed Strafford, and forced a civil war on England. Precisely what Pym meant ultimately to achieve is still the subject of heated controversy, primarily because he died in 1643 before his plans came to fruition. It is consequently impossible to know whether he meant to create a constitutional monarchy or a republic, or simply to harness Stuart absolutism. But there is no question that he was an outstanding politician, a clever diplomat, and a Machiavellian manipulator of men. He had an uncanny sense of timing, an abiding hatred of Arminianism, and wisdom enough to use the social unrest of the artisan and apprentice ranks of the London citizenry in carefully planned demonstrations that worked to Parliament's advantage.

Parliament first rid the country of the king's "evil" advisers, whom it blamed for the maladministration during the eleven no-Parliament years. Justice Finch, the hated defender of ship money, and Secretary Windebank, who was charged on seventy-four counts with aiding Catholics, fled to the Continent. Francis Cottington, both Chancellor of the Exchequer and Master of Wards, gave up his lucrative posts rather than his life in a successful attempt to placate Parliament. But these men were objects of lesser scorn than either Laud or "Black Tom" Strafford, whom the Commons made scapegoats of its anger toward the crown. Broken by an arduous life of work, and bent by the weight of Puritan criticism, Laud went to the Tower for treason, spent four years there without giving an inch to his enemies, and died by execution in 1645. Strafford enjoyed no such period of grace. Pym was worried lest Strafford's efforts to bring charges against the Puritan leadership of secretly negotiating with the Scots should succeed. Moreover, the Puritans deeply resented his efficient but autocratic administration in Ireland, which had not seen such a capable royal servant since the days of Poynings. Strafford was accused of having advised Charles to use Irish troops to suppress the opposition, an allegation that Parliament was unable to prove. He was indicted for treason, but Pym could not make the indictment stick during the protracted trial the following spring. But Strafford nevertheless died at the hands of Parliament, purportedly for having undermined the fundamental laws of the realm. He fell victim to a legislative device called a bill of attainder an act that did not require proof of guilt. Charles did nothing to help Strafford: he would not interfere in Parliament's judicial affairs, and he at last signed the bill because the London mob threatened the queen and his children.

During the spring and summer of 1641, Parliament destroyed the bastions of divine-right monarchy and provided for its own perpetuity. It passed the Triennial Act, which ordained that Parliament must meet at least once every three years whether the king called it or not, thereby making it impossible for him to rule without it. Ship money, distraint of knighthood, and other unparliamentary taxes were declared illegal. Tunnage and poundage was granted to Charles for only a few months with the stipulation that only Parliament could legalize its collection. The prerogative courts of Star Chamber and High Commission were abolished, as were the Councils of the North and of Wales. Victims of the courts, such as Prynne and John Lilburne, were released from prison. Parliament also debated at length the structure and government of the Church, a discussion that illustrates the basic differences of view over religion within the "country party." The canons issued by Laud were abolished, but no decision was reached whether to reform the Church along Calvinist lines, do away with bishops, or simply harness their authority. Catholic persecution was intensified by requiring churchwardens and constables to report known and suspected recusants in every parish in and around London. In the same summer Charles visited Scotland to muster popular support against Parliament, and a worried Pym sent commissioners to watch him lest he raise a Scottish Royalist army. Meanwhile Pym laid the basis for the establishment of a militia to protect London and Parliament against a Royalist reaction by taking advantage of a fortuitous Irish rebellion, the implications of which he cleverly manipulated to Parliament's advantage.

The rebellion, though ferocious and bloody, did not actually endanger Parliament or help Charles, but it did arouse the London mob and provide Pym with another argument for creating an army. The atrocities committed in Ireland have been grossly exaggerated, and the causes of the revolt had little directly to do with affairs in England. There had, of course, been religious differences among the Irish since the "plantation" of Protestants in the Pale of Ulster by James I—and there were still the clannish social, political, and economic rivalries that had plagued the country for centuries. The native Irish, some of whom were Protestants, resented absentee landlords who controlled valuable land, and the stern administration of Strafford during 1633–40. He superintended Irish commerce, suppressed recalcitrant peers, collected heavy taxes, and ruled by martial law. But he also put Ireland on a sound financial footing, drove the Jesuits underground, rid the seas of pirates, and kept the peace. The rebellion of 1641 was a result of a half century of English absolutism, against which both Irish Catholics and Protestant Ulsterites rose on Strafford's departure. Marauding bands pillaged, murdered, and destroyed property. While their wrath was directed primarily at English and Scots Protestants, native Catholic

Irish were not left unmolested. Though the estimates of casualties from battle, hunger, and disease vary greatly in contemporary accounts, probably no more than five thousand perished.

The foremost contemporary historian of the period, Clarendon, remarked that the rebellion "proved of infinite disadvantage to the king's affairs which were then recovering new life." There seems to have been increasing support for the king at this point, many Englishmen, even in Parliament, feeling that, since the tools of divine-right monarchy had been broken, Parliament should now compromise with Charles. But Pym had no intention of stopping there, and the Irish rebellion made it possible for him to regain enough support to secure the adoption of the Grand Remonstrance in November, 1641. This document, approved by an unimpressive majority (159–148), itself an indication of strong Royalist sentiment, is an important one for British constitutional history. In it, Parliament enumerated about two hundred grievances and attacked a new group of advisers (Sir John Culpepper, Edward Hyde, and Edward Nicholas), Church government, the queen and her coreligionists, and the judges in an effort to win back the support of moderates who were drawing closer to Charles because they found Pym's ideas extreme. Apparently Pym intended either to destroy the episcopacy altogether or at least to reduce its authority in the Church, for one article in the Remonstrance, perhaps its most significant point, reads: "we desire there may be a general synod of the . . . divines of this island; assisted with some from foreign parts [Scottish Presbyterians?], professing the same religion with us, who may consider . . . good government of the church, and present . . . their consultations unto the parliament . . . thereby to find passage and obedience unto the parliament." It obviously had decided to assume responsibility for the tenets and government of the English Church even though statutory law vested that responsibility in the crown in Convocation. The ultimate result of this proposal was the Westminster Assembly, which met intermittently for several years beginning in 1644. Lengthy and detailed discussions among episcopal Puritans, Separatists, and Presbyterians failed to reach a compromise, so that episcopalianism prevailed after the Restoration. It is also apparent that the radical faction in Parliament meant to depart from the traditional constitution of England. Therefore, rather than closing the gap between moderate and radical elements, the Remonstrance aggravated it so that many of the moderates ceased to support Pym's goals.

At long last Charles decided to be firm with Parliament. He reasoned that it meant to impeach Henrietta for advancing Catholicism and for advising him to enlist the aid of an Irish army. Henrietta, furious and defiant, badgered him to "pull those rogues out [of Parliament] by the ears." Charles stormed angrily into Commons with an armed guard ready to arrest Pym, Hampden, Holles, Haselrig, and Strode, but they had escaped moments earlier. The Speaker, by now no longer the spokesman of the crown, would not reveal where they had gone and the Lords refused to consider their impeachment. Two months later, in February, 1642, Parliament passed the Militia Ordinance (technically not a statute because Charles did not sign it), which created a Parliamentary army. The Puritan leadership justified this unconstitutional action by divining that Parliament's decisions "hath the stamp of royal authority although his Majesty, seduced by evil council, do in his person oppose or interrupt the same." As Charles could not recognize this principle without destroying the whole fabric of monarchic authority, he despaired of compromise and left London, never again to return until he stood accused of treason in 1648.

Pym then discarded the mantle of dutiful obedience to Charles by pushing through Parliament the Nineteen Propositions. They ordained essentially that high-ranking advisers to the crown could hold office only with Parliament's consent; that Charles must sign the Militia Ordinance; that his children must have teachers and spouses acceptable to Parliament; and that all enemies of the kingdom, including Catholics in the House of Lords, must surrender their posts. Under threat of such terms, Charles had little alternative but to fight. He therefore summoned loyal subjects to rally round his standard at Nottingham on August 22, which act formally instituted the first Civil War.

No single factor nor fundamental principle can satisfactorily explain the causes of this Civil War. An older generation of Stuart historians ascribed it to a constitutional struggle between a progressive Parliament and a conservative monarchy over financial, religious, legal, and foreign affairs. They also cited such abrasions as the king's alternating stubbornness and laxity, the aims of the Puritans, governmental corruption, censorship of the press, and so forth. They were right up to a point. More recent scholarship has suggested economic and social causes involving rivalry between officeholders and office seekers, conflict between urban middle classes and the aristocracy, and other theories based on class conflict, usually relating to the gentry. There is a measure of truth in all these. Virtually everything already discussed about legal, political, religious, economic, and social issues of the period had a bearing on the ultimate catastrophe of civil war, but it should not be assumed that it was inevitable; even during the strained relations of 1640-42, cool heads sought compromise. Yet the crown and Parliament, in pursuing their individual interests, went so far down the road from the fork of 1640 that neither could turn back in the spring of 1642, and it became almost impossible to negotiate on any rational basis.

Men have little trouble deciding between antithetical alternatives such as freedom or servitude, but Englishmen in the 1640s faced no such clear-cut alternatives in choosing between the Roundheads and the Cavaliers. Some, for reasons peculiar to themselves, were already committed by 1642, but many others stopped short in the midst of blood and pain to justify their support of Parliament, the crown, or neutrality. There were no fixed lines of support by class or region for either camp. Professor Trevelyan has written that the war was waged by "two small minorities," and that in 1642 "not half the nation, nor half even of the gentry, had been induced to support . . . king or Parliament." Whether men fought for the king or for Parliament, or refused to fight at all, depended on many variables. In general, however, the upper gentry and aristocracy, most of whom were Arminians or at least Episcopalians, became Royalists. Their greatest strength lay principally in the north and west of England, and chiefly in rural areas. Parliamentary support came largely from the professional and mercantile classes in urban areas, especially of southeast England and East Anglia. But even here there can be no sweeping generalization, for, while Cambridge, London, and Norwich, for instance, supported Parliament, Durham and Oxford sided with the king. The only nearly universal support that Charles got from any group came from the Catholics who, though victims of Laud's system, preferred it to Puritanism or Presbyterianism.

The Civil War in the 1640s was in some ways similar to the Wars of the Roses in the 1460s. Large armies, supported by satellite units operating on the periphery, rolled across the land county by county attacking enemy strongholds or fighting battles decided in a single day. No one can travel through England's heartland without noticing iron gates and stone walls that still bear the marks of war. All Englishmen faced heavier taxes, higher prices, and shorter provisions, and anguish at the loss of a friend or relative, but otherwise the civilian population did not generally suffer. Towns like Birmingham in 1642 and Leicester in 1645 were besieged, and important country houses became strongholds or military headquarters; yet few towns were either depopulated or devastated. Casualty lists on both sides were long, more soldiers probably dying from disease and complications from wounds than from mortal blows in battle.

The campaigns of the war cannot detain us long. Skirmishes occurred at many points across the country soon after the mobilization of the Royalist army. Charles hoped to capture London quickly, but the Parliamentarians stopped him, thereby forcing his retreat to Oxford. With the advent of spring in 1643, he organized a three-pronged attack on London, with armies commanded by the Earl of Newcastle, Sir Ralph Hopton, and Prince Rupert, Charles's nephew, moving toward the capital from Oxford, from the southwest, and from the north. Hopton and Newcastle broke through the Roundheads' lines, but later became bogged down against stiff opposition. Charles had lost the initiative and never regained it, even though his Cavaliers dominated the fighting for the succeeding year. Royalist armies sallied forth from garrison towns in the two following springs, without lasting gains. Charles and his Council of War, comprised of Cottington, Hyde, Culpepper, Nicholas, Digby, and a bevy of colonels and captains, settled down in Oxford to direct Cavalier regiments. The first important battle was fought, indecisively, at Edgehill, where Prince Rupert's thirteen thousand men engaged those of the Earl of Essex on September 23, 1643. The Cavaliers suffered heavy casualties, and like the Confederates in the American Civil War, they could ill afford to lose men because they could not replace them.

The Cavaliers' slight military edge in the early months could not offset Parliament's advantages. It had a bigger and better-provisioned army, the support of the navy (which cut off whatever chance Charles had of getting Irish or Continental help), and more money. The rich counties of the southeast, which Parliament controlled, yielded more taxes and supplies than the counties held by the Royalists. The Parliamentarians also confiscated the Royalists' property or compounded with them for it, and benefited from trade with Continental friends. Though at first the Cavaliers had better commanders in Rupert and Newcastle, Parliament soon came up with their superiors in Lord Fairfax and Oliver Cromwell. Cromwell rose rapidly from a command of sixty men in 1642 to a command of eleven hundred men a year later. His regiment was composed of fundamentalist Protestants (mostly Independents) led by hand-picked officers, some of whom were relatives or friends of Cromwell and shared his moral convictions. Although the regiment was not nearly as free of drunkenness, swearing, and gambling as some of Cromwell's admirers would have us believe, he did mold his men into a God-fearing and rigorously trained fighting unit. These "Ironsides" fought for principles rather than for pay, were armed with pistols, swords, and breastplates, and more than once turned battles in Parliament's favor. Cromwell's leadership also helped to offset the temporary confusion that arose late in 1643 because of the deaths of Pym and Hampden.

In December, 1643, the Scots and Parliamentarians signed the Solemn League and Covenant, prescribing "the reformation of religion . . . in doctrine, worship, discipline, and government . . . and that popery and prelacy should be extirpated." This alliance, which the Scots believed would result in the institution of Presbyterian Church government in England, proved disastrous for Charles in 1644–45. Following his victory at the Battle of Marston Moor in July, 1644, Cromwell conquered northern England, assisted by the Earl of Leven's Scotsmen. Another Parliamentarian triumph at Newbury in the same year drove the Royalists from Somerset, Wiltshire, and Hampshire. A potentially dangerous power struggle between the civil and military leaders on Parliament's side might have helped Charles but for the Self-Denying Ordinance that deprived all members of Parliament (except Cromwell) of military command and led to the reorganization of the army (thereafter known as the New Model Army) under the command of Fairfax and Cromwell. Several skirmishes in 1645 and the heavy Cavalier defeat at Naseby in June broke the Royalists' resistance. Thereafter Charles had no choice but to capitulate. He surrendered Oxford to Fairfax in June, 1646, and sought asylum with the Scots army camped at Newark. The Scots welcomed Charles because they hoped to get his consent to the Solemn League and Covenant; Charles, on the other hand, used this to bargain for Scots help against Parliament. When they could not come to terms, the Scots turned him over to Parliament and withdrew across the Tweed. Parliament imprisoned Charles at Holmby House in Northamptonshire and drew up peace terms embodied in the Propositions of Newcastle (January, 1647), which he refused to accept on the grounds that Parliament meant to deprive him of all meaningful authority.

Meanwhile Parliament and the New Model Army disagreed on government and religion. By permitting Cromwell to create a truly national army out of the militia of the several county associations that had hitherto comprised the Parliamentary forces, Parliament had given birth to an efficient political force as well as a military machine. The Self-Denying Ordinance had also contributed to the cleavage between Parliament and the New Model Army, in effect separating military leadership from political leadership. The New Model Army consisted of fundamentalists of several sects, mostly Independents or Congregationalists, but also Seekers, Anabaptists, and Levelers, whose chaplains and pamphleteers disseminated their ideas without interference from Cromwell. Consequently the army contained all the elements of political and religious radicalism in the country. As freedom of worship within the regiments was permitted, the troops had no wish to agree to enforced religious conformity, as the Presbyterian-dominated Parliament would have liked. Parliament and the army differed on three basic issues: (1) Parliament sought to make peace with Charles to the exclusion of the army, which, having actually won the war on the battlefield, insisted on having a part in the peace settlement; (2) officers and men agreed that there should be latitudinarianism in religion and a new government based on a broad franchise and frequent Parliamentary elections, while Parliament wanted religious conformity and a restricted franchise; (3) Parliament hoped to disband the army at the earliest opportunity, without paying the large arrears in soldiers' wages, while the army refused to disband for fear that Parliament would ignore its religious and political aims and make good their intention not to pay the troops.

To strengthen its position against Parliament, the army took Charles prisoner and brought him to its headquarters at Newmarket. Several proposals for resolving the differences between crown and country emanated from the rank and file, among them the radically democratic ideas of John Lilburne's Levelers, who advocated social equality, land reform, religious toleration, and low franchise qualifications coupled with frequent Parliamentary elections. But the terms that the army finally asked Charles to accept were much more moderate. The Heads of the Proposals, composed by Henry Ireton, Cromwell's son-in-law, called for biennial Parliaments, Parliamentary control of the army and the appointment of the crown's councilors, and a lenient settlement with Royalists over their confiscated property. Charles nonetheless rejected these terms because he believed that he could regain all his former power by playing off one against the other the Scots Covenanters, the army, and Parliament, thereby destroying the opposition's unity. He managed to escape a few months later to the Isle of Wight and made a treaty with the Scots, who deserted Parliament on his promise to establish Presbyterianism for three years.

The continuing friction between Parliament and the army on the one hand, and the alliance between the Scots and Cavaliers on the other, led to the second Civil War in the summer of 1648. By a strange twist of circumstances, Cavaliers, Scots, and English Presbyterians allied against the New Model Army, which easily defeated them in a few weeks. Cromwell met stubborn resistance in southern Wales and Yorkshire, and Fairfax felt the sting of Royalist fervor in Kent and Essex, but in the end the New Model Army destroyed the opposition at the Battle of Preston (Lancashire) in mid-August. Cromwell captured Charles, imprisoned him at Windsor Castle, and occupied London. When the Presbyterian Parliamentarians refused to bring charges against the king, a troop led by Colonel Pride purged 143 of them from Parliament, leaving only about 50 Independents, derisively called the Rump.

During the troubled years since 1643, Cromwell had tried to steer a middle course between the army and Parliament. He wanted to avert any settlement that would radically alter England's traditional constitution. So he had sought to limit, not destroy, monarchy. But, by 1649, Charles's utter intransigence forced him to change his mind. The Rump, subservient to Cromwell, abolished the House of Lords and set up a commission of 135 men to try Charles for treason, murder, and the perversion of fundamental laws. As no judge dared to do so, Sergeant John Bradshaw presided over the crowded court in Westminster Hall. Charles refused to answer the charges on the grounds that no court had the authority to try him. When he could have spoken, he would not; later, when he wished to speak, he could not. Despite threats and other pressures, Cromwell eventually could induce only fifty-nine regicides to sign the death warrant. Thousands came to watch Charles's execution on a crude scaffold erected on Whitehall in front of the Banqueting Hall, where he had often held council meetings. Comforted and supported only by Bishop Juxon, Charles made a stirring speech that few heard amid the clamor of the crowd. As the executioner's ax dealt the mortal blow, many onlookers groaned; others dipped their handkerchiefs in his blood; few fully realized the import of what had been done that thirtieth of January, 1649. A shadowy figure was seen lingering beside Charles's coffin that night, mumbling "cruel necessity," but it was too late to salve the conscience of Cromwell who had caused the execution of a man with whom he had romped as a boy thirty years earlier at his uncle's estate in Huntingdonshire.

The day after the execution, Commons declared that, as monarchy had proved inconsistent with the liberty and public welfare of Englishmen, it should be abolished, a proclamation that was formalized with the institution of the Commonwealth in the following May. The Council of State, whose membership frequently changed during the next four years, originally consisted of forty-one members drawn from the Rump and the army. These councilors worked efficiently and dutifully through committees not unlike those of the old privy council, and carried on the day-by-day operations of government. Behind them stood the Rump and the army, both subservient to Cromwell who, though he held no special status or title in the new scheme of things, nevertheless wielded consummate power. The young republic faced serious domestic and foreign threats that demanded immediate resolution. Cromwell feared the intentions of radical republicans like the Fifth Monarchy Men* as well as the Royalists, whose ranks were swelled by the popular reaction against the execution of the king. Furthermore, both Ireland and Scotland rallied to the support of Charles II, and tension mounted between England and the Netherlands over commercial rivalry in America and the East Indies and the political asylum that the Dutch gave to Royalists.

Ireland had slipped into anarchy upon the outbreak of rebellion in 1641. Native Irish peers such as the Duke of Ormonde and Protestant Scots-Irish landlords supported the king in the Civil Wars and refused to recognize the new republic. Cromwell therefore invaded Ireland with twelve thousand men, who attacked the fortress town of Drogheda and slew virtually all of its garrison. This massacre, and another at Wexford, induced the other coastal towns to surrender, a fact that has led some to condone Cromwell's barbarism. He believed, no doubt sincerely, that the Irish were a sinful, irresponsible, and backward people who respected only force and could not be reasoned with. Whether he honestly felt that he acted merely as the instrument of divine judgment against the heretical Irish rebels can never be answered to everyone's satisfaction. There can be no doubt, however, that his settlement in Ireland set the course of its history for the next two centuries. He might have chosen several alternatives, such as the reinstitution of the Tudor-Stuart system of imperial rule through a cadre

* A sect of religious fanatics who believed that Christ would soon come to establish the fifth universal monarchy as foretold in the Book of Daniel (chapter 2), and that it was their duty forcibly to remove existing governments from His way.

of administrators, or the eviction of Irish from the Pale and the settlement of the area by Englishmen. Instead, he had the Rump pass a statute in 1652 that transferred about two-thirds of the land to English Protestant landlords, many of whom never lived on their land, forced the migration of Irish peasants to poorer land, and rigorously reimposed the anti-Catholic penal laws. If the English landlords and merchants in Ireland benefited by trade and the protection of English law, the vast majority of the Irish were ultimately reduced to abject poverty by a ruling class unsympathetic to their economic plight and hostile to their religion. Consequently the condition of the Irish steadily deteriorated until the nineteenth century, when English and Irish statesmen eventually resolved the problems the Cromwellian settlement had helped to create.

Scotland, though also rebellious, did not suffer such severe punishment. Cromwell felt that the Scots had simply gone astray in supporting Charles II, who had insincerely promised to accept Presbyterianism in order to win their support, while they hoped to use Royalist help to establish their religion in England. Cromwell defeated the Scots Royalist rebels at Dunbar in September, 1650, and a year later to the very day ended their rebellion by routing them at Worcester, where Charles II narrowly escaped capture through the help of Catholics, who hid him until he fled to France. Cromwell dealt leniently with the Scots, for though they resented the presence of English administrators and troops, they were allowed freely to practice their religion, and few lost either their lives or their lands.

The first Dutch war (1652–54) climaxed a half century of commercial rivalry in which English trade generally suffered at the hands of superior Dutch seamanship and initiative. The early Stuarts had not developed a firm colonial policy, with the result that the Dutch soon dominated the carrying trade to Asia, Africa, and America. Although Charles I had used ship money partly to strengthen the fleet, it could not compete in trade or war with the more numerous and swift vessels from the Netherlands. Cromwell, cognizant of the weakness of the fleet, added ships to it and secured the passage of the Navigation Act of 1651, by which goods imported into the British Isles had to be transported in English ships manned by English seamen —a clear challenge to Dutch mercantile supremacy. The war, which began when the Dutch refused to salute English ships in the Channel, went badly for the latter in 1652, but the New Model Navy held its own in several furious engagements and gradually built its strength through the administrative reforms of Admiral Robert Blake. His tight blockade of Dutch home ports so crippled their economy that they came to terms in 1654. They promised to lower their flag to England's in the Channel, to make monetary retribution for the Amboyna Massacre of 1623 and for English shipping damaged or lost in the war, and to offer no further refuge to Royalists.

Unsuccessful on the battlefield, English Royalists tried diplomacy and intrigue against the Commonwealth. Charles II and his court lived in exile at several towns, including Brussels, Paris, and Rouen in France and the Spanish Netherlands. Royalist diplomats tried without appreciable success to enlist the military support of foreign powers or at least to secure loans to sustain the exiled government. To this end, in 1649 Charles sent Edward Hyde and Cottington to Spain. They were received coolly by Philip IV who, understandably uncertain about how long the Cromwellian regime might last, and fearful of its naval power, at first refused recognition to either side, and later declared for the Commonwealth. Hyde and Cottington encountered great difficulty obtaining even a house in Madrid, received vague replies from the Spanish Council of State to their many entreaties for money, and left after almost two years of fruitless negotiation. The pope offered much sympathy but little money. Even the French, who had serious internal problems with the Fronde, could not be relied on despite the urgent pleas of Henrietta Maria.

The Royalists in England organized a badly directed and generally ineffective underground movement that had little to do with the eventual restoration of Charles II in 1660. Several dissident factions could not agree how best to fight Cromwell. The Louvre group, centered around Henrietta and Henry Jermyn in Paris, sought an alliance with the Scots Presbyterians in the hope of inspiring an invasion of England. Older Royalists like Hyde, Nicholas, and Ormonde favored a conspiratorial policy that they hoped would undermine the strength of the Commonwealth and win the allegiance of moderates from all parties. A third group, the Swordsmen, led by Rupert, staged a number of uprisings, the most important being Penruddock's in 1655, none of which did much damage. Their poor organization, insufficient support, and the extraordinarily effective spy network founded by John Thurloe, Cromwell's secretary of state, defeated every attempt to overthrow the republic. When the restoration of Charles II did come, it owed more to the country's dissatisfaction with military dictatorship than to the Royalist conspiracy.

Having suppressed Royalist intrigue and defeated the Dutch, Cromwell drifted into war with Spain, first in America and then in Europe. The Thirty Years' War had created a new power configuration on the Continent, with Sweden, France, and the Netherlands gaining most by it, and Spain had been seriously weakened. France and Sweden offered no serious threat to the Commonwealth because they were essentially land powers, but Spain still had a very large fleet that could successfully exclude English commerce from much of the New World. Furthermore, Spain and France were at war over two provinces bordering on the Pyrenees, and while England stood to gain little by helping the French, it had a great deal to gain at the expense of Spain while it was engrossed in the French war. Additionally, Philip IV had not been able to control his Portuguese subjects since the outbreak of their war for independence in 1640, and they were giving aid and comfort to Rupert's Royalist fleet. Cromwell also seems to have had ambitions to emulate Elizabeth's feats on the Main. For these reasons he sent a fleet commanded by Admiral Sir William Penn, the Quaker's father, who captured Jamaica. Another fleet seized Spanish treasure off Cadiz and destroyed a Spanish squadron off the Azores. Early in 1657, England and France jointly attacked Dunkirk, which fell within the year. Dunkirk and some West Indian islands remained in English hands as a result of the Treaty of the Pyrenees (1659).

Meanwhile Cromwell had encountered difficult domestic problems. He had as much trouble as Charles I had had in meeting satisfactorily the objections of restless elements opposed to what they considered to be his arbitrary, ill-defined rule. Although he had been most tolerant of sectarianism in the New Model Army, he showed little patience after 1648 with the moderate Levelers' program or that of their most radical wing, the Diggers, a communitarian sect led by Gerrard Winstanley, who urged sweeping agrarian reforms and social equality, or with the "radical" pietist sects like the Family of Love and the Seekers, whose simple religion and socialistic practices harmed no one. The Rump Parliament had strongly supported Cromwell since 1649, but by 1653 it displeased him so much that he contemptuously dissolved it and summoned another Parliament known as Barebone's, after the name of one of its members. It proved to be more cooperative than its predecessor by constructing a new governmental organization embodied in the Instrument of Government (December, 1653), the only written constitution England has ever had. Called the Protectorate, this government lasted until the resignation of Richard Cromwell, Oliver's son, in 1659. The constitution gave Oliver Cromwell veto power over legislation passed by Protectorate Parliaments, the first of which was composed of 141 members chosen by the Council of State from a slate of nominees proposed by trustworthy Congregationalist churches. Except for the legalization of divorce, an innovation traceable to John Milton, this Parliament accomplished little. The Instrument of Government additionally provided religious toleration for all Christians except Catholics, Arminians, and some pietists. Although Cromwell extended a welcome hand to a colony of Jews from Holland in 1655, he sometimes harassed sects whose views he considered inconsistent with Independency or political stability. Being of the gentry himself, and distrustful of essentially popular government, he made certain that political influence remained in the hands of wealthier, propertied individuals by granting the franchise only to those with an annual income of at least £200.

During the next three years, Cromwell called Parliament infrequently, ruling for lengthy periods by executive decree. He adhered to the statutory requirement that it should meet at least triennially and remain in session for a minimum of five months, but he often ignored its recommendations, scolded it, and expected its complete cooperation, especially in authorizing taxes. Admittedly the Rump Parliament in 1649–53 had exercised very great power, but it was power based not so much on its own authority as on the force of the New Model Army, which backed it. The Parliaments after 1653 were weaker than those before 1642. Generally speaking, Cromwell's relations with Parliament were hardly cordial. He believed Parliament to be an essential part of the government, and entertained the hope that it and he would work closely together. Yet his own attitude of authority as the Lord Protector, and his denial of Parliamentary sovereignty caused strained relations. Just like the early Stuarts, Cromwell had definite ideas about what Parliament ought to do, and outlined a legislative program for it to consider. When it turned to issues of its own choosing, however, Cromwell simply dissolved it, again according to precedents set by the early Stuarts. Parliament was not happy with the implementation of Protectorate government. For instance, the second Protectorate Parliament (1656–58), composed largely of republicans, disliked the military rule by major-generals (instituted in 1655 by the Protector to control unrest) in the ten districts into which England was divided. The major-generals were nominally only commanders of the militia, but in reality they enforced Cromwell's strict moral code by suppressing innocent recreation as well as the theater, drunkenness, and licentious-ness. The country might not have reacted so negatively to the militant repressions of the major-generals but for their high-handed treatment of the rank and file, many of whom, though formerly pro-republican or neutral, began to have second thoughts about condoning a military regime that used methods for which Charles I had been denounced.

The general unrest over the Puritanism of the major-generals seriously undermined the strength and popularity of the Protectorate. Many came ardently to desire an end to military absolutism, arbitrary executive decrees, high taxes, and the reinstitution of the traditional forms of the English constitution—monarch, Commons, and Lords. Since Cromwell appeared to members of Parliament to be already playing the part of king, they sought to make him one through a provision in the Humble Petition and Advice (1657). But he refused the crown for three reasons: he feared that his supporters in the army would not brook the restoration of monarchy; he realized that the scope of his authority would be greatly narrowed by being king; and he was not born to the purple. But he accepted the other provisions. These extended Commons' authority by allowing it to seat its members and to approve appointments by the Protector to an upper House composed of about fifty of his friends and relatives. Commons also could reject nominees to the newly created privy council, which supplanted the Council of State. Even to the extent that Cromwell could name his successor, the structure of the amended Protectorate government bore a remarkable resemblance to the old monarchic government. Soon afterward, Cromwell quarreled with Parliament again, dismissed it, and ruled for the next few months by executive prerogative. Inexorably, the country had gone virtually full circle through moderate reform, radicalism, conservatism, and reaction since 1641. It appeared to many to be only a matter of time before monarchy would be restored. And that day was hastened by Cromwell's sudden death on September 3, 1658.

Richard Cromwell, his eldest surviving son, succeeded to the Protectorate and ruled for only about eight months. He was amiable, cultivated, and at first generally accepted by the Parliamentary and army leaders. But he showed no understanding of the disruptive parties whom his father, by the strength of his military record and remarkable personality, had barely managed to control. Anti-Protectorate republicans and Presbyterians set to work to modify the government immediately after their old enemy had died. Richard moreover had no appreciable experience in politics or soldiery, and his right to rule was based solely on Oliver's deathbed nomination. In character Richard was as negative as his father had been positive, and he acted more like a comfortable country squire than the leader of a government that owed its very existence to the military. As Professor Tanner has aptly phrased it, "Oliver was Protector because he had been Lord General; Richard was only Lord General because he was Protector."

The reaction against him began within a few weeks. In the fall of 1658, key Army officers organized meetings that resulted in a petition calling for the reorganization of the army's high command and the separation of the civil and military authority of the Protector, the lord generalship going either to Charles Fleetwood or John Lambert. Richard summoned the third Protectorate Parliament in the hope of securing its support against the army, but the members, far from helping him, became obdurate and proposed constitutional reforms designed to make him a puppet. He therefore dissolved Parliament in April, 1659, and held office without much actual authority until his resignation the following July. Virtual anarchy prevailed from the dissolution until the intervention of General George Monck early in 1660.

This subordination of civil to military authority was repulsive to moderates of all parties. Unwilling to condone military dictatorship, Monck, commander of ten thousand soldiers in Scotland, led them to London and restored Parliament as it had been before Pride's Purge (the expulsion of Presbyterians from the Long Parliament in 1648)—in other words, a Parliament composed principally of Presbyterians and constitutional monarchists. He probably had no thought then of recalling the Stuarts, but he soon realized that this was the only means of restoring order. Accordingly, the Long Parliament retired and another assembly, known as the Convention (because Parliament could be called only by a king), accepted the Declaration of Breda from Charles II. He promised to respect Parliament's settlement of religious, constitutional, and property issues, to pardon all rebels except the regicides, and to pay arrears in soldiers' wages. He triumphantly entered London, the trusty Edward Hyde at his side, amid the general rejoicing of his subjects on May 29, 1660, his thirtieth birthday.

Although the Declaration of Breda imposed no constitutional restrictions on Charles II, and restored the traditional government of king, Lords, and Commons, it is a mistake to think that he received the crown as it had been in Charles I's day. The nation had gone through a traumatic experience that had altered many of the premises to which it had subscribed in, let us say, 1640. The Puritan Revolution had wrought fundamental changes in English society, not all of which can be explored fully here. Many of the thirty thousand pamphlets, broadsides, tracts, and books published in this period discussed issues such as pacificism, social equality, woman suffrage, millenarianism, land reform, religion, Sabbatarianism, and so forth. These writings not only laid the basis for future implementation of such ideas, but they also created a popular press, including the English newspaper, and a taste for reading. Authors contrived every conceivable political system, among them a fresh approach to democracy, which had germinated under the frost of authoritarianism and dictatorship. Political agitation had toppled divine-right monarchy, created a republic, and, despite the interlude of the Restoration, later helped to inspire the Revolution of 1688.

8

The Later Stuarts, 1660–1714

The peaceful restoration of the Stuarts under the accommodating conditions set forth in the Declaration of Breda sustained the convictions of General Monck and the Convention "Parliament" that Englishmen would gladly trade civil disorder, military autocracy, and Calvinist restraints for political stability, constitutional monarchy, and freedom under law. From his landing at Dover to his entry into London on his birthday, May 29, 1660, Charles II received an enthusiastic welcome, complete with bell-ringing, flag-waving, blazing bonfires, and cheering crowds. He enjoyed his finest hour the more because he had spent nine difficult years in exile in France and the Low Countries, feared for his life, groveled for money to support his court, and endured the insults of Cromwellian republicans. If the strain of those years had lined his heavy, swarthy face, with its thick lips, drooping eyelids, and bulbous nose, the fugitive's life had hardened his tall and athletic body, sharpened his wit, strengthened his will, and taught him the wisdom of compromise. Affable, garrulous, tactful, and shrewd, Charles was undoubtedly the gayest and most popular Stuart monarch. Neither the advice of condescending councilors nor the pangs of personal scruples swayed him from the lesson learned from his father's execution—that disputes with Parliament or any other powerful faction must be averted. But if he avoided quarrels wherever possible, he knew how to be firm without offending. He tended to be lazy, preferring pleasure to business, but he could work hard when circumstances warranted. He loved hunting, tippling, dancing, and the theater, where he met the mistresses who, with aristocratic courtesans like the Ladies Portsmouth and Castlemaine, bore him at least fourteen illegitimate children. Though full of devilment, he had a fine mind, which grasped domestic and foreign policies that he successfully manipulated to his advantage. He also promoted scientific inquiry that led to the establishment of the Royal Society in 1662, encouraged the naval reforms of Samuel Pepys, and took a keen interest in colonial and commercial affairs. That he was as popular at death as he had been in 1660, despite the vicissitudes of a troublesome reign, owed much to his policy of expediency and the fact that he symbolized the spirit of gay relief shared by his subjects now that the tensions and pressures of the Interregnum were at last ended.

Charles II did not inherit the partiality of his two royal predecessors for a meddling alter ego. He tolerated for only six years the scrupulous, restraining advice of his prissy, dogmatic, argumentative councilor Edward Hyde, earl of Clarendon, and preferred ministers of average talent who shared his views. Hyde, who had served since 1640 as a toothless tiger beside the throne, deserved the honors that Charles at first heaped upon him, not the least of which was the important connection made with the royal family by the marriage of his daughter, Anne, to James, duke of York. Hyde sincerely believed in the subordination of Parliament to the king's will and the supremacy of Anglicanism, but Charles nonetheless forsook him in 1667 when such convictions threatened his popularity. As for the other councilors, Secretary Sir Edward Nicholas and the Lord Lieutenant of Ireland, George Monck (later duke of Albemarle), were able enough. Elderly Royalists such as the Duke of Ormonde and the Duke of Southampton, who became Lord Treasurer despite his ineptitude, were rewarded for loyalty, and gay blades like the second Duke of Buckingham received lucrative sinecures. Finally, there was the young Presbyterian, Sir Anthony Ashley Cooper (later earl of Shaftesbury), whose ambition first led him into association with the older Anglican Royalists and later pushed him into opposition to the crown over religion and foreign policy.

Charles agreed at Breda to let Parliament resolve disputed questions of confiscated Church and Royalist property, religion, punishment of rebels, and the disposition of the army. Accordingly, the Convention, which sat until late December, 1660, pardoned all rebels except the regicides; thirteen of them were executed, and others drew prison terms, paid fines, or escaped into exile. The radical republican Sir Henry Vane, though he had not signed Charles I's death warrant, likewise suffered death, and the remains of Cromwell, Ireton, and Bradshaw were disinterred and hanged symbolically at Tyburn. Parliament dealt leniently with property holders, allowing purchasers of Royalist estates to keep them, but returning to the Church and Royalists their confiscated property. The army and navy, arrears fully paid, dispersed quietly, leaving only five thousand of Monck's Scots Guards as the nucleus of a new standing army. The Convention also declared illegal all acts passed since January, 1642, but re-enacted laws that had abolished the king's feudal revenues and privileges such as wardship, validated civil marriage, and confirmed the Navigation Act of 1651. The Convention dated the beginning of Charles II's reign from the moment of his father's death, and left the most troublesome issue of religion for the succeeding Parliament to settle.

The newly elected Cavalier Parliament (1661–79) was strongly reactionary, sensitive about its traditional rights, and angry at the Protestant Nonconformists, whom it blamed for the country's troubles over the previous twenty years. It therefore refused to honor Charles's promise of religious toleration of all Protestants. The Presbyterians in the Convention "Parliament" had arranged the Savoy Conference with the Anglicans, but it failed to formulate an advantageous compromise for the numerous Calvinist sects that had sprung up during the Interregnum. The moderate Anglicans, who controlled the Cavalier Parliament, therefore re-established the supremacy of the Anglican Church by restoring bishops to the House of Lords and by passing, between 1661 and 1665, four statutes known as the Clarendon Code, even though the Chancellor was not responsible for drafting them. As these laws restricted the political and religious activities of thousands of nonjurors, who refused to take the required loyalty oath, Presbyterians, Baptists, and Congregationalists were driven into opposition to the crown's religious policy.

The Clarendon Code included the Corporation Act (1661), the Act of Uniformity (1662), the Conventicle Act (1664), and the Five Mile Act (1665). The first statute required municipal officeholders to renounce the Presbyterian Covenant, take communion annually in the Anglican rite, and swear an oath of allegiance to the crown. The Act of Uniformity enjoined the use of the prayer book upon all clergymen in the Anglican Church, which forced Calvinist ministers out of the Establishment. The statute also denied abjuring clergy the right to administer the Anglican sacraments, demanded an oath of allegiance to the Anglican Church and the crown, and required the licensing of teachers. The Conventicle and Five Mile Acts forbade Nonconformists from holding religious services attended by five or more persons (except members of a family), and prohibited their ministers from coming within five miles of their former parishes in any city, town, or borough. These restrictions forced Dissenters to move into the country, where islands of Catholic worshipers had already found refuge.

The Cavalier Parliament also completed the financial settlement with the crown begun by the Convention. The most abrasive issue between king and Commons in prerevolutionary times had been Parliament's reluctance to authorize adequate subsidies for the operation of the national government, which had led Charles I to levy unparliamentary taxes. The Convention in 1660 therefore guaranteed Charles II £100,000 annually in return for his surrender of customary feudal dues and services such as purveyance. But this sum was obviously insufficient to meet even the king's ordinary expenses, which had usually averaged five or six times that amount in the 1630s. To arrive at an equitable sum, Parliament carefully investigated the monetary needs of the crown and promised to pay Charles II another £200,000 annually, most of which it expected to raise by subsidies and property taxes. But, as the Parliamentary grant usually fell short of the guaranteed amount over the next few years, Charles sought other means of getting money, not only because he found it impossible to operate the government on the actual grant, but also because non-Parliamentary sources of revenue made him less dependent on the Commons. For this reason partly, he married the unattractive and dull Portuguese Catholic princess, Catherine of Braganza, an alliance which yielded about £800,000, commercial advantages in Portuguese territory, and the ports of Bombay and Tangier.

In 1665–66 the twin catastrophies of plague and fire stunned London and the southeast. The bubonic plague, a highly contagious and deadly disease that had frequently ravaged the population since the Black Death in 1348–49, spread rapidly with terrible consequences. A few cases appeared in 1664, but that was not unusual in any year of the seventeenth century, when larger urban centers were rarely free of the pestilence; at least a half-dozen outbreaks of epidemic proportions had killed thousands in London during the previous forty years. The disease spread most quickly during warm weather, when the black rats, on whom the lice carrying the lethal infection fed, could more easily multiply amid the crowded, filthy conditions in which most of the metropolis' half-million residents lived. As usual, the authorities ordered fires burned to purify the air, which they believed carried the disease; slaughtered scavengers (dogs, cats, and pigs), which were the natural enemies of the rats; and carted away from cross-marked houses the carbuncle-ridden victims of the plague for burial in lime-covered common graves. Between May and November, 1665, when cold weather brought some relief, the pestilence killed almost a hundred thousand persons in London. It affected mainly the poor who lived in the slums and could not afford to leave the city. Many Anglican clergymen escaped, but scores of Nonconformist ministers and Catholic priests remained to give medical aid and spiritual comfort to the stricken. But they could not stem the tide of death, which left hundreds of homes vacant, brought business to a standstill, and made heroes of humanitarians immortalized in Daniel Defoe's *Journal of the Plague Year* (1722) and the diaries of Pepys and John Evelyn.

The pestilence had not yet run its course when a horrendous fire in 1666 reduced most of the oldest section of London within the Roman walls to smoldering ruins. The fire, which probably began in a baker's shop in Pudding Lane on September 2, was blown by a dry, easterly wind toward the heart of the city. Flames and smoke rising hundreds of feet into the air swept through thousands of homes, more than eighty parish churches, the Inns of Court along Fleet and Holborn streets, and St. Paul's Cathedral. Temporary quarters for evacuated families were set up on the northern perimeter of the city, and the king, his brother James, and General Monck personally supervised the primitive fire-fighting techniques and managed to save the Tower and the buildings west of Temple Bar. This destruction of about 440 acres of London and Westminster, though a great calamity, proved to be a blessing in disguise. The fire leveled the worst slums of the ancient city, which was rebuilt in brick and stone largely through the efforts of the renowned architect, Sir Christopher Wren, whose work on St. Paul's and many other churches still stands as a monument to his genius.

The Restoration did not alter the basic structure of English foreign policy, which led to two Dutch wars and an unpopular Anglo-French neutrality pact during the reign of Charles II. The long-standing commercial rivalry with the Dutch had continued after the cessation of hostilities in 1654, and the recognition of the Protectorate by Spain did not endear it to Charles or Clarendon. England quickly demonstrated to Holland and Spain that it meant to challenge their mercantile supremacy through its own mercantilist system by confirming the 1651 Navigation Act, which Parliament strengthened in 1660 by including in the British carrying trade additional American imports like tobacco and sugar. English colonization and commerce were expanded in several ways: the establishment of the Hudson's Bay Company in 1670 opened the riches of the fur trade in northern and western Canada; the Anglo-Portuguese marriage treaty required Charles to render military aid against Spain and gave England Bombay, which broke the Dutch trade monopoly in India; a small English expedition easily captured the Dutch colony of New Netherland in 1664, from which the colonies of New York and New Jersey were formed; and an English proprietary company founded Carolina, adjacent to Spanish Florida. While Charles opposed Spain and Holland, Louis XIV of France courted England's friendship. Except for a brief period in 1666 during the second Dutch war, Anglo-French amity continued throughout Charles II's reign. Louis came of age in 1661 and immediately laid plans for the expansion of his frontiers at the expense of Holland, Spain, and Austria. Charles gained a great deal by keeping England out of the Continental struggle, for Louis paid him handsome annual subsidies to remain neutral.

England went to war with Holland in 1665 over commercial rivalry, the conquest of New Netherland, control of the Channel and the western Mediterranean sea lanes (England held Tangier), and the raid on the Dutch fort on the Gold Coast of West Africa. This naval war, which involved hundreds of ships commanded by Prince Rupert and Albemarle for England and Michael DeRuyter for Holland, was fought principally in the Channel and North Sea. The Royal Navy defeated the Dutch in June, 1665, off Lowestoft despite heavy losses, and valiantly held off a superior Dutch fleet in the costly Four Days' Battle a year later. At that time France entered the war on Holland's side, forcing England to divide its fleet, but Louis refused to risk the loss of his ships on the high seas and kept them at anchor. Peace feelers had already gone out in June, 1667, when DeRuyter daringly sailed up the Medway and the Thames as far as Gravesend, sinking or disabling dozens of men-of-war and merchantmen riding at anchor, and throwing London into a panic, made worse by the plague and the low morale of English sailors, who had not been paid for months. England lost the war but won the peace made at Breda in July, 1667. It confirmed the conquest of New Netherland in exchange for England's surrender of a few West Indian sugar islands.

Despite this favorable treaty, the country was in an ugly mood, for the navy had been unable to prevent the Dutch sailing into the

Thames, and the Dissenters, who deeply resented the restrictions of the Clarendon Code, interpreted the plague and fire as divine punishment on a wicked and sinful government. Needing a scapegoat, Charles let Clarendon take the full brunt of the criticism. Parliament drew up articles of impeachment charging that the Chancellor had made unwise treaties, bribed public officials, and treasonously laid the country open to defeat caused by naval unpreparedness. Charles made no effort to save his trusted adviser, whose counsel had begun to irk him. Clarendon went into exile in France, where he wrote the *History of the Rebellion,* the best Royalist account of the Civil War.

There followed a reorganization of the membership of the privy council, the new members of which had in common only their dislike of the ousted Chancellor. The initials of the five key councilors—Clifford, Arlington, Buckingham, Ashley Cooper, and Lauderdale—formed the word Cabal, a name by which the council was known from 1667 to 1673. None of them were committed to Anglicanism: Clifford and Arlington were covert Catholics; Buckingham and Lauderdale were nominal Presbyterians; and Ashley Cooper was a staunch Presbyterian. All except Ashley Cooper were second-raters whom Charles could easily dominate.

Charles showed increasing sympathy for Catholics not only because of personal inclination to the Roman Church and his marriage to a Catholic princess, but also because of his brother's conversion to Catholicism in 1670. He tried to extend religious toleration to Catholics as well as Protestant Dissenters, but the Clarendon Code prevented it, and Parliament, having refused to accept the Declaration of Indulgence (1672), passed the Test Act (1673), which excluded Catholics and Dissenters from public office by requiring officials to take communion annually in the Anglican rite, and to renounce transubstantiation. Charles should therefore have known that the country would not tolerate pro-Catholic policies. Yet, without informing Parliament, he had secretly arranged a treaty with Louis XIV at Dover, promising, in return for subsidies, to join France in a war against Holland, and to establish Catholicism as England's state religion whenever the time seemed appropriate. The clandestine and public articles of this treaty contradicted England's obligations, made in 1668, to assist the Dutch and Swedes against France.

The Anglo-French alliance forced England into an unpopular third Dutch war in 1672. Charles had not expected that Louis would march against the Low Countries so soon, or that his subjects would criticize an attack on their old enemies. Parliament grudgingly doled out money to outfit the fleet, which engaged the Netherlanders in several bloody but indecisive battles in the Channel and mouth of the Scheldt River, engagements that the French fleet conspicuously avoided. The French land assault across the Dutch frontier compelled the brave defenders to flood their country by breaking the dykes. When it became apparent to Charles that Englishmen regretted their half-hearted support of Louis, and that there was little to gain by continuing the war, he quickly signed the Treaty of Westminster (1674). Its chief advantage for England lay in the collapse of Dutch mercantile supremacy and the advancement of English naval superiority, especially in the Channel and North Sea. Samuel Pepys' reorganization of the Royal Navy's key personnel and administration, and the naval architect Anthony Deane's rebuilding of the fleet, did not change the weary lot of the ordinary seaman, but they strengthened England's foremost fighting arm on the eve of the great colonial wars with Spain and France during the succeeding century.

The outcry in Parliament against the Declaration of Indulgence and the French Catholic alliance wrecked the Cabal, which was replaced by another group of less-qualified councilors, chief of whom was Thomas Osborne, earl of Danby. Rooted in the old allegiance to Anglicanism and strong monarchy, he set out to construct what amounted to a rudimentary "party" organization based on the liberal exercise of patronage, bribery, intimidation, control of elections and votes in Parliament, and unparliamentary means of raising revenue. Because Parliament included strong opponents of royal policy, it was seldom called, and its wishes were generally ignored by the crown. The preservation of the alliance between the crown on the one hand, and the Cavalier gentry, nobility, and Anglican clergy on the other, which had resulted from the Civil War and the Restoration settlement, most particularly the Clarendon Code, became the watchword of Danby's administration. The Whigs (whose nickname came from the term applied to the Scottish Covenanters who had resisted the ecclesiastical reforms of Charles I), headed by the Earl of Shaftesbury until 1681, ranged themselves against this entrenched Tory oligarchy (Tory originally meant an ignorant Irish outlaw). The constitutional historian Sir David Keir convincingly makes the point that the origins of the Whig party are to be found in the Civil War. Not a few of those who had been Parliamentarians and had acquired Royalist property between 1642 and 1660 were in responsible positions throughout the country after the

Restoration by virtue of their superficial conformity to Anglicanism. Under Charles II, Whig associations and political clubs like Shaftesbury's Green Ribbon Club in London thrived in the emerging industrial and commercial centers of the country, such as Birmingham, Bristol, and Yarmouth, where many Dissenter sects also founded their own schools, churches, and presses to disseminate religious and political ideas. There consequently existed in the generation before the Glorious Revolution a rudimentary Whig organization both in and out of Parliament. Within it the outnumbered Whigs labored to decrease the power of the Anglican Church, win religious toleration, and limit monarchic authority, all of which might be possible if they could successfully exclude King Charles's Catholic brother James from the throne. Charles inadvertently strengthened the Whigs by doing what he could to silence them, as when he dissolved Parliament in 1679 to save Danby from possible impeachment and to prevent James's exclusion, both of which issues developed in part from the popular hysteria generated by the Popish Plot.

This hoax was contrived by two malcontents, Titus Oates and Israel Tonge, who sought notoriety and financial reward by laying before the privy council in September, 1678, forty-three charges alleging that Catholics intended to assassinate Charles II, establish a Jesuit-dominated monarchy under James, and massacre Anglicans and Dissenters. That Danby and most of the councilors and members of Parliament believed these lies can be explained only in relationship to the century-long fear of Catholic intrigue, and to the credulity of a generation that commonly believed in the powers of magic and witchcraft, blamed Catholics for starting the fire of London, and viewed the plague as a punishment from God. Oates, a failure at virtually everything he undertook and a convicted perjurer, had been expelled from Cambridge University and two Catholic seminaries at Saint-Omer and Valladolid. He was also a defrocked Anglican priest. His close association with the Catholic clergy gave him an intimate knowledge of their names, descriptions, and organization, facts that lent credibility to his false accusations. Tonge passionately hated Jesuits and spent his spare time concocting theories about their nefarious intentions.

Oates and Tonge made a deposition regarding the truth of their charges before Sir Edmund Berry Godfrey, a respected London magistrate, whose murdered body was later discovered on the northern outskirts of the city, face down, transfixed with his sword, and bearing the marks of strangulation. Who killed Godfrey remains an unsolved mystery. Oates naturally accused the Jesuits, and implicated Queen Catherine, whom he charged with attempting to poison Charles. Oates also sent his hirelings to testify to the truth of these charges before the council and Parliament. Shaftesbury and his Whig followers believed them, and fanned the flames of religious fanaticism. During the next five years Lord Stafford, a lawyer named Langhorne, and eight priests, including Oliver Plunkett, the last English Catholic priest to be martyred, all of them innocent, were brutally executed. Hundreds of others, including four peers, who had staunchly supported the exiled Royalist government against Cromwell, served long imprisonments. The reaction against these excesses finally came in 1684, by which time Oates had been exposed. He went to prison, was released by William III after 1689, and died in penury in 1705. King Charles saw through his lies, admitting as much to intimates, but he dared not interfere for fear that the secret article of the Treaty of Dover (the restoration of Catholicism in England) might be bared and that any attempt to intervene on behalf of the innocent victims would further alienate the already angry Parliamentary opposition.

A new Parliament met in March, 1679, after what was probably the first general election fought in England roughly along party lines, during which the names of the two parties, Whigs and Tories (which stuck until Liberals and Conservatives replaced them in the nineteenth century) came into wide use. The primary election issue was whether James should be excluded from the throne. The electors returned many Whigs. Shaftesbury immediately introduced a bill to exclude him, which Charles quashed at first by removing James from the council and other posts, and later by dissolving two successive Parliaments. The 1679 Parliament also brought impeachment proceedings against Danby for treasonous complicity with France and governmental corruption. It is curious that the Whigs, because of whom innocent men had been executed in connection with the Popish Plot, should also have been responsible for passing the Habeas Corpus Act, which protected prisoners against the consequences of a bill of attainder by requiring that they be formally indicted by a bill of particulars and speedily brought to trial or released.

Charles employed every tactic to forestall Whig efforts to limit the crown's authority, even to the point of making Shaftesbury president of the council for a short time. But the king's efforts were in vain, and he dissolved the Parliaments of 1680 and 1681 in rapid succession. He faced one crisis after another in the dangerous years from 1679 to 1683. Angry mobs paraded against papists, the French alliance, and the heir apparent, and the country tottered on the brink of civil disorder. The Whigs formed more political clubs and made plans to place either the Calvinist William of Orange, Stadtholder of Holland, who had married James's daughter Mary, or the king's illegitimate son, the Duke of Monmouth, on the throne at Charles's death. A fictitious story was circulated of a Whig plot to kill Charles and James at the Rye House in Hertfordshire while they were journeying between London and Newmarket. The plot allegedly miscarried when the king's party traveled later than expected. Charles took vengeance on the supposed conspirators: although Shaftesbury escaped into exile and died in 1683; Algernon Sidney and Lord Russell were executed; the Earl of Essex committed suicide in the Tower. With their deaths the Whig opposition temporarily collapsed for want of effective leadership, which allowed Charles the opportunity to revoke the Charter of London and replace some Whig municipal and county administrators with trustworthy Tories. The country gradually forgot about the exclusion bills and returned to normal, and Charles was able to rule without Parliament for the rest of his reign because of subsidies from Louis XIV. Consequently the Anglican Tory oligarchy had firm control of the nation when Charles died on February 6, 1685, as a result of a stroke. Father Huddleston, the Benedictine who had helped him escape following the Battle of Worcester in 1651, received him into the Catholic Church shortly before his death. The throne passed at once to the Catholic James II. While, on the surface, the succession appeared tranquil, the Duke of Monmouth plotted to overthrow him.

There is no better example of Englishmen's respect for hereditary monarchy than the general acceptance of James II, whom many suspected of wishing to enhance the interests of his Church, after more than a century of Protestant ascendancy. His chief support came from moderate Anglican Tories and his coreligionists, who numbered no more than an eighth of the population, as well as from the Anglican hierarchy and Parliament, at least three-quarters of whom were loyal. The new king's personality certainly did not endear him to his subjects. James II was a plodder who worked very hard and had no time for frivolity. He had the stubbornness of James I and the moral scruples of Charles I, and like them, he lacked the wisdom to compromise, or abandon those policies that provoked widespread opposition. Humorless and blunt, he pursued a policy designed to Catholicize in form, faith, and administration a nation that was overwhelmingly committed

to Protestantism. The result was ultimately to turn his Anglican sup
porters against him and to cause the Revolution of 1688. As Bishop
Burnet wrote in his monumental history of the period, "A great king,
with . . . a great treasure and powerful allies, fell all at once, and his
whole strength, like a spider's web, was . . . broken at a touch."

At his coronation, James promised to support the Anglican Church,
but he soon showed that his promises were meaningless. He brought
pressure on justices of the peace and other local dignitaries to make
sure that only reliable moderates would be returned to Parliament. He
allowed the public celebration of the Catholic Mass in royal chapels,
released Catholic prisoners, and appointed mostly Catholic privy councilors, including the Jesuit Edward Petre. He renewed the French alliance and took more seriously than Charles II the promise of French
help to reinstitute Catholicism as the state religion. Yet most Englishmen were unaware of these developments, and James's strength actually
grew during the first year of his reign. The abortive rebellions of Monmouth and the Earl of Argyle in England and Scotland undoubtedly
augmented royal authority in the summer of 1685.

Several prominent Whigs, including Argyle and Monmouth, had managed to escape to the Netherlands following the discovery of the Rye
House Plot. Four months after James's accession, Argyle led a small
band of rebels to Scotland, where he expected to find strong support
against the king among Presbyterian clansmen. His plan was to draw
the English army north, leaving London undefended against a simul-
taneous uprising by Monmouth in the western counties of England.
But Argyle got very little help except in his home county of Argyle-
shire, and his followers (those who did not desert or simply fail to
show up) were cut to pieces. He was captured, imprisoned in Edinburgh Castle, and executed. The locale of the rebellion for many miles
around Inverary was subsequently devastated by the king's troops,
and hundreds of Scotsmen were butchered, branded, fined, or transported to the penal colonies.

Argyle's rebellion was a side show compared to the initially formidable threat posed by Monmouth, who, though accompanied by less
than a hundred men at his landing in Dorsetshire on June 11, 1685,
expected a large part of the nation to rally round him. His estimate of
support was based on the fact that most of the agricultural and business element of the west country were Dissenters who, despite Charles's
pronouncement that Monmouth could never be king because he was
an illegitimate son, had greeted him warmly as the "Protestant Duke"

and the heir apparent on his tour in 1679. But the situation had changed between 1679 and 1685, for James was by then the duly constituted and anointed king, whom legalistic and religious Englishmen were reluctant to help depose. Moreover James was already in middle life, would probably rule for only a few years, and had not yet indicated that he intended to suppress Nonconformity. Furthermore, Monmouth alienated many Whig aristocrats by issuing an absurd proclamation accusing James II of being a tyrant, murderer, and usurper who had lit the fire of London, assassinated Essex in the Tower, and poisoned Charles II. Monmouth also said he could prove his legitimacy and that, while awaiting Parliament's decision whether to make him king, he would be content with the title of captain-general. Although thousands enlisted in his army, and several towns gave generously of their supplies to sustain it, many of his men later deserted in the face of the king's advancing army.

As the rebel forces marched to Taunton and Bristol, Parliament declared Monmouth a traitor. After several inconsequential skirmishes won by the rebels, the main units of Monmouth's and the king's armies clashed at Sedgemoor in Somersetshire in early July. The battle was decided in the king's favor before noon, by which time Monmouth had already taken flight for his life, leaving his followers to be slaughtered in battle, executed on the spot, or thrown into prison. The king's men combed the countryside in search of him and found him quivering with fear in a ditch. He demanded to see James, got his wish, and supinely begged for his life. He denied having issued a proclamation or having sought the throne, and blamed others for seducing him into rebellion. Turning a deaf ear to Monmouth's pleas for mercy, James sent him in chains to the Tower and ordered his execution.

James might have soothed the passions of the Dissenters by pardoning all but the rebel leaders, but instead he took stern reprisal against them in a series of trials known as the "Bloody Assizes," conducted by Judge George Jeffreys. The guilty and innocent, some of whom were tried merely for association with rebels or suspicion of treason, were prosecuted by this ambitious man, who doled out sentences liberally. Although historians since George Macaulay have painted him as a black heart, he was not so cruel as he has generally been portrayed. Even so, he badgered witnesses, admonished juries, and attempted to discredit the Nonconformists, sentencing dozens of persons to death and ordering others to be fined or sent to the penal colonies. Jeffreys had previously served the crown faithfully by prosecuting those accused of complicity in the Popish Plot and in 1685 he carried out James's orders to the letter. The king was so pleased with his work that he was immediately appointed Lord Chancellor. It should not be forgotten, however, that the rebels had committed treason, for which the penalty was death, and that harsh sentences were by no means bizarre in the seventeenth century.

James's actions after the "Bloody Assizes" left no doubt of his intention to browbeat Parliament, the courts, and the council into accepting what amounted to monarchic absolutism supported by Tory extremists, many of whom were Catholics. While there certainly is truth in the argument that James sought to enhance Catholicism by replacing Whig and opposition Tory officeholders, such actions also raised serious constitutional questions. Opposition to him therefore arose as much from political as from religious grievances. He made permanent the temporary army of thirteen thousand men raised to fight Monmouth, alleging that it would discourage further rebellion, but Parliament suspected that this army, camped on Hounslow Heath, was intended to intimidate it. When it strongly objected to the army's continuing existence, James dissolved Parliament. He also dismissed nonpartisan judges and councilors, and appointed docile, compliant men in their places. He overrode the Test Act by granting dispensations to Catholic officers, and successfully upheld their commissions before magistrates whom he had admonished beforehand to be cooperative, even though only Parliament had the legal right to alter statutory law. He revived the hated Court of High Commission, abolished by Parliament in 1641, in order to impress his will upon recalcitrant Anglican and Nonconformist clergymen, and appointed Catholic priests to several episcopal seats. He even violated the institutional independence of the universities. While the Fellows of Magdalen College, Oxford, were in the process of choosing a new president, James ordered them to elect an incompetent Romanist. When they nonetheless chose their own Protestant candidate, the king set aside the election and expelled the Fellows. Finally, he issued two Declarations of Indulgence that extended religious toleration to Dissenters as well as to Catholics, but the Dissenters were not so easily convinced that James actually believed in freedom of conscience and suspected with good reason that it was a cheap trick to win their support.

James subsequently learned to his surprise that the principle of freedom of conscience could be turned to his disadvantage. Probably acting as much out of moral conviction as out of sympathy for Parliament, whose will the king was disregarding, seven Anglican bishops, including Archbishop William Sancroft of Canterbury, prepared a petition asking that the clergy not be forced to read the second Declaration of Indulgence in the parish churches. James rejected the petition and scolded the bishops, but very few clergymen read the Declaration on the appointed Sunday (May 7, 1688). This rebuff angered James so much that he accused the distinguished bishops of libel and sent them to the Tower. The news of their incarceration stirred the country, Anglicans and Nonconformists standing together against the king's violation of the ancient right of petition. The intensity of this popular reaction on behalf of the bishops ensured their acquittal, for even servile judges dared not attempt to sway the jury or press for a conviction. When the jury returned a verdict of not guilty, the spectators in the crowded gallery responded with a deafening cheer, jubilant Londoners jammed the streets to light bonfires and ring bells, and even the troops at Hounslow Heath celebrated. It was of enormous consequence for the future that, by attacking the status of the Anglican hierarchy, James had alienated the one remaining political force that had theretofore supported him. With only the Catholic leadership, which was by no means strong, still loyal to him, nothing but the sanctity of the monarchy protected him from virtually all the rest of the country. Before long even that thin shield was battered down by the political coalition of the Tories and Whigs in favor of William of Orange.

Public opinion had turned sharply against James, but his subjects did not expect him to reign much longer. He was fifty-six years old and sickly, and his throne would pass at his death to either Mary or Anne, his Protestant daughters, who had married respectively the Protestant Princes of the Netherlands and Denmark. This situation suddenly changed when Queen Mary of Modena, whom James had wed in 1673, gave birth in June, 1688, to a son, who would certainly be reared a Catholic, thereby perpetuating the Catholic dynasty for at least another generation. It mattered little at this juncture whether Englishmen believed the wild rumor that the baby was not the actual son of Mary and James, but a child smuggled into the palace in a warming pan to deceive the nation.

About the time of the prince's birth, seven leading nobles and gentry, representing both Whigs and Tories, secretly invited William of Orange to invade England for the "preservation of liberty" and his wife's place on the throne. The signatories, the Duke of Devonshire, the Earls of Danby and Shrewsbury, Bishop Henry Compton of London, Richard

Lumley, Henry Sidney, and Edward Russell, the last of whom carried the message to William, assured him that nineteen-twentieths of the nation, the army at Hounslow Heath, and the authorities of London would support him. William hesitated at first, recognizing that it was always dangerous to rely on the loyalty of rebels, some of whom had reneged on their promise to support Monmouth. But when it became apparent to him that not only the leading English politicians, but also virtually all the princes of western Europe, except his bitter enemy Louis XIV, favored the invasion as a first step toward marshaling the resources of England against France, he shared his plans with the Dutch States-General and spent four months in military preparation. Despite Louis's warning that something was afoot, James blindly ignored the threat to his throne until it was too late. Meanwhile most noblemen, some of them councilors, secretly joined the rebels. James finally realized late in September that the invasion was imminent, but by that time his efforts to mollify the hostility of his subjects were fruitless.

William dispatched a proclamation to England stating the *raison d'être* for his invasion before the "Protestant wind" carried his six hundred ships and fourteen thousand troops safely past the Royal Navy to an unopposed landing at Torbay in Devonshire on November 5. The Dutchman declared that he meant only to protect Mary's interests and abide by the wishes of a freely elected Parliament to fix the succession. He charged James with repeated violations of fundamental laws: interference with the courts; overriding of Parliamentary statutes; suppression of municipal and university franchises; and intimidation by means of a standing army, which included the Earl of Tyrconnel's Irish troops. William wisely said nothing of his own ambitions for the English throne, which, together with the honesty and moderation of his proclamation, undoubtedly helped to assure a bloodless revolution. The west country greeted him warmly as he went from Torbay to Exeter. James ordered his army to Salisbury, but recalled it before encountering the enemy when most of the troops deserted to William with their commander, Lord John Churchill (later duke of Marlborough). The queen fled to France with her infant son in the midst of this crisis, which brought James an ultimatum from William that he meant to carry out his promises. Without hope of successfully resisting William's advance toward London, deserted by virtually everyone, and convinced that imprisonment and execution awaited an overthrown king, James made for France. He threw the Great Seal into the Thames, thinking naïvely that without it Parliament could not legally be summoned. But soldiers apprehended him at Dover, and returned him to the capital where William later purposely "permitted" him to escape. James left England on December 23, never to return. Until the last of his direct line died in the early nineteenth century, the Catholic Stuart pretenders spent their lives in fruitless efforts to recover the English throne.

William of Orange, like William of Normandy, Henry Bolingbroke, and Henry Tudor, deposed a reigning monarch by force of arms and wisely left the disposition of the throne for others to decide. Accordingly, free elections for the Convention (Parliament could be summoned only by royal writ) were held in January, 1689. Its members offered the throne jointly to William and Mary after William made it clear that he would not be content to be merely the consort. Mary, a dutiful wife of great beauty and personal charm, gladly retreated into his shadow, though she governed the country efficiently during the long periods while he was abroad.

William III and Mary II accepted the throne under the conditions defined in a Declaration of Rights, which Parliament enacted into law, with minor emendations and additions, in October, 1689, as the Bill of Rights. It provided for a Protestant monarchy and fixed the succession in turn on the heirs of William and Mary, on her sister Anne and her heirs, and finally on the relatives of William of Orange. The other principal provisions were: that only Parliament could authorize taxes and a standing army in peacetime; that the right of petition to the crown for redress of grievances was the privilege of any subject; that Parliament should be freely elected and often convened; that it should enjoy freedom of speech; and that the crown could not set aside any Act of Parliament. The justification for these provisions was embodied in a long preamble that enumerated the specific transgressions of James II.

Inherent in the Bill were the doctrines of social contract and justifiable revolution, which John Locke (1632–1704) defined in his *Essay on Civil Government* and *Second Treatise on Government*. He held that monarchy owed its right to rule neither to God nor to heredity, but to free men endowed with unalienable rights to life, liberty, and property. When, in the state of nature, men themselves could no longer protect their possessions and preserve their natural rights, they vested governmental authority in a king on condition that he rule justly for the common good. Should he violate these terms unilaterally, his subjects were released from their contractual obligation of obedience and could overthrow the government in order to preserve their property and rights. Locke's theories therefore not only absolved the rebels of 1688 of culpability in deposing James; they also provided, along with those of Montesquieu, Rousseau, and Jefferson in the next century, the philosophical basis for the American and French revolutions.

Locke also advocated religious toleration and the separation of Church and state in his *Essay on Toleration,* in which he argued that the government should not impair freedom of conscience or compel religious conformity. King William added his authority to Locke's because he strongly opposed persecution and owed a debt to the Dissenters, who had been largely responsible for the revolution that brought him the English throne. He accepted the episcopal system because, even though a Calvinist, he had no choice under statutory law, but he tried quietly to counter vestiges of Arminianism by appointing Latitudinarian bishops to dioceses that fell vacant. Very few Catholics suffered from the disabling penal laws; most returned to the accustomed secret practice of their religion at isolated centers served by priests, who in turn were subject to John Leyburne, the third vicar apostolic in England since the early seventeenth century and one of a series of vicars that ruled the Catholic community until the re-establishment of Catholic bishoprics in 1850. The Catholics had not really expected freedom of worship and were therefore not disappointed when Parliament granted the Nonconformists that right in the Toleration Act of 1689. It relieved all laymen except Catholics, Unitarians, and Jews of the proscriptions in the penal laws on condition that they took the oaths of allegiance and supremacy. Nonconformist clergymen were likewise relieved if they additionally subscribed to the Thirty-nine Articles, which few of them were willing to do. These concessions did not extend to their sitting in Parliament or serving in the armed forces. After 1727, however, Parliament annually passed enabling legislation that allowed Dissenters to hold public office, although it was unwilling as yet to abolish the Test Act. The Toleration Act also excused Quakers from taking the oaths, but many nevertheless emigrated to Pennsylvania, which William Penn had founded in 1681.

Freedom of the press was also furthered by the Revolution. The volume of printed matter of all types had steadily swelled since the invention of movable type printing in the mid-fifteenth century. The greatest impetus in England came from the Puritans, who employed the printed word to the fullest advantage in disseminating ideas. Their tracts, pamphlets, broadsides, and newsbooks (newspapers) appeared at an astounding rate during the Civil War and Interregnum, despite censorship that made it criminal to publish anything without a license, a law which John Milton labored unsuccessfully to have repealed. Popular craving for news spurred the publication of newspapers on a regular basis beginning in the 1640s. Censorship was continued by Charles II, and Chief Justice William Scroggs enforced it under James II against anyone who criticized the government. William III wisely abolished censorship in 1694 so that henceforth authors could freely express their opinions. The government was stoutly criticized in the press by both Whigs and Tories during the 1690s, and literary freedom sometimes degenerated into literary license under Queen Anne, when periodicals became common topics of discussion in coffeehouses.

The 1688 Revolution made England a better place for most persons because of the destruction of absolute monarchy, the shifting of the balance of power to Parliament, and religious and literary freedom, but contention between king and Parliament, and between Whigs and Tories, certainly did not cease. Only the enmity to James II had temporarily united political factions that otherwise had little in common. They resumed their accustomed bickering in 1689 over control of Parliament, finance, and England's role in the war against Louis XIV. The Whigs expected William to be their champion if not their spokesman in the new order of things, but he refused to be a puppet to any group. He upheld his promises and observed the limitations on his authority defined in the Bill of Rights, but he never stopped trying to preserve what was left of royal prerogative against the inroads of Parliament, which the Whigs dominated for most of the reign.

Neither Whigs nor Tories cooperated fully with William once the jubilation over the deposition of James II had worn off and men returned to the everyday business of government. William's character and aims did not inspire loyalty in England. Consumed by hatred for Louis XIV, whom he had battled unceasingly since the early 1670s, he drove his crippled and asthmatic body to the breaking point in his determination to destroy the power of France. He never became acculturated to the English way of life, and rarely appeared in public, preferring the solitude of country houses to the bickering of politicians in London. Each spring he gladly traded the tiresome deliberations at the council table, in which he had no genuine interest unless they related to his military plans or prerogatives, for the battlefield on the Continent.

At first he tried to heal the wounds of revolution by appointing representatives of both political factions to a coalition council, namely

Danby, Nottingham, Shrewsbury, and Godolphin. This arrangement pleased no one. The Whigs resented William's refusal to punish the Jacobites, while the Tories never gave him their wholehearted loyalty, particularly after the death in 1694 of Queen Mary, and dragged their feet in the war effort. William was driven for these reasons into the arms of the Whig Junto (1693–97), a five-man clique led by Sir John Somers, who saw to it that the Commons granted the money needed for the war, and wrung from William several important concessions as the price of cooperation. He therefore signed two important statutes, the Triennial Act (1694), by which Parliamentary elections had to be held at least every three years, and the Treason Act (1697), which protected Whigs against false charges of treason. Henceforth the accused was entitled to see the bill of indictment, have benefit of attorney, and be confronted by witnesses, whose testimony was admissible only if they had actually seen the treasonous act. William confided in the Junto only when absolutely necessary and relied principally on the advice of unofficial counselors like the Dutchman William Bentinck (later earl of Portland), and Sunderland, who, to stay in power, frequently changed his political principles.

During the six months between the invasion and the coronation of William and Mary, the armies of Louis XIV smashed across the frontier of the Palatinate and ravaged its fields and towns. This attack, one of the most brutal in modern history, thrust Europe into the War of the League of Augsburg (1689–97). The coalition powers had to manage for the first year and a half of the war without the leadership of William III, who remained at home to deal with rebellions in Scotland and Ireland.

Representatives of the Scottish estates had convened in Edinburgh at William's invitation to recognize his succession, in return for which they obtained the recognition of Presbyterianism as the state Church. The Protestant Lowlanders concurred with this settlement, but the Highland clansmen generally remained loyal to James II and Catholicism. Since the days of the Popish Plot, which had repercussions in Scotland, the political situation there had been delicate, and Argyle's rebellion had added to the dissension. In 1689 several clans, notably the Gordons and the Macdonalds of Glencoe, banded under the leadership of John Graham of Claverhouse, Viscount Dundee, to resist the Edinburgh settlement. Major-general Hugh Mackay marched against them but was trapped and defeated at Killiecrankie Gorge in a wild charge of three thousand screaming Highlanders in which Claverhouse died. As no one of comparable ability continued the resistance, it gradually diminished, although it did not disappear altogether until the last of the Jacobite clan armies was cut to pieces at Culloden moor in 1746.

The Irish Jacobites proved far more dangerous to William. Resistance centered mainly in the army of Richard Talbot, earl of Tyrconnel, James II's lord lieutenant, who threatened the Scotch-Irish Protestant Ulsterites and provided the old king with men and arms for a possible counterrevolution against England. An Irish insurrection began shortly after William and Mary ascended the throne. The rebels overran the southern two-thirds of the country, slaughtered settlers in outlying regions within the Pale, and prepared to besiege Londonderry, behind whose walls the Protestants took refuge. James landed in April, 1689, at Kinsale near Cork to take personal command of the assault. Louis XIV could not spare many men to aid James, for he needed them for the war against the Empire, but he did provide four hundred officers, weapons, and the service of the trusted diplomat Count d'Avaux, who watched James and regularly reported his actions to Louis. The attack on Londonderry lasted for three months, at the end of which time an English force relieved the beleaguered and starving garrison.

When William realized that he was in danger of losing Ireland altogether—the rebels had already declared its independence and officially restored Catholicism—he led an army of thirty-five thousand men to Ulster, where, on July 1, 1690, he won a decisive victory on the banks of the Boyne River. His success forced James's return to France, but its principal significance lay in the triumph of Protestantism. The Presbyterian Orange Lodges in English-speaking parts of the Empire-Commonwealth have since celebrated his victory in much the same fashion as the Irish commemorate St. Patrick's Day.

The rebellion, which dragged on for another year, was concluded by the lenient Treaty of Limerick (October, 1691). It provided essentially that the Irish should enjoy virtual religious freedom by the suspension of the penal laws, and be allowed to retain their land and titles. Those who wished, out of loyalty to James II, to emigrate to France were free to do so, and about twelve thousand availed themselves of this opportunity. However, Parliament nullified the treaty. It re-established Anglicanism as the Irish state Church and reactivated the penal code, which forbade Catholic worship, made felons of priests and nuns, excluded Catholics from public offices, most educational institutions, and some learned professions and skilled trades, and denied them the right to own land. These provisions subjected the vast majority of Irish to a small ruling class, reduced them within a few years to wretched poverty, and nearly destroyed the country's economy. The same disabilities were extended to the Scotch-Irish Presbyterians in 1704; thereafter many emigrated to America.

The Irish and Scottish rebellions kept William in the British Isles until the spring of 1691, while Louis overran the Palatinate, Savoy, and Catalonia in northern Spain. The signatories of the League of Augsburg (established in 1686)—Austria, the Palatinate, Sweden, Spain, Bavaria, Saxony, and the Netherlands—counted on William's leadership and English sea power and money to counterbalance the huge French army of 300,000 men and navy of ninety warships stationed at Brest and Toulon. England had more at stake in the long run than the other coalition powers. Jean Baptiste Colbert, the Sun King's indefatigable chief adviser to 1683, had balanced the budget, encouraged industry and commerce through government subsidies and strict mercantilism, built a formidable navy, and brought Canada under direct royal administration in 1663. Thus strengthened, France sought to fill the power vacuum created by the collapse of Spain and coveted by England. The war provided England with the opportunity to destroy French naval power, to seize some of her colonies, to maintain the independence of the Low Countries and Spain, and to expand the northern boundary of New England. No wonder Parliament poured 150,000 men and nearly £40,000,000 into the war effort.

King William's War in America initiated more than a hundred years of Anglo-French colonial rivalry. Louis's preoccupation with European affairs had hurt New France, which had not yet recovered from the exploitation of a succession of monopolists who cared only for profits from the fur trade. The brilliant administrations of Jean Talon and the Count de Frontenac strengthened the colony somewhat, but the ten thousand *habitants* along the St. Lawrence River and in Acadia were no match for the American colonial militia and their Iroquois allies. William Phipps easily captured Port Royal in Acadia in 1690, although he was unable to take Quebec, whose garrison subsequently tried to carry the war into New England while withstanding repeated Iroquois raids all along the frontier.

France won the initial victories on land and sea in Europe. Louis XIV concentrated his fleet in the Channel and forced a fight with the Anglo-Dutch armada commanded by the Earl of Torrington off Beachy Head on June 30, 1690. Torrington had first retreated in the face of the advancing French flotilla rather than run the risk of defeat, which would lay England open to invasion while its army was with William in Ireland. Though no coward, he thus became the scapegoat for the country's sense of shame and was court-martialed. During the next two years the French army defeated William at Mons and Neerwinden and captured the fortress at Namur.

The tide turned slightly in the coalition's favor in 1692. France failed to follow up its victory off Beachy Head with the result that the Admiralty seized the opportunity to strengthen the fleet, which managed to forestall the planned French invasion of England in a spectacular triumph off La Hogue in a five-day battle commencing on May 19, 1692. Despite the loss of a large Anglo-Dutch mercantile convoy in 1693, England's timidity in not attacking the main French fleet anchored at Brest, and the failure of Admiral George Rooke to gain control of the western Mediterranean by blockading the French squadron at Toulon, the coalition made some headway when William recaptured Namur in 1695 and held the line of defense along the Spanish Netherlands–Holland border. As neither France nor the coalition could prevail against the other, and as both were exhausted by the long war, they made peace at Ryswick in 1697. More a truce than a permanent settlement of differences, the treaty simply provided for the mutual restoration of territory captured since 1679, and Louis's recognition of William as England's legitimate sovereign.

The war had been extremely costly for England; so costly, in fact, that the normal sources of revenue ran out. During most of the seventeenth century, when Parliament granted too few subsidies, or taxes became excessively burdensome, the crown frequently went to merchants or other wealthy men for loans at interest rates ranging up to 14 per cent. Joint-stock companies, the corporation of the City of London, the goldsmiths of Lombard Street, and many private investors had often loaned the crown money. As no distinction was made between the indebtedness of the crown and the indebtedness of the state, technically all national government income and expenditure was the king's responsibility. There was therefore no national debt, even though at any given time the crown owed hundreds of thousands of pounds to many investors. But the crown found it increasingly difficult to meet its financial obligations, not only because there was no sinking fund from which to draw funds to amortize debts, but also because any substantial increase in expenditure, such as in war, put a heavy strain on its financial resources. For these reasons, in 1692, Parliament secured a loan of £1,000,000 apart from the crown in order to pay for the war, thereby incurring a national debt for the first time.

The practical wisdom of consolidating the national debt and the crown's debt as well as of having a central agency from which the government could draw loans at favorable interest rates led to the creation of the Bank of England in 1694. The Scots financier and member of Parliament William Paterson conceived of the scheme, which was implemented by the ambitious treasurer, Charles Montagu, earl of Halifax. It provided for the establishment of a joint-stock company comprising about 1300 subscribers who raised £1,200,000, which it loaned to the government at 8½ per cent interest. The bank could employ its capital for private investment and issue bills of exchange and paper money, which were widely used as legal tender. The bank stood on shaky ground for the first few years, and it competed for loans with other institutions such as the Tory-dominated Land Bank (founded in 1696), but it survived numerous crises to become one of the strongest and most stable financial organizations in the world.

In 1697 England had too many selfish politicians and too few objective statesmen. As a result the Whigs and Tories worked at cross-purposes with the king. Welcome as the peace of Ryswick had been to William, he realized that Louis XIV would never be satisfied with a stalemate. Accordingly, William cautioned Parliament not to impair the country's military preparedness, but it would not listen, for it believed that he had sacrificed England's resources for the sake of his homeland. Now that the war was over, Parliament hurried to reduce the standing army to 7000 men in England and 12,000 in Ireland, and forced William to cashier his Dutch Guards and Dutch councilors. Parliament's dislike of foreign advisers showed itself in its recovery of the Irish estates William had granted them. Parliament also tried, repeatedly but unsuccessfully, to exclude his supporters and friends (derisively called placemen) from the Commons. Under such circumstances, it is not surprising that the king trusted neither the Whigs nor the Tories and relied instead on a few close friends and his own good judgment in running the government. The tension between William and Parliament increased when, in the election of 1698, the Tories and anti-Junto Whigs were returned to Parliament in greater numbers. Since the old-line Whig Junto had come to power on the basis of their control of the Commons, these Tories and Whigs demanded that this principle be applied to their advantage in the privy council. Consequently one after another of the Junto resigned, and Tories and Independent Whigs replaced them. It mattered little to William by that time which faction controlled the council, for he could not depend on either Whigs or Tories. The Tories, although happy in 1688 at the overthrow of James II, soon wearied of William, who was neither English nor Anglican at heart. Whatever grudging support they gave him resulted from their affection for Queen Mary. When she died in 1694, there was no longer any reason for them to conceal their great displeasure with a monarch who openly favored the Dissenters and plunged England into a foreign war that brought only higher taxes. The Tories opposed not only war and Nonconformity, but also the Bank of England, controlled largely by the moneyed Whig interests. Whereas the Tories drew their greatest strength from the ranks of the gentry and country parsons, the Whigs were composed principally of the Nonconformist town clergy, the commercial and financial interests of the country, and the smaller landowners. If the Tories had some semblance of unity born of religion, property, and tradition, the Whigs were without recognized leadership and suffered from factionalism. They had only three things in common: they craved personal advantage through control of public office; they disliked William's European point of view and foreign advisers; and they tried to weaken monarchic authority. The old-line Whigs of Shaftesbury's day had had their moment of triumph with the success of the Revolution, and they were the beneficiaries of William's generous patronage. By 1699, however, the charm of the Revolution had worn off, and with Tories in control of most national offices, the Whigs lost ground in Parliament. The Tories were to remain in the ascendancy until after Anne assumed the throne.

Her accession was part of the Act of Settlement of 1701, by which Parliament assured the continuation of the Protestant monarchy. The Act provided that, should William die without direct issue, the throne should pass to Anne (James II's younger Protestant daughter) and her heirs, and then to the Electress Sophia of Hanover (granddaughter of James I) and her children. Since William, aging and ill, was not likely to remarry, and Anne had recently lost the last of her seventeen children, the Act practically guaranteed that the Hanoverians would ultimately inherit the throne. Such an arrangement was acceptable to William, the Tories, and the Whigs. Since Sophia was quite old and would not likely become queen of England, her son, George Lewis, would be the first Hanoverian monarch of England. William liked him because he was a proven soldier and a bitter enemy of France. The Whigs liked him because he was a Lutheran—essentially a Dissenter. The Tories, having no alternative but the Catholic Stuart Pretender, had to be satisfied. They made certain that George would not do them disservice, however, by writing into the Act of Settlement two provisions that required that he become a member of the Anglican Church and that England should not be obliged to enter into a foreign war in the interests of his Continental possessions without the consent of Parliament.

Meanwhile England had gone to war again with France. The key to peace in Europe after 1697 had lain in the settlement of the succession to the Spanish throne so that neither France nor the Empire could, by securing it, upset the balance of power. King Carlos II, called "the Bewitched" because of physical deformities, mental aberration, and repulsive habits, had confounded his physicians who had predicted his imminent death for more than thirty years. As he would surely die soon without a direct heir, the princes of Europe scurried to snatch the vast dominions of the Spanish Hapsburgs in the Old and New World. Louis XIV and Emperor Leopold, both related to Carlos by marriage, proposed as his successor Philip of Anjou and Archduke Charles respectively. Since France and the Empire would rather have gone to war than to allow the other's candidate to succeed to the Spanish throne, William III and Louis agreed privately that the Spanish Empire should be partitioned: Prince Joseph Ferdinand of Bavaria should get Spain and its American possessions; Charles should have Milan; and Philip was promised the kingdom of Naples and Sicily. In this first Partition Treaty (1698), William managed to prevent a union of France and Spain or the Empire and Spain, and kept the Spanish Netherlands out of French hands. But a second treaty became necessary when Prince Joseph died in 1699. Without consulting Carlos, Leopold, or the English Parliament, William and Louis agreed that Archduke Charles should inherit Spain and most of its dominions except those in Italy, which Philip would get. But shortly before his death in November, 1700, Carlos willed all his dominions to Philip on condition that the thrones of France and Spain should never be united. Louis thereupon declared that Philip could succeed to the French throne, seized the fortresses on the Dutch border, and recognized the Pretender, "James III," as English king (James II had died in September, 1701). The Tory-dominated Parliament impeached Whig ministers for being parties to the secret partition treaties, but later accepted the fact that only a war could stop French aggression, and therefore allowed William to join the Low Countries and Austria (and later Prussia and

Savoy) in the Grand Alliance, and to raise an army of forty thousand men. The War of the Spanish Succession had scarcely begun when William died in March, 1702, after a fall from his horse at Hampton Court.

"Good Queen Anne," middle-aged, fat, and old-fashioned, was the last and probably least able Stuart sovereign. A homebody, Anglican, and English-born, she met the basic requirements set down in the provisions of the Act of Settlement, but little more. Despite such admirable qualities as affection, moral virtue, generosity, loyalty, and forbearance, and even though her subjects generally respected her, she has received few compliments. Dour, sluggish in mind and body, credulous, and naïve, she was devoted to High-Church Anglicanism, disliked Dissenters, hated Catholics, and subscribed privately to divine-right monarchy. She favored Tory political principles and blindly followed the advice of close friends, among them John and Sarah Churchill, duke and duchess of Marlborough, who took advantage of her trust and munificence and shaped her thinking more than did the privy council, which she infrequently consulted. She would have benefited from a forceful and talented consort, but George of Denmark was of little help. It was of him that Charles II once remarked: "I have tried Prince George sober, and I have tried him drunk, and drunk or sober there is nothing in him."

While Anne reigned, Marlborough forged England's fortunes on the battlefield as commander-in-chief of the Anglo-Dutch forces. This remarkable strategist, one of the greatest soldiers of a nation that has produced many, had a kaleidoscopic career. The scion of a family of middling status and several generations of public service, he rose rapidly from near obscurity in the 1670s by dint of politic conduct, good looks, a persuasive manner, and political intrigue. He saw action at sea and in Holland under Charles II, served James II against Monmouth, but deserted the Stuart for William III in 1688. He expected rewards from the Dutchman and severely criticized him when they were not forthcoming. William accused him of treason for corresponding with James II, and banished him from court, but later recalled him to help negotiate the Grand Alliance. Theoretically and traditionally a Tory, the duke nonetheless preferred to work with the Whigs because they supported the war more enthusiastically. He played up to Queen Anne, built Blenheim Palace with the thousands of pounds from the public Treasury that she gave him, and yet treated her arrogantly and presumptuously. His avarice is said to have surpassed even his craving for fame and honors, and the Tories, who disliked the war and despised the duke, accused him of clipping his troops' pay and taking bribes from army contractors, for which, rightly or wrongly, Anne cashiered him in 1712. Although allegedly miserly, petulant, and haughty, he nevertheless brought England the great victories by which France was crushed.

Little need be said about the other principals in the cabinet and Parliament, for the leaders of the two parties, plotters and self-seekers for the most part, generally put their personal interests above those of their country. They schemed for office and favors and against each other, and, when there was time, gave thought to the conduct of the war. Until 1705, when the Whigs captured control of the privy council, the war effort lagged because of quarreling between the Tory Commons and the Whig Lords, and because of disagreement between councilors who were convinced that England should fight principally at sea, and others who reasoned that Louis XIV could be beaten only on land. Finally, the moderate Tories, led primarily by Sydney and Treasurer Godolphin, struggled to overcome the negativism of ultraconservatives like the earls of Nottingham and Pembroke, secretary of state and president of the council respectively.

When Marlborough led his army to Flanders in 1702 to relieve the pressure of French advances along the Meuse and Rhine River lines, Prince Eugene of Savoy, the brilliant general of the Austrians, had already carried the war into the Po Valley of northern Italy. Marlborough captured Liége and Bonn; and Admiral Rooke, though unable to take Cadiz, sank a large Spanish treasure fleet at Vigo Bay. These initial victories were practically annulled, however, by the defection of Bavaria to the French, who planned to march on Vienna and knock the Empire out of the war. Eugene immediately withdrew north of the Alps, but the French army stood between him and his capital. Marlborough acted swiftly in this crisis. He hurried down the Rhine Valley and through Bavaria to help Eugene and the Margrave of Baden break through the French vise. Near the village of Blenheim, on the north bank of the Danube, the allies triumphed on August 13, 1704, in a battle involving more than 100,000 men. This victory, one of the greatest in English military annals, saved the Empire, forced Bavaria to quit the war, and drove the French west of the Rhine. On the same day Admiral Rooke bested the French navy at Málaga, and a month later English marines easily captured the strategic fortress of Gibraltar. From that day until World War II, when air power undermined the importance of naval bases, England controlled the western Mediterranean, thereby guaranteeing the safety of trade routes to the Middle East and Asia.

Blenheim silenced the wagging tongues of hostile Tories, improved the stock of the pro-war Whigs, and convinced the English that the French could be vanquished. Although the Whigs won the election of 1705, Marlborough and Godolphin still dominated war policy by virtue of their command of the army and the Treasury. Tories like Robert Harley (later earl of Oxford) and Henry St. John (later Viscount Bolingbroke), and several Whigs, notably young Robert Walpole, replaced the conservative High-churchmen on the privy council. This reshuffling of the council in favor of moderation in politics and vigor in war ensured that sufficient supplies would be voted for the war, and forestalled repeated efforts by the extremist Tories to ruin the Whigs by excluding them from high public office through the already twice-rejected Occasional Conformity Bill.

Politicians also considered political union with Scotland during these first critical war years. The two kingdoms had shared monarchs since 1603, yet each had retained its political institutions, legal system, and religion. Such dissimilarities were magnified by Scotland's backwardness in agriculture, industrial production, literature and science, and social welfare. Scotland also had only about a fifth of England's population. The Scots therefore felt the more conscious of their national characteristics, Parliament, and Presbyterian religion, which might be endangered by union with their larger, stronger, and more aggressive southern neighbor. Conversely, Englishmen, understandably proud of their achievements, were loath to admit a poorer, less advanced people to their commercial advantages. Such considerations notwithstanding, reasonable men on both sides of the Tweed envisioned the gains to be realized by each kingdom through a political union. Several factors worked toward that possibility: (1) Anglo-Scottish relations had improved since Cromwell's time because of the presence of thirty Scots in the Rump Parliament, Scottish support for the restoration of Charles II, the collapse of Argyle's rebellion in 1685, and the acceptance of William III four years later; (2) so long as Scotland remained independent, the Jacobites and French could use it as a springboard into England; (3) the Whigs feared a negative reaction from the Scots to the anticipated Hanoverian succession; and (4) the Scots finally realized that the alternative to union was economic stagnation.

Widespread poverty, the bleakness of the country, lack of natural resources, insufficient capital, famine in the 1690s, and the barrier of the English mercantilist system combined to depress the Scottish economy. Scottish commercial interests nevertheless tried to establish colonies and expand their markets. All these ventures failed. The best-known is the Company of Scotland for Trading to Africa and the Indies, the so-called Darien Company, which failed in three attempts to found a permanent settlement in the Isthmus of Panama at a loss of £200,000 to its stockholders. The colonists died like flies from shipwreck, fever, oppressive heat, and Spanish bullets; their Bibles and woolens understandably found no market among illiterate and naked savages. English investors and politicians boycotted the company, refused to help the distressed colonists, and condemned the Scottish intrusion into Spanish territory, which endangered the Anglo-Spanish alliance. The Scots, naturally angry, retaliated in the Act of Security (1704), which provided for the succession of the Protestant Scottish royal family on Anne's death unless an advantageous political and commercial relationship should be concluded with England. The anti-Presbyterian, Tory-dominated English Parliament retaliated with the Aliens' Act (1705), barring Anglo-Scottish trade until Scotland consented to union.

Despite riots and protests in both capitals, wisdom and moderation prevailed among the English and Scottish commissioners who had been negotiating a union treaty since 1702. Its terms were ratified by the respective Parliaments in January and February, 1707. They were: (1) that the two Parliaments should merge, Scotland being represented by forty-five members in the Commons and sixteen peers, elected by the Scots aristocracy, in the Lords; (2) that the Scots should assume a small proportion of the English national debt; (3) that they should be compensated for the losses at Darien by a cash payment of £400,000 and free-trade privileges with England; and (4) that the United Kingdom, symbolized by the Union Jack, should be named Great Britain. The treaty worked no immediate miracles on the Scottish economy and did not measurably strengthen England, but both peoples profited in peace and war in the long run.

Meanwhile major interest centered on the war. Except for the Spanish people's refusal to accept Archduke Charles in place of King Philip V despite a bloody campaign in 1705–8 that brought the allies to the gates of Madrid, they prevailed on all fronts. Marlborough returned to the Netherlands to win the battles of Ramillies (1706), Oudenarde (1708), and Malplaquet (1709). He decimated the French northern army, forced Louis XIV to weaken French arms in northern Italy by withdrawing soldiers to the Dutch frontier, and temporarily destroyed

French morale, which had already been weakened by famine, heavy taxes, and long casualty lists. In these years the British fleet also vanquished the French squadron at Toulon and captured the island of Minorca. In America, where the war was named after Queen Anne, the Canadians successfully resisted English raids across the St. Lawrence frontier, and repulsed a naval expedition against Quebec. Port Royal and all of Acadia, which the English had taken in the last war but relinquished in the peace, again fell into their hands in 1710. New France might well have been conquered but for the council's preoccupation with the Continental war; several English regiments arrived at Boston in 1711, too late to do any good.

The war in Europe might have ended in 1709 had Louis been willing to accept the unconditional surrender of all his territorial gains since the 1670s. But, to the dismay of the exhausted Dutch, the Whigs, egged on by Marlborough, insisted on pushing the war to the ultimate advantage for England, despite growing agitation in official and popular circles for peace. So it dragged on needlessly for another four years. The French somehow stiffened their resistance, and the Tories, taking full advantage of the popular outcry for peace, overthrew the Whigs and Marlborough. The war had raised taxes, pushed the national debt to alarming heights, and seemed chiefly to serve Marlborough's personal ambition. Opposition intensified when he promised, in the Barrier Treaty (1709), to surrender the hard-won frontier fortresses to the Dutch upon the conclusion of peace, and later asked Anne to make him captain-general for life. She would not, but the Tories nevertheless feared that he was aiming for military dictatorship and worked toward his overthrow. Meanwhile Abigail Hill, better known as Mrs. Masham, a Tory sympathizer, replaced Sarah Churchill as Anne's confidante, and did wonders in completing the queen's alienation from the Whigs, which was made easier by the overwhelming Tory victory in the elections of 1710.

The Tories doubtless profited in these elections from the unfavorable public response to the impeachment of Dr. Henry Sacheverell, an intemperate and bigoted Anglican priest who had already made something of a reputation as a severe critic of the Dissenters. On Guy Fawkes Day, 1709, he delivered a polemical sermon in St. Paul's, in which he excoriated the Whigs and Dissenters as warmongers, heretics, and revolutionaries. His remarks assumed greater importance than they deserved because of the current political crisis over the continuation of the war. In fact, the sermon, widely disseminated in print, aroused so much animosity toward the war and the Whigs that Lord Treasurer Godolphin decided to try Sacheverell before the House of Lords, the highest court in the land. The Whigs charged him with impugning the legality of the Revolution of 1688, discrediting the extension of religious toleration granted by Parliament to the Dissenters, and accusing the Whig high command of working to overturn the British constitutional system. The Whigs blundered by prosecuting Sacheverell, as the action lent further credence to the oft-repeated Tory charges of Whig extremism. The trial, held in February and March, 1710, was closely followed by courtiers and commoners alike: the queen openly showed her sympathy for the Tories and the accused, and never missed a session; demonstrators crowded against the doors of Westminster Hall by day; and rioters roamed the streets and desecrated Dissenter chapels at night. Sacheverell was found guilty by the slim margin of seventeen votes, but he was given a very light sentence, merely being deprived of the right to preach for three years.

As the elections had given the Tories a majority of about two to one in the Commons, Anne invited Robert Harley to form a Tory government that included Henry St. John, seemingly his close friend but actually his secret rival for power, and mostly moderate Anglicans. Harley realized that little was to be gained by railing against the Dissenters on religious grounds, but most of the Tory members of Parliament did not share the sense of toleration that sprang from his once having been a Nonconformist Presbyterian. These extremist members of Parliament hoped to repeal the Toleration Act, expel all Whigs from office, no matter how insignificant, and prosecute the Whig leadership for criminal maladministration and embezzlement of government funds. As Harley was a typical organization man with a flair for placating the discordant elements within his party, he managed to keep the hotheads under control despite inflammatory pamphlets like Jonathan Swift's *The Shortest Way with Dissenters*. But, when a disgruntled secret service agent stabbed Harley in 1711, forcing him to spend many months in convalescence, St. John captured control of the dissident Tories. Although ostentatious and raucous in personal conduct, St. John nevertheless commanded a large following also among avid High-Church parsons and squires, whose support increased his political power to the point where it rivaled Harley's when the latter returned to active life, newly raised to the earldom of Oxford.

All the Tories had one thing in common, however, and that was a desire for the speedy conclusion of peace with France. Marlborough fell from his lofty position in 1712 when they accused him of criminal manipulation of public funds. With their antagonist out of the way, they first gradually curtailed England's military activities and later withdrew English troops altogether, leaving the Dutch and the Austrians to fight on alone for another year. In 1713, England and the Netherlands made peace with France at Utrecht. Philip V was permitted to keep the Spanish throne on condition that he forsook his claim to the French succession. The frontier fortresses remained in Dutch hands as promised, and England acquired Nova Scotia, Newfoundland, and Rupert's Land in Canada, and Gibraltar and Minorca in Europe. England additionally won the asiento, the exclusive right to supply Spanish America with African slaves. Since Austria was given the Spanish Netherlands (today's Belgium), and England held Gibraltar and Minorca, English sea power was unchallenged in the Channel and western Mediterranean.

Even before peace had been signed, the extremist Tories in Parliament, encouraged by St. John (later Viscount Bolingbroke), sought to perpetuate their power and to cripple the Whig opposition through disabling legislation. The Tories first passed the Occasional Conformity Act (1711), which stipulated that Dissenters convicted of practicing their religion, despite their previous legal conformity to Anglicanism to qualify for office, should be fined and dismissed. The Schism Act (1714), Bolingbroke's brainchild, continued proscription by forbidding Dissenters to operate schools or to teach in them. The House of Lords, which had been abolished in 1649, but was reinstituted at the Restoration in 1660, also worried the Tories because, since 1688, it had been a Whig stronghold. It was not only that the Lords had as much legislative authority as the Commons, except in matters of finance (and continued to have it until 1911); it also enjoyed the traditional role of being an appellate court in civil cases, and accordingly had tried persons in public life accused of serious crimes, most recently Dr. Sacheverell. Hence the Whig-dominated Lords were a continuous threat to Tory officeholders. They therefore convinced Anne to ennoble twelve new Tory peers, thereby erasing the Whig majority. Finally, the Tories raised property qualifications for members of the electorate so as to debar the less opulent Whigs, and imposed a stamp tax on printed matter in order to make it more difficult for Whig authors and publishers to disseminate Whig literature.

While the Tories were taking these steps to crush their opponents, Bolingbroke and Oxford were locked in a bitter power struggle for control of the party. Oxford, still sickly, indecisive, and less popular than Bolingbroke among the rank and file, attempted to blacken the latter's reputation with charges of corruption. In this he was unsuccessful, and he also failed to counter Bolingbroke's intrigues to gain the full confidence of Anne and Parliament. In turn, Bolingbroke had sponsored the Schism Act not only to weaken the Whigs, but also to embarrass Oxford, once a Nonconformist, who still had many Presbyterian supporters. Foremost in Bolingbroke's mind, however, was his concern about his future in the event that the queen, ill since 1712, should die. He reasoned that he must be in a position at her death either to swing the country in favor of the Catholic Stuarts, with whom he was treasonously corresponding, or to dictate terms to the Hanoverian successor. He came close to success. At his importuning the queen dismissed Oxford in July, 1714, but she died unexpectedly four days later (August 1), shortly after she had made Charles Talbot, duke of Shrewsbury, Treasurer. As he had the support of the two most influential councilors, the dukes of Argyle and Somerset, who abhorred Bolingbroke, the latter lost control of the privy council. When one after another of the councilors spoke out for King George I (Electress Sophia had died before Anne), Bolingbroke had no choice but to join in the chorus. But he had acted too late. George, knowing his opposition to the Hanoverian succession and lust for personal power, demanded his resignation, got it, and landed in England in mid-September, by which time Bolingbroke had fled to France to lay plans for Jacobite rebellion.

9

The Early Hanoverians, 1714–1760

The two most significant constitutional developments beginning after the Glorious Revolution and continuing into the eighteenth century were the increasingly important role of Parliament and the evolution of the cabinet system. Parliament's standing may be inferred from the fact that, from 1689 to 1714, the crown rejected only five bills approved by the Commons and Lords. After the Bill of Rights (1689–90), no English monarch could legally exercise autocratic power. In Macaulay's words, the Revolution of 1688 decided once and for all whether "the popular element . . . in the English polity" should be subordinated to monarchy or be allowed to develop freely, "and to become dominant."

But if 1688 ushered in a new era in the evolution of the English constitution, two centuries were to pass before Parliamentary democracy prevailed. Less than a hundred aristocratic families dominated Parliament in the eighteenth century. They controlled a large proportion of the membership in Commons by reason of their ownership of borough tenements and the severely restricted franchise, and by exercising their traditional right to nominate certain members. The House of Lords was composed of temporal peers and twenty-six ecclesiastical peers. Although the crown created additional peers from time to time, noble family representation in the Lords had not changed substantially for centuries, sons succeeding to their fathers' places generation upon generation. As the nobles controlled much of England's land and wealth, many were understandably loath to see constitutional, economic, or social changes that might threaten their dominance. By 1714, however, the Lords had surrendered considerable authority to the Commons, especially in matters of finance. All money bills had customarily originated in the Commons, and were then sent to the Lords for passage. After 1689, this was often *pro forma*, for, although Commons had admitted as late as the 1670s that the Lords could amend or reject money bills, the latter rarely did so. As a matter of fact, Commons carefully guarded its prerogative in finance and discouraged amendments of money bills in the Lords by simply setting aside those that the Lords had altered, and sending up entirely new bills that often embodied the amendments. It is true that the Lords occasionally rejected money bills during the seventeenth and eighteenth centuries, but the fact that after 1671 the only formal division on a money bill in the upper House occurred in 1763 is proof that it generally respected the wishes of the Commons in finance. The Lords, however, had the right to alter or reject money bills or any other bill until the Parliament Act of 1911.

The House of Commons was composed of about 560 members from 1714 to 1801, when the Anglo-Irish political union added another one hundred members. Scotland and Wales sent sixty-nine members to Commons, the remainder sitting for English counties, boroughs, and universities. Approximately 80 per cent of the English members represented boroughs. For a number of reasons, however, Commons in 1714 was far from truly representative of the British people, and was, indeed, less so than it had been two centuries before. Enclosure, urbanization, improved transportation, population growth, and industrialization in the Midlands caused shifts in population concentrations that rendered less meaningful the old basis of representation in Parliament. The Tudors and early Stuarts had greatly increased the size of the Commons, adding 180 members between 1509 and 1685, sometimes in recognition of boroughs as important urban centers; more frequently to augment the crown's influence in Parliament. As the crown paid little or no attention to the principle of popular representation in creating these nomination boroughs, certain geographic areas came to enjoy disproportionate representation while other more heavily populated areas had no representation whatsoever. Furthermore, after 1485 many members of Parliament were not residents of their constituencies.

The disproportionate representation of some areas as compared with others became more pronounced during the early eighteenth century, owing partly to the limitation of the franchise in the counties to forty-shilling freeholders (those whose land returned an annual income of at least forty shillings) and to closed corporations in the boroughs (principally councilors and tenement owners). In addition, by 1714, many members sat for constituencies that had long since lost most, and in one case all, of their inhabitants. Examples of such "rotten" boroughs and "pocket" boroughs (where the few who could vote were said to be in the "pocket" of the patron or proprietor) were Old Sarum, a ghost town in Wiltshire, and several in Cornwall. The latter, for instance, sent forty-four members to Parliament, many more than did metropolitan London, whose population of about 675,000 in 1714 was at least five times larger than Cornwall's. Disproportionate representation was even more marked in the Scottish constituencies, where only a few thousand electors of the total population of 1,500,000 determined the forty-five members returned to Parliament. Several rather large English Midland towns whose population increased greatly because of the Industrial Revolution, had no representatives in Parliament until the early nineteenth century.

Another constitutional development after 1689 was the evolution of the cabinet (from the Latin *camera,* meaning a small room), whose development to 1714 was mentioned in the previous chapter. After 1660, the crown began to consult officially, but privately, a select group of councilors rather than the full, unwieldy privy council, about important matters of state. Consequently the cabinet, without legal foundation, gradually evolved into the crown's principal consultative body. The Cabal of Charles II and the Junto of William III are examples of rudimentary cabinets. By the latter's reign, it had become more or less customary also for cabinet officers to be of the same political party as the majority of the members of Parliament. This practice was established by the accession of George I. His cabinets, numbering usually about fifteen people, included his foreign advisers as well as important office-holders like the two principal secretaries of state, the Lord Chancellor, president of the council, and the Lord Privy Seal, the Chancellor of the Exchequer, the lord lieutenant of Ireland, the secretary for Scotland, and the paymaster-general. The chief of the cabinet, who during the eighteenth century often held a portfolio connected with finance, became known as the prime minister even though this title admitted of no definition in statutory law. Critics of Sir Robert Walpole, often considered Britain's first prime minister, not unjustifiably labeled him thus in order to denote a certain authoritarianism reminiscent of the French chief ministers, Richelieu and Fleury. Walpole undeniably dominated the political arena and manipulated Parliament and the cabinet, but one should not infer from this that he or any other eighteenth-century prime minister independently exercised anywhere near the authority that Benjamin Disraeli and William Gladstone were to in the nineteenth. The Hanoverian kings exerted strong influence in government; if they necessarily paid deference to cabinet chieftains for practical political reasons, they surrendered not one iota of their princely prerogative. Even if one were to admit that the prime ministers enhanced their authority at the expense of the crown under the first two Georges, such advances were virtually eliminated by the firm rule of George III until 1783. The concept of the prime minister's being responsible only to Parliament, without more than polite consideration of the wishes of the monarch, is a relatively recent development of the last century.

Apart from these seminal constitutional developments, Great Britain underwent other changes during the early eighteenth century. One of these was an increase in population. Granted that it is hazardous to guess at the population of England and Wales before the first official census of 1801, some rough guidelines can be suggested. The population in 1714 was somewhat under 6,000,000. It advanced slowly from 1689 to 1760, when it stood at about 6,750,000, rose more rapidly from that year to 1780, and increased sharply in the following decades. It was approximately 9,100,000 in 1801. The spectacular rise in population during George III's reign was due to factors that are not yet fully understood and about which demographers have disputed at great length. Even if historians had all the baptism and burial records of Anglican parishes, they would not have a complete set of statistics, for not only were births and deaths sometimes unrecorded, but similar statistics concerning large numbers of Dissenters and Roman Catholics were never kept. The best evidence suggests that the population growth after 1760 was caused as much by a decrease in the death rate, particularly among infants and young adolescents, as by a substantial increase in the birth rate resulting from earlier marriages, and consequently earlier and more frequent pregnancies. Other factors have been suggested, especially improved hygiene, medical discoveries such as smallpox vaccine, the gradual recession of the plague, and a reduction in the consumption of gin by the lower classes because of restrictive legislation on its manufacture after 1743. Greater agricultural productivity likewise had something to do with longevity and fertility; the application of agricultural techniques invented by Jethro Tull and "Turnip" Townshend and the animal husbandry of Robert Bakewell increased the amount of food available. Improved diet helped people to withstand better the rigors of cold, damp, and disease that earlier had sent so many to graves prematurely. Crop failures were also less frequent and

PRINCIPAL TOWNS AND PRODUCTS OF ENGLAND
1746

1 CATTLE	7 SHEEP	13 CHEESE	19 COPPER	25 HOPS
2 COAL	8 HORSES	14 BUTTER	20 POTTERY	26 FRUIT
3 CORN	9 WOOL	15 STONE	21 HARDWARE	27 TIMBER
4 MINES	10 WORSTEDS	16 OATS	22 LINEN	28 ROPE
5 IRON	11 SHIPS	17 METALS	23 SILK	
6 TEXTILES	12 FISHING	18 SALT	24 CIDER	

less severe by the later eighteenth century, and therefore deaths from malnutrition and starvation were fewer.

In 1714 most Englishmen still lived on farms or in hamlets and small towns. The urbanization of England was neither widespread nor rapid before the onset of the Industrial Revolution. How little most towns had grown in the two centuries after 1500 may be illustrated by the fact that during the reign of Henry VIII there were at least thirty towns with 5000 to 10,000 persons; in 1714 there were not many more with comparable numbers. The heaviest concentrations of population at the turn of the eighteenth century were in the southwestern, southeastern, and northwestern counties. East Anglia and certain south-central counties like Hampshire either lost residents or failed to grow between 1660 and 1714. Northern counties like Northumberland, Cumberland, and the West Riding of Yorkshire were still sparsely populated. The acceleration of industrialization in the Midlands, which will be described in a subsequent chapter, drew some people north, especially after 1760. Metropolitan London, the bustling center of trade, commerce, law, and government, continued to bulge during the eighteenth century, growing from 675,000 inhabitants in 1700 to nearly 1,000,000 in 1760. The next largest towns at the turn of the century, each with about 30,000 persons, were Bristol, Norwich, Liverpool, and Glasgow. The expansion of overseas and coastwise trade can be deduced from the growth of Liverpool's population from about 4000 in 1662 to 60,000 in 1760, when another important port, Bristol, had 100,000 residents. In 1760, about a dozen provincial towns each had about 20,000 inhabitants. The future industrial centers of Birmingham, Sheffield, Leeds, and Nottingham each had no more than 5000 persons in 1714. Therefore, as the national population grew after 1760, so did the towns. The early nineteenth century witnessed an enormous growth of urbanization; after 1871 the majority of British citizens were born in cities.

The complexities of the social structure in England and Wales, the gradations within each class, and variations in status are as difficult to determine as the population. Class was ordinarily related to titles, genealogy, skills, income, and so forth. Gregory King, a demographer writing in 1688, compiled a table in which he noted the number of families, the heads of families' "Ranks, Degrees, Titles, and Qualifications," and their average annual family income. The importance of income in establishing social status is obvious, as is the enormous gulf that existed between the middling and lesser gentry, businessmen, entrepreneurs, and professionals on the one hand, and the laboring people of town and country (servants, cottagers, and the like) on the other. Professor T. S. Ashton has shown that, although one should not die in a ditch in defense of King's accuracy, his table nevertheless indicates important approximations. Ashton reckoned that 25 per cent of the national income went to only 3½ per cent of the population in 1688; 50 per cent to 18 per cent; and only 17 per cent to 60 per cent of the population. Not unexpectedly, therefore, the largest average incomes, £3200 and £1300, were enjoyed by the 186 temporal and 26 ecclesiastical peers respectively. The income of the gentry (baronets, knights, esquires, and gentlemen), numbering about 16,400 families, ranged between £280 and £880 annually. Some 8000 small merchants (averaging £198) and 10,000 lawyers (£154) were not far behind financially, and did much better than the 10,000 clergymen (who averaged £61 annually) or 40,000 freeholders "of the better sort" (£91) and 120,000 freeholders "of the lesser sort" (£55). The income of hundreds of thousands in the lower classes fell off sharply, ranging from an average of £38 for 60,000 artisans' to £6 10s. for 400,000 cottagers' and paupers' families.

Although English society at the Hanoverian succession was still firmly structured along class lines, such lines were not so sharply defined as they were on the Continent. There was considerable mobility both within and between classes. After the middle of the sixteenth century, and particularly during the first half of the seventeenth, the rigid exclusiveness of the aristocracy had broken down to the extent that some men of other backgrounds attained noble rank. Notable examples were Lord Cottington, Archbishop Laud, Lord Strafford, and the Earl of Bristol, each of whom advanced to a class higher than that of his father. The important role played in finance and politics by seventeenth-century merchants attests to their rising respectability as well as to the importance of trade and commerce. The economic and social gains of the gentry in the century before 1640 have been well established by several historians, though they do not agree as to how much importance should be placed on this fact as a cause of the Civil Wars. Whether by dint of hard work, education, talent, patronage and preferment, or the accumulation of wealth, Englishmen often managed to climb a rung in the social scale. Moreover, the Puritan Revolution provided many with an opportunity to purchase at very reasonable cost the sequestered land of Royalists, and these purchases were confirmed at the Restoration. As ownership of land still counted as a basis of social status, the acquisition of estates was a measure of social importance. Therefore the aristocracy, in losing their hereditary lands, gave up wealth and social status to the squirearchy and gentry. As titles and money were not always bedfellows, marriages between the families of aristocrats and squires, or between merchants and gentry, were not uncommon. A titled nobleman not infrequently "sold" a son in a marriage bargain with a rich merchant, whose daughter brought a substantial dowry. By the early 1700s, and increasingly as the century wore on, the accumulation of wealth through business was no longer considered an impediment to genteel status. Since money, whether from land or business, was concentrated in the hands of the aristocracy, gentry, and mercantile and professional classes, the vast majority of Englishmen in 1714 were still chained to a life of hard work, little pay, and marginal subsistence. Sons and daughters of such families could not often pull themselves up by their bootstraps, regardless of their talents and industry. But, though the working classes sometimes suffered from hunger, privation, and other social evils and discomforts, they ordinarily managed during the eighteenth century to acquire more possessions and enjoy more amenities than their forefathers had two or three generations earlier.

The splendid houses and rich fields of peers and squires dotted the English countryside. They lived comfortably, supporting their opulent tastes by rents and mercantile investments. In most cases their country houses had been in their families for centuries, and as travel was difficult, uncomfortable, and often made hazardous by highwaymen and bad roads, they were often situated near provincial and market towns. Such smaller urban centers supplied goods and services and sold agricultural and manufactured commodities produced by the surrounding area. Unlike the Squire portrayed by Henry Fielding in *Tom Jones* (1749), not all squires lived carefree lives of wenching, deer hunting, and revelry. If the upper classes frequently enjoyed their dogs, goose riding, horse racing, bear baiting, and gambling, they also took a keen interest in the affairs of their lands and communities. As their forefathers had done, they went up to Parliament, took their turns as sheriffs and justices of the peace, and fulfilled their roles as respected leaders of their districts. Their sons went to Oxford and Cambridge —no longer the great intellectual centers they had been in earlier times —if not to take a degree, then at least to learn the ways of a gentleman. Eldest sons eventually inherited their fathers' titles and lands, while second, third, and fourth sons filled those church, military, and government posts, both at home and in the colonies, that were open to them. In essence, the way of life of the upper classes resident in the country had not changed substantially since the late sixteenth century.

The yeomen and tenant farmers, numbering, according to King, about 310,000 families at the turn of the eighteenth century, who either owned their land or held it by some type of lease, formed the agricultural "middle classes." Their holdings varied from a few hundred to a few dozen acres, and the kind of crops they planted and livestock they kept varied from place to place, depending on local demand for their surplus yield. Some yeomen were financially as well off as squires —and occasionally better off. They did not, for instance, grumble nearly as much as the squires about land and hearth taxes. These farmers usually sold the staples required in their immediate neighborhood at the town market and thereby got the hard cash they needed to meet their expenses and to gratify their tastes in a society that had not yet gone over entirely from a barter to a money economy. Most farms produced a variety of food, including wheat and rye south of the Trent, barley in Wales, and oats in northern England and Scotland, as well as beef, pork, mutton, and milk and cheese. The researches sponsored by the Royal Society and the Dutch agronomists, who pioneered rotation of crops and turnip and clover cultivation by which fields might be chemically revitalized and herds of cattle kept over the winter, encouraged scientific farming among some. Tull's seed-planter and Bakewell's successful breeding of beef cattle in Leicester-shire also increased agricultural productivity. Leicester and Lincoln-shire sheep were bred not only for mutton but also for wool to feed the hungry textile industry. Scientific methods of farming, publicized in Arthur Young's books based on observation of methods employed throughout western Europe, had revolutionized agriculture by the turn of the nineteenth century. Even so, it is difficult to believe that such improvements were widely adopted until well after the Napoleonic Wars. As Professor Lipson has suggested, quoting Arthur Young, if new techniques were mentioned to a Buckinghamshire farmer, "he laughs at you for a theorist."

The cottagers and agricultural laborers, numbering about 775,000 families and more than 2,500,000 persons in 1714, made up the bulk of the rural lower classes. The cottagers worked pitifully small plots of land rented from landlords on whose property lay clusters of shabby cottages, many without floors or glass in the windows. They could afford to keep no more than a cow or two or some fowl and subsisted marginally on what their few acres and vegetable gardens provided. The economic level of the laborer deteriorated during the eighteenth century. He either worked steadily for some landlord for only a few pounds a year, or traveled about seeking work wherever he could find it. As laborers were plentiful, wages were low. The enclosure movement, particularly in a belt running from the southwest through the Midlands to the northeast, which had been slowly taking land from the small farmer since the later Middle Ages, but slackened during the last half of the sixteenth and seventeenth centuries, was vigorously resumed in the eighteenth. Enclosure by agreement or by Act of Parliament deprived tenant farmers and cotters of more than 5,000,000 acres in the century after 1714. While it is true that some of this land was reclaimed from the wild, many smaller farmers were deprived of their livelihood, and cotters and agricultural laborers especially after 1760 were driven into the slums of industrial towns. But enclosure had beneficial results also: it helped to destroy the wasteful open-field system, provided more food, and increased the amount of land under cultivation. The degree to which the spread of industrialization and urbanization affected the mercantile and working classes will be described later.

Not only scientific farming, but science in general took great strides during these years. Although some still distrusted the seemingly occult ways of the biologist, chemist, mathematician, and physician in the late seventeenth and eighteenth centuries, their discoveries alleviated suffering, made the wonders of the human body and the universe more intelligible, and greatly enlarged the sum of knowledge and put it to practical use. Science became respectable during the seventeenth century and revered in the eighteenth: its practitioners no longer had to fear the restrictions and punishments of Church and state as they had in medieval and earlier modern times; the methodology of research developed by Bacon and Descartes improved the unsatisfactory technique of trial and error under which Copernicus, Galileo, and da Vinci had labored; society craved a better life and gained confidence in its ability to achieve it; and scientists, encouraged by learned societies that sponsored symposia and harvested the independent investigations of their members for publication in journals, no longer toiled in isolation from their fellows at home or abroad. As a result, the scientifically adolescent world of Galileo matured into the complex, rationalistic, and mechanistic world of Sir Isaac Newton.

At the close of the sixteenth century Europeans knew little more about the anatomy and functions of the human body than had Hippocrates or Galen, diseases were often viewed as visitations by God upon a sinful people, and treatments were largely inadequate and sometimes harmful. Surgery was performed without the benefit of effective anesthetics and was a gruesome business that tortured the patient and often killed him, if not by imperfect techniques or pain, then by postoperative infection. Physicians' remedies often did little to cure disease, and preventive medicine was practically unknown. Childbirth and ordinary illnesses like fevers, agues, smallpox, and measles killed three of every eight children before they reached puberty. At a time when isolation and cleanliness in connection with contagion were inadequately understood, disease in one person frequently led to the deaths of entire families in the neighborhood.

William Harvey (1578–1657), physician to Charles I, built his research on the studies of the Fleming Andreas Vesalius, who taught anatomy at the University of Padua before the former's birth. Harvey dissected living animals and human cadavers in order to study the structure and function of vital organs and the circulation of the blood, holding that it fed the tissues of the body. He revolutionized anatomical study by proving that the heart was a pump that squeezed blood into the arteries both by way of the pulmonary system through the lungs and of the circulatory system through the rest of the body. Although he uncovered few new facts, for Galen and Vesalius had already explained much about circulation, and did not understand the capillary system, he did more to explain the general function and routes of the arteries and veins than anyone else, and thereby laid the basis for further study in the next two centuries. Harvey also studied insects with the help of microscopes invented by Robert Hooke (1635–1703) and others, which enabled an English botanist named Nehemiah Grew (1641–1712) to establish the principle of plant fertilization by observing stamens and pistils. Continentals, notably Malpighi of Bologna and Leeuwenhoek of Holland, first sketched the structure of tissues and muscular fibers and saw bacteria and blood corpuscles. Hooke and Richard Lower (1631–91) proved that air is heterogeneous, implying what others like Joseph Priestley (1733–1804) later proved to be the existence of oxygen, which burned off carbon dioxide and thereby purified the blood as it coursed through the lungs.

These were important discoveries by eminent scientists, but the name Sir Isaac Newton (1642–1727), the foremost English scientist of the seventeenth and eighteenth centuries, captures the imagination. He dabbled even as a boy in Lincolnshire in the construction of mechanical devices, studied mathematics and optics at Trinity College, Cambridge, and became professor of Mathematics there at the age of twenty-seven. His intense interest in optics resulted in the construction of a reflecting telescope and experiments with light and prisms. As early as 1665, while he was sitting out the plague at his country home, his mind turned to the motion of celestial bodies. After years of reflection, failures, and ridicule, he published his conclusions about the universal law of gravitation in a book entitled *Mathematical Principles of Natural Philosophy* (1687) that astounded the world and assured his fame. His ideas revolutionized the concept of the universe as drastically as has the splitting of the atom and space exploration in this century.

The Polish astronomer Copernicus had proved the heliocentric theory and observed the seemingly circular orbits of the planets, the moon, and comets, following essentially the conclusions of Aristotle, based on ideas borrowed from Pythagoras, who conceived of the universe as composed of bodies that plotted concentric circles around the earth. Two centuries after Copernicus, Galileo observed that these bodies followed elliptical orbits, and pondered, although he was never able to explain, what force drew them away from natural linear paths. Newton finally concluded that this force, applicable to all matter in the universe, was gravity. His law of universal gravitation explained that "bodies attract each other with a force which is inversely proportional to the square of their distance apart." Using this principle, Newton calculated the masses of the sun, moon, and planets, determined their orbits mathematically, explained the rise and fall of tides, and computed the revolution of the earth on its own axis. The effect of Newton's law was immediate and profound, as every student of eighteenth-century philosophy, theology, and literature is aware. Not until the time of Albert Einstein was the intellectual community again so mesmerized by the charm of cosmology.

Although Continental scientists set the pace in biological, chemical, and botanical discoveries in the seventeenth and eighteenth centuries, Englishmen registered important achievements in these and related fields. Robert Boyle (1627–91), an eminent chemist and one of the founders of the Royal Society in 1662, developed an air pump by which he could measure not only the pressure of gases, but also the effect of air pressure. This enabled later scientists to predict the effect of high altitudes on bodily functions and to understand the influence of pressure on weather, important particularly for seafarers. Thomas

Newcomen and James Watt also adapted this principle to pumps that drew water from shallow mines and drove pistons on steam engines. Henry Cavendish (1731–1810), another notable chemist and physicist who spent a large part of his fortune on experiments with gases and electricity, continued Priestley's work on the properties of hydrogen and oxygen in pure water, only to be cheated of his triumph by the publications of Lavoisier in 1783 on the same subject. Finally, mention must be made of Edward Jenner (1749–1823), a Berkeley physician whose experiments led to the development of a vaccine drawn from cows suffering from the pox.

Most of these discoveries were unknown, of course, to the generation of George I (1714–27), who reached Greenwich after a journey from Hanover on September 30, 1714, about seven weeks after Anne's death. The death of Electress Sophia, an octogenarian of extraordinary charm and poise, shortly before Anne, had robbed Britain of a colorful monarch. It acquired instead an obstinate, sensuous, and vulgar Teuton of fifty-four who detested pageantry, avoided the public, was accustomed to having his own way, and frequently indulged his physical appetite with two German mistresses, Ehrengard von Schulenburg (duchess of Kendal) and Charlotte Kielmannsegge (countess of Darlington). Because they were the objects of the king's affection, they enjoyed the attention of English courtiers and politicians who quickly learned that they controlled royal favors. But if these cunning and influential ladies easily twisted George around their fingers, others found him pigheaded, petty, and often cruel, even toward his family. George divorced his wife, Sophia Dorothea, in 1694 and imprisoned her in the Hanoverian Castle of Ahlden for thirty-two years. He distrusted and was jealous of his son, George Frederick, and treated him basely. Although the king was clever, courageous, a fine diplomat, and devoted to detail as only Germans can be, he displeased the English. He has been adversely criticized by contemporaries and historians alike as a dullard, who generally paid little attention to British affairs unless they related to the interests of Hanover or to the royal prerogative. The provincial and nationalistic English had trouble warming up to a king who made no serious effort to adjust to their way of life, who bothered to learn no more than a few words of their language, and who made no bones about his intention to exploit English resources for the sake of Hanover.

It would be a mistake, however, to label George I a mere cipher. Although he did not interfere inordinately in the work of his principal councilors, they dared not make policy without his consent. Too much has been made of the king's inability to speak English (in connection with the growth of the cabinet system and the office of prime minister), for, like most members of the cabinet, he spoke French fluently. His apparent lack of interest at cabinet meetings, or frequent absence from them, was as much the result of the press of other business as it was of a language barrier. Not even Walpole, who conspired for power with the Prince of Wales against the king, and virtually had his way in managing the country and Parliament during his ministry from 1721 to 1742, escaped an occasional scolding by George I and George II.

The Whigs enjoyed predominance under George I and George II, not simply because they staunchly resisted the restoration of the Catholic Stuarts and had been primarily responsible for the Act of Succession which led to the Hanoverian accession, but also because George I subscribed more easily to their principles and policies than to the Tories'. Consequently, the latter were politically eclipsed in 1714 and languished in the shadow of the Whigs for forty-five years. That is not to say that the Whig councilors consistently enjoyed the exclusive confidence of the king: he usually had one or two Tories in his cabinet and relied heavily on the advice of Hanoverian friends such as Baron Bothmer and Andreas Bernstorff. Of those closest to the king by reason of high office in the privy council, Charles, Viscount Townshend (principal secretary for foreign affairs to 1717, and again from 1721 to 1730), Earl Stanhope (chief minister and principal secretary for western and southern European relations and the colonies to 1721), and Sir Robert Walpole (paymaster-general to 1717, and prime minister, 1721–42) were the most influential. Many of the older councilors in the early cabinets of George I, such as Halifax (Lord Treasurer) and Shrewsbury (Lord Chamberlain), were holdovers from Anne's council, did not exert much weight on governmental policy, and died within a few years of the Hanoverian succession. Younger men, few of whom were of first-rate ability, replaced them and generally agreed with the wishes of Walpole, who completely dominated politics during the 1720s and 1730s. Not only in the major departments of the national government, but in the county and borough governments as well, many Tories suspected of sympathy for the Stuarts were dismissed from office. Loyal Tories, especially among the squirearchy and Anglican priesthood, generally kept their posts.

George's easy accession to the British throne was challenged in 1715 by the Jacobites (supporters of the Old Pretender, James Edward Stuart [1688–1766], styled James III). Fervent and courageous though they were, the Jacobites had slim chance of victory. It was not that there were not enough Catholics from the Irish bogs and Scottish Highlands, or opponents of the Anglo-Scottish union of 1707, or English emigrés in the garrets of Paris (to which Bolingbroke, and later Ormonde, both Jacobites, had fled) ready to die for the Stuarts; rather, it was that most Englishmen and Scots, mindful of the unconstitutionality of James II's acts, and the finality of the Glorious Revolution and the 1701 Settlement Act, were content with a Protestant monarchy. In addition, the Jacobites were woefully deficient in organization and planning; the leaders in England, France, and Scotland failed to coordinate their efforts; and the death of Louis XIV (1715) deprived them of any chance of French military support. Finally, the rebel leadership was incompetent and failed to muster a sustained offensive in the early weeks of the uprising.

The Earl of Mar, supported initially by the Mackintoshes, Grants, Camerons, and Gordons, gathered a small band of clansmen at Braemar in August to proclaim Prince James king. Other clansmen joined him shortly afterward to launch successful assaults against Perth and Fife. But loyalist troops repelled attacks on Fort William and Inverary, prevented the rebels from crossing the Firth of Forth by securing Sterling Castle, Edinburgh and Leith, and dispersed the clansmen as well as the vagabond army of Jacobites from northern England. The latter, after a brief foray into Scotland, fell back to Preston and were easily defeated. Had Mar acted decisively in the first weeks rather than temporizing while he awaited James's arrival, and had the popular and powerful Duke of Atholl lent his support instead of betraying rebel plans to the English, the outcome of the "Fifteen" might have been different. Defeat in Scotland was matched by the inability of Ormonde, who crossed from France twice, to raise more than a handful of Devon men. James himself did not reach Scotland until January, 1716, by which time Mar was preparing to retreat to Dundee. James realized that his cause was hopeless and left within the month for France. Thereafter it was only a matter of rounding up the traitors.

Their punishment was light. A few Scots lost their estates; several hundred were deported to the West Indies; and only two of the ringleaders (Derwentwater and Viscount Kenmure) and twenty-six of the rank and file were executed. The rest, many of whom were never tried, returned peaceably to their homes to nurse their pride and grumble about English tyranny. Prince James continued to call himself the legitimate monarch of Britain, but the princes of Europe virtually ignored him. Only misdirected patriotism among the Scots kept the flame of Jacobitism alive for another generation until it was finally extinguished in 1746.

This threat to Whig hegemony as well as sound practical considerations such as concern about lack of continuity in the conduct of foreign affairs arising from triennial elections and too frequent changes in government personnel, led to the passage of the Septennial Act in 1716. It lengthened the term of Parliaments from three to seven years, which remained unchanged until the 1911 Parliament Act reduced it to five years. It also prolonged the Whig hegemony during the first critical years after the Hanoverian succession. The Whigs pushed through the bill in the face of strong opposition from the Tories, who had introduced a similar measure in Queen Anne's reign only to lose out because of Whig dissent. Rather than run the risk of an election in 1718, which might have weakened his support in the Commons, Stanhope thought it simpler and safer to prolong the life of the existing Parliament. The Whigs were also anxious to strengthen their position abroad.

The restoration of Britain's traditional alliance system after the territorially disruptive Treaty of Utrecht became the principal aim of Stanhope's foreign policy. That he managed to achieve it despite major obstacles arising primarily from dynastic rivalries among the European powers is testimony to his great diplomatic skill. One can easily imagine the difficulty of concluding simultaneously Anglo-Austrian and Anglo-Spanish alliances when Emperor Charles VI was sulking over the loss of Spain and refusing to recognize Philip V as its legitimate ruler. Moreover, if Britain hoped to preserve amity with the United Provinces, which were pressing for an alteration of the Treaty of Utrecht in accordance with Britain's promises in the 1709 Barrier Treaty (not entirely satisfied in 1714), she had to mediate the dispute over the frontier fortresses lying between Holland and the Austrian Netherlands. Renewal of the prewar trade agreements with Spain was also urgently required in order to sustain the level of British commerce as well as to satisfy the merchants and landowners who were the backbone of the Whig party. Furthermore, only an accommodation with France would forestall her support of the Jacobites.

Stanhope attained most of these objectives in 1714–16. He successfully mediated the Austro-Dutch differences over the frontier fortresses and convinced Austria to sign the Treaty of Westminster (June, 1716), by which the signatories' mutual territorial and commercial privileges and rights were guaranteed. The treaty also confirmed Charles VI's possession of Majorca in the western Mediterranean, and promised the neutrality of the British navy should Charles attempt to snatch Sicily from Savoy, which had acquired it over Austria's strong objections in 1714. The strength of the British navy also had significance for Spain. Elizabeth Farnese, the second wife of Philip V, had ambitions for her son in Hapsburg Italy, and British friendship was a precondition of the fulfillment of her plans. Consequently the Spanish renewed the prewar trade treaties with Britain and officially recognized the Hanoverian succession. Despite frequent Spanish violations of these commercial concessions, and clashes with English smugglers on the high seas, Anglo-Spanish peace persisted until 1739. Britain and France reached an understanding in 1716, the latter reconfirming the succession of George I and forcing the withdrawal of Prince James to Rome.

These alliances assumed greater significance in the light of Britain's indirect and half-hearted involvement in the Great Northern War. This protracted struggle in northeastern Europe between Charles XII of Sweden and Peter the Great of Russia and their allies developed from circumstances in which England had no interest other than the Baltic trade. But, as Hanover was vitally concerned with the outcome of the war, and as the King of Great Britain was also Elector of Hanover, it was almost impossible for England not to become involved. It was a touchy business, not only because George believed that the presence of Russian troops in Mecklenburg endangered the security of Hanover, but also because Denmark, Hanover's neighbor, became a major theater of war. While it is true that England's Baltic trade, essential to the shipbuilding industry, was in jeopardy, that consideration weighed less heavily on the king's mind than his ambition to acquire the duchies of Bremen and Verden. It should also be appreciated that, while Hanover had treaties with Denmark and Prussia, which obliged her to assist them against Sweden, England was bound by an alliance of 1700 to help Sweden. Hanover's allies expected George to deploy the British navy in the Baltic, but, to do so, he and Stanhope had to make it appear that the actions of Britain and Hanover were entirely unrelated, else they would have violated the section of the Act of Settlement that specifically forbade a foreign-born English monarch to use his adopted country's resources for the benefit of his Continental possessions. Accordingly, George ordered British ships into the Baltic ostensibly to protect commercial interests and secretly instructed their captains to help his allies wherever possible. In the end George got Bremen and Verden, English commerce was protected, and Denmark, Russia, Prussia, and Poland were left to pick over the carcass of the once-powerful Swedish empire.

The pretext by which George had employed British sea power to Hanover's advantage did not deceive Townshend and Walpole, who strenuously objected to such an obvious subterfuge, especially when they were powerless to alter the king's policy while he, Stanhope, and the Earl of Sunderland (who did his utmost to undermine George's confidence in Walpole and Townshend) were directing foreign policy from Hanover. Townshend and Walpole also resented the German advisers' meddling and the fact that George had refused to permit his son, Frederick, to exercise effective regency powers in his absence. The king, jealous of and spiteful toward his son and daughter-in-law, the beautiful Caroline, who was popular among young English politicians and *bons vivants,* specifically forbade the prince to approve Parliamentary bills or have anything to do with foreign affairs. As Walpole and Townshend had ingratiated themselves with the prince and his circle of friends and had voiced their objections to the king's wily manipulation of English interests, they were driven into opposition to Stanhope and Sunderland. This split the cabinet into two factions and resulted in the dismissal of Townshend and Walpole. It also led Walpole to set about molding his own faction in Parliament.

The cabinet crisis left Stanhope, Sunderland, and the German advisers in control of the government until 1721. However much one might wish to sympathize with Walpole's position, it cannot be said that Stanhope had neglected his responsibilities. On the contrary, he settled the serious differences between Austria and Spain, thereby creating the Quadruple Alliance of Britain, Holland, Austria, and Spain in 1718. Charles VI surrendered his hollow claim to the Spanish throne and exchanged Sardinia for Sicily. Queen Elizabeth Farnese was contented by Austria's promise that her son would inherit the duchies of Tuscany and Parma when the incumbents died. At home, Stanhope attempted and failed to put through a Peerage Bill that would have prevented the king from appointing more than six new English peers to the House of Lords, by which it was hoped to prevent the strengthening of the opposition Whigs should Prince George succeed to the throne. He did, however, persuade Parliament to rescind the objectionable Occasional Conformity and Schism Acts in 1719, which, though never widely enforced, had been a dagger at the throats of Whig Dissenters.

The defeat of the Peerage Bill gave Stanhope and Sunderland cause to fret over the Walpole faction's mounting strength in Parliament. Since the split in the cabinet over foreign policy, Walpole had won to his point of view many of the rank-and-file Whig members, and had likewise gained the confidence of the few Tories in Commons so that he commanded a substantial following wherewith to combat the government's policies. There were no serious differences between Walpole and Stanhope over political principles or the alliance structure that helped to ensure peace on the Continent; Walpole was merely aiming to so increase his political power that Stanhope would have no choice but to restore him to the cabinet. The friendship of Walpole and the heir apparent strengthened his hand immeasurably among those English members of Parliament who resented Stanhope's pro-Hanoverian policy and the influence of the German advisers. As a matter of fact, Stanhope himself began to have misgivings about playing second fiddle to the Germans at court. He therefore concluded that, given his precarious position between the Walpole faction on the one hand, and the German faction on the other, it would be safer to make an accommodation with the former. Accordingly, in 1720 he brought Townshend and Walpole into the cabinet as president of the council and paymaster-general respectively.

Admitting that Walpole's faction was strong, it is hard to see how he could have unseated Stanhope by 1721 without the advantage of the financial crisis that followed the bursting of the South Sea Bubble. The heavy cost of the War of the Spanish Succession had greatly increased the national debt, much of which had been underwritten at interest rates as high as 9 per cent by the Bank of England, the East India Company, and several private investors. As the debt had climbed to almost £50,000,000 (1711) and the government needed more money, the Earl of Oxford, never happy about doing business with the Whig-dominated Bank, founded the South Sea Company. It sold stock to raise a capital of £9,000,000, which it loaned to the government at 6 per cent interest plus a substantial annual commission for managing the stock. When Britain acquired the right to the asiento trade in the Treaty of Utrecht, the Company assumed control of it; but in the ensuing years it paid virtually no attention to trade and became more deeply involved in finance. In the six years from

1713 to 1719 it assumed a larger proportion of the debt and made a handsome profit for its stockholders. By 1719 the Company held about £11,500,000 of the total national debt. The profits of the Company had been so great, and demand for its stock had increased so much that in 1720 it approached the government with a plan to assume the remainder of the debt, amounting to about £31,000,000. It proposed that the Company convert the debt by exchanging South Sea stock for annuities and government stock in order to underwrite a loan at 5 per cent, and to pay the government about £7,500,000 for the privilege of assuming its liability. As the prospect of having only one creditor at lower interest rates than it could get with others was too appealing to turn down, Parliament approved the scheme in the spring of 1720. Many small investors—landed aristocrats, squires, gentry, merchants, and members of Parliament—poured their savings into South Sea stock. The wild demand for the stock caused it to skyrocket from £128½ per share in January, 1720, to over £1000 in mid-July. At the same time, numerous joint-stock companies—some of them perfectly legitimate operations, and others formed for such ludicrous purposes as the manufacture of a perpetual motion wheel and "for carrying on an undertaking of great advantage, but nobody to know what it is," gained handsomely as a result of the popular craze for making easy profits.

Suddenly, despite government efforts to curb the creation of shaky joint-stock companies and to punish deceitful stockbrokers who duped the public into investing in hairbrain ventures, the stock market crashed. South Sea shares tumbled from £1000 in July to £135 in November. Smart investors made fortunes overnight by buying low and selling high, but most investors, unaware of the risk involved in purchasing the oversubscribed South Sea stock, kept their shares until it was too late to recover their investments. The outcry over the collapse of the Company was immediate and violent. The public, spurred on by members of Parliament and others who had lost their savings, demanded and found scapegoats in Stanhope, Sunderland, the elder James Craggs (postmaster-general), and John Aislabie (Chancellor of the Exchequer), who bore the brunt of the blame. At this critical juncture Walpole, who already had something of a reputation as a financial wizard, had warned the country of the Company's instability even while he himself owned some of its stock, and had not been a member of the cabinet long enough to have become associated in the public mind with the crash, was asked to find a solution. His ability to do so, primarily by convincing the

Bank of England to assume most of the debt at a heavy loss to Company shareholders, gained for him great popularity and opened the door to political power. He was also fortunate in that Stanhope died after a vicious verbal attack on him in the Lords; the elder Craggs allegedly committed suicide; Aislabie resigned the chancellorship and was sent a prisoner to the Tower; and Sunderland, dismissed from the cabinet, died in 1722. With Walpole's old adversaries either dead or disgraced, the road to a bright future lay open to him.

Walpole (1676–1745, later Lord Orford), a man of abundant ability in finance and administration, assumed control of the cabinet in 1721 and dominated the course of British affairs until fatigue, ill health, and a political crisis caused by war with France in 1742 forced his retirement. Corpulent, choleric, and ruddy, this brilliant orator and manager of men rose from a locally prominent family of Norfolk squires to become a member of Parliament, paymaster-general, and first Lord of the Treasury. His inordinate ambition and lust for power gave him the patience to erode the stubbornness of opponents, ingratiate himself with the king, the Tories, and rank-and-file Whigs, and manage both Parliament and his colleagues in the cabinet; and if it was necessary to achieve his objectives, he was not above using intimidation or bribery. He enjoyed the confidence and support of the crown, for George I respected him, and Queen Caroline of Anspach was grateful to him for his defense of her husband against the old king in the three years after 1717. Walpole was not a prime minister in the technical sense, and, indeed, resented his enemies' use of the term, which was intended derisively, but he controlled the Whigs on the floor of the Commons and in the smoke-filled anterooms, gained their support through a liberal application of patronage, and gave the Tories, particularly the squires and Anglican parsons who had enormous influence in the country districts, a sense of security and personal freedom. He weathered crisis after crisis with the aplomb of a captain sure of the capabilities of his ship and crew, standing defiantly on his bridge in the face of a raging storm. Most significantly, with the help of Stanhope's alliance system, he kept England at peace for two decades during which he concentrated on finding solutions to domestic problems.

Although Walpole could rest easier in the knowledge that by 1722 many of his early antagonists had perished, and that young colleagues in the cabinet like the brothers Henry Pelham and the Duke of Newcastle initially defended his views, he realized the dangers inherent in his position. In the first place, he had to prevent George I from involving Britain once more in the labyrinth of Continental politics, and thereby possibly inducing Spain, France, or Sweden to lend support to the Jacobites. It was partly his fear of the Jacobites that led him to strike at the Catholics by imposing on them a ruinous land tax of five shillings in the pound, pardon Bolingbroke so as to rob him of an excuse for stirring Jacobite rebellion, and have Francis Atterbury, bishop of Rochester and dean of Westminster, and his accomplices tried for treason in 1722 for plotting to restore Prince James. Lastly, Walpole felt that he had somehow to dispose of John Carteret, a former colleague of Stanhope's who had managed to hold his secretaryship of state after the 1721 crisis largely because King George liked his pro-Hanoverian conduct of foreign policy. As simply dismissing Carteret would have antagonized George, Walpole induced the king to send him to Ireland as lord lieutenant to settle serious problems respecting the coinage and the exalted claims of the Irish House of Lords as a court of ultimate appeal, and to establish a cotton industry.

Walpole expended some time and effort in thwarting Spain's attempt to oust Britain from Gibraltar, but his talents and energy were directed primarily to trade and finance. He had temporarily salvaged the country's credit following the collapse of the South Sea Company, but the increasing cost of government, the burden of meeting annual interest payments of over £3,000,000 on the national debt of £54,000,000, and amortization of the principal on the debt strained the resources of the government. It had relied heavily on land taxes since the days of William III, but the squires and landed aristocrats, many of whom were disgruntled Tories, grumbled about high taxes and would not tolerate increases. In order to gain their support, Walpole gradually reduced the land tax from four shillings to one shilling in the pound between 1721 and 1733. But he had to find other sources of income to make up for this loss of revenue. He did so by stimulating overseas trade and effecting customs reform.

Operating within the framework of the mercantile system, Parliament in 1721 abolished or drastically reduced export duties on over a hundred commodities manufactured in Britain, and admitted duty-free about forty categories of raw materials imported primarily from the American colonies. Walpole also granted subsidies to certain manufacturers who had difficulty realizing profits in the production of goods like refined sugar and silk, which suffered from heavy foreign competition. Yet Walpole was no prototype of the free trader; he often bowed to pressure from special mercantile groups such as the West Indian sugar planters, whose demand for protection he met in the Molasses Act (1733), which levied high duties on sugar, rum, and molasses exported by Spanish, Dutch, and French West Indian planters into the American colonies. He also maintained the high import duties on staples such as tea, coffee, chocolate, and tobacco and angered most Englishmen by imposing a heavy tax on salt.

Customs reform greatly stimulated the import and export trade and nurtured the shipping industry. The reduction of the land tax in 1732 to one shilling in the pound as well as losses in revenue because of extensive smuggling (the government captured over two hundred ships and prosecuted about two thousand smugglers in 1723–33) had, however, sharply reduced the receipts of the Exchequer. To increase revenue without resorting to unpopular higher land taxes, and to make smuggling unprofitable, Walpole introduced his excise bill of 1733. That this was a prudent and equitable measure there can be little doubt, but it aroused a storm of opposition. Merchants feared, probably without justification, that government agents would peer into every nook and cranny of their businesses, thereby interfering with trade and reducing profits. They had strong spokesmen in Parliament, not only among the Hanoverian Tories and opposition Whigs like William Pulteney and Bolingbroke, whose paper, *The Craftsman*, had bitterly attacked Walpole's policies since 1726, but also among members of his own faction. The bill would have extended the system of bonded warehouses instituted by Walpole a decade earlier. Tea, coffee, and chocolate were at that time subject to storage in warehouses operated by the government without prepayment of excise duties until the goods were either sold on the home market, when the duties were collected, or shipped abroad duty-free. Walpole hoped to include wine and tobacco in this system, but, when the bill was defeated on the first reading, he dropped it rather than provide the opposition with an excuse to demand his resignation.

We also owe the conception of the sinking fund to Walpole. At his suggestion in 1717, this device for amortizing the principal on the national debt, which has since been widely adopted by many countries, was inaugurated by Stanhope and continued by his successors. Stanhope and Walpole earmarked certain taxes for deposit in the fund which, between 1717 and 1742, reduced the debt by about £9,000,000. It could have been reduced even more had they not frequently dipped into this nest egg to meet current operating expenses rather than increase taxes.

Walpole concentrated his efforts on the smooth operation of his administration and the consolidation of his political power, but he did not neglect foreign affairs for which his brother-in-law, Townshend, was primarily responsible until they quarreled in 1730. The maintenance of peace by means of the Quadruple Alliance became the watchword of Walpole's foreign policy. He quickly discovered that peace was never easy to keep while George I reigned, for the king had a penchant for becoming involved in German affairs. When he died of a stroke while journeying to Hanover in 1727, Walpole scurried to gain the support of his successor, George II (1727–60). Walpole did win his friendship and confidence, but it was not easy, for, like his father, he never forgot his attachment to Hanover and was equally ready to employ English resources in its interests. He also listened more attentively to the complaints of merchants and members of Parliament such as Viscount Cobham and the Earl of Chesterfield, who were hostile to Walpole for having dismissed them from office for opposing the excise bill. But nonetheless George stood by his chief minister until 1742, despite frequent criticism by the opposition of England's timidity in not taking firm action against Spanish encroachments on the British West Indian trade and wrongs against British sailors. George was prone to fits of anger and pride, and to hasty decisions that strained Walpole's tact and patience. But the latter understood the king's uncertainty and gullibility and, with the help of the queen and liberal doses of firmness and cajolery, generally managed to dissuade him from positions that he was initially unwilling to alter. George helped Walpole to sway Parliament to the support of his foreign and domestic policies and winked at governmental corruption proved by the opposition. After the death of Caroline in 1737 and the outbreak of war two years later, Walpole's position gradually deteriorated.

Against his better judgment Walpole abandoned his peace policy because of heavy pressure from the Parliamentary opposition, who bared case after case of Spanish cruelties and treaty infractions in pursuit of the Spaniards' right to seize contraband goods on British merchantmen in violation of the asiento and in an effort to break the Spanish trade monopoly in the West Indies. Spanish infractions of British personal and property rights and barbarities toward British seamen languishing in Iberian jails were not uncommon, but, after all, the Spanish were fighting for economic survival against large financial deficits, corruption in government, inflation, and a serious decline in their world trade. Walpole found it impossible by 1738 to convince the king and the opposition that the negotiation of a new Anglo-Spanish trade treaty was preferable to war in satisfying the numerous demands of merchants for redress of grievances. When Walpole threatened the Spanish with war, they paid nearly £100,000 in damages, but they refused to surrender their right to enforce the limitations of the asiento in Spanish home and colonial waters and to impound ships and men involved in smuggling.

The sentiment for war mounted steadily early in 1738, when Captain Robert Jenkins, a smuggler, appeared before Parliament. He recounted how, eight years earlier, the Spanish had boarded his vessel in the West Indies, maltreated his crew, hanged him from the yardarm, and torn off one of his ears. He kept it wrapped in a box and produced it dramatically to show the startled Commons. He demanded retribution, which Commons was only too willing to make by war.

The initial jubilation of Londoners, who lit bonfires and rang bells at the news of war the following October, soon turned to gloom because of the heavy losses suffered in the next two years. Admiral Edward Vernon successfully broke the Spanish defenses at Porto Bello, Panama, in November, 1739, but the expeditions against Cartagena (in New Granada) and Santiago de Cuba, characterized by heavy mortality from wounds and tropical disease, bickering among the commanders, and foolish tactics, were dismal failures. Although events had borne out Walpole's prediction in 1738 that "they may ring the bells now, but before long they will be wringing their hands," these costly setbacks inspired attacks on Walpole by the "Boy Patriots," the younger members of the opposition. Led by William Pitt (later earl of Chatham), Richard Grenville (later Lord Temple), and George (later Lord) Lyttelton, who allied with old Jacobites like Sir William Wyndham and angry politicians like Cobham and Chesterfield, they formed a powerful faction in Parliament, and their biting criticism of the conduct of the war and the corruption of the Walpole administration stemmed as much from personal political ambitions as from concern for the nation's welfare. The group gained prestige and power from the support of Prince Frederick (1707–51), the heir apparent. Like his father before him, he quarreled with the king following a vitriolic debate in Commons over the amount of his maintenance allowance (Walpole siding with the king against the opposition) and a silly squabble at the time of the birth of the future George III (1738), which resulted in the alienation of Frederick from court and his alliance with the Boy Patriots. Walpole, greatly fatigued and ill with a disease that was to kill him in 1745, fought back hard and weathered several Parliamentary votes of no confidence and strong criticism by the king and some cabinet members.

But with power gradually slipping from his hands, he reluctantly led Britain into the War of the Austrian Succession (1740–48), precipitated by the unfaithfulness of Frederick II of Prussia (d. 1786). As Emperor Charles VI had no son, he had taken in 1713 (renewed in 1725), by means of the Pragmatic Sanction, which Britain and other major European powers signed, the precaution of obtaining their promise to respect the territorial integrity of the Austrian Hapsburg dominions upon the succession of his heir, Maria Theresa (d. 1788). Frederick the Great, whose father had created the strongest army in Europe, ignored his country's pledge to Austria and carried on the Hohenzollern family tradition of territorial aggrandizement at the expense of weaker neighbors, by allying with France, Spain, Saxony, and Bavaria to dismember the Hapsburg Empire. Maria Theresa, for all her ability and fortitude, could not alone repel such a mighty military machine and consequently lost most of Silesia to Prussia in the first year. In order to prevent the resurgence of French power, maintain the Continental balance of power, weaken Spain, guard British commercial ties with the Austrian Netherlands, and protect Hanover, Britain entered the conflict on the side of Austria in 1741 without formally declaring war until 1744.

Walpole succumbed to the public clamor for war in 1741 as reluctantly as he had in 1739, when George II persuaded him to remain at his post. But the elections of 1741 left Walpole with a bare majority in Parliament, and opposition to him had mounted so fast that he felt constrained to resign the following February. George honored him with a peerage and continued to rely on his sage advice. The burdens of the prime ministership in that crucial hour devolved on John Carteret (Earl Granville), a brilliant classicist but a poor politician. He made a few changes in the cabinet, bringing in the brothers Henry Pelham and the Duke of Newcastle, and some Hanoverian Tories and Boy Patriots. But Carteret failed to please anyone, and in 1744, on Walpole's recommendation, the king replaced him with Pelham. Pelham, a taciturn plodder with enough ability to make do, and not at all like his fiery, pompous, and corrupt brother, ran the government for the next eleven years. Old adversaries of Walpole, such as Pulteney and Spencer Compton, and Newcastle of course, were Pelham's chief aides. William Pitt, the most talented politician of the day and an articulate critic of Walpole, got no cabinet appointment because George II resented his vociferous opposition to large-scale British troop commitments in support of Hanover.

The British Continental campaigns were confined almost entirely to the Low Countries, where the Dutch and Hanoverians fought as allies, and though generally successful were unprofitable in the long run. As well as heavily subsidizing Maria Theresa with £500,000 and supporting her cause with British-paid Hessians, the English and their allies fought two major battles, at Dettingen (June, 1743) and Fontenoy (May, 1745). In the first George II himself commanded the field army, the last English monarch to do so. He demonstrated amazing courage, encouraging his men and fighting alongside ordinary soldiers, and his presence undoubtedly had a salutary psychological effect on the troops and increased his popularity at home, but the English victory at Dettingen was attributable more to the faulty strategy of the French and to English bravery than to the king's generalship. The military position of the allies deteriorated during the next two years. Frederick II again invaded Bohemia and Silesia, and French troops commanded by the brilliant Marshal de Saxe pushed deep into the Low Countries, forcing Holland into the war. A large army defeated the combined English, Dutch, Austrian, and Hanoverian forces at Fontenoy. Shortly thereafter, following a victory over the Austrians, Frederick II withdrew from the war and signed the Treaty of Dresden (1745).

Britain continued to fight France on the high seas and in the colonies until the Peace of Aix-la-Chapelle in 1748. The navy did not distinguish itself. Thomas Mathews, commander-in-chief in the Mediterranean, had the opportunity to destroy the combined Franco-Spanish fleet bottled up in Toulon (February, 1744), but let it slip away because of confusion in battle plans. The Channel fleet under Sir John Norris did somewhat better; while it never engaged the French Brest fleet, it maintained command of the narrow seas, thereby preventing a planned invasion of England. In America the English colonials, without the help of British regulars needed more desperately in Europe, attacked the massive fortress of Louisbourg on Cape Breton Island, the only part of old Acadia left to France after the Treaty of Utrecht. Fearful of French privateers sallying forth from the fortress, which the brilliant military engineer, Vauban, had begun in 1720, Governor William Shirley of Massachusetts sent four thousand raw militiamen under William Pepperell in Commodore Warren's squadron to besiege it. As its walls were well-nigh impregnable, the colonials bombarded and blockaded the fortress for six weeks until the starving garrison capitulated in June, 1745, in the only significant battle of King George's War, as the War of the Austrian Succession is called in America. The French and British also clashed in India without decisive result, as we shall see below. The Treaty of Aix-la-Chapelle finally ended the war in all theaters. More a truce than a lasting peace, and broken within a decade, Aix-la-Chapelle gained nothing territorially for Britain or her colonies. It temporarily restored the asiento trade but otherwise reinstituted the *status quo ante bellum* with France, which got back hard-won Louisbourg and retained the Old Northwest to the consternation of New Englanders and ardent imperialists like Pitt. Viewed in historical perspective, this struggle was but one of several phases in the Anglo-French conflict from the outbreak of the War of the League of Augsburg in 1689 to the conclusion of the Napoleonic Wars in 1815. The most important aspect of this protracted confrontation, as succeeding pages will prove, occurred in the colonies of America and India and resulted in the maturation of the far-flung British Empire.

Events of ominous implication but little lasting consequence meanwhile drew the government's attention to a domestic crisis. Charles Edward (1720–88), the dashing elder son of the Old Pretender, seeing the bickering among the selfish Whig politicians, British troop concentrations in Flanders, and an Anglo-French war in progress, conceived the moment propitious for another rising to restore the Stuarts to the British throne. Only thirty years had passed since the Fifteen, but in that time the Jacobite zeal of most Scots had waned as the commercial prosperity they enjoyed under the Hanoverians grew. Even the Highlanders' sentimental attachment to the Stuarts had dwindled substantially and was more of a nationalistic affectation than a vibrant political ideal. Bonnie Prince Charlie, who landed at Eriskay in northwest Scotland in late July, 1745, with only seven companions, was therefore doomed to the fate of his father.

The Young Pretender made surprising progress during the summer, owing largely to the lack of capable military leadership of British regulars in Scotland, and the initial success of the rebel army, which swelled ultimately to nearly six thousand men. Leading his followers past the smaller force of Sir John Cope, who had blundered in abandoning Sterling Castle to move northward to Fort Augustus and Inverness, Prince Charles reached Perth in early September. There his principal general, Lord George Murray of Atholl, took command, and pressed on to Edinburgh, which capitulated after slight resistance on the seventeenth. Although most of the Lowlanders did not share the Highlanders' loyalty to Charles, he was in nominal control of Scotland despite his loss of the north and Aberdeen, and the neutrality of the isolated Western Isles. The crushing defeat and virtual annihilation of Cope's forces near Prestonpans on the coast road between Edinburgh and Aberdeen at dawn on September 21 encouraged Charles to invade northern England. He reconcentrated his army at Dalkeith, crossed the border on November 3, and captured Carlisle after a brief siege. The rebels then advanced to Derby (December 4), but decided to retreat on hearing of an approaching army led by Marshal George Wade and the Duke of Cumberland, the king's second son. The farther the rebels advanced into England, the more anxious they were to leave, and local inhabitants refused generally to aid them.

The Jacobite retreat to Glasgow, Sterling, and finally to Inverness during December and January, 1745–46, is a dismal record of gradual collapse brightened only by their victory over General Henry Hawley at Sterling and concluded by the final spirited battle of weary Highlanders against Cumberland's army on the rain-soaked moor at Culloden. Here, the prince's forces were routed in less than an hour, and the battered remnants of the proud rebel army fled to Inverness, where Cumberland butchered some of them. About 1200 Scots perished that bloody day. Bonnie Prince Charles left the scene at the last moment consistent with safety and gradually journeyed to the west coast where, five months and many harrowing escapes later, he boarded ship for France. In 1788 he died a hopeless drunkard in Rome; the direct Stuart line perished with the death of his brother, Henry, in 1807.

After Culloden Cumberland killed many of the rebels and burned their farms in a ferocious vendetta that the Scots understandably have never forgotten or forgiven, earning for himself the name of butcher. Parliament punished the rebel leaders, many of whom escaped abroad, by confiscating their estates, abolishing Scotland's archaic feudal social order, and depriving Highland chiefs of their authority. It also aroused further antipathy by forbidding Highlanders to wear tartans or serve in their own regiments. Pitt reversed the latter order during the Seven Years' War, and kiltie-clad Scots fought bravely for General Wolfe on the Plains of Abraham.

Before we consider this most important of Britain's wars for the expansion of empire, certain aspects of domestic history under Pelham must be mentioned. Despite the fact that the opposition had come to power partly on the strength of its criticism of Walpole's corrupt faction, Pelham's government did nothing to reduce corruption. If we take Newcastle, the Duke of Bedford, or the Earl of Sandwich as typical of his subordinates, in fact they compounded it. Party organization, if it existed at all in the modern sense, degenerated into more pronounced factionalism, lust for power, personal ambition, and compromise for gain. The king himself was not above political chicanery, condoning bribery, manipulation, and double-dealing for the sake of an electoral majority, a bill, or a policy. No one seemed willing to halt the spiral of corrupt politics: Walpole, after 1742 the honest broker and elder statesman, was dead; the Tories were divided and powerless; and Pitt and other potential reformers were grossly outnumbered in Parliament and relegated to inconsequential posts.

Under such circumstances one would not expect of the Pelham administration any outstanding legislation. Several acts passed under Pelham's leadership had social significance, notably Hardwicke's Marriage Act (1753), calendar reform (1752), a bill concerning the status of Jews (1753), and an Act regulating the production and consumption of death-dealing raw gin. The Marriage Act struck a sensible blow at the practice of impromptu, evasive, or convenient marriages without witnesses by often unscrupulous and derelict parsons, very often in taverns or the Fleet Prison in London. Henceforth the law required publication of bans and a formal ceremony conducted by a licensed Anglican priest before witnesses. The calendar was updated by adding eleven days and beginning the New Year at January 1 instead of March 25, a switch from the old-style Julian reckoning of time to the new-style Gregorian, in use throughout virtually all of western civilization since the papal reform of 1582. The Act for easier naturalization of Jews was repealed within a year because of the traditional prejudice against them.

Pelham also made some financial reforms and sought to perpetuate his faction's power. He consolidated the national debt of about £79,-000,000 and by 1757 had lessened the government's financial burden by getting bondholders to accept a reduction in interest rates from 4 per cent to 3 per cent. He was able to do this because of the increased public confidence in government credit in the expansive war economy. But such confidence was endangered by the death of Frederick, Prince of Wales, in March, 1751. Fearing that his political friends might try to dominate the heir apparent, George, who was only ten when his father died, and force him to dismiss the Pelham brothers, the latter successfully pushed through Parliament a regency bill. It provided that in the event of George II's death while his grandson was still a minor, a regency council headed by the Duke of Cumberland should govern. In the end, however, the bill was pointless, as George III was of age when his predecessor died in 1760.

Meanwhile European powers again drifted inexorably toward war. The dull and inconclusive War of the Austrian Succession had satisfied only Frederick the Great and Maria Theresa, who realized the goals for which they had gone to battle—respectively, Silesia and the recognition of her inheritance of the Austrian dominions. Europe languished in an uneasy state of armed neutrality from 1748 to 1756 while the colonial conflict between France and Britain grew in intensity. British interests on the Continent centered on the maintenance of the balance of power, primarily against France and secondarily against Prussia. Austria, on the other hand, feared France less than Prussia and felt certain that because of Hanover England would remain faithful to its alliance. But, as Austria sought the restoration of her power in the Germanies at Prussia's expense, and Britain fretted more about the intentions of France, the existing alliances ceased to have meaning. Consequently Britain and Prussia drew together while Britain and Austria moved apart. These tendencies toward new alliances became rigid when Prince Kaunitz, the Austrian chancellor, reversed the three-hundred-year enmity between his nation and France in a treaty so startling that historians have named it the Diplomatic Revolution. The Franco-Austrian entente abruptly ended any chance for Anglo-Austrian friendship: there was no coming to terms with a nation allied with Britain's colonial rival in America and India. Meanwhile Britain signed a defensive alliance with Russia and the Convention of Westminster with Prussia (1756).

British interest in India began in the 1580s, when the Levant Company financed trade expeditions to the subcontinent, and intensified under the aegis of the East India Company chartered by Queen Elizabeth in 1600. In the earlier seventeenth century, English entrepreneurs attempted to gain a firm foothold in Southeast Asia, the East Indies, and India, in competition first with the Portuguese, and later with the Dutch, who largely supplanted Portugal. The Dutch dominated the Indian trade to such an extent that, as late as the 1660s, English factors admitted Dutch control of a substantial part of the Indian and South Seas market. At the turn of the eighteenth century less than two thousand Englishmen, including dependents, lived in enclaves on both coasts—Calcutta, Madras, Bombay, and Surat—where they erected forts for storage and refuge against both the Dutch and Indians. They sought to keep on friendly terms with native princes, frequently winning their cooperation through liberal bribes of money and gifts. The increasing independence of rajahs and viceroys following the collapse of the Great Mogul Empire after the death of Aurungzeb in 1707, played into the hands of the Dutch, English, and French, the last of whom had recently entered the Indian market. Although theoretically subject to the Moguls, most of whom after Aurungzeb were corrupt and ineffective rulers, local princes partitioned the Empire into practically or entirely autonomous principalities, the most important of which were the Mahratta Confederacy, Oudh, and Bengal in the north, Nizam's Dominions in the central interior, and Mysore and the Carnatic in the south. The French East India Company had been founded under Louis XIV, gained a foothold at Pondicherry south of Madras, and Chandernagor in Bengal, and grew powerful in the first two decades of the eighteenth century. They replaced the Dutch, whose Indian and American colonies and trading stations collapsed as a result of their commercial wars with England in the mid-seventeenth century and their massive struggle for survival against Louis XIV.

In 1744, to take advantage of the anarchy in the Mahratta Confederacy, Mysore, the Carnatic, and the Nizam, then being ravaged by wars between petty princes, France declared war on England. By that time both the French and the English East India companies had successfully extended their purely commercial ventures into political hegemony in their dependencies. The English Company, which earned more than £2,000,000 in profits for British merchants and stockholders in 1710–50, was encouraged by Parliament to expand its military and legal authority into the hinterland. The French did likewise, and the inevitable clash of interests provoked war. France was fortunate to have in its service Joseph Dupleix (1700–73), who was appointed governor of Pondicherry in 1741. He was a brilliant administrator and devoted imperialist who was anxious to add India to the French crown. Since his arrival in 1720, he had been busy befriending nawabs (native rulers), intervening in their affairs, replacing them if they resisted French demands, and training a native army officered by Frenchmen. As there was no need to disguise his ambitions after 1744, Dupleix launched a combined land and sea attack on Madras, which capitulated in June, 1746. The French would have kept all the Carnatic but for the Treaty of Aix-la-Chapelle that required their surrender of Madras in exchange for Louisbourg in Canada.

Dupleix continued to implement his plans for control of India during the lull in Europe in 1748–56. The resumption of hostilities in India in 1750 was occasioned by his intervention in the disputed successions of rival nawabs in the Carnatic and the Nizam, resulting in the establishment of French puppet regimes that endangered British interests. This time, however, the East India Company had a soldier as capable as Dupleix to guard its welfare. Robert Clive (1725–74) had come to Madras in 1744 at the age of nineteen after an unhappy and dissolute adolescence, during which he had displayed an uncontrollable temper and a suicidal tendency. This inconspicuous youth, who was ignored by his superiors, fought courageously in defense of Madras in 1746 before being captured and briefly imprisoned at Pondicherry. When Dupleix threatened to conquer the Carnatic two years later, Clive, whose remarkable abilities as a soldier had by then been rewarded with an army commission, led a successful assault on its capital at Arcot, and in 1752 unseated the French puppet, Chanda Sahib, after the battle at Trichinopoly. As Clive had not been content in India, he decided to exploit his military reputation by standing for Parliament, but he failed to win a seat, depleted his modest savings, and returned to India to make his fortune. Meanwhile the French authorities erred grievously by dismissing Dupleix for his failure in the Carnatic. His successor was repulsed throughout the south, which became virtually a British province.

These events in India, though of momentous consequence to Britain, probably interested Englishmen less than the death of Pelham in March, 1754. He had governed the country well through mastery of Parliament and the smooth operation of administrative machinery, but his death left a gap that George II had no trouble filling. It was virtually a foregone conclusion that Newcastle should succeed his brother: the king liked and trusted him; he had wide political experience and knew how to manage the Commons; and he had helped to formulate policies to Hanover's advantage. His being a peer, however, excluded him from the Commons, where vital business requiring a high-ranking cabinet spokesman was conducted. Newcastle searched for a member of Parliament to serve that purpose, and made the worst choice imaginable. There were several able candidates whom he might have picked: the Scotsman William Murray, a party legal expert; Henry Fox, a fiery debater and frequent critic of the Pelham administration who was a close friend of Cumberland's; and William Pitt, who had tried unsuccessfully to placate the king by supporting Pelham. All gained cabinet posts, but none got the Commons leadership, which went, illogically, to a talented but politically inexperienced diplomat named Sir Thomas Robinson. He soon proved unable to sway the Whig backbenchers and was replaced. Meanwhile Newcastle failed to manage his cabinet and it split into factions. Henry Fox resigned the principal secretaryship after a quarrel with the prime minister; Pitt disliked being merely paymaster-general, criticized Newcastle's ineffective foreign policy (which had failed to stop Frederick the Great's invasion of Austria, suffered the shock of the Black Hole of Calcutta, and lost Minorca and Oswego, all discussed below), and was dropped from the cabinet; and other talented administrators like Grenville and Henry Legge, Chancellor of the Exchequer and vice-treasurer of the navy respectively, resigned in the wake of similar criticism. Hardwicke, Lyttelton, and other unimaginative cronies of Newcastle remained in the reshuffled cabinet, but its unpopularity and ineffectiveness, as well as the growing conviction that only Pitt could restore British honor in wars on three continents, compelled the king, who tried every means to avoid it, to appoint him chief minister in November, 1756. Except for three months in the following spring, Pitt held office until October, 1761.

Only firm adherence to his convictions and the sting of his skillful oratory had prevented Pitt (1708–78, later earl of Chatham), son of a prosperous merchant, from attaining supreme political power before the age of forty-seven. He had been selfish, factious, and overbearing as a young man sent to Parliament from the pocket borough of Old Sarum, but he grew into an incorruptible, fearlessly frank, and brilliant administrator. He had a nasty temper, abundant self-confidence, astounding vigor despite a painful case of gout, and a stern countenance that disarmed opponents. There was no mistaking the tall man with the generous aquiline nose and deep-set eyes that glowed like hot coals when he was angry or speaking passionately. Then, according to his granddaughter, "nobody could look at him in the face." He ranks among the finest orators in the history of Parliament. No faction could count him a friend, and party allegiance sat on him lightly. Long a bitter critic of costly commitment in Continental affairs for the sake of Hanover, he was convinced that Britain's future lay in the colonies. He set his sights on unconditional victory over the French in America, supported Clive in India, and helped Frederick the Great weaken France in Europe. He also reorganized the armed forces, put efficient and capable young officers in command, and made certain that they received adequate supplies. Although Pitt left no mark on domestic legislation, he had qualities of mind and character that transcended the pedestrian politics and diplomacy of his day and aimed at enlightened statesmanship.

Pitt assumed office six months after the declaration of war against France in Europe (May, 1756) and two and a half years after the outbreak of hostilities in America (May, 1754). Of the two theaters, America was by far the more important. The French in Canada and the English colonials had glared suspiciously at each other over an undefined boundary that stretched across half the continent from the Atlantic to the Mississippi. Since the establishment of Canada as a royal province in 1663, a succession of able governors, intendants, and bishops had put the colony on a sound economic basis. They had encouraged immigration and large families that increased the population to 65,000 by 1754. They had also sent Jesuit missionaries and hardy explorers into the upper Great Lakes, and the Ohio and Mississippi valleys all the way to the Gulf of Mexico, and built a chain of fortresses at key points like Lake Champlain, the Sault, and the future sites of Kingston (Ontario), New Orleans, St. Louis, and Pittsburgh.

These forts threatened to contain the settlement of English colonials east of the Appalachian Mountains at a time when they had begun to trade profitably in the hinterland of what later was called the Old Northwest, comprising the territory bordered by the Appalachians, the Ohio, the lower Great Lakes, and the Mississippi, all of which they claimed by right of original sea-to-sea charters. The economic, political, and social development of the English settlements since the Restoration had been phenomenal. The thirteen colonies (the last, Georgia, was established by royal charter in 1733 as a social experiment devised by James Oglethorpe) had 1,250,000 persons, including about 250,000 slaves. Thriving commercial centers had grown at Philadelphia, Boston, New York, and Charleston despite the restrictive Navigation Acts and the ineptitude of the colonial office and its agents in America. Whether farmers, craftsmen, professionals, or merchants, the American colonials were eager for victory over their French counterparts.

A quick glance at a map of North America in 1754 would suggest that the French were in a commanding geographical position, but their actual control of the interior was tenuous. Militarily they had the advantages of a fine militia based on the seignorial system and supported by well-trained and experienced veterans of the European wars, central command under the governor at Quebec, and deep respect for authority. The English colonials, on the other hand, were hampered by differences among thirteen separate governments, lack of sympathy for their problems in London (the Pelham and Newcastle ministries paid them little attention), and a poorly trained and organized militia that had previously refused to fight beyond its colonial borders and had little support from British regulars, whose officers generally lacked both zeal and ability. Therefore the outcome of the struggle was by no means a foregone conclusion.

The French and Indian War began over a dispute in the Ohio country. In 1749 some Virginians had formed the Ohio Company, which acquired a huge tract of land and the right to trade and colonize in the upper Ohio River area. Their agent, Christopher Gist, explored it and brought in a few settlers who were soon followed by Pennsylvania fur traders. This alarmed the French, who strengthened their forts at Niagara and Detroit and erected others, among them Fort Duquesne at the confluence of the Allegheny and Monongahela rivers. Virginia Governor Robert Dinwiddie countered by sending the young surveyor George Washington to learn the French plans and advise them that they had trespassed on Virginia territory. As they refused to withdraw, Dinwiddie sent Washington with 150 militiamen into the region, where they erected Fort Necessity before being driven out in a skirmish with 1500 French and Indians. These developments led Newcastle to dispatch a thousand regulars commanded by the stubborn, elderly General Edward Braddock to Virginia early in 1755. Without experience in frontier warfare or sense enough to heed Washington's advice on tactics, he led about 1900 regulars and militia toward Fort Duquesne, and was intercepted by the French before reaching it and defeated at the Battle of the Wilderness, where he and 1400 of his men perished. New Englanders, supported by Indians and a handful of regulars, balanced these reverses by victory at the Battle of Lake George (September) and occupation of the west shore of the Bay of Fundy across from Nova Scotia (where Halifax had been founded in 1749 to offset Louisbourg). The French Acadians of Nova Scotia, ignored for generations by their countrymen at Quebec and now considered a security risk by the British governor, were arrested, herded onto ships, and transported to the four corners of the thirteen colonies. Most of their farms were burned, and few of the 6000 to 10,000 exiles ever returned to their Canadian homeland.

The year 1756 was black the world over for the British. The western Mediterranean island of Minorca fell first. As the cabinet was worried about a French invasion of England, it kept the main body of the navy in the Channel, and sent Admiral John Byng in command of an undermanned and poorly equipped squadron to relieve the French siege of Port Mahon. Byng went reluctantly, encountered the French fleet that was guarding the rear of its besieging army, and retreated after deciding in consultation with his officers that he could do nothing to help the beleaguered English garrison. His dismal return to Portsmouth embarrassed Newcastle and angered Parliament and the merchants, who demanded the admiral's head for surrendering Minorca and thereby imperiling British trade. Though Newcastle was clearly to blame for this failure, Byng was court-martialed and executed for cowardice in the face of the enemy. Three months later (July), Suraja Dowlah, the Bengalese pro-French nawab, stormed the fortress of the East India Company at Calcutta, promised its valiant survivors leniency if they capitulated, and then allowed them to be suffocated to death in the stifling heat of a small cell called the Black Hole. Finally, Montcalm, the brilliant new governor of Canada, outwitted the dilatory and incompetent English general (Loudoun), and captured Forts Oswego and George. He thus removed the British threat to the French settlements along the upper St. Lawrence. King George was therefore forced to agree with Pitt that the government had been guilty of mismanagement.

Not even Pitt's administrative genius could transform defeat into victory overnight. The British consequently suffered further reverses in 1757 and early 1758 while he was busy reorganizing the forces and putting new life into the supply lines to America, Europe, and India. Fort Henry fell to Montcalm in August, 1757, and a British assault against Ticonderoga was repulsed with very heavy casualties. In Europe, Frederick's Prussians fought alone against the overwhelming superiority of the combined Austrian, Russian, and French armies, lost the Battle of Kolín, failed to prevent the French invasion of Saxony, and withdrew from Bohemia. Meanwhile the Duke of Cumberland's Hanoverian army lost to the French at Hastenbeck, abandoned Hanover, and agreed to disband. Clive provided the only ray of hope when, in January, 1757, his army of one thousand English and two thousand sepoys (native troops) recaptured Calcutta and pursued Dowlah's forces to Plassey, where Clive decisively defeated them in June.

The tide finally began to turn in Britain's favor late in 1758, and crested in all three theaters of war in 1759. Clive consolidated British strength in Bengal, attacked the French forts in the Carnatic, and had by 1761 forced the French to abandon their headquarters at Pondicherry. In America, Generals Amherst and Wolfe, typical of the fresh young talent recruited by Pitt, took Louisbourg while Colonel Bradstreet and General Forbes captured Fort Frontenac and Fort Duquesne. Pitt devised a bold scheme to attack Canada from three directions: Amherst was to advance up the Lake Champlain–Richelieu River route to Montreal by way of Ticonderoga and Crown Point; another English army was to proceed toward Montreal from the west via Niagara; and Wolfe, though gravely ill, was to lead nine thousand men transported in ships commanded by Admiral Saunders, who knew the fog-shrouded St. Lawrence, to the citadel at Quebec. The dramatic story of Wolfe's conquest of the Canadian capital at the cost of his life and that of Montcalm on the Plains of Abraham in September, 1759, is familiar enough not to need description here. With the fall of Montreal shortly thereafter, Canada in its entirety became a part of the British Empire. Meanwhile, in Europe, the renewed strength of the navy foiled French plans to invade England. Led by Admirals Boscawen and Hawke, the navy defeated the French fleet at Quiberon Bay, blockaded the major French ports, and carried supplies and money to help Frederick humble the Austrians and force Russia's neutrality. Thus the Year of Victories, 1759, set the pattern for the remainder of the war.

The war was concluded in 1763 by the Treaty of Paris. France surrendered to England all of Canada, including Acadia (Nova Scotia) and Cape Breton Island, but retained the right to fish for cod on the Grand Banks off Newfoundland as well as possession of the islands of St. Pierre and Miquelon in the Gulf of St. Lawrence. England also acquired the French West Indian islands of Dominica, Tobago, Grenada, and St. Vincent, but, to the dismay of the English sugar planters in the Caribbean and their friends in Parliament, who thought the acquisition of any sugar island more important than the entire frozen wasteland of Canada, France kept Haiti, Guadaloupe, and Martinique. England also kept Hanover and Minorca, acquired Florida from Spain in return for Cuba, and procured the French slave depot at Senegal in Africa. The *status quo ante bellum* was restored in India, with the stipulation that the French dismantle their fortifications and withdraw their garrisons. In 1768, however, the French East India Company collapsed and the reorganized British Company, buttressed by support from the home government, became masters of much of India.

But the two principals in the English war effort, Pitt and George II, did not enjoy the fruits of victory. George had died on October 25, 1760, and was succeeded by his grandson, George III, a contentious man with a mind of his own who forced Pitt out of office in favor of his friend, John Stuart, Lord Bute. The king and Bute were so anxious to conclude the war speedily that they demanded less from France and Spain than the overwhelming British victory warranted. Spain, for instance, though it had entered the war late on the French side and lost Havana and Manila to the Royal Navy, kept Cuba and the Philippines. Nevertheless, the series of events that had begun to shape the boundaries of the British Empire in 1689 had finally matured in 1763. Thereafter Britain remained at peace for twelve years, while George III tested the significance and endurance of the Glorious Revolution and the growth of cabinet and Parliamentary authority.

10

The Reign of George III to 1793

George III succeeded to the throne in October, 1760, at the age of twenty-two and ruled through a personally tragic and internationally tumultuous period of sixty years in which the Industrial, American, and French revolutions transformed contemporary society. So much has been written about his boyhood, character, intentions, and policies that an accurate assessment of his reign is difficult. Generations of capable historians have been trapped by the seeming logic of the Whig interpretation of history, an aspect of which emphasizes the iniquity of authoritative kings and their supposedly corrupt councilors since the early seventeenth century as opposed to an essentially righteous and allegedly victimized Parliament that struggled to break the chains that fettered liberty. George III and his ministers from 1760 to 1782, most of whom were Tories, have been given a bad press that originated in the untruths and half-truths first enunciated by their opponents and kept alive by later historians. Since the 1930s, however, the massive researches of eminent scholars like Sir Lewis Namier, J. H. Plumb, Herbert Butterfield, and Romney Sedgewick have forced a sweeping revision of the standard Whig interpretation of George III's reign.

The old standard interpretation, in its most extreme form, went something like this. George, a backward and dutiful child, was tied until early manhood to his ambitious mother's apron strings, during which time she trained him in the art of kingship. His bedtime stories consisted of excerpts from Bolingbroke's *Patriot King*, a primer for strong kings. As soon as he could, George III dismissed the Whig ministers because he believed them to be factious, self-interested, and corrupt politicians bent on limiting the royal prerogative, and restored incompetent and sometimes traitorous Tories (some of whom had been

Jacobites) to high office, appointed a succession of dim-witted marionettes as chief ministers, and grossly mismanaged governmental affairs at home and in the Empire. As a result, the American Revolution succeeded, splitting the Empire that the Whigs had labored assiduously to create. In the meantime George attempted to restore absolute monarchy, subvert the constitution, destroy personal liberty, and humble Parliament. That he failed in this wicked design, and that Britain and its Empire did not entirely crumble was due to the perspicacity and lofty aims of William Pitt the Younger, Edmund Burke, Charles James Fox, and others. They stopped George and once more set Britain on a true course to democracy.

This reasoning contains an element of truth, but it has been grossly distorted to accommodate the Whig point of view. What sort of man was George III? Clever or cunning he certainly was not, though he was a capable monarch. In 1761, he married the stodgy Charlotte of Mecklenburg-Strelitz, who made a man of him and with whom he cohabited out of a sense of duty to produce numerous heirs to the throne. George, heavy-faced, bug-eyed, and thick-lipped, had difficulty even as a child concentrating on any task for very long. He could not read until the age of eleven. His love for his mother and close attachment to Lord Bute was not unusual for a child, much less for one who felt insecure, was possibly retarded, suffered several periods of mental aberration after 1765, and disliked making decisions. His need for reassurance and constant advice from trusted friends was a weakness that he overcame after his marriage. George liked to convey a strong image, but he was often uncertain of himself, and an alter ego like his mother or Bute or his wife was a comfortable crutch on which to support his flagging courage at crucial moments. He had admirable qualities—he loved his family, took responsibilities seriously, and adhered faithfully to the precepts of the Anglican Church—but he was also arbitrary and narrow-minded. He alienated his subjects, could not get along with a succession of able chief ministers or many members of Parliament, and never learned the meaning of compromise.

Unlike his three predecessors, George III wanted to be an integral part of the government. He refused to take a back seat to any chief minister and, in fact, ran the government with a firm hand until the catastrophe of the American Revolution. His ministers during that time were not permitted to manage affairs as George I and George II had allowed Walpole, Pelham, and Newcastle to do. But there was nothing unconstitutional in George III's insistence on making policy personally, for the crown was still the fountainhead of all legal authority, and the office of prime minister had not yet assumed constitutionally those independent powers that were to characterize it in the next century. Although there was a great deal about his personality and politics that gave umbrage to his subjects, the first English-born Hanoverian monarch had no such scheme as that the Whig historians have ascribed to him—to subvert the constitution, or reinstitute absolutism, thereby destroying what Parliament and the cabinet had achieved since the Revolution of 1688–89.

George was finally able to dismiss the Whigs by 1770, after which the Tories had the ascendancy until 1830. He did so because to him the Whigs represented the system of corruption, factionalism, and selfish opportunism that characterized politics from Walpole to Newcastle. These characteristics weakened the Whigs and played into the king's hands during the 1760s and 1770s. The issues that had originally united them—opposition to the policies of Charles II and James II, the achievement and perpetuity of the Protestant monarchy, and the profitable conclusion of the War of the Spanish Succession—had become meaningless by the mid-eighteenth century; these goals had been realized, but new ones had not been formulated. The present concept of party as a political organization that formulates platforms, supports candidates for election, and hopes to implement programs by legislation was almost unknown in the eighteenth century. Whig politicians consequently went their separate ways in search of power and privilege and the means to implement private and factional aims such as control of Parliament and financial and other reforms. The most distinguished, able, or powerful Whig leaders gathered support in and out of Parliament, kept its allegiance through friendship, control of rotten and pocket boroughs, bribes, bargaining, and the distribution of an extensive patronage at both national and local levels. Leaders of Parliamentary factions vied for the prime ministership, cabinet posts, and royal favor. Both Whigs and Tories included several factions, each having distinct aims and principles. Party labels sat lightly on the backs of members of Parliament who frequently voted against their factional leaders' wishes, crossed party lines, or gave their support for a variety of reasons to one or another policy or bill.

The Tories had been eclipsed politically for a long time. Their heyday had been the period from the Restoration to the death of Anne. They generally supported a strong executive against the encroachments on it by the legislature, and the preservation of traditional religious, economic, and social institutions against Dissenters, businessmen, and reformers of one kind or another, and fought for power with the Whigs. The latter took advantage of the internecine struggle between the Oxford and Bolingbroke factions, which had the upper hand when George I became king in 1714, and profited from the association of some Tories with the Jacobite rebellions in 1715 and 1745. The Tory factions recovered some strength by proving the corruption of the Walpolian system, but they made little headway because George II distrusted them. They were uncertain about principles and at George III's accession were fraught with as much factionalism as the Whigs. As George hated the Whigs, the Tories were the only alternative. If they were to retain power, they had to carry out his wishes or suffer the consequence of dismissal. This is precisely what happened from 1761 to 1783, when a succession of Tory ministries, interrupted only twice by nominal Whig governments headed by Grenville and Chatham, collapsed. George III himself was a master of political manipulation, developed a following in Parliament called the "King's Friends," reasserted his legal place as head of the government, and temporarily halted the development of the cabinet system and ministerial responsibility to Parliament. The lack of political organization among either Whigs or Tories enabled him to be in effect his own prime minister for twenty-three years.

George III became king in the middle of the Seven Years' War, which by that time had turned in favor of Britain and her allies. Yet his subjects were weary of casualty lists and heavy taxes and misunderstood Pitt's monotonous pleas for total victory. They demanded peace, the sooner the better, and so did the king. Therefore the great war minister lost the confidence of his colleagues, his countrymen, and his king, and resigned in 1761. It was practically a foregone conclusion that the king's tutor and friend, the Tory Lord Bute (1713–92), who had been a cabinet member since 1755, would succeed Pitt. Bute concluded peace as quickly as possible. It has already been pointed out that while Britain obtained a great deal of territory, it amounted to much less than many believed she rightly deserved. The treaty was consequently unpopular in Britain: the Whigs complained of Bute's acceptance of terms that Pitt had rejected in 1759; Parliament became suspicious of collusion between Bute and George III, and some members of Parliament made wisecracks about the prime minister's Scottish ancestry. Bute, ill and harried by gibes, catcalls, and rotten vegetables hurled at him by irate Londoners, resigned early in 1763.

George III had difficulty finding an able Tory with influence in Parliament to succeed Bute because Whig factions still controlled it. He settled reluctantly on the nominal Whig George Grenville for several reasons: Grenville headed the largest faction in the Commons; his brother-in-law, Pitt, though still piqued at being asked to resign on the eve of victory, agreed not to oppose the new ministry; Grenville had been a member of Whig cabinets before 1763, but he had not been closely associated with the old Whig power structure characteristic of the Walpole, Pelham, and Newcastle administrations, and had quarreled earlier with Pitt, whom George III heartily disliked. Moreover, should Grenville falter, Bute was ready to give advice (which he did until he and the king disagreed in 1766 over the reappointment of Pitt and the membership of the cabinet). The Grenville ministry lasted only until 1765, but in that short time it was forced to face the damaging criticisms of John Wilkes and others, provoked the American colonies, and alienated the king by passing the Regency Bill.

Wilkes, the son of a middling London merchant without wealth or an impressive genealogy to aid him, rose to notoriety almost overnight by publishing a series of scurrilous attacks on the government's foreign policy, the conduct of the king's ministers, and the role of monarchy in a journal entitled *The North Briton Review*. Hitherto Wilkes's only advantage had been the help that powerful factionalists like Lord Temple and the rakish Earl of Sandwich had given him. In 1763, with Temple and Pitt at his side, this arrogant, uncomely, fulminating member of Parliament for Aylesbury, who had more gall than talent and could match insults with the best, stirred a hornet's nest that neither the king nor Grenville, who became prime minister in the midst of it, had sense enough to let lie. In No. 45 of his *Review* (April, 1763), Wilkes took to task in uncompromising terms a speech from the throne in which the unpopular Treaty of Paris was defended. He denounced its terms, censured Bute, then the prime minister, for accepting them, ridiculed his Scottish ancestry, accused the Tories of maladministration and Jacobitism, and reminded George III of his solemn responsibility to his subjects to appoint honorable and dutiful ministers.

These charges infuriated George III, helped to force Bute's resignation, and provided the Parliamentary opposition with a rallying cry against royal policies. Apparently convinced that the punishment of Wilkes would enhance the crown's prestige and silence the opposition, George instructed the secretary of state to arrest the authors, publishers, and printers of No. 45 by authority of a general warrant, an order for arrest that specified no one by name. Consequently Wilkes and forty-nine others went to prison on a charge of seditious libel. As the legality of a general warrant, which had occasionally been employed in the past against printers, was questionable, Lord Temple secured a writ of habeas corpus from Chief Justice Charles Pratt of the Court of Common Pleas, a friend of Pitt. Pratt ordered Wilkes's release on two grounds: that a general warrant was illegal and that a member of Parliament was immune from arrest for libel. This favorable decision threw the London mob into a frenzy of jubilation, for they interpreted the exoneration of Wilkes as a stroke for liberty. It also cast the king in the worst possible light, and forced him to use underhanded means to trap Wilkes. Spies dogged him, a friend of the king seriously wounded him in a duel, and royal agents discovered among his private papers an obscene burlesque of Pope's illustrious *Essay on Man*. Whether Wilkes wrote the *Essay on Woman* is problematical, but he did have it printed for private distribution among his coarse friends. On this flimsy evidence, Commons having meanwhile expelled him, the crown instituted a libel suit against him in the Court of King's Bench. When the case was heard, he had already fled to France to escape punishment and to recover his health. He remained in France for four years.

Although politicians did not dream of the consequences of the new defense policy that Grenville introduced, it was the most significant issue facing his ministry in 1763. The Treaty of Paris made Britain the strongest colonial power: its dominions stretched from the Mississippi to the Ganges and from the Arctic Ocean to the Equator. Except for Spanish Louisiana and a few French islands, the Union Jack flew over much of North America. But the French intended to recover their lost territory, and hostile Indians, many of whom had been allies of France in the late war, roamed the trans-Appalachian region. Grenville's solution to this problem raised a furor that initiated events culminating in the American Revolution.

He regarded a uniform Indian policy as essential if conflict between tribesmen and colonials was to be avoided and trade with the back country was to prosper. The thirteen separate American colonial governments had differed previously on so many issues that the likelihood of agreement on an Indian policy was remote. The record of the colonies' participation in the wars since 1689 was discouraging, and the French and Indian War had been no exception. The militia had frequently refused to fight beyond their colonial borders, had expected

British regulars financed by the imperial government to defend them, and had demanded reimbursement for most of their military expenses. Merchants grew rich from smuggling sugar, indigo, coffee, and other goods from the West Indies in violation of the trade acts, and had even traded with the enemy in wartime.

Colonials also had begun to cross the Atlantic watershed into the Ohio and Kentucky country several years before the outbreak of war in 1754, and larger numbers of former militiamen who had seen its rich land followed them after the war. Their settlements threatened peace with the Indians of the region, with whom British commissioners had made treaties promising that colonials would not trespass west of the Alleghenies. This and other factors led the tribesmen in 1763 to band together under Pontiac, the Ottawa chief, for attacks on western forts from Niagara to Detroit. Grenville therefore decided that a moratorium should be put on westward expansion, as Indian agents in the field had suggested earlier. The Proclamation of 1763 forbade settlement west of the Appalachian watershed and ordered homesteaders already there to abandon their farms. The Americans deeply resented and apparently misunderstood the intent of this temporary expedient at a time when the imperial government allowed the newly conquered French Canadians to keep their seignorial system, Roman Catholic religion, social customs, and civil law. Such leniency was the more objectionable to the Americans because of their long commercial, religious, and territorial rivalry with the Quebeçois.

The defense of the sprawling British Empire since 1689 had cost a great deal of money. England's colonial wars, financed largely by British taxpayers of the landed, professional, and mercantile classes who either sat in Parliament themselves or had powerful spokesmen there, had helped to enlarge the national debt by 1763 to about £130,000,000. Hitherto the cost of American defense had been borne in peacetime primarily by the colonials, and in wartime by the imperial government. But the colonials, for reasons such as particularism, ennui, niggardliness, and lack of genuine interest in Empire problems, had rarely fulfilled their military obligations to the satisfaction of the imperial government. Grenville therefore reasoned that they should pay part of the cost of supporting a permanent garrison of ten thousand British regulars. But Grenville realized that attempts by Pitt and others to collect taxes in the colonies had been unsuccessful because of smuggling, and the laxity, inefficiency, dishonesty, and absenteeism of customs agents, some of whom stayed in Britain and hired substitutes, and that it had cost more to collect the duties than the money realized from them. What he failed to foresee, however, was the distinction that the Americans made between duties imposed to raise revenue, and duties that simply regulated commerce. The Sugar Act of 1764 was lenient, though Parliament expected that it would bring in more revenue than the expired Molasses Act, which had not been closely enforced. The Sugar Act largely duplicated the provisions of the Molasses Act except that the duty was cut in half and new duties were placed on West Indian items including pimentos and coffee. The Stamp Act of 1765 stipulated the use of government stamps on virtually all legal documents, ship's papers, and printed matter.

The Americans stoutly resisted the new duties. They refused to pay them, continued to smuggle goods from the West Indies, mistreated customs and stamp agents to the point that many resigned, made Non-importation Agreements, and argued at the Stamp Act Congress in October, 1765, at New York that it was illegal for Parliament to tax them unless they had representation in it. This came as a shock to Grenville even though he had expected some opposition. The Sugar Act had purposely been made more lenient than the Molasses Act, and, before the passage of the Stamp Act, Grenville had asked the colonial assemblies whether they had any objections to it and, if so, what alternatives they might suggest. With but one or two exceptions, the Americans did not bother to reply.

Neither the cabinet nor Parliament took kindly to the Americans' sensitivity to direct taxation. In fact, it struck most British politicians as novel and bizarre, for colonials had never been entitled to direct Parliamentary representation, and large blocks of British taxpayers had no direct representatives in Parliament, and yet they did not grumble. Notwithstanding the argument of the American James Otis in a pamphlet entitled *The Rights of the British Colonies Asserted and Proved* that it was unconstitutional to tax Americans without the consent of their representatives, British constitutional theorists had long held the view that all members of Parliament, regardless of the individual constituency for which they sat, collectively represented and guarded the rights of all British subjects, whether in England or in the colonies. Most Americans, on the other hand, had been accustomed to direct legislative representation in their colonial assemblies and simply did not see the British viewpoint. They also apparently believed that the Stamp Act, which required payment directly into the Exchequer in hard currency, scarce at the time, was but the first in a series of punitive taxes aimed at weakening them economically when they were struggling against the effects of a dwindling postwar market, the restrictions of the mercantilist system, and the shortage of specie. It is also indubitably true that, although Americans received support from sympathizers in Parliament, notably Pitt, Charles James Fox, and Edmund Burke, most British politicians felt that the leaders of the more than two million colonists were naïve, backward bumpkins who knew next to nothing about self-government or finance. Such paternalistic attitudes undoubtedly blinded officials to the growing political and economic maturity of the Americans and hurt whatever chance they had at Westminster for a fair hearing of their grievances. Nor did most politicians realize that, during the period of neglect of colonial problems by the Pelhams, the Americans had grown accustomed to regulating their own internal affairs, and had been moving rapidly toward what mid-nineteenth-century theorists called responsible government. They had advanced beyond the point of accepting per se the dictates of the imperial government that had lost touch with their problems, cared little about their aspirations, and still viewed them primarily as consumers of British manufactures, decided what they might produce and with whom they could trade, and expected them to pay a third of the cost of their defense when they felt perfectly capable of defending themselves. Although American political leaders admitted the sovereignty of Parliament over the colonies, they had reached a stage of development that was inconsistent physically and psychologically with dependent status and were eager to make their own decisions.

Grenville resigned in 1765 in the wake of popular and Parliamentary criticism of his handling of American defense policy and the prosecution of Wilkes, which backfired and lost him the invaluable support of Pitt and the Newcastle Whigs. Grenville also had no patience with the king and would not cooperate with him during his first mental lapse. George III, who ran hot and cold with virtually everyone, developed an intense dislike of Grenville that was vented on the occasion of the latter's innocent indiscretion in excluding the king's mother from a list of prospective regents (enumerated in the Regency Bill) in the event that he again lost his sanity. Pitt should have been the logical successor to Grenville, but George III would not have him. He therefore appointed another Whig, the young, able, but inexperienced Lord Rockingham, who pieced together a makeshift cabinet composed of Newcastle, his friends, and younger politicians like the Duke of Grafton and Charles James Fox. Pitt's refusal to accept a post hurt the new ministry and it lasted less than a year. All it succeeded in doing was to rid the country forever of general warrants and to repeal the Stamp Act. By that time not only the old party affiliations but factional loyalties as well had broken down so that any semblance of orderly political organization was shattered. In such a crisis the king, knowing Pitt's hatred of cliques, and confident that he could rely on the Great Commoner's deep respect for the crown if not his affection for the crowned head, finally convinced him to form a cabinet. Although they had often disagreed on policy and as often exchanged polite barbs, they shared an abhorrence of factionalism and corruption that was sufficient to bridge their differences.

Pitt, whom George III elevated to the earldom of Chatham, felt confident that he could make right his predecessors' wrongs. But the task proved too much for him. Primarily because of poor health induced by a lifetime of ceaseless labor, he took the Lordship of the Privy Seal, a sinecure, and allowed his admirer and protégé, the Duke of Grafton, to be titular head of cabinet. Tormented by gout and nervous prostration that kept him away from his desk for nearly two years, Pitt resigned in 1768. During this time his physical infirmities and dispiritedness sapped his strength and quenched the zeal that had formerly sustained him, captivated his audiences, and unnerved his opponents. As he was unable to devote careful attention to the issues he set out to resolve, namely the advancement of British influence throughout the world, the humiliation of France and Spain as colonial powers, and the solution of the American defense problem, these devolved upon his cabinet appointees, principally Grafton, the Earl of Shelburne (secretary of state in charge of colonial affairs), and Charles Townshend (Chancellor of the Exchequer), all talented and unjustly maligned administrators who unfortunately made serious blunders in America that Pitt's closer supervision might have averted.

Spain's possession of South America and several Caribbean islands, and French footholds in the West Indies, Newfoundland (the fisheries), and India, as well as their combined strength in Europe through the Family Compact that allied their Bourbon governments, worried Pitt. The Duc de Choiseul, Louis XV's able chief minister, resented his country's losses in the Seven Years' War and made plans to recover them, by invading England if necessary. He realized that Britain could be humbled only at sea, and for this reason he doubled the size of the French navy, drastically reorganized its administrative and service personnel, and mustered what was left of the country's nearly exhausted financial resources. Charles III, the Spanish monarch, detested Britain and was eager to help France destroy its commercial and naval superiority in the hope of recovering Minorca and Gibraltar.

Whether Britain could forestall the fulfillment of these plans was by no means certain in 1766–70. Parliament repeatedly cut defense budgets. The American colonies seethed with discontent. The East India Company had insufficient resources to resist a French attack in India. Colonial administration was fraught with corruption, absenteeism, mismanagement, and negligence. Despite these weaknesses, Pitt and his cabinet did what they could to bolster British defenses at home and abroad. They built additional ships, erected coastal fortifications, and strengthened Fort Pensacola in Florida as a bulwark against French and Spanish power in the West Indies. They also sent a British garrison to the Falkland Islands to avert the expansion of Spanish control over them. But Pitt failed to prevent the French invasion and annexation of Corsica, which threatened British naval supremacy in the western Mediterranean, to collect payment of ransom from Spain for Manila, or to force the demobilization of Dunkirk, the last two being issues left over from the Peace of Paris.

British successes or failures in thwarting French and Spanish ambitions hinged partly on the reaction to its policies by the principal Continental powers that had been its allies in the late war. For one reason or another, Pitt's overtures to Russia, Prussia, Sweden, Denmark, and the United Provinces for the establishment of a Grand Alliance against the Family Compact fell on deaf ears. Russia was then preoccupied with eastern European affairs, and later (1772) joined with Prussia and Austria to dismember Poland. Prussia was wrestling with economic problems, seemed unmoved by the resurgence of French power, and was piqued at Britain for deserting its alliance in 1762 by making separate peace with France. Friendship with Denmark, Sweden, and the United Provinces, all weak powers, was little help without the cooperation of the before-mentioned great powers, and a *rapprochement* with Austria was beyond hope. Therefore Britain, stripped of virtually all the Continental alliances on which it had relied for a hundred years to divert French and Spanish attention from the colonies, stood alone against their still formidable military might.

As France and Spain hoped to take advantage of continued discontent and possible revolution in the American colonies, the solution to this vexing problem was of the utmost importance. The repeal of the Stamp Act, coupled as it was with the equally offensive Declaratory Act, had not salved the Americans' irritation, and serious differences in the Grenville and Chatham cabinets over the extent to which the colonials should be forced to comply with the Trade and Quartering Acts lessened the chance of a sensible and mutually satisfactory settlement. The crisis over the Stamp Act had no sooner passed than another arose as a result of a request by General Thomas Gage, British military commander in the thirteen colonies, that the New York Assembly fulfill its obligations under the Quartering Act to supply and house his troops. When, early in 1766, the Assembly refused to comply fully with the request and, in the following December, declined to make any appropriations whatsoever, it was prorogued by command of Parliament, the order to take effect on October 1, 1767. This decision had come hard. Shelburne, generally a friend of the colonials, had been unable to make a decision about New York's recalcitrance without the approval of Pitt who, because of poor health, was unable to give it careful attention so that the decision finally had been reached primarily through the insistence of Townshend. He was also responsible for the imposition of new import duties (June, 1767) applicable to the colonies on tea, glass, lead, paints, and paper and added another measure that eased the collection of the duties by means of writs of assistance, vice-admiralty courts, and customs commissioners stationed at Boston and elsewhere. In doing so, Townshend took into account colonial sensitivity to internal taxation as well as the loss of nearly £500,000 in revenue in Britain because of a reduction in the land tax. These Acts, clearly intended to raise revenue rather than to regulate commerce, stirred protests from several New England assemblies and led to the formation of new Nonimportation Agreements and revolutionary associations.

Thereafter the American colonial and imperial governments drew farther apart. Parliament insisted that it had every right to legislate for the colonies while the latter, ably defended by spokesmen such as Samuel Adams of Boston and John Dickinson of Pennsylvania, argued with equal logic that, although Parliament could do so, it was nevertheless unconstitutional to impose duties primarily for revenue or to deny the right of assembly for opposing them, as in the case of New York. The situation grew tenser when the Sons of Liberty began to drill in anticipation of a possible war and, in February, 1768, Adams and the Massachusetts House of Representatives sent out a circular letter, advising the other twelve colonial governments of their efforts to resist the new duties and asking that they do likewise. Additional Non-importation Agreements covering ports from Boston to Charleston hurt English mercantile interests to such an extent that in April, 1770, the North ministry repealed all the duties except the one on tea.

The Pitt-Grafton ministry had also to contend with the return of Wilkes early in 1768 on the eve of the general elections to Parliament. He expected help from Grafton and Pitt, but, as they were then ministers of the crown, they dared not give it, although Lord Temple lent a hand. Wilkes therefore fell back on his enormous popularity with the London mob, which still regarded him as the champion of liberty against the "tyranny" of George III. Wilkes's portrait hung in the London Guildhall; several towns passed resolutions honoring him; others gave him money; and his name inspired cheers among the discontented. Sentiment for Wilkes was to a considerable extent a manifestation of a reaction against the crown and its ministers in an uneasy time of unemployment, high prices, and poor harvests that bred widespread unrest, strikes, looting, and rioting, especially in London. Wilkes became a national hero simply because he dared to criticize royal policy and its agents.

Despite his outlawry and conviction of libel in 1764, Wilkes stood for Parliament in the City of London, lost, but was shortly thereafter elected for Middlesex. This was possible because the election period covered several days and varied from district to district by as much as two weeks. His election posed a legal question for the Commons and a threat to royal policies. George surely would be affronted by Wilkes's admission should the Commons decide to seat an outlaw and a libeler. As Parliament would not convene until the following November, Wilkes voluntarily surrendered to the authorities in the hope of removing these impediments. Justice Mansfield of King's Bench returned a verdict that rescinded the outlawry but upheld the conviction for libel, and sentenced Wilkes to imprisonment for twenty-two months. As he had considerable support in the Commons and had strengthened his popular image as a martyr by going to prison, the crown would have been well-advised to let the matter die. In refusing to do so, it brought on a political crisis that damaged its prestige, helped Wilkes, and increased opposition to the government. The king put pressure on his friends in the Commons, got them to refuse to seat Wilkes even though he could not have been legally excluded on the libel conviction alone, and censured him for another piece of scurrility that he had written in prison. Undaunted and unabashed, he was elected twice more by Middlesex, and each time was refused his seat. Finally, despite the fact that the crown's candidate received only a minority of the votes cast in a fourth Middlesex election, that man was admitted over Wilkes, the winner. It must have irked George III that, after Wilkes was released from prison, he served a term as Lord Mayor of London, was elected to Parliament in 1774 and seated without opposition, and later succeeded in having expunged from the *Journal of the House of Commons* the record of his crimes and exclusions.

Meanwhile the Grafton ministry had collapsed in January, 1770, amid the clamor of opposition to colonial policy, the Wilkes case, popular unrest, and Pitt's condemnation of all three. Although pale and weak, he emerged from retirement to accuse Grafton of betraying their friendship, to excoriate the Commons' subversion of the popular mandate in the Middlesex elections, and to condemn the Townshend duties. Pitt thereby unwittingly threw in his lot with numerous other and often less capable or sensible government critics who formed an opposition of heterogeneous elements of English society from members of Parliament to unemployed draymen. Although they lacked any semblance of organization, they maintained a more or less constant resistance to the policies of the North ministry.

Lord Frederick North (1732–92), the last in a succession of Georgian chief ministers without the courage to resist the overbearance of the king, replaced Grafton and held office for twelve troublesome years during which he repeatedly offered his resignation only to be dissuaded as often by the king. A corpulent, lethargic, and homely man who was uncomfortable in the limelight and disliked heavy responsibility, North had had considerable governmental experience since 1759 in the Treasury office before becoming paymaster in Chatham's second ministry and Chancellor of the Exchequer following Townshend's sudden death in 1767. Despite admirable virtues such as affability, loyalty, and domesticity, and a flair for administration, North has received harsh treatment from Whig historians, possibly because he followed George III's lead in provoking the Americans to the point of revolution and in slyly manipulating the Commons, which during his ministry included about two hundred "King's Friends." Revisionist historians have lately attempted to burnish North's much-slandered name, which resulted not so much from what he did as from what he did not do. He had considerable ability, but rarely measured up to it. He conceived his role as merely that of king's agent for government business in the Commons, whose prestige fell in proportion to its unwillingness to act independently of the crown. North was at his best when managing the Commons, which is precisely why George III kept him on for so long. He was careful also never to stir the volcanic depths of the king's explosive temperament which meant, of course, that he gave in to George, and hence remained on cordial terms with him. George III and North proved an unbeatable combination that weathered the best the opposition could muster against them until the catastrophe of British defeat in the War of the American Revolution brought North's downfall and George's surrender of personal political hegemony.

North inherited the invective heaped on the Grafton ministry and the crown by the author of the *Junius Letters,* which appeared regularly between 1768 and 1772 in the *Public Advertiser,* one of several anti-government London newspapers. The identity of Junius has never been established positively, but it has been assumed he was Sir Philip Francis, Pitt's underling in the War Office and later the vilifier of Warren Hastings. The *Letters* are notable for their intimate knowledge of public business, superb style, and malicious sarcasm, which has rarely been equaled in the annals of British political literature. Junius found sadistic pleasure in the misfortunes of his adversaries, for he rejoiced over the agonizing death of the princess dowager, the infidelity of Grafton's wife, and the waywardness of one of George's sons. The *Letters* cover a variety of topics including Wilkes, American taxation, representative government, popular unrest, gossip, and defamation of character. The most famous one (December 19, 1769) splattered the king with such cold-blooded venom that it led to the trial before Justice Mansfield of the publisher and printers in lieu of the author, whose anonymity protected him. Mansfield ruled that editors could be prosecuted only for printing libelous news, not for the libel itself, and juries in that and similar trials refused to find the accused guilty of it.

Contemporaries might well have thought the country at the brink of civil war. Wilkes, Junius, and other critics inflamed the passions of the mob that milled uncontrolledly in the streets, committed acts of violence against persons and property, and even threatened North's life. As the London civic authorities generally sympathized with the opposition, they did little to quell the disturbances, which forced the crown to use troops to restore order with billy clubs and bayonets, thereby adding credence to popular outcries against government repression. Meanwhile saner critics in the Commons were laboring more effectively. Foremost among them were Edmund Burke (1729–97) and Charles

James Fox (1749–1806), young close friends of often identical political views who were beginning to make their marks in political circles. Burke, the Dublin-born son of a lawyer, was a gifted orator and articulate political theorist who first entered public life as Lord Rockingham's secretary in 1765 after several years as editor of the *Annual Review.* Imbued with a deep sense of moral purpose, he was moderate, constructively critical, and circumspect except with regard to the interests of his family, for whom he unashamedly sought political favors. His sympathies lay from the first with the American colonials, whom he defended in the Stamp Act crisis and in their opposition to the Townshend duties. In 1770 he authored some *Thoughts on the Causes of the Present Discontents* in which he argued that politicians had drifted from the noble, principled goals of party into factionalism; that the king had contributed to the collapse of party organization by using patronage to win friends and thereby subverted the British constitution; and that the restoration of party, which he mistakenly assumed had actually existed since the Glorious Revolution, together with economic reform, would restore the delicate constitutional balance between the crown and Parliament and eradicate corruption. Fox also sided with the Americans and was a constant thorn in North's side. A large man without many scruples, Fox frequented gambling tables where he squandered a fortune bequeathed by his famous father, Henry Fox, Lord Holland. The younger Fox was such a jovial and endearing rake, however, that he won many friends who quickly learned that beneath his carefree frolicking lay the keen mind and tenacity of a statesman. His charming personality, family background, and connections with the aristocratic Whig families that comprised most of the Rockingham faction started him on a political career that was enhanced by his intimate friendship with the Prince of Wales and his uncommon oratorical talents.

The early years of the North ministry were marked by a succession of provocative domestic issues which it easily overrode because George III controlled a comfortable plurality in the Commons and because the opposition was too badly divided to offer more than willy-nilly resistance. The ministry's baneful dismissal of popular outcries over the Middlesex election issue and the *Junius Letters* lowered its prestige but did not alter its political mastery. Accusations of government corruption were legion, but George III nevertheless kept control of the lower House by liberal gifts of money and of offices to those who supported his proposals, and by taking away honors, posts, and pensions from those that opposed them. He also weathered the severe criticism that arose over the indiscretion of three members of the royal family. The Duke of Cumberland, his brother, was a convicted adulterer who secretly married the widow of a Yorkshire squire. Another brother also wed a commoner, the illegitimate granddaughter of Sir Robert Walpole; George's sister, the queen of Denmark, was banished to Hanover by her husband for committing adultery. George III, impeccably virtuous in his own private life, took steps to ensure that no other scandals would besmirch his family name and to protect the blood line from further pollution by commoners. Parliament passed the Royal Marriage Act (1772), which forbade the marriage of any descendant of George II before the age of twenty-five except by the king's permission, and required the approval of the privy council after that age, with at least a year's notice of intent to marry. The opposition tried to kill the bill on the grounds that George III had no right to regulate the personal lives of his relatives, but he carried it through Parliament by threatening to take reprisal on members who voted against it.

The opposition did manage to make constitutional reforms that lessened the crown's influence in Parliament. The Election Act of 1770 entrusted decisions in disputed Parliamentary elections to a committee of fifteen members chosen largely by lot, thereby overthrowing the old system by which decisions were reached in the committee of the whole. The purpose of the reform was obviously to forestall a recurrence of the Middlesex elections fiasco. A second reform, which arose from a dispute between newspapers and Parliament that involved several lawsuits, resulted in Parliament's tacit permission for public reporting of its debates. This decision broadened freedom of the press and rendered members of Parliament far more susceptible to public criticism. The publication of division lists (the equivalent of yeas and nays) in the Commons and Lords was not permitted legally, however, until 1836 and 1857 respectively.

These reforms, important though they were at the time, were mere pinpricks to the North ministry as compared to colonial problems. Aside from North's reform in 1773 of the British East India Company's governance of India and a serious dispute with Ireland, both discussed below, the American colonies commanded most of its attention. Parliament's repeal of all the Townshend duties except the one on tea had only temporarily lessened the radical coloniais' anxiety over taxation or their determination to resist any form of British domination. Although leading Americans like Benjamin Franklin and John Dickinson cautioned moderation in the belief that independence would come peacefully as a consequence of colonial economic growth and greater political maturity, other colonials, who were representative of all classes from backwoods farmers to sophisticated lawyers, demanded immediate satisfaction of their grievances against the imperial government, by revolution if necessary, and scoffed at British attempts at conciliation.

Hotheads like Samuel Adams spurred them on, as did newspapers from Boston to Charleston. In some communities like Boston and Newport, Rhode Island, where the presence of customs houses and Admiralty courts provoked public resentment, British soldiers came to blows with colonials. In March, 1770, for instance, there occurred the so-called Boston Massacre in which the guard stationed at the Customs House killed four or five Americans after severe provocation. Afterward the soldiers were successfully defended by John Adams. Another incident occurred on the Atlantic shore near Providence, where a British revenue cutter, the *Gaspee*, which had run aground, was burned by a crowd of Rhode Islanders who got off scot free when a board of inquiry failed to get evidence on which to convict them. Nor did Americans take kindly to the defamation of Franklin's character in an investigation of the Whateley Letters, which the governor and his subordinate in Massachusetts had written in 1773–74 to Thomas Whateley, a member of Parliament who strongly resisted American opposition to taxation. The letters subsequently fell into Franklin's hands and he forwarded them as a point of information to the Massachusetts Assembly. Its petition for removal of the Massachusetts officials was reviewed by the privy council which, instead of taking the issue seriously, made a mockery of American attitudes and humiliated Franklin. Meanwhile some influential Americans including Patrick Henry, Thomas Jefferson, and Samuel Adams organized intercolonial Committees of Correspondence to formulate plans to stir revolutionary sentiment and to lead the revolution itself should circumstances warrant.

In the midst of such mutual distrust and recrimination, the North ministry blundered badly in imposing a tax on tea in May, 1773. The tax was intended to serve a triple purpose: to maintain the principle that Parliament could legally legislate for the colonies; to help to defray the cost of American defense; and to aid the East India Company whose English warehouses were crammed with surplus tea largely because Americans refused to buy it, which put the Company in financial straits. It had customarily brought its tea to England where it paid a tax and reshipped the tea to America where another tax was levied.

The government relieved the Company of its duty in England and authorized it to collect a threepenny tax per pound from American consumers. Under this arrangement the colonists could buy tea at a retail price lower than either the price of smuggled tea or the price in England, where consumers paid a heavy twelvepenny tax per pound. North undoubtedly had the interests of the Company uppermost in mind, but he was also not unaware of the king's insistence that "there must be one tax to keep up the right." The Americans interpreted the purpose of the tax in the latter sense. When the cargo of tea reached Boston aboard the *Dartmouth,* a band of men arrayed as Indians boarded her on December 16, 1773, and heaved it overboard. Tea shipped to other American ports either lay unpurchased or was returned to England. This news infuriated the king and North and irritated Chatham and Burke who, like several moderate American leaders, suggested voluntary reparation before taking reprisal. But Parliament would not listen to such conciliatory talk and, taking cognizance only of the king's instructions in favor of punishment, at once passed the four Coercive Acts, known in America as the "Intolerable Acts." The first, which closed the port of Boston on June 1, 1774, to all commerce, threw thousands out of work and caused a serious food shortage. The Massachusetts Government Act amended the colony's charter by forbidding special town meetings, augmenting the governor's authority, and transforming the colonial council from an elective to an appointive body, the net result of which was to deprive the colony of a great deal of independent political authority. The third, an Act for the Impartial Administration of Justice, empowered colonial governors to transport Americans accused of murder to England for trial on the ground that local juries would be too subjective in determining innocence or guilt. The fourth, the Quartering Act, applicable to all the colonies, allowed military commanders to requisition buildings to house their troops.

The Quebec Act of 1774, although technically not part of the coercive program, was regarded in the American colonies as equally "intolerable." Consistent with the leniency shown the French Canadians since the conquest of 1760, Parliament, upon the recommendation of Canadian Governor Sir Guy Carleton, established a permanent government in Canada that permitted them to keep their religious and economic institutions and social customs. Such concessions to a conquered people against whom the thirteen colonies had for long been fighting, seemed manifestly unfair to them. Their greatest displeasure arose, however, from an article of the Act which extended the boundary of Quebec Province south to the Ohio River, an area to which several colonies had claim by virtue of their original charters and into which American settlers had moved in substantial numbers. It was therefore paradoxical that an administrative decision by the North ministry that was eminently just and sensible for the Canadians, and that later ensured their loyalty to Britain during the American Revolution, was one of its contributing causes.

There probably had been a point at which compromise on the American question was still possible, but by 1774 that point had been passed. The colonials had talked a good case in opposition to British taxation and, before long, they talked themselves into an attitude that ruled out compromise. Of course, the road to war was hardly a one-way street. The British were often ignorant of the intensity of American feelings, gave little serious consideration to their grievances, were unwilling to face the fact of their growing economic and political maturity, made ill-advised decisions, and went along with George III's refusal to consider compromise. Perhaps the succession of ministries after 1764 misjudged the effectiveness of the conscious minority of radicals, patriots, indebted landowners, merchants, smugglers and others who underwent a metamorphosis of attitude from simple resentment of British overbearance to a desire for independence. The imperial government had repeatedly and almost uniformly backed down in the face of American hostility to its tax reforms. Taxes were undoubtedly at the root of dissent that had many offshoots but, by 1774 it had become merely a primary excuse for rebellion that in all likelihood would have erupted sooner or later regardless of what Britain tried to do to avert it.

The Coercive Acts by which the North ministry had hoped to overpower American resistance backfired and impelled the colonies into combined action. Delegates from twelve colonies, mostly radicals chosen by Committees of Correspondence, met in the First Continental Congress at Philadelphia in September and October, 1774, to plan a course of action. The debates that centered on the Coercive Acts and means to overcome them showed that revolutionary sentiment was not confined to those directly affected by them nor to the lower and middle classes, but that it had supporters in every part of America who were representative of all social classes and economic levels. Voting by colonial units rather than individually, a system that destroyed the influence of the few conservatives present, the Congress adopted the Suffolk Resolves (the work of a committee in Suffolk County, Massachusetts), which proposed the following actions: that the Coercive Acts were unconstitutional and should be disobeyed; that the colonies form and arm militia; that Nonimportation Agreements be renewed; and that the British government take cognizance of their Declaration of Rights and Grievances in which they stated the colonial case against taxation without representation in polite but firm and uncompromising language. In effect the Congress, speaking authoritatively if not officially for all disgruntled Americans, set its face resolutely against Britain by issuing what amounted to a warning of sterner action should the Intolerable Acts not be quickly repealed.

North interpreted the Declaration as it had been intended, but his eleventh-hour attempt at conciliation was not seriously considered by the Americans and was weakened by an unsympathetic Parliament that rejected the impassioned pleas for moderation by Burke and Chatham. The most that Parliament would allow was the right of individual colonial assemblies to approve regulatory taxes levied under their own authority to pay for defense and the costs of colonial administration. Meanwhile Massachusetts and other colonies prepared for rebellion. General Gage, operating under permissive authority from the secretary of state to compel the observance of the Coercive Acts, and confronted with the threat of armed rebellion, dispatched Major Pitcairn's troops to Concord, Massachusetts, to confiscate a cache of rebel arms. Met by a much smaller band of militia at Lexington (forewarned by Paul Revere and others), Pitcairn repeatedly ordered their dispersal, but as they did so, someone fired a shot that set off volleys from both ranks. The British later seized the arsenal at Concord, but their return journey to Boston was marked by heavy casualties from American snipers. Shortly thereafter the colonial militia began the siege of Boston.

The rebellion soon degenerated into full-scale war whose ultimate outcome no one on either side could predict in the spring of 1775. Within a few months, however, it became clear that only complete independence from Britain would satisfy the radicals and secure widespread support. The Second Continental Congress at Philadelphia in May strengthened revolutionary sentiment and created a continental command for George Washington, who transformed a makeshift militia into a respectable army that forced General Howe to withdraw from Boston to Halifax and attacked Canada in a two-pronged invasion up the Lake Champlain–Richelieu River corridor. Although the invasion failed, it proved American military capabilities and raised colonials' morale. Morale was further heightened by Thomas Paine's electrifying pamphlet *Common Sense* (January, 1776), in which he laid aside the sham of personal loyalty to George III whom he called the "Royal Brute," blamed him personally for American troubles, suggested the absurdity of nearly three million people being politically dependent, and advocated independence. It was formally declared six months later. The Declaration's argument in defense of the natural rights of man and its accusations against George III, particularly the violation of the "social contract" with the American people, relied heavily on the ideas of European theorists like Locke and Rousseau and was as much an attempt to win foreign sympathy for the revolution as it was a *raison d'être* for independence.

The military history of the revolution, while fascinating in itself and vital to the study of American history, can here be discussed but briefly. Despite the disparity in population between Britain and the thirteen colonies and Britain's technological and financial superiority at the beginning of the war, both belligerents labored under serious handicaps. Britain had an experienced army of between 30,000 and 40,000 regulars including German mercenaries, but the problem of supplying them by transports taking from three to nine weeks to cross the Atlantic was never satisfactorily solved. The British profited to some extent from the military and financial support of American Loyalists, but relatively few actually bore arms and the others, hampered by the close surveillance of their communities and harassed by their patriotic neighbors, were either unwilling or unable to lend much assistance. The British also faced the difficulties of the vastness of the fighting front stretching along the coast from Maine to South Carolina, for it forced the deployment of troops in small numbers and made troop concentrations for battle exceedingly difficult. They exhibited an inadequate knowledge of American topography and were unaccustomed to fighting the kind of frontier war familiar to the enemy. The military leadership of Generals Howe, Burgoyne, and Clinton was adequate but unimaginative and often timid, and Lord Cornwallis, although more aggressive and able, proved inadequate to the task. Finally, the British had control of American waters until 1778 simply because the colonies had no navy to speak of. Elsewhere, however, the Royal Navy was kept busy trying to counter repeated threats to the Empire and shipping by France, Spain, and Holland, which took advantage of the revolution to declare war on their old colonial and commercial rival in the hope of recovering their colonies and a larger share of world trade.

The Americans had an equal number of problems. Although man for man as capable marksmen as the British and equipped with more accurate rifles, they lacked experience, adequate training and discipline, and generally refused to serve long-term enlistments. Washington, although nominally in command of as large an army as that of Britain, could never be certain of an adequate force at any time and in the winter of 1776–77 led only three thousand shivering and hungry men. American officers were no better strategists than their English counterparts: certainly neither Ethan Allen, Horatio Gates, Nathanael Greene, nor even Washington made reputations as brilliant soldiers. They lost as many battles as did the British officers, yet they were able to muddle through tight situations on which the enemy failed to capitalize. Strong French military and financial support after 1778 and the bravery of foreign officers like Lafayette, Pulaski, de Kalb, and von Steuben aided the revolutionary cause and won sympathy for it in foreign capitals.

The first two years of the war produced no significant gains on either side. Howe, assisted by Burgoyne and Clinton, stiffly resisted the siege of Boston for almost a year and won the bloody Battle of Bunker Hill (June, 1775) before evacuating his forces to Halifax the following March. The theater of war shifted thereafter to the Middle Atlantic colonies. Howe occupied New York City after successfully assaulting Staten Island and Long Island and compelling Washington to withdraw, first to Manhattan and later, in October, 1776, to White Plains, where the British took the fort and pursued the enemy across New Jersey to the Delaware River. Howe and Cornwallis then retired to winter at New York, leaving small Hessian and British garrisons at several New Jersey towns. Seeing his opportunity to counterattack when the enemy was weakened, Washington recrossed the Delaware, captured Trenton in a surprise attack in late December, and outsmarted Cornwallis, who had hurried to meet him, at Princeton in January, 1777.

The Americans broke the stalemate in October, 1777, at Saratoga, the turning point in the war. The British surrender at Saratoga resulted partly from an apparent lack of coordination between Burgoyne and Howe, to whom Lord Germain, secretary for war, had sent separate and conflicting instructions. Burgoyne had visited England over the winter of 1776–77 to seek approval of a plan for a decisive northern campaign aimed at knocking New England out of the war. It called for a pincer movement by two large armies, one moving down from Canada by way of Lake Champlain to the upper Hudson River and the other up from New York City through the Hudson Valley for a merger at Albany. That done, the British could concentrate their forces in the Middle and South Atlantic colonies where American strength was weaker. Germain authorized the northern campaign but also sanctioned Howe's attack on Philadelphia in the mistaken belief that it was of great strategic value despite the frontier character of a war that was not seriously affected by the control of cities. Having taken Philadelphia, Howe was then to join forces with Burgoyne at Albany. Burgoyne began his march in June and advanced according to plan, but the expected help from Howe never materialized. Howe's fifteen thousand troops were delayed by Washington, who forced the Battle of Brandywine Creek, in early September so that the assault on Philadelphia was delayed by two weeks, and afterward attacked the British post at Germantown. This delay spelled defeat for Burgoyne. He met stiff resistance all along his advance but pressed on despite supply problems and the hazards of the wilderness in upper New York, to which his troops were unaccustomed. On October 13 he was surrounded by a much larger American force at Saratoga and forced to surrender. Four days later he signed a humiliating agreement by which close to six thousand British soldiers were taken to Boston and transported to Britain on condition that they would never again serve in America.

The significant American victory at Saratoga had even greater political consequences. Lord North at once made peace overtures to Silas Deane and Franklin, who were in Paris negotiating a treaty. He later sent commissioners headed by the Earl of Carlisle to Philadelphia with a truce proposal already approved by Parliament. Considering its earlier intransigence, Parliament made surprising concessions by agreeing to suspend the American revenue Acts passed since 1763 and to impose no new taxes so long as the Continental Congress accepted a reconciliation. But Congress rejected the commissioners' repeated requests for a conference and unofficially informed them that it would discuss nothing short of complete political independence and the withdrawal of all British troops. American firmness sprang partly from the confidence created by Saratoga and partly from the ratification of two treaties with France in February, 1778.

While there was some prerevolutionary sentiment in France, its decision to ally militarily and commercially with the colonies was based more on the opportunity such an alliance presented to crush British power than on sympathy for the American cause. The treaties provided for French military and financial assistance, a mutual favored-nation agreement that opened the ports of the signatories to each other's goods, a guarantee against making separate peace with Britain, and a recognition of each other's exclusive territorial interests in America and the West Indies. This alliance, obviously of enormous help to the Americans, transformed a civil war within the Empire into a world war that strained British resources to the limit, forced Britain to divert money and ships from the American theater, and closed lucrative markets to British goods, which in turn weakened its already strained economy. In addition, to make matters worse, in 1779 Spain declared war on Britain, and Holland did likewise the following year. Several northern European states including Sweden, Denmark, and Russia formed the League of Armed Neutrality, by which they subscribed to the rule laid down by France that neutral ships carrying noncontraband goods to belligerents were not subject to seizure. Britain was caught on the horns of a dilemma, for it could not accept this rule without lending assistance to the colonies, which benefited from trade with Baltic countries, yet it dared not resist the rule forcibly for fear of losing Baltic markets and supplies and making new enemies.

The Franco-American alliance forced the transfer of most British fighting ships stationed in American waters to the English Channel to counter the threat of French invasion, and to the West Indies to guard British territories and commerce from French men-of-war and American privateers. In 1779 a French fleet cruised defiantly in the Channel and the British garrison at Gibraltar withstood a long Spanish blockade. In the following year the French captured Dominica, Grenada, and St. Vincent in the West Indies despite the stiff resistance of Admiral George Rodney's fleet. French ships generally encountered little opposition along the American coast, ran several British blockades to land troops, and induced General Howe to evacuate his men from Philadelphia and Newport. Having been repulsed in the north, General Clinton, Howe's successor as commander-in-chief, and Cornwallis moved the center of British activity late in 1778 to the southern colonies where American forces were weaker and Loyalist sentiment was believed—erroneously—to be strong. The British won numerous small battles of little significance in Georgia, Virginia, and the Carolinas from December, 1778, to May, 1780. Savannah and Charleston, South Carolina, also fell to British arms before Nathanael Greene could stop the spiral of American defeats. Meanwhile Clinton moved thirty thousand men north to New York and Rhode Island to wage campaigns against Washington's undernourished and bedraggled troops, and to prepare for the anticipated landing of several thousand Frenchmen commanded by Count Rochambeau.

Cornwallis remained with less than two thousand men to hold the Carolinas against repeated American attacks. As the Americans were being supplied and reinforced from Virginia, he moved north into its back country. Fearful, however, of straying too far from his supply line at the coast, he concentrated his expanded army of seventy-five hundred on a peninsula between the York and James rivers called Yorktown. Anticipated reinforcements led by the defector Benedict Arnold were intercepted by Washington's combined American and French army, which took a position blocking Cornwallis's rear while Admiral de Grasse, fresh from victory over the British in the Battle of Chesapeake Bay, barred Cornwallis's escape by sea. Trapped and outnumbered two to one, Cornwallis surrendered on October 19, 1781. Sporadic fighting, principally in the south, continued for another year, but the war was practically over after Yorktown. At sea the Royal Navy took a beating in 1781–82 at the hands of the French and Spanish who captured St. Kitts and Tobago in the West Indies, West Florida, and Minorca in the Mediterranean.

These reverses brought down the North ministry, which had been losing support in Parliament since Saratoga. North had offered his resignation in 1779 but had stayed on at George III's insistence and bore the brunt of steadily mounting criticism of the war. The king, blind to the hopelessness of victory, tried to prolong the war while North, sensitive to mounting sentiment for peace, resigned in March, 1782, after defeating a no-confidence vote in the Commons by a margin of one vote. Despite the king's objections to Rockingham, whose Whig followers had pushed through a resolution in 1780 that "the influence of the Crown had increased, is increasing, and ought to be diminished," he was nevertheless invited to form a ministry. Fox and Shelburne joined it as foreign secretary and home secretary (responsible also for the colonies) respectively, and immediately quarreled over which of them should direct the peace negotiations that began in May, 1782. They also differed over peace terms: Fox wished to recognize American independence immediately and to write separate treaties with the United States and France; Shelburne believed that American independence should be a part of an over-all peace settlement lumped together in one treaty. Rockingham therefore had to make the most of a difficult situation by continuing the war in the hope of winning a victory or two that might strengthen Britain's position at the bargaining table. Admiral Rodney provided one at the Battle of Les Saintes Islands in April, 1782, which saved Jamaica for the Empire, and the Mediterranean fleet provided the other by relieving the Spanish siege of Gibraltar. But the Fox-Shelburne quarrel, other domestic problems discussed below, and the king's obstructiveness prevented Rockingham from doing more.

The death of Rockingham in July, 1782, relieved George III of an unwanted minister whom he had reluctantly appointed when Shelburne refused to serve. Political instability continued for another year and a half under two short-lived ministries—that of Shelburne and the Fox-North coalition—before William Pitt the Younger ended it in December, 1783. Fox did not succeed Rockingham because he was a constant critic of strong monarchy and was therefore unacceptable to the king. Shelburne, who served until February, 1783, was less objectionable to George III because of his cautious defense of monarchic prerogatives and his denunciation of factionalism and corruption. His administrative skills and superior intellect commanded wide respect, but his self-righteousness and zeal for reform alienated many members of Parliament without whose support no ministry could long survive. Fox ruined Shelburne's chances for ministerial longevity by refusing to accept a cabinet appointment and did what he could to impede peace negotiations. Shelburne concluded a preliminary treaty with the Americans in January, 1783, but, despite Parliament's acceptance of its terms *in toto* several months later, the opposition forced Shelburne to resign by rejecting them. Fox and North then forgot their differences long enough to conclude final peace treaties with France and the United States.

The Treaty of Paris with the United States, and the Treaty of Versailles with France and Spain were both signed on September 3, 1783. In the first, Britain recognized the independence of the United States and the extension of its boundaries to the Mississippi and the Great Lakes; admitted American fishing rights on the Newfoundland banks and in the Gulf of St. Lawrence; and agreed that both nations might freely navigate the Mississippi. The Americans promised that Congress would "recommend" to the state legislatures the full restoration of confiscated or destroyed Loyalist property. In the second treaty, Britain confirmed France's possession of the islands of St. Pierre and Miquelon in the Gulf of St. Lawrence, and ceded the right to cure fish in the region, several West Indian islands including Tobago, Senegal in Africa, and trading rights in India. Spain acquired Minorca and East and West Florida. The Anglo-Dutch treaty of 1784 granted Britain the Dutch trading posts in India and admitted British trade to the Malay Archipelago.

While waging the American war, Britain had had to face an agonizing religious problem at home, agitation for home rule in Ireland, and a serious administrative problem in India. The religious problem was highlighted in the Lord George Gordon riots of 1780. At the time, the people of London were in an irritable mood occasioned by unemployment, hunger, and the agitation produced by Wilkes, the *Junius Letters,* and the American Revolution. In addition, although nearly a century had passed since the last large-scale Protestant animus toward Catholics had been openly displayed, the embers of anti-Catholicism still smoldered in fervent Protestant hearts. The Roman Catholic Church in England had lost ground during the eighteenth century, and many of its members, no longer widely subject to religious persecution, had lost the zeal that persecution often inspires in a minority. As the number of practicing Catholics gradually declined, they tended to congregate in rural districts or smaller urban communities in the west and north especially, where private chapels in the country houses of Catholic aristocrats served as centers of worship. London contained many Catholics, but it was no longer the hub of Catholic life as it had been in the seventeenth century. So long as Catholics made no issue of their religion, they could be reasonably certain that the local authorities would not invoke the penal laws against them.

The situation suddenly changed when the North ministry proposed to set aside the prohibitive religious oaths required of officeholders and others since the early seventeenth century, ostensibly to allow Catholics to serve in the army when recruits were sorely needed for the American war. Parliament therefore passed the Catholic Relief Act (1778), by which Catholics might become eligible for military service simply by taking an oath of fidelity to the king. The Act also allowed other Catholics who took the oath to inherit and purchase property legally, freed them from menacing informers who had collected £100 for evidence leading to their conviction as recusants, and abolished imprisonment for life as the penalty for contumacious recusancy. When, however, in 1779 Parliament applied this law in Scotland, it led to riots among Presbyterians in Glasgow and Edinburgh, and the formation of a Protestant Association that had an English branch under the presidency of Lord Gordon. He presented a petition to Parliament against leniency to Catholics in June, 1780, amid the clamor of a huge crowd that he aroused at St. George's Fields (Southwark) with inflammatory language. The crowd became a mob that terrorized metropolitan London for six days during which Catholic chapels were desecrated, members of Parliament and other innocent bystanders were threatened, manhandled, and in some cases killed, and the residences of Catholic ambassadors and government officials burned and looted. No one was safe from harm unless he wore the blue ribbon symbolic of antipopery. The riots, which killed nearly five hundred persons and destroyed or damaged hundreds of private homes and public buildings before the king's guard could quell them, began simply as an outburst of religious bigotry but ended as a social revolution against class privilege, wealth, and governmental complacency toward the welfare of thousands of underprivileged persons. As a result of the riots, Gordon went to prison, where he died in 1788; nearly two dozen rioters were executed; and Parliament overwhelmingly rejected the Association's petition.

The threat of Irish rebellion was no less serious than the reality of the American Revolution even though its importance was eclipsed by the North ministry's understandable preoccupation with the thirteen colonies. The Irish government had not changed substantially since the enactment of Poynings's Law in the 1490s, which subjected the Irish to an alien English administration headed by a lord lieutenant responsible to the crown. Ireland had its own Parliament, but the British Parliament could rescind its laws even as it could legislate for Ireland. Since the days of Sir Thomas Wentworth in the 1630s, English repression and retribution had become household words among the Irish peasants. They were forced to pay tithes to the wealthy Anglican Church while they worshiped in wattle chapels, languished in poverty, paid rack rents that enriched absentee English landlords who generally watched coldly as their tenants starved or signed themselves into indentured servitude to escape their miserable lot. Jonathan Swift struck close to the mark when he suggested sarcastically in the *Modest Proposal* (1727) that the Irish could survive by eating their children.

Nearly four million Irish Catholics and Protestant Ulsterites quietly accepted their subordination during most of the eighteenth century, but in the 1770s a few angry Protestant members of the Irish Parliament (Catholics were excluded from it) voiced repeated protests against Ireland's servile status and economic plight. The American Revolution heartened them because it proved that the use of force by a dependent people could win significant concessions from the mother country. What the Americans did, therefore, the Irish threatened to do.

The opposition to British trade regulations that forbade wool exports except to England and all business with the colonies, and encouraged the development of the linen industry because it enriched British merchants instead of helping millions of Irish farmers, was begun by two Irish politicians—Henry Grattan and Henry Flood. They took advantage of the Anglo-French conflicts of 1778 that resulted partly in a threat to Ireland by enemy ships and the growth of an Irish militia, an informally raised force of citizens that numbered nearly eighty thousand men by 1781. Fearful lest Irish grievances might lead to revolution and possible alliance with France, the Irish Parliament repealed some of the obnoxious penal laws, and the British Parliament granted relief to the Irish economy by opening the colonies to Irish goods, which were also admitted into England either free or under lower duties. Grattan and his colleagues were dissatisfied with these concessions and threatened to resort to force unless Britain conceded Ireland home rule. The British Parliament therefore repealed Poynings's Law and an Act of 1719 that had empowered it to make laws binding in Ireland. This Act of Repeal (1782) granted the Irish Parliament legislative independence subject only to the executive approval of the lord lieutenant. This arrangement, although far from ideal because it did not remove economic restrictions and discrimination against Catholics holding public office, lasted until 1801, when Ireland was united governmentally with England in the same manner that Scotland had been in 1707.

The difficulties in India, unlike the economic and constitutional problems in Ireland and America, arose primarily because of the inability of the East India Company to govern the subcontinent under the terms of its antiquated charter, which had been renewed without substantial alteration every generation since 1600. Considering its limited resources, heavy responsibilities, and lack of adequate military aid from home, the Company had done remarkably well in keeping Indian affairs under reasonable control despite endemic civil wars, changing alliances, and the interference of Portuguese, Dutch, and French rivals. The Company, originally a purely commercial organization that reaped handsome profits for English shareholders, had been forced into exercising governmental and judicial authority in consequence of the home government's apathy, the need to control Indian magnates in order to keep the law and order essential to good business, and the Anglo-French colonial struggle, which had left a vast Indian territory in British hands.

As the government formulated no definite colonial policy for India, and as the Company could not effectively rule it, authority devolved upon corrupt Company administrators called nabobs, who administered their remote districts like petty feudal princes. Because their salaries were low and their authority great, most nabobs could not resist the temptation to exploit their positions for personal profit. After a few uncomfortable years in the hinterland, most of them could retire to a life of ease in England on the fortunes made from graft, gifts, and rake-offs. When Clive returned to India as Company governor in May, 1765, he did what he could during a short administration of eighteen months to eradicate corruption and exploitation. His reforms reduced such practices and rid the Company of its worst officials, but they, as well as the Company directors in England, fought him tooth and nail. He suggested to the directors that salaries of Company officials should be greatly increased in order to lessen the temptation for easy profit. When the directors refused, he established a salt monopoly without their permission, using the profits to augment the salaries of officials from himself down to the lowest clerk in proportion to their rank. But bad health forced Clive's return to England, whereupon the directors repudiated his reforms and thereby inadvertently encouraged Company men to return to their corrupt ways.

Faced with the fact that a Parliamentary committee of inquiry had substantiated Clive's charges of maladministration, and that the civil wars in Bengal and Oudh had sharply reduced the Company's revenues, North secured the passage of the Regulating Act of 1773. This Act reformed the Company's administrative structure and put it under the supervision of the British government. It provided for an executive composed of a governor-general assisted by four councilors responsible to the Company directors. They in turn were required to submit their accounts semiannually for audit by the Treasury and to report regularly on military and political affairs to the secretaries of state. The Act also established a supreme court of four judges to which Indians might appeal for redress of grievances and forbade Company officials to accept presents or engage in private trade.

Warren Hastings (1732–1818), an Oxfordshire man whose twenty years of Company service in India had transformed him into an Anglo-Indian in style as well as behavior, served as governor-general from 1774 to 1785. His awesome responsibilities included implementation of the Regulating Act, mastery of the delicate political relationship between the Company and native princes, and the institution of radical reforms. An able and impatient imperialist, he attacked problems fearlessly and did not mind stepping on sensitive toes. He at once alienated the executive council, particularly Sir Philip Francis, who later ruined him, but he also made remarkable progress that might have permanently stabilized Indian administration had it not been for the political and military complications inspired by France during the American Revolution. The French aggravated the existing animosity between the Company in Bengal and the powerful Mahratta Confederacy in the west and south, which Clive had kept at bay by an alliance with Oudh, a buffer state between Bengal and central India. For a variety of reasons that cannot be discussed here, the Mahratta chiefs headed by Sindia and supported by French troops attacked Oudh, Bengal, and the Carnatic in a war that lasted until 1782 without conclusive result. The conflict cost Britain a great deal of money and reduced Company profits; so much so, in fact, that Hastings had to resort to extorting money from native princes, which in turn led Councilor Francis, whom Hastings had wounded in a duel, to charge him unjustly with profiteering. Hastings retired to England in 1785, having kept India in the Empire at great personal sacrifice and against heavy odds. He had organized the Indian revenue for the first time on a definite basis and had created the public offices and services of Bengal. But feeling against him in England was strong, and at the instance of some Whigs, chief of whom was Burke, he was impeached by the House of Commons. The trial in the Lords dragged on intermittently for several years before he was at last acquitted. He retired to his home an impoverished and ruined man. Like Clive, who had committed suicide in 1774, Hastings had saved India but lost his good name.

Five years before the trial began, the manifest impracticality of certain sections of the 1773 Regulatory Act led to consideration of a more lasting and effective India bill. Friction between Hastings and the council at Calcutta, to which he was responsible under the existing law, and the report of a Parliamentary committee that investigated the workings of the Indian administration led Fox to introduce an India bill in 1783. The Commons passed it, but the Lords, intimidated by George III's threats of reprisal against anyone who supported it, voted against it. There was also strong suspicion among Fox's opponents that he intended by his bill to enhance his power and perpetuate his coalition ministry with North. The Fox bill would have included the appointment of seven principal councilors for a four-year term as part of the bill itself; that is, Parliament, where Fox had a clear majority, would have had the initial right to name them, obviously from among his friends. It also appeared that these councilors would take Fox's recommendations for distribution of patronage in East India Company positions so that, in effect, he could personally control Indian affairs. The acrimonious debate over the India bill provided George III with the opportunity he had awaited to rid himself of Fox and North, and both were asked to resign.

William Pitt then formed a ministry at the king's invitation despite his lack of a Parliamentary majority. Fox at once raised the question of the constitutionality of this arrangement in order to force the resignation of the ministry, but Pitt stayed on until the 1784 elections returned his supporters in much larger numbers. Almost immediately thereafter, Parliament passed the India Act by which India was governed until the Sepoy Revolt of 1857. The dual role of the Company and the government was prudently recognized in the measure. Civil and military affairs became subject to a six-member Board of Control appointed by the crown and resident in England, while authority over commerce and control of the patronage remained in Company hands. The Company also could appoint, with the king's approval, the governor-general and his chief subordinates. As much of the difficulty arising from the old law stemmed from bickering between the governor and the executive council, the new relieved the governor of having to follow its advice. The Act certainly did not eliminate corruption nor ensure a faultless administration, but it recognized the Company's traditional commercial interests and gave the government the chance to rule with integrity and justice in India.

The ministry of William Pitt lasted with only one brief interruption for seventeen years—a period of exciting political controversy, economic reform, and the French Revolution. It is true that Pitt's meteoric rise to headship of the state at the age of twenty-four was partly attributable to his father's great reputation, yet he had enough ability to stand alone. A dutiful and precocious boy, he applied himself to his studies at Cambridge more assiduously than others of his social class, and from the winding streets of Cambridge went to the walled quadrangle of Lincoln's Inn, where he was admitted in due course to its select company. As he had been reared in an intensely politically-oriented household, it was practically inevitable that he himself should choose a political career. He entered Parliament in 1780 and at once attracted attention as a convincing orator and clever bargainer. North and Rockingham offered him cabinet posts, but he refused them because he distrusted political extremism, whether Whig or Tory; Pitt more easily subscribed to Shelburne's principles, essentially neither Whig nor Tory, and served a short term as Chancellor of the Exchequer. The Fox-North ministry, a coalition of Whigs and Tories, forced him into opposition and the limelight over the abortive India bill, and inaugurated a feud that ended only with the deaths of Fox and Pitt in 1806. Their sparkling oratorical exchanges in the Commons enlivened the debates and became the topic of public discussion.

Pitt enjoyed the confidence of the country and the support of the crown during a great ministry in which he fulfilled his responsibilities with consummate devotion and uncommon energy. A man of high principles and unquestionable chastity in his personal life, he literally worked himself to death at the age of forty-six. His patience at crucial times overrode the disappointment he felt when his bills went down to defeat. His government cannot be credited with passing much significant legislation, but his steady control of administrative procedures and his financial reforms helped to stabilize politics and strengthen the economy on the eve of the war with France in which Britain played the banker and the merchant to her European allies. Pitt respected reformers like the abolitionist William Wilberforce, and though he was not successful, he sought in 1788 to abolish the lucrative African slave trade. In the same year, when George III again lapsed into insanity, Pitt defended the royal authority and thereby prevented the Whigs from making the reckless and dissolute Prince of Wales the regent. Admittedly Pitt made blunders and used his position to personal and party advantage: he refused to face the dangers inherent in French revolutionary ideas until it was almost too late; he suppressed personal liberty in the 1790s through the Sedition Acts and suspension of habeas corpus; he nullified the Whig majority in the Lords by inducing George III to ennoble over sixty Tory peers mostly from the *nouveaux riches;* and he relied on the king's influence to maintain a majority in the Commons. Pitt's critics also accused him of leaving the country in political disorder and vulnerable to French invasion at his death as well as of dropping important bills he had sponsored when they encountered strong opposition that threatened his position. Nonetheless, Pitt restored a semblance of party discipline by marshaling formerly conflicting interest groups—reformers, important London authorities, old aristocratic landed families, and exponents of Adam Smith's theory of laissez faire—into the core of a fresh Tory party, an achievement that no politician since Walpole had been able to accomplish. Pitt also restored the dignity and independent judgment of the prime minister and the cabinet.

Most of Pitt's legislative program failed. His efforts to abolish the evil slave trade, involving transportation of about forty thousand Africans to the colonies annually, collapsed in the face of the greedy self-interest of Liverpool and Bristol slave traders, West Indian planters, and their spokesmen in Parliament. He hoped to establish commercial union with Ireland in order to improve its struggling economy and increase revenue in England, but this too floundered on the objections of English manufacturers fearful of competition. In 1783 Pitt had contemplated enlarging the electorate to include copyholders, and redistributing the seats in Parliament by transferring the representation from thirty-six rotten boroughs to London and some heavily populated counties that were grossly underrepresented. Parliament repeatedly rejected these proposals, and Pitt's poor health, strong opposition from his own followers, and the national fear of granting political reforms in view of what transpired in France during the Revolution prevented him from making further attempts to amend the representative system. The country did benefit, however, from Burke's Place Act (1782), which disfranchised certain civil servants in the finance and postal branches of government whom the crown customarily appointed and expected to vote for its candidates. Beyond that no electoral reform was accomplished until 1832.

Like Walpole, Pitt is remembered best for financial reforms. The American Revolution had added £115,000,000 to the national debt, which stood at £240,000,000 in 1783. Much of it was encumbered by heavy interest payments that ate up about two-thirds of the annual budget, impairing the government's ability to pay off the principal. Pitt therefore resolved to reduce government expenditures, increase revenue, and provide a better way of amortizing the debt. Part of the debt was funded, but the customary means of doing so, sale of bonds to privileged parties without competitive bidding or public advertisement, inevitably raised interest rates. Pitt ended this practice and henceforth the government marketed bonds to the highest bidder at lower interest rates to the Treasury. By additionally lowering tariffs on commodities such as tea (the duty on it was cut to one-tenth the former rate); discouraging smuggling by the Hovering Act, which allowed seizure of suspicious ships lying offshore; imposing excise taxes on popular items like tobacco and wines; and levying new taxes on necessities like hats, candles, paper, carriages, and windows, Pitt nearly doubled the annual revenue. His careful investigation of financial operations also revealed a large floating debt of almost £22,000,000, about a quarter of which had been incurred recently, while most of the rest had been carried on the books of several departments without payment in some cases for as long as thirty years. In addition to the institution of an up-to-date bookkeeping system and the subjection of every department to annual audit, Pitt liquidated the floating debt by paying £2,000,000 owed to the Bank of England, selling bonds worth £6,000,000 to satisfy new debts, and consolidating the remainder of the floating debt with the accumulated national debt, which he gradually lowered by means of the sinking fund. Pitt's fund differed from Walpole's (see Chapter 9) in that Pitt used surplus revenue rather than special taxes to raise at least £1,000,000 annually and invested it in bonds earning compound interest. The earned increment could then be applied to the payment of the principal on the debt. The plan worked well for a few years and collapsed only because of Britain's enormous expenditures during the French Revolutionary and Napoleonic wars.

Pitt, who had studied Adam Smith's *Wealth of Nations* and believed in his advocacy of a freer world market made possible by the abandonment of mercantilist restrictions and the adoption of lower tariff schedules, did his utmost to promote these ideas. The loss of the American colonies had dealt a heavy blow to an economy that was undergoing rapid expansion due to the Industrial Revolution. If Pitt's financial system was to work, new markets had to be cultivated, for increased trade and increased revenue went hand in hand. It was an achievement of no mean consequence that Pitt overcame French animosity by arranging the Eden Treaty (1787), which provided for the mutual exchange of goods at very low tariff rates—the French accepted British cotton and iron products and sent its wines to England. As Britain's manufacturing techniques were superior to those of France, its goods easily undersold competitive French goods so that Britain got much the better of the bargain. The French Revolution unfortunately destroyed this commercial connection and prevented Pitt from making others, but at the same time Britain, although expending huge sums of money on the French war that began in 1793, also profited handsomely in consequence of it.

The dramatic events leading to the French Revolution are too familiar to warrant repetition here. British politicians watched with mixed feelings as the moderate proposals of the Third Estate gradually hardened into full-scale reaction against the old regime. Most Englishmen cheered the overthrow of the feudal institutions by which the absolute monarchy and the vacuous aristocracy had kept the mass of Frenchmen in servility. The sweeping legislative changes of the National Constituent Assembly, notably the Declaration of the Rights of Man, struck the British as a righteous rectification of long-standing injustices. A wave of enthusiasm swept over English liberals, who proposed constitutional and social reforms and established prorevolutionary clubs. But the execution of Louis XVI and his wife and the cruelties perpetrated in the Reign of Terror (1793–94) horrified the British, causing a sudden *volte-face* of opinion that appeared to justify the warning sounded by Edmund Burke in his *Reflections on the Revolution in France* (1790).

Burke's views had a greater impact on European attitudes about the Revolution than had those of Arthur Young, the peripatetic author of *Travels in France* (1791), who described more accurately the true state of French society in 1789. Burke's critics and members of his own party reproved him for apparently betraying the principles he had advocated in defense of justice for the Irish and the Americans, but he was not really inconsistent. His argument that the British government had violated the accepted social order in the two earlier cases was the very reason for his denunciation of French revolutionaries. According to Burke, they had denied their heritage by violently destroying their traditional institutions instead of relying on orderly, gradual processes. In other words, instead of repairing their house, the revolutionaries tore it to the ground, sweeping away the good with the bad.

Meanwhile the major Continental powers, much less inclined than Britain to favor the collapse of a governmental system that was not far different from their own, watched the course of the Revolution with grave misgivings. The unsuccessful attempt of the French royal family to flee France and their capture in Varennes in June, 1791, resulted in their virtual imprisonment in Paris and alarm in European capitals. Although most Frenchmen were too much concerned with the dazzling progress of their revolution to pay any attention to foreign affairs, the Girondists, moderate radicals in control of the Legislative Assembly, favored a foreign war as a means of abolishing monarchy. Louis XVI likewise encouraged a war in order to free himself from his impossible predicament, and the *émigrés*, who had fled to Austria,

Prussia, Holland, and England, naturally agreed with him. Touched by their appeals, conscious of his relationship to Marie Antoinette (a daughter of former Austrian Empress Maria Theresa), and a strong advocate of absolute monarchy, Emperor Leopold II joined Frederick William II of Prussia in the Declaration of Pillnitz (August, 1791), in which they suggested a coalition of European states to stop the revolution and restore the authority of the French monarch. With a small army of *émigrés* and others poised in the Rhineland, and the Austrian emperor talking war against the revolution, the Legislative Assembly protested and, getting no satisfaction, almost unanimously declared war on Austria in April, 1792. Prussia immediately sided with Austria. The French armies marched on Savoy and occupied the country west of the Rhine. Within a year virtually all Europe became involved in a war that lasted with but two brief interruptions in 1802 and 1814 until Napoleon's defeat at Waterloo in 1815.

Britain, although allied with Prussia and Holland since 1788 in what Pitt considered a purely defensive arrangement, had no desire to get involved in Continental affairs. A European war would surely increase the debt and bring little benefit; it would interrupt Pitt's efforts to build the economy, improve administration, and strengthen his party; and it would destroy the commercial treaty with France at the cost of handsome dividends. Pitt was essentially a peacemaker: he had labored assiduously to keep the peace in Europe, preventing the partition of the Swedish kingdom by Russia and Denmark, but failing to settle the differences between Russia and Turkey that led to war in 1787. No one in Britain save a few extremists wanted a French war, neither Pitt, nor Parliament, nor merchants and industrialists, nor George III, who cautioned his prime minister not to become entangled in French internal affairs. But the revolutionaries forced Britain into war by victories in the Austrian Netherlands that threatened Holland, by declaring the Dutch Scheldt River open to international navigation (thereby threatening Dutch independence and flaunting an agreement that Britain had signed to keep the river closed to foreigners), and finally by offering military assistance to revolutionaries in any European country. Such hostile acts raised serious doubts in Pitt's mind that the French radicals would be content with only the control of their homeland. In his agony of indecision, Pitt temporized until the execution of Louis XVI raised such an uproar in Britain that it severed Anglo-French diplomatic relations. In an act that sensible men could only have considered irresponsible, on February 1, 1793, France declared war on Britain, which brought into action its enormous resources in finance, industry, and sea power that were to prove the deciding factor in the wars until Napoleon's final overthrow.

11

Industrial, Social, and Cultural Change, 1750–1830

The British have long been justly famous as manufacturers and traders of wares that they have exported to the four corners of the world. In the early sixteenth century, they began in a small way to industrialize and to seek new markets to sustain the economy in a growing nation that even then outproduced domestic needs. As Professor John Nef has ably shown, the first significant industrialization in England occurred in the hundred years after 1540, by which time it had established its primacy in mining and heavy industry. In terms of invested capital, the number and range of business firms, the variety of small concerns employing a dozen or so laborers, the utilization of natural resources, and the hundreds of patents awarded for new processes and inventions during that period, England's artisans, capitalists, and entrepreneurs laid the basis for much greater industrialization in the eighteenth century. By that time some politicians and economists, whose theories will be considered later in this chapter, had begun to argue convincingly against the restrictive mercantilist system.

Such attitudes resulted from the gradual quickening of industrial and commercial momentum that has often been somewhat misleadingly called a revolution. Arnold Toynbee, the late nineteenth-century economic historian, was among the first to coin the phrase "industrial revolution" to dramatize the technological changes that occurred between 1760 and 1850. As late as a generation ago, some historians still spoke of *the* industrial revolution as though there had been no industrialization in Britain before the reign of George III. Recognizing that economic and social changes occur very slowly, scholars have since proved the folly of parceling economic developments into neat chronological periods, and have therefore questioned the use of the term *revolution* to describe economic changes that originated much earlier than 1760 and are still going on. Revolution connotes suddenness and fundamental alteration of basic institutions, ideas, or techniques. While there is justification for calling some of the developments to be discussed hereafter revolutionary, one must remember that the transition from the domestic to the factory system, the growth of an urban industrial proletariat, the displacement of labor by machinery, mass production instead of individual craftsmanship, and the substitution of mechanical power for human and animal power did not come about overnight, and the old systems and techniques went on existing side by side with the new. Nor did industry replace agriculture as the nation's primary occupation until the twentieth century. The vast majority of the British people earned their livelihood from the land in 1800, and at least half still lived in the country fifty years later. Moreover, factories, which some have argued were in existence since the reign of Henry VIII, did not spring up everywhere during George III's reign, and most of the machines in them were still made of wood until the early nineteenth century. Consequently one should not view the so-called industrial revolution as a radical departure from economic activity prior to 1760, but as a period of acceleration in the pace of industrial and technological change.

What made the century after 1760 appear more dramatic than it actually was were the effects of artificial power, greater employment of natural resources, larger capital investment, wider markets, and the social impact on the industrial proletariat. Before the eighteenth century, industry had depended on human power and rushing water to turn machinery. For most of human history, industry had connoted *manufacture* in the original meaning of the word—to make by hand. Mass production was practically unknown and universally distrusted, and the worth of individual craftsmanship was duly recognized and appropriately rewarded. The tools and techniques of the seventeenth century gradually succumbed to new machinery and skills in the eighteenth, but their impact took considerably longer than one might surmise to affect a society not yet trustful of whirling gears and bursts of steam. Nor should one unduly extol the accomplishments of eighteenth-century industrialization or bemoan its effects on the face of the land or the lot of the urban classes. The factories belching smoke and soot and the row upon row of dingy dwellings, which

Charles Dickens described so well, did destroy in many places the pastoral beauty of clean, green, and tidy country villages. Disease ruined the health and grime covered the bodies of laborers in mills and mines. Low wages and high prices combined to impoverish many families and chained them to a life of drudgery in dismal factories and squalid neighborhoods. Hard work and improper nourishment stunted children, fathers toiled fifteen hours a day and often died or were maimed in industrial accidents, and mothers frequently labored in factories while struggling to care for their families. On the other hand, the ultimate results of industrialism were beneficial to labor, capital, and the nation as a whole, and society gradually became acclimatized to the stresses and strains of the new way of life. The evils that our forefathers created by mechanization and the factory system in some cases still exist, but they are the price mankind has had to pay for the sake of material comfort. Reformers from that day to this have constantly sought to shorten working days, increase wages and improve conditions in industry, provide education and cultural benefits for the working man, care for the sick and the indigent, and beautify cities. While their aims have never been fully realized, neither have they been merely voices crying in the wilderness.

Why did industrialization develop earlier and more rapidly in Britain than on the Continent? Primarily because England had a more stable social and political order and a sounder banking system that provided a healthy climate for economic growth. Furthermore, the territorial expansion of the Empire in the eighteenth century brought Canada, India, Australia, and many smaller colonies within Britain's commercial system, and the substantial population growth after 1760 required accelerated production to meet larger domestic needs. And, though Britain's involvement in the colonial wars and the gigantic Napoleonic struggle (see the next chapter) was very costly, its economy adequately supported the expense, and entrepreneurs and industrialists gained handsomely by supplying military and consumer goods to their allies. These exports were transported by a large mercantile fleet and were protected by the powerful Royal Navy. Britain likewise had essential raw materials such as iron and coal, without which no industrial society could thrive, a damp climate essential to the textile industries (dry thread broke easily in machines), and wealthy capitalists anxious to increase their earnings. Such advantages would have been wasted, however, without the inventiveness and energy of the British people themselves.

The foremost characteristic of the industrial revolution was the factory system. In the domestic system, artisans worked in their homes with raw materials provided by entrepreneurs, who also sometimes owned the tools and machines. They paid the artisans for their labor and sold the finished products. It was a short step from controlling the raw materials and selling the products to supervising the entire operation from start to finish under one roof. Consequently, the domestic system gradually gave way to the factory system in which large and costly machines were housed in separate buildings in which the workers, who lived nearby, often in tenements built and operated by management, worked for specified wages and hours. Such factories were frequently built in districts near the sources of raw materials: iron and steel mills in the Midlands, and textile mills near the north-country sheep farms and along the Mersey River, where ships from the United States and India unloaded their cargoes of cotton.

New and speedier techniques of processing raw materials or extracting metals resulted from important inventions that cannot all be individually considered without tiring the reader with an endless list of names. We shall therefore be content to summarize the major developments in the manufacturing and extractive industries, remembering always that technical improvements were being achieved simultaneously in smaller industries like pottery, linen, pewter, glass, and brewing.

The value of coal for domestic and industrial use was recognized in the eighteenth century when the supply of wood fuel became scarce and the price of timber consequently rose. About the time of Elizabeth's accession, the coal fields of Newcastle, the Midlands, and Scotland yielded about 225,000 tons annually, most of which was shipped by sea to London. Coal replaced timber in the salt, glass, soap, and brewing industries. Not much coal was exported until after 1709, when Parliament rescinded the heavy duty on it. The enlarged foreign market (France and Italy had little coal, and the German collieries in the Ruhr Valley were not developed until the 1820s) and the expansion of the metallurgical industries at home, which successfully shifted from wood fuel to coke, encouraged coal mining and made it feasible to relocate ironworks near coal fields in the north after the forests of Gloucestershire and the southeast had been depleted. By 1750, coal mining in Yorkshire, the Midlands, and South Wales yielded about 5,000,000 tons annually, and a century later it had grown to nearly 60,000,000.

Insufficient ventilation, lack of mechanical lifting devices, and drainage problems kept mines shallow until the early eighteenth century.
Sixteenth- and seventeenth-century mines were seldom deeper than
three hundred or four hundred feet and employed on the average less
than fifty men. In those days simple methods of expelling putrid air
and noxious fumes from underground mines were developed, such as
the employment of boys operating fans and fires to force air up shafts.
Much later, in 1815, Sir Humphry Davy invented the safety lamp
which, together with the introduction of mechanical ventilating fans
(about 1840), not only helped to prevent fatal explosions, but also
permitted the sinking of much deeper shafts, in some cases down to
fifteen hundred feet. Little could be done to ease the grueling labor
of colliers using pickaxes and shovels (a steam boring machine was
invented in 1813, but it was not widely used), or to reduce the danger
to miners from the use of blasting powder to loosen the mineral. Nor
was anything done to help the children who hauled coal tubs along
wooden rails on their hands and knees through narrow passages and
then climbed long ladders to the surface with sacks of coal strapped
to their backs. Cast-iron rails replaced wooden rails underground by
about 1800; above ground, horses hauled heavy coal wagons on rails
to rivers and canals for loading on flatboats that carried the coal to
neighboring markets or to ports like Newcastle for transport to London
and abroad.

Steam as a source of power had been known since about 1650, and
in 1698 a Devonshire army officer named Thomas Savery had built
a steam engine that was used to drain water from mines. In 1706,
Thomas Newcomen, a blacksmith and landowner, invented a cum-
bersome and expensive steam engine that burned thirteen tons of coal
daily in driving an upright piston housed in a five-foot cylinder. When
steam forced the piston upward, the cylinder was cooled, creating a
partial vacuum that brought the piston downward again. The piston
was attached to a beam that turned a water pump used for drainage.
Newcomen's device was not widely adopted except at larger coal mines
and in some water works because of the amount of fuel it required;
there were less than 150 in use by 1775, by which time the horsepower
had been increased from twenty to seventy-five. James Watt (1734-
1819), son of a western Scottish shopkeeper and a brilliant mathematician and mechanic, first became interested in steam power when, in
the employ of Glasgow University as an instrument maker, he was
required to repair a Newcomen engine. He soon realized the power

wasted by using most of the steam to heat and cool the cylinder, and, in 1769, patented a horizontal steam engine in which steam pressure controlled both the forward and backward thrusts of the piston. With the financial backing of the Birmingham manufacturer Matthew Bolton, and the technical assistance of the master ironworker John Wilkinson, Watt perfected and marketed his engine at great profit. The value of Watt's machine was its adaptability to motion. Whereas the Newcomen engine could be connected only to a crankshaft, Watt's was connected to wheels and gears so that it could power machines in the textile and pottery factories and iron foundries, and haul up minerals at mines. Later, the rotary motion generated by the Watt engine was applied by Robert Fulton to steamboats (1807) and by George Stephenson to locomotives (1825), which, in time, revolutionized transportation.

The iron industry became important after the Darby family in Lancashire perfected the use of nearly-pure-carbon coke made from coal. This relieved ironworkers from reliance on charcoal produced from scarce and costly timber. In the sixteenth century, iron forges were located primarily in the southwestern counties and the Sussex and Kent Weald, where ore and wood were plentiful. But the wood eventually ran out, and the iron mines (even after the discovery of fresh deposits in Cumberland and the Midlands) did not yield sufficient ore to supply even domestic needs by 1700. Thereafter pig iron had to be imported from the Baltic countries. Since pig iron was brittle and contained impurities that had to be burned out in forges heated to very high temperatures, which coal could not produce, the development of high-carbon coke by Abraham Darby (d. 1717) and his son at Coalbrookdale was of the utmost importance to the growth of the iron industries. They, along with the Wilkinsons and Walkers of Yorkshire, laid the basis for the modern iron and brass industries in England, just as John Roebuck did at the Carron Ironworks in central Scotland. Despite the costliness of having to import most pig iron from Sweden, Russia, and Spain, foundries multiplied rapidly during the war years from 1740 to 1815, when weapons and ammunition were manufactured in large quantities. The iron industries also benefited from Wilkinson's application of steam power to blast furnaces in 1776, and the patenting in 1783 by the Lancashire foundryman Henry Cort of processes for rolling and puddling pig iron in the production of malleable iron, obviating the necessity of repeatedly hammering and heating the metal to increase tensile strength. As a result, the production of iron ore was increased from about a half-million tons in 1800 to ten times that amount by 1850. Wrought iron served society in a number of ways, among them the manufacture of boilers, ship plates, and machinery, as well as bridge construction. The first iron bridge spanned the Severn River in 1787.

Steel had been laboriously produced since the Middle Ages, but the significant development of the industry had to await the inventive mind of Henry Bessemer (1813–98). Improvements in the tensile strength of steel (wrought iron with a quantity of carbon added), which can be finely sharpened, bored, and polished, were made about 1740 by a Doncaster watchmaker, Benjamin Huntsman, who introduced the crucible method. This technique, in which carbon was added to molten malleable iron in clay crucibles, produced higher quality steel more quickly than the time-honored process of laying pieces of charcoal on repeatedly heated iron. But the work was slow and yielded only small amounts of steel. Despite the demand for it from the Sheffield cutlery shops and the cannon foundries, steelmaking remained a small industry until Bessemer, son of a French immigrant artisan and self-taught ironmaster, devised a way to make high-grade steel from phosphorus-free iron ore in greater quantity and at far less cost than the old process. Midland towns like Sheffield, Nottingham, and Birmingham sprang up around the steel foundries and dominated the European steel market. The steel men of South Wales and Clydeside in Scotland were not far behind.

The remarkable progress of the metallurgical industries was matched by the continued growth of woolen manufacturing and other textile industries. Wool had been the mainstay of English economic life for centuries. Earlier chapters have shown how the production and processing of wool had significantly affected British society since the fourteenth century. Wool had created the Flanders market, sustained the Merchant Adventurers, and contributed to the decay of manorial villages and the feudal system. It had also encouraged the enclosure movement, provided millions of pounds in crown revenue, helped to sustain the domestic system, and provided employment for thousands of workers. Wool, which had been the heart of financial prosperity in East Anglia and the southeast, spread into the southwest during the sixteenth century, and occupied much of the spare time of farm families in virtually every English and Scottish county by 1700. By the mid-eighteenth century, England exported nearly twenty times more woolens than cottons. Despite several statutes that protected the woolen manufacturers against competition by the cotton industry, which Flemish Protestant refugees had introduced in England during Elizabethan times, the latter grew along the Mersey River in Lancashire as well as in Renfrewshire and Dumfriesshire in Scotland. By 1830, Manchester had won the nickname Cottonopolis. Cotton goods were at first expensive because of high tariffs on raw cotton imports and the cost of transporting cotton from the Middle East, India, and the West Indies, which provided short-staple cotton fibers that often broke in the spinning machines. By the late 1780s, however, the tariff had been lowered, machinery had greatly increased the output of cotton goods, and long-staple cotton from the black belt of the United States was imported at reasonable prices. Raw cotton imports rose from about 3,000,000 pounds in 1750 to 56,000,000 pounds in 1800. In the same period the value of cotton exports rose from £45,000 to £7,000,000. Linens had long been made in northern Ireland (Ulster), and were also manufactured in small quantities in Lancashire and southern Scotland, but English- and Scottish-made linens were hurt by the freer Anglo-Irish trade relations following the political union of 1800, as well as by the fact that cotton was used for the same purposes as linen. Silk weaving never reached the production level of either wool or cotton simply because few could afford to buy silks, but towns like Macclesfield and Leek in Lancashire and the Spitalfields section of London became centers of the small English silk industry. All these textile industries profited at the turn of the eighteenth century and for many years thereafter from the skill and capital of thousands of French Huguenot artisans, who emigrated to England following Louis XIV's revocation in 1685 of the Edict of Nantes.

Considering the vital importance of textiles to the nation's economy, it is not surprising that inventors turned their minds to ways of speeding up their manufacture. The initial problem was the slowness of spinning; it took the work of ten spinners to keep one weaver busy. In 1733, John Kay invented the flying shuttle, a device in which hammers drive the shuttle through the warp. Kay thus made it possible for one weaver to produce as much wide cloth as four weavers had formerly been able to, but the widespread fear among weavers that it would throw them out of work discouraged the adoption of the flying shuttle for a generation. In 1767, James Hargreaves mechanized spinning with his spinning jenny, which initially spun eight threads simultaneously, and later eighty threads. Richard Arkwright, who began his working life as a barber and ended up a millionaire bourgeois, in 1771 patented the water-frame, a spinning machine turned by water power that produced better thread of pure cotton (earlier most cotton thread contained some linen for strength) by passing the fibers through two tight-fitting rollers, thereby making thread suitable as warp. In 1780 the Bolton (Lancashire) weaver Samuel Crompton constructed his famous "mule," which was based on the spindle idea of Hargreaves and the rollers of Arkwright. Crompton's produced much finer thread than earlier spinning machines, and did it more quickly. The Kent clergyman Edmund Cartwright built a power loom in 1785 that enabled weavers to keep up with the now speedier spinning of thread, and the American Eli Whitney invented the cotton gin, which mechanized the formerly long and laborious task of separating seeds from lint. Hence, by 1800 the entire operation, from cotton pod to the finished cotton cloth, could be performed on machines that even a child could operate.

Industrialization made more of an impact on Scotland than on England. Dramatic increases in production, particularly in the iron, steel, textile, and shipbuilding industries were characteristic of economic growth in southwestern Scotland during the later eighteenth century, when the smaller industries, such as distilling and brewing, and chemicals and toolmaking, developed rapidly. The total effect of Scottish industrialization was to augment its wealth to a level roughly on a par with England in proportion to their populations and resources. At the same time, between 1750 and 1830, the ratio of rural dwellers to townsmen was reduced from 4 to 1 to 3 to 1, and the national population of Scotland rose from about 1,250,000 in 1750 to more than 2,000,000 in 1820.

The remarkable thrust of commerce and industry in Britain as well as the increase of agricultural productivity demanded improvements in transportation in order to move large quantities of food, raw materials, and finished products economically and rapidly between distant parts of the country. Modes of travel and transport had not changed since the Norman Conquest. Horse-drawn, springless wagons and pack horses had plodded for centuries over muddy, pot-holed roads, and shallow-draft flatboats still plied rivers and streams that inconsiderately flowed along channels far from mines, factories, and markets. To be sure, there were some firm cobblestone roads, but most highways, particularly around the new commercial centers of the Midlands and the southwest, were unable to withstand the erosion of weather and wheels and frustrated traveler and carrier alike. At four or five miles an hour, with stops for rest and nourishment, it required fourteen days by coach to journey from London to Edinburgh, and shorter trips took proportionately as long. There were, however, some express runs connecting major cities: that between London and Bristol covered the distance in about two days. Pack horses and wagons could carry heavy loads, but only at the risk of becoming stuck in mire, and most bulk weight like coal and ore was conveyed wherever possible by water. Complaints about poor roads were legion; Parliament and the local authorities were painfully aware of them, but no one seemed willing to pay the heavy cost of improvements. Since 1555, each parish had been legally bound to keep its roads in good repair, but few parishes fulfilled their responsibilities to the letter of the law.

Improvements were made at long last toward the end of the eighteenth century because of the demands of industry, but neither the government nor the taxpayers financed them. Instead, by 1815, Parliament had authorized more than a thousand turnpike companies to construct or rebuild about twenty thousand miles of toll roads. Many of the new thoroughfares were designed by the brilliant Scottish engineers John Macadam (d. 1836) and Thomas Telford (d. 1834), who had small fragments of granite pressed down firmly with heavy rollers over firm bases of crushed rock. This method of construction, known as macadamizing, is still used today on country roads, although it has been replaced by blacktopping and cement on major highways. The new roads speeded stagecoach travelers on their way, reduced shipping costs by cutting travel time, and quickened mail delivery.

The feverish construction of canals, the first of which was a twelve-mile canal that the Duke of Bridgewater had dug in 1761 between his coal mine at Worsley and Manchester, proved the practicality of economical inland water transportation. The canals were so successful that the private companies that built most of them made profits of up to 200 per cent on their initial investment. Canals were linked with navigable rivers and roads wherever possible, often necessitating locks to equalize water levels. By the 1840s, when railroads replaced canals as the major means of transport, there were well over three thousand miles of canals in England and Scotland. The longer ones were usually constructed in shorter sections by several different companies (and often varied in width and depth). They joined London to the Midland cities of Birmingham, Manchester, and Liverpool with feeder canals connecting smaller centers with the main line, cut England in two between the rivers Mersey and Trent, linked the Don and Severn rivers from Birmingham to Bristol, and traversed the country in Scotland between the Firth of Forth and the Clyde. As canal transport was only about half as costly as land transport, agriculturalists and industrialists used it to great advantage; so too did the men seeking work in northern factories. Canals are still used in some parts of England, and bargemen, the last of an independent breed, can yet be seen steering their trains of flatboats through narrow ribbons of still water.

Watt's steam engine gave birth to the railway industry, which has faithfully served Britain and the rest of the world since the 1820s, only to be undercut in our day by the ubiquitous automobile and truck. In the early seventeenth century, long before the application of steam power to rotary motion, draymen had driven coal wagons over crude wooden planks from collieries to rivers, and later over iron rails laid atop the planks. By 1760, iron rails deep in mine tunnels had eased the burden of children who pulled coal tubs along them to shafts. These were also railways, but without the flanged wheels invented by William Jessop in 1788 or the mechanical driving power that made the railroad the speediest form of transportation yet devised. Exactly who first constructed a working locomotive in Britain is uncertain, although the Cornishman William Murdock is said to have built a small one in the 1780s, and the mining engineer Richard Trevithick is reported to have done likewise at the turn of the century. The earliest locomotives were very slow, but they were put to some use around collieries. The honor of constructing the first practical locomotive belongs to the self-educated engineer George Stephenson (1781–1848), whose "Blucher" chugged along at the then amazing speed of ten miles an hour to the astonishment of onlookers and the fright of livestock that ran off at the sight and sound of clicking wheels and flying sparks. In 1825, the first regular line opened between Stockton and Darlington, and in 1830 a second linked Manchester with Liverpool, by which time the Stephenson engines had attained speeds of thirty miles an hour. Although another fifty years were to pass before the sections of the country were connected by rails, and mechanical problems like air brakes and couplings had been solved, the railway age had begun. In the 1830s and 1840s, steamships began to ply the oceans and the electric telegraph revolutionized communications.

Industrialization and improved transportation combined to transform sleepy villages and small towns into crowded hubs of urban life, into which poured thousands of families in search of work. The center of population gradually shifted northward during the latter eighteenth century. After 1760, the Midlands grew much faster than the south, although in no county of England and Scotland did the population drop, which indicates the phenomenal growth of population. From 1760 to 1800 it increased by 50 per cent in England and 65 per cent in Scotland. In 1700, except for Cheshire, no English county north of the Trent River had a population density of over 100 persons per square mile; a century later all the Midland counties had at least 150 per square mile, and Lancashire and the West Riding of Yorkshire, whose populations had grown during the eighteenth century from 240,000 to 670,000 and from 245,000 to 580,000, respectively, had over 260 persons per square mile. Some towns, for instance Swindon and Crewe, the latter of which had 200 residents in 1840 and 18,000 in 1870, were virtually created by the railway industry, while iron, steel, and textile towns grew apace. Between 1770 and 1830, Manchester rose from 30,000 inhabitants to 240,000, while its neighboring town of Bolton, a mere country village in 1750, had 17,000 by 1800. Birmingham, Leeds, and Liverpool each had a population of more than 60,000 by 1810, and numerous Lancashire and Warwickshire towns had at least 15,000. Some of the new townsmen had moved up from the south, but the number who migrated long distances was relatively small. Most industrial workers had simply moved into the cities from the surrounding countryside, where the population was also growing, or had emigrated from Ireland. In 1805, 10,000 Irish lived in Manchester alone.

Because there are so many variables, it is practically impossible to generalize accurately about the social and economic effects of industrialization on the laboring classes. Wages in relation to the cost of living and employers' profits, as well as working conditions, differed widely from industry to industry and from region to region. How well or how poorly the workers fared also depended on the attitude of factory and mine owners and the community's sense of social responsibility. Many workers were proletarians, that is to say, without property and completely dependent on daily wages. They had no legal rights against exploitation by the owner class, and victimization under these circumstances was not uncommon. Other workers enjoyed better wages and working and living conditions. Analysts of industrial society have tended very often to choose extreme examples to prove the inhumanity of the machine age, and cases of extreme hardship are certainly not difficult to find. There were not a few colliers who toiled in intense heat, ankle deep in water, for eighteen hours a day in return for £10 or £15 a year, but others made £35 or £40. Five- and six-year-olds labored six days a week from 5 A.M. to 8 P.M. in textile mills. There were likewise cases of half-naked women hauling coal and even giving birth in mine tunnels, of children who were mangled in textile machines when they fell asleep from utter exhaustion, and of teen-agers dwarfed by arduous work and improper nourishment. On the other hand, skilled laborers in the iron, pottery, steel, and brewing industries, for instance, commanded wages of twelve to fifteen shillings a week, were treated decently because their employers could not do without them, and frequently did not work more than ten hours a day. Factory owners like the Crowley family of Lancashire, mindful of their workers' welfare, hired physicians, enforced rules against drunkenness and immorality, and encouraged arbitration to settle labor disputes. Other firms advertised high pay, good company housing, and travel reimbursement for those willing to migrate long distances for employment. Even in the cotton industry, in which the economic and working conditions were among the worst in the country, the mill hands' lot varied greatly. The factories of David Dale at New Lanark were exemplary in their beneficent treatment of workers and their families, who lived in a clean town in comfortable, low-rent housing provided by the company, and had schools operated by the owner. Another entrepreneur, Samuel Oldknow, saw to it that his workmen had meat and fresh fruit daily. It must be admitted, however, that these were exceptional cases in a society in which too many industrialists argued that the good of mankind at the expense of profits was bad business. Man, they held, was necessarily subordinate to the machine and had to suffer the consequences of that relationship. Whether the work in mines and mills was harder on workers than the domestic system or agriculture had been is open to serious question. One wonders, for instance, whether the sheer monotony of repeatedly doing the same simple chores in a dingy factory for seemingly endless hours at marginal wages did not do more harm to the spirit and health of workers than the dust and grime, the demands of unreasonable overseers, or the fatigue that were an inescapable part of their daily lives. Such conditions had always been the lot of employees, even under the guild system, but the days when men were individually respected for their skills and enjoyed a modicum of personal freedom and leisure died in the eighteenth-century factory and were not revived until labor unions managed to re-elevate the dignity of their members through strikes and collective bargaining.

W. L. Lecky, one of the shrewdest economic historians of the last century, carefully studied wages and prices in the eighteenth century and concluded that, while the working conditions and the social status of laborers often deteriorated, their standard of living steadily rose. Taking 1700 as the index year at 100 per cent, Lecky determined that laborers in London had a cost of living index of 94 per cent between 1714 and 1763, while their real wages (the buying power of money in relation to the cost of living) climbed to 118 per cent. The real wages of representative Lancashire workers in the same period averaged 130 per cent. He also showed that the average wages of workers in three industrial regions rose markedly. Workers in London earned on the average £25 annually in 1770 and £30 in 1790; in the west country the average wage climbed from £17 10s. to £20, and in Lancashire from £11 5s. to £26 5s. Such figures include highs and lows in wages, of course; many laborers were more poorly off while others were better off. In addition, there was the ever-present fear of unemployment, fluctuations in wages and prices because of depressions and inflation, and so forth. Moreover, no adequate provision was made for thousands of indigent, aged, sick, and unemployed workers. The Elizabethan Poor Law (1601), which was frequently amended during the seventeenth and eighteenth centuries, was still the basic social legislation at the turn of the nineteenth century. It charged parish overseers with the responsibility of caring for those unable to do for themselves, provided workhouses in which orphans, the able-bodied aged, and the unemployed might be gainfully occupied, and prescribed punishment for vagrants and vagabonds. But the record of public welfare in the country's ten thousand parishes appears to have been inadequate. Parish residents were obliged to support the needy through special levies, but there is no indication that overseers did more than the minimum for the benefit of lifelong residents, much less for strangers stranded in unfamiliar neighborhoods and in need of homes and work. Compassion and social responsibility were alien to many Englishmen in the eighteenth-century—and to their progeny —until the state assumed in the twentieth century the administration and cost of public welfare. But despite this sorry state of affairs, some politicians, reformers, and industrialists showed concern for human misery, and, before the social legislation of the mid-nineteenth century, acts were occasionally passed to provide medical, educational, and social benefits for women and children employed in mines and factories. Nevertheless such reforms fell short of what today would be considered the minimal standard.

In addition to the industrial urban proletariat, the economic changes created a new breed of energetic capitalists, many of whom had risen from humble origins to become factory and mine owners. There had always been men of this sort, of course (the Tudor and Stuart periods are full of such examples), but rapid industrialization in the later eighteenth century set them apart as a distinct social class roughly on a par with the upper gentry, and, in a few cases, with the landed aristocrats. Their rising importance may be gauged by the number of them whom Pitt the Younger and Lord Liverpool made peers in the period from the 1780s to the 1820s. Like the agricultural upper classes, the industrial aristocracy built sumptuous houses on the outskirts of factory towns, sent their sons to the universities and the Inns of Court for training and the cultivation of social connections that prepared them for careers in the law, the armed forces, the Church, and business. The businessmen also controlled local patronage and elections to Parliament, and they frequently dominated municipal government. As their wealth increased, so too did their political power and their agitation for more representation in Parliament. The latter was partly realized in the Reform Act of 1832, which redistributed some seats in Commons to the new industrial centers (see Chapter 13). Industrialists can no more be lumped into categories as favoring or opposing this or that principle of reform or traditionalism than any other group—but, in general, many of them advocated reform of the representative system, were concerned lest social reform would strengthen the working classes, supported liberalization of the fiscal and commercial systems, and advocated freer trade relations and a minimum of governmental interference with business.

The industrialists who argued in favor of laissez faire, the antithesis of the outmoded and restrictive mercantilist system that was still the economic policy of Britain, had been converted to the doctrines of Adam Smith, author of the famous *Wealth of Nations* (1776). Born at Kirkcaldy, Scotland, and educated at Glasgow and Oxford universities, Smith accepted in 1752 the chair of moral philosophy, which included economics, at Glasgow University. He left this post in 1764 for extended travel on the Continent, where he met prominent rationalists like François Quesnay and Anne Robert Turgot. They were physiocrats, economic theorists who argued that all wealth stemmed directly from the land, and that the only true producers in the economy were farmers, miners, and foresters. Industrialists and merchants were "sterile" producers, who merely processed and distributed the wealth and derived most of the profit from it. Contending that any governmental interference with the natural laws of supply and demand would disrupt the cycle of production, processing, and distribution, the physiocrats urged that industrialists and merchants should not be hindered—laissez faire—and that any sort of mercantilist restraints or attempts to stimulate artificially a favorable trade balance by legislation was inimical to natural economic development.

The physiocrats greatly influenced Smith's views on economic liberalism. Unlike the mercantilists and physiocrats, however, he believed that neither gold nor land, but labor was the basis of wealth, and that the value of commodities should be reckoned primarily by the labor that went into their production, whether on farms or in factories. The industrial bourgeoisie and merchants played a vital part in manufacturing and distributing the finished products. The prevailing mercantilist view that competition from foreign states was harmful to the national economic welfare of Britain was untrue, Smith said, for national economies are in fact closely dependent on each other so that the free exchange of goods in the international market according to natural laws of supply and demand benefits all without injury to any. He contended that, except for punitive tariffs aimed at forcing high-tariff states to open their ports to British goods, all trade barriers—customs duties, trusts, monopolies, price regulations, and restraints on colonial industry and trade—should be abolished. He believed that mercantilism also kept food prices high, to the particular detriment of the working classes and domestic agricultural growth, and necessitated the development of industries in Britain, although the country lacked the special labor skills and raw materials required to make them profitable enterprises. The division of labor according to men's special talents, Smith added, would of itself create individual wealth, and the collective productivity of hundreds of thousands of workers would naturally enrich the nation. Such views were enchanting to some politicians, including Prime Minister William Pitt, who tried to put them into practice in a commercial treaty with France in 1787 (see p. 324), but the concept of free trade was so alien to the British mind that it did not win wide acceptance until the mid-nineteenth century.

Smith's economic theories applied to agricultural productivity as well as to industrial output at a time when the growing population of Britain led the government to regulate exports and imports of corn (a generic term including all grain cereals—wheat, rye, barley, oats, and maize). From time to time since the fourteenth century, the crown had attempted to stimulate exportation of corn. In 1689, for instance, Parliament had passed the Corn Bounty Act, under which exporters of corn were paid subsidies to sell it abroad at domestic prices. This policy continued until 1773, when a new Corn Law was passed to discourage the exportation of corn because the growing population and occasional poor harvests had brought surpluses dangerously low. When domestic corn ran short, large quantities of foreign corn were imported, flooding the market and lowering prices, which was disadvantageous to home producers, who had strong spokesmen in Parliament. Periodically after 1773, therefore, Parliament enacted new Corn Laws, which imposed duties on foreign corn and other regulations in order to keep prices at a fixed level. The law of 1804, for instance, prohibited exports when the price of domestic corn rose above fifty-six shillings a quarter (eight bushels), and allowed imports so long as domestic producers got at least sixty-three shillings a quarter. While in principle the Corn Laws ensured that the British people would always have a sufficient supply of grain at fairly stable prices, and while home growers neither got rich nor were impoverished by those laws, they tended also to inflate prices to the advantage of the landed proprietors who produced most of it. The Corn Laws were consequently unpopular with industrialists, who argued that they forced them to pay higher wages, and with the working classes, who blamed them for the high price of bread. This was especially the case in hard or troubled times—during the Revolutionary War and most of the Napoleonic Wars (1793–1815), when little corn was imported; and during famine years in the depression of 1816–19 (all discussed in the following chapter). The Corn Law of 1815 forbade corn imports until the domestic price reached eighty shillings a quarter, and was obviously intended to support the inflated grain prices of the preceding war years. The government of Lord Liverpool, recognizing the hardship and social unrest created by crop failures in 1825, proposed to institute a sliding scale of tariffs on corn that would promote imports when the domestic price was high, and discourage them when it was low. Parliament rejected this bill, but during the succeeding ministry of the Duke of Wellington it passed an almost identical bill. Sir Robert Peel's ministry repealed the Corn Laws in 1846.

Some politicians and theoreticians obviously disagreed with Smith's formula for prosperity. Economists including Thomas Malthus, David

Ricardo, Jeremy Bentham, and John Stuart Mill advanced their own proposals for improving the commonweal or predicted misery for the masses if present trends continued unchecked. Malthus, a Hertfordshire clergyman and economics teacher, argued in his *Essay on Population* (1798) that, as the population of Britain was growing much faster than its supply of food, man would be reduced to starvation unless some national catastrophe like famine, war, or disease intervened to reduce the population. Nothing should be attempted by the government, he said, to try to improve the workers' standard of living because this would tend to enlarge the population; hence workers should be paid only enough for mere subsistence and they should be persuaded to marry later and exercise voluntary restraint in procreation. Malthus' arguments had an appeal in a society whose population had grown by 50 per cent in only forty years, but they had serious flaws: he mistakenly reckoned that socioeconomic conditions were immutable and failed to take into account either man's ingenuity in providing the necessities of life or the possibility of exchanging industrial goods for foodstuffs in international trade. The banker David Ricardo, likewise a prophet of gloom, believed that profits from invested capital in industry and agriculture would gradually diminish. He said this was particularly true of rents, which he defined as the cost of using land or other natural resources. He contended that the town worker would always be kept poor by the operation of the "iron law of wages," i.e. wages would tend to remain at the subsistence level, because of an oversupply of workers and an undersupply of jobs. Since this situation was permanent, society should not bother to try to improve public welfare by social and economic legislation, for that would tend to increase the population still further and compound the evil of unemployment. Bentham and Mill were the strongest advocates of the school of thought called utilitarianism, in the spirit of which much of the reform legislation of the Victorian period was passed. Bentham, a jurist, tireless traveler, and *raconteur*, proposed that it was the government's duty to promote laws for "the greatest happiness of the greatest number," and that all laws should be measured by the yardstick of whether they decreased human misery. As the workers could not help themselves, and their employers often would not aid them, it was the government's business to assure that the economy grew steadily, that job security and freedom from want was guaranteed to every worker and his family, and that gross social inequities were rectified. Mill, a philosophical and legal scholar and sometime civil servant and member of Parliament, contended in his *Principles of Political Economy* (1848) that workers had no choice but unemployment in the capitalist system unless they were willing to accept low wages and their employers' conditions of employment. He agreed with Bentham that the government must do everything possible to diminish human misery and ignorance, but he emphasized that the state must never intrude upon personal liberty or become patriarchal. He believed men should be free to order their lives as they chose, but that this was possible only if they had a measure of financial security and an adequate education. Appeals by Mill and other utilitarians helped to create a favorable milieu for the socioeconomic reforms of late Georgian and early Victorian Britain.

Britain was fertile ground for the spades of humanitarians. While many of the landed aristocracy and industrial bourgeoisie enjoyed their country estates, fox hunting, cricket, gambling, port wine, and fat mutton, prisoners were being treated like caged animals in inhumane prisons, whipped and pilloried in public squares before jeering crowds, dangled from gibbets at Tyburn and the Old Bailey, and victimized by the harsh criminal code. About two hundred crimes, many of which are today only misdemeanors, were punishable by death. The insane were crammed into filthy common cells at Bedlam and other institutions that provided amusement for Sunday strollers.

Neither the penal code nor prison conditions had changed since Elizabethan times. To our society, which shudders at the thought of hanging or electrocuting even hardened criminals, it is shocking to learn that stealing a sheep, a piece of linen, or forty shillings, pickpocketing, felling a tree in a garden, or catching fish in another's pond were all punishable by death. Yet more heinous crimes, such as attempted patricide, wounding with a knife, arson, perjury, and housebreaking, were only misdemeanors in the late eighteenth century. Petty theft, rioting, disorderly conduct, and a host of other relatively minor offenses called for transportation to the penal colonies in the West Indies and Australia, and thousands of debtors, many of them victims of abject poverty, were imprisoned for years. Fortunately some juries, recognizing the inhumanity and sheer illogic of the criminal code, recommended mercy or refused to convict, and thereby saved lives. Crowds eager to catch a glimpse of a tormented man on the scaffold took pleasure in his pain. More than four hundred executions occurred in Middlesex alone during Lord North's ministry (1770–82).

Considering the deplorable state of most prisons—filthy, vermin-ridden, hellholes where debtors and women were cast into common cells with murderers—the executed may have been more fortunate than the inmates who, until the 1780s, had to pay fees to the jailer for admittance and discharge, for straw for a bed, and even for food, and higher fees for simple privileges like a walk in the fresh air, a lice-free cell, or privacy. Prisons like the Old Bailey (Newgate), the Compter, and the Fleet in London, or those at Derby and Bedford in the provinces, were dilapidated structures, many of which had been built in the sixteenth century or earlier. Not uncommonly, jails were built over or near open sewers or putrid streams that flooded the lower cells, filled prisoners' nostrils with the stench of offal, and bred diseases like typhus, tuberculosis, and jail fever. Aged and sick prisoners were sometimes left to die without aid, and spiritual comfort was not regularly provided. When the common jails were full, rotten hulks anchored in the Thames swallowed up the overflow.

Prison reform was a long time in coming. Some private citizens, mostly Methodists and Quakers, did what they could to ease the lot of prisoners, and prison reform societies like the London Missionary Society and the Church Missionary Society raised money and dispensed charity to them. Other persons promoted legislative reform by shocking Parliament with evidence of barbarity and unconcern. Foremost among them were John Howard, high sheriff of Bedford, Sir Samuel Romilly, solicitor general in 1806, and the Quaker gentlewoman Elizabeth Fry. Howard led the way, beginning in 1773, by visiting prisons on both sides of the Channel to prove that English jails were worse than the notorious Bastille. Although public apathy repeatedly frustrated him, he did manage to stop the collection of jailer's fees, secured legislation providing some privacy, regular labor, and educational training for inmates, and induced some town administrations to build new prisons. Romilly convinced Parliament to reduce by a few the number of crimes punishable by death, but most of his bills were rejected, as were the reforms proposed by Elizabeth Fry, who founded an organization in 1817 to assist women prisoners in Newgate. Their strenuous efforts accomplished pitifully little and the prisons and the criminal code in 1820 were not substantially different from what they had been sixty years earlier. Among the Tory reforms of the 1820s, however, were some sponsored by Home Secretary Sir Robert Peel that provided decent accommodations and treatment for prisoners and cut the number of crimes punishable by death by about a half.

Romilly, Fry, and others likewise labored assiduously to erase the blight of the slave trade, which English shipowners from Bristol and

Liverpool had pursued since the late sixteenth century, and which had been greatly encouraged by the Treaty of Utrecht (1713), which guaranteed England a monopoly of the slave trade between Africa and Spanish America. The slavers either bought and sold Africans, most of whom were victims of tribal wars or had been captured by dealers in human flesh, or transported them to the New World, bringing back cotton, sugar, and other goods in the return voyage. Many of the slaves, locked below decks without proper ventilation, food, or much water during a long voyage of several weeks, died en route or as a result of mistreatment. Several million slaves were conveyed to the West Indies and America in 175 years. In Sir Robert Walpole's time, British slavers carried, on the average, 75,000 to 100,000 slaves annually, and, even with the interruption of the American Revolution, the average was about 40,000 to 50,000 in the latter part of the century. Liverpool-based merchantmen brought a total of nearly 400,000 slaves to the West Indies in 1783–93.

Aside from the Quakers, few raised their voices before the mid-eighteenth century against the barbarous and inhuman treatment of slaves in the so-called middle passage, which was the middle link in the trade from Britain to western Africa, from there to the New World, and then back to England. Because of the profits made by manufacturers who shipped goods to Africa on the first leg of such journeys, many of them condoned slavery and ignored its immorality. By the early years of George III's reign, however, the influence of John Wesley and the evangelical movement began to be felt and numerous abolitionist societies and organizations were established for the betterment of conditions among slaves. Headed by men like Granville Sharp, Thomas Clarkson, and William Wilberforce, they informed the British public of the horrors of the middle passage and the barbarous treatment of slaves in the West Indies, and advocated the abolition of the slave trade. Wilberforce (d. 1833), the independently wealthy son of a Hull merchant, member of Parliament for Hull and later Yorkshire, and the close friend of Pitt the Younger, spent his entire adult life struggling to help the slaves. In 1787 he founded the Society for the Abolition of the Slave Trade, and in the following year, largely because of his influence, a government committee studied the evidence of cruelty and deprivation among the slaves and recommended some improvements that Parliament later enacted into law. Pitt did what he could to help Wilburforce achieve abolition, but Parliament, which included able spokesmen for the Liverpool and Bristol slavers and the mercantile interests in

England and the West Indies, hamstrung their efforts and repeatedly blocked antislavery legislation.

The excesses of the French revolutionaries made all reform in England unpopular and suspect, with the result that the movements for the abolition of the slave trade and for emancipation of slaves were effectively checked until the early nineteenth century. Charles James Fox and the reform Whigs, along with the Clapham Sect, a group of conservative Anglicans who instituted a movement that stressed traditionalism in Christianity and dispensed charity through the Church Missionary Society (founded 1797) and the British and Foreign Bible Society (1804), espoused the abolitionist cause. It was largely owing to Fox that the Act which abolished the slave trade in 1807 was passed. Thereafter the struggle to abolish slavery itself continued. A milestone had been reached when, in 1772, Chief Justice the Earl of Mansfield ruled in the case of the slave Somerset, who had sued for his freedom when his master brought him to England, that slaves automatically became free once they touched English soil. But notwithstanding this important decision, slavery continued—with bloody results in the insurrections of the 1790s in the French and British West Indies (discussed in the next chapter). After the end of the Napoleonic War in 1815, and the serious economic and social unrest of the postwar period, the Tories began a reform movement that the Whigs continued after 1830. One result was the abolition of slavery throughout the Empire in 1833.

Industrialism deeply affected the lives of the proletariat, widened the gulf between them and the upper classes, created a multitude of social and economic problems, and raised questions of morality, justice, and charity. Many workers and their employers looked to organized religion for answers to these important questions, but the powerful and wealthy Anglican Church had difficulty answering. While society had undergone traumatic changes, the liturgy, tenets, attitudes, and range of responsibility of the Established Church had varied little since the Restoration in 1660. The seventeenth-century disputes between Anglicans and Dissenters no longer raged, and Anglicanism slipped into complacency. But new foes like secularism, opportunism, and a deism that practically deified rationalism, loomed large before the Anglican divines in the eighteenth century. Scientists and philosophers disputed traditional doctrines based on the Scriptures and supernatural causation. Industrial workers often lost faith in a seemingly unconcerned Supreme Being. Businessmen, drunk with the heady wine of profit that brought physical comfort, began to identify themselves with a mechanistic and ordered universe that had been devised, created, and then practically abandoned by the impersonal, unprovidential God of deism. These challenging developments demanded swift consideration by concerned and imaginative clerics, but the Anglican Church had too few of them.

The Restoration settlement had re-established the primacy of Anglicanism, but the Revolution of 1688 ultimately worked to the Church of England's disadvantage by legalizing Protestant Dissenter sects. The Glorious Revolution, a Whig victory in Church and state, brought latitudinarianism in its wake, augmented the political importance of the Dissenters, and helped to destroy the mutually beneficial connection between the crown and the state Church. Notwithstanding Queen Anne's deep devotion to the Anglican Church and her efforts to promote higher standards among the clergy by selecting only trusted High-churchmen for hierarchic posts, Anglicanism lost both parishioners and prestige. The signs of the times were plain to see in 1717, when George I, an Anglican by necessity but a Lutheran at heart, dissolved Convocation, which, together with the crown, had formerly governed the Church. Thereafter Parliament played a more vital role in helping the supreme governor of the Church of England to rule it.

Moreover, the Anglican hierarchy came increasingly under the influence of politicians, first under the Whigs to 1760, and afterward under the Tories. Although the involvement of prelates in politics was hardly novel—it had been going on since the beginning of Christianity in England—the influence of the prelates, twenty-six of whom sat in the House of Lords, was exploited more frequently for political advantage in the eighteenth century. Usually fewer than 150 of the approximately 225 temporal and ecclesiastical peers entitled to sit in the Lords attended Parliament in any session. Since many votes in the Lords were close, the twenty-six votes of the prelates assumed great importance. Moreover, the bishops were obliged to attend Parliament at Westminster for several months each year, usually from late October to May or June, a responsibility that kept them away from their diocesan duties for long periods, and left too few weeks to deal with them properly. Consequently the bishops' visitations of parishes were often infrequent and hurried; candidates for ordination to the priesthood were sometimes inadequately examined by bishops, who licensed them without knowledge of spiritual or intellectual shortcomings that closer scrutiny would have bared; and confirmations were delayed in some parishes by as much as four years. In addition, bishops were expected to help elect party candidates, which took time and money, and they were overburdened with visitors and social fetes. As the expenses of most bishoprics were greater than their income, incumbents sought translation from poorer dioceses like Bristol and Oxford, which returned annual revenues of £450 and £500 respectively, to richer sees such as Durham and Winchester, which were worth £6000 and £5000. Episcopal preferments, as well as preferments to other higher ecclesiastical offices such as prebendary, canon, dean, and royal chaplain, depended more on the candidate's family background, social connections, and political views than on administrative ability or spiritual strength. All things considered, too many prelates got preferments because they were politically acceptable to the party or faction in control of Parliament and the cabinet. While there were some devoted, spiritually sincere, and industrious hierarchs, too many neglected their responsibilities either by choice or because of the press of secular affairs, or simply succumbed to the pleasures of life. Their presence tended to weaken public confidence in the Anglican Church.

Some vicars and curates had as little spirituality, scholarly interest, and administrative talent as their superiors. Laziness, drunkenness, and irresponsibility were not uncommon among the lower clergy. For a number of reasons, the Established Church did not attract many outstanding men to the priesthood. One was the difficulty of rising through the ranks to high office unless one had the qualifications mentioned above. Many young men from poorer families, who had managed to complete a few terms at Oxford or Cambridge by serving the gentlemen commoners (sons of the gentry and aristocracy) as servitors, battelers, or poor scholars, were forced by lack of funds to leave the university before taking their degrees in order to earn a living. The Anglican priesthood was a convenient way of doing so. These clergy frequently lacked theological training and a spiritual vocation; indeed, some could scarcely remember the number of Articles professed by the Anglican Church (thirty-nine), much less what tenets they contained. Curates, pastoral assistants to vicars, were in most cases doomed to a life of poverty without hope of advancement to higher-paying benefices. Of the 10,000 benefices in England during the eighteenth century, only about 6000 provided an annual revenue of over £50, and more than 1200 yielded less than £20. Curates without much experience sometimes administered parishes for absentee vicars who held two or more benefices. Instances of pluralism were fairly common even though a Tudor statute (21 Henry VIII, cap. 13) and the forty-first canon of the Canons of 1604 had expressly forbidden any clergyman to hold an additional benefice unless his original one provided an income under £8. Pluralism and shoddy administration inevitably damaged the spiritual quality of the Church.

On the other hand, the career of Samuel Wesley, vicar of Epworth Parish in Lincolnshire, who reared and personally educated eighteen children on an annual income of £45 or £50, is evidence enough of the devotion, learning, and sacrifice of some Anglican priests. At his knee, John and Charles Wesley, the founders of Methodism, learned Greek and Latin and read the theological, philosophical, and historical works that prepared them for further study at Oxford University and arduous lives of preaching and humanitarianism. John Wesley (1703–91) was reared in a society that questioned the divine origin of Christianity, revelation as a source of faith, the truth and efficacy of the Bible, miracles, and other axioms of religion. Both the Anglican and Calvinist denominations (such as the Congregationalists and Presbyterians) were rebuked by rationalists like David Hume, author of *An Enquiry Concerning Human Understanding* (1748), who rejected miracles as irrational and contrary to the immutable laws of nature, and argued that creation was the only revelation by God, if indeed He existed at all. Skeptics, rationalists, deists, and Unitarians abounded in the early eighteenth century. Against their denunciations, the traditionalist Anglicans generated a counterattack in the pulpits, the pamphlet press, and the meetings that became an integral part of the evangelical movement. This movement, which reached its apogee after 1815, began quietly in the 1730s, and had great appeal for the middle and upper classes, which espoused its emphasis on personal religion and humanitarian work among the oppressed lower classes. The Clapham Sect, mentioned earlier, was a typically evangelical association, as were the several Bible and missionary societies. Evangelicalism inspired hundreds of devotional works, giant religious rallies, and fervid discussions at the fireside, helped to spread Methodism, and played an immensely important role in promoting the socioeconomic reform legislation of the nineteenth century.

Methodism, a reform movement akin to evangelicalism within the Anglican Church, spawned in the hearts of the Wesley brothers and about a dozen of their friends, who formed the "Holy Club" while students at Oxford in the 1720s. They were greatly influenced by a book entitled the *Serious Call to a Devout and Holy Life* (1728), written by the Northamptonshire recluse William Law, formerly a fellow at the university and private tutor to Edward Gibbon, the eminent historian of Rome. Reminiscent of Thomas a Kempis' *Imitation of Christ* (composed in the fifteenth century), Law's work appealed to the conscience, asking men to live a Christlike life of devotion, study, and Christian brotherhood. More eighteenth-century teachers and students could have profited by reading it. Too many ignored their studies, gave or attended pedestrian lectures, and wasted time in pursuit of pleasure. One could not expect educational standards to be high in a society that counted social connections and personal adornment more important than learning. The Wesley circle, on the other hand, met regularly to study the Bible and the classics, took Communion and confessed their sins regularly, and did what little their annual allowances of about ten pounds would permit for the poor, the sick, the imprisoned, and the orphaned. Frivolous fellow students ridiculed their methodical way of life, and, as has so often been the case with a minority, its detractors provided a name—Methodists—that has long outlived them.

The spark of pietism (emphasis on personal spiritual conversion to Christ) that burned in the breasts of the Wesley brothers ignited the faith of thousands of persons on both sides of the Atlantic and eventually spread throughout the world. Following a disheartening experience as missionaries in James Oglethorpe's colony of Georgia, the Wesleys returned to England in 1738 to preach the doctrine of personal salvation by faith inspired by God, a view they had acquired from Law as well as some Moravian Brethren they had met in America. Thereafter they traveled the length and breadth of Britain, preaching generally in fields to huge audiences that were moved to tears by their zeal and eloquence. Methodism appealed most to the oppressed lower classes—the colliers, factory hands, and simple craftsmen—who had lost confidence in the pious platitudes of Anglican divines. It attracted men seeking a rationale of life to sustain them through daily trials because it appealed to the heart, not the mind.

While the Wesleys preached in London and the north, their friend George Whitefield (d. 1770), the volatile, erratic son of a Gloucestershire tavern keeper, stumped the industrial areas of the southwest, delivering simple but electrifying homilies in the finest tradition of evangelism. Despite the biting sarcasm of circumspect Anglican clergymen, who derided the Wesleys' methods, generally refused them permission to preach in churches, and scoffed at their repeated professions of allegiance to the parent Church, Methodism continued to grow. It also survived a quarrel between Whitefield and the Wesleys that caused a schism within the movement. After a time the Methodists inevitably separated administratively and doctrinally from Anglicans, who insisted on subscription to the Real Presence in communion, episcopal rule, and canonical training and ordination of the clergy. Methodist chapels served by unordained ministers sprang up around the country, congregations rejected episcopal sovereignty, and parish, provincial, and national meetings and conferences in the tradition of the synodal and conciliar systems replaced the customary Anglican pyramid of ecclesiastical authority. By 1797, when the new Church had some 100,000 members, the last link between the Wesleyan Methodists and the Anglicans was broken.

12

Reaction and Reform, 1793–1830

The French Revolution (1789–99) profoundly affected British domestic affairs, for it retarded political and social reform for a generation and endangered civil liberty. The transition from monarchy to republicanism in France caused frequent debates in the British Parliament and press, widened the gulf between reformers and the conservative government of Pitt, and entrenched the Tory oligarchy. Hopeful men with genuinely humanitarian ideas as well as political opportunists like Fox who, although sympathetic to some reform, sponsored it primarily to regain political power, had tried for decades to reform Parliament and rectify social inequalities. They accomplished pitifully little largely because Pitt, who initially helped them, wearied of promoting lost causes against strong aristocratic conservative opposition, and because the excesses of the Revolution made reform in Britain unpopular. Most responsible segments of British society recognized, even if they did not wish to support, the urgency of moderating the severe criminal code, abolishing the slave trade, correcting the abuses in the electoral and representative systems, relieving economic distress among the lower classes, and encouraging a measure of religious freedom for Roman Catholics. Despite insufficient support to effectuate their proposals, the reformers made a start, and few questioned their motives before 1793. While their aims were radical in that they would have modified traditional social and political practices, the means by which such aims were promoted were peaceful and orderly. But after the Revolution began, the authorities unfortunately made the mistake of associating French radicals, who had overturned their social order, with British reformers, who never intended to upset basic institutions. As a result, in the 1790s the reactionary Tory oligarchy repressed the reformers in the mistaken belief that they were a threat to national security and the established social order. While in 1789 many Englishmen supported the ideals of reform symbolized in the French Revolution, by 1793, when Britain and France went to war, reform and dissent had become seditious words and their exponents were regarded as dangerous malcontents.

It is difficult to see what there was about the reformers' goals that suggested sedition, for while some pamphleteers did relate French problems vis-à-vis the lower classes to circumstances in Britain, and others said some startling things about the oppressions of the governing class, the reformers generally conducted themselves moderately and peacefully. The three best-known reform organizations were the London Corresponding Society, the Society of Friends of the People, and the Society for Promoting Constitutional Information. The first, composed of skilled tradesmen and shopkeepers, wished to broaden the franchise among townsmen in order to increase popular representation in Parliament. The second society, founded in 1792, was made up mostly of Whig followers of Fox, and advocated reform of Parliament by the abolition of patronage, the reduction of high franchise qualifications, and an increase in the representation of heavily populated districts as a means of breaking the Tory monopoly of government. The third, a vehicle for bourgeois opinion, took a moderate position embodying most of the proposals of the other two. Youths, romanticists, artisans, craftsmen, hungry workingmen—mostly neither poor nor rich—joined other reform societies in the hope of remedying what they believed to be grievances perpetrated by the governing class, and corresponded with French revolutionary clubs about idealistic proposals that might institute a new social order in Britain.

Agitation for reform sometimes led to rioting, as it did at Dundee, Birmingham, and Sheffield in 1791–95. In some cases, however, the riots were begun by reactionaries who feared for their property and privileged status. Often, unrest was directly related to high prices and famine. The war reduced trade in grain which, together with a scarcity of grain resulting from a succession of bad harvests, forced up prices to a point where the poor could not afford to buy bread. The price of wheat, for instance, rose from 54s. a quarter in 1791 to 90s. 4d. in 1796, the year after the worst famine in recent memory. This understandably led to bread riots throughout the country and denunciations of the government, which was unjustly blamed for inflation. In short, the reform societies and the spontaneous riots among hungry men were not rooted in sedition nor were they a serious threat to the upper classes.

The latter nevertheless closed ranks in the belief that the unrest was aimed at overthrowing the social order, and that any concessions to the agitators might break the barrier that separated privileged society from the masses.

For this reason, Pitt's government passed statutes that restricted civil liberty and resulted in the prosecution of hundreds of allegedly seditious persons. Pitt and Parliament were certainly not alone in their conviction that patriotism should be equated with support of the government: by 1793 there were far more antirevolutionary clubs than reform societies, and except for occasional demonstrations in some large cities in the south and in the economically depressed areas of Scotland, the country as a rule raised no objection to the government's attempt to legislate political conformity. At first Pitt was satisfied with the issuance of a proclamation in May, 1792, that outlawed "seditious" meetings and publications. In the following December, however, he ordered the militia to make ready for possible rebellion. In 1794, Parliament suspended habeas corpus over the strong opposition of Fox and his Whig followers, who unsuccessfully resisted what was a clear denial of personal rights, allowing the government to detain suspects indefinitely without trial. The next year Parliament passed two laws, the Seditious Meetings Act and the Treasonable Practices Act, which empowered the courts to sentence to transportation to the penal colonies anyone who spoke against the king or the government, criticized the fundamental institutions of the country, or tried to pressure Parliament into enacting reforms.

The enforcement of these statutes was left to the local magistrates, some of whom conducted witch-hunts for "Jacobins" or republicans— names given to anyone sympathetic to even moderate reform. While it is true that many of the accused were acquitted, dozens of others were given stiff penalties that can be explained only by the seeming panic that gripped the upper classes. In Scotland, Lord Braxfield did his utmost, even to the point of browbeating jurors, to convict any and all accused of sedition. Thomas Muir, an officer of the Glasgow Society of the Friends of the People, was sentenced to transportation to Botany Bay (Australia) for fourteen years, as were scores of others. Juries in London, however, could not be so easily swayed, so that the government's attempt to convict a dozen leaders of the reform societies failed after three of them—Horne Tooke, John Thelwall, and Thomas Hardy —were acquitted. Nevertheless, in some towns house-to-house searches uncovered suspected radicals and revolutionaries, who were sentenced to stand in the pillory, fines, imprisonment, or transportation to Botany Bay simply for criticizing the war or advocating greater social equality and popular representation. Repression drove the reformers underground with the result that the sedition trials tapered off—only to be revived in 1798–1800, when the corresponding societies were suppressed and the infant labor unions were outlawed by the Combination Acts of 1799–1800 as conspiracies to restrain trade. Many unions continued to exist, however, under the guise of benevolent societies, and in 1824 Parliament rescinded the Acts, thereby enabling workingmen to bargain for shorter hours and higher wages.

Although Britain went to war with France just ten years after concluding peace with the Americans, the army was nevertheless ill-prepared to cope with the remarkable strength of the French citizen army. In 1783, in accordance with the traditional British conviction that standing armies in peacetime were dangerous and costly, Pitt immediately reduced the army to 17,000 men. This was defensible in that Britain scrupulously avoided Continental entanglements in the following decade. As late as 1790, the army numbered only about 20,000. By 1792, however, Parliament, over the objections of Pitt, who disliked increasing the armed forces or the taxes to support them, had gradually authorized increases in the army's numerical strength by the addition of 35,000 infantry and cavalry and 20,000 mercenaries from Hanover and Hesse. These increases were financed primarily through existing resources rather than through taxation. With the onset of war, the army was substantially enlarged, but, even so, in 1794, it consisted of approximately 75,000 regulars and 90,000 militia, far below the strength of Continental armies. In addition to its numerical weakness, abuses such as purchases of commissions to the rank of colonel, inadequate pay, poor rations, and inefficient recruiting techniques sapped its effectiveness and morale. Moreover, until the Duke of Wellington's Peninsular Campaign late in the war, the government wasted the army in costly and futile expeditions in the Low Countries, along the French and Spanish coasts, and in the West Indies.

The navy, on the other hand, was better equipped and more effective than at any time in the previous century thanks to the administrative reorganization by Charles Middleton, comptroller of the navy in 1778–90. As Pitt had little interest in the Continental struggle being waged by his allies, and aimed rather at enlarging the Empire at French expense (thereby following essentially his father's policy in the Seven Years' War), the navy was vital to his plans, and consequently had his support. Although conditions of naval service were as dreadful as ever (flogging, rotten food, cramped quarters, arrears in pay), and led to mutinies at the Nore and Spithead in 1797, British seamen fought valiantly. That there were relatively few major battles at sea from 1793 to 1814 was due to the manifest superiority of British fire power and tactics, and the timidity of the French admirals, who kept their ships at anchor rather than run the risk of further defeats like those at Camperdown and Trafalgar. The navy also kept supply lines open: British control of the seas protected commerce, and commerce enabled Britain and its allies to persist even after Napoleon had conquered most of Europe.

At the commencement of the war with France in 1793, Britain allied with Austria, Prussia, Holland, Spain, Sardinia-Piedmont, and several smaller German states in the First Coalition (1793–97). The alliance was weak not only because of rivalry between Austria and Prussia over the second and third partitions of Poland in 1793 and 1795, but also because of the apathy of Holland and the military weakness of Spain and the lesser Hapsburg dominions. The loosely organized allies planned an uncoordinated attack on France on four fronts, the British (27,000 men, mostly German mercenaries) and Dutch advancing from the Austrian Netherlands, the Piedmontese crossing the Italian Alps, the Spanish moving over the Pyrenees, and the Austro-Prussians marching across the upper Rhine. These armies, with a total strength of 300,000 men, were to converge on Paris in the hope of swiftly concluding the war. All indications pointed to certain victory: the Girondists and Jacobins were at one another's throats in the French Assembly; the country was in a state of political and financial disorder; rebellions had erupted at Lyons, Toulon (which surrendered to the British in 1793), and in the Vendée, the district around the Loire estuary, among townsmen and peasants hostile to the radicalism in Paris. Revolt also had rocked the French West Indian colony of Santo Domingo, where Negro slaves had massacred their masters in 1791, permitted the British to occupy Port-au-Prince in 1793, and organized a republic under the inspired leadership of Toussaint L'Ouverture. In addition, the French army was disorganized. But the situation had changed completely before the end of the year. The Jacobins had overturned the Girondists in June, restored order through the Reign of Terror, smashed the rebellions in Lyons and the Vendée, recaptured Toulon, and repulsed the invaders on all fronts with the powerful conscripted army raised by War Minister Carnot.

The years 1793–95 were disastrous for the allies in Europe. The Austro-British campaign in the Low Countries failed miserably. Rather than follow the general plan devised by the Austrian General Coburg for an advance on Paris following the capture of the French barrier fortresses, the Duke of York, the inept commander of the British army, separated his forces from the main army in a futile attempt to win a popular victory at Dunkirk. Coburg's advance had also been stopped cold with the result that the northern assault collapsed. During 1794, the French steadily advanced into the Austrian Netherlands, forcing the British to withdraw across the Dutch frontier, then into Flanders, and finally to the Hanoverian border by early spring, 1795. After the British retreat, Holland became a French puppet state for the remainder of the war. The British Mediterranean fleet commanded by Lord Hood once again took Toulon, but the revolutionary forces recaptured it within the year with the help of an unknown artillery lieutenant named Napoleon Bonaparte. The British attempted to send aid to the Royalist sympathizers in the Vendée, but they were suppressed before the expeditionary troops could land. As Prussia was more interested in territorial aggrandizement in Poland, it withdrew most of its soldiers from the Rhine frontier to eastern Europe and concluded peace with France in April, 1795; Spain did likewise the following summer. Britain and Austria were therefore left to battle the enormous armies of the Republic, which sustained its only military reversals at the hands of the Hapsburgs in northern Italy in 1794–95.

The army's shameful performance in the Low Countries was offset by the navy's distinguished victories over French fleets, which finally took refuge in home ports rather than risk total annihilation. Except for a disastrous expedition to Quiberon in 1795, the navy won repeated victories. It captured the Cape of Good Hope, Malacca, and Ceylon as well as Corsica, at whose port of Ajaccio the Mediterranean fleet was thereafter based. Lord Howe successfully engaged the Brest fleet, destroying half its ships in a five-day battle on the high seas during May–June, 1794, called "The Glorious First of June," though the grain-laden French merchantmen from America that the French men-of-war had gone out to protect managed to slip by. The Mediterranean squadron commanded by Sir John Jervis, including a ship captained by Horatio Nelson, forestalled the merger of the French and Spanish navies (Spain had by that time defected to France) by defeating the vastly more numerous Spanish flotilla off Cape St. Vincent in February, 1797. Finally, Admiral Adam Duncan, after blockading the Dutch ships off

Texel, decisively defeated the Dutch in the Battle of Camperdown in the following October. These victories did much to dispel the gloom of Englishmen who were weary of defeats and suffering from successive years of famine.

During these same years Henry Dundas (Viscount Melville), secretary of war, promoted the conquest of the French West Indian islands at the cost of 40,000 British lives. As these islands, particularly Santo Domingo, were vital to the French economy and would be of untold advantage to British trade, Dundas and Pitt reasoned that their conquest would enhance the popularity of the government in a period of unrest and greatly injure France. Early in 1794, taking advantage of insurrections of Negro slaves against their French masters in several West Indian islands, British regulars occupied parts of Santo Domingo, and Tobago, Guadeloupe, Martinique, and St. Lucia. Seizure of the islands proved to be no problem, but holding them was another matter. The French forced the evacuation of Guadeloupe, and the native rebels, who considered the British as offensive as the French for failing to abolish slavery, began a general counteroffensive on all the islands. The rebels, led by Toussaint L'Ouverture, in 1795 began attacks on British garrisons in Santo Domingo that lasted for three years. Most of the soldiers who escaped the vengeance of the natives fell victim to yellow fever and other diseases, which decimated the West Indian army. When it had been reduced to less than 2000 men, Pitt dispatched Sir Ralph Abercromby with 17,000 reinforcements, but two-thirds of them were blown back by contrary winds and never reached their destinations. Thousands of others were subsequently sent as replacements. Abercromby established headquarters at Barbados and sent units to Grenada, St. Lucia, and St. Vincent to keep the rebels under control. Wounds and disease took a heavy toll in these campaigns, which occupied more trooops than Wellington commanded in the entire Peninsular Campaign a decade later. By 1798, Santo Domingo had to be evacuated, leaving Britain in possession of only Tobago, St. Lucia, and Martinique. The fruitless expenditure of so many lives and supplies, and so much money in the West Indies proved the folly of Pitt's insistence on concentrating upon the colonial struggle rather than the Continental war; unlike other British wars since 1660, the outcome of the struggle was finally determined in Europe. So long as Pitt was prime minister, however, British commitments on the Continent were minimal.

Weakened by the withdrawal of Prussia and the defeat of Holland

and Piedmont by the French revolutionary armies, the First Coalition collapsed altogether in 1797 when Austria, reeling from the crushing offensive generated by Napoleon along the Italian frontier, capitulated in the Treaty of Campo Formio. Three French governments had ruled since 1793—that of the Jacobins, the Thermidoreans, and the Directory—the last of which held power tenuously until Napoleon's *coup d'état* in 1799, which resulted in his appointment as First Consul and, in the next year, as sole Consul and virtual dictator of France. His meteoric rise to the command of all the revolutionary armies, and ultimately to the emperorship in 1804, is a remarkable record of duplicity, uncommon administrative ability, ambition bordering on the maniacal, boundless energy, and audacious military tactics. His commanding personality mesmerized the nation and transformed mere boys into fierce soldiers eager to proselytize for the ideals of revolutionary France throughout Europe.

Until the formation of the Second Coalition in 1799, Britain stood alone against the mighty Republic and constantly faced the threat of French invasion until the victory at Trafalgar in 1805 lifted the danger. The Directory had hoped to launch an invasion of England supported by the united French, Dutch, and Spanish fleets, but British naval triumphs at Cape St. Vincent and Camperdown in 1797 forced the postponement of the plan for which Napoleon had massed a huge army and flotilla at several Channel ports. Instead, at Napoleon's insistence, the Directory decided to strike a mortal blow at British commerce (which in turn supported its military expenditures and some of those of its allies) by conquering the Middle East, a vital link in the British lifeline to India. Never one to shrink from the impossible, Napoleon planned to take Egypt, cut a canal from the Mediterranean to the Red Sea, and lead his army to India. Sailing from Toulon, his armada of about three hundred ships crammed with forty-three thousand soldiers evaded Nelson's squadron then cruising in Neapolitan waters, seized Malta from the Knights of St. John who had ruled it since the Crusades, and disembarked at Alexandria. The French easily overwhelmed the Mamelukes, the ruling oligarchy, at the Battle of the Pyramids (July, 1798), but Nelson hurried to the eastern Mediterranean where he sank the bulk of the French transports in Aboukir Bay on August 1 in the Battle of the Nile, thereby hermetically sealing the French army in Egypt. The inhospitable climate, lack of supplies, and several defeats by an Anglo-Turkish force gradually sapped French strength and prevented Napoleon's reduction of the stronghold of Acre.

Meanwhile the Second Coalition (1799–1801), composed principally of Britain, Austria, and Russia, won important victories on several fronts but could not dislodge the French from Holland and Switzerland or push them beyond the Rhine frontier. The Directory's inability to cope with the Allied offensive and Napoleon's impatience with a course of affairs in which he was bypassed and plotted against, induced him to run the risk of evading the British blockade and to return to France. Leaving thousands of troops to die in the desert, he hurried to Paris to organize the *coup* of February, 1799, that resulted in his being named First Consul.

Napoleon's return immediately turned the tide against the Coalition, and, in the following two years, the British managed only to recapture Malta and force the evacuation of Egypt and Syria. Britain and Austria had nothing but trouble with their fickle ally, Russia, whose demented czar, Paul, drew his forces from the projected Anglo-Russian invasion of Holland. While the Austrians were being driven from Italy in the Marengo campaign, more British lives were fruitlessly wasted in raids on Spanish ports, expeditions to Minorca and Sicily, and the Anglo-Turkish offensive in Egypt that tied up sixteen thousand regulars and cost General Abercromby his life.

In 1801 the belligerents, exhausted by nearly a decade of war, talked peace. Napoleon was in a commanding position. He had pushed the Austrians back to within fifty miles of Vienna and had forced them to sign the humiliating Treaty of Lunéville (1801) following his overwhelming victory at Hohenlinden. The czar not only abandoned his allies, he also formed a League of Armed Neutrality composed of Sweden, Denmark, Prussia, and Russia, which threatened Britain's vital Baltic trade and necessitated the bombardment of Copenhagen. By that time the Coalition had died, as had Pitt's government, which had resigned over the issue of Catholic emancipation in Ireland. The only road left to Britain was peace; fortunately, France needed a respite from war just as desperately. The news of the final ratification of the Treaty of Amiens (March, 1802) sent Englishmen into a delirium of joyous celebration. Peace alone was the cause of their rejoicing, for the British had little to show for their sacrifices, not least of which were the heavy taxes they paid and the £334,000,000 added to the national debt since 1793. The treaty confirmed most of France's Continental conquests and gave Britain only Ceylon and Trinidad. Had the truth been known—that Napoleon had no intention of keeping peace for long—Britain would have been wise to spend the interval of two years before the formation of the Third Coalition girding itself for another French onslaught.

Pitt's government had been preoccupied with serious matters other than the French war and the domestic problems it had created. Foremost of these was the continuing unrest in Ireland. Its grievances over religion, land, industry, and trade (recounted in Chapter 10) had not been removed by the legislative independence grudgingly granted by the North and Rockingham ministries in 1778–82. Catholics could neither vote nor sit in the Irish Parliament, which was controlled largely by English patrons who owned the tenements and dictated the votes of their electors. The mass of the peasantry still suffered from rack rents, primitive agricultural methods, famine, and the oppression of the stewards who controlled the affairs of the absentee landowners, and of the land speculators, whose sole interest was in profits. Irish industry, which might have put the country in a sound financial condition had trade been free, was stifled by the Navigation Acts that stipulated what could be manufactured and with whom trade might be conducted. They also forced the Irish to export foodstuffs desperately needed at home, and to produce commodities that did not help the plight of the peasants. Finally, although several of the most offensive penal laws had been rescinded, Irish Catholics and Presbyterians had to pay tithes to the Established Church, which they could not afford and which the affluent Anglicans did not need.

Parliament granted Ireland legislative independence in 1782 and other minor economic, political, and religious concessions in the following decade. Largely because of Pitt's genuine concern for the Irish, as well as the ominous threat of rebellion that hung over the island, the Corn Laws were relaxed to admit its grain at lower customs rates. In 1793, Catholics holding life leases on land were granted the franchise. Catholic students were admitted to Trinity College, Dublin, and to the professions, which, except for medicine, had formerly been closed to them. Moreover Catholics were allowed to serve as justices of the peace and jurymen. But these concessions, although a significant break-through at least for the Catholic gentry, satisfied neither them nor the Anglo-Irish Presbyterian Ulsterites, for the English ruling oligarchy's dominant position in trade, landholding, patronage, and social status remained unchanged. Despite the fact that Irish industry and trade, particularly in wool, cotton, glass, sugar, and grain, thereafter grew steadily under the impetus of industrial mechanization and thereby helped to improve the Irish economy, the Dublin Parliament and the leaders of the Catholics and Presbyterians still resented the English. It was clearly and repeatedly demonstrated during the 1780s and 1790s that what the Irish really wanted was political and personal freedom from dependence on the English oligarchy.

The Irish began a policy of general resistance to the English on all issues, which took a radical turn in the formation of revolutionary associations soon after the outbreak of the French Revolution. The two best known were the Society of United Irishmen, founded at Belfast in 1791 by the lawyer Theobald Wolfe Tone, who hoped to unite all Irishmen in the struggle for political independence, and the Defenders, an underground organization of Catholic peasants who terrorized the countryside. A third organization, the Orange Lodges (named after William of Orange) was composed of Presbyterian irreconcilables bent on keeping Catholics out of power.

By 1795, Wolfe Tone had come to the conclusion that the only hope of achieving Irish independence lay in an alliance with revolutionary France, which, of course, was eager for any opportunity to weaken Britain. His decision undoubtedly resulted from the dismissal of Earl Fitzwilliam, whose term as Lord Lieutenant of Ireland (January to March, 1795) was cut short by the Pitt ministry's disapproval of his outspoken intention of effecting complete Catholic emancipation as soon as possible. Pitt privately agreed with Fitzwilliam, but he knew that such precipitous action, without the necessary groundwork, would alienate the English Anglican oligarchy, disturb the militant Presbyterians, and interrupt the gradual process of reform that he had in mind. It would also infuriate George III, who had an almost paranoiac hatred of Catholics. Fitzwilliam's dismissal therefore had the result of convincing the Presbyterians that London, not Dublin, controlled Irish affairs. It also annoyed the Catholics, whose hope of relief from religious stigma was shattered by the seeming duplicity of the government, which honestly had not expected the Lord Lieutenant to advocate full emancipation. Riots and insurrection followed: Catholic Defenders harassed the English and Orangemen in night raids; Orangemen closed ranks against Catholics; Pitt searched for a solution short of independence; and Wolfe Tone plotted with the Directory in Paris. In return for a Franco-Irish alliance of sorts, the French, in December, 1796, sent troops to invade Ireland in conjunction with a large army of Irish peasants, but heavy weather prevented a landing. The British victory at Camperdown the following year discouraged another attempt until late summer, 1798, when two small detachments of

Frenchmen unsuccessfully raided the Irish coast during the waning weeks of a fierce rebellion. The rebellion, which had been provoked by the imposition of martial law, curfews, house-burnings, and barbaric punishments aimed at restoring order, involved mostly Catholic peasants, who, without organization, adequate leadership, or effective weapons, were an easy prey for the government militia that overwhelmed them at Vinegar Hill (June, 1798) and put their houses and fields to the torch.

The rebellion convinced Pitt that the only solution was political union between England and Ireland on the same basis as the Anglo-Scottish union a century earlier. On this issue, sides were immediately taken: Lord Cornwallis and Viscount Castlereagh, the chief administrators in Ireland, as well as the Catholic aristocracy and priesthood, agreed with Pitt. On the other hand, a number of English members of Parliament and the Irish Protestant Parliament (which feared the consequences of the Catholic emancipation that originally came with the proposed plan of union) joined the king in opposition. Eventually, by assuring Anglicans that the Established Church would not be disestablished, by judicious use of pro-union propaganda, by promising to disrupt neither the existing franchise qualifications nor the system of Irish patronage, by bribery, by sacrificing emancipation, and finally by setting aside the king's objections and threatening to resign, Pitt convinced the London and Dublin Parliaments to pass the Act of Union (1800). It provided for the dissolution of the Irish Parliament, trade and monetary concessions to Ireland, continuation of the Established Church, and the island's representation in the united Parliament by thirty-two Irish peers (including four bishops) and one-hundred Irish members of Parliament.

Pitt's victory had come hard and not without damage to his popularity and support in both England and Ireland. The Irish Protestant upper classes—mostly merchants, former members of Parliament, and professionals—who, a decade earlier, had supported political reform, now opposed the union for fear they would lose their controlling position. And many Catholics, aristocrats as well as commoners, were disappointed by Pitt's inability to include Catholic emancipation in the arrangement. They had been led to assume that emancipation and the abolition of tithe payments to the Established Church would result from the union. Although Pitt had not definitely promised that they would, he urgently felt the necessity of both, for he realized that otherwise the union, which aimed at settling the Irish question, would not accomplish its purpose. But when he broached the subject privately in the cabinet in the autumn of 1800, the news leaked to the king, who immediately raised so much objection on the grounds that emancipation would violate his coronation oath to preserve the Anglican Church that, in February, 1801, Pitt resigned. The subject was not again mentioned until the late 1820s, and then only under the threat of another insurrection.

Henry Addington (later Viscount Sidmouth, 1757–1844), a conservative, retiring, and thrift-conscious former Speaker of the Commons, replaced Pitt. Except for Castlereagh, his cabinet consisted of second-raters chosen more on a basis of personal friendship than of talent. His ministry had little Parliamentary support initially and nothing like the party following enjoyed by Pitt. Had it not been for the conclusion of peace within a year of the government change-over, which pleased the upper classes who were weary of high taxes and the payment of large subsidies to Continental allies, and Pitt's sense of loyalty in supporting Addington, his term in office would have been very short. For the time being, the country willingly made do with him, appreciating his abolition of Pitt's unpopular income tax and sharing his conservative attitude toward such social and political reforms as abolition of the slave trade and Catholic emancipation. Accordingly, in the elections of 1802, additional pro-Addington members were returned to Parliament. While Addington's policies—speedy restoration of a favorable trade balance, reduction in government expenditures, and financial reform to reduce the huge national debt and improve government credit—were sensible in peacetime, they were foolhardy during the uneasy interlude between the Wars of the Second and Third Coalitions. Parliament knew of Napoleon's preparations for an invasion of England and accurately evaluated his assertion that peace could be maintained only if Britain surrendered Malta, Egypt, and the French Indian forts in accordance with the 1802 treaty. Members of Parliament therefore opposed Addington's sharp reduction in the numbers of soldiers and sailors in the regular forces and reliance upon an enlarged militia of inferior quality as provided in the Militia Acts of 1802–3. When Addington finally recognized the danger from France, and led the country into war in May, 1803, it was no better prepared to cope with the enemy than it had been in 1793. Moreover, even after the war was renewed, Addington did not appreciate the gravity of Britain's position. Unlike the situation in 1793, when it had entered the war in order to contain the spread of revolutionary doctrines and uphold the independence of threatened allies, Britain now stood alone in a life-and-death struggle for national survival. Until Britain joined Russia and Austria in the Third Coalition (1804–5), nearly a year after declaring war on France, it was forced to keep a defensive posture that depended upon the navy's ability to prevent Napoleon's flat-bottomed transports from crossing the Channel.

Parliament refused to accept such a vulnerable posture, and Addington, who had not been able to step out of Pitt's shadow, resigned for want of support in April, 1804. Although ill and weary from a lifetime of work and worry, Pitt answered the call of his half-mad king and anxious countrymen and served until 1806, when death relieved him of his awesome responsibilities. As usual, he put his confidence in Britain's allies, and was disappointed by them a third time. Instead of carrying out a plan to invade England, Napoleon suddenly marched his huge army diagonally across France for a surprise attack on Ulm (October, 1805), where he encircled and captured the bulk of the Austrian army. A few weeks later he cut the Austro-Russian army to pieces at Austerlitz, which resulted in the French occupation of Vienna and the Austro-French Peace of Pressburg. Pitt, who had been elated with Admiral Nelson's victory at Trafalgar a few days earlier, was filled with gloom at news of Austria's collapse.

In March, 1805, in the final stages of preparation for the English invasion, Napoleon had formulated a plan to enable his unwieldy flotilla to cross the Channel without fear of the British navy. He had dispatched Admiral Villeneuve's Toulon fleet to the West Indies, certain that Nelson's Mediterranean squadron would pursue it. Villeneuve was to rendezvous at Martinique with French captains already in Caribbean waters, elude Nelson, and hurriedly return to Spain. There, Villeneuve's enlarged fleet was to join the Spanish fleet for a voyage northward to the Channel, where, together with the Brest fleet, they could command the narrow seas and permit the French army to cross safely. Initially all went according to plan: Nelson did follow Villeneuve to the Caribbean, missed him, and raced back to Gibraltar. As Napoleon had scrapped the invasion by that time, he ordered Villeneuve to Toulon. But Nelson caught him off Cape Trafalgar, and sunk or captured most of the Franco-Spanish fleet. Although the battle cost Nelson his life, it forced the enemy's ships into harbor for the rest of the war and forestalled any further attempt to invade Britain. Two months later Pitt was dead.

As Pitt had no peer as Parliamentary leader and party chief, and had successfully carried on the government with the support of the king's friends, mercantile interests, Tory landed aristocrats, and the Duke of Portland's moderate Whigs (who had generally voted with the government out of disapproval of Fox's radicalism), there was no one capable of stepping into his shoes. In consequence, the new ministry, mistakenly called the Ministry of All Talents (1806–7), was a hodgepodge of factional leaders including Addington, Portland, Fox, and Grenville. William Wyndham, Baron Grenville (1759–1834), a nephew of the former prime minister, became first Lord of the Treasury and nominal chief behind Fox until the latter's death in September, 1806. The Pittites, the strongest faction in Parliament, would not support the Fox-Grenville ministry and it consequently accomplished little. Fox labored to make an honorable peace, but Napoleon refused to consider it. He had humbled the Austrians and more recently the Prussians, who had entered the war when the French occupied neighboring Hapsburg dominions. The Prussians, like the Austrians, sued for peace. The Fox-Grenville ministry did make two significant reforms. The first strengthened the army by abolishing the volunteer system on which Pitt had relied, and substituted a system of compulsory military training for all men of military age, who could then be inducted into the regular army or be retained as militia in the home guard, which was improved and enlarged. The second reform, sponsored by Fox shortly before he died, was the abolition of the African slave trade as of January 1, 1808. Grenville subsequently tried unsuccessfully to amend the law excluding English and Scottish Catholics from commissions in the armed forces, but when George III opposed him, Grenville had to resign. A succession of three Tory ministries—those of Portland (1807–9), Spencer Perceval (1809–12), and Lord Liverpool (1812–27)—carried Britain through the dangerous years of the Continental system, the Peninsular Campaign, the American War of 1812, and the final collapse of Napoleonic hegemony in 1815.

The defeat of Austria and Prussia left only Britain and Russia (Naples and Sweden were inconsequential allies) in the Third Coalition, and the temperamental and idealistic Alexander I soon abandoned it as well. Although his army had been stalemated at Eylau and defeated at Friedland (1807), it was certainly not broken, and it could have taken the field had not the Treaty of Tilsit intervened in July of that year. Alexander's decision to come to terms with Napoleon was logical. The czar rightly suspected that Pitt's death would stop the payment of British subsidies. He realized the folly of attempting almost singlehandedly to stop the French advance which, if it succeeded, might cost Russia its territorial ambitions in Poland. He also knew that the British navy could be of little help in a land war, and that the British army, whose inefficiency had been demonstrated in fruitless expeditions during 1805–6 to the Middle East, the Elbe River, and Naples, could not be relied upon. Furthermore the Treaty of Tilsit, which confirmed Napoleon's conquests and promised Russia's cooperation in the Continental system (see below), also provided for French assistance against the Turks, who had declared war on Russia. Tilsit posed a new threat to the British Baltic trade, rich in essential naval stores. Primarily for that reason, but also to prevent a union of the French, Danish, and Russian fleets, which would imperil British naval supremacy, a squadron bombarded and looted Copenhagen and carried off the Danish fleet. The shelling of civilians and the burning of the town angered many Britons, but the government obviously had had no alternative.

Unable to invade England and too weak to challenge its naval supremacy, Napoleon, master of all Europe except Spain and Portugal, set his clever mind to the task of destroying his only remaining enemy. That contemptible nation of shopkeepers and artisans, he reckoned, was so dependent on its export trade that an ironclad embargo against all British and colonial goods would surely wreck its economy and force its surrender. So it was that Napoleon instituted the Continental system, issuing the Berlin Decree in November, 1806, and the Milan Decrees the next year, in which he declared a blockade of all European ports from the Baltic to the Adriatic (eventually extended to include Spain, Portugal, and Russia). In addition, neutral ships were forbidden to carry British goods or to touch at British ports. Britain countered by a series of Orders in Council, establishing a blockade of France and her allies and threatening neutrals who traded with them. Neither the British nor the French fleets could hope to enforce a tight blockade, but the British had a better chance of doing so simply because their naval supremacy made it impossible for the French fleet to close all major European ports. Nevertheless French privateers did a great deal of damage to British merchantmen.

The effects of the Continental system on Britain and the French Empire are important, for, although Britain did eventually suffer considerably because of it, the system hurt Britain less than it did France. Prior to 1810, the French blockade of French, Dutch, and Baltic ports did not markedly affect British exports: what trade was lost on the

Continent was easily recovered by new markets in the United States, South America, and British North America (Canada). According to Professor J. M. Thompson, the French embargo did not seriously hinder British trade. The fact is, the total value of British-made exports to the Continent fell by only about £4,000,000 in both 1807 and 1808 from what it had been in 1806, and the value of colonial products re-exported from England rose from £10,000,000 in 1805 to nearly £13,000,000 in 1810. Moreover, the value of British exports to American markets (B.N.A. and U.S.A.) greatly increased until the Americans placed an embargo on British goods on the eve of the War of 1812. Thompson further points out, however, that the Continental system did hurt trade in 1810–11, when the total value of home-produced goods exported sank from £50,000,000 to £35,000,000, and the domestic market became glutted with excessive imports in commodities such as flax, sugar, coffee, and raw silk, causing a serious depression, gold shortages, reduced wages, industrial layoffs, and riots in several cities. At the same time, shortages in timber and grain, normally imported from Scandinavia, hurt British shipbuilding and caused food shortages and higher prices. But ultimately, aided by the French defeats in the Peninsular and Russian campaigns, Britain managed to survive the economic warfare by promoting new markets and breaking the effectiveness of the Continental system in Portugal, Spain, and north-central Europe.

As for France, the system backfired. Her allies and subject nations, particularly Denmark and Prussia, long accustomed to buying better quality and cheaper British goods, simply refused to go without them. Such goods, imported through Portugal and Spain or smuggled into German Baltic ports, found their way to all parts of the Empire. Discontent among the subject peoples became so rampant that Napoleon finally resorted to granting licenses exempting certain ports and merchants from the system. Indeed, as the French Empire simply could not meet consumers' demands, it began secretly to import British goods even through French ports. The system created most discontent in Austria and Prussia, which by 1809 began to resist French hegemony, and it ultimately constrained the French to invade Russia, which would no longer enforce the embargo.

Reaction on the Continent against Napoleon appeared first in Portugal and Spain and spread to Austria and Prussia. Britain quickly seized the advantage. Its efforts to assist these states were led by two outstanding members of the cabinet, George Canning, the foreign minister (1770–1827), and Lord Castlereagh of the War Office (1769–1822), who, though bitter personal enemies, strengthened Britain's diplomatic and military posture until their respective resignations in 1809 and 1812. In 1807, neither Portugal nor Spain had yet been overrun by Napoleonic armies, Portugal being an ally of Britain and Spain of France. Spain, ruled by the imbecilic Charles IV but actually controlled by the crafty chief minister Godoy, had been of little help to France. Its economy, supported by masses of poverty-stricken peasants still bound essentially to serfdom, and dependent upon the inflationary importation of precious metals from its exploited American colonies, tottered on the brink of collapse. Moreover, Portugal was an open window in an otherwise tight European fortress committed to the enforcement of the Continental system. Napoleon therefore decided to conquer Portugal, but as Britain's control of the seas made a naval attack hazardous, he had first to occupy Spain, whose decadent royal family was overthrown and replaced with Joseph, the Emperor's brother. The French attack on Portugal and Spain in 1807–8 came off smoothly: General Junot, supported by pro-Bourbon Spanish troops, occupied much of Portugal, although he failed to prevent the escape of the Portuguese regent and fleet to Brazil. The French army also occupied northern and western Spain as far as Madrid. But the invasion at once stirred the Portuguese and Spanish peasants, who established revolutionary councils and organized scores of militia units that fought ferociously against the French in Portugal and the Spanish provinces of Catalonia and Andalusia, and appealed to Britain for help.

The Portland ministry responded immediately, dispatching an army under Sir Arthur Wellesley (later Duke of Wellington, 1769–1852), which disembarked at Mondego Bay, Portugal, early in August, 1808, hurried toward Lisbon, and defeated Junot's forces at Vimeiro. With Junot in retreat, the high command at London became embroiled in a silly dispute over seniority in the army that resulted in Wellesley's replacement ultimately by Dalrymple. He blundered and raised a furor in popular and official circles at home by concluding the Convention of Cintra (August 30) in which he agreed to carry captured French troops back to France in British transports. Sir John Moore, a courageous soldier, then assumed command of the British forces in Portugal and immediately led his men toward Madrid, which the Spanish rebels had recently taken. This turn of events brought Napoleon to Spain at the head of 225,000 men, who recaptured Madrid and most of the north, thereby imperiling the Spanish peasant army trapped within his net. Moore acted swiftly in this crisis: with only 30,000 men to match the French, he turned northward from Salamanca to cut Napoleon's communication lines, forcing him to divert attention from the Spanish rebels. Moore fought two successful engagements at Benavente and Corunna while falling back toward the coast. His bold maneuver, which cost him his life, saved his own troops from annihilation, took the strain off the beleaguered and grossly outnumbered Spanish militia, and temporarily halted the French counteroffensive.

Wellesley replaced Moore the next year and, until 1813, engaged in hard fighting against about 350,000 troops that Napoleon needed more urgently on the Austrian and Russian fronts. Although the Allies considered the Peninsular Campaign less important than the campaigns in central Europe, the outcome of the Napoleonic War in the years 1808 to 1813 was determined in Spain. Wellesley faced many obstacles, including the numerical superiority of the French, the lack of organization and effective leadership among the Spanish rebels, the harshness of the climate and terrain, and the initial inadequacy of the British army. He overcame all these problems, restored a measure of honor to an army that had scarcely won a significant battle in fifteen years, and emerged from the war a national hero. This young, handsome, and cultured soldier had already made an enviable military record in India. His zest for leadership and the tidiness of his mind inspired his troops and transformed them into a disciplined, efficient army of professionals. Historians have generally been critical of Wellington's command of men and of his character, although they all admit that he was a superb soldier. Admittedly he had a typical eighteenth-century aristocratic haughtiness and felt a deep repugnance for social and political reform, as his later political career proved. He has also been accused of being ill-mannered, bad-tempered, and aloof, as well as unsociable, sullen, opportunistic, and something of a libertine. While there is undoubtedly substantial truth in these allegations, they have certainly been exaggerated. This soldier, politician, and statesman, for all his personal foibles, deserves from posterity the kind of respect that those under his command heaped on him during a campaign in which he gave the lie to the invincibility of the French revolutionary army.

The only significant British victories in 1808–12 were won in the Iberian Peninsula and in several expeditions in the central and eastern Mediterranean. At home, while the British people suffered some economic hardship, Parliament bickered over political reform, and over

Prince George who, because of George III's insanity and blindness, became regent late in 1810. Abroad, the fleet, supported by the army, triumphed at Sicily, Corfu, and the Ionian Islands. In the summer of 1809, Lord Chatham led forty thousand troops in an attack on Walcheren Island off Antwerp in the vain hope of helping the rebellious Austrians by diverting French troops. The expedition failed to capture Antwerp, suffered heavy casualties largely because of malaria, and withdrew ignominiously in December, having captured only Flushing. Meanwhile Wellington struggled to hold a defensive line along the Torres Vedras near Lisbon against the encroachments of French armies commanded by Marshals Ney, Soult, and Massena, which prowled about Spain's western frontier and finally crashed through into Portugal as far as Coimbra. Helped by Portuguese rebels led by British officers, who harassed the French in guerrilla warfare and periodically broke their advances, Wellington began to win victories such as Fuentes de Oñoro and Ciudad Rodrigo in 1811-12. When the French fell back into Spain, Wellington followed. By means of many raids and a few pitched battles and sieges, he at first consolidated his position in the south and then drove the French into the Pyrenees. Although the fighting continued until April, 1814, when Wellington captured Toulouse and Bayonne in southern France, the British had won the Peninsular Campaign by the time Napoleon had invaded Russia in June, 1812.

The deceptively virile Napoleonic Empire began to crumble internally some years before the disastrous invasion of Russia, and the succeeding Allied counteroffensive destroyed it. Rebellions in Portugal and Spain and the nationalistic resurgence in central Europe endangered French hegemony as early as 1807. Whether the Empire could withstand this rejuvenation among its vassal states and Russia's sudden intransigence in 1811 was problematical until at least 1813. While the Empire's fate thus hung in the balance, Napoleon, furious over Alexander I's proclamations throwing open Russian ports to trade and imposing duties on the importation of French goods in violation of the Continental system, in June, 1812, invaded Russia with 400,000 men. After taking Smolensk and Borodino, Napoleon pushed on to Moscow, where he fully expected to receive the Russian surrender. He waited in vain. Gentle fall soon turned to bitter winter. His army, far from its supply lines, shivered for want of adequate clothing and shelter (much of Moscow had been burned) even as deep snow covered the land and froze what grain still stood in the fields. Finally Napoleon left for Paris, abandoning his men, scarcely 30,000 of whom survived.

The failure of the Russian invasion led to the formation of the Fourth Coalition, composed of Britain, Prussia, Sweden, Russia, and Austria. While the Russians harried the remnants of the retreating French forces, Napoleon amassed a conscripted army of a quarter million men, who defeated the Allies at Dresden. But the Allies launched a counter-offensive that decimated the French host at Leipzig in October, 1813. Britain took no part in this campaign as its troops could not be spared from the Spanish front. Its subsidies, however, helped to sustain the Allies, and Castlereagh hurried between capitals urging an invasion of France. Three Allied armies crossed the Rhine, moved relentlessly toward Paris, and took it easily in March, 1814. Two weeks later the emperor signed the preliminary peace at Fontainebleau with representatives of Austria, Prussia, and Russia. It provided handsome financial settlements for the Bonaparte family, required no payment of indemnities, and sent Napoleon into honorable and confortable exile on the island of Elba. In the following May, the Coalition signed the First Treaty of Paris with Louis XVIII, the restored Bourbon king. It reiterated the provisions of Fontainebleau, set French boundaries as they had been in 1792, united Holland and the Austrian Netherlands (Belgium), and gave Britain Tobago and St. Lucia. It did not require, despite British insistence that it should, an indemnity. The Allies also laid plans for a meeting at Vienna beginning in September to settle the manifold territorial and political questions Napoleon's conquests had created.

Since 1812, Britain's attention had been divided between Europe and North America, where it had been drawn into an unwanted war with the United States, stemming from the inadequacy of the 1783 Treaty of Paris and a controversy over the maritime rights of neutrals. That treaty had granted the Americans sovereignty over the Old Northwest, but the British, taking full advantage of the treaty's vagueness as to the time of withdrawal, and arguing that the Americans had not settled the Loyalists' claims or paid the debts owing to British merchants, refused to evacuate their forts from Lake Champlain to Michilimackinac. These were only convenient excuses: actually, the British intended to control the valuable fur trade as long as possible, make provision for the Indians to whom they had granted lands by treaties that were not considered in the American peace settlement, and possibly to repossess this valuable territory. The American Confederation government was too weak to press the issue. But after the ratification of the Constitution that established a firm union, the Republic insisted that the British withdraw, threatened to curtail Anglo-American trade, and sent the military into the Ohio country in the early 1790s to defeat the Indians, whom the Americans believed were being aided and abetted by the British from Canada.

The Americans also complained bitterly of British violations of their neutral rights in maritime trade. Anglo-American trade had greatly increased after the American Revolution despite costly British import duties and Britain's insistence that only British ships carry American goods. Following the onset of the Anglo-French war in 1793, the French, fearing that the British navy would interrupt French trade with its West Indian colonies, allowed American ships to carry goods between the islands and France. Consequently Britain at once imposed the so-called Rule of 1756, which stipulated that trade closed to a nation in peacetime could not be opened to such a nation in wartime, and subjected American ships to search and seizure, continued to impress American seamen into British naval service, and confiscated dozens of cargoes, construing contraband in the widest possible sense. When diplomatic exchanges and a brief embargo on foreign trade failed to stop interference with American shipping, President Washington dispatched John Jay to England to negotiate a settlement of all Anglo-American differences. In the resulting Jay Treaty (1794), Britain agreed to withdraw from its western forts, participate in joint commissions to define the Nova Scotia–Maine boundary, satisfy Loyalists' claims, and determine damages for confiscations of ships and cargoes. The two countries also signed a most-favored-nation commercial treaty for a term of twelve years. However, Britain refused to admit American ships to Canadian and West Indian ports.

During the following decade American relations with both Britain and France verged on the brink of war. From 1798 to 1801, the United States and France fought an undeclared naval war resulting from French depredations on American ships and other insults, among them the famous XYZ Affair. British captains continually challenged American ships on the high seas, impressed seamen unable to prove their American citizenship, and seized cargoes carried directly from the French West Indies to France. British Judge William Scott's decision in the *Polly* case (1800) meant that only those ships that had landed West Indian goods in an American port and paid duties, and then re-exported them to France, were free to trade with Britain's enemies.

Two basic decisions by the British government created strong antipathy among Americans: the broad interpretation of what constituted contraband and a denial that free ships make free goods. Later British court rulings and clashes at sea worsened Anglo-American relations. In the case of the *Essex* (1805), for instance, the court reversed the decision reached in the *Polly* case, and decreed that West Indian goods to be free from confiscation by British men-of-war must clearly be intended for shipment only to the United States.

Napoleon's Continental system and the retaliatory Orders in Council closed all European countries except Turkey and Sweden to American shipping and led to more seizures of American ships and impressment of seamen. Naval clashes like that between the *Leopard* and the American frigate *Chesapeake* in 1807 (and another between the *Little Belt* and the *President* in 1811) angered the American government. It first imposed an embargo against trade with any foreign country and later passed the Nonintercourse Act, which sealed American ports against goods from Britain, France, and their colonies. The resumption of trade with France after Napoleon's abrogation for Americans of the Berlin and Milan Decrees late in 1810 aggravated Anglo-American relations. By that time Congress, heavily influenced by Anglophobe members called War Hawks, was urging the seizure of Spanish Florida and Canada. An uprising led by Chief Tecumseh, which General Harrison crushed at Tippecanoe in November, 1811, added credence to the War Hawks' allegations that the British were arming Indians in order to impede American westward expansion and to maintain control of the fur trade. Even so, the War Hawks' thirst for war was not shared by the industrialists and merchants of the Northeast whose prosperity depended on trade with the West Indies and Canada, and probably would not have been slaked but for the long and bitter dispute over maritime rights.

President Madison declared war on Britain in June, 1812, only weeks before the British cabinet decided to rescind its Orders in Council so as to avert a conflict that it did not want and could scarcely afford in view of the continuing battle in Europe. The Americans, many of whom also objected to the war, erred in believing that the Canadians would welcome liberation from the yoke of British oppression. Canadians, on the contrary, felt loyal to the government that had respected their customs and religion, and willingly defended their homeland. The Maritime Provinces of Nova Scotia and New Brunswick, linked commercially with New England and protected by the British navy, enjoyed an unprecedented period of prosperity and never saw an American soldier. Upper Canada (Ontario), which had been settled mostly by Loyalists and recent American immigrants, stoutly resisted several American invasions out of gratitude to the generous British government that had doled out land and supplies in hard times, respected their religious views, and trusted them with a measure of self-government in the Constitutional Act of 1791. That Act, promoted by Governor Lord Dorchester and sponsored in Parliament by Pitt, had amended the 1774 Quebec Act to take into account the interests of English-speaking, Protestant Canadians. It reaffirmed the supremacy of the Catholic Church and the seignorial system in Quebec, and divided Quebec Province into the two provinces of Upper and Lower Canada, each of which was given an assembly elected under broad franchise qualifications and a legislative council appointed by the governor.

Although the military events of the war had little effect upon the Treaty of Ghent (December, 1814) that concluded it, they aroused deep feelings of resentment among Canadians, who, having had virtually nothing to do with provoking the war, nevertheless suffered most because of it. At the outset, the Americans seemed certain to be the victors. Canada had only 400,000 inhabitants defended by a small but well-trained militia supported by a few thousand British regulars. They faced a seemingly stronger nation of nearly 8,000,000 people over an indefensible thousand-mile frontier. Canada was not so vulnerable, however, as these facts would imply. The American army never exceeded 35,000 men; recruitment drives generally failed; New England strongly opposed the war and actually traded with the enemy; and the rest of the country was at best lukewarm to it. On the other hand, the Canadians exhibited intense patriotism, willingly served in the militia, respected governmental authority, and had able leaders like Prevost, Brock, and Tecumseh.

The Americans in 1812–13 were unable to muster a sustained offensive against Canada. They launched a three-pronged attack aimed at Fort Malden (Amherstburg), Niagara (thence to York and west to London), and Montreal and Quebec. All three invasions failed. General Hull crossed from Detroit and issued a proclamation of liberation to the Canadian people, but soon withdrew across the Detroit River and surrendered the fort under threat of attack by militia supported by Tecumseh's Indians. The small American force on the Niagara frontier, which the New York militia refused to join, advanced as far as Queenston before being hurled back by Sir Isaac Brock, who lost his life in the engagement. The troops in upper New York moved into Lower Canada above Plattsburgh, but retreated before encountering the enemy. Similar expeditions against the same points in 1813 were only slightly more successful, owing partly to Perry's victory in the Battle of Lake Erie, which resulted in temporary American control of the lower Great Lakes and an offensive against Upper Canada. Harrison's army recaptured Fort Detroit, forced the British to evacuate Fort Malden, and pursued them to victory at Moraviantown. On the Niagara frontier, an American force was stopped cold at Stony Creek, and a third army, advancing on Montreal in two columns, was repulsed by Canadian *habitants* and some regulars at Chateaugay and Chrystler's Farm near Cornwall. Meanwhile the Americans burned the village of York (later Toronto), the capital of Upper Canada.

The fighting quickened and reached a climax in 1814. The Americans once more invaded at Niagara, took Fort Erie, and advanced to Lundy's Lane, where a small but bitter battle was fought with heavy casualties and claims of victory on both sides. After an inconsequential American incursion up the Richelieu Valley, Prevost, heavily reinforced by seasoned veterans recently arrived from Europe, attacked in the vicinity of Plattsburgh but had to withdraw after an American naval victory on Lake Champlain had made his position vulnerable. In the summer, British sea power and the arrival of troops from Europe seriously threatened the United States. Until then, despite the British naval blockade of the American coast that severely curtailed trade and led to several engagements between individual ships, New England and the Middle Atlantic states had not been subjected to many British attacks by sea. But the clear British naval superiority not only permitted occasional raids against American coastal towns; it also resulted in the capture of Washington (August, 1814) and the burning of its public buildings, including the White House, in retaliation for the destruction of York the previous year. Thereafter, except for Jackson's crushing victory over General Pakenham in the Battle of New Orleans (January, 1815), which was fought without knowledge that peace had been signed, the war gradually ground to a halt.

The Treaty of Ghent, like the war itself, accomplished next to nothing. It restored the territorial *status quo ante bellum* and established commissions that later made the Rush-Bagot Agreement (1817), which disarmed the Great Lakes, and the Convention of 1818, which granted Americans fishing rights in Canadian waters and defined the boundary along the forty-ninth parallel from the Lake of the Woods to the Stony

Mountains. But the treaty said nothing about impressment or the maritime rights of neutrals, the issues over which the war had been fought. It is ironical that while neither Britain nor the United States gained anything substantial by going to war, Canada had. Canadians had borne the brunt of invading armies and sustained casualties and heavy property losses. The crisis of war had forced them to forget at least temporarily their ethnic differences, which hitherto had pitted merchants against farmers, and Catholics against Protestants. The united war effort aroused a tinge of national feeling and purged them of sympathy for American republicanism. The Canadians also became more conscious of their ties with Britain and its monarchy and Parliamentary system. Therefore, despite occasional quarrels thereafter between English and French-speaking Canadians, interprovincial rivalry, perturbation at the imperial Parliament's seeming indifference to their problems, and the minor rebellions of 1837 and the resulting Durham Report aimed at correcting the issues that had caused them, by 1849 the Canadians developed a system of responsible self-government. Canada's transition from a totally dependent crown colony to a sovereign nation provided a prototype for colonial governmental evolution in the Empire-Commonwealth.

Three months before the end of the American war, Castlereagh had joined representatives from most European nations and principalities at the Congress of Vienna to reconstruct the map of Europe and consider other questions relating to the final peace settlement with France. The gay capital of the Austrian Empire was a proper setting for the round of parties and celebrations that preoccupied the princes and statesmen, whose frivolity and distaste for business during the early weeks of the Congress exemplified a general easing of tension following Napoleon's exile to Elba. But they gradually got down to work, for they were anxious to return home where enormous problems delayed or caused by the war awaited their attention.

The major decisions reached at Vienna resulted from negotiations restricted almost entirely to Britain, Prussia, Russia, and Austria, although the lesser powers did a great deal of spadework in committees. These decisions are so well known that they need not be repeated except as they related to British interests. The Great Powers generally agreed that legitimate governments overthrown by Napoleon should be restored; that the states which had borne the heavy cost and casualties of the war should somehow be compensated; that buffer states should be established and strengthened against French military resurgence; and that the balance of power—allowing no state or combination of states to endanger the others—should be ensured.

Britain was less concerned than its allies in negotiating along these lines, for the war had provided ample opportunity to expand the Empire, and the territorial acquisitions were confirmed at Vienna. Britain had acquired St. Lucia, Tobago, and Trinidad in the Caribbean, Mauritius and Ceylon in the Indian Ocean, Malta and the Ionian Islands in the Mediterranean, Guiana in South America, the Cape Colony in Africa, and Heligoland in the North Sea. Moreover, Lord Mornington, Wellington's brother and governor-general of India in 1797–1805, had seized the last Dutch and French trading posts as well as huge blocs of Indian territory in a war against the sultan of Mysore and his ally in the Carnatic. Such substantial British gains made it difficult for Castlereagh to argue convincingly that Prussia and Russia should not be given what they wished—Saxony and the duchy of Warsaw. He would have preferred Prussian compensation in the Rhineland, where a watchful eye could be kept trained on the French frontier, and feared what Russia's acquisition of the duchy might do to the stability of central Europe. However, when Alexander I and Frederick William III threatened to fight before surrendering their demands, Castlereagh conceded. Of the rest of the Vienna settlement, he and Wellington (who succeeded him in the negotiations in March, 1815) were most pleased by the union of Holland and the Austrian Netherlands, for this new state provided a buffer against French expansion and ensured that a friendly power controlled the southeastern shore of the Channel.

When the Congress was nearing conclusion and some of the representatives had already departed, news came of Napoleon's escape from Elba. He had landed in southern France, gathered an army as he traveled toward Paris, and occupied the throne quickly vacated by Louis XVIII. Thus began the Hundred Days from March 1 to June 15, 1815, during which time Napoleon struggled to overthrow the overwhelming might of his resolute enemies. As most of the British soldiers released from the Spanish campaign had gone to America, and other units had been disbanded, Wellington commanded only about 35,000 British and Hanoverian troops in occupation of the Netherlands. Marshal Blücher's 120,000 Prussians and 60,000 other Germans were quartered nearby. Napoleon planned to defeat those forces before falling on the unprepared Austrians, thus averting the union of the three armies. He crossed the Netherlands' frontier on June 15, defeated Blücher on the sixteenth, and attacked the combined Anglo-Dutch-Hanoverian army drawn up defensively on a ridge overlooking Waterloo near Brussels. The French almost won the day in deadly assaults against Wellington's lines before the timely arrival of Blücher's reinforcements. At nightfall, thousands lay dead or wounded and the French were in disorderly retreat. Paris capitulated three weeks later when Napoleon surrendered himself to a British squadron, which ultimately took him to the desolate island of St. Helena in the south-central Atlantic, where he died in 1821.

The shock of the Hundred Days convinced the Great Powers that France must be punished and that international safeguards should be established to guarantee peace. Accordingly, the Second Treaty of Paris (November, 1815) provided that France was to surrender territory on its northern and eastern frontiers, losing millions in population, pay a huge indemnity, and be occupied by Allied armies for three years. The Great Powers also joined two associations—the Holy Alliance and the Quadruple Alliance. The Holy Alliance was the brain-child of Alexander I, the naïve and aberrant Russian czar, who asked all European rulers to conduct their foreign policy according to Christian moral precepts and to abjure war as an instrument of national policy. Castlereagh considered this mystical nonsense and refused to join the Alliance, although most nations except the Papal States and Turkey did join, more out of courtesy to Alexander than out of conviction that moral precepts alone could prevent future wars. While treaties were generally respected by nations not yet committed to a philosophy of *Realpolitik,* they were more effective and lasting when buttressed by military power. The Quadruple Alliance among Britain, Prussia, Russia, and Austria, which had as its initial purpose the preservation (by force if necessary) of the settlements reached at Vienna, was consequently a more practical organization for peace-keeping. Although it had disintegrated by 1824 for reasons that will become clear later, the balance of power it helped to create carried over into the next generation of Europeans, who did not become involved in a major war until 1854.

The Alliance unfortunately degenerated into a tool of reaction dominated by Metternich of Austria. The signatories convened only four times—at Aix-la-Chapelle (1818), Troppau (1820), Laibach (1821), and Verona (1822)—in each instance but the first (when France, having fulfilled its obligations under the Second Treaty of Paris and settled down under the Bourbon monarchy, was admitted to the Alliance), it used its military power to suppress popular revolutions in Portugal, Spain, and Naples. In 1820 Britain withdrew from the Alliance in protest against the Protocol of Troppau, which obliged signatories to intervene forcefully in the domestic affairs of nations whose conservative governments were threatened by liberal revolutions. Thereafter Britain became an interested observer of Continental affairs, doing what it could to ensure that military intervention by the Great Powers did not result in permanent occupation. For reasons of commercial interest or strategic defense, however, Britain did become involved in the Greek revolution against Turkey and the Latin American revolutions against Spain.

The Liverpool ministry, in power since 1812, welcomed the pacification of Europe but not the domestic problems that followed in its wake. To the comfortable and satisfied ruling classes, largely removed by social status, wealth, and prerogatives from the adversities that faced ordinary Englishmen, Britain in 1815 appeared economically sound and politically stable. It had fought a successful and honorable war that brought new colonies, commercial prosperity, and greater international prestige. But this mirage of affluence and social tranquillity quickly faded, and there appeared the specter of economic depression, famine, and forceful agitation for reform. By the end of 1816, Britain, though it had neither been invaded nor scarred by the long war, like its allies was fraught with internal dissent.

The roots of the depression lay in the war years. The national debt, which Pitt had considered dangerously high in 1785, had soared by 1815 to nearly £900,000,000, and the government had difficulty meeting even the interest. The needs of war had expanded industrial and agricultural productivity far in excess of normal peacetime demand at home and abroad. Exports, imports, and the lucrative carrying trade, which had grown substantially despite the Continental system and the American war, fell off after 1815 by as much as 15 or 20 per cent. European nations that had depended almost entirely on British industrial output during the war, no longer needed military supplies and either could not afford to buy British goods or erected high trade barriers to keep them out. The war years had also seen a rapid growth in population without comparable increases in food production. The latter was attributable to backward agricultural methods, increased enclosure of arable and common land, and the restrictive Corn Laws, which kept food prices high. The factory system had triumphed over the time-honored handicraft method, particularly in the textile industry, and had put men out of work. The already oversupplied labor market was further glutted by veterans returned to civilian life and migrations of farm workers to overcrowded industrial centers like Birmingham, Sheffield, and Manchester. All these factors combined to precipitate factory shutdowns, business bankruptcies, an agricultural slump, layoffs of industrial, mine, and farm workers, wage reductions, and food shortages.

The deplorable results of the depression accentuated old grievances among the working classes and reformers and deepened their hostility toward a government that did pitifully little to ameliorate the distress. The Perceval and Liverpool ministries had done their best to suppress political reform since 1810, and they were equally insensitive to social welfare during the post-1816 depression. The reform movement, stifled by repression in the 1790s, was revived in the last years of the war by a small but popularly-supported group of members of Parliament led by Sir Francis Burdett and another clique outside the government including William Cobbett, "Orator" Hunt, and John Cartwright. Like Wilkes before them, these men captured the public imagination as champions of political democracy, social welfare, and personal liberty, and laid the foundation for broader-based agitation.

The government at first responded to the reformers' appeals by taking harsh reprisals. In 1810, Burdett published a public letter in *Cobbett's Weekly Register* in which he excoriated the government for imprisoning the president of a debating society who had criticized an action of the Commons. The Speaker ordered Burdett's arrest for libel, but he resisted it behind the barricaded doors of his house. An angry crowd rallied to his defense and blood was spilled before soldiers could take him to the Tower. Cobbett, who also went to prison for criticizing the cabinet, had in addition criticized the regent for dissolute behavior and squandering twice the amount of his annual allowance.

Loosely related to these events in the capital, and indicative of the rising tide of popular discontent, were the rash of riots, machine-breakings, demonstrations, and public meetings in the industrial north by skilled workers and laborers called Luddites. As the depression deepened, these disorders multiplied and spread to other parts of the country. Although rioters went to prison, to the penal colonies, and to the scaffold, their trials only provoked more rioting, deeper popular anguish, and occasional violence. Prosecutions of authors and publishers of allegedly seditious literature and another suspension of habeas corpus (for the last time in English history), though bitterly contested, usually resulted in acquittals by juries that understood better than the government apparently did the widespread misery that was at the root of popular outbursts and criticisms in the press. The government sometimes used troops to quell rioters and disband peaceful demonstrations, like the march from Liverpool to London by a group of petitioners called Blanketeers, who merely intended to present grievances to Parliament. But the best-known instance of the use of force occurred at a huge rally of workers and their families at St. Peter's Fields, Manchester, in August, 1819. They had gathered peaceably to hear speeches, but the local magistrates assigned militia and cavalry to stand by in case of trouble. When the speeches became inflammatory, the magistrates ordered the speakers' arrest, but the crowd at once began to mill around the militia moving toward the platform, and the cavalry rushed in to free them. They killed eleven and injured several hundred in the confusion of unsheathed swords and trampling horses. This Peterloo Massacre, as the victims' friends called the incident (the cavalry involved had fought at Waterloo, hence the allusion), distressed the cabinet but did not divert it from its intention to enforce the law.

The government's hand was strengthened by Parliament's passage in 1819 of the Six Acts. In general, these laws prohibited collection of weapons, maintenance of private militia, and mass meetings held for the purpose of arousing public opposition to the government, and imposed a higher stamp tax on newspapers which, if found to be seditious, might be confiscated. Except for the indirect censorship of the press and prohibition of free assembly, these were moderate measures of considerably less bite than the repressive laws enforced during the previous twenty-five years. They were, however, more successful, for they came at a time when the country was finally crawling out of depression to economic normalcy. With better times popular outbursts gradually subsided, and the shocking Cato Street conspiracy in February, 1820—an attempt by a few radical republicans led by Arthur Thistlewood to murder the cabinet and abolish monarchy—that was discovered before harm was done was atypical of national attitudes.

The old King George III, blind, deaf, and insane for years, died on January 29, 1820. His eldest surviving son, perhaps no worse than the other five, succeeded him as George IV (1820–30) at the age of fifty-eight. No English monarch in modern times inspired less public confidence or caused greater scandal to the royal family. As a handsome lad with cherubic cheeks and a della Robbian smile, he had learned politics from his close friend, Charles James Fox, whose wit, heady pursuit of pleasure, and quarrels with the king he also emulated. His affairs with a variety of mistresses distressed his father as much as did his drinking and gambling and his secret but illegal marriage in 1785 to Mrs. Fitzherbert (no member of the royal family could marry before the age of twenty-five without the government's consent). The substantial allowance Parliament provided burned holes in his pockets and was never enough to cover his enormous debts: in 1786 he owed £250,000; by 1794, £600,000. In the next year, simply to extricate himself from debt, he yielded to an arranged dynastic marriage (the earlier one had been annulled) to the doughty Caroline of Brunswick, whom he ignored practically from the first, and who, refusing to live with him, left in 1814 for the Continent. From time to time—in 1788, 1801, and 1804—as the king slipped in and out of insanity, Prince George prepared to take the regency, which he finally assumed in 1810. When at long last his father died, George IV no longer really cared. A lifetime of indulgence had left him dissipated, corpulent, prematurely aged, and indifferent toward responsibility. He was not a wicked man—far from it. Generosity, charm, and honesty were typical of him, but he was not the sort of monarch who appealed to industrialists and working aristocrats upon whom the future depended. His name had for too long been a byword for irresponsibility, and his subjects could not admire a king more concerned with collecting art and rebuilding royal palaces than in attending to the nation's business.

Donning royal purple did not change him. A few months after his accession, he asked the cabinet's help in procuring a divorce from Caroline, which required an Act of Parliament. Caroline, no pillar of virtue, brazenly returned to England in June, 1820, to claim her rightful place as queen. Another wife, even another queen with her record of marital infidelity, might have been met with silent contempt. But, although the country did not condone her conduct, George's dastardly treatment of Caroline and his sordid personal life turned public sympathy in her favor. As both Houses of Parliament and the press discussed the spicy details of her life, most of which were grossly exaggerated, her supporters multiplied. Liverpool, utterly insensitive to the public's attitude, managed to squeeze through the Lords a bill of pains and penalties that granted the divorce and deprived Caroline of her title. But opposition to the bill in the Commons was so strong that the ministry simply gave up the fight. The cabinet soon realized that it had blundered by identifying itself with the king's ignoble interests, and never fully recovered the public's confidence so long as Liverpool remained prime minister. As for Caroline, she continued to press for her rights, doing whatever she could to capitalize on her popularity. Although she had no legal right as queen-consort to be crowned, she nevertheless embarrassed everyone by appearing outside Westminster Abbey on coronation day in June, 1821, only to be turned away. Her untimely death the following August settled a problem that otherwise could have been solved only by the king's unlikely change of heart. When he learned of her death, he celebrated it by getting drunk.

Traditionally, cabinet changes had followed monarchic successions, but George IV retained the prime minister and practically all his cabinet, and in doing so, badly disappointed the Whigs. Since Pitt's reorganization and revitalization of the Tory party in the 1780s, the Whigs had been almost completely shut out. Various Whig factions, loosely led since Fox's death by Earl Grey (1764–1845) and Lord John Russell (1792–1878), had been seriously hurt by their oblique association with radicalism and their promotion of such constitutional and social reforms as an extended franchise, Catholic emancipation in England and Scotland, the elimination of electoral abuses, and moderation of the criminal code and penal system. While their program won substantial support among Protestant Dissenters, merchants and manufacturers, and other moneyed and professional interests in London and the industrial Midlands, the Whigs could not win a Parliamentary majority so long as the Tories controlled the patronage and kept franchise qualifications narrow.

The Tories, the spokesmen of political conservatism, the Established Church, and the landed aristocracy, had the advantages of longevity in office (and the control of local governmental offices that it brought), the influence of the royal Household, and the favorable reputation gained from having waged successful and profitable war. But the character of the party had begun to change. Although the high command still rested in the hands of old-line conservatives like Lord Eldon and Liverpool, younger and more liberal-minded Tories like Frederick Robinson, William Huskisson, and Robert Peel were brought into the cabinet in 1822–23. They had cut their political teeth in the political and economic environment of the French revolutionary and Napoleonic periods and had seen how strongly the rank and file in the country had combated the old-guard attitudes and privileges of the Tory oligarchy. Although these younger men were unwilling to subscribe to the radical proposals of left-wing Whigs, they realized the urgency of reforming archaic governmental and social institutions.

But their sensible proposals to modernize trade, finance, and the law would never have gotten off the ground without the permissive authority granted the cabinet by George IV. The king was still constitutionally the head of the government, and the prime minister and his colleagues were still his principal servants appointed, insofar as Parliament would allow, to execute his wishes. The extent of the cabinet's authority was by no means settled by George IV's accession, as has sometimes been supposed. While its license to act independently of the crown was clearer in practice than it had been, say, a century earlier, it had not yet replaced the king as the actual sovereign executive power. That day was a half century away. How much authority the cabinet might exercise therefore depended on the will of the king, and, to a lesser extent, on the personality and political support of the prime minister. George III, for instance, had frequently brought his authority to bear on the course of politics. The first Grenville and Rockingham had been forced out of office. Fox, the leader of the moderate Whigs, alienated George III and consequently never became prime minister. The Younger Pitt's earlier career was repeatedly stymied by the king. The American Revolutionary War continued despite the opposition of most of the cabinet. Neither Pitt nor the second Grenville could pass a Catholic emancipation bill over the king's objections. But Pitt's ability to assert his character and develop a strong Parliamentary following, and the failure of George III to continue his energetic personal influence in politics combined to augment the practical authority of the prime minister, and that of the cabinet. The strong leadership generated by Pitt strengthened the cabinet's hand and gradually led to an expansion of its independent authority during the nineteenth century.

While the character of the crown and cabinet were undergoing these subtle changes, so too were both Houses of Parliament. The Commons, composed of about 650 members by 1800, had not yet been reformed. Elections often were decided by patronage and royal influence, particularly in "rotten" and "pocket" boroughs. The members still primarily represented property interests rather than people. But the increasing power of political parties, the diminishing intervention of the crown in the late eighteenth and early nineteenth centuries, and, above all, the pressure of public opinion tended to moderate the Commons' attitude toward reform. The lower House had occasionally taken modest steps to rectify electoral corruption and sometimes asserted independent judgment against the wishes of the crown and the Lords. Although the Commons rejected proposals to update the representative and electoral systems no less than seven times between 1818 and 1826, it willingly adopted important economic reforms. Finally, when piecemeal measures to remedy particular governmental evils proved inadequate, the Commons removed the worst of them in the Reform Act of 1832 (discussed in the next chapter). The character of the Lords also underwent some alteration. The increasing authority exercised by the lower House since the seventeenth century, although never sufficient to override firm opposition in the Lords, tended to weaken the solid conservatism of the upper House. In the eighteenth century, the Lords, with about 360 members, had represented almost exclusively the great landed families. Neither the Commons nor the Lords saw any reason to alter the established social and political order. But, whereas the Commons toward the end of the century began to react to demands for reform, the Lords, far more amenable to royal influence, which was often inimical to change, set its face resolutely against any substantial alteration of the *status quo* for fear that liberalization in any form would diminish the privileged position of the upper classes. However, the creation of 165 new peers during the Pitt and Liverpool administrations tended to weaken the upper House's solid conservatism. Many of the new peers had had business and professional backgrounds and were consequently more closely identified with the new order of things and less hostile to reform than their traditionalist-minded colleagues. Nevertheless, the Lords remained essentially unreformed until the eve of World War I.

Students often associate economic and social reform with the Whigs, largely because of their agitation in Parliament from Wilkes to Burdett, but it should be remembered that the earliest reforms were enacted during the Tory ministry of Lord Liverpool. Foremost among the liberal Tories in his cabinet after 1822 were Chancellor of the Exchequer Robinson, President of the Board of Trade Huskisson, and Home Secretary Peel, each of whom was to some degree a financial expert. Consequently the Liverpool ministry is best known for its revision of the commercial system, which until that time was based on the outmoded Navigation Acts. Although some modifications had been made in these laws that permitted only British ships manned by British crews to carry foreign goods to Britain or its colonies, it became increasingly obvious to the cabinet that an essentially protectionist policy aimed initially at combating the Dutch and maintaining tight trade connections within the Empire was not only unprofitable, but harmful to

British world trade. Aware of the enormous expansion of British productivity, which could not be absorbed entirely at home or in the colonies, and cognizant of the protectionist philosophy adopted after 1815 by several European states only just commencing their industrialization, Huskisson (1770–1830) determined to amend the Navigation Acts. In accordance with his plans, Parliament reduced tariff schedules across the board on items such as silk, books, iron products, and minerals; the tariffs on cotton, wool, and linens were drastically cut to 10, 15, and 25 per cent respectively. Parliament also simplified the enormously complex tariff laws, reducing their number from 1100 to 11. These reforms stimulated industrial growth, greatly increased Britain's share of world trade, and augmented national revenue. But lest it be falsely concluded that the Tories had suddenly adopted free-trade principles, it must be emphasized at once that they were tariff reformers, not tariff abolitionists, and that the amended trade Acts remained in force until mid-century.

The Tories made other financial reforms in the 1820s. While Huskisson reorganized the archaic accounting system, Robinson reconstituted Pitt's old sinking fund by basing it henceforth only on annual surplus revenue instead of on revenue raised by taxes specifically earmarked for deposit. Robinson also reduced the principal on the funded national debt by about £6,000,000 annually, and so arranged the budgets for 1823–26 that the government could afford to abolish the onerous salt and window taxes. In 1820–25, partly due to these Tory reforms, the country enjoyed such a degree of prosperity that the economy became dangerously inflationary. Cheap money and high profits encouraged irresponsible business expansion and loose banking practices among the hundreds of small provincial banks and the powerful Bank of England. Partly for these reasons, the country slipped into the commercial crisis of 1825–26, marked by numerous bank failures, falling prices, and business bankruptcies, which abruptly terminated government plans for further economic reform and showed the need of strengthening the banking system. Accordingly, Parliament passed legislation forbidding the issuance of notes under five pounds and permitting the establishment of joint-stock banks more than sixty-five miles outside London, or in the capital itself so long as these banks issued no notes. This enabling legislation led to the creation of many large joint-stock banks (about fifty by the eve of World War I), with branches in hundreds of towns throughout the country. Unlike the Bank of England, which dealt primarily with big business and the

government, these banks welcomed small deposits and loaned the accumulated capital to business, thereby encouraging continued national
economic growth. Unfortunately, as we shall see in Chapter 13, their
eagerness for profit led them to speculate unwisely with the result that
dozens collapsed in the 1830s, necessitating further governmental controls on banking.

Meanwhile Sir Robert Peel (1788–1850) was grappling at the Home
Office with the iniquities and barbarities of the criminal code and
penal system, discussed in the previous chapter. This great Tory reformer, son of a wealthy Lancashire cotton merchant, entered Parliament in 1809 and, despite his youth, had already served as under-
secretary for war and the colonies and chief secretary for Ireland before
becoming Home Secretary in 1822. Over the next five years, and in
a second term in 1828–30, building upon the agitation for penal reform begun by Sir Samuel Romilly and Sir James Macintosh, who
had bared some of the worst atrocities of the criminal code, Peel drastically altered it. He abolished the death penalty for half the two hundred felonies punishable by hanging, stopped the use of government
spies formerly planted among labor unions and radical societies to
gather incriminating evidence, did away with benefit of clergy in criminal cases, and revised the marriage laws. He also improved jail conditions by providing trade instruction, allowing religious consultation,
and seeing to it that both the prisoners and their cells were kept clean
and supplied with necessities. In 1829, Peel replaced the elderly and
inefficient London watchmen with a professional police force that at
last offered some protection from gangs of thieves and cutthroats and
kept the peace during riots, strikes, and demonstrations.

To erase the unfavorable impression created by coercive measures
during the French war, the Tories also tried to improve labor and
management relations. The evils generated by the industrial revolution had brought to a head the long-standing grievances of workers
over long hours, low wages, and intolerable working conditions. Despite more than forty statutes forbidding the formation of trade unions
on the grounds that they were conspiracies in restraint of trade, they
nevertheless multiplied, often under the guise of benevolent societies.
Labor riots, one of the earliest of which occurred in the 1760s among
the Spitalfields (London) silk weavers because the government had
fixed wages, became more common as industrialism quickened. Strikes
and riots erupted not only in times of unemployment and low wages,
but also in good times, because of high profits and high prices without

commensurate wage increases, as was the case during the postwar depression and the succeeding period of prosperity. In order to solve this vexing problem, the Tories first repealed the Spitalfields Act and another law forbidding emigration of artisans. And, with the help of Francis Place, a former tailor and member of Parliament for Westminster, Parliament finally repealed the Combination Acts in 1824–25. Henceforth trade unions might legally agitate peacefully for shorter hours and higher wages. This permissive legislation unfortunately brought on a rash of strikes and labor riots in 1825, forcing the government to pass another Combination Act which, while not denying the legal status of the unions, imposed stiff penalties on workers or employers who threatened or actually used force to achieve their aims. But it was a long time before the unions realized their goals, not because they lacked zeal, but because they associated with radical political movements that alienated Parliament and vexed the governing classes. The effectiveness of the trade-union movement therefore dates from the late nineteenth century, when labor leaders joined with Fabian socialists to form the Labour party.

The Tory reform was temporarily halted in February, 1827, with Lord Liverpool's paralytic stroke. A power struggle ensued in the cabinet between two Tory factions led by Canning and Wellington. Eventually George IV made Canning prime minister despite his advocacy of Catholic emancipation and support of Caroline during the divorce debates. Canning controlled a majority in the Commons and primarily for that reason got the appointment, but Tory party unity was smashed by the quarrel with Wellington's followers, and the few months left of Canning's life (he died in August, 1827) witnessed a Parliamentary split over revision of the Corn Law of 1815, which had forbidden importation of grain until the domestic price had risen to eighty shillings a quarter. A serious crop failure in 1826, causing high prices and famine, led Canning to introduce a measure that would have lowered duties on grain imports in proportion to rising domestic prices, but Wellington managed to kill it in the Lords. Ironically, faced with a similar situation after he himself had become prime minister in January, 1828, Wellington convinced Parliament to pass a similar bill.

Wellington's ministry of less than two years, while differing little in personnel from Canning's, was heavily influenced by the Duke's conservative attitudes toward reform. But logic and justice, as well as strong Parliamentary support for repeal of the Test and Corporation Acts, and for relief for Catholics from their lingering political disabilities, forced these reforms on the cabinet. The Test and Corporation Acts, passed during Charles II's reign, had excluded Protestant Dissenters from governmental and military positions. But in practice Dissenters managed to hold positions in government, for although Parliament was unwilling to repeal the Acts, from 1727 on it did annually pass a law enabling them to hold offices and exempting them from the prescribed penalties for doing so. Membership in the Dissenter churches grew rapidly during the eighteenth century, and so many Dissenters held local and national offices and service commissions that the continuation of the Acts was widely recognized as plain nonsense. Accordingly, despite the opposition of Wellington and others in the cabinet, a bill to repeal them, introduced by the Whig Lord John Russell, was passed in 1828. Agitation for Catholic emancipation originated among the Irish and quickly won sympathy in England following the repeal of the previously mentioned Acts because it failed to exclude an oath against transubstantiation required of all members of Parliament. As Catholics held transubstantiation to be a cardinal tenet of faith, they could not sit in Parliament.

Daniel O'Connell (1775–1847), an Irish lawyer of extraordinary size, oratorical talent, and tenacity, took up his coreligionists' cause. Catholic emancipation became a burning issue in 1828 when O'Connell, duly elected to Parliament for county Clare, was refused his seat because of religion. His exclusion received wide publicity and embittered the Irish. Wellington was personally reluctant to change the law, but he knew that it would be foolhardy to create a martyr. Moreover, to the petitions he received from influential members of both Houses in favor of O'Connell, there was added the cautious warning of Peel and the gentle persuasion of George IV that Catholic emancipation could no longer be delayed. Conservative and mostly Anglican peers and members of Parliament fought the bill tooth and nail, but Wellington's defense of it in the Lords (for fear of Irish rebellion), and Peel's influential support in the Commons carried the measure through Parliament.

The qualifications written into the Catholic Emancipation Act (1829) had the unfortunate effect of realienating the Irish. They were admitted to all the political and civil rights enjoyed by other British subjects, and were permitted to hold any office except those of monarch, Lord Lieutenant of Ireland, secretary of Scotland, and Chancellor of England or Ireland. In place of the Oaths of Allegiance and Supremacy, officeholders henceforth were required only to swear to be loyal to the crown, renounce the pope's temporal authority in Britain, and respect the Protestant religious and political settlement. But, in order to discourage the return of too many Catholics to Parliament, the franchise qualification in Ireland was raised from forty shillings to ten pounds. Moreover, as the Act was not retroactive, O'Connell's exclusion stood, thereby necessitating another election in county Clare, which he easily won. Such restrictions provoked the Irish instead of erasing their lingering dissatisfaction with the Act of Union. Wellington thereby harnessed his successors with the vexatious problem of Irish demands for home rule.

The last year of Tory dominance, while without significant domestic developments except the death of George IV in 1830, brought to a successful conclusion a decade of fruitful diplomacy initiated by Canning, who in 1822 had replaced Castlereagh at the Foreign Office. Canning's principal concern centered around the Latin American revolutions against Spain and the Greek war for independence against the Ottoman Empire. Following the intervention by the Quadruple Alliance in 1823 on behalf of the Spanish monarch, Ferdinand VII, he had asked its help in suppressing the revolutions in Mexico, Chile, Colombia, and elsewhere led by San Martín, Bolívar, and Iturbide. In order to forestall such intervention, Canning had approached Richard Rush, the American minister to Britain, with a proposal for a joint Anglo-American declaration of recognition of the new Latin American republics. Canning made the overture partly because of a desire to stifle the Alliance's repeated tampering with liberation movements, and partly in the hope of cornering at least a portion of the Latin American commercial market, formerly closed by Spain. But the Americans, imbued with a spirit of transcendentalist nationalism that rejected any connections with the old country, decided finally to refuse the British offer. They then proclaimed the Monroe Doctrine unilaterally in the certain knowledge that the British navy would buttress the bold American pronouncement that the United States would go to war to protect the independence of the new republics. Canning failed to identify the common interests of Britain and the United States, but he had won the good will of Mexico, Colombia, Bolivia, and the other new states, which readily opened their ports to British goods.

The Greek revolution (1821-29) also commanded Britain's close attention, for any change in the Balkans or the eastern Mediterranean could adversely affect its naval supremacy and trade as well as endanger the balance of power, particularly if Russia made good its threat to intercede. The Ottoman Empire, although vast and seemingly strong, was actually fraught with administrative corruption, bigotry toward the Christian minorities, and a rising spirit of nationalism among the subject peoples. In March, 1823, Canning recognized the belligerency of the Greeks, and, in effect, their independence. He did so not simply to protect British economic enterests in the region, to gratify the strong pro-Greek sentiment among Englishmen responsive to Lord Byron's stirring words, or to strike a blow against the smug Quadruple Alliance, but also to guarantee that, should Russia intervene, Britain would have the right to prevent the creation of a Russian dependency in Greece.

Despite Britain's recognition, the Greek cause went from bad to worse, particularly after the arrival in 1824 of Egyptian troops under Ibrahim Pasha, a son of the sultan's vassal, Mehemet Ali. The situation had grown so serious by 1827 that, after the sultan had repeatedly refused to mediate, Britain, France, and Russia formed an alliance to assist the Greeks, with an understanding that none of the signatories would seek to enhance its political authority or economic interests in Greece. When further attempts at moving the sultan to peace failed, a combined British, French, and Russian fleet commanded by Sir Edward Codrington destroyed the Turko-Egyptian fleet at Navarino in October, 1827. This escalation from diplomacy to successful war, consummated after Canning's death, greatly pleased ordinary Englishmen, but embarrassed Wellington, annoyed the king, and resulted in Britain's withdrawal from the conflict. Wellington did what he could to restore peace, but when it came it was not a result of British diplomacy, but of the force of arms by France and Russia, whose armies fought alongside the Greeks. The Treaty of Adrianople (September, 1829) concluded the war, while at a conference in London the following February, Britain, France, and Russia declared and guaranteed Greek independence.

13

Domestic Reform and Imperial Growth, 1830–1865

The death of the unloved George IV on June 26, 1830, brought his brother William (1765–1837) to a throne he had never expected to inherit. Although none of the six sons of George III merited by their conduct their countrymen's respect, the accession of William IV at the age of sixty-four suited the British better than the base and cruel Ernest, duke of Cumberland (George III's fifth son, king of Hanover, 1837–51), who otherwise would have been the English king. William at least liked people, and enjoyed playing the role of a bourgeois king. He attracted crowds on his frequent strolls through the streets of London and amused them with witty remarks on the lawn of Windsor Castle, his favorite residence. He had had little administrative experience beyond a brief term as Lord High Admiral during Canning's administration, and was therefore unaccustomed to and unnerved by heavy responsibilities. His rough manner and coarse language resulted from the years he had spent at sea, beginning when he was a boy. The "Sailor King" was good-natured, moderately industrious, and comfortably corpulent. His marriage in 1818 to Adelaide of Saxe-Meiningen (1792–1849), a charming, comely, efficient, and steady woman whose two children had died before she became queen consort, helped William bear his burdens with equanimity and exercise restraint in temper and language.

Britain had changed markedly since William IV had been a carefree boy. As the preceding chapters have demonstrated, the forces loosed by industrialization, most importantly political radicalism and popular demands for social and economic reform, had greatly undermined the stable and orderly world of the eighteenth-century agricultural ruling oligarchy that had had things its own way since the Revolution of

1688. But in 1830 it still controlled both Houses of Parliament, county and town government, the Established Church, and most of the nation's wealth. As if encased in glass houses apart from the restless clamor of discontent that gripped most of the working classes, and rather indignant at the rising prestige and prosperity of the new industrial bourgeoisie, the landed aristocracy and gentry peered out condescendingly at the strange new world that had evolved in less than two generations. They saw riots erupt with disturbing frequency, radicals in Parliament calling repeatedly for political reforms, humanitarians pleading for social justice, evangelists pricking men's consciences, and industrialists demanding a greater share in government. Reform had been in the air for fifty years, but the French revolutionary and Napoleonic wars had provided an opportunity for traditionalists to squelch it by equating it with sedition and treason. After the war, the Tories, goaded by the liberal Whigs, realized that a measure of social and economic reform was the only alternative to Parliamentary defeat, and they consequently accomplished a great deal in the 1820s. Once the floodgates of reform had been opened, they could not be closed, for a widespreading tide of popular agitation for further social and political change swept over the country. Above all, the industrial bourgeoisie, not satisfied with what they had gained financially by economic legislation, now demanded political recognition commensurate with their rising importance.

Circumstances in England and on the Continent in 1830 dramatically demonstrated the urgency of reform. In July, a popular French revolution overturned the Bourbon absolutism of Charles X and brought the "Citizen King" Louis Philippe to the throne. In August, Belgian insurgents rose against their Dutch governors, and smaller rebellions occurred in several states of the Germanic Confederation. These outbursts, partly aimed at destroying the absolutist governments established at the Congress of Vienna, deeply affected the attitudes of both British workingmen, who approved them, and the upper classes, who viewed them with consternation and apprehension. If revolts could take place in France or Hesse, why not also in Britain? The workers dared not hope for the franchise, for that would have been a pipe dream in 1830, but they were eager that the government should at long last recognize and remedy their oppressions. Meanwhile the industrial bourgeoisie could not help but compare their political role with that of their counterparts in France, and the liberal Whigs were pointing accusing fingers at the conservative Tory ministry of Wellington, which had steadfastly refused to consider political reform. The Tory economic reforms of the 1820s and the generally prosperous times since 1826 had helped to quiet unrest. But in the autumn of 1830, encouraged by Continental events, agricultural laborers and factory hands were up in arms over low wages, high prices caused by a market depression, unemployment, and harsh enforcement of the Poor Law by parish overseers. Kentish farm workers rioted first, breaking machinery, setting grain ricks afire, looting, and occasionally attacking unpopular employers and local officials. The rioting then spread into Sussex and Hampshire, into Berkshire and Buckinghamshire, and finally into Northamptonshire. The disorder died as quickly as it had risen, but it did pinpoint popular dissatisfaction with the ruling classes.

The death of George IV had automatically dissolved Parliament and necessitated a general election. As a result of the split in the Tory party occasioned by the Catholic Emancipation Act, and because of their opposition to further reform, approximately fifty conservative-minded members of Parliament lost their seats to others more favorably inclined to political reform. Wellington, prime minister since 1828, and spokesman for the aristocracy, believed that Britain had the best possible governmental system yet devised and saw no reason to alter it. But he was forced to resign when the Commons hotly contested his terse statement that no reform would be entertained while he controlled the administration. Earl Grey (1764–1845), a gentle septuagenarian of grace and ability who, with Lord John Russell, had led the Whigs since Fox's death in 1806, formed a coalition ministry of outstanding men, most of whom were later to have distinguished political careers. Grey could not ignore the Tories and consequently named a number of Canningites to the cabinet, notably Charles Grant (Board of Control), Lord Melbourne (Home Office), and Henry Temple, Viscount Palmerston (Foreign Office). The others were either old-line Whigs like Edward Stanley (Ireland), Lord Althorp (Exchequer), and Sir James Graham (Admiralty), or radicals such as Lord Henry Brougham (Chancery), who had championed the abolition of slavery, extension of the franchise, and other popular causes. Their diverse political attitudes kept them apart on several issues, but they agreed wholeheartedly on the necessity of reforming the electoral system. Grey therefore resolved to achieve it, and the Commons was with him.

That gross abuses existed in the electoral and representative systems has been shown in earlier chapters. Nevertheless a few points here will help to refresh the reader's memory. The overwhelming majority of the British people had no voice in the national government. Since great cities like Halifax, Leeds, Manchester, Birmingham, and Sheffield did not have borough status, they had no direct representation in the House of Commons. The distribution of seats in the Commons had not changed since 1688 even though the concentrations of population and the social class structure had. Scotland had only forty-five members of Parliament, one more than Cornwall, despite the fact that the population of Scotland was eight times larger. The one million residents of metropolitan London had less than one-fourth the number of members of Parliament that Cornwall had. Old Sarum in Wiltshire, customarily cited as the worst example of misrepresentation, had become a ghost town by the mid-seventeenth century because of the growth of its neighbor, Salisbury, but it still returned two members. Bath in Somersetshire, where only the mayor, aldermen, and common councilors could vote for members of Parliament because of local charter provisions, was a glaring example of the highly restricted franchise. Franchise qualifications varied widely from town to town, depending on the terms of their charters, but in the counties the franchise was uniform—the possession of a forty-shilling freehold, a requirement first introduced in 1434 and still in effect in 1830. Of the 513 members of Parliament for England and Wales at the beginning of the nineteenth century, nearly 200 had been elected in each instance by less than a hundred voters. Of the 405 members returned by the 203 Parliamentary boroughs, only 74 sat for boroughs north of the Trent River, where the most spectacular population increases had occurred since 1760. About 150 aristocrats, by virtue of tenement ownership and right of nomination, controlled the election of about 250 members, and the crown controlled many more. In addition, certain seats in the Commons could be purchased; intimidation of voters by local magnates was easy because voting was oral; and illegal voting (registration was not required before 1832) was not uncommon. Of the 16,000,000 people in the United Kingdom in 1830, less than 450,-000 could vote.

Early in 1831, Lord John Russell introduced a comprehensive Reform Bill to remedy some of these evils. While the Bill disappointed the liberal Whigs, who had hoped for the secret ballot and a Parliamentary term of five years (it was then seven years), it did propose to redistribute 168 seats to underrepresented and unrepresented areas. This was to be achieved by depriving sixty boroughs of less than 2000 residents of both their seats, and by taking away one of the two seats in

each of forty-seven other boroughs that had between 2000 and 4000 inhabitants. The Bill further proposed to extend the franchise to all men
in boroughs according to a uniform standard: those owning or renting
a house for which the annual rent was ten pounds excluding taxes. In
the counties, in addition to the forty-shilling freeholders, the franchise
would be granted to copyholders (holders of long-term leases) paying
ten pounds annual rental and to wealthier tenants paying fifty pounds
a year. When, on the second reading of the Bill in the Commons, it was
very nearly defeated, Grey asked William IV to dissolve Parliament in
order to put the issue before the country. The elections to the new Parliament returned the Whigs in much larger numbers. Russell immediately reintroduced the Bill, which easily passed the required three
readings in the Commons, only to have the Lords reject it. The Lords,
who had had things their own way for centuries, and who feared that
the Bill would jeopardize governmental stability and their own hegemony, seconded the words of Wellington: "I confess that . . . I cannot
see what is to save the Church, or property, or colonies, or union with
Ireland, or, eventually, monarchy, if the Reform Bill passes."

What Wellington and his aristocratic colleagues failed to appreciate
was that the country would not abide the Bill's defeat. When the Lords
rejected it, rioting broke out in the Midlands, south, and west, not
only among those who had expected to get the franchise under the
Bill (they stirred up opposition, but did not themselves generally riot),
but also among the economically depressed, who simply resented the
ruling classes' apparent indifference to the demands of the middle classes
for political change. Crowds smashed windows in Wellington's house,
burned the Duke of Newcastle's mansion at Nottingham, rioted in
Bristol, London, Worcester, and Coventry, and hanged bishops in effigy.
Parliament adjourned while the rioting ran its course. Early in 1832,
when it reconvened, Russell introduced an amended Reform Bill aimed
at placating the Lords, who again defeated it despite the near civil
war that their rejection of the previous bill had caused. Grey then
asked William IV to create enough new peers to make it possible to
override the opposition, but the king refused, forcing the prime minister's resignation despite his strong support in the Commons, and turned
to Wellington. But Wellington was unable to form a government, and
William therefore had no choice but to accede to Grey's wishes. When
the Lords learned of the king's intention to enlarge the upper House
by one hundred members, they capitulated, although most of the Bill's
opponents either stayed away or refused to vote on it. This signal Whig

triumph greatly enhanced the prestige of the prime minister's position, and demonstrated the Commons' ability to overcome the opposition of the Lords.

Although the Reform Act was no political panacea, it was a firm step forward in weakening the aristocratic oligarchy. The statute is complex and only its essential features may be given here: (1) it disfranchised fifty-six rotten boroughs and reduced from two to one the members of Parliament sitting for thirty other boroughs; (2) certain boroughs with more than two members before 1832 lost one or two of them; (3) the 143 seats surrendered by these boroughs were redistributed as follows: English and Welsh counties acquired 65 additional members, Scotland 8, and Ireland 5, while 44 seats were given to twenty-two new boroughs, mostly industrial centers in the Midlands; (4) in addition to the freemen who kept the vote, the franchise was uniformly extended to urban householders paying or receiving an annual rental of ten pounds, and, in the English and Welsh counties, apart from the forty-shilling freeholders, the copyholders and tenant farmers paying fifty pounds rent annually were enfranchised; (5) Scots farmers with property returning ten pounds a year, and Irish farmers paying twenty pounds rent, were also entitled to vote.

The Reform Act did not create a democratic political system, but it did benefit the middle classes of town and country, strengthen the cabinet's position, and help to free the Commons from great pressure by the Lords and the crown. The electorate of the United Kingdom was enlarged to about 800,000 and thus more people had representation in Parliament, but the principle that it represented property instead of people had not been changed. The rural and urban property qualifications were still high enough to exclude the industrial proletariat, smaller farmers, and agricultural workers. The vote remained in the hands of the landed aristocracy and gentry, but the addition of yeomen farmers, the industrial bourgeoisie, and about 10 per cent of the craftsmen to the roster of voters destroyed the upper classes' virtually exclusive control of politics. The abolition of most of the rotten and pocket boroughs also helped to weaken the influence of the upper classes, which, along with the crown, had formerly controlled the election of many members of Parliament. The House of Lords lost not an iota of its constitutional authority, but the Commons, whose members sat by choice of the electorate instead of by hereditary right, and who were therefore sensitive to popular demands, thereafter more easily withstood pressure from the Lords. Although the crown continued to intervene indirectly in Parliamentary affairs until well into the twentieth century, the prime minister, whose authority was rooted in a Parliamentary majority based at least broadly on the will of the electorate, could more easily strike off on roads that the Lords or the crown could not easily block. Hence the practical political predominance of the Commons that was recognized in the Reform Act augmented the independence of the prime minister. On the other hand, because the Act was a compromise between old and new political philosophies, it disappointed political radicals and the working classes. They had hoped for equal electoral districts, the secret ballot, annual or at least triennial Parliaments, and much lower franchise qualifications, but they were denied even a faint voice in government. The Act also impressed a lesson on the Tories over whose objections it had been carried. Thereafter they came to realize that a reconciliation with the principle of political reform was the only alternative to defeat at the polls. Still, in the 1830s, the Tories were unwilling to go much beyond what the Act had done. Peel, the Tory leader in the Commons, admitted as much in the Tamworth Manifesto during the elections of 1835: "I consider the Reform Bill a final and irrevocable settlement of a great constitutional question." But the turn of events during the next generation forced the Tories to alter their concept of finality.

The social, economic, and political legislation promoted by the Whig ministries during the four years following the Reform Act was an enormous achievement. The abolition of slavery and the Factory Act, both passed in 1833; the Poor Law Amendment Act of 1834, which actually reduced the amount of relief given to the needy; and the Municipal Corporations Act of 1835, which remodeled and standardized local town government, did little to enhance the welfare of the working classes, whose agitation had laid the basis for these laws, but, except for the Poor Law, they were nevertheless a giant step forward in remedying gross evils.

For fifty years, men like Wilberforce, Fox, Clarkson, and Brougham had striven to emancipate the slaves in the British colonies. The Whigs, now occasionally called Liberals, had shown sympathy for abolition, but the Tories or Conservatives, representing the vested financial interests of merchants and planters, had repeatedly frustrated it. Lord Durham and Lord Brougham, strong abolitionists in Grey's cabinet, at last put through—with the help of humanitarian societies, Dissenter sects, Claphamite Anglicans, and public anxiety over frequent slave insurrections in the West Indies—an Act to emancipate the slaves. It provided for gradual emancipation as well as compensation to the slave-owners and a period of partial control over the freed slaves during which they were to become accustomed to caring for themselves. Thus the law decreed that slavery should cease on August 1, 1834, and that the owners should receive a total of £20,000,000 outright from the government and the part-time services of their former slaves, who were obliged to work three-quarters of each week for seven years (five years for household slaves). During this period their employers had to provide them with food and shelter. Children under six and those born after the effective date of the statute were to be freed at once.

Having freed the slaves in the colonies, the government next sought to ameliorate the working conditions of the "white slave" children in the factories and mines. The Factory Act amended earlier Acts of 1819 and 1825, which had prohibited the employment of children under nine in cotton mills, outlawed nightwork, limited the working day for those under sixteen to twelve hours, and stipulated regular hours for meals. The Act of 1833, applicable to minors in all textile factories, limited the work week for children from nine to twelve to forty-eight hours (no more than nine hours a day), with two hours daily of educational instruction; and, for those between thirteen and eighteen, sixty-nine hours.

As early as 1832, the Whigs began to consider in committee the amendment of the inadequate, improperly enforced, and extremely costly Elizabethan Poor Law of 1601, which had been amended somewhat in 1722, 1782, and 1796. Under Elizabeth, Parliament had recognized the principle of the collective responsibility of each parish to care for its aged and infirm as well as for the healthy but unemployed poor. The administration of the Poor Law had been given to overseers of the poor together with the churchwardens, who were empowered to levy local taxes sufficient to meet local needs. During the eighteenth century, when, due to the changing economy, high prices, and market fluctuations, the ranks of the poor greatly multiplied, Parliament broadened the scope of poor relief. Gilbert's Act of 1782, for example, led to the so-called "Speenhamland system," according to which the parish authorities drew on the parish rates to pay employed workers earning low wages a subsidy (varying with the cost of bread) sufficient to sustain their families. This system undoubtedly helped the poor, but it did not solve the basic problem of poverty. Moreover it increased the cost of support, sometimes encouraged laziness and indifference, and did a disservice to workers who were not poor enough to warrant help, but who still lived on bare subsistence wages. Injustice was compounded by the haphazard and indiscriminate judgment of the parish overseers, who had the right to choose which families should receive allowances, whether or not such families by their demonstrated sense of responsibility, industry, or genuine need really deserved help. Furthermore, since employers realized that the government would subsidize low-income families, they tended to resist demands for higher wages. The cost of supporting this system rose constantly, and by 1820 the poor rates cost parish taxpayers about £8,000,000 annually. The financial burden became so heavy in some parishes that groups of them banded together to share the administrative expenses.

For good reason, therefore, the Poor Law of 1834 reorganized the administration of relief and tightened the restrictions governing its implementation. The basic guideline of this Act was that no one who had a standard of living comparable to that of the lowest wage-earner in the district should be given relief. The Poor Law administration for the whole country was centralized in the hands of three commissioners, with Boards of Guardians, consisting of elected representatives and justices of the peace for each union of parishes, responsible for implementing the law. The central commission, which could arrange parish unions, require the establishment of workhouses, and devise rules to handle the sturdy poor as well as the infirm, the orphans, the sick, and the insane, carried out its responsibilities well, although in the process it incurred severe criticism from those who believed only in the principle of self-help. Ultimately, however, the effectiveness of the new system, which discontinued relief for the able-bodied and created a scale of allowances for different levels of poverty, depended on the judgment of the local boards. Most Boards of Guardians did a good job of enforcing the regulations, but others paid little attention to the necessity of distinguishing between the mentally deranged, the orphaned, and the disabled and infirm poor, who were sometimes herded together in the more than six hundred workhouses that became the scandal of Victorian society, as the novels of Dickens clearly show. The hardheartedness of some Guardians was matched by the harsh and occasionally brutal treatment of workhouse inmates—conditions that the Chartists (see below), humanitarians, several religious sects, and the press repeatedly assailed without significant result until much later in the century. But, in general, the new Poor Law, despite its shortcomings and inequities, was a welcome substitute for the old system, which had gotten completely out of hand and could not have been continued except at the extreme financial sacrifice of local rate payers.

Meanwhile Grey's ministry had been replaced by that of Lord Melbourne (1834), and thereafter by the equally brief Conservative government of Sir Robert Peel. Grey had resigned over the issue of tithes, a tenth of every family's produce or income. Englishmen resented the tithe, but not as much as did the Irish Catholics, who had to pay the tithe to the Established Church, whose annual revenue in Ireland was nearly £1,000,000. The Irish population of about 8,000,000 included some 6,500,000 Catholics, most of whom were poor tenant farmers paying high rents and living in abject poverty. The payment of the tithe to the state Church was a double tax, since the Irish were obliged in conscience also to support their own churches and clergy. This was therefore a grave hardship on an already poverty-stricken people. Many Irish families simply refused to pay the tithe or to listen to any compromises proposed by Parliament, and they engaged in rioting and looting to the distraction of their English overlords. Tied to the tithe question was the larger and potentially more dangerous one of repeal of the Act of Union, which Daniel O'Connell had tirelessly promoted since the insult of his disputed election to the Union Parliament in 1828. He had marshaled block support among most of the Irish members of Parliament at Westminster. Despite Grey's efforts to appease the Irish by abolishing first fruits and some bishoprics and sinecures in the Church Temporalities Act (1833), and later that year to force the pacification of Ireland through the Coercion Act that temporarily suspended habeas corpus and instituted martial law, the Irish continued to resist the tithe and to agitate for repeal of the Union. Unable to find a solution to the Irish problem, Grey resigned (1834), and was succeeded by Lord Melbourne. But he was only a stopgap prime minister whom William IV disliked and asked to resign after only four months in office. Peel replaced Melbourne in November, 1834, but his ministry lasted only until the following April. It included traditionalist Tories like Wellington, Lord Lyndhurst, and Lord Aberdeen, and was Conservative both in name and in its attitude toward political reform. Peel asked the king to dissolve Parliament in the hope of increasing his strength in the general election of 1835, which nearly doubled the number of Conservatives in the Commons, but the perennial issue of Ireland once more aroused bitter debate and forced Peel's resignation (1835). Thereafter Melbourne formed his second ministry, which, though little stronger than the first, managed to stay in office until 1841 partly because Queen Victoria was fond of him, and partly on Peel's sufferance. Four issues during his ministry must be considered briefly—the Municipal Corporations Act, the tithe, the Bedchamber question, and working-class unrest.

The basic system of British urban government had not changed substantially for centuries. In Norman and Angevin times, when most of the cities and boroughs had received their charters of incorporation, authority was vested in a mayor and council chosen by a fairly broad electorate. Town government was generally representative of at least the guildsmen and property-owners, but was gradually undermined by public apathy and the dominance of a few local families of wealth and influence. Consequently, by the eighteenth century, many towns were controlled by an oligarchy who rotated public offices among themselves (or permitted life tenure on the council), manipulated public funds for private advantage, owned most of the property, determined the election of members of Parliament, and often neglected to provide adequate public services and necessities such as housing, poor relief, sewers, roads, and health protection. There were significant differences in the forms and practice of local government, and corruption and inequity were widespread. As a result, Parliament passed the Municipal Corporations Act (1835), which revoked the charters of the smaller boroughs and standardized governmental organization in 178 English and Welsh boroughs. Authority was vested in a mayor, aldermen, and councilors. Male taxpayers resident in the towns for at least seven years were entitled to vote for members of the council, two-thirds of whom were elected for terms of three years and one-third for six years, one-third standing for election each year, thereby ensuring continuity of personnel. The council in turn chose the mayor and the aldermen, and appointed local heads of departments in charge of municipal services. The town budget was subject to annual audit. Magistrates appointed by the Lord Chancellor controlled the administration of local justice. These basic institutions of town government have not changed to this day, although obviously the range and scope of public services have expanded because of the complexities of twentieth-century urban society.

The idea of reducing the income of the Church of Ireland by abolishing some benefices, and the possibility of substituting some kind of land tax for the tithe, were rejected by O'Connell. During Melbourne's second ministry, when he needed the support of the Irish members to hold his majority in Parliament, he arranged a compromise with O'Connell known as the "Lichfield House Compact." In return for Irish support and silence on the issue of repealing the Act of Union, Melbourne promised to enact legislation to reduce the franchise qualifications, reform municipal government in Ireland, and apply some of the surplus revenue of the state Church in Ireland to secular uses. He kept his word on the franchise and town government (both Acts comparable to the reforms of 1832 and 1835 for England and Wales), but the Lords rejected the appropriation of Church revenue for secular purposes, although they did pass the Tithe Act of 1838, which transferred the payment of tithes from the Irish tenants to their landlords. Meanwhile Stanley had resigned as Irish secretary and was replaced by Lord Morpeth, who permitted his under-secretary, Thomas Drummond, to administer the country. He did away with martial law and other coercive measures, admitted Catholics to the constabulary and magistracy, and promoted economic growth. Hence the Melbourne ministry temporarily settled the Irish problem, though it periodically troubled virtually every succeeding prime minister until Britain gave Eire its independence in 1924.

William IV died on June 20, 1837, and was succeeded by his eighteen-year-old niece, Victoria, daughter of George III's fourth son, Edward, duke of Kent, and Victoria Mary of the German House of Saxe-Coburg. Victoria (1837–1901) had been trained since early childhood in the art of queenship. After the duke's death in 1820, the duchess had seen to her daughter's future: the princess learned history, languages, philosophy, and manners from her tutors, but her long life on the throne alone could instruct her in politics. She was plump, plain, and just under five feet tall. Her moon-shaped face, with its sparkling blue eyes, small mouth, and medium-brown hair combed in a consummately unflattering style, rather typified her girlish innocence and naïveté. She was not without spirit and zest for life, but her mother's heavy hand had kept them dormant. The duchess never allowed her daughter to forget that she would one day be the queen. Victoria was the essence of propriety—circumspect, industrious, self-assured— whether having breakfast with the prime minister in her apartments or delivering a speech from the throne in Parliament in a high, clear, and expressive voice. She always took her responsibilities to heart, worried like a mother about her subjects, and had a keen interest in government business. In 1840 she married Prince Albert of Saxe-Coburg-Gotha, a capable, stolid, but essentially kindly man who exerted great influence behind the scenes as the queen's constant companion and consort. They were very close, and his untimely death in 1861 at the age of

forty-two left her wretchedly alone. For some ten years thereafter she
became a recluse, garbed in mourning and refusing to appear publicly
until Benjamin Disraeli managed to draw her out again into the world
of the living. Even so, she was lonely, introspective, troubled, and often
crusty with her ministers. Her reign was so long that the ideals and
mores of her youth belonged to a world that died long before she did.

But these sad years were far away for young Victoria, who gloried
in her new regal station and authority. Her uncle, King Leopold of
Belgium, had warned her against subscribing to radical ideas and
advised the retention of the Melbourne ministry. Leopold also sent
Baron Stockmar to give her counsel, but it was Melbourne whom she
liked best. The prime minister, a courteous, soft-spoken gentleman
with old-world charm, more than three times Victoria's age, represented
to her a kind of father image. They got along famously, and he took
what advantage he could of her genuine affection to offset his party's
weakness in Parliament. Peel's Conservatives gave him no rest. Their
numbers had increased in the recent elections, practically overturning
the slim majority Melbourne had achieved through his tenuous alliance
with O'Connell. Hence Conservative criticism of Chartism, the Anti-
Corn Law League, the operation of the new Poor Law, and the rebellions in Canada and Jamaica assumed very great importance and ultimately forced Melbourne's resignation in 1839.

Peel was ready to assume control of the government, much to
Victoria's chagrin because she did not like his cold, stiff, and aloof
manner. Their mutual animosity came into the open when she absolutely refused to accept Peel's demand that certain ladies of her bedchamber be replaced by his nominees. Peel was within his rights,
for with Victoria's reign the day had arrived when the British
sovereign could neither dismiss the prime minister without the consent
of Parliament nor refuse to accept his appointments to the cabinet or
the royal Household. Since 1783, the prestige of the prime minister had
gradually grown, primarily because his authority rested increasingly on
his support in Parliament. With the increase in the prestige and authority of the prime minister there went a firmer party allegiance and structure. Hence the prime minister's authority rested on the control of
Parliament by members of his party, who, at least theoretically, represented the British people. Accordingly, resistance by the monarch to
the legitimate proposals of the prime minister was tantamount to opposing the wishes of Parliament and the country. It is therefore understandable that, when Victoria rejected Peel's demands, he refused to

form a ministry and she gratefully turned again to Melbourne, who remained in office for another two years.

The Melbourne ministry had a new lease on life. The government had improved the postal system so that a letter could be sent anywhere in the United Kingdom for a penny, and had given a little financial support to elementary education, which was placed under the surveillance of a committee of the privy council. The government had also allowed the printing of division (voting) lists of the House of Commons. Yet, important though they were, these things did nothing to ameliorate the hardships of the working classes.

Since the late eighteenth century, the working classes had staunchly supported Whig proposals to amend the electoral and representative systems because they believed the party of Fox, Grey, and Russell would do more for them than would the party of Liverpool, Wellington, or Canning. But the Reform Act of 1832 had been a great disappointment to the workers because it did almost nothing to meet their grievances. When the Whigs passed reform after reform in the 1830s, few of which did anything substantial to improve the social and economic welfare of the working classes, the latter lost faith in Parliament. Their attitude was perfectly understandable. After all, Peel had made it clear in the Tamworth Manifesto that the Conservatives had had enough of reform for the present, and so too had "Finality John" Russell, who remarked more than once that the reforms of 1832 should be sufficient forever.

The grievances of the working classes, such as the stringency of the Poor Law that stopped outdoor relief for lower-income families (the Speenhamland system), long hours of labor, low wages, unhealthy working conditions, and frequent economic recessions, had not seriously interested the government. Hence the workers began to take matters into their own hands. In 1834, for example, thousands in London, annoyed that they were required to work fourteen or sixteen hours a day, staged a massive demonstration. Agricultural laborers in the south likewise rioted and demonstrated against long hours and low wages. Some of the demonstrators were members of newly formed trade unions, which had sprung up after the repeal of the Combination Acts in 1824. William Lovett, Robert Owen, and John Doherty had spearheaded the unionization of workingmen on a national basis, building upon the efforts of several local organizers, notably the idealist-humanitarians Richard Oastler of Yorkshire, Thomas Cooper of Leicester, and Feargus O'Connor, the Irish editor of the radical Leeds newspaper, the *Northern Star*. Doherty had formed a union for cotton workers in 1829, and in the following year founded the National Association for the Protection of Labor, which, though unsuccessful in creating a single national union of all skilled workers, did encourage the establishment of unions among colliers, potters, and others. The national unionization of all workers was also the exalted aim of the utopian socialist Robert Owen (1771–1858), a Welsh mechanic and self-made man, who had become the philanthropic proprietor of a cotton mill at New Lanark, Scotland. He built what was then an ideal industrial community with healthful residences, educational facilities, and playgrounds for his workers and their families. Although he hoped to establish dozens of model cooperative communities for industrial workers and farmers, the two he did found at New Harmony (Indiana) and Queenwood (Hampshire) failed. Undaunted, Owen tried his hand at trade unionism, and in 1833 helped to found the Grand National Consolidated Trades Union, which enrolled over a half million skilled and unskilled workers on farms and in factories. These unions encountered strong opposition from entrepreneurs and the government (by authority of the revised Combination Act of 1825, discussed in Chapter 12), and did not last because they struck recklessly, rioted, ran into financial difficulties, and lost members because of intimidation by employers, government prosecutions, and hard times.

The infant union movement survived only in the smaller craft unions in certain skilled industries, but it helped to lay the foundation for extragovernmental, extra-Parliamentary agitation for further political reform. The failure of trade unionism as a political force led to Chartism. William Lovett, who in 1836 had founded the London Working Men's Association, which patterned its program after the proposals first made in the 1780s by John Cartwright and Horne Tooke, drew up the People's Charter, which a convention of representative workers meeting in London in 1839 subsequently approved and presented to Parliament in a petition. Signed by more than a million Chartists, it asked for annual Parliamentary elections, equal electoral districts, salaries for members of Parliament, abrogation of property qualifications for election to Parliament, universal manhood suffrage, and the secret ballot. Parliament rejected the petition out of hand. Perhaps this reaction to an essentially democratic document might have been expected. After all, the Reform Act had not abolished every pocket borough, did not prevent further corruption or violence in elections, and sustained the view that property ownership still largely determined political power. The aristocratic oligarchy, though somewhat muted by the enfranchisement of the middle classes, was slow to surrender its prerogatives and no petition could destroy them overnight.

Not all the Chartists of 1839 subscribed to Lovett's peaceful methods. There were firebrands like Feargus O'Connor, Julian Harney, and John Frost, who believed that massive demonstrations, riots, strikes, and even violence were the only effective weapons against the obdurate government. The failure of peaceful petition therefore led to an attempt at force. Colliers, ironmongers, and factory hands were stirred into unwise, sometimes bloody, and generally fruitless resistance to their employers, local officials, and Parliament. The worst disturbances were at Newport in Monmouthshire, where government troops, in quelling the rioters, killed about twenty-five. This aspect of Chartism, scarred by sedition and violence, helped to destroy the movement, though it survived for a few more years, with a particularly active period in 1841–42, following a bad harvest that caused food shortages, high prices, and more unemployment. Another petition, signed by about three million persons, was presented to Parliament, which rejected it by an overwhelming majority. By 1848, Chartism was all but dead, but the political reforms it had proposed were ultimately enacted into law during the next century.

Allied to Chartism, but different in that it was essentially a middle-class movement started by radical members of Parliament, was the Anti-Corn-Law League, founded in 1836. Its staunchest supporters were Richard Cobden, a rich Manchester merchant, and John Bright, a manufacturer and gifted orator. The intent of the organization was obvious: to arouse sufficient public feeling against the Corn Laws to force the government to repeal them. The Corn Laws, regulating the price of grain, had worked a hardship on the lower classes as well as on the industrialists. The latter contended with convincing logic that the laws benefited primarily the landowners, but hurt industry, which was eager to produce and sell quality goods on the world market to nations that would purchase them on condition that they in turn could sell their surplus grain and raw materials in Britain. Hence the Corn Laws, viewed in this context, were a hindrance to industrial growth and trade. The industrialists also argued that wages were high enough, *if* food prices were lowered by repeal, but that the higher food prices caused by the Corn Laws forced up wages, which cut profits. Cobden, newly elected to Parliament, and Charles Villiers, a long-time champion of repeal of the Corn Laws, led the fight in the

Commons and were greatly assisted by public pressure through the now usual demonstrations, public meetings, and pamphleteering. This induced Peel, whose Conservatives had gained a majority in 1839 and finally brought down the Melbourne ministry in 1841, to lower the sliding scale of tariffs that had regulated the exportation and importation of grain since 1828. Total repeal, as will be discussed later in this chapter, did not come until 1846.

Domestic unrest during the Melbourne ministry was matched by unrest in the colonies of Canada and Jamaica. In 1774, Sir Guy Carleton, governor of Canada, was instrumental in securing the passage of the Quebec Act, which guaranteed the French colonials their social and legal institutions as well as the seignorial system. As a result, Quebec had remained loyal to the Empire during the American Revolutionary War. Thereafter about forty thousand Loyalists from the United States emigrated to Canada. Some settled in the towns of Quebec and Montreal. Others took up a new life in the hinterland of Nova Scotia and in the western part of Quebec Province, creating the provinces of New Brunswick (1784) and Upper Canada (Ontario), which was separated administratively from Lower Canada (Quebec) according to ethnic or racial lines by the Constitutional Act of 1791. This Act laid the basis for the troubles that ensued in the next forty-five years, primarily because it left a small but outspoken English-speaking minority of merchants and professionals in Lower Canada, and led to the control of Upper Canada by the so-called Family Compact, an oligarchic clique of townsmen, mostly officials, officers, and clergymen, centered at Toronto. The government of each province was vested in a governor, an appointed council, and an elected assembly.

In Lower Canada, the governor and a majority of the council were English while the assembly was almost entirely French. The English wanted greater legal recognition, costly internal improvements, and governmental support of trade and industry. The Catholic French, mostly farmers, were unwilling to raise taxes to support these projects and feared that the English would put an end to their way of life. The assembly, led since 1815 by the moderate reformer Louis Joseph Papineau, also wanted French judges and control of the council. A serious quarrel over finance developed between the governor and the assembly during the 1830s.

Thousands of American immigrants had settled in Upper Canada between 1783 and 1812. Most had taken up farming in the rich Thames Valley. They gradually came to resent the overbearance of the

Family Compact for several reasons: (1) it controlled most of the land through speculative operations that forced up land prices and limited the amount of unencumbered arable land available for private purchase, while at the same time no clear policy had been established for registering land titles; (2) it promoted necessary but costly internal improvements that provided little advantage to back-country farmers, who were expected to help pay for them through higher taxes; (3) as many of the farmers were Methodists, they disliked the domination of the Anglican Church, religious discrimination, and the existence of the Clergy Reserves—land set aside for the support of the Anglican priesthood. Consequently a reform party arose in the assembly. It was composed of Methodists led by Reverend Egerton Ryerson, followers of the moderate constitutionalist Robert Baldwin, and a few radicals headed by William Lyon Mackenzie.

In both provinces, therefore, there arose a desire for legislative independence (then termed responsible government), a desire that was encouraged by Lord Grey's reforms in England and by the liberal administration of President Andrew Jackson in the United States. When neither the British Parliament nor the Canadian administrators would do anything to correct popular grievances, armed rebellion broke out in both provinces late in 1837. It was centered principally around Montreal and the Niagara frontier and involved only a few hundred persons, who were easily suppressed by the local constabulary and militia. But though the rebellions failed, they did induce the imperial Parliament to investigate the causes. To this end Melbourne sent Lord Grey's son-in-law, "radical Jack" Durham, to Canada in 1838 to appraise the situation. He was fatally ill, and his investigation was brief and incomplete, but he did pinpoint the difficulties arising from the "racial" issue, religious and political minority rights, and governmental cliques. Early in 1839 the Durham Report, a cardinal document of Canadian history, was filed at the Colonial Office. Based on its recommendations, Parliament passed the Act of Union (1840). It united Upper and Lower Canada into the single Province of Canada (Nova Scotia, New Brunswick, Prince Edward Island, and Newfoundland being administered individually as crown colonies for the present) and vested authority in a governor-general assisted by an executive council and a two-house legislature composed of an appointed legislative council and an elected assembly having equal representation from each of the old provinces. The Act did not resolve all the political problems of Canada, for the fundamental differences between the French and

English colonists remained, and indeed were perpetuated by continuing the Roman Catholic religion, civil law, and the seignorial system (until 1854) of the French-Canadians. The Act did lay the foundation, however, for the achievement of responsible government by 1849 through the cooperation of coalition ministries of the principal French- and English-speaking parties, and through the enlightened administration of Governor-General Lord Elgin (1848–54), who did not play favorites in politics and encouraged party development. Responsible government, which was also soon attained in two of the Maritime Provinces, led in turn to the Confederation of Canada as an independent dominion within the Empire in the British North America Act of 1867.

As in Canada, so too in Jamaica, the largest and richest British colony in the West Indies, trouble had arisen over a financial quarrel between the governors and the assembly, but there it was worsened by the social and economic effects of emancipation in 1833. England had captured Jamaica from Spain in 1655. From the first the colony had depended on slaves to work the rich sugar plantations and was a base of operations for English piratical raids on the Main against Spanish and French merchantmen during the colonial wars of the eighteenth century. The number of slaves on the island grew rapidly: the ratio of blacks to whites in about 1750 was approximately 12 to 1; a century later, when the total population had risen to 500,000, the ratio was nearly 28 to 1. Many of these slaves were primitive people only a step removed from the jungles of Africa. The supply of slaves had constantly to be enlarged because of death, sickness, and a low birth rate. They were subjected to harsh rule by stewards who managed the absentee landlords' estates with more concern for profits than for the welfare of workers. Slave insurrections were not uncommon, and because the whites were constantly in fear of their lives, authorities often proclaimed martial law. In the later eighteenth century, because of disease, hurricanes, loss of the American market, and interference with trade during the French revolutionary and Napoleonic eras, the planters experienced hard times. After the Emancipation Act of 1833, despite the apprenticeship system, many freed slaves refused to live on the plantations or to work for their former masters. Social unrest became endemic and no measure of legal enforcement could quiet the colony.

From the early days, Jamaica had had a loosely representative political system headed by a governor. A two-house Parliament composed of a legislative council and an assembly, elected by less than two thousand voters among the officer, merchant, and planter class, was dominated by a small but powerful clique that so mismanaged the colony's finances that the Melbourne ministry first decided to amend the constitution and later to suspend it. When the imperial Parliament did so by a margin of only a few votes, there arose a government crisis in which Melbourne resigned (1839). But, when Victoria and Peel quarreled over the Bedchamber question and Peel would not form a ministry, Melbourne returned to office. The Jamaican constitution was then restored, and the unstable political, economic, and social conditions on the island went unreformed until 1865, when, because of a combination of heavy taxes, Negro insurrection, and oligarchic rule, the colonial secretary, Edward Cardwell, abolished the representative system and placed the colony under the authority of a governor and an appointed council. Hence, in Jamaica, there had occurred a political evolution practically opposite to that which had been taking place in other parts of the Empire, namely, the gradual attainment of responsible government.

Meanwhile, settlements in Australia and New Zealand were prospering after an inauspicious start. The aborigines had lived in Australia for centuries, but European contact dates only from the seventeenth century, when several Portuguese and Dutch explorers skirted the northern and eastern coasts in search of spices and gold. One of them, the Dutch Captain Abel Tasman, in the employ of the Dutch East India Company, in 1642–44 discovered Van Diemen's Land (Tasmania) and New Zealand, and charted part of the eastern Australian coastline. Like others before him, he was disappointed by what seemed a barren, unproductive, and impoverished land unworthy of exploitation. Apparently the first Englishman to sight Australia was William Dampier. In two voyages between 1688 and 1701, he gave the lie to gloomy accounts of the Continent and publicized his discoveries in widely read books. Thereafter Britain practically forgot Australia for nearly a century when, in 1768, Captain James Cook, son of a laborer and an ordinary seaman who had risen through naval ranks, went to Tahiti to observe the planet Venus and look for the mysterious "southern land." He landed in the spring of 1770 at Botany Bay near the present city of Sydney, a region he named New South Wales.

What to do about Cook's discovery was another matter. In 1779, one of his shipmates, Sir Joseph Banks, suggested to Parliament the possibility of using New South Wales as a penal colony, a substitute for the southern American colonies to which criminals had previously been transported. Accordingly, the Home Office agreed in 1786 to transport approximately 750 prisoners, nearly a quarter of whom were women, to Botany Bay under the command of the crusty and atheistic former naval officer, Arthur Phillip, who was the colony's first governor. Together with civil and military personnel, a minister, and the prisoners, he disembarked at Sydney Cove the following year. They were strangely unprepared to cope with the inhospitable environment: supplies were inadequate, no one had remembered to bring plows, and food ran short. For several years the colony depended for survival on supplies sent from Britain or traded by American and East India Company ships. By the turn of the century, however, business establishments had been founded, freed convicts and the military and civil officers had squatted on the land, merino sheep and cattle had been imported, and a semblance of civil order had been established after years of riots, drunkenness encouraged by the rum trade, and food shortages.

Gibes about the criminal heritage of the Australian people have long irked them but cannot be denied. Many of the women had been prostitutes, and most of the men were felons, but others were victims of the harsh criminal code that prescribed long imprisonment for petty offenses like debt and vagrancy. Despite the convicts' aversion to work and the apathy natural to their circumstances, they were kept busy tilling the soil, laying roads, and constructing buildings. In 1790, a thousand additional convicts arrived, some with trade skills and a modicum of farming experience. Many more, including a few hundred free settlers, later came to New South Wales, Victoria, South Australia, and Queensland. By 1840, when the Home Office officially ceased transporting criminals to New South Wales (it continued to send some to Van Diemen's Land for another twenty years), there were about 130,000 white settlers in Australia. To the smaller farms and sheep stations of freed convicts, retired soldiers, and civil servants were added the larger holdings of enterprising men like John Macarthur, who diversified farming, imported large flocks of sheep, and founded towns in the hinterland. Next to Governor Phillip, who had returned to England in 1792, Governor Lachlan Macquarie (1809–21) did most to stabilize and expand the colonies through strict law enforcement, promotion of individual farming, and resettlement of convicts. He also introduced large-scale wool production. Additional colonists were attracted to Australia in 1851 by the discovery of gold in Victoria and New South Wales and by the prospect of profitable sheep and cattle farming. In 1860 the country had more than a million inhabitants.

Meanwhile the first English colonials, encouraged to emigrate by a colonization society founded in 1830 by Gibbon Wakefield, a philanthropist and empire-builder who believed that only sturdy, honest men should be allowed to emigrate, had landed in New Zealand in 1839 to build a new nation on groundwork previously laid by Anglican missionaries. Unlike the Australian aborigines, who had simply moved inland when the colonists came, the more advanced Maoris resented the intrusion of missionaries, whalers, seamen, and farmers who took their land and imposed an alien political and social system that threatened their way of life. They therefore went to war in 1844-45, slaughtering some of the settlers ,at Wairau, and made peace only when Governor Sir George Grey promised to stop English seizure of Maori land. When the treaty was broken, a second Maori war began in 1860 and lasted for ten years until the two peoples were reconciled through the recognition of Maori land titles and joint participation in government.

The governmental development of the colonies in Australia and New Zealand was nearly identical to that in Canada, which had become the prototype for the whole Empire. Once the initial problems of settlement in Australia had been mastered and the several colonies had become solvent, responsible government developed rapidly. At first the governor had had absolute military, civil, and legal authority, but in 1823 trial by jury could be safely introduced and an executive council nominated. As the urban officer–civil servant–bourgeoisie class controlled the council, it frequently quarreled with the rural, former convict, and free immigrant class that demanded a share in the government. This ultimately forced the council to admit to its membership a few elected representatives, who in turn quarreled with the governor over finance and demanded recognition of legislative control of domestic affairs through a ministry supported by an elective majority in a lower House. Accordingly, through the Imperial Act of 1850, New South Wales was permitted to establish an elected lower House, party organization matured, and ministerial responsibility was granted. The other Australian colonies of Victoria, South Australia, Queensland, and Tasmania (Western Australia's wilderness had been abandoned to the aborigines) likewise had written constitutions by 1859 embodying the principle of ministerial responsibility. In New Zealand, which had been ruled under the guidance of the New Zealand Company and

Anglican missionaries by a governor and a legislative council, the steady growth of population and economic prosperity led to the establishment of an elected assembly in 1846. When the company relinquished its authority in 1851, a new constitution was written that brought responsible government into force four years later.

Few Englishmen had the vision to appreciate that the destiny of Britain lay in the growth of its far-flung dominions, and consequently paid less attention to them than to the revolutionary events that between 1815 and 1848 periodically inflamed parts of Europe and the Near East. The reactionary decisions reached by the major powers at Vienna were inconsistent with the liberal ideology that outlived the French Revolution. As has been shown, military intervention by the Quadruple Alliance had checked these forces during the 1820s. The successful Greek and Latin American wars of independence, however, helped to destroy the Alliance, although not the balance of power which it had created. The overthrow of King Charles X in 1830 in France touched off a second round of revolutions in Belgium, Italy, Germany, Poland, and Spain that culminated in the unsuccessful but ultimately salutary revolutions of 1848.

The architect of British foreign policy during this period was Henry Temple, Lord Palmerston (1784–1865), an elfish-looking man with a twinkle in his eye. The scion of an independently wealthy family, he had been educated at Cambridge in the tradition of Tory conservatism and had served in successive Tory cabinets from 1809 to 1830 when, because of his association with the Canningites, he sided with the Whigs. Although he abhorred the idea of social and economic reforms on behalf of the working classes, he did believe in a measure of political change short of enfranchising them. He became foreign secretary in the midst of the Belgian revolution of 1830 and served in that capacity in every Whig government thereafter until 1855. Afterward, except for ten months, he was prime minister until his death. Some have tried to make a statesman of Palmerston, but that would be stretching the bounds of eulogy too far. He always played the game of diplomacy close to his chest, delighting in taking action first and deliberating later. He had a penchant for sensational, *ad hoc* decisions that brought the country to the brink of war more than once, but his consummate diplomatic skill and enormous self-confidence helped him to wriggle out of these delicate situations. Except for Melbourne, who let him have his way in practically everything, Palmerston annoyed every prime minister by his overbearing manner and seeming flippancy in dealing with sensitive foreign powers, and drove Victoria and Albert to distraction. The saving grace of this remarkably energetic and cocksure bachelor was that his policies succeeded, bringing his nation the respect of the international community and himself the accolades of his admiring countrymen.

A case in point is the Belgian revolution of 1830. Castlereagh had helped at Vienna in 1815 to arrange the political union of Belgium and Holland, an arrangement pleasing to the British because it established a friendly power across the Channel. The Belgians, mostly Roman Catholics and either French- or Walloon-speaking, had not possessed the economic advantages enjoyed by the Dutch, resented their over-lordship, and consequently rebelled shortly after the French revolution of July, 1830. The rebellion threatened to escalate into a European war when Prussia, Austria, and Russia sided with the Dutch and offered military assistance, and Britain and France, after consultations between Palmerston and Talleyrand (ambassador in London), supported Belgian independence. Palmerston would have preferred no alteration of the *status quo*, but, recognizing that the situation had gone too far, he believed compromise preferable to a general war. He therefore mediated the crisis through a series of conferences among the Great Powers, the Netherlands, and Belgium that resulted in the recognition of Belgian independence early in 1832. The Dutch, understandably anxious about such questions as the apportionment of the national debt and the liberal constitution written by the Belgians in 1831, refused to accept their independence, and did not do so until 1839. Nevertheless Belgium was declared an independent state whose neutrality was guaranteed by the Great Powers. Victoria's uncle, Leopold of Saxe-Coburg, became its first monarch.

In 1831, while Palmerston was negotiating the pacification of the Belgian insurrection, he became alarmed by a Near Eastern crisis provoked by the Egyptian pasha, Mehemet Ali. Disappointed by the Turkish sultan's ingratitude following Egyptian intervention in the Greek rebellion of the 1820s, Mehemet Ali sent an army headed by his son, Ibrahim Pasha, to wrest Arabia and Syria from the weak Ottoman Empire, of which Egypt was a restless member. The Egyptian army overwhelmed the Turks and threatened to take all Asia Minor and possibly even Constantinople itself. This turn of events deeply interested all the major powers: Austria disliked any territorial alteration; Russia, long interested in establishing hegemony over the Dardanelles and the Black Sea, threatened to intervene on behalf of the Turks;

France, anxious to weaken British authority in the eastern Mediterranean, had helped Mehemet Ali with advice and arms; and Britain could not tolerate either a French protectorate over Egypt or Russian control of the Ottoman Empire. When Palmerston failed to respond to the Turks' appeal for help, they turned to the Russians, who signed with them the Treaty of Unkiar Skelessi (1833), which guaranteed Turkey Russian help in the event of attack and required the sultan to close the Dardanelles if any power attacked Russia. Although this treaty temporarily settled the Near Eastern crisis and allowed Egypt to keep Syria, it greatly annoyed Palmerston, who rightly saw in it a vast increase of Russian influence in the Near East. But his efforts to have it rescinded failed.

Mehemet Ali went to war again in 1839, to secure recognition of his hereditary position in Egypt and possession of Syria. The Turks were again routed by Ibrahim and demoralized by the unstable political situation caused by the death of the old sultan and the accession of his youthful and inexperienced son. When several members of Melbourne's cabinet cautioned against direct British intervention in the Near East, Palmerston resorted to diplomacy. He brought pressure on Louis Philippe to withdraw French support of Mehemet Ali and gained a consensus among the major European powers on the preservation of Turkish territorial integrity. The scheme worked marvelously: Louis Philippe ultimately backed down; Metternich naturally agreed to the recognition of a principle he had championed since 1815; the Prussian Frederick William III, who had sent military advisers to help the sultan, followed suit; and Czar Nicholas I, although anxious to dominate the Turks, realized that Unkiar Skelessi had made far more enemies than friends. They signed the Treaty of London (1840), obliging them to force Mehemet Ali to withdraw his army from Asia Minor. Although obstinate at first, he changed his mind when an Anglo-Austrian fleet bombarded his troops in Syria and an English force captured Acre. He consequently surrendered Syria, Arabia, and Crete, retired to Egypt where his authority was confirmed, and agreed to pay the customary annual tribute to the sultan. Meanwhile the signatories had also agreed to the Straits Convention (1841) whereby they promised that none of their warships would penetrate the Dardanelles or the Bosphorus while Turkey was at peace.

Few could have justifiably questioned Britain's right to intervene in eastern Mediterranean affairs to defend its political and economic interests. But many argued against Britain's going to war with China in

1839–42, ostensibly to protect its nationals, but actually to force the regularization of Anglo-Chinese diplomatic and commercial relations. The French, Dutch, English, Portuguese, and Americans had traded privately with Chinese merchants since the late eighteenth century. A few years before 1833, when Parliament abolished the East India Company's profitable monopoly of the China trade, the Chinese government had taken the first steps to stop the traffic in Turkish- and Indian-grown opium that was destroying its workers' health and hurting the economy by draining the country of silver with which the Chinese merchants paid for the drug. As these mild measures failed to discourage smuggling by private English merchants, the Manchu government early in 1839 clamped down on the opium traders of several nations by confiscating and destroying large stores of opium worth millions of pounds and inflicting severe corporal punishment on the guilty merchants. British trade representatives, who had replaced Company agents in 1833, had done what they could to curtail smuggling and to negotiate a commercial treaty aimed at opening Chinese ports to British industrial goods even while they underwent personal indignities at the hands of an isolationist government that resented any contact with the Western world. When the indignities and penalties multiplied, war ensued. It was of short duration: the British seized Canton and gained control of the Yangtze River, thereby forcing the Manchu to sue for peace. The Treaty of Nanking (1842) formalized Anglo-Chinese diplomatic relations; required the Chinese to pay an indemnity equal to the value of the goods they had destroyed; ceded Hong Kong to Britain; and opened the ports of Shanghai, Canton, Ningpo, Amoy, and Foochow to British trade. Oddly, no mention was made of the traffic in opium, which continued illegally until a later treaty (1860) authorized the importation of opium subject to tariffs.

On Lord Melbourne's resignation in 1841 Sir Robert Peel (1788–1850) became prime minister. Tory-bred, Tory-educated, and Tory-trained in politics under Lord Liverpool, Peel had had much administrative experience as secretary for Ireland and in the Home Office, where he had made a reputation in the party by creating a metropolitan police force and amending the criminal code. With Wellington in the House of Lords, Peel had become Conservative leader in the Commons during the ministries of Grey and Melbourne. Despite his reserved manner, he made friends and attracted strong support from able backbenchers such as William E. Gladstone, Edward Cardwell, Lord Dalhousie, Sidney Herbert, and Benjamin Disraeli. Son of a wealthy textile manufacturer, Peel understood the problems of business and the temper of its leaders, whose attitudes he championed during his second ministry. His forte was finance; his tidy mind grasped essentials and retained sticky details, and if he was not a brilliant orator, his colleagues were never befuddled by an unclear presentation of the facts. Above all, he was forthright in personal relationships and intellectually honest. His countrymen might well have expected little by way of reform from a man who had resisted Catholic emancipation, fought the Reform Act of 1832, and enunciated traditionalist political doctrines in the Tamworth Manifesto. Yet he felt grave misgivings about traditionalist views that aroused strong opposition from a battery of critics including the Chartists, Anti-Corn-Law Leaguers, utopian socialists, free-traders, and the underprivileged of town and country. That the banking system, tariff schedules, and large annual budgetary deficits demanded immediate remedy Peel had no doubt, but he realized that to tamper with these sacred cows of the protectionist Conservatives would make him their enemy. He nevertheless went ahead—at the cost, as it proved, of his popularity, leadership, and party unity.

The gravest issue facing Peel in 1841 was the budgetary deficit. An economic depression, the effect of the Corn Laws, a succession of bad harvests, and declining trade had combined to plunge the country into a serious financial crisis. Melbourne's efforts to reduce the deficit by raising customs duties by about 5 per cent across the board had not succeeded. Peel believed that high duties prevented business expansion and reduced government revenue, and pointed as proof to the increased revenue that had followed tariff reductions in 1824–25. He therefore wrote the budget of 1842 with this principle in mind. It reduced tariffs on approximately half the dutiable articles, admitting raw materials at only 5 per cent duty and finished products at 20 per cent. Peel admitted that government income would be cut for the time being, but declared that in the long run the tariff reduction would stimulate trade and increase public revenue. In order to tide the government over, he had Parliament pass an income tax of sevenpence in the pound on incomes over £150. This tax was intended to be temporary—to last for four years—but it was extended for three more in 1845 and periodically thereafter so that it became a fixture. When his reforms produced a surplus by 1844, Peel was encouraged to reduce the tariff even further in the budget of 1845, which removed it completely from most raw materials, abolished virtually all export duties, retained the income tax, and increased inheritance and real-estate taxes. He also raised excise taxes on articles such as spirits, sugar, tobacco, and paper. It was with understandable pride that Peel reported to the Commons in January, 1846, on the success of these commercial reforms: the value of exports from the United Kingdom had risen in 1842–44 from £47,000,000 to £58,000,000 while customs revenue increased by about £100,000 annually. Peel could therefore argue convincingly that the principle of high protection was inimical to the best interests of the nation. It is no wonder that several Midlands cities erected statues in honor of this champion of the industrial and commercial classes.

With their interests as well as the financial stability of the country in mind, Peel undertook to tighten government control of banking. Early in the eighteenth century, Parliament had forbidden any financial organization having more than six partners to engage in banking, but allowed them to issue their own paper currency. In 1826, an Act sponsored by Peel had permitted the creation of joint-stock banks anywhere more than sixty-five miles from London (this geographic restriction was removed in 1833) and certified their right to issue paper money. Country banks with numerous branches and not much experience mushroomed all over the country. Many of them failed due to unwise speculation and insufficient reserves: about eighty had collapsed in 1825 and fifty-five more during the inflationary years immediately preceding the 1836 depression. As early as 1810, the government, concerned about deflation, had investigated the operations of the country banks that were found to be issuing paper currency far in excess of their gold reserves. Consequently Peel had sponsored an Act in 1819 that required these banks to redeem on demand their paper money for gold, hoping that this would force them to back it with specie. But the banks continued to circulate more paper than they had backing for in bullion so that, when financial crises arose, as in 1825 and 1836, many failed along with the business firms that depended on them for credit. The situation was aggravated by the drain of gold reserves to the United States through trade and the collapse of many of the Jacksonian "pet banks" with whom British merchants did business. These bank failures provided Peel with the opportunity to tighten government controls over irresponsible banking practices through the Bank Charter Act (1844). It stipulated that the Bank of England might issue paper to the amount of £14,000,000 for the present, and more later so long as it was supported by bullion, three-quarters of which had to be in gold. Provincial banks already circulating paper could continue to do so but could not enlarge their issues. The notes of defunct banks would be assumed by the Bank of England and new provincial banks were forbidden to print paper money. Although the Bank of England later found it necessary occasionally to exceed the limit of its paper over bullion reserves, and country banks continued to circulate paper money until 1921, the Act did stabilize banking practices and was a safeguard against inflation.

Peel's thoughts turned more easily to finance than to social welfare, but he was not unmindful of the deplorable working conditions among women and children in mines and factories. How bad these conditions were, the Commons learned from two reports of the commission on children's employment in 1842 and 1844. Young mothers worked underground along with five- and six-year-olds hauling coal tubs; children were apprenticed to tradesmen without pay, schooling, or care for their health; whole families worked and made only enough to subsist. These reports, together with the persuasiveness of Lord Ashley, author of the Factory Act of 1833 and the object of recrimination by the propertied class, who fulminated against governmental interference in business, resulted in remedial legislation. The Mines Act (1842) forbade employment underground of boys under ten and of all women. The Factory Act (1844) restricted the working day of children between nine and thirteen to 6½ hours, or to alternate full days (they were to attend school half-time); prohibited children under thirteen from working at night; and limited daily working hours of women to twelve. Both bills met strong opposition in Parliament despite the pleas of Home Secretary Graham, the agitation of Disraeli and his followers (the "Young Englanders"), and Lord Ashley's eloquent speeches. Their principal opponents were members of the so-called "Manchester school," free-traders and champions of individualism led by Cobden and Bright, who denounced these Acts as injurious to free enterprise and heretical to the doctrine of self-help, so popular among Victorians. To secure passage of the bills, Peel had to threaten to resign. In 1847, Parliament went a step further by passing the Ten Hours Act, which forbade employment of women or young persons aged thirteen to eighteen for more than ten hours a day. Over the next generation the provisions of this law tended to be applied to men as well, the ordinary working day running from six in the morning to six in the evening with two hours allowed for meals.

While Peel struggled with budgets, banks, and Factory Acts, Britain came dangerously close to war with the United States over border incidents and the delineation of the Canadian-American boundary.

Since the Revolutionary War, Americans had been accustomed to viewing Canada as an object of territorial expansion. If the War of 1812 had temporarily discouraged them, the acquisition of Florida from Spain, the Louisiana Territory from France, and Texas from Mexico had whetted the appetites of expansionists who, in the 1830s, invented the slogan "manifest destiny" to rationalize their conviction that the Stars and Stripes should fly over all North America. Mackenzie, leader of the Rebellion of 1837 along the Niagara frontier, had gotten sympathy and material aid from members of the hunters' lodges that had been organized in the northern border states from Michigan to Vermont. They raided Canadian territory at several points, including Niagara, where the American ship *Caroline* supplied Mackenzie's rebels on Navy Island. When Canadian troops burned her on the American shore, one of her crew was killed. Alexander McLeod later boasted in a Buffalo tavern that he had killed the American, and was arrested. Britain demanded his release. President Van Buren did what he could to convince the New York authorities to comply, and eventually McLeod was exonerated. The case called into question the security of the unguarded frontier that prompted the British to send reinforcements and build a chain of forts along the lower Great Lakes, and heightened Anglo-American hostility. At the same time American lumberjacks and Canadian potato farmers raided each other's settlements in the Aroostook Valley, part of the territory on the Maine–New Brunswick border that had been in dispute since the careless definition of the boundary in the Treaty of Paris (1783). While Congress and the Canadians prepared for war, British and American officials set their geographers to work searching old maps to prove whether there actually did exist one "St. Croix River" and the "highlands" mentioned in the treaty. Finally, when neither side could prove its case and the Americans had refused the arbitration of the king of the Netherlands, Peel sent Lord Ashburton, who had an American wife and was a friend of Secretary of State Daniel Webster, to arrange a treaty to settle all outstanding Anglo-American differences. The resulting Webster-Ashburton Treaty (1842) awarded Canada five-twelfths of the disputed territory and obliged Britain to pay Maine and Massachusetts £150,000 each in compensation. Not often mentioned, but more important in the long run than the territorial settlement, was a clause that provided for the extradition of either Canadian or American criminals who sought safety across the border, except those whose "crimes" had been political. Thus Britain, long the asylum for political refugees from the European continent, extended that privilege to Canada.

In 1846, another crisis arose over the Oregon territory. The Webster-Ashburton Treaty had settled the northeastern boundary, and a convention had defined the border from the Lake of the Woods to the Stony (Rocky) Mountains at the forty-ninth parallel, but who owned the land between the mountains and the Pacific had not been determined. American settlers had followed explorers and traders over the Oregon Trail to the Pacific Northwest and laid claim to the region, as did explorers like Captain Cook, agents of the Hudson's Bay Company, and a few hardy pioneers. The disputed territory lay along the Pacific coast between latitudes 42° and 54°40', which Spain and Russia had relinquished by treaty with the United States in 1819 and 1824 respectively. As the region was rich in timber, salmon, furs, and farmland, neither the United States nor Britain was willing to surrender it lightly. That the Americans meant to have it, President Polk made perfectly clear in his campaign slogan of "fifty-four forty or fight." But as neither country wanted war, both agreed to extend the boundary to the Pacific along the forty-ninth parallel, allowing Britain to keep all of Vancouver Island. The convention did not please Canadians, who were beginning to believe what events repeatedly proved later—that the interests of the home country took priority over Canada's interests whenever Britain and the United States quarreled. Canada had in the twenties received preferential treatment in the matter of grain exports to England. Hence the repeal of the Corn Laws, which almost destroyed the Canadian milling industry overnight and caused the ruination of about half the business firms in Montreal by 1849, pleased Canadians even less.

Peel had been moving in the direction of free trade since his assumption of office in 1841, and in 1846 he climaxed his public career by abolishing the Corn Laws. Several factors and circumstances impelled him toward this momentous decision. His commercial reforms in 1842–45 had reduced the tariff from Huskisson's high of about 30 per cent to 10 per cent, with most raw materials on the free list. The economic benefits of these reforms to the nation as a whole had been significant; they brought the country out of the depths of depression of 1841–42 to moderate prosperity by 1844, with a consequent increase in public revenues and a reduction of the budgetary deficit. Peel also realized that the operation of a sliding scale, which reduced duties on corn during times of agrarian shortages, as in 1826, 1828, and 1842, had been beneficial to the working classes, whose low wages, which remained the same through poverty and plenty, could buy cheaper and therefore more bread. Moreover the Anti-Corn-Law League, led by Cobden and Bright, who also represented the Manchester School of free-traders in Parliament, had argued convincingly for some years that trade with agricultural nations was discouraged by high tariffs on foodstuffs. Evangelicals, utopian socialists, and humanitarians had assiduously compiled evidence to prove that the working classes were the real victims of high food prices, bad harvests, and market depressions. Chartists and trade unionists likewise became interested in the relationship between low wages and high prices in terms of the workers' standard of living. And Peel himself put his finger on the best argument against the Corn Laws, in a speech before Parliament in January, 1846, when he maintained "that the argument in favour of high protection on the ground that it is for the benefit of a particular class, is untenable." It was clear to Peel, as it was to all reasonable men, that the hardship imposed on the common people for the economic welfare of a few hundred landowners was inconsistent with logic and justice.

But arguments based on logic, justice, and a mountain of evidence that the Corn Laws increased the burdens of the working classes would probably have been insufficient to abolish the precious privilege of the landed interests of the Conservative party without the concurrent calamity of the Irish famine. Famines were hardly novel in Ireland: its peasants had endured them for centuries, most recently in 1831 and 1837, but the famine of 1845–46 was something else again. A disease that rotted potatoes in the field had first been noticed on the Isle of Wight in late summer, 1845, and spread to other sections of England and Ireland. The next year brought a second failure of the potato crop due to a wet spring and cold autumn. About half of Ireland's 8,000,000 inhabitants, 1,250,000 of whom earned less than three shillings a week, and another 2,250,000 of whom were unemployed for half the year, absolutely depended on potatoes for survival. The destruction of both the English and Irish crops for two successive years therefore resulted in widespread hunger, disease bred by malnutrition, the starvation of tens of thousands, and the emigration of many more to England, the United States, Canada, and elsewhere. The reports of experts who visited the fields and fens of Ireland corroborated Peel's suspicions about the sorry plight of the peasantry. He knew then what must be done, regardless of the consequences to himself or the party: "The remedy is the removal of all impediments to the import of all kinds of human food—that is the total and absolute repeal forever of all duties on all articles of subsistence."

It quickly became apparent that Peel would have to overcome the entrenched protectionism among some of his colleagues in the cabinet and in Parliament. In a series of cabinet meetings held between October 31 and November 6, 1845, Peel outlined his program to ameliorate conditions in Ireland. He proposed that a number of public works should be inaugurated by the government to provide the unemployed Irish with work, and that an Order in Council should suspend the Corn Laws with the proviso that Parliament should be quickly summoned to consider their amendment. These proposals split the cabinet, only Lord Aberdeen, Sir James Graham, and Sidney Herbert siding with the prime minister. Meanwhile the Whig leader, Lord John Russell, long an advocate of some protection, published a letter in which he came out wholeheartedly in favor of free trade, thereby practically forcing the Conservatives to agree or face defeat. When Peel, in another series of cabinet meetings during late November and early December, failed to win the unqualified support of his colleagues, he offered his resignation to the queen. She invited Russell to form a ministry, but, failing to secure Peel's pledge that the Conservatives would support repeal, and lacking a Parliamentary majority, Russell declined. Hence Peel returned to office.

As expected, repeal encountered stiff opposition in Parliament among protectionist Conservatives led by Benjamin Disraeli. In the midst of catastrophe in Ireland, mass meetings in the industrial centers sponsored by the Anti-Corn-Law League, and hundreds of petitions pouring into Parliament either for or against repeal, it convened in January, 1846, and for the next four months the lower House listened to impassioned debates. Peel proposed a bill that would lower many tariffs and gradually reduce the sliding scale of duties on grain over the next three years so that by 1849 they would only be nominal. Many protectionists immediately accused Peel of betraying his own party. Others were ready to agree to a temporary suspension of the Corn Laws to meet the Irish emergency provided that protection would afterward be restored. But hard-core protectionists as well as Peel realized that there was no repairing the gap in the high wall of tariffs on foodstuffs once it had been breached. It was all or nothing, and now. Hence the protectionists and free-traders locked horns in a struggle of the utmost consequence. In the end more than half the

Conservatives voted against the Corn Bill, which passed the Commons with Whig support on May 15 by 327 votes to 229. The Lords followed suit in June, largely because Wellington sided with Peel.

Peel's singular victory in converting Britain to the principle of virtual free trade, which dominated the economic policy of the country for the remainder of the nineteenth century, had immediate consequences for the prime minister and the Conservative party. On June 26, the very day the Lords approved the Corn Bill, the protectionist Conservatives, Irish members of Parliament, and a few others combined to defeat Peel's Preservation of Life Bill by which he intended forcibly to restore order in several Irish counties where violence had accompanied economic distress. This defeat forced Peel's resignation and replacement by Lord John Russell (1792–1878), whose Whig ministry lasted until 1852. More importantly, the issue of free trade had split the Conservatives into factions that did not reconcile their differences until 1868. About a hundred members of Parliament called the Peelites, including Cardwell, Herbert, Goulburn, Graham, Gladstone, and Aberdeen, remained loyal to the principles of free trade and economic reform enunciated by their fallen leader, who never held office again and died from an accident in 1850. The Manchester School group often voted with the Peelites, for they were for free trade, which they believed would lead to international peace and commercial growth. Both groups increased their strength in the 1847 election, which generally went against the protectionists. The remaining Conservatives, who were in the majority, had no effective leader in the Commons. They nominally followed Lord George Bentinck, who had the sort of social and educational credentials to please pedigreed and club-minded Tories, but neither the political sagacity nor the organizational and oratorical brilliance of young Disraeli. The latter pulled the strings while Bentinck lent a fashionable air to the party, yet neither man could claim unqualified leadership. Most Tories resented Bentinck's support of a bill in 1847 (not passed until 1858) that would have permitted Jews to sit in Parliament without taking the required oath "on the true faith of a Christian." They also looked askance at Disraeli, the author of two socially critical novels, a former radical, and a man whom many did not trust. Although protectionists were willing to rally around a man of his obvious talents, they disliked the fact that he was the son of a businessman who had nominally converted his Jewish family to Christianity. However, when Bentinck's death in 1848 robbed the party of its ornament, even fussy Conservatives had to recognize

Disraeli's *de facto* leadership. Nonetheless, he had to serve a long apprenticeship as leader in the Commons and share cabinet control on three occasions with Lord Derby (in the ministries of 1852, 1858–59, and 1866–68) before becoming prime minister in his own right. By that time (1874) he was already past seventy and nearing the end of a brilliant career.

The Whigs gave the appearance of greater unity under Lord John Russell, but they too were troubled by factionalism, especially between the old-line Whigs and the liberals in the party. The latter had gained strength in the general election of 1847, which was held on the eve of a money-market crisis that forced the Bank of England to violate the restrictions on paper money imposed by the Bank Charter Act, hurt the economy, and worsened conditions among the working classes. It also aroused middle-class opposition to the income tax and Chartist agitation for educational, social, and political reform. Russell had to straddle the fence on many issues so as not to alienate traditionalist Whig friends or displease the combination of Peelites, liberals, and Irish upon whose support his slim majority in the Commons depended. But although he welcomed their support, he refused to form a coalition ministry and was consequently unable to pass much legislation. That he managed under these trying circumstances to cope with the Irish famine, suppress Irish rebellion, enact the first Public Health Act, and repeal the Navigation Acts was no mean accomplishment.

His immediate problem was the Irish famine, which had reduced the nation to starvation and death. Despite massive importation of grain, government loans to Irish landowners and parochial authorities, and a large public works program that stimulated the economy and provided employment for many, the desperate Irish rioted and looted. Hotheads in Parliament, called the "Young Ireland" group, became impatient with Daniel O'Connell's methods of peaceful persuasion and resorted to open rebellion against the coercive measures of the British government. The rebels organized a paper republic in 1847 under the high-born Smith O'Brien, raised a bedraggled force of hungry peasants who looted, shouted blasphemies at the British constabulary, and fought a few skirmishes with them. The police easily put down the rebels, who suffered the inevitable consequences of imprisonment or deportation to the penal colonies. Although Ireland required sweeping economic, social, and religious reform, the Russell ministry was satisfied with an attempt to ease the land problem in the Encumbered Estates Act (1849), which merely substituted greedy Irish landlords for greedy English landlords, forced up rents, caused more evictions of peasants, and heightened Irish hatred.

At home Russell's government did somewhat better in the legislative field by enacting three laws, the first of which, the Ten Hours Act, has already been discussed. Largely because of the persistence of Edwin Chadwick, one of the Poor Law commissioners who spent ten years collecting evidence on the health hazards of slums, rubbish heaps, and inadequate sanitation systems, Parliament passed the Public Health Act (1848). It created a national General Board of Health with authority to organize local boards and inspect local health conditions. This statute laid the foundation for state support of public health that has grown into the system of nationalized medicine. Since the modification of the commercial system in the 1820s, nothing had been done about the lingering mercantilism embodied in the Navigation Acts. Tariff reforms since 1823 had rendered them practically meaningless and the repeal of the Corn Laws had also undermined the Canadian milling industry centered at Montreal, where some merchants were driven to the conclusion that political union with the United States was the only alternative to economic stagnation within the Empire. Primarily for these reasons, between 1849 and 1853, Parliament repealed most of the Navigation Acts.

In addition to economic problems, Russell's ministry faced serious religious developments in the Oxford Movement and an attempt to re-establish Roman Catholic dioceses in England. Thoughtful Anglican clergymen had long been exercised about the indifference of their Church to the great social and economic issues of the day, the spiritual apathy at every level of the priesthood, and the hierarchy's preoccupation with personal and political matters at the expense of diocesan responsibilities. Despite the important contributions of the evangelicals in reviving a measure of faith among the laity, the state Church languished in conservatism and had not undergone any significant administrative reform since the seventeenth century. It lacked elasticity and missionary zeal and had lost ground to the Presbyterians, who outnumbered Anglicans in Scotland, and to the Methodists, whose ranks had grown from 100,000 in 1790 to 500,000 in 1840. The number of Catholics had also increased, though not nearly as much as had those of the Dissenters. In addition to converts, Catholicism profited by the emigration of many Irish to Gloucestershire, Lancashire, and the western Lowlands of Scotland to find work or to escape the famine. Even with them, Catholics composed only 3 or 4 per cent of the country's population, but they had able leaders in such vicars apostolic (administrative heads that had substituted for bishops since the late seventeenth century) as Nicholas Wiseman, William Ullathorne, and Henry Manning. They maintained colleges such as Oscott and Ushaw, and had considerable influence in some industrial communities, especially in the Midlands. On the other hand, despite repeal of the penal laws, and the Catholic Emancipation Act, their religion still cost them social position, jobs, and opportunities for advancement in an overwhelmingly Protestant society.

The Oxford Movement began in the early 1830s among a small circle of Anglican priest-scholars at the university. They sought to identify the Anglican Church more closely with the pre-Reformation Christian Church, to prove the validity of their priesthood's apostolic succession, to improve the quality of the hierarchy, and to promote greater devotion to the liturgy and the sacramental system. The principal exponents of these views were John Keble, Edward Pusey, and John Henry Newman, who wrote dozens of tracts that seemed to some High-churchmen dangerously close to the Roman Catholic position. Keble and Pusey remained loyal to the Anglican communion, but Newman (1801–90) searched so deeply into Christian tradition and his own conscience that he was eventually driven into a position inconsistent with Anglican doctrines. In 1845 he became a Catholic convert and was put in charge of helping many other Anglicans who had turned Catholic and who experienced various disabilities because of their conversion. The Oxford Movement not only encouraged some conversions to Catholicism, it also enriched the tradition of the Anglican Church and helped to advance spirituality among its clergy.

This movement had scarcely run its course when the nation learned in September, 1850, of the re-establishment of Catholic dioceses by order of Pope Pius IX. Wiseman became a cardinal and archbishop of Westminster, and twelve suffragan bishops were appointed to head the new dioceses. The papal decree led to anti-Catholic riots in many cities; Parliament was incensed over this "effrontery" and demanded counteraction that took form in the Ecclesiastical Titles Act (1851), which made it unlawful for Catholic clergymen to accept hierarchic titles based on British place names and prescribed penalties for anyone who implemented the pope's order. But the government did not enforce the statute, and twenty years later it was repealed.

Although the Russell ministry hoped to avoid implication in Continental affairs, it fell in 1852 as a result of Palmerston's cavalier conduct of foreign policy. His attitude during the revolutions of 1848 was almost entirely sympathetic to the revolutionaries. This pleased most of the British public immensely but annoyed Russell and angered Queen Victoria, who resented not being consulted by Palmerston and naturally sympathized with her fellow monarchs. A detailed discussion of Palmerston's reaction to each of the revolutions is beyond the scope of this brief account, but it might be mentioned by way of example that he did everything possible short of direct intervention to promote the unifying forces in Italy, and sent a British fleet to the Dardanelles to help the sultan override the threats of war mouthed by Austria and Russia in consequence of his having granted Louis Kossuth and other Magyars asylum in Turkey following the suppression of the Hungarian revolution. The only important exceptions to Palmerston's eager support of popular movements may be seen in the actions he took, in concert with France and Spain, to sustain Portuguese Queen Maria on her throne in 1846 for the sake of English commercial interests, and his defense of the rights of a Portuguese Jew named Don Pacifico, a British subject since his legal residence was at Gibraltar, whose home in Athens had been ransacked by a mob. When in 1850 Don Pacifico appealed to the Foreign Office for help in securing damages, which the Greek government had refused to give him, Palmerston ordered the fleet to seize Greek ships. This bold maneuver offended the Conservatives, perturbed the Russians, who regarded any British operation in the eastern Mediterranean with suspicion, and temporarily ruptured Anglo-French diplomatic relations. France had offered its good offices, Russell had accepted the offer, but Palmerston intervened before the French had acted. When Parliament demanded that he account for his actions, he did so in a speech that not only successfully defended his conduct in the Don Pacifico incident, but also traced the history of foreign policy under his administration since 1830. Whatever the Conservatives thought of his rationale, patriotic Englishmen rallied to his defense in response to his premise that the government should defend the rights of every British subject, wherever he lived. But despite Palmerston's popularity, Russell was embarrassed by the Opposition's harangue against the ministry's brinkmanship and responded scrupulously to the queen's injunction that no further dispatches should be sent without her prior knowledge. Palmerston, however, simply ignored Victoria's wishes: he informed the diplomatic corps in London that he approved Louis Napoleon's overthrow of the Second French Republic in December, 1851, and thereby provided Russell with the opportunity he had been seeking to ask for his foreign minister's resignation. Three months later Palmerston worked his wiles in Parliament to defeat Russell's militia bill and had his revenge in securing the fall of Russell's ministry.

Lord Stanley (Lord Derby after 1851) formed a Conservative government that lasted only a few months. Its principal ministers, save for Disraeli, Chancellor of the Exchequer and leader in the Commons, were unimpressive administrators without the comfort of a Conservative majority. Disraeli scarcely had time to compose and present the budget that continued free trade before the general election of 1852 again returned more Whigs (now often referred to as Liberals), radicals, and Peelites than Conservatives, and Derby had to surrender the seals of office. Lord Aberdeen, formerly foreign secretary under Peel, became prime minister of a coalition government. Aberdeen collected a star-studded cabinet, almost half of whose members were Peelites. The cabinet included Gladstone (Exchequer), Graham (Admiralty), Palmerston (Home Office), Russell (Foreign Office), and Newcastle (War and Colonies)—so much talent that men of Cardwell's consummate abilities had to accept secondary rank. This ministry lasted only about two years. The team generally worked well together, but prima donnas like Russell and Palmerston disliked sharing the stage and soon took to quarreling between themselves and with Aberdeen about foreign policy and a reform bill to lower franchise qualifications that Russell had proposed. Furthermore, Britain, which joined France and Turkey against Russia in the Crimean War in March, 1854, made so little headway in the fighting that the press began an incessant attack on Aberdeen and Newcastle, ultimately bringing down the government. Lord Palmerston's first ministry (1855–58) carried the war to a successful if not altogether satisfactory conclusion.

The Crimean War was caused primarily by the long-standing rivalry between Russia and the Ottoman Empire and the belief shared by Britain and France that the czar intended to dismember his weak neighbor. Russian control of the Balkans and Asia Minor would greatly endanger Britain's naval position in the Mediterranean. France had more proximate interests to protect. In 1740, the sultan had granted French Catholic religious orders the exclusive right to control the sanctuaries in the Holy Land associated with the life and passion of Jesus. Toward the end of the eighteenth century, however, largely because of religious indifference, the French had relinquished their places to Greek Orthodox priests. But, in 1852, under pressure from Emperor

Napoleon III, who glimpsed an opportunity to advance his prestige, the Porte transferred the holy places back to the French. Czar Nicholas I then intervened. He demanded not only that the Greeks should be reinstated, but that the Porte should formally acknowledge Russia's right to defend Greek Orthodox interests throughout the Ottoman Empire. On the Porte's refusal, Russian troops occupied the Balkan principalities of Moldavia and Wallachia to force Turkey's hand. Nicholas cared not a whit what the French thought of his action, for to him Napoleon was an upstart and a charlatan, but British attitudes were another matter. On the basis of conversations with Aberdeen during a visit to England in 1844, Nicholas had surmised that Britain would not challenge Russian intervention in the Balkans. But regardless of what Aberdeen may have said in 1844, in 1853 he was definitely opposed to such action, as was plainly stated during talks that year between Nicholas and the British ambassador at St. Petersburg. Nicholas suggested then that if Britain closed her eyes to Russian intervention, it might have Egypt, Crete, and Cyprus for itself. Such a course of events, Nicholas assured the ambassador, was preferable to the ultimate and inevitable parcelization of the Empire through nationalistic movements.

Britain might have avoided this unnecessary war had the Aberdeen cabinet and the British ambassador to the Porte followed a uniform policy. Aberdeen, hoping for peace, believed that the several powers of Europe might bring pressure on Turkey to concede Russia's demands on the holy places. But neither Palmerston nor Russell trusted Russia to withdraw from the principalities if Turkey did so. Moreover, Ambassador Stratford Canning in Constantinople, who had a grudge against Nicholas for having refused in 1833 to accept his appointment as ambassador to Russia, worked at cross-purposes with Aberdeen by counseling the sultan to reject Russian offers of settlement. Consequently, when Nicholas refused to evacuate the principalities, Turkey declared war in October, 1853.

Little fighting occurred during the early months of the war, although the destruction of the Turkish fleet at the cost of four thousand Turkish lives in the Battle of Sinope established Russian naval superiority in the Black Sea. But it was short-lived. An Anglo-French fleet broke the Straits Convention of 1841 by penetrating the Dardanelles several months before the Allies entered the war, following Russia's refusal to evacuate the principalities. Except for some naval action in the Baltic, the French and British fought most of the war in the Crimea, a promontory on the northern coast of the Black Sea where stood the mighty fortress of Sebastopol, impregnable from the sea and heavily gunned and garrisoned on the landward side. The Allies, consisting initially of 30,000 French troops, 20,000 British, and 7000 Turks, laid siege to the bastion while another Turkish force battled the Russians along the Danube, forcing them ultimately to withdraw from Moldavia and Wallachia. The siege of Sebastopol dragged on through the bitter winter of 1854–55 and until the following September. British newspaper correspondents, notably W. H. Russell of the *Times,* sent back the gory details of futile allied assaults and Russian counterattacks, long casualty lists, and criticism of administrative and military irresponsibility that strangely captivated the public, who had had no taste of war since 1815 and viewed it as a romantic adventure. Battles like Alma, Inkerman, and Balaclava (immortalized in Tennyson's "Charge of the Light Brigade") were characterized by allied assaults on Russian entrenchments, hand-to-hand fighting, and heavy losses on both sides. Thousands more died less conspicuously from dysentery, cholera, or infections from wounds. All suffered from the inadequacy of supply and transport as well as lack of coordination and efficiency among administrators at the War Office, Home Office, Treasury, and Office of the Master-General of Ordnance, causing division of authority and shortages of munitions, food, clothing, and medicine in the front lines. But for the ministrations of Florence Nightingale and her nursing assistants, which helped to inspire the establishment of the Red Cross, many more soldiers would have perished.

The Crimean War proved the deficiency of the British army, which Wellington, the Commander-in-Chief, despite his immense military prestige, had done next to nothing to remedy. Consequently tactics, weapons, and discipline had not changed since 1815, and the British were fortunate in being able to field even a halfway adequate army. Moreover *pax Britannica* had lulled the country into woeful apathy toward things military. Parliament echoed this attitude by doling out money sparingly, more to the navy than to the army, but to neither in terms of need. The enlisted men, whose uncomfortable uniforms had not changed since the Peninsular Campaign, got a shilling a day from which expenses were deducted, leaving them usually about threepence. They were considered expendable, were ill-treated, and had fewer civil rights, filthier living accommodations, less public respect, and a higher death rate from disease than the working class and the pardoned criminals from whose ranks they were drawn. Good men rarely joined the army, which willingly took anyone of bad character on the premise that rigid discipline and corporal punishments would make such men into soldiers. The officers, most of whom were of the gentry and aristocracy, left much to be desired. Promotions were impossible beyond the rank of captain without the proper family background and enough money to purchase a commission from a retiring officer anxious to continue a life of leisure. Army careers offered younger sons of the nobility enough pay, social prestige, and ease of life to attract as many scoundrels as honest men, few of whom bothered to learn much about tactics or were experienced in battle. Despite the lessons of the Crimean War, nothing was done to remedy army abuses until Cardwell's sweeping reforms in 1868–71.

Six months after public criticism and internal dissension brought down Aberdeen's ministry in favor of another headed by Palmerston, the fall of Sebastopol, the eagerness of Napoleon III to end the war, and the succession of Alexander II (1855) to the Russian throne led to peace negotiations that culminated in the Treaty of Paris (1856). In addition to the belligerents—Britain, France, Turkey, Russia, and Sardinia-Piedmont (whose seventeen thousand troops had won Camillo di Cavour a place at the conference table to promote Italian unification)—Austria and Prussia were represented as interested parties in European affairs. Foreign Minister George Villiers, earl of Clarendon, was Britain's principal negotiator. For all its sacrifice—twenty-five thousand lives and £50,000,000—Britain gained pitifully little unless one concedes Palmerston's point that the prevention of the partition of Turkey by Russia was worth a war. In addition to the mutual restoration of Russian and Turkish territory, the signatories agreed to respect Turkish territorial integrity and not to send their warships through the Straits into the Black Sea, which was to be neutralized. Moldavia and Wallachia were placed under the trusteeship of the Great Powers, thereby guaranteeing that the Danube would remain an international waterway. Finally, and probably most importantly, considering the trouble these issues had formerly caused, the signatories agreed to a declaration that abolished privateering, protected even enemy-owned goods (except contraband) on neutral ships in wartime as well as neutral goods on belligerent merchant ships, and held that only effective blockades were legally binding.

In addition to the prosecution of the Crimean War, Palmerston enlarged British commercial rights in China, pursued a strong policy against Russian encroachment in Persia and Afghanistan, and suppressed the Sepoy Mutiny in India, only to lose office in 1858. These foreign and imperial problems overshadow the domestic affairs of his ministry. Under the circumstances, it is hardly surprising that he is not remembered as a legislator. Yet the admission of Jews to Parliament (1858), the skillful way in which he handled the financial crisis of 1857 (caused principally by overspeculation in foreign investments) by allowing the Bank of England to ignore the paper money restrictions of the Bank Charter Act, and the passage of the India Act (1858), transferring control of Indian affairs entirely to the British government, were hardly inconsequential achievements.

In October, 1856, Chinese authorities at Canton boarded the *Arrow*, a ship owned by a Hong Kong merchant but having British registry, arrested some of the crew on a charge of piracy, and refused to release them until the British bombarded and occupied Canton. These events inaugurated another Anglo-Chinese war lasting until 1860, in which Britain and France cooperated in military expeditions from which the Americans and Russians also benefited commercially. After Palmerston had overridden Parliamentary censure of the British action at Canton by winning the election of 1857, he sent troops to Tientsin, a port city near Peking. They forced the Chinese to conclude the Treaties of Tientsin (1858) with the four foreign governments, opening the Yangtze River to foreign commerce, permitting alien merchants to travel in the hinterland, and allowing them to trade in eleven additional coastal cities. When the Chinese hesitated in ratifying these treaties, British and French troops destroyed the Manchu Summer Palace near Peking, inducing the Chinese to sign the Convention of Peking (1860), which increased the amount of the indemnity owing to British and French merchants, added Tientsin to the eleven cities opened to foreign commerce, admitted opium as a legal import subject to tariffs, and ceded part of the Kowloon Peninsula (opposite Hong Kong) to Britain. To protect these concessions, some British troops under the command of Captain Charles Gordon (later General Gordon of the Sudan) helped the government suppress the Taiping Rebellion (1850–64), a popular movement against autocratic rule and foreign encroachments.

The roots of the Anglo-Persian War (1856–57) lay in the attempt by the shah of Persia to annex the territory of Herat, situated within the borders of Afghanistan on the strategically important route into the Northwest Province of India, and Russia's encouragement of Persian aggression with an eye to controlling Afghanistan. The shah had attacked Herat in 1837 but was repulsed by its ruler with the help of British military advisers and the intimidating presence of a British squadron in the Persian Gulf. Despite an 1853 Anglo-Persian agreement to honor Herat's territorial integrity, the outbreak of the Crimean War afforded the shah the opportunity to invade Herat on the grounds that it was being threatened by the Amir of Afghanistan. Britain consequently took military action. While a British fleet patrolled the waters of the Persian Gulf, Sir James Outram's army of five thousand regulars and sepoys hurried from Bombay to win two decisive victories over the Persians. Persia agreed to terms in March, 1857, relinquishing any claim to Herat and Afghanistan, promising to consult Britain on any further problems in the area, and thereby in effect foreswearing cooperation with Russia against Afghanistan as a first step into India.

Shortly after the settlement of these Persian troubles a bloody mutiny broke out among more than 200,000 native troops in the British army that ended the historic hegemony of the East India Company in India. We last glanced at Indian events during the trial of the Bengalese governor, Warren Hastings, who had attempted to expand British authority over states neighboring the dominions along the eastern coast and to deal with difficult problems arising from the unsettled political conditions in Oudh, Mysore, and the Mahratta Confederacy. No governor could have been expected to cope easily with the dual authority in India created by Pitt's India Bill of 1784, which had vested political control of Indian affairs in a Board of Control and left trade and some administrative authority in the hands of Company directors at London, both agencies responsible to Parliament. But, despite Hastings' recall and disgrace, his successors, notably Lord Cornwallis (1786–93), Lord Wellesley, Wellington's elder brother (1798–1805), and Lord Dalhousie (1848–56), followed his example almost to the letter. The aggressiveness of native rulers forced them into wars that resulted in English annexation or outright control of most of the Indian states. The governors also emulated Hastings by making alliances with other states whose princes permitted the British to dominate their military and foreign affairs so long as they retained domestic jurisdiction. Any important decision by the governors without the approval of the Board of Control at London violated the intent of the India Act, but political crises, French intervention in native affairs during the Napoleonic War, and the invasion of British-held territory left no time for consultation or indecision. Furthermore, the governors effected social and economic reforms in both the Company and its territories that frequently aroused Indian resistance simply because the changes they proposed threatened to undermine centuries-old customs rooted in superstition or the Hindu and Moslem religions.

The administrations of Cornwallis and Wellesley are notable for economic reform and the beginning of a new series of Anglo-Indian wars that lasted until 1856 and brought virtually all of India into the British Empire. Cornwallis improved the Company's operations by raising the salaries of its officials in order to discourage dishonesty, and by tightening law enforcement through local courts in which English judges presided. He also settled the troublesome Bengalese land problem. All land belonged to the state and landholders paid rent (really taxes) on it. But a small group of tax-farmers had gained so much authority in their districts that Cornwallis decided to certify their actual ownership of the land, thereby distressing the tenant farmers who worked it. He also responded quickly to aggression by Sultan Tipu of Mysore, whose father Hastings had fought in the First Mysore War, an indecisive confrontation that had embittered Tipu. Consequently Cornwallis allied with Hyderabad and the Mahrattas in the Second Mysore War (1790–92), as a result of which Tipu ceded half of his state to the allies and paid an indemnity of £3,000,000. When Wellesley succeeded Cornwallis, Britain and its Allies in Europe were waging war with Napoleon, who had invaded Egypt and hoped to march through Persia to India. As expected, Tipu, again under French pressure, renewed his aggression, inducing Wellesley to make a treaty with Hyderabad that made it a British protectorate. Tipu was defeated and Wellesley annexed Mysore, the Carnatic, and Tanjore. A new threat arose shortly thereafter in the Mahratta Confederacy, where a civil war had followed the death of the chief minister and disagreement among the several chiefs over his successor. Seeing an opportunity to enhance British authority in central India, Wellesley sided with one of the chiefs—fortunately the victorious one—defeated his rivals, and in 1802 concluded a treaty that made most of the old Mogul Empire a British protectorate. Since this war had endangered Bengal's northwest frontier, Wellesley annexed most of Oudh's frontier provinces along the Ganges River from the cities of Cawnpore to Delhi. Oudh itself fell to the British in 1856.

Pitt recalled Wellesley in 1805 because he had exceeded his authority by meddling in the affairs of neighboring states that could not thereafter be effectively governed by the Company. Yet his successors carried on the same policy for the remainder of the nineteenth century. The governors, confronted by repeated political crises and wars among Indian states, succumbed to the irresistible temptation to take advantage of them with an eye to annexation. While ambition, greed, and imperialistic ideals undoubtedly played a role in Anglo-Indian foreign policy, it may also be true that it was the governors' response to circumstance that eventually made all of India a British possession. So it was that Lord Moira (1814–23) fought a war against the fearless Gurkha tribesmen in 1814–16 that quieted the unrest on the Nepal border and established British forts in the foothills of the Himalayas. He was also drawn into the last of the Mahratta wars (1817–18), which colored the vast territories between the Vindhya Mountains and the Indus River British red. Heretofore only Punjab and Sind in the northwest had escaped British encroachment. As the Russians had become active in Persian and Afghan affairs in the 1830s, and threatened to extend their influence in northwest India, General Charles Napier contrived a pretext to annex Sind, and the Sikhs of Punjab lost their independence in 1848 when they violated British territory.

Not every British governor spent his days poring over battle tactics. Lord William Bentinck (1828–35) and Lord Dalhousie made significant, albeit indigenously unpopular, reforms that contributed to the natives' disenchantment with British rule. Bentinck, a Whig idealist of the school of Grey and Durham, introduced the English language in Indian schools, encouraged Indians to enter the civil service, helped to inspire an air of gentility in garrison life by allowing officers to bring their wives to India, and suppressed the Thugs, murderous highwaymen and plunderers who had long terrorized the countryside. Bentinck also helped missionaries to spread Christianity, and, with the assistance of the famous historian Thomas Macaulay, revised the Indian penal code. Lord Dalhousie's administration was among the most memorable in Anglo-Indian history. In addition to annexing Oudh, he built railways and telegraph lines, laid roads and dug canals for irrigation, discouraged infanticide and human sacrifice in religious ceremonies, improved the postal system, and systematized the educational system under a department of public instruction.

Most Indians resented these changes, even though they were undoubtedly changes for the better, and discontent among Hindus and Moslems, who clung tenaciously to their ancient superstitions and religious tenets, exploded into bloody rebellion in May, 1857. Not long after Lord Canning had replaced Dalhousie as governor, the British began to manufacture cartridges, greased with the fat of pigs and cows, the caps of which had to be bitten off before they could be used in the new Enfield rifle. As cows were sacred to Hindus, and Moslems refused to touch pork, which they considered to be unclean, many sepoys would not use the cartridges and were court-martialed and imprisoned. This precipitated a mutiny at Meerut near Delhi that touched off rioting and murders throughout the Ganges Valley. The rebels seized Delhi and established a provisional government, followed by months of heavy fighting between some 200,000 sepoys and 40,000 British regulars, principally in the state of Oudh and at Cawnpore and Lucknow. The fate of the British forces might have been worse but for the loyalty of the monotheistic Sikhs of Punjab, who had no scruples about pigs and cows, and of the sepoys in the south, who were rushed north to help suppress the rebellion. Although it continued in places for two years, by late autumn, 1857, most of the mutineers and rioters had been suppressed by staunch British resistance and brutal punishment.

The mutiny sounded the death knell of the British East India Company. Parliament had long realized that the exercise of dual authority by Company and government was not an effective way of dealing with enormous administrative, social, and economic problems. Palmerston consequently introduced the India Bill of 1857, which the Conservatives had no trouble getting through Parliament the following year. The Act transferred the government of India to the crown, represented by a viceroy, and replaced the Board of Control by a secretary of state with cabinet rank. The minister was assisted by a fifteen-member advisory council, a majority of whom had to have resided in India for at least ten years.

The Crimean and Chinese wars as well as the Sepoy Mutiny and differences within the Liberal cabinet forced Palmerston to resign, but he resumed office ten months later when the second Conservative ministry of Derby and Disraeli could not overcome the lack of a Parliamentary majority. Until Palmerston's death in 1865, foreign affairs dominated his attention once again because of problems arising from unification movements in Germany and Italy and the American Civil War. Palmerston demonstrated anew his lifelong commitment to the preservation of the Continental balance of power by tacitly encouraging the Italians to cast off the yoke of Austrian oppression, and by reminding the major European powers not to meddle in affairs that the Italians should be allowed to resolve independently. The Prussians, on the other hand, posed a strong threat to central European stability, particularly after Otto von Bismarck became chancellor in 1862, because

German unification under Prussian control could be achieved only by forcing Austria out of Germanic affairs and by stealing from Napoleon III the ethnically divided and minerally rich states of Alsace and Lorraine. Although Palmerston did not live to see either the Austro-Prussian (1866) or Franco-Prussian (1870–71) wars, he did glimpse the inevitable outcome of Bismarck's shrewd diplomacy in the duchies of Schleswig and Holstein, situated at the base of the Danish peninsula. The complexity of the Schleswig-Holstein question may be gauged from one of Palmerston's oft-quoted remarks: only three persons in Europe understood it, the dead prince consort, an insane German professor, and he himself—and he had forgotten it. The duchies, partly Germanic and partly Danish, had long had political, legal, and economic ties with Denmark and Germany. Holstein, in addition to being personally united to the Danish crown, was a member of the Germanic Confederation established in 1815. When the duchies rose in rebellion in 1848 under Prince Frederick of Augustenburg, the great powers intervened. The result of this intervention was the Treaty of London (1852) by which Frederick renounced his claim to the duchies in return for monetary compensation, and which recognized the eventual succession of Prince Christian of Glücksburg to the throne of Denmark and the duchies so long as he promised not to alter the status of the duchies. When Christian IX succeeded to the throne in 1863, he announced his intention to annex Schleswig. Despite Palmerston's and Russell's efforts to settle the issue by diplomatic negotiations, Prussia and Austria jointly went to war against Denmark in 1864. If the cabinet did not realize that much larger stakes were involved—Bismarck's plan to provoke another and more significant confrontation with Austria—it undoubtedly sensed that the days of Palmerstonian diplomacy were over.

The Civil War in the United States posed graver problems for Britain. The issues that drove the Southern Confederacy from the federal Union in 1861 interested the English almost as much as it did Americans. But most Englishmen underestimated the complexities present in American society on the eve of the war. It was not simply a matter of the aristocratic South versus the industrial North, rich landowners versus poor factory workers, a congressional power block versus a conscious minority, or even slavery versus freedom. Both the British working classes and aristocracy tended, however, to view the struggle in black and white terms, and to identify themselves with one or the other of the belligerents, the aristocrats and some industrialists sympathizing with their counterparts in the Southern States while the urban workers and most men of the middle class equated their situation with that of the workers and entrepreneurs in the North.

The immediate issue confronting the cabinet was the practical wisdom and propriety of recognizing the Confederacy at the risk of alienating the Union, which consistently refused to admit the South's belligerency, much less its separate national existence. The cabinet decided to follow a policy of neutrality. It issued a proclamation on May 14, 1861, applicable throughout the Empire, cautioning British subjects to lend no martial aid to either belligerent, and in doing so tacitly recognized the Confederacy's existence. Palmerston, Gladstone, and others made no secret of their sympathy for the South and seriously considered formal recognition until the Battle of Antietam (September, 1862), an indecisive Union victory that emboldened Lincoln to issue the Emancipation Proclamation, which freed only those slaves behind Confederate lines. Afterward the cabinet and the greater part of the country held to a position of legal neutrality but leaned heavily in favor of the Union.

The Civil War also deeply affected sections of the British economy dependent on American cotton. Too much has been made, however, of King Cotton diplomacy by Confederate agents in London. The Union blockade of Confederate ports severely cut back cotton imports and threw thousands of mill hands out of work in Lancashire and Clydeside, but cotton stores in Britain were not depleted by the autumn of 1862 when the government's sympathy turned toward the Union. As a matter of fact, wheat imports from the American North and West were as important to the British economy as cotton. It was therefore not cotton shortages that prevented British recognition of the Confederacy so much as it was Palmerston's uncertainty until 1863 as to which side might win, and his reluctance to back a loser.

Ugly incidents at sea and along the Canadian border raised tempers on both sides of the Atlantic. The first occurred in 1861, when an American warship stopped the British packet *Trent* and removed two Confederate emissaries bound for England. This violation of neutral rights on the high seas outraged the cabinet and very nearly caused war until Lincoln's conciliatory letter soothed British tempers. A series of crises developed as the result of the construction by Scottish shipbuilders of several unfitted and unarmed privateers for the Confederacy. When finished, ships like the *Alabama, Florida,* and *Shenandoah* plundered Union vessels. At war's end, the American government demanded damages of the British, who grudgingly agreed, in 1871, to pay an indemnity of $15,500,000. A third controversy involved the running of the Union blockade by British privateers, who violated the neutrality proclamation and risked international war for the sake of personal profit. Finally, Canada's proximity inevitably caused incidents along the border, provoking American accusations of Canadian treachery and encouraging loose talk in the American press and Congress in favor of annexing Canada. Moreover, while the Confederacy complained to the Canadian authorities about the "underground railway" that secretly transported thousands of slaves through the North across the border, the Union accused Canadians of harboring and assisting Confederate agents as well as deserters from the Union army. The threat of American aggression against Canada, particularly in the immediate postwar period when the Irish Fenian Brotherhood was active, forced Britain to enlarge greatly its military establishment along the border at a time when the British public and Parliament were complaining about the enormous cost of keeping troops in colonies that were perfectly capable of defending themselves. The last British redcoat left Canada in 1871.

The year of Palmerston's death, 1865, marks the end of a fascinating era of domestic reform and imperial growth that had begun with the Tory reforms of the 1820s. But a new era was already visible on the horizon. The age of aristocracy, of privilege, and of Whigs, Tories, and Peelites was in its death throes; the age of Gladstone, Disraeli, and Parnell, of rapid industrialization and imperialism, and of the common man was at hand.

14

Aspects of Later Victorian Life and Thought

The Great Exhibition of 1851 opened by Victoria and Albert in the barrel-vaulted, iron and glass Crystal Palace in Hyde Park, London, drew nearly six million visitors, who marveled at the wonders of industry, art, and nature gathered there from all over the world. More than half the exhibits at this first truly world's fair were British, demonstrating the material prosperity, the industrial might, and the inventive genius of mid-century Victorians. The Exhibition might well have suggested to thoughtful onlookers the rapid ascendancy of the industrial and commercial bourgeoisie and the fading grandeur of the great aristocratic families, whose long day of power and privilege was slipping inconspicuously into twilight. The aristocrats had dominated the eighteenth century and were still rich and puissant in the nineteenth, but they were no longer supreme in Parliament, uppermost in local government, or the only social paragons of their communities. To a substantial degree, they had been replaced in positions of power by the wealthy and energetic entrepreneurs, whose self-satisfaction, born of an understandable pride in their high achievements during the previous hundred years, was typical of the attitudes of middle-class Victorians. Like them, most Englishmen believed in the ultimate perfectibility of mankind through the application of science and technology, political reform, economic growth, and high moral standards. If some Victorians had grown conservative and complacent toward social injustice because of wealth and comforts, others still preached the virtues of hard work, devotion to duty, religious faith, and social responsibility. The self-made man was greatly admired by Victorian society: in fact, Samuel Smiles' *Self-Help* (1859), demonstrating how dozens of prominent men had achieved wealth and fame by making the most of their talents, was one of the most popular books of the day.

But a humanistic and humanitarian philosophy also permeated Victorian society in the half-century preceding the First World War and colored attitudes toward politics, imperial growth, and social welfare. Thus the exortations of reformers like Bentham and Mill, apostles of social welfare and government action to extirpate misery and ignorance earlier in the century, finally bore fruit. The prospect of ameliorating social problems and extending political rights to the masses had become a real one. The country had made remarkable progress in those areas since the Napoleonic era. The basic power structure in the national and local governmental systems had been altered by the great Reform Act and the Municipal Corporations Act. The restrictive and discriminatory Navigation Acts and Corn Laws had been swept away. Factory and public health legislation had improved conditions among the working classes. Some of the worst evils in the land, including the Draconian criminal code, slavery, the exploitation of women and children by industry, and legislative discrimination against the evangelicals and Catholics had been remedied by 1865. The later Victorians continued to reform the government and society, particularly through electoral reform and public welfare measures, and brought about in Britain by the eve of World War I an essentially democratic political system, an enlightened program of social welfare, and a viable economic system that was capable of competing with the industrial states of Europe and America, supporting the financial burden of an expanding empire, and sustaining continued commercial growth. In some cases these accomplishments were realized only after struggle with the monied classes, who were not always anxious to share their affluence with less fortunate countrymen and were fearful of extending political power to the workingman.

Foremost among the politicians who shaped Britain's destiny in these years were Benjamin Disraeli, William Gladstone, and David Lloyd George. The several ministries of later Victorian England faced serious problems, not the least of which were the economic slump of the great depression (1873–86), the Boer War, the international crises that led to World War I, and a chronic quarrel with Ireland over home rule.

Population and commerce expanded at an accelerated pace during the later nineteenth century. The population of the United Kingdom (excluding Ireland) increased between 1871 and 1911 from 26,000,000 to 41,000,000 despite the widespread use of new contraceptive methods, smaller middle-class families, and emigration that annually averaged 90,000 in the seventies and 200,000 in the eighties because of the economic depression. Although life expectancy remained fairly low (forty-five or fifty years), the birth rate was steady at about 35 per 1000 because the working classes continued to have large families. The death rate fell to about 22 per 1000 by 1850, and to about 17 per 1000 in 1900 as a result of better working conditions, more and better food, and higher standards of health and sanitation. In the forty years after 1870 iron production rose from seven to ten million tons; coal output from 118,000,000 to 264,000,000 tons; and merchant shipping from 6,000,000 to 11,000,000 tons. The cotton industry, the most important in the country during this period, grew by about 25 per cent in 1890–1910 after recovering from the serious setback during the American Civil War and falling prices in the depression. The new chemical, petroleum, electrical, and engineering industries helped to lay the basis for even greater industrial expansion during World War I. Over-all, exports mounted from £250,000,000 in 1870 to £430,000,000 in 1910, while imports, mostly raw materials and foodstuffs, swelled in the same period from £300,000,000 to £680,000,000.

The extension and improvement of transportation facilities contributed significantly to economic growth. The railways had attracted nearly £250,000,000 in invested capital by 1850, when there were about 6500 miles of track. By 1870, 15,000 miles of track had been laid, and nearly 24,000 by 1910. Railway expansion not only facilitated the movement of goods at a fraction of the former cost, it also lessened the provincialism and immobility of people who were generally unaccustomed to traveling more than a few miles from home. As railway travel was cheap (a penny a mile), speedy (sixty miles per hour in 1900), and convenient, even poorer working-class families could take advantage of weekend excursions into the countryside and to the seashore. Shipping grew apace. Most of the mercantile fleet before 1860 was composed of wooden sailing ships; afterward an increasing number of ships were built of iron or steel and were fitted with steam or turbine engines and screw propellers. The changing character of the mercantile fleet could be seen when the steamship *Great Eastern* was built during the heyday of the graceful clipper ships. Completed in 1858, she was 680 feet from bow to stern, had steam engines and paddle wheels, could accommodate 4400 passengers and crew, and carried enough coal for the round trip between London and Bombay via the Cape of Good

Hope (the Suez Canal opened in 1869). The total tonnage of the merchant fleet increased from 3,600,000 in 1850 to 11,000,000 in 1910. In the same period the total tonnage of ironclads grew from 168,000 to 10,200,000. Sixty per cent of the world's steamships in 1900 were British-owned.

Meanwhile the telegraph had greatly speeded communications. Telegraphy was perfected by Samuel Morse, but it had been conceived by a Scotsman as early as 1753 and advanced in the 1830s by the mechanical inventions of Charles Wheatstone and W. F. Cooke. The first telegraph line in England (between London and Slough) had been opened in 1844, and the length and breadth of the country was subsequently crisscrossed by lines and poles. John Brett laid a telegraph cable in 1851 across the Channel to the Continent, and in 1866 the American Cyrus Field linked Britain and North America. By 1870, the telegraph spanned in an instant the enormous distances between England, the Middle East, India, and remote eastern Siberia. Thanks to Marconi, wireless telegraphy (radio) was employed ship-to-shore in 1899, and two years later radio signals were beamed across the Atlantic for the first time.

Towns grew along with industry and communications. Industrial centers spawned giant metropolitan districts, swallowing up neighboring communities. Such was the case in Lancashire, for example, where Manchester engulfed Stockport, Oldham, Bolton, and Salford; in the West Riding of Yorkshire, where Huddersfield, Halifax, and Wakefield merged with Bradley and Leeds; along the Tyne and Clyde rivers where houses and factories crowded the banks for miles; and throughout metropolitan London, which grew from a population of 958,000 in 1801 to 2,350,000 in 1851, and to 4,500,000 by 1911. This rapid urban growth occurred without much attention being given to town planning or adequate public utilities. Many communities at mid-century still had unpaved and improperly graded roads, poor street lighting, inadequate sewage systems, and impure water. Prior to the Municipal Corporations Act of 1835, lack of money and technical skills as well as the reluctance of the wealthier citizens, who controlled municipal government, to improve dilapidated neighborhoods where factory workers lived, little was done to promote urban development. Thereafter the town councils could do considerably more with the money they gained from special tax levies. Housing became a particularly vexing problem in growing industrial communities where low-rent dwellings were in great demand but short supply. It was, therefore, difficult to clear away slums without dispossessing thousands of families who could not afford to move. Nevertheless decayed housing was demolished and new structures were built in many cities by authority of the Artisans' Dwellings Acts of 1868 and 1875. In the process of developing new neighborhoods, councils laid out parks and playgrounds that working-class families could enjoy more often because of an improved standard of living and more leisure resulting from shorter working hours. The Public Health Acts of 1848 and 1866 enabled councils to employ medical officers, provide genuine hospitals instead of the pesthouses in which the victims of contagious diseases had formerly been confined, and make improvements in sewage, water, and lighting systems. Improvements such as these were more common in larger metropolitan centers like Liverpool, Birmingham, and London than they were in smaller towns, many of which were still characterized at the beginning of the twentieth century by narrow streets, crowded conditions, and row upon row of identical red brick duplexes. Even today one need only ride the train through the Midlands or visit the older sections of Glasgow or Newcastle to appreciate how little urban conditions have changed since 1900.

Urban working-class families shared to some degree the prosperity enjoyed by the upper classes during most of the later nineteenth and early twentieth centuries. There were no significant fluctuations in either prices or wages in the forty years after the inflationary Napoleonic period. But the two decades after 1850 were a time of unexampled economic growth during which real wages rose about 10 per cent more than prices, which also remained fairly high. These good times resulted from rapid industrial expansion, a significant growth in the volume of exports, the discovery of gold in California and Australia, which inflated the economy, and the heavy foreign demand for British products during the Crimean, Austro-Prussian, and Franco-Prussian wars. Wages remained high until 1877 and then dropped slightly for about ten years, but not nearly as much as did prices. Over-all, wages rose in the later nineteenth century by nearly 50 per cent. According to one authority, who used a base of 100 in 1850, the index of wages advanced to 156 by 1874 and fell to only 148 by 1886. The great depression (1873–86), caused primarily by industrial overproduction, a succession of poor harvests, and increased foreign competition in foodstuffs, depressed food prices, which in turn lowered prices for most other commodities.

Agricultural interests did not fare nearly so well in later Victorian

England. Although there had been several market depressions before 1846, each of which temporarily lowered prices, agricultural productivity had increased because of the demands of a rising population and the protection that the Corn Laws gave against foreign foodstuffs. The gloomy predictions of landowners that repeal of the Corn Laws would ruin agriculture were not borne out for a quarter of a century. Farm prices rose between 1846 and 1854 and then leveled off for nearly twenty years, during which time agriculture grew rapidly. The fifties and sixties were years of heavy capital investment in farming, some diversification into dairy farming and stock breeding, and greater use of machinery and chemical fertilizers. Scientific methods of farming together with the installation of drainage systems led to an increase in the acreage under cultivation, but the improvements also increased production costs. Farming was still a paramount industry at mid-century. Until 1870, the land provided employment for more workers than did any other industry. A government survey in 1874 showed that half the land in England was owned by less than 7500 people, but the other half was held by small farmers, each having less than three hundred acres of improved land. Of this latter group, nearly 100,000 worked farms under fifty acres. Consequently any depression affecting farm prices was bound to have serious repercussions on the rest of the economy. As far as farmers were concerned, the principal causes of the depression in the seventies and eighties were their inability to recover from poor harvests from 1873 to 1882, and the flooding of the British market by cheap foreign wheat and meat. The rapid extension of the railroad into the American West after the Civil War encouraged American farmers to plant additional millions of acres in wheat that could be moved easily and cheaply from the prairie lands to the Atlantic seaboard. Larger and faster freighters likewise cut the cost of transportation between American and English ports by nearly 80 per cent in the thirty years after 1860. The construction of refrigerator ships in 1880 enabled Australian and South American packers to ship beef and mutton to the British market. Since land prices and wages in the New World were lower than in England, where capital investment and higher wages forced up production costs, the English farmer could not undersell foreign food imports. For these reasons agricultural prices tumbled steadily and the acreage given over to grain crops declined by nearly 50 per cent in the last quarter of the century. But the depression was not altogether harmful for agriculture because it forced farmers to diversify (relying more on poultry farming, fruit, fresh meat, hops, and potatoes than on grain), to employ more scientific methods, and to guard against overproduction. The government encouraged the growth of truck farming, which in turn increased the number of smaller farms by the turn of the century. These remedies enabled English agriculture to survive foreign competition, but conditions about 1900 were still nowhere nearly as prosperous as they had been in the early seventies. Farmers did not really begin to recover the losses sustained during the many years of hard times until World War I, when a serious cutback in imports encouraged the growth of domestic production. By that time, however, farm income accounted for only about 7 per cent of the gross national income.

The application of scientific discoveries to many practical uses in industry and agriculture profoundly improved the way of life, the comforts and conveniences, and the physical well-being of Victorians. If the evolutionary hypotheses of Sir Charles Lyell, Herbert Spencer, and Charles Darwin pricked their moral sensitivity and appeared to be challenging the bases of Christianity, the greater part of society welcomed scientific advances that provided tangible benefits like electricity, aniline dyes, synthetic products, the internal combustion and diesel engines, anesthesia, X rays, and protection against septic infections. Scientists also explored the mysteries of the universe and the human body, and made important discoveries in atomic physics, thermodynamics, bacteriology, geology, botany, and biology. Along with continued scholarly progress in established fields like chemistry, the new disciplines of archaeology, anthropology, psychology, and sociology were being developed. Scientific research was encouraged by the establishment of modern laboratory facilities by the Royal Philosophical Institution (founded in 1799), which sought to apply scientific advances to mechanical devices useful in agriculture and industry, the University of London, the British Association for the Advancement of Science (1831), and the Royal College of Mines (1851).

It would be tedious if not boldly venturesome to attempt to summarize the manifold scientific achievements in the nineteenth century on even a national basis. We must therefore be content to mention only a few of the more important British scientists in three or four fields and to suggest what practical and philosophical effects their work had upon society. The discoveries of chemists and physicists may be taken as examples of the application of pure scientific research to practical uses. The development of lighting, for instance, is a fascinating story. Private householders in the seventeenth and eighteenth centuries had hung out lanterns on moonless nights. In 1792, William Murdock extracted illuminating gas from raw coal (as well as coal tar from which perfumes, explosives, fertilizers, and dyes were manufactured). As a result of his work, gas companies that supplied coal gas for street- and house-lighting were established in the 1810s and 1820s in London, Liverpool, Edinburgh, and other large cities. The Cornishman Sir Humphry Davy, in addition to studying the effects of gases like nitrous oxide and chlorine, invented the safety lamp for miners (1815) and the arc light (1841). Meanwhile the investigations of Europeans such as Volta, Galvani, Ampère, and Ohm laid the basis for the electrical industry. The principal English scientist in this field was Michael Faraday, who in 1830 and 1831, respectively, invented electroplating and the first electric dynamo, which led to the development of the electric motor, electric lighting, and the electric telegraph. James Clerk Maxwell further developed Faraday's work in electromagnetism by proving the similarity between oscillating electric discharges and light waves. Electricity as a source of illumination became practical in the 1870s through the invention of the incandescent filament bulb (1876) by the Scottish physicist Joseph Swan, and its improvement by Thomas Edison.

Maxwell and J. P. Joule contributed to the theory of the conservation of energy and its conversion into heat. In 1890, Joseph Thomson proposed the electron theory. The schoolmaster John Dalton made basic discoveries in atomic theory early in the nineteenth century. This not only proved the molecular and atomic composition of matter, but also enabled scientists to analyze chemical compounds and to write formulas of chemical substances. A standardized table of atomic weights was adopted in 1860 at the International Chemical Congress at Karlsruhe. British chemists like Charles Macintosh and Thomas Hancock were likewise involved in the production of rubber for commercial uses and of agricultural fertilizers, wherein Sir John Lawes was most important. While Europeans and Americans in the 1840s were devising effective methods of inducing complete anesthesia with ether, chloroform, and nitrous oxide, Joseph Lister had great success in the 1860s in preventing septic infections through the use of a solution of carbolic acid.

These discoveries in chemistry, physics, and medicine notwithstanding, the paramount scientific achievement of the century was probably the development of the hypothesis of human, animal, and plant evolution by natural causes. Lyell, Darwin, Spencer, T. H. Huxley, and Alfred Wallace each worked in this important area. The concept of evolution had not originated with them, of course, for Greek philosophers had suggested it broadly centuries earlier, and more recently so too had the eighteenth-century *philosophes.* The geologist James Hutton, author of *Theory of the Earth* (1795), had argued that the configuration of the earth's crust had been molded over many millenniums through natural forces. Lyell then proposed in his *Principles of Geology* (1830–33) that volcanoes, earthquakes, the flow of rivers, and the passage of time rather than divine creation explained the earth's physical characteristics. Thirty years later, he indicated in *The Geological Evidences of the Antiquity of Man,* which was based on an examination of artifacts deposited in the earth's substrata, that man had evolved over a very long period. Archaeologists later uncovered human fossils and artifacts that apparently corroborated Lyell's thesis and forced them to push back the origin of mankind a million years. Darwin, Huxley, and Spencer were concerned with the evolution of plant and animal life, and later of man himself. The essential facts of Darwin's life are commonly known: his medical and theological studies at Edinburgh and Cambridge universities; his employment as botanist aboard the *Beagle* that took him to South America and the South Seas; and his observations of various but apparently related species of animal and plant life in different regions of the world. He set down his evolutionary hypothesis on the *Origin of Species* in 1842, but did not publish it until 1859, a few months after he had read the manuscript of the unheralded naturalist Wallace, whose ideas closely paralleled his own. In 1871, Darwin extended evolution to include man.

The publications of these two scientists (Wallace's *Contributions to the Theory of Natural Selection* appeared in 1870) and those of their popularizers, principally Spencer and Huxley, provided a scientific basis for the theory of evolution, which had been under consideration for many years. Put in the simplest terms, Darwin held that all forms of animal and plant life have developed from a remote but common source and have evolved into many different species. Certain species died out while others survived, not because of inherent intelligence or design, but through certain physical characteristics which, being different from the norm, gave them an advantage over their enemies in the struggle for existence. To quote Darwin, "variations, however slight and from whatever cause proceeding, if they be in any degree profitable to the individuals of a species, in their infinitely complex relations to other organic beings and to their physical conditions of life, will tend to the preservation of such individuals, and will generally be inherited by the offspring. The offspring, also, will thus have a better chance of surviving. . . . I have called this principle . . . Natural Selection." Over many generations covering thousands of years, these advantages became so pronounced that entirely new species developed, accounting for the many kinds of animals and plants now extant.

Darwin's popularizers took key phrases such as "struggle for existence" and "natural selection" and applied them broadly and somewhat unscientifically to situations in human society, especially in fields such as ethics, sociology, psychology, and international relations. In his ten-volume *Synthetic Philosophy* (1860–96), Spencer applied the principle of "the survival of the fittest," a phrase that he coined, to an evolutionary process affecting all matter, living and inorganic, and he maintained that some unknowable power guided it. At best, this was a statement of agnosticism, for Spencer never admitted the existence of God. (Neither, for that matter, had Darwin, for he, like other empirical scientists, had long since disassociated his discipline from the rationale of medieval Scholasticism whereby science was made to serve the interests of theology.) Huxley went further and attempted to discredit belief in God and in Christian morality on the basis of the new evolutionary hypothesis. In works such as *Man's Place in Nature* (1863), he argued that man had evolved from a primitive, baser form of life, that the Bible was unhistorical, and that God did not exist. Christianity was therefore a hoax that had been contrived from pagan and Judaic elements, as was also Christian morality, sin, and the relationship of man's free will to either salvation or damnation after death. Huxley's attack on the fundamental teachings of Christianity found considerable support, primarily among the professional and mercantile bourgeoisie that had gradually been falling away from belief in dogmatic religion.

The pragmatic attitudes to which "social Darwinism" led (including the imperialist justification of the exploitation of peoples and natural resources in Africa and Asia on the grounds that it was the duty of civilized society to assume the burden, to borrow Kipling's phrase, of advancing the interests of backward and heathen brethren), although not entirely based on the evolutionary hypothesis, profoundly affected moral standards. Religion still colored Victorian life and manners, and the Anglican and evangelical churches had large memberships, but spiritual fervor gradually waned in the later nineteenth century. It was not that the Victorians were irreligious or complacent in spiritual matters, for practically the opposite was true. Religious controversy among fundamentalists, freethinkers, and latitudinarians had not been so fervent since the seventeenth century. Churches were filled to over-flowing. Many believed in the literal truth of the Bible and read it avidly. Fundamentalist Protestants, High-Church Anglicans, and Ro-man Catholics denounced Spencer's and Huxley's views and rejected altogether the materialistic evolutionary hypothesis. Evolution had a greater impact on fundamentalists, whose religious beliefs relied more heavily, if not exclusively, on a literal interpretation of the Bible, than on the Catholics, who in addition to the Scriptures based their doctrines on canon law, revelation, and the decrees of the ecumenical councils. Materialistic evolution as well as other allegedly pernicious doctrines of the new social and political order were condemned by Pope Pius IX in the *Syllabus of Errors* (1864). Yet for many of the industrial and mercantile bourgeoisie, as well as for some of the literary giants of the century, formal adherence to the principles of Christian morality had become more of an affectation or an outward show of social acceptability than of religious conviction. Respectability, a word that covered a multitude of sins in Victorian England, required that the family attend church on Sundays, and that for the rest of the day noth-ing more strenuous than a pleasant stroll through the park or the diges-tion of a heavy meal should be attempted lest one's neighbors should think one untoward and immoral. In one sense, respectability meant that a person should demonstrate his Christian beliefs through proper social conduct, and in another sense, that the good Christian prospered be-cause he was circumspect, law-abiding, and industrious. Otherwise for many Victorians religiosity and respectability had no relationship. If Sabbatarian restraints dictated one's activities on Sunday, the working week need not be wasted in hearing lengthy sermons or helping less fortunate neighbors. Secularism also scarred the face of Victorian mo-rality. The growing emphasis on material comfort and the divorce law of 1857 that took divorce out of the ecclesiastical courts and made it the subject of a civil suit, for instance, as well as the abolition of Church rates in 1868 and the disestablishment of the state Church in Ireland and Wales, in 1869 and 1914 respectively, indicates not only the weak-ening of the Established Church but also the increasing belief that it had no right to dictate personal conduct. The broad range of secular ac-tivities and interests among all classes of Victorians likewise weaned churchgoers away from church functions. Cheap newspapers, maga-zines, and novels, sports like cricket and soccer, and weekend trips into the country by railroad and bicycle, among other things, left less time to attend services or to read the Bible.

Secular interests not only competed with religion, they made salvation in the hereafter seem less appealing than the pleasant realities of this world. The Churches were therefore forced to put on new dress to hold their members and to recruit new ones. The public image of the Established Church, for example, had undergone substantial change, not simply because evangelicalism, the Oxford Movement, and the challenge of science and materialism helped to alter the views of its disciples, but also because the needs of the age had changed. Greater attention had to be paid to the urban lower classes, many of whom had rejected eighteenth-century clerical conservatism and complacency toward great social questions. Anglicans, Methodists, Catholics, and many other denominations joined in the race to win followers from the growing ranks of workers by seeking them out in their own neighborhoods.

The Anglican Communion comprised three broad groups. The High Church or Anglo-Catholic party, following the traditionalist view, stressed the sacramental system, dogma, historic ties with the pre-Reformation Christian Church, and the liturgy. The Broad Church or Latitudinarian party minimized formal worship and doctrinal niceties and approached religion from a rationalist and humanitarian viewpoint that some of its critics regarded as Christian socialism. Its adherents, among whom were some of the literary giants of the century—Frederick Maurice, Charles Kingsley, and Benjamin Jowett—eschewed the supernatural elements of Christianity and sought to reconcile its basic tenets with the new scientific discoveries of Lyell and Darwin. The evangelicals who remained within the national Church instead of joining one of the Protestant fundamentalist sects comprised the Low Church party. They adhered to a literal interpretation of the Bible in all matters of faith and morals, kept dogma and ritual to a minimum consistent with the Thirty-nine Articles and the ecclesiastical canons, diligently practiced Sabbatarianism, and shut their minds to the radical ideas of freethinkers.

Outside the Established Church were the evangelical Protestants—Methodists, Presbyterians, Congregationalists, Baptists, Quakers, and others—who stressed in varying degrees the importance of personal experience of guilt for sin and of man's reconciliation to God through faith and repentance. They put trust in the authority of the Scriptures as against canons, decrees, or reason, and upheld the virtues of churchgoing, preaching, and private family prayer. The Catholics, still a small proportion of the population, enjoyed a revival because of the conver-

sions resulting from the Oxford Movement, but they were essentially a
tightly knit and rather exclusive society in most larger towns, where
they built new chapels and supported their own schools at all levels.
Although a few Catholics had distinguished diplomatic, legal, or medical careers, they generally played a minor role in government and the
learned professions. Notwithstanding the Catholic Emancipation Act
(1829) and the re-establishment of Catholic dioceses (1850) which
did away with the last legal restraints imposed upon Catholics in earlier
times, they were not entirely free from discrimination practiced by some
of their Protestant neighbors. The Roman Church benefited from the
leadership of the Jesuits as well as three successive archbishops of Westminster—Henry Manning, Herbert Vaughan, and Francis Bourne—
who dominated English Catholic affairs from the mid-nineteenth century to 1935, founded numerous parishes, and erected the still-
unfinished Westminster Cathedral in central London.

In Scotland a branch of the Presbyterian Church had broken away
in 1843 as a result of a long-standing dispute over the appointment of
ministers to parishes. The general practice within the Scottish Church
had been to recognize the right of the patron who held the endowment
to a church to nominate an incumbent when the position fell vacant.
Led by the theologian Thomas Chalmers, nearly five hundred ministers, about a third of the Presbyterian clergy, seceded from the parent
Church over the right of an individual congregation to choose its own
minister, and formed the Free Kirk of Scotland. In 1900, this Church
united with another dissenter sect to establish the United Free Church.

This democratization of Presbyterian Church government in Scotland was matched by a similar movement within Methodism in England, where, in 1877, Jabez Bunting succeeded in reconstituting the
Wesleyan Conference by including an equal number of clergymen
and laymen. The Salvation Army, founded in 1865 at London by William Booth, its first general, sent ministers and social workers into the
slums of the larger cities to open hostelries to combat drunkenness,
immorality, depravity, and despair with Christian charity, soup kitchens,
and ample doses of private counsel and public preaching. Missionaries
representing many denominations went also into the African colonies
to proselytize and to Europeanize the heathen and often culturally
backward natives, although in doing so, they often inadvertently
paved the way for economic exploitation and political domination by
less reverential fellow countrymen.

15

Liberalism and Imperialism, 1865–1914

From 1865 to the coming of World War I, liberalism took on two forms: political and economic. By the former was meant constitutional government, an extension of the franchise, and guarantees of civil, religious, and political liberty for the individual. Economic liberalism stressed individual freedom also—freedom of trade, freedom from government interference or regulation, freedom of competition, and the protection of private property rights. Until the end of the nineteenth century these were the cardinal principles of the Liberal party, the party of manufacturers, bankers, merchants, professional men, and many artisans. By the early years of the twentieth century many Liberals had become convinced that it was necessary for the country to return to the mercantilism of the seventeenth century. The Liberal party, therefore, abandoned its former insistence on laissez faire in the economic field, and began to advocate the regulation of business and industry, and to sponsor social reforms with an eye to the improvement of the lot of the common man. Hence it was the Liberal party that secured the enactment of old-age pensions, unemployment insurance, educational reforms, and the limitation of the hours of labor.

The Conservative party, on the other hand, was the champion of all that was traditional in English life: the crown, peerage, Established Church, and the Empire. While not opposed to "progress," it had generally stood for the *status quo* and contented itself with tidying up laws already on the statute books. When in office, its chief interest lay in imperial and foreign affairs, while the Liberal party was chiefly concerned with domestic affairs. By the end of the century, a strong capitalist element had joined the Conservative ranks and captured control of the party. It then became the party of the landed aristocracy *and* of capital, and soon abandoned its time-honored adherence to the *status quo*. Its members urged the enactment of legislation to improve the social and economic conditions of the workingmen, but at the same time refrained from using the "radical" methods of the Liberal party. In short, they became the champions of what has been called Tory Democracy.

By the 1880s industrial Britain needed more supplies of raw material to feed its hungry mills and factories, more foodstuffs for a rapidly increasing population, and wider markets for its surpluses of capital and manufactured goods than were provided by the home and European markets. Along with other European nations, none of which wished to become a "dumping ground" for another's goods, Britain joined in the scramble for colonial possessions in the backward areas of the world —particularly in Asia and Africa, teeming with tropical and subtropical products now desired by the Western world. In this manner, Britain, which had since 1815 been anti-imperialistic, now joined in the "New Imperialism."

The Liberal party did not approve this new departure in national policy and, down to 1914, usually opposed participating in the race for colonies. On the other hand, the Conservatives were strong advocates of empire building and successfully pushed forward the acquisition of many new colonies and spheres of influence in the years prior to World War I.

The developments and ideas described in the previous chapter should convey something of the iconoclasm of Victorians who challenged the bases of many traditional attitudes and institutions. The political developments from the death of Palmerston to 1914 were no less remarkable inasmuch as they culminated in the creation of a democratic society that the bulk of the British people only a few decades earlier had considered to be impossible. Palmerston, no friend of political reform, had dominated governmental affairs to such an extent that numerous attempts since the Reform Act of 1832 to broaden the franchise by including the intelligent working classes had repeatedly gone down to defeat in Parliament. The lack of political reform was also partly attributable to the *ennui* of the working classes themselves, who made no serious effort to support it on an organized basis following the failure of the last Chartist agitation in 1848. Liberal-minded leaders of both parties nevertheless believed, whether for altruistic or practical political reasons, that the enfranchisement of the artisan class could not be long delayed.

Palmerston's death in 1865 eased the road to reform. At that time both the Liberal and Conservative parties were being reorganized and regenerated under the leadership of Disraeli and Gladstone. They managed their parties in the House of Commons during the ministries of Russell (1865–66), who was created earl in 1861 and elevated to the House of Lords, and of Lord Derby (1866–68), who was nearing the end of a long if colorless career. Gladstone, son of an affluent Lancashire merchant and West Indian planter, was a towering, elegant, and grizzly-looking gentleman with a sonorous voice. He had been educated in the proper Tory environment of Eton and Oxford, where he took the highest scholastic honors and sharpened his oratorical skills as president of the Oxford Union. Bowing to his father's wishes, he forsook a career in the Anglican Church to stand successfully for Parliament in 1832. During the succeeding thirty years he held increasingly more important posts in the government, most of which were related to finance. In 1834–35, Peel appointed him junior Lord of the Treasury and colonial under-secretary, and in 1843, after two years as vice-president of the Board of Trade in Peel's second ministry, Gladstone joined the cabinet as president of the Board of Trade. The turning point in his long career came in 1846 over repeal of the Corn Laws, when he followed Peel in secession from the Tory party and gradually worked his way into Whig-Liberal party ranks. As Chancellor of the Exchequer in the fifties and sixties under Aberdeen and Palmerston, Gladstone established a reputation as an outstanding financier and demonstrated in his budgets his deep concern for the welfare of the working classes and the industrial bourgeoisie by reapportioning the tax load so that the greatest burden was borne by those most able to carry it. He was never at a loss for words. If even his friends sometimes wearied of his circuitous argumentation and profuse verbiage, they had nothing but praise for his amazing vitality, hard work, scrupulous morality, and active mind. Although he did not pass up an opportunity to strengthen and expand the Empire, his deepest concern lay with the pressing problems of the modern industrial state and its teeming masses of workers, and with Ireland. His principal political support derived from the industrial and commercial entrepreneurs, the liberal-minded aristocracy and squirearchy, and the rank and file of the urban working class.

To what has been mentioned in a previous chapter about Disraeli's Judaic heritage, his family's nominal defection to Christianity when Benjamin was only a boy, and the crucial role he played in the stormy debates over the Corn Laws, there should be added some account of his legal studies at Lincoln's Inn, his publication of several socially critical novels that became best sellers, and three unsuccessful attempts in the early thirties to win a seat in Parliament, which he finally achieved in 1837. Despite the lack of prominent family connections, wealth, and a socially acceptable higher education, all of which were to some degree essential qualifications for aspiring young politicians in the Tory party, he overcame the political purgatory of a long apprenticeship. His sharp wit, brilliant speeches, strength of character, political acumen, and intense personal pride and ambition swept aside the gibes and sneers of Tory and Whig critics, who ridiculed his outlandish habits of dress (he liked frills, lace, and gaudy trousers and waistcoats), his Hebraic physiognomy, affected mannerisms, and sense of the dramatic. He served three Derby ministries as Chancellor of the Exchequer and Tory leader in the Commons, rebuilt the shattered pieces of the party following the secession of the Peelites in 1846, and ultimately achieved in 1868 a lifelong dream of becoming prime minister. Disraeli did not share Gladstone's passionate concern for the welfare of the common man, but he had the political sagacity to realize that his party could not stand for long on the spindlelegs of the declining aristocratic families. He therefore reasoned that the Conservatives must ultimately enfranchise the artisans in the hope of counterbalancing the pro-Liberal industrial and commercial bourgeoisie. He also believed that businessmen could be wooed into the Conservative party if he could prove to them that it could expand trade by enlarging the Empire and acquiring new markets.

The Russell ministry (1865–66) was immediately confronted by several troublesome questions. It suppressed the urge to follow Palmerston's policy of meddling in the Schleswig-Holstein question and thereby set the pattern of nonintervention in Continental affairs that obtained until the Congress of Berlin in 1878. As we have already seen, Russell's government dealt successfully with the Negro insurrection in Jamaica (Chapter 13) and reversed the island's evolution toward responsible government, which was commonly encouraged in other parts of the Empire. Ireland, quiescent since the awful famine of the forties, once more caused trouble following the organization of the Fenian Brotherhood and the Phoenix National and Literary Society, whose members committed acts of violence and plotted to overthrow British rule. At home, the Russell ministry faced a critical agricultural problem caused by a recurrence of the cattle plague (more serious than that of 1745–57), which killed about 6 per cent of the beef stock in England in 1865–67 at an estimated loss to farmers of £3,500,000. Russell had greater success in dealing with the commercial crisis of 1866, which had begun with the collapse of a discounting firm named Overend, Gurney, and Company, that had liabilities of £19,000,000. The crisis bankrupted several large speculative enterprises, caused a run on the banks, and forced the Bank of England to violate the Bank Charter Act of 1844.

These problems notwithstanding, Russell and his lieutenant, Gladstone, directed their primary attention to the enactment of a reform bill. In the thirties, "Finality Jack" Russell had solemnly declared that the Reform Act (1832) had settled the franchise and Parliamentary representation question for all time. Twenty years later he repented of his heresy and henceforth undertook to enlarge the electorate by enfranchising the intelligent artisans. Between 1852 and 1860, Russell introduced three of the five reform bills aimed at lowering the property qualification for voters and at the same time allowing those with a higher education or extensive property to cast more than one vote in Parliamentary elections. Parliament rejected all these bills. The prospect of enacting a reform bill in 1866, however, looked brighter than ever. The Liberals had a comfortable majority in Parliament and the support of the entrepreneurial class as well as of trade-unionists and other workers' associations that had been aroused from their apathy by the sparkling oratory of John Bright. One of the main arguments employed since 1832 by the opponents of reform, principally Conservatives but also a hard core of old-line Whigs, against enfranchising any of the working classes (the same argument that defeated the bill in 1866), had been that they had insufficient education, wisdom, and political experience to be trusted not to upset the fundamental balance of the British constitution. These traditionalists ignored the fact that there had been no serious agitation by the working class since the collapse of Chartism in 1848, and that more of them had had a rudimentary education by 1866 than was the case in 1832. Forthright Liberals reminded the traditionalists, however, that it was illogical for a nation to subscribe on the one hand to a social and economic philosophy of laissez faire, and to continue on the other hand the injustice of permitting barely a fifth of England and Wales' adult male population of more than five million to vote, or to fail to recognize that the apportionment of Parliamentary seats in 1832 had been outdated by the rapid growth of the underrepresented industrial towns and cities.

The moderate reform bill introduced by Gladstone in 1866 would have created 400,000 new voters, about half of whom were artisans. It was badly drafted and far too radical to please either the Conservatives or some forty reactionary Liberals, led by Robert Lowe and called Adullamites because of Bright's remark that they reminded him of Saul's discontented subjects who sought asylum with King David in the Cave of Adullam. Lowe, who while resident in Australia had learned to distrust the ten-pound household franchise proposed by Gladstone and his colleagues, succeeded in amending the bill to a point where it was no longer palatable to the Liberals. The heart of the opposition's argument was the belief that the enfranchisement of the urban workers would ultimately lead to a pure democracy in which the irresponsibility of the ignorant and venal elements of society would destroy liberty and overturn the mastery of those who by breeding, education, property, and experience should properly govern the kingdom. The Adullamites and Conservatives joined forces to defeat the bill and to force Russell's resignation.

In June, 1866, Lord Derby became prime minister for the third time even though he lacked a Parliamentary majority and the Adullamites refused to support his government. Disraeli once again became Chancellor of the Exchequer and Conservative leader in the Commons. Between Derby's assumption of office and the meeting of Parliament the following February, the force of public opinion, which was to play an increasingly important role in influencing government policy, prompted Disraeli to sponsor a reform bill in order to take, in the public's eyes, the credit that properly belonged to the Liberals. The onrushing tide of working-class discontent in 1866–67 was fed by several rivers that breached the dam of Parliamentary intransigence. First, the failure of the 1866 bill had gravely disappointed the lower classes, who believed more firmly than ever that only by broadening the franchise could they muster sufficient strength in Parliament to outvote those traditionalists who had so often ignored their grievances. Second, the trials of some unionists who had caused trouble at Sheffield and Bradford in 1866, called into question the legal status of the smaller trade-unions in Lancashire and Yorkshire. A governmental commission of inquiry upheld the legal right of the unions to urge higher wages and shorter hours, thereby reaffirming the principle established by statute in 1825. The trade-unionists nevertheless held conferences in London, Birmingham, Manchester, and elsewhere at which fiery speeches were made criticizing Parliament's refusal to pass a reform bill, the trials, and general government mismanagement. Third, the financial crisis of 1866, which bankrupted firms and caused unemployment, reminded workingmen anew of the hardships that they had suffered in consequence of unsound financial practices and speculative business. Last, and most important, violence flared in London on July 23, 1866, resulting in the trampling down of the fence at Hyde Park by an angry crowd of workers whom the cabinet had locked out and forbidden to assemble.

Such demonstrations in behalf of reform and against the Conservative leadership convinced Disraeli that he should at once introduce a reform bill. Accordingly, in March, 1867, shortly after the opening of Parliament, he had one ready for consideration. It was more liberal than any of the previous bills proposed since 1852 and consequently met stiff opposition. Disraeli repeatedly assured the lower House that, despite the bill's seeming liberality, safeguards were built in, such as the stipulation that householders must have lived in their lodgings for at least two years and have paid the poor rates. Hence, he declared, only a fourth of the new electorate would be composed of the working classes, and the nobility and the middle class would still control three-fourths of the votes cast in Parliamentary elections. He therefore assured the House that by no stretch of the imagination could the reform bill be construed as leading to anything like a popular democracy or endanger the existing power structure. As expected, some Conservatives fought the bill, and three members of Derby's cabinet—Lord Carnarvon, General Jonathan Peel, and Lord Robert Cecil (later marquis of Salisbury and prime minister)—resigned over it. The principal opposition, however, came from the Liberal ranks. Gladstone picked the bill to pieces in an effort to reduce the minimum financial qualification for urban householders to five pounds, and Lowe's Adullamites rejected the measure out of hand. After months of heated debate and frequent amendment that liberalized several sections of the bill, it passed the Commons as well as the Lords, which received it apathetically and made no serious effort to prevent its enactment.

The Representation of the People Act, or the Second Reform Act (August, 1867) as it is usually called, added nearly 940,000 electors to the existing roll of just over 1,050,000, and extended the franchise to practically all adult male residents of Parliamentary boroughs. Every householder who had lived in his lodgings for a year and paid the nominal poor rates or who rented a residence worth ten pounds annually without furnishings obtained the right to vote. So too did country residents, either landowners or life tenants, whose land returned at least five pounds a year, or short-term tenants who rented land for twelve pounds or more a year, providing they paid the customary taxes. The Act also redistributed some seats in Parliament without altering its size, along roughly the same lines followed in 1832. Eleven smaller boroughs lost their representation and each of thirty-five other boroughs surrendered one seat. The fifty-two seats thus freed were reassigned as follows: Manchester, Liverpool, Leeds, and Birmingham acquired a third seat; eighteen other boroughs gained one seat; the counties picked up a total of twenty-five seats; London University received one seat; and the Scottish universities together gained two. Irish representation was unaltered. The Act, although a milestone on the road to universal manhood suffrage, was liberal without being revolutionary. The agricultural laborers, who were without land or whose lodgings were too poor to meet the minimum financial qualification, and the poorest industrial workers, whose rent was less than ten pounds, were the chief segments of the male population overlooked, but they too received the vote less than twenty years later.

While British politicians thrashed out the particulars of the Second Reform Act, the Canadians had been considering the feasibility and wisdom of a confederated union of the several provinces of British North America. The union of Upper and Lower Canada into the Province of Canada in 1840 had helped to stabilize political differences between the English- and French-speaking Canadians, but it had not brought, as Lord Durham hoped it might, any appreciable lessening of the ethnic, religious, and commercial dissimilarities between the two sections of the province. Nevertheless, a succession of coalition ministries representative of the moderates of both groups had proved the workability of responsible government. Immigration, principally from England and Ireland, boosted the Province of Canada's population to about 2,500,000 in 1861, while industrial and commercial growth in the St. Lawrence Valley and lower Great Lakes encouraged a railroad boom in the fifties and sixties that linked the Atlantic ports of New England with Montreal, Toronto, and Windsor. Representative government had also developed in the Maritime Provinces of Nova Scotia and New Brunswick, which had a combined population of nearly 600,000 in 1861 and a thriving economy based on fishing, lumbering, shipbuilding, and farming. In Prince Edward Island, with only eighty thousand residents in that year, there was dissension between the colonists and absentee landowners, who dominated politics, commerce, and the land. Newfoundland, not even created a crown colony until 1824, had only a few thousand inhabitants, had few developed natural resources except fish and timber, and lagged far behind the provinces on the mainland. British Columbia, tied commercially to the northwestern American states and separated from eastern Canada by 2500 miles of wilderness, had attracted only fur traders, sailors, and a few stalwart colonists until the discovery of gold in 1856 along the Fraser River transformed the trading posts at Victoria and Vancouver into boom towns. In 1858, British Columbia became a crown colony.

The foremost issue in British North America during the sixties was political confederation, which seemed difficult of achievement because of the widely separated and largely independent-minded provinces and colonies, whose inhabitants feared what national union might do to their parochial interests. By 1865, several factors converged to make it apparent that confederation should be delayed no longer. First, the Anglo-American animosity bred by the American Civil War demonstrated to Canadians the weakness of their defenses against the gigantic military power to the south, especially in view of the fresh round of annexationist talk by influential Americans, the Fenian raids, and the possibility of Canadian involvement in war over the unsettled *Alabama* claims. The Civil War had also shown Canadians what could happen when regional differences went unresolved, and when a constitutional system permitted individual states to exercise undefined residual powers. Second, the abrogation in 1866 of the Canadian-American Reciprocity Treaty of 1854, a treaty that had greatly encouraged Canadian commercial growth, impressed upon Canadians the necessity of developing their domestic industries so as to survive against the protectionist commercial policy of the United States and the free market of Britain. Industrial development and economic self-sufficiency could best be achieved under a national government. Third, the regional isolation and parochial interests of the Maritimes were being broken down by better transportation and improved communication with the Province of Canada. One of the preconditions of national union was the latter's promise that an intercolonial railway connecting Halifax with Montreal and Toronto would be built if Nova Scotia and New Brunswick agreed to confederation. Fourth, the fathers of confederation recognized that only by the speedy completion of a transcontinental line could distant British Columbia be induced to join the dominion rather than gravitate toward the United States. Such a massive enterprise could not be undertaken without substantial assistance from foreign investors, who would naturally be reluctant to underwrite the railway without some assurance of the political stability that would accrue from national unity. Fifth and last, in 1864, the radical parties in the assembly of the Province of Canada had reached an impasse with the Conservative ministry and agreed to join a coalition ministry only on condition that it should work toward national union.

The immediate events leading to confederation began in September, 1864, when the legislators from Prince Edward Island, Nova Scotia, and New Brunswick met at Charlottetown, Prince Edward Island, to discuss a possible union of the Maritimes so as to facilitate railroad construction and encourage commercial expansion. It soon became apparent to leaders such as Joseph Howe and Charles Tupper (Nova Scotia) and Samuel Tilley (New Brunswick) that provincial self-interest would prevent any chance of uniting the Atlantic Provinces. Fortunately several politicians from the Province of Canada, including George Brown, John A. Macdonald, and George E. Cartier, had attended the Charlottetown meeting as observers. When Maritime union collapsed, they invited the delegates to attend a conference at Quebec City the next month to consider a national union. Despite the Maritimes' fear of being engulfed by the more populous and prosperous Canadian province, and long arguments over educational, religious, and financial questions, as well as over representation in the federal Parliament's House of Commons and Senate, the thirty-three delegates agreed to the Quebec Resolutions, which specified the constitution of the proposed confederation. After the provincial legislatures of Ontario, Quebec, New Brunswick, and Nova Scotia had ratified the constitution, a delegation headed by Macdonald took it to Westminster. Parliament quickly passed the British North America Act (March, 1867), Canada's constitution, with less interest by members of Parliament, according to Professor Edgar McInnis, than they paid to a new dog tax considered immediately after the Canada Act. The Dominion of Canada formally came into being on July 1, 1867. Manitoba joined it in 1870, as did British Columbia and Prince Edward Island in 1871 and 1873 respectively. The completion of the transcontinental Canadian Pacific Railway in 1885 opened the prairie lands to settlement and led to the creation of Alberta and Saskatchewan in 1905. Newfoundland, Canada's tenth province, joined the confederation in 1949.

Lord Derby, old and ill, resigned in February, 1868, and was succeeded by Disraeli, who held office for only ten months—during which time Parliament passed reform bills for Ireland and Scotland similar to the Second Reform Act and sought a solution to the Irish problem. This was provoked anew in 1865 by the revolutionary acts of the Fenian Brotherhood (a militant organization, operating in Ireland, England, and the northern United States, which sought to win Irish independence through terrorist acts against the British authorities in Ireland and England, and through raids along the Canadian border). The Fenian raids in Ireland and England were quickly suppressed and were followed by numerous trials for treason and felony. Gladstone took the Conservatives to task for their inability to cope with the revolutionaries except by the usual repressions, and brought such pressure to bear on Disraeli that he submitted the issue to the country in a general election. The voters showed their sympathy for Gladstone's concrete proposals for pacifying Ireland by removing the sources of its grievances, and were not deceived by Disraeli's obvious policy of expediency in promoting the Reform Act. The country consequently returned them to Parliament in substantial majority, thereby providing Gladstone with a popular mandate to reform British administration in Ireland.

Gladstone's first ministry (1868–74) concentrated on finding a solution to the Irish problem. The Fenian raids, which had broken the relative tranquillity in the island that had prevailed since the great famine and the collapse of the "Young Ireland" movement for home rule in 1848, focused the attentions of Englishmen on the genuine grievances of the Irish and aroused their sympathy toward them. What has been said in previous chapters about Irish discontent over the land question, the favored status of the Established Church, and British administration was as true of the nineteenth century as it had been of the seventeenth, except that the problems had become more serious and Irish tempers had grown shorter. The efforts by a succession of British ministries to satisfy the Irish—the economic benefits that accrued from Anglo-Irish union, the removal of political impediments on account of religion, the governmental commissions sent to Ireland to study the land problem, and the financial assistance provided during the famine, for example—did not slake Irish thirst for greater concessions and eventual national independence. Hindsight suggests that Gladstone was naïve to believe he could rectify overnight the accumulated grievances of three centuries of British domination among a people whose hatred of their overseers had become practically hereditary, but he moved forward as though he could do just that. In 1898, at Gladstone's death, the Irish question still hung in the balance, yet he had accomplished more to settle it than anyone else since the six-teenth century.

Gladstone first moved to disestablish and partially disendow the Church of Ireland. He recognized the injustice and illogic of forcing Irish Catholics, who were obliged by conscience to support their own Church, to pay tithes to and maintain the Established Church when barely an eighth of the population were Anglicans. While the Catholics worshiped in often shabby and overcrowded chapels, the great Angli-can cathedrals and comfortable parish churches stood largely empty. The poverty of thousands of Irish families, for whom the payment of double Church rates frequently meant the sacrifice of sustenance itself, was compared unfavorably with the affluence of the Irish Prot-estant Church, which had an endowment valued at £16,000,000 and an annual revenue approximating £700,000. Despite the unequivocal opposition of the queen and all but one of the bishops in the House of Lords, Parliament passed an Act (1869) that disestablished the Church of Ireland as of January 1, 1871, recognized the legal status of the Catholic, Anglican, and Presbyterian Churches as well as the right of a parishioner to support whichever Church he chose, and divorced the Establishment from any connection with the government in Ire-land. The Act also permitted the Anglican Church to keep its church property and approximately half its endowments. The other half, amounting to £8,000,000, was deposited in a fund that was used during the following generation to subsidize Irish education, alleviate poverty, and encourage industrial and agricultural improvements.

An equitable settlement of the Irish land question, to which Glad-stone turned next, proved a far more perplexing problem because of the complexity of the system of land tenure. In England and Scotland, most of the land was held by tenants, the terms of whose leases had been carefully specified. They paid a fair rent agreed upon with the landlord, who customarily did not violate the lease and compensated them for whatever improvements they made. This was essentially true also in Ulster, but it was not the case in the rest of Ireland. The Irish tenants worked small farms whose land had been exhausted by overuse and by lack of crop diversification and fertilization. They were entirely at the mercy of their landlords, who, concerned about profits and knowing the scarcity of arable land, frequently charged exorbitant rents against which the tenant had no recourse but personal complaint. Because of the limited opportunities for industrial employment and the scarcity of land, the Irish tenant, unlike his English counterpart, could not easily move into town or relocate on another farm. Hence, he either paid the high rent demanded by the landlord or was evicted. Irish landlords also generally refused to compensate tenants for improvements, with the result that over the years farms had seriously deteriorated. Following the great famine, some landlords consolidated their holdings into larger farms, thereby dispossessing more tenants, who had no recourse whatsoever under the law.

In order to remedy these conditions, Parliament passed the Land Act (1870), which stipulated that a tenant, upon leaving his farm, was entitled to compensation for improvements he had made so long as they had increased the market value of the land, and to sue for damages if evicted for any reason, provided that he had conscientiously paid his rent. The Act also empowered courts to review complaints of high rents and allowed tenants first option to purchase their farms should the landlord decide to sell, with a provision that the government would loan the purchase price on very favorable terms. But though on paper it ameliorated the Irish tenants' plight, this legislation unfortunately brought few changes. A few thousand tenants did buy farms with government loans, but others who took their complaints to court found the judges generally in sympathy with the landlords, who consequently continued to raise rents, evict tenants without just cause, and ignore the provisions of the Act regarding compensation for improvements. And while on the one hand Parliament sought to help the Irish, on the other it aroused their ire by enacting another coercive measure, which authorized the police to search private homes for weapons and to enforce a curfew, as well as to forbid possession of firearms except by license.

Finally, in 1873 Gladstone decided to reorganize Ireland's system of higher education. In 1845, under Peel, there had been founded the so-called "Godless Colleges" at Cork, Limerick, and Belfast, which had been affiliated in 1850 with the Queen's University. The creation of these new colleges, called "Godless" because they were forbidden by statute to teach theology, broke the monopoly over higher education in Ireland exercised by the Anglican Church, which controlled Trinity, the only other college (except for Maynooth College, an indigent Catholic seminary). As Gladstone believed that the Queen's Colleges were inferior, and that the opportunities for higher education open to Catholics were inadequate, he introduced the Irish education bill (1873). It proposed to abolish the Queen's University and affiliate the other colleges with Trinity College at Dublin, thereby creating a truly national university that would be the only degree-granting body in the country. Since the university was to be entirely nondenominational, and hence would have no chair in theology, the bill aroused opposition in all quarters: Irish Protestants (Established Churchmen) disliked the secularization of Trinity College; English Nonconformists refused to countenance a system in which teachers could be dismissed for offending their students' religious scruples; Catholics would not join any system that "mixed" Catholics and Protestants, and intended to keep their own Catholic University, founded in 1854. Parliament consequently defeated the bill. In 1879, however, the Conservatives successfully carried through a similar measure that created the Royal University of Ireland and established scholarships for worthy students regardless of their religion.

Gladstone had had more success with the Education Bill (1870), which had been drafted largely by William Forster, his Quaker vice-president of council. Educational opportunities had lagged far behind other achievements in Victorian England. Elementary education before 1833 had been almost entirely in the hands of Churches. In that year, however, the government had instituted the practice of modestly subsidizing a number of Church-related schools, and several succeeding governments raised the figure in steps until, by 1860, it was nearly £1,000,000. The government inspected the subsidized schools and assisted in their management. The archdiocese of Canterbury appointed some clerical inspectors, and some lay inspectors worked through the interdenominational British and Foreign School Society. Shortages of teachers were remedied by establishing normal schools, twenty-five by 1851. Even so, insufficient subsidization and the inability of the Church-related and public schools to meet the needs of the rapidly expanding population pointed up the inadequacy of the existing educational system. In 1870, only 2,000,000 of the 4,500,000 English children of school age were enrolled in elementary schools. About half these pupils attended schools that were not subject to inspection and had received no government grants. Children from poorer families had difficulty obtaining even a few years of formal instruction.

The Education Act established a national system of nonsectarian elementary schools under the supervision and management of elected school boards. The denominational schools were not disturbed, provided they met minimal standards and adequately served local needs. Where no schools existed, the school boards were empowered to build and staff them through local taxation. Attendance at the board schools was not compulsory (until 1880), but the boards might require children under thirteen to attend. The Act further forbade religious instruction of any kind in the tax-supported schools, although it might be provided on a voluntary basis outside the regular school day. Parents able to do so were required to pay fees, but poor children could attend free of charge. This Act, along with another of 1891, which made elementary education free for all pupils, reduced illiteracy from 20 to 2 per cent by 1900.

Until a proper foundation had been laid at the elementary school level, no serious thought could be given to improving secondary education, which was limited to the sons of the bourgeoisie and nobility until well into the twentieth century. The grammar schools, some dating back to the sixteenth century, had seen better days. They were endowed institutions for the ' most part, and their curriculums were frozen by immutable statutes that forbade the teaching of subjects such as the natural, biological, and social sciences. The "public" schools (private in the American sense) differed from the grammar schools in three major ways: they took in boarders, trained their pupils to be athletes and gentlemen as well as scholars, and generally were alive to new pedagogical techniques and trends, which they superimposed upon the basically classical curriculum. To the time-honored public schools of Winchester, Canterbury, and Eton were added the nineteenth-century foundations of Uppingham, Shrewsbury, Birmingham, King's, and the like, which taught practical subjects like drafting and science. Beginning in the 1820s, there was a rapid growth in adult or continuing education for working-class families beyond the elementary schools, through the foundation of Mechanics' Institutes and Working Men's Institutes, where for a nominal fee one could hear evening lectures on cultural and technical topics or use the amply stocked reading rooms and libraries.

Educational opportunities such as these were particularly significant in a society that did not subscribe to the principle of higher education for the masses. University education was, until late in the century, the prerogative of the wealthy and the privileged. Only two universities —Oxford and Cambridge—existed until the early nineteenth century. Until 1870, when Parliament abolished religious tests for university degrees, students could not matriculate at Oxford without subscribing to the Thirty-nine Articles of the Anglican Church, nor could Nonconformists at Cambridge obtain a degree or hold scholarships without doing so. Gradually, scientific advances, the demands of industry, and criticism from freethinking scholars forced both universities to broaden their archaic curriculums by including natural science, law, medicine, biology, and other new "ologies." The entrance requirements at Oxford and Cambridge, their limited facilities, the demands of a changing society, and the needs of Nonconformists led to the creation of the so-called "red brick" or provincial universities. The University of London opened in 1828 and grew rapidly following its federation with King's College on the Strand seven years later. The Anglican-endowed University of Durham, devoted principally to theological and related studies, opened in 1832. Victoria College (later Manchester University) was founded in 1851, and full-fledged universities developed from the medical schools at Sheffield, Leeds, and Birmingham. Although these new institutions did not ignore the humanities and social sciences, they concentrated on scientific and technical subjects. There were added in due course the universities of Reading, Liverpool, and Bristol. Without them, worthy students, especially those from working-class families, would have wasted their talents in less meaningful occupations. The ancient Scottish universities of Aberdeen, Edinburgh, St. Andrew's, and Glasgow admitted students more freely than Oxford or Cambridge and charged lower fees so that more Scots managed to take university degrees than was the case in England. It has been said that this weakened the quality of higher education in Scotland, but if this were true, Scottish professors would not have attained the enviable reputations they earned in the nineteenth century, and English school boards would not have preferred Scottish over English teachers.

While Gladstone's first ministry is remembered best for Irish and educational reforms, his administrative, legal, and army reforms were no less important. Imprisonment for debt, which had inflicted harsh injustice on countless victims of poverty for five hundred years, was finally abolished in 1869. The Secret Ballot Act (1872) freed voters from the intimidation of superiors, who had in the past often forced them either to accede to their wishes in Parliamentary elections or suffer reprisals such as loss of employment or domicile. In 1871, largely in order to avert further labor-union troubles like those that had erupted in 1866 in the north, Parliament affirmed the legality of labor associations whether or not they engaged in practices to restrain trade. At the same time, however, a second law prescribed penalties for picketing, molestation of nonunionists, damage to property, and other practices commonly associated with strikes. By executive decree in 1870,

Gladstone undercut the spoils system (patronage) in all departments of the civil service except the Foreign Office (which continued to make appointments and promotions on ephemeral qualifications like social class, family background, and personal influence) by basing appointments and advancements on competitive examinations, a system that had worked well in the Indian Civil Service for seventeen years. Henceforth career government servants lent a measure of stability and continuity to policies and procedures in departments whose chiefs changed with virtually every new cabinet. The reorganization and modernization of the army in 1868-73, executed by Secretary for War Edward Cardwell, reversed practices followed in the military in some cases since Stuart times. He first placed supreme authority over the army in the hands of a civilian war secretary to whom the professional commander-in-chief was accountable. Second, on the conviction that the country could not afford to maintain a large standing army, he lowered the customary term of enlistment from twenty-five to six years of regular service and six years in the reserves. The smaller force was to serve as a nucleus, and the much larger army needed in wartime could be recruited from the trained reservists. Third, in order to save the expense of keeping redcoats in the self-governing colonies, an issue that had long irked the taxpayer in England, British regiments were withdrawn altogether from Canada, New Zealand, and Australia, and the number of troops in the Cape Colony was substantially reduced. Finally, despite strong opposition in Parliament, Cardwell, by means of a royal warrant, abolished the purchase of commissions, which henceforth were awarded on the basis of merit.

Gladstone also remodeled the judiciary. Legal experts such as Jeremy Bentham and Walter Bagehot, novelists like Dickens (especially in *Bleak House*), and the ordinary citizens who had lost their patience and savings in protracted litigation, had long urged the reorganization and simplification of the national system of courts. Beginning in the 1820s, Parliament had appointed commissions to study the system with an eye to clarifying and expediting its procedures, standardizing its terminology, and eliminating overlapping and conflicting jurisdictions. Their recommendations had been enacted into law piecemeal without much significant alteration of the courts' structure and independent authority. A major breakthrough came in 1857, when cases involving wills and marriages were transferred from the ecclesiastical courts to the new secular courts of probate and divorce. But inconsistencies, delays, and complexities remained in the courts of common law, the admiralty court, and the Chancery court until the passage of the Judicature Act of 1873, which reorganized these courts as the Supreme Court of Judicature. It was composed of two branches—the High Court of Justice and the Court of Appeal. The High Court had three divisions: Chancery; King's Bench (including all the old common-law courts); and Probate, Divorce, and Admiralty. The judges could employ the rules of either common law or equity, whichever suited the circumstances best; in case of conflict, equity should prevail. These courts heard both criminal and civil suits in the first instance. Five Lords Justices of Appeal (plus the Lord Chancellor, the Lord Chief Justice, and the President of the Probate, Divorce, and Admiralty division of the High Court, who were ex officio members) constituted the panel of judges in the Court of Appeal. It heard appeals from any division of the High Court and was intended to replace the House of Lords as the final appellate court. But the Appellate Jurisdiction Act (1876) routed appeals in civil suits through the Court of Appeals to the Lords, which remains to this day the highest tribunal in the United Kingdom. Litigants might appeal criminal cases to the Lords on condition that they had secured a writ of error. A criminal court of appeal was later interposed between the High Court and the Lords.

Notwithstanding the remarkable record of reform achieved by the first Gladstone ministry, the electorate turned out the Liberals in 1874. Discontent among several important political groups showed up after 1871 in the defeat of Liberals in almost every by-election. The army reforms provoked adamant opposition in Parliament and among the army and its partisans. The Nonconformists resented Gladstone's efforts in an early draft of the Education Bill to require catechetical teaching in rate-supported schools, subject only to a conscience clause, and the increased government grants to Anglican schools. Landowners, long responsible for managing local government, were incensed over the establishment of a Local Government Board, which assumed the management of public health, the Poor Law system, and the business of the Poor Law districts. Publicans, a well-organized body, resented the oppressiveness of an Act of 1872 that stiffened penalties for drunkenness and shortened the business hours of public houses (taverns). Many High-churchmen regarded as traitorous Gladstone's disestablishment of the Protestant Church of Ireland and the abolition of religious tests at Oxford and Cambridge. Trade-unionists were disappointed by both the Liberals' indifference to social legislation and the stringency of the Trade Union Act of 1871. Businessmen and farmers blamed the Liberals for trade reductions and the economic slump that began in 1873. Finally, Gladstone had silenced the British lion in foreign relations. Compared with Palmerston's firm intervention in world affairs, the Liberal policy of aloofness and nonalignment was widely interpreted by the electorate as retrenchment at the cost of national honor. The Foreign Office's indifferent effort to dissuade Bismarck from launching the Franco-Prussian War in 1870, for example, and Britain's submission in 1871 to Russia's repudiation of the neutrality clauses relating to the Black Sea in the Treaty of Paris (1856), damaged the nation's image abroad and weakened Gladstone's reputation at home. The public had been appalled, moreover, by his supine concession to American demands in the Treaty of Washington (1871) that provided for the settlement of the *Alabama* claims arising from the Civil War. In addition, there was dissension in the cabinet.

A superb politician of Disraeli's caliber naturally took full advantage of this public dissatisfaction and rode the crest of the electoral tide that swept the Conservatives into office in 1874 with a comfortable majority of fifty seats. Conservatives profited from the criticism that ordinarily befalls the party in power as well as from the national reorganization of their own party. In 1867, Disraeli had created the National Union, designed to build party strength at the local level among the newly enfranchised skilled workers. He tightened party organization three years later by coordinating the work of local Conservative associations through a central office in London. The Liberals, preoccupied with their programs, did not learn the worth of grassroots politics until it was too late to counteract Conservative strategy. The experience of defeat in 1874 led Gladstone to establish in 1877 the National Liberal Federation to encourage the formation of local Liberal associations.

In the election, Disraeli had pledged a modest program of social reform. Although the Conservatives had censured Liberal legislation as precipitous and radical, they themselves were soon caught up in a fresh round of legislation aimed at promoting the welfare of the workers. Accordingly, in 1875–78, they enacted public health, housing, labor, merchant marine, and education laws that buttressed Disraeli's creed of Tory Democracy. A Public Health Act codified the health and sanitation statutes passed since 1848 and created urban and rural sanitary districts supervised by borough councils, boards of guardians, or boards of health, whichever served local needs best. An Artisans' Dwellings Act empowered town councils to demolish slums and construct suitable housing. A Trade Union Act rescinded the labor laws of 1871, authorized peaceful picketing, and defined, on essentially the same basis as that applicable to individuals, the very few instances in which trade-unions could be held liable for criminal conspiracy. Collective bargaining was also legalized: this, along with other guarantees, secured the position of the unions until 1901, when the Taff Vale decision in the House of Lords (discussed later) once more jeopardized unions by holding them financially responsible for damages resulting from strikes. A Merchant Shipping Act, promoted by a member of Parliament named Samuel Plimsoll, authorized the Board of Trade to guard seamen's lives by condemning unseaworthy ships and outlawing overloading. The Factory and Workshops Act (1878) consolidated the earlier laws on the subject. It regulated sanitation and safety standards in both textile and other factories; fixed employment hours and mealtimes for children under fourteen years of age, "young persons" aged fourteen to eighteen, and all women; made provision for holidays and part-time education of employed children; required certificates of health before children under sixteen years of age could be employed; and stipulated that all industrial accidents must be reported to an inspector of factories. Finally, an education act forbade the employment of children under fourteen without proof of their having been to school, and empowered school attendance committees in districts not having school boards to compel pupils' attendance.

Not satisfied merely to cement the new relationship between the Conservatives and the wage-earners through social reform, Lord Beaconsfield (Disraeli accepted the title from his grateful queen in 1876) set out to make Britain once again a meaningful force in the European community, to define and strengthen colonial boundaries, and to outdistance the French, Germans, Russians, and other imperial powers in the race for new colonies in Africa and Asia. He commenced this bold adventure by obtaining the largest single block of shares in the Suez Canal Company. The interest evidenced by the British in the affairs of Egypt and the Isthmus of Suez had grown steadily since Napoleon's invasion in 1798. We have noted earlier the repeated British intervention in support of the Turkish Empire, of which Egypt was a virtually autonomous unit, and the lengths to which Palmerston and others went to guarantee the independence of the eastern Mediterranean theater against Russian and French encroachment. Britain consequently watched closely the construction of the Suez Canal, built

largely with French and Egyptian funds by the engineer Ferdinand de
Lesseps, which was opened in 1869. Since the Canal shortened the sea
route between London and Bombay by nearly five thousand miles and
the travel time by steamer by more than three months, the strategic
importance of that region in peace and war assumed great proportions.
The Khedive of Egypt, Ismail, a colossally extravagant and irresponsible
fellow who owned a plurality of the shares in the company that had
dug the Canal, went bankrupt in 1875, owing to financial mismanagement and ruinous loans from a number of European bankers. Unable
to extricate himself from his enormous indebtedness, he offered to dispose of his shares to the highest bidder. Disraeli, without bothering to
consult Parliament and thereby run the risk of missing a golden opportunity, at once arranged privately to purchase in the name of the
British government the khedive's 176,602 shares (about 45 per cent of
those outstanding) for £4,000,000. Parliament subsequently approved
the transaction, which paid handsome financial dividends to British
stockholders, gave Britain a foothold in northeastern Africa, and
strengthened British sea power. Disraeli then capped his first monumental triumph in foreign affairs by having Parliament bestow on
Victoria the title Empress of India.

Meanwhile a crisis that threatened the territorial integrity of Turkey
had arisen in the Balkans and eventually led to the Russo-Turkish
War of 1877–78. Pushed by Austria and Russia, both of which had
territorial ambitions in European Turkey, the Christian subject peoples of Bosnia and Herzegovina, resenting Turkish misrule and an
extremely unfair tax system, rebelled in 1875 against their Mohammedan overlords. The revolt spread to Bulgaria and Salonica, where
Moslem landlords' atrocities against Christian peasants shocked the
sensibilities of the Great Powers and provided the Russians with an
excuse to intervene. While the French, German, and British Mediterranean squadrons hurried to Turkish waters and Serbia and Montenegro rose in support of their Slavic neighbors, Russia and Austria
secretly agreed that Austria should acquire Bosnia-Herzegovina in return for its neutrality in the event of a Russo-Turkish war. Although
the Turkish atrocities incensed Englishmen and led Gladstone to
publish a passionate pamphlet entitled *Bulgarian Horrors and the Question of the East*, Disraeli, who had dispatched Foreign Secretary Salisbury to warn the sultan of Britain's displeasure over the situation and
to use his good offices at a conference of the Great Powers at Constantinople, refused to intervene for fear of a confrontation with Rus-

sia. Consequently, when Turkey refused to heed the advice of the delegates in the belief that Britain would come to her aid in the end, Russia declared war in April, 1877, and in a few months smashed the Turkish army.

The Treaty of San Stefano (March, 1878) ended the war but aroused the apprehension of the Great Powers. The treaty ceded to Russia a broad belt of territory on the eastern shores of the Black Sea, created a large, autonomous Bulgarian state under temporary (two years) Russian military occupation, and made Bosnia-Herzegovina an autonomous area under Austrian administration. The treaty therefore appeared likely to make Russia the dominant power in the Balkans, a situation wholly unacceptable to Britain because of the Russian threat to Constantinople and the Straits, and Russian expansion in the Middle East and along the approaches to India. Germany, too, feared further complications at a time when Bismarck was striving to arrange a European balance of power that would leave him free to concentrate on the domestic problems that arose after German unification in 1871. At the instigation of Lord Beaconsfield and Bismarck, British, German, Austro-Hungarian, Russian, French, Italian, and several Balkan Slavic delegates convened at the Congress of Berlin in June. Britain and Austria gained most by the settlement, and Russia, confronted by massive opposition to San Stefano, had no choice but to capitulate. The most important features of the Berlin settlement were: (1) Bulgaria was cut to two-thirds of the size proposed in the Treaty of San Stefano; (2) Austria-Hungary was permitted to "occupy and administer" Bosnia-Herzegovina, which technically remained part of the Turkish Empire; (3) Russia kept only the Bessarabian provinces of Rumania, while the rest of it, together with Serbia and Montenegro, was accorded independence. A separate Anglo-Turkish convention signed in June, 1878, provided for British guarantees of the territorial integrity of Asiatic Turkey in exchange for British occupation of Cyprus, subject only to the payment of an annual subsidy to the sultan. Beaconsfield returned triumphantly to London, having achieved, as he told the cheering crowd, "peace with honour."

But peace and honor were more difficult to maintain in Afghanistan. As we saw in Chapter 13, the British had twice repulsed Russian advances in Persia and Afghanistan in order to protect the northwestern Indian frontier. Even so, the Russians had gained a strong foothold in vast areas south of Lake Balkhash and the Aral Sea, and in southwestern Turkestan, and continued to press diplomatically and militarily into

Afghanistan, which Britain sought to control as a buffer state between the Russian Empire and the Punjab. In 1878, however, when the Amir of Afghanistan cordially received a Russian delegation but refused a similar courtesy to one sent by the Viceroy of India, Lord Lytton, Lytton dispatched more than thirty thousand troops to expel the Russians and compel the amir to accept a permanent British embassy in his capital. The amir fled with the Russians to Turkestan and died shortly afterward. His son, faced with a British army of occupation, recognized permanent diplomatic relations with Britain and agreed to allow the Foreign Office to direct Afghanistan's foreign policy in return for military protection against the Russians and a large annual subsidy. But, in 1880, a series of palace revolutions that eventually brought a hostile amir to the throne led to an Anglo-Afghan war, which Gladstone pursued reluctantly and with indifferent success until spring, 1881, when the British evacuated the capital and recognized Afghan independence. Over the next twenty-five years, troubles between Britain and Russia frequently erupted along the Russo-Afghan frontier, which the British with great difficulty managed to control. Finally, in 1907, an Anglo-Russian accord obliged the signatories to honor the territorial integrity of Afghanistan, placed its foreign affairs under British control, and admitted Russia on an equal basis with Britain to trade in the country.

The British electorate again demonstrated its fickleness in the general election of 1880. Beaconsfield, although old and chronically ill, had given the wage-earners more advantages than they had expected when they supported the Conservatives in 1874. He had also revived by a stirring foreign policy reminiscent of the Younger Pitt the glory of conquest and international pre-eminence that the Britons had come to expect of their governments since Elizabethan times. Had Beaconsfield held the election in 1878 following the Congress of Berlin, the country would doubtless have rallied to the Conservative standard. By 1880, however, troubles beset him on all sides. A serious agricultural depression, explained earlier, had severely damaged the nation's economy and foreign trade. Many factory workers lost their jobs or went on strike. Taxpayers resented the heavy military expenditures in the Afghan and Zulu wars (see below), which forced Sir Stafford Northcote, Chancellor of the Exchequer, to raise the income tax and other taxes, and to make costly short-term loans to meet the mounting financial deficit. Moreover, Disraeli displeased the Nonconformists who, although not entirely satisfied with the Liberal policies of the previous government, nevertheless had to admire Gladstone's strict sense of morality. Gladstone's remarkable vigor, unweakened by the weight of more than seventy years, played a crucial role in the elections, particularly in the Midlothian district of northern England and southern Scotland, where he spoke to thousands about Conservative sins and Liberal virtues. Finally, a new home rule movement in Ireland led by Charles Stewart Parnell (1846–91) had risen from the ashes of Fenianism to plague the Conservative government through its use of obstructionist tactics in Parliament.

The second Gladstone ministry (1880–85), like the first, plunged into the sea of Irish discontent. The Liberal victory of 1880 had pained Queen Victoria, whom Beaconsfield had mesmerized into believing that all things Liberal were inherently untrustworthy. She was now obliged to accept Gladstone, whom she did not like, and, a year later, death removed Beaconsfield, whom she did like. The cabinet included old and able friends of Gladstone like Forster, who accepted the crucial portfolio of secretary for Ireland, and younger but experienced politicians, such as Joseph Chamberlain (1836–1914), president of the Board of Trade, whose governmental and educational reforms as mayor of Birmingham had already won him a national reputation.

Although some Irishmen continued to shed English and their own blood for the cause of an independent Irish republic, repeated instances of violence since the union of 1800 had not altered the fact of British rule. The Young Ireland and Fenian movements, committed to terrorism, had not only been unsuccessful; they had also provoked from Westminster a series of retributive measures that further complicated the Irish problem. The Irish leadership in Parliament, faced with the dilemma of its inability to obtain repeal of the union, and with the ineffectiveness of armed resistance, organized the Nationalist party, which formally split with the Liberals in 1877. Led initially by the unobtrusive Protestant Ulsterite Isaac Butt (d. 1879), the Nationalists sought to achieve the compromise of home rule—the establishment of an independent and sovereign Parliament for Ireland. The home rulers' methods were fundamentally peaceful, but much violence among radicals in Ireland accompanied the party's efforts at Westminster to induce Parliament to grant its demands. When it became apparent, during Disraeli's last ministry, that the government would not satisfy them, they employed their collective strength to vote against every government bill, thereby obstructing the legislative process.

The Nationalists took on new life under the leadership of Parnell, who, considering his heritage, seemed a most unlikely candidate for

Irish leadership. Protestant, Cambridge-educated, a landowner, and the son of an English father and an American mother, this stalwart, inscrutable, and clever member of Parliament for county Meath stands as tall as O'Connell in the annals of Irish history. He had entered Parliament in 1875, and rose in only two years to the leadership of sixty-five colleagues in the Commons committed to repeal of the Act of Union. His influence ranged far beyond the halls of Westminster: he was president of the Home Rule Federation in Great Britain and first president of the National Land League in Ireland; although not in sympathy with their principles, he had close friends in the Irish revolutionary brotherhood based in Paris, and in the Clan-na-Gael and other Irish-American nationalist organizations, which gave him $200,-000 during his triumphal American tour in 1880.

Gladstone had little success during the campaign in arousing the sympathies of the British electorate to the chronic Irish land problem, but his heart was set on resolving it. The agricultural depression that gripped England had even more serious consequences in Ireland, where sharp reductions in productivity and trade inflicted the accustomed miseries on the oppressed Irish tenants. Confident that the English would not help them, in 1879 they founded the Land League, which sought to abolish rack rents and drive the landlords off the land, thus leaving it to the occupants. The League's guiding force was Michael Davitt, a long-time Fenian terrorist who had been in half a dozen English jails for treasonous and felonious acts, and who wanted both an Irish republic and agrarian socialism. Encouraged by the League, the Irish rioted in protest against evictions. Parliamentary pressure mounted against Gladstone, urging him to take immediate action to keep the peace, and he consented to another coercion Act (1881), which empowered the lord lieutenant to imprison without trial or bond anyone suspected of treasonable acts or conspiracy against landlords. As a consequence, Parnell, his lieutenant, John Dillon, and others were imprisoned.

In April, 1881, Gladstone introduced an Irish Land Bill aimed at satisfying what Parnell had called the three F's—fixed tenure, fair rent, and free sale. These principles were designed to abolish short-term leases, set reasonable rents, and allow tenants to sell their leases. The Act also created a land court which, upon appeal from either landlord or tenant, might set a fair rent for fifteen years during which time the tenant could not be evicted except for delinquency in rent. Tenants were given the extraordinary privilege (considering the fact that they did not own the land) of selling their leases at their own price, provided that the landlord was given first option to buy them. Finally, the government offered to lend tenants up to three-quarters of the purchase price should they wish to buy their farms, and to grant loans for improvements. The Act was generous but ineffective. The Nationalists disliked it because the land court too frequently decided in favor of the landlords; the radical revolutionaries were dissatisfied with anything short of complete independence; and influential members of Parliament were alienated by what they considered rash action aimed at placating traitors. Unfortunately for Gladstone, the prognosis of further trouble made by the Act's opponents was realized. The imprisonment of Nationalist and Land League leaders set off a reaction in Ireland in the form of violence and sneak attacks on British officials, and led to tenant refusals to pay rent until Parnell and the others were released. Gladstone did his best to allay their fears. He freed the prisoners and appointed the liberal-minded Lord Frederick Cavendish chief secretary for Ireland, the effective administrative subordinate to the Lord Lieutenant. But when the situation seemed to be settling down, the brutal murder of Cavendish and his under-secretary, Thomas Burke, in Phoenix Park, Dublin, in May, 1882, shocked all England and tore open the wounds that Gladstone had sought to heal.

The murderers were caught, tried, and hanged. That they were proven to be revolutionaries whom Parnell had spurned carried little weight with Englishmen, who unjustly held him and his moderate Nationalist friends up to scorn. In response to public pressure, Parliament suppressed the Land League, adopted new measures to override Irish obstructionist tactics, and passed the Crimes Act (1882). This empowered the British administration in Ireland to substitute three judges for juries in important trials in which the juries would surely side with the accused. Undaunted, Parnell founded the National League to replace the Land League and continued to encourage peaceful resistance through boycotts and intimidation of landlords.

The Irish question had consumed virtually all Gladstone's attention, but the respite that followed the grave events of 1882–83 afforded him the opportunity to promote another of his favorite programs: reform of the electoral and representative systems. It will be recalled that the Reform Act of 1867 had enfranchised practically all the urban workingmen and tenants in the country, but had overlooked the agricultural laborers. To remedy this situation the Liberals sponsored and passed the Reform Act of 1884, which extended the franchise to agricultural laborers on the same conditions as had been set for town laborers in 1867, thereby adding some two million voters. Therefore, except for a few thousand domestic servants and others who paid no rent, manhood suffrage had been achieved. The Bill nearly foundered in the House of Lords, a Conservative stronghold, where Lord Salisbury mustered substantial and almost overwhelming opposition until Gladstone struck a bargain with him that obliged the Liberals to redistribute the seats in the Commons. Accordingly, the Redistribution Act (1885) freed seats by abolishing separate Parliamentary representation in boroughs of less than 15,000 inhabitants, and by limiting to one member the representation of boroughs under 50,000. By allocating the freed seats to other constituencies, some of which were newly created, the House of Commons was increased by twelve members to 670. Except for a few very large towns, which remained two-member constituencies, the country was divided into one-member constituencies of roughly equal population. Hence a new principle had been adopted, that of representation by population rather than by communities.

Lord Beaconsfield had bequeathed to Gladstone a bag of troubles in Afghanistan, Egypt, and South Africa (see below), which forced him into an imperialist posture inimical to his party's interests and his own convictions. In 1882, in consequence of an Egyptian nationalist uprising to expel foreigners, a British squadron shelled Alexandria and British troops occupied Egypt, an action that led to serious complications in the Sudanese region of the upper Nile. Once the British army had ended the rebellion, Gladstone dispatched Sir Evelyn Baring (later Lord Cromer) as consul-general with instructions intended to stabilize the political situation, after which, it was hoped, the troops might be speedily withdrawn. In 1881, however, the Mohammedan religious fanatic, Mohammed Ahmed, who styled himself the Mahdi (Messiah or Guide), had begun a rebellion of thousands of Sudanese tribesmen, who had been for years the victims of Egyptian carpetbaggers. The Mahdi terrorized the countryside, besieged several Egyptian fortresses, and in 1883 cut to pieces an Anglo-Egyptian army commanded by the British officer Hicks Pasha. These developments confronted Gladstone with the difficult decision of whether to abandon the Sudan altogether or to make a stand against the Mahdi. Gladstone did not wish to add Sudan permanently to the Empire, but the high command in London and British authorities in Egypt were anxious to settle the problem one way or another. He finally consented in an unguarded moment to allow an expeditionary force under General Charles Gordon, who had been governor of the Sudan in the 1870s, to support the Anglo-Egyptian garrisons along the upper Nile, with instructions either to evacuate them or to make peace with the Mahdi. Upon reaching the area, Gordon decided on his own authority to crush the rebels, but they trapped him at Khartoum in January, 1885, butchering him and his men only two days before a relief column under Lord Wolseley reached the bloody scene. The incensed British public accused Gladstone of waiting until too late to decide whether to send supporting troops; the infuriated queen scolded and humiliated him; and the House of Lords censured his government. Thereafter Anglo-Egyptian troops abandoned the Sudan south of Wadi Halfa for twelve years.

Although Gladstone had managed with great difficulty to hold his own against mounting opposition to his Irish policy from Conservative and Nationalist ranks, his failure to match Beaconsfield's success abroad severely damaged his reputation and public confidence in his administration. On the face of it, Gladstone resigned in June, 1885, over the budget, which called for higher taxes at a time of continuing economic depression. But actually, the government's inability to settle the Irish problem, the massacre at Khartoum, the indecisive British position vis-à-vis Afghanistan (see above), and the intransigence of the Nationalists rendered his ministry ineffective. Lord Salisbury, who had succeeded to the Conservative leadership upon Beaconsfield's death in 1881, reluctantly accepted office at the queen's insistence even though he lacked a Parliamentary majority and had no assurance of the Liberals' cooperation. Salisbury remained prime minister only until January, 1886. It took him several weeks to form an acceptable cabinet that included old faces such as Northcote (Treasury) and R. A. Cross (Home Office) as well as aggressive newcomers like Lord Randolph Churchill, leader of the renegade, liberal-minded Conservatives in Parliament (India Office). A future prime minister, Arthur James Balfour, Salisbury's nephew, was named president of the Local Government Board. With the Parliamentary session rapidly drawing to a close, the Conservatives passed only one significant law, an Irish Land Act written by Lord Ashbourne (Chancellor of Ireland), and negotiated beforehand in secret conferences between Parnell and Lord Carnarvon (Lord Lieutenant of Ireland), thereby ensuring the support of the Nationalists. The Act released £5,000,000 from the Irish Church fund to finance loans to Irish tenants at 4 per cent to purchase their farms over a mortgage period of forty-nine years. This legislation marked a departure from the Conservatives' former insistence upon coercion:

indeed, some influential cabinet-rank Conservatives began to believe that home rule was the only solution to the Irish problem, and frequently said so in public addresses.

The general election of December, 1885, returned the Liberals in numbers exactly equal to the combined strength of the Conservatives and Nationalists. The Liberals obtained a majority over the Conservatives, which brought Gladstone into office for the third time since 1868, but the votes of the eighty-six Nationalists, if ranged against him, could obstruct Liberal legislation. For this reason as well as his conviction that home rule should be delayed no longer, he let it be known that he would introduce such a measure immediately upon the opening of Parliament. The Parnellites at once announced their support of Gladstone's administration, and in April, 1886, the government confidently introduced the first home rule bill, which proposed to create a separate Irish legislature (the word Parliament was not used) at Dublin. It was to consist of two bodies or orders: one composed of twenty-eight peers plus seventy-five members elected by selected constituencies, the other of 206 members elected by the existing constituencies. The legislature's powers were to be restricted to domestic affairs, with matters involving the armed forces, peace and war, religion, trade, and customs and excise regulated by the imperial Parliament at Westminster. The bill was defeated on the second reading largely because of defection from Liberal ranks, and it split the party. Even before it had been introduced, Liberals including Lord Northbrook, Lord Hartington, George Goschen, Sir George Trevelyan, and Joseph Chamberlain announced their refusal to support it. In all, ninety-three Liberals voted against the bill and then formed the Liberal Unionist party, dedicated to the preservation of imperial unity. Gladstone consequently resigned in August, 1886.

The second Salisbury ministry (1886–92) immediately backtracked on the Irish problem even though his previous Conservative government had leaned toward conciliation and some high-ranking party members were voicing sympathy for home rule. While professing an intention to alleviate economic distress and social injustice, Salisbury declared that Parliament should govern Ireland so firmly, consistently, and honestly, that within twenty years the Irish would be content to accept decisions that Parliament reached. What they needed, he added, "is government—government that does not flinch, that does not vary; government that [they] . . . cannot hope to beat down by agitations [and] . . . that is not altered in its resolutions or its temperature by the party changes which take place at Westminster." The agent whom Salisbury chose to implement this policy was Balfour, the new chief secretary for Ireland. A sluggish, introspective, and cultured man of thirty-eight who had been practically indifferent to public affairs since entering Parliament in 1875, he surprised everyone, on the one hand by rigorously enforcing the law against Irish extremists, and on the other by ensuring that the Ashbourne Land Act and other remedial legislation designed to alleviate poverty and to right injustice were carried out. His four-year administration is known best for the Criminal Law Amendment Act which, unlike all the earlier coercion laws, was meant to be permanent (the earlier laws had been limited to one or two years). Passed early in 1887, it authorized the British authorities in Ireland to outlaw nationalist associations, to place "disturbed" districts under martial law, and to try alleged conspirators before resident magistrates.

That Parliament passed this harsh law owed much to the scandal involving Parnell's alleged sympathy with Irish revolutionaries, particularly those responsible for the Phoenix Park murders. The *Times* of London published several scathing articles entitled "Parnellism and Crime," including letters purportedly written by Parnell condoning the murders. He at once denied having written them and demanded a Parliamentary inquiry as to their authorship. Parliament refused, but named a commission to study the issues raised by the *Times*. It discovered that a derelict Irish journalist had forged and sold the letters to the newspaper. This, plus the commission's exoneration of Parnell, enabled him to win a libel suit against the newspaper and to sustain his honor. But tragedy befell him in 1890. He was named corespondent in a divorce suit that shocked the sensibilities of Victorians, destroyed any chance of his continuing to lead the Nationalists, and may have contributed to his death at forty-six in October, 1891. His successor, John Redmond, repaired the break in the Nationalist party by the turn of the century and carried on the struggle for home rule.

In addition to the usual preoccupation with Ireland and the light-hearted celebrations honoring Queen Victoria's Golden Jubilee in 1887, Salisbury was concerned with reforming local government in England and Wales. Since the passage of the Municipal Corporations Act (1835), Parliament had enacted several measures creating local agencies to regulate elementary education, housing, the Poor Law, licensing, police, and the like. These agencies operated for the most part almost entirely within urban areas, and practically nothing had been done to reorganize county government, which was still essentially in the hands of overworked justices of the peace. This was remedied in the County Councils Act (1888), which transferred practically all administrative duties in the counties to locally elected county councils, leaving the justices of the peace with only judicial functions. In addition, the Act bestowed county borough status on sixty-one cities and boroughs, which became self-governing areas with status equal to that of the counties. New counties like London were created, for example, but others such as Yorkshire and Somersetshire remained territorially as they had been. Further local government reform came in 1894 as a result of the Local Government Act, which established councils to manage urban and rural districts that were administrative subdivisions of the county and were subordinated to the county councils. Rural parishes were also recognized as units of local government, confirming what had long been the case, but making them subordinate parts of the rural districts wherein they lay.

Since the Parliament had been elected in 1886, its statutory term of seven years was rapidly coming to a close. Salisbury therefore decided to submit his record to public scrutiny in a general election in 1892. It was refreshing, for a change, that the election had not been provoked by a government crisis, party confrontation in Parliament, or dissension within Conservative ranks. On the whole, the Salisbury ministry had been quite successful: Ireland was quieter than it had been for years, and the country had gradually been returning to economic normalcy after nearly two decades of hard times. Gladstone, although eighty-three, infirm, and weary of a public life that had spanned the entire reign of Victoria, once more carried the Liberal standard. He had not forgotten home rule: in fact, the hope of securing it made it worth-while for him to postpone his retirement. The electorate, on the other hand, was weary of Irish problems and anxious to forget them. The Grand Old Man triumphed again, largely because of support in Scotland and Wales, but he did not gain the substantial majority he had fought so hard to win. Counting the Nationalists' support, he had a majority of only forty seats.

The fourth Gladstone ministry (1892–94) proved to be his last, and it ended on a sour note. He personally introduced the second home rule bill (1893), which differed from its predecessor on only one significant point: in addition to the creation of an Irish legislature, it proposed to allow eighty Irish members to sit in the imperial Parliament, limiting their participation solely to Irish affairs. The House passed the bill (many members voting for it because they knew the Lords would defeat it), but, as expected, the Lords rejected it by 419 votes to 41. Defeated once more, and with his strength and hope practically spent, Gladstone resigned early in 1894. He died four years later and received the stately funeral, the public tribute, and the burial in Westminster Abbey that his long career merited.

He had dominated the Liberal party to such an extent that his retirement created a power vacuum, which was filled rather unsatisfactorily by Lord Rosebery (1847–1929), who had served in three Gladstone ministries at the Home and Foreign Offices, but who disappointed the party's high expectations of him. He lasted as prime minister for only fifteen months (1894–95) and was under constant harassment by Conservatives and Liberal Unionists. To be sure, any Liberal prime minister would have been hard-pressed, for the party lacked an appealing legislative program. A program had been drafted in 1891, which included home rule, tax reform, pay for members of Parliament, and curtailment of the power of the House of Lords, but powerful interests in the country were ready to defeat those aims. Ireland for the moment was a dead letter. Belief in free trade was waning because of mounting competition from other industrial states. The country looked with greater interest on solutions to social and economic problems, and on imperial growth and international relations. Hence, lacking broad public appeal, defeated on home rule, divided, and without strong leadership, the Liberals languished in limbo while the Conservatives held office under Salisbury (1895–1902) and Balfour (1902–5). They passed legislation on behalf of the factory workers, approved Australian federation (1900), quarreled with the United States over the Venezuela boundary, strengthened imperial unity, enlarged the Empire in Africa, fought the Boer War, and competed with Germany and its allies in world trade, armaments, and diplomacy. Finally, the newly formed Labour party began to challenge the hegemony of the two traditional parties.

Britain had made great strides toward political democracy, and for more than a century had led the world in industrial growth, but it lagged behind countries like Germany in social reform. Although the government had passed numerous laws since mid-century to improve the physical well-being and comfort of the workers, much remained to be done. Moreover it was insufficiently realized that self-help could be carried only so far, and that eventually the state must exert its influence and expend a greater proportion of the national budget to alleviate poverty arising from circumstances beyond the workingman's control. Governmental and private studies made in the 1880s and 1890s showed that at least a third of the factory workers lived on marginal incomes derived entirely from weekly wages. When their income stopped even for a few weeks because of unemployment, sickness, or industrial accidents, their families suffered. Perhaps 10 per cent of the working class even in the best of times lived in squalid, overcrowded housing and were undernourished and diseased. Heavy unemployment during the depression years forced a greater national attention to social problems, as did the labor riots and strikes, particularly the London dock workers' strike of 1889, which aimed at ensuring regular work at sixpence an hour and pay for overtime.

Critics of society's seeming indifference toward the economically underprivileged were increasing in number, but traditionalists in both parties regarded them in the 1890s in much the same way that their forefathers had viewed the evangelists of political reform a century earlier. Far from being revolutionaries or radical rabble-rousers, many of the critics were moderates who passionately believed in social reform. Lord Randolph Churchill (father of Sir Winston), Joseph Chamberlain, and Charles Booth, author of *Life and Labour of the People in London* (1891–1903) and one of the earliest advocates of old-age pensions, may be counted among the moderates. It is true, however, that some of the critics were socialists who had read Karl Marx's *Capital* (1867) or who had been impressed by socialist success in France and Germany. English socialism has roots dating from at least the seventeenth century, and the utopian and Christian socialists (typified by Robert Owen and Charles Kingsley) had had some impact in earlier Victorian times, but modern British socialism dates from the 1880s. Its disciples ranged from the Marxian journalist H. M. Hyndman, the author of *A Textbook of Democracy: England for All* (1881), to the idealist William Morris, one of the founders of the Social Democratic Federation, who wanted to turn back industrial society to the halcyon days of the medieval craft guilds. Trade-unionists, particularly the unskilled workers, believed in a measure of socialism. The hard years of the depression had made them distrustful of their employers and caused them to lose faith in the willingness of the traditional parties to do anything meaningful in their behalf. Membership in trade-unions had grown sharply in the latter half of the century, and the Trades Union Congress, a national confederation of labor unions that had held its first annual meeting in 1868, had 1,500,000 members by 1892.

In that year the Congress secured the election of the Scottish miner Keir Hardie as the first Labour member of Parliament, but none of the twenty-six candidates sponsored by Hardie's Independent Labour party was elected in the general election of 1895. Finally, the Fabian Society, founded in 1893 by Sidney and Beatrice Webb, and including such brilliant figures as the playwright George Bernard Shaw, the historians H. G. Wells and G. D. H. Cole, the future prime minister Ramsay MacDonald, and Annie Besant, who had organized the London match girls, advocated the gradual democratization and socialization of Britain by peaceful legislative processes. They argued against the evils of capitalism that encouraged wasteful competition for profit and in favor of nationalizing the land and large industries such as the railroads and other means of transportation and communication, coal, electricity, and banking. Only by these means, they felt, could there be realized equal economic welfare among all classes. Under the aegis of the Trades Union Congress, in 1901 the Independent Labour party, the Social Democratic Federation, and the Fabian Society joined forces to form the British Labour party. Its influence was first sharply felt in the election of 1906, when twenty-nine Labour candidates were returned to Parliament.

In the 1890s, however, the days of Labourite power lay far in the future, and social reformers had not yet broken down the traditionalism of the Conservatives who had all but forgotten Disraeli's Tory Democracy. Salisbury and Balfour were preoccupied with world affairs and were not anxious to pass much social legislation. Nevertheless, in view of what has been said about the plight of the workingman, it will be appreciated how beneficial was the Workmen's Compensation Act (1897), which made employers liable for damages arising from industrial accidents not caused by the employee's own carelessness. Should the employer dispute a claim for compensation, he bore the burden of proof in court. In 1900, these benefits were extended to cover agricultural workers. In 1901, the Conservatives codified the numerous factory Acts passed since the Factory and Workshops Act (1878) and added several new features. The most important provisions of the 1901 Act were that children under twelve could not be employed in factories, and that those thirteen and older could be hired only on condition that they were in good health and had had at least a modicum of formal education. Safety devices and health precautions were required to protect workers against infection and industrial accidents. "Young persons" and women could be employed for no more than between fifty-five and one-half and sixty hours, depending on the industry. The Education Act (1902) created a ministry of education with authority over all tax-supported elementary, secondary, and technical schools, whether secular or denominational. Religious instruction might be given, but no one could be compelled to attend these sessions. The county borough and urban district councils (established in 1888) replaced the local school boards, which were abolished where they still existed, and had the right to oversee curricular matters through school managers. The councils were also to ensure that secondary and technical schools were provided where none existed or to supplement training provided by them. The Licensing Act (1904) empowered local authorities to close public houses in districts having too many for the public welfare, and provided funds to compensate publicans who lost their licenses for that reason.

The last few years of Victoria's reign, climaxed by her proud Diamond Jubilee in 1897, were clouded by intense international rivalry bordering on war. A dangerous dispute between the United States and Britain occurred in the 1890s over the disputed boundary between British Guiana and Venezuela. The issue went back to 1840, when the British surveyor, Sir Robert Schomburgk, had carefully plotted a boundary that the Venezuelans refused to recognize. Over the succeeding several decades they held to another boundary that included nearly one-half of Guiana's jungle wilderness. The British did not press the matter until the discovery of gold in 1893 in the disputed territory. When it appeared that they might attempt to force their will on Venezuela, the United States intervened. President Grover Cleveland forcefully argued that the boundary should be arbitrated by an international commission, but Lord Salisbury refused to accept such a settlement. There followed a succession of communiqués, the most important of which was a statement by Secretary of State Richard Olney that intervention by Britain in Venezuelan affairs would be a breach of the Monroe Doctrine, and an equally strong rebuttal by Salisbury, stating that Britain regarded the Doctrine as a dead letter. Cleveland then took matters into his own hands by proposing to Congress in 1895 that the American government appoint a commission to settle the dispute unilaterally, realizing, of course, that war with Britain might result. Salisbury kept calm and preserved the peace, for he did not wish to risk war at a time when Britain was quarreling with the Boers of South Africa. Moreover, considering the increasing tension with Germany (discussed below), Britain could ill afford to alienate the United

States, whose trade and friendship were vital to British interests. Accordingly, Salisbury consented to arbitration by a panel of two Americans, two Britons, and one Russian, who, in October, 1899, unanimously decided in favor of the British claim.

Meanwhile the Foreign Office was becoming alarmed at the turn of events in Europe. Before his retirement in 1890, German Chancellor Bismarck had skillfully engineered a treaty system that linked Austria-Hungary and Italy defensively with Germany in the Triple Alliance of 1882. He had also managed to maintain close ties with Russia, which had earlier joined Germany and Austria-Hungary in two Three Emperors' Leagues. (The first, concluded in 1873, had broken down following the affront to Russia at the Congress of Berlin [1878]; the second had collapsed as a result of a Balkan crisis in 1885 that Bismarck prevented from escalating into a general war.) Despite serious rivalry in the Balkans between Russia and Austria, he had made a treaty with Czar Alexander III in 1887 for a period of three years, a treaty that Kaiser William II refused to renew in 1890. So long as Bismarck controlled German affairs, he succeeded in his diplomatic goal of isolating France in order to deter the French from trying to recover Alsace and Lorraine, acquired by Germany in 1871, and to forestall Russian aggression against Germany's eastern frontier and territorial aggrandizement at the expense of Austria in the Balkans. But Bismarck's successors allowed France and Russia to slip through the curtains by which he had isolated them. They allied defensively in 1894, primarily as a precaution against aggression by any member of the Triple Alliance. None of these alliances directly affected Britain, whose only formal commitment in Europe was the defense of Belgian independence, which had been guaranteed by treaty in 1839. All the British prime ministers since Disraeli had followed a policy of nonalignment and nonintervention in European affairs.

This isolationist policy suited the leaders of both political parties inasmuch as they believed that Britain's strength lay in the military and economic resources of the Empire. Therefore, rather than become entangled in the web of European politics in which Britain had no immediate concern, they made an effort to strengthen the bonds uniting Britain and its Dominions through imperial conferences, the first of which convened in London in 1887. The colonial and Dominion representatives considered questions of imperial defense and commercial and social relations, and were reminded by the Colonial Office of their responsibilities to the mother country. Several colonies, although irked by Britain's condescending attitude toward them, agreed to share in the cost of strengthening the navy. Subsequent conferences held in Ottawa (1894) and in London (1897) discussed closer communications, inter-Empire preferential trade treaties, the abrogation of commercial treaties with states outside the Empire, and the establishment of a permanent imperial council to promote imperial federation (essentially a customs union). The principal advocate of federation was Colonial Secretary Joseph Chamberlain, who was anxious to promote trade within the Empire and to involve the colonies more directly in military defense. Several Dominions agreed to give money or to supply ships for the navy, but Canada refused to do either because it feared losing its identity in a combined "British" fleet.

The reluctance on the part of some colonies to support the military aspects of federation to the extent that Britain had suggested, and on the part of Britain to adopt a protectionist commercial policy of primary advantage to the colonies were factors that convinced Salisbury's ministry to abandon its policy of "splendid isolation." Other factors, of course, weighed in that decision. One was the increasing trade rivalry with Germany, which was at the heart of most other aspects of Anglo-German antipathy. Germany was rich in natural resources vital to a flourishing industrial system. Its entrepreneurs and scientists employed the newest mechanical devices and business techniques. It had an abundant supply of cheap skilled labor that produced high-quality goods respected the world over. High German tariffs excluded British-made goods while German merchandise flooded the free-trade markets of Britain and its possessions and often undercut the price of British goods in foreign markets. Moreover Germany was a fledgling but aggressive imperial power that had established colonies in German East Africa, German Southwest Africa, and Togoland and the Cameroons on the north shore of the Bay of Guinea. The Germans had also acquired several important islands in the Pacific archipelago and spheres of economic influence in southeastern China. In these regions the Germans competed with British interests, and they had encouraged the South African Boers to resist British encroachments in the Transvaal and Orange Free State. After 1900 the Germans made menacing gestures toward the French territories in northwest Africa. A third factor was Germany's announced intention at the turn of the century of constructing a railway between Berlin and Bagdad. If completed, it would have afforded Germany the opportunity to exploit the economic resources of the Near East, jeopardize British commercial and military interests in that area, and threaten British naval supremacy in the Indian Ocean. Finally, anti-British feelings were stirred in several European capitals by the Boer War. For these reasons and others that arose in the decade prior to World War I (discussed in Chapter 16), when successive British gestures toward a reconciliation with Germany came to naught, Britain sought closer relations with France, Russia, and Japan.

Before considering these treaties, mention must be made of some aspects of Britain's role in the partition of Africa and the complications this created with the other colonial powers. There is no need to recount the oft-repeated theories about the causes of New Imperialism after 1870, for the Christian missionary movement, economic exploitation, nationalism, the effect of imperialism on the prestige of political parties, altruistic humanitarianism, and the like are familiar even to casual students of modern European history. English interest in Africa dated from the early seventeenth century, when joint-stock companies sent ships and explorers to the Guinea Coast, the Red Sea, and the southern shores of the Mediterranean. More than a century and a half passed, however, before Britain gained its first permanent possession in Africa by wresting from France the settlements along the Senegal River during the Seven Years' War (1756–63). This encouraged the growth of the immensely profitable African slave trade, considered earlier, as well as of gold mining in the Gold Coast Colony. By 1815, because of the depletion of gold and the abolition of the slave trade (1807), the Bay of Guinea settlements ceased to be important to the British economy, although slavery continued illicitly well into the 1840s. By that time British attention in Africa had shifted to the Cape Colony, acquired from the Dutch during the Napoleonic War, and to exploration of the interior. By 1870, much of Africa had been traversed by traders, missionaries, and explorers from several European states. British explorers played a significant role in unveiling the secrets of the Dark Continent. In 1791, for example, Major Daniel Houghton penetrated the basins of the Gambia and Senegal for five hundred miles. During the next thirty years Mungo Park, John Peddie, and J. H. Tuckey followed the course of the Niger and the lower Congo rivers. In the 1820s, Captain Hugh Clapperton crossed the Sahara and discovered Lake Chad. Before 1840, others had tracked through the wilderness of the Sudan, Abyssinia, and the upper Nile. Under the auspices of the Royal Geographical Society, Captains Richard Burton and John Speke explored parts of Somaliland, and, in the 1850s, discovered Lakes

Tanganyika and Victoria. Meanwhile other explorers pushed northward from the Cape Colony into Natal, Mozambique, and Bechuanaland. The most famous African explorer was David Livingstone, a Lanarkshire textile worker as a young man, who in 1841 went to Bechuanaland with a hard-won medical degree to serve as a medical missionary for the London Missionary Society, one of several Christian philanthropic organizations that established medical stations in East, Central, and South Africa. He mastered native dialects, befriended numerous tribes, and charted vast stretches of the interior of Portuguese Angola, along the Zambezi River, and in the upper Congo basin. In 1866–72, he discovered the Murchison Cataracts, Victoria Falls, and Lake Nyasa. He died while striving to trace the course of the vast Congo River system, a task which the American journalist, Henry Stanley, who "found" the allegedly lost Livingstone in 1871, completed in the late 1870s. Tribesmen bore Livingstone's corpse hundreds of miles from the upper Congo to Zanzibar, and a grateful nation transported it to England for burial in Westminster Abbey.

The race for colonies in Africa inevitably produced clashes. Before 1900, Britain had several confrontations with the French, Germans, Boers, and tribesmen. Two of these—with France at Fashoda on the upper Nile and with the Boers in South Africa, who were encouraged by the French and Germans to resist British encroachments on their territory—may be taken as examples. It will be recalled that British troops suffered casualties when the Mahdi revolted in the Sudan, after which Britain evacuated Sudanese territory for about ten years. By the mid-1890s, it was becoming apparent that the French intended to enlarge their dominion at the eastern fringe of the Sahara by occupying the Sudan. This brought an Anglo-Egyptian army under Sir Herbert (later Lord) Kitchener back to Khartoum, which he captured in 1898. Meanwhile a small French force had hurried to Fashoda, situated at the headwaters of the White Nile, and had claimed the region for the Third Republic. Kitchener at once marched south, confronted the French, and forced their withdrawal. The difficulty was settled by an Anglo-French agreement that demarcated their respective spheres of interest.

The troubles with the Boers began in the early nineteenth century. In 1652, the Dutch East India Company founded Capetown, which over the next two centuries grew into a thriving port surrounded by farms owned by Dutch, German, and French colonists called Boers (or Afrikaners). The British captured the Cape in 1795 and secured international recognition of their control over it in 1814. At that time about twenty-five thousand Boers, fiercely independent farmers who disliked the regulations introduced by the British, were scattered over about a hundred thousand square miles. Boers and British got along badly from the first, but particularly after 1823, when the British tried to enforce Sabbatarian restraints, ameliorate conditions among the Boers' Hottentot slaves, and enforce their law. The abolition of slavery in 1833 particularly irked the Afrikaners, who objected to it on principle and also thought the rate of compensation insufficient. When the Colonial Office granted the Cape Colony limited representative government in 1833, the Boers were practically ignored, as was their effort to share in the profitable export trade. For these reasons the Boers began to migrate across the Cape's northern frontier. This Great Trek (climaxed in 1837–38) led ultimately to the establishment of the two small Boer republics of the Orange Free State and the Transvaal, which were carved from the rich grasslands at the cost of hundreds of Boer lives in wars with the Zulus and Matabeles. In order to gain a seaport (Durban), the Boers attempted to create a third state in Natal, but the British blocked them and annexed it in 1843. Troubles between tribesmen and Boers, and encouragement from British missionaries, philanthropists, and government officials in South Africa led the Colonial Office to annex the Boer republics in 1848, but that rash action was reversed in 1853. Repeated gestures toward reannexing the republics, however, as well as the discovery of diamonds in 1867 in southern Bechuanaland, occupied by Afrikaners, led to still another crisis, which culminated in the Cape Colony's annexation of the diamond fields. In 1877, Parliament passed enabling legislation for a union of the South African states, Boer as well as British. In that year the Transvaal was annexed, infuriating the Boers and plunging Britain into a sanguinary war with the Zulus in which the Boers were already involved. Once the Zulus were beaten, the Boers demanded the retrocession of the Transvaal, and when the British offered them only colonial status, they went to war in 1880–81. Boer victories, notably at Majuba Hill (February, 1881) in northern Natal, forced the British to agree to the Pretoria Convention, which granted the Afrikaners complete self-government within the Empire.

During the next fifteen years, British rule was gradually extended northward into Bechuanaland and the region northeast of Natal. Cecil Rhodes, who had come to South Africa in 1870 and made millions in the diamond mines, and who dreamed of a Cape to Cairo railway through a solid block of British territory, persuaded the Colonial Office to establish a protectorate over Bechuanaland (1885) and to give his chartered South Africa Company control of the Rhodesian territory northeast of the Boer republics. Imperialist action of this kind worried the Boers, as did the intrusion of thousands of Uitlanders (Outsiders) in consequence of the discovery of gold in 1886 on the Witwatersrand near Johannesburg in the Transvaal. The Uitlanders soon outnumbered the Boers two to one and demanded equal civil rights; the Boers overtaxed them, refused to allow them to vote or stand for office, and passed other discriminatory legislation that produced hard feelings, leading the Uitlanders to appeal to the British government for protection. The president of the Transvaal, Paul Kruger, pro-German and an Anglophobe since his participation in the Great Trek, believed that the British intended to annex the Boer states. He had good reason to suspect their intentions. In December, 1895, Dr. L. S. Jameson, one of Rhodes's lieutenants, had made a raid into Johannesburg, but had failed to carry off a military *coup d'état,* which forced Rhodes to resign the governorship of Cape Colony and brought Kruger a congratulatory telegram from Kaiser William II. Kruger alleged that Colonial Secretary Chamberlain had engineered the plot, and, although the latter's complicity in it has never been definitely established, the Afrikaners were convinced of it. Encouraged by the Germans and fearful of British intentions, Kruger rejected British offers to mediate the Uitlanders' complaints and, in October, 1899, declared war.

Historians have meticulously studied the Anglo-Boer War of 1899–1902, but its true causes will probably never be explained to everyone's satisfaction. Certainly the long and bitter duel between British and Boers since 1814 must be taken into account. Otherwise scholars disagree. Did the British hope to annex the Boer states outright or to include them in a South African confederation? Was Chamberlain involved in the Jameson raid? How much stock did the British put in the economic gains to be had from the gold and diamond mines? Did public opinion on both sides force the politicians into war? Would Kruger have backed down if Britain had made concessions? Historians have asked these and other questions without arriving at many conclusions. It is true, however, that it took 350,000 British troops to defeat a heroic Boer army of 40,000 at a cost to Britain of £250,000,000 and 30,000 lives. Much of the world, including a significant minority in England led by the rising Liberal leader David Lloyd George, opposed the war on the grounds that Britain had conducted herself badly in her policies toward the Boers, and several Dominions grudgingly gave the mother country only token military support. The Boers proved courageous soldiers, crack shots, and experts in guerrilla warfare, the more so because the enemy destroyed their farms and imprisoned their families in detention camps where thousands perished. They were never technically defeated, even after they lost their two capital cities, but overwhelming odds and exhaustion forced them to the peace table, where the equally weary British accorded them the respect that their magnificent effort warranted. The crown annexed the two republics, but it paid the Boers £3,000,000 in compensation for property losses, recognized their language on an equal basis with English, and promised them self-government at the earliest opportunity. The Transvaal obtained home rule in 1906; the Orange Free State in 1907. In 1910, they joined the Cape Colony and Natal in the Union of South Africa, which proved its loyalty to Britain in World War I under the leadership of Jan Christian Smuts.

Colonial rivalry in the Far East was also intense. Mindful of protecting the interests of India and Australia, the Foreign and Colonial Offices anxiously watched the rebellious natives on India's northwest frontier, French expansion in Indo-China, and tension among Russia, China, and Japan over Korea and southeastern China, where the Americans, British, Germans, Russians, and French increased their shares of the China trade by enlarging their spheres of economic influence. The British managed with great difficulty to maintain a foothold in China, and acquired important colonies including the Fiji Islands (1874), northern Borneo (1884), Burma (1885), and much of New Guinea (1886). They also controlled the lion's share of the China trade until the Sino-Japanese War (1894–95) bared the Chinese Empire's weakness and precipitated a rush by European powers to share in the spoils. The Russians, supported by France and Germany, forced Japan to withdraw from Manchuria, and for this aid to China received rights in the important harbor of Port Arthur. The Germans were given economic control of the Shantung peninsula and a lease of Kiaochow. The French built railways into the mining country of Kwangsi and Kwangtung provinces. The British also profited, obtaining ninety-nine-year leases of the port of Weihaiwei (opposite Port Arthur) and the Kowloon peninsula (opposite Hong Kong) as well as the reaffirmation of their economic privileges in the Yangtze Valley. Even so, they feared the results of further partition of China and for that reason supported the United States in proposing the open door policy, an agreement

among all the interested nations except Russia to refrain from excluding any nation from trade in areas controlled by them. Although this
policy helped to allay imperialist fever, Chinese nationalists had already
been provoked to the point of rebellion against all foreigners. In 1900,
these "Boxers" (a colloquial translation of the name of an organization
called the Society of Harmonious Fists) slaughtered embassy and con-
sular officials, missionaries, and converts to Christianity. This brought
a multinational expeditionary force to Peking to restore order, which
was kept until the outbreak of the Russo-Japanese War in 1904.

The inflammatory world situation described in the preceding pages
forced Britain to seek allies. The United States was first approached,
but, despite its gratitude to Britain for helping to forestall European
intervention in the Spanish-American War, it had no intention of becoming ensnared in problems outside the Western Hemisphere. Britain
also approached the Germans in a series of talks in 1899-1902 between
Chamberlain (later replaced by Lord Lansdowne) and the German
ambassador in London, Paul Hatzfeldt. These failed because of Germany's new naval building program and its desire for additional territories. It felt confident with good reason: it had what seemed to be
a good military alliance system; it had made giant industrial and colonial strides; it had the strongest army on the Continent; and it began in
1897 to build a powerful navy that soon challenged Britain's two-power
standard (under which the Admiralty tried to maintain a navy equal
in strength to the naval power of any two other Great Powers). The
Admiralty consequently spent during the next decade vast sums of
money on a new fleet of speedier, larger, and deadlier battleships like
the *Dreadnought,* launched in 1906.

Britain's overtures to Japan, France, and Russia succeeded. The
Anglo-Japanese Alliance (1902) provided that if either signatory went
to war in the Far East (presumably against Russia), the other would
remain neutral. It thus allowed the Japanese a free hand against Russia
and enabled Britain to withdraw most of its ships and troops to other
theaters of possible conflict with the assurance that Japan would protect
the colonies in the Far East. Britain next negotiated the Entente Cordiale with France in 1904. The reasons behind the Anglo-French *rapprochement,* which marked a significant departure in British policy
toward France (only six years earlier they had nearly gone to war over
the Sudan), are too complex to explain fully. The death in 1901 of Victoria, who was Kaiser William II's grandmother and sympathetic toward
Germany, brought her son, Edward VII (1901-10), to the throne. Hav-

ing frequently visited France and come to appreciate its cultural tradition, he hoped for greater Anglo-French understanding. Salisbury, both prime minister and foreign secretary, had had so much difficulty with Frenchmen in Africa, Indo-China, and elsewhere that he had grown to dislike them. At his resignation in 1902, Lord Lansdowne, a Francophile, took over at the Foreign Office. French and English businessmen urged their governments to reconcile their differences for the sake of trade, and the military in both countries saw virtue in an alliance against the Central Powers. Finally, both signatories had interests to guard in North Africa: Britain in Egypt and the Sudan, and France in Algeria. Accordingly, France surrendered whatever claims it had in Egypt while Britain promised not to interfere with French desires to establish a protectorate over Morocco, which Germany preferred for economic reasons to see politically independent. The Anglo-Russian Entente (1907) is explainable in terms of business and the two nations' long rivalry in Persia and Afghanistan. The discovery of vast reserves of petroleum in Persia about 1900 attracted Russian and British drilling concerns. Britain won the greatest concessions from the shah, but Russia also acquired a share of the oil fields. Moreover, having been beaten in the Russo-Japanese War, Russia was anxious to avoid further conflict. Consequently, Russia and Britain took from Persia (which had no say in the decision) spheres of influence, the northern part becoming a Russian sphere, the southern part a British sphere, and the middle part a neutral zone in which both promised not to seek special economic concessions. Russia also promised not to threaten India and to recognize British control of Afghan affairs, and both agreed to stay out of Tibet.

In 1905, the Liberals took advantage of waning Conservative support to force Balfour's resignation. Both his and Salisbury's administrations had been preoccupied with foreign affairs, which had not gone well, and they had practically ignored the public clamor for social reform. The new prime minister, Sir Henry Campbell-Bannerman (1836–1908), former war minister under Lord Rosebery and Liberal leader in the Commons, chose a cabinet of progressive, bright administrators, the most important of whom were Herbert Asquith (Exchequer), Sir Edward Grey (Foreign Office), David Lloyd George (Board of Trade), R. B. Haldane (War Office), and Herbert Gladstone, the former prime minister's son, who assumed the crucial post of Home Secretary. It was crucial because the Liberals won the election of 1906 with the largest majority of any party since 1832 on the strength of a forthright platform that proposed to disestablish the Anglican Church in Wales, uphold free trade (the Conservatives, increasingly concerned about the trade rivalry with Germany, now favored tariffs), abolish plural voting in Parliamentary elections, make tax reform, pay members of Parliament, pass an Irish home rule bill, and reform the House of Lords. In addition, the Liberals hoped to enact education and labor legislation. Much of this program was adopted into law before World War I.

Campbell-Bannerman inherited a difficult situation with the trade-unions. They had recently found new strength in an association with the infant Labour party, but their hard-won rights were once more challenged in the famous Taff Vale decision in the Lords (1901), which had ruled in favor of the Taff Vale Railway in southeastern Wales, against which the railway union had struck in August, 1900. Since the Lords held the union responsible for damages caused during the strike, it ultimately had to pay the railway company £23,000. The union had appealed the case to the Supreme Court, which ruled that the trade dispute legislation of 1871-76 (see pp. 474-475 and 476-478) protected unions only against criminal suits, not civil suits, for which they might still be liable for damages. The Liberals, concerned lest workingmen throw their votes entirely on the side of the new Labour party, were anxious to placate them. They therefore passed the Trade Disputes Act (1906), which immunized unions against claims for damages arising from strikes and affirmed their right to picket peacefully. Parliament also adopted other measures to assist workers. The Workmen's Compensation Act (1906) extended the disabilities under which laborers earning under £250 annually might be compensated to include occupational diseases, and added other occupations to the long list covered by the 1897 Act. In 1908, a Mines Act gave colliers an eight-hour day.

The Liberals made even more sweeping social reforms under Asquith (1852-1928, later earl of Oxford and Asquith), who succeeded Campbell-Bannerman upon his resignation in 1908 and remained in office until 1916. A member of Parliament since 1886, a noted jurist and free-trader, and a cabinet member at various times since 1892, he courageously attacked educational, unemployment, and housing problems. For example, despite the Lords' efforts to reduce government expenses, the Liberals passed the Old-Age Pension Act (1908), under which both men and women workers over seventy, provided their annual income did not exceed £31 10s., were entitled to collect a weekly allowance of from one to five shillings. The Labor Exchange Act (1908), sponsored by Winston Churchill, then a junior minister in the government, established a national employment service under government auspices. Through the efforts of John Burns, the first Labour member of any cabinet and president of the Local Government Board, Parliament passed the House and Town Planning Act (1909), which empowered local officials to demolish dilapidated buildings, erect suitable dwellings, and repair unsanitary houses at the owner's expense. The Trade Boards Act (1909) stipulated that those employed in four of the so-called "sweated industries" (those that paid wages insufficient to enable their adult employees to maintain a minimal standard of living) should receive a living wage fixed by local boards composed of employers, employees, and appointed members. The original Act covered chain-making, tailoring, mechanical lace-finishing, and paper box-making; subsequent legislation in 1913 and 1920 extended its benefits to nearly fifty other industries. An Act of 1907 aided small farmers. Since the depression of the 1880s, because of heavy competition from foreign grain, many farms under fifty acres had been incorporated into larger farms, and the number of smaller farms had steadily declined. The government had therefore begun to encourage truck farming as a means of diversifying agriculture, and to that end Parliament had enacted a law in 1892 that authorized local officials to buy land from large landowners who had refused to partition their holdings and to sell it in small parcels. The 1907 Act put more teeth into the law by transferring this operation to the central government.

The Liberals had less success with educational reform. In 1906–8, they passed legislation that provided lunch money to impoverished elementary pupils and protected children and juvenile delinquents from mistreatment in industrial schools and reformatories. The Liberals and Labourites also hoped to amend the Education Act of 1902, which had offended Nonconformists by continuing governmental grants to the Anglican voluntary schools. Since this aid was provided through local school taxes, many Nonconformists preferred to go to court rather than pay them. The Liberals therefore introduced a new bill that proposed to continue state support to the Anglican schools, but only if religious instruction was barred during the regular school week and if none of the schools used the funds to support catechetical teaching on weekends. The Commons passed the measure with the support of more than two hundred Nonconformist members, but the Lords rejected it.

The Lords also blocked passage of bills to abolish plural voting and to reduce the number of licensed public houses. Voters were entitled to cast ballots in any constituency in which they owned property, a practice made easier by the fact that elections were held on different days in various constituencies. This gave a decided advantage to property owners and was widely regarded as undemocratic, but the Conservative-dominated upper House refused to surrender a privilege that had long benefited the Tories. The licensing bill (1908) likewise foundered in the Lords, which rejected the proposal to revoke thirty thousand liquor licenses (with compensation to vendors) over a period of fourteen years, after which time licensing was to be controlled by local option.

For centuries the Lords had been a powerful political body. Despite repeated efforts since the late eighteenth century to harness its authority, it had come through the reform era unscathed. As its membership was based on hereditary right, it was not subject to the popular will. Primarily for that reason, as well as because the Lords had often frustrated the passage of Liberal legislation, all the Liberal prime ministers since Gladstone first took office in 1868 had proposed that the Lords' authority should somehow be limited. The idea was overwhelmingly supported in the Commons and among the electorate. The Lords' blockage of key legislation since 1905, and particularly its disapproval of the budget of 1909, brought on its own downfall. At the center of the controversy over the budget was Lloyd George (1863–1945), a stern, erratic son of a Welsh teacher who, because of his father's early death, had had to struggle to become a lawyer. He entered Parliament in 1890, committed to do something meaningful in behalf of the common man. This avid opponent of Tory imperialism and irreconcilable enemy of the landed aristocracy was appointed Chancellor of the Exchequer in 1908 by Asquith.

The Liberal budgets since 1906 had been commendably frugal, but Lloyd George's so-called People's Budget, designed to make war on poverty and against the privileged, called for much heavier government spending on old-age pensions, and other social-service obligations underwritten by the central government, at the same time that the country was paying for the naval build-up resulting from the arms race with Germany. Lloyd George estimated that unless additional sources of revenue were found, the deficit for the coming fiscal year would increase the national debt by £16,000,000. Being a free-trader, he rejected the Conservatives' suggestion that the additional revenue be raised through higher tariffs. Instead, he proposed to tax the wealthy, particularly large landowners, by imposing higher taxes on unearned increments (the increased value of real estate, especially idle land, determined by a national survey of all land, which would show the profits made over the original purchase prices) payable when the property was inherited or otherwise changed hands; on large incomes over £3000 with a supertax on income over £5000; and on holders of liquor licenses. The land taxes aroused the strongest opposition, but Lloyd George was determined to impose them, not only to raise revenue, but also to assist the owners of small farms. Some property owners were holding their land in the hope of making more profit in a period of rapidly mounting land prices; others had converted arable land into expansive lawns, hunting preserves, golf courses, and the like. Such practices were nearly as common in metropolitan areas like London, where property owners refused to sell land badly needed for housing until prices rose, as they were in rural areas. As we have already seen, the government had since 1892 passed legislation to induce landowners to part with some of their holdings. Lloyd George's proposal was aimed at forcing them to sell or lease the land by taxing it so heavily that it would be too expensive to keep.

The Commons passed the budget on November 4 by 379 votes to 149; the Lords rejected it by 350 votes to 75. Since the seventeenth century, when England fought a civil war partly over the Commons' right to initiate money bills, the Lords had rarely challenged that right, and whenever the upper House had attempted to amend such bills, the Commons had thrown them out and sent up new bills, often incorporating the Lords' suggestions but preserving its control over finances. Hence it was the practice that the Lords could neither initiate money bills nor amend them, but simply approve or reject them. Not a single money bill had been challenged by the Lords since 1860. For these reasons the Commons was provoked by the upper House's attempt to amend the budget. But the Lords argued that this budget was not essentially a money bill, for it included provision of funds and tax measures designed to circumvent the earlier defeat of several Liberal bills, as for example the licensing bill. The Commons, on the other hand, argued that the Lords' action was unconstitutional, and Asquith decided to put the issue to the country in a general election, which would serve as a popular referendum on the budget. The election of January, 1910, was indecisive, for neither Liberals nor Conservatives gained a clear majority, forcing Asquith to carry on a coalition ministry composed of Liberals, Labourites, and Irish Nationalists, although the Lords finally agreed to pass the Budget Bill in the spring of 1910. The death of Edward VII in May automatically dissolved Parliament and necessitated another election in the following December which brought essentially the same results. As it was thought untoward to immediately confront the new monarch, George V (1910–35), with what had become the most important constitutional crisis since 1688, the coalition ministry decided to postpone action on a bill introduced the previous February to reform the House of Lords. Accordingly, Asquith delayed until June, 1911, by which time he had secured King George's promise that, if the Lords rejected the Parliament Bill, he would create enough new peers to override its opposition. Recognizing that further resistance was hopeless, the Lords passed it in August, 1911.

The Parliament Act abolished the Lords' right to veto money bills passed by the Commons by stipulating that they would become law one month after their introduction in the Lords regardless of its action on them. It further stipulated that bills other than money bills, if passed by the Commons in three successive sessions over a period of at least two years, would likewise automatically become law irrespective of what the Lords did. Finally, the Act fixed the statutory term of Parliament, formerly seven years, at five. At the same time Parliament enacted legislation granting £400 annual salaries to all members. This was done primarily to assist the Labourites, who had formerly been supported with trade-union funds until the Osborne case (1909) declared this practice illegal. Save for the admission of women to the franchise, an issue hotly debated before World War I (discussed in Chapter 16), these two Acts completed the century-long struggle to attain popular democracy. After 1911 the Lords could delay but not block the passage of any measure—but, as we shall see, its role in the twentieth century has been far from inconsequential.

The Liberals enjoyed a very good year in 1911, for, in addition to their singular triumph over the Lords, they passed the National Health Insurance Act, designed to protect workers against unemployment through accident or illness. It provided health insurance on a compulsory basis for all manual laborers between sixteen and seventy. Funds used to provide weekly allowances and free medical attention for no more than twenty-six weeks were raised by assessing men fourpence a week, women threepence, the employer threepence, and the government twopence. The Act also provided, on a limited basis, some unemployment insurance for workers in industries particularly prone to layoffs. That section of the Act was intended to be experimental and applied at first only to a few industries such as the building trades, iron foundries, sawmills, and shipbuilding. The unemployed were to receive seven shillings a week for up to fifteen weeks from a fund raised by assessing workers and their employers twopence halfpenny a week.

In all the agitation for Liberal reform since 1906 the figure of Lloyd George looms large. He was also the guiding spirit behind the disestablishment of the Anglican Church in Wales in 1914. At a time when the Irish were once more agitating for home rule, a topic that can more conveniently be discussed in the following chapter in connection with the Irish war effort, the Welsh were reminded that the Protestant Church of Ireland had been disestablished and partially disendowed in 1869. Like the Irish, the majority of the Welsh were non-Anglican, but, in addition to supporting their own Nonconformist chapels and clergy, they had to contribute tithes to the Church of England. The Liberals had several times attempted to relieve the Welsh of this burden, especially since 1893, but each time Victoria, a devout adherent of the Established Church, had managed to check their efforts with the help of Conservative High-churchmen. But the Commons passed the disestablishment bills in three successive sessions in 1912–14, each time over the objection of the Lords. The third time the bill came under the provisions of the Parliament Act and consequently became law with the king's assent in September, 1914. The Act separated from the Church of England the four Welsh dioceses and deprived their bishops of their seats in the House of Lords. Henceforth contributions to any Church became voluntary, and the Anglican Church was disassociated from the government in Wales. Certain Anglican endowments were transferred to create a fund from which monies were subsequently drawn to support educational and other public services. As the world war had by then begun, however, enforcement of the law was suspended, first for one year, and then until the consummation of peace.

While Parliament had been preoccupied with domestic affairs, the Foreign Office watched apprehensively as the machinations of the Great Powers on the Continent led the world into the most horrendous war ever inflicted upon mankind. We have already considered some of its remote causes. How they developed and why they resulted in a world war must be our next concern.

16

World War I and Its Legacy, 1914–1929

For most of the nineteenth century, Britain was the strongest world power by virtue of its command of the seas, its vast empire, and its industrial and commercial predominance. Exploiting this dominant position, it had also been the major arbiter of international problems in accordance with the principles of the balance of power and its policy of "splendid isolation," which meant the avoidance of entangling alliances and military dependency on other powers. But the rise of Germany and France as military, commercial, and colonial powers, the division of Europe by 1894 into two armed camps through the alliance and alignment systems, dangerous incidents like that at Fashoda in the Sudan, world-wide antipathy toward Britain as a result of the Boer War, and the increasing reluctance of the Dominions to sacrifice their interests in favor of plans such as Joseph Chamberlain's imperial federation, forced Britain to reconsider its isolationist foreign policy. Truth to tell, in 1900 Britain had no friends among the Great Powers. Business, colonial, and naval rivalry had alienated the French and Germans, and the British had long quarreled with the Russians over the spoliation of the Ottoman Empire and the Middle East. Furthermore, although Britain generally supported the Europeans' commercial interests in the Far East, it could not rely on the support of Russia, France, or Germany in the event of war in that area. Accordingly, the Foreign Office at first sought to ease tensions with Germany and its allies and, when that policy failed, made treaties short of outright military commitment with France, Russia, and Japan. Having done so, in the decade preceding World War I the Foreign Office continued to act as an "honest broker" in attempting to settle recurrent and increasingly explosive international incidents in the hope of averting widespread European war.

Intense international rivalry bordering on anarchy characterized the decade preceding World War I. A succession of crises beginning with Morocco in 1905 and culminating in the eleventh-hour attempts to avert war in July, 1914, marked the tortuous road to Armageddon. Such a state of European affairs was in itself not unusual. Earlier sections of this book have described how Britain and Germany responded to their colonial, naval, and commercial rivalry; how French and German tempers had flared over the perennial issue of Alsace-Lorraine; and how Austro-Russian competition in the Balkans had brought those nations to the brink of war. One could far more easily infer from these circumstances that World War I was inevitable than appreciate that it might have been averted or at least localized if one or another of the Great Powers had modified or moderated its demands. But war as an instrument of national policy was still a vital part of the statesman's stock in trade. Accordingly, Europeans generally believed that any war fought over Alsace-Lorraine, Morocco, the Balkans, or other trouble spots would be of short duration and limited in theater and in objectives.

To many people, Europe seemed no more bellicose in 1905 or 1910 than it had been for most of the later nineteenth century. The Great Powers had often quarreled, yet they had managed to avoid catastrophe. They had all at one time or another intruded into the affairs of weaker states to keep the peace, end a war, rewrite a treaty, stop a revolution, or acquire economic advantages. This situation was little different in the early twentieth century except for one very important element—the blind intransigence of the heads of government whose shortsightedness, selfishness, and refusal to compromise rendered a peaceful settlement of national differences nearly impossible. A few statesmen, some Britons among them, recognized the peril of war at the last moment and tried, though unsuccessfully, to avert it.

Many books have been written about the causes of World War I. Most of their authors have attempted to ascribe war guilt to this or that power or combination of powers. Most scholars, however, have been content to argue that, in varying degrees, all the belligerents were involved one way or another in the machinations that led to the war. While its causes will probably never be explained to everyone's satisfaction, it is well to remember its results—that World War I cost the belligerents nearly $275,000,000,000 in property losses; that 65,000,000 soldiers fought in the war; that 22,000,000 men were wounded; and that almost 9,000,000 were killed in the fighting.

Britain's decision to sign the Entente with France in 1904, a decision that reversed a half century of British policy in Europe, was a fateful one. On the face of it, it seemed a harmless-enough treaty: Britain recognized France's interests in Morocco and France forswore any claim on Egypt. But the agreement angered Germany, which had investments in Morocco and therefore wanted to protect the latter's independence. The Great Powers customarily notified one another of arrangements such as those concluded in the Entente. Britain notified Germany officially, but France failed to do so. Hence Germany took it as a diplomatic affront and responded accordingly, the more so because German economic interests were jeopardized by France's overt efforts to introduce economic reforms designed to make the sultan a French puppet. Moreover, French intervention in Morocco violated the multilateral convention signed in Madrid in 1880, where the Great Powers had agreed that Morocco's status should not be altered without international agreement. For these reasons, as well as because Germany hoped to drive a wedge between France and Britain, thereby destroying the Entente Cordiale, in March, 1905, Kaiser William II visited Tangier, where he made a characteristically blunt speech in behalf of Moroccan independence. War talk ensued for a few weeks during which time Britain stood staunchly behind France. War was averted largely through the good offices of the United States, which arranged arbitration of the dispute at the Algeciras Conference in January, 1906. All the powers there, except Austria, were ranged on the side of France, and, consequently, the diplomats agreed to create an international Franco-Spanish police force to regulate trade through eight Moroccan ports and a Moroccan bank whose stockholders were predominantly French.

The first Moroccan crisis had apparently been resolved amicably, but it had serious consequences. Since France had gained the advantages, the Germans felt humiliated and angry. Their anger mounted when French marines were sent to Morocco in 1907 on the pretext that native riots endangered the lives of French citizens. The Moroccan crisis had also drawn the ties between Britain and France closer. Although they misunderstood feeling in England, the French were led to assume that Britain would fight on France's side in the event of war with Germany. This French attitude was encouraged by British military leaders who, in 1905–6, 1911, and 1913, held conversations with their French counterparts to map offensive and defensive plans against the possibility of an unprovoked German attack against France through Belgium. While the British signed no written pledges, the French concluded that the conversations amounted to a moral obligation on the part of the British to help them should occasion arise. Britain's agreement in 1907 with Russia (France's military ally), which defined the signatories' territorial spheres of influence in Persia and generally cleared the air between them, further helped to coalesce Anglo-French interests and to range Britain more clearly against Germany. At the same time the Germans began to voice grave concern over what they believed to be a British attempt to encircle them through the French and Russian treaties, opposition to the Berlin-Bagdad railway scheme, and naval build-up. Although the Germans probably read too much into the aims of British diplomacy, which were essentially nonmilitary and nonaggressive, their attitudes assumed greater importance than the facts. The facts were that Britain had simply honored its treaty obligations in the Moroccan crisis; that Foreign Minister Sir Edward Grey had not committed Britain to the defense of France; and that, in 1908 at least, there was no formal joint military agreement obliging the landing of British forces in France in the event of a German war. However, as the European situation grew more serious through the Balkan crises in 1908–9 and 1912–13, the British cabinet came to feel that the country's interests lay with France should war come. In 1914, consequently, although Britain need not have helped France, to do otherwise, as Grey pointed out to Parliament, would leave the British people "isolated, discredited, and hated; and there would be before us nothing but a miserable and ignoble future."

Austria's annexation of Bosnia and Herzegovina in 1908, in violation of the Congress of Berlin (1878), had no material effect on the status of the two states, which Austria had administered since the Congress, but it was an affront to Russia, which had consistently opposed Austrian expansion in the Balkans. The situation might have touched off an Austro-Russian war but for Germany's support of Austria, Russia's unpreparedness, and the refusal of both Britain and France to support Russia in the Balkans. Hence the Russians backed down and Austria retained the territories. Britain's reluctance to intrude in an area in which it had no vital interests to protect is understandable, but France's refusal to assist Russia needs a word of explanation. There were two factors involved. The first was France's decision not to interfere in Balkan affairs in view of the more pressing danger of provoking Austria's ally, Germany; the second stemmed from an understanding reached between France and Germany over Morocco in 1909, which temporarily eased tensions by admitting Germans to equal economic opportunities.

France's failure to live up to this agreement led to the second Moroccan crisis in 1911. In that year, arguing that the sultan had not maintained order, the French landed troops at Fez. When Germany protested this violation of the Algeciras accord and complained of France's ignoring the promises it had made in 1909, the French turned a deaf ear. The German government consequently sent a warship, the *Panther,* to the closed Moroccan port of Agadir (May, 1911), ostensibly to protect German businessmen (although there were none there), but actually to save face, to deter further French inroads in Morocco, and hopefully to gain colonial compensation elsewhere. Although publication of diplomatic papers has since made it clear that neither France nor Germany would have gone to war over Morocco in 1911, that fact was not then known. A war that seemed imminent was averted when Germany recognized France's protectorate over Morocco so long as it did not interfere with German business interests, and, in return, France ceded some territory in French Equatorial Africa to Germany.

War had once more been averted, but the crisis had heightened tensions between Germany on the one hand, and France and Britain on the other. Anti-German sentiment quickened in France and England, and drew them closer together. Grey had taken a strong stand during this crisis, warning Germany not to make exorbitant demands in Morocco or attempt to arrive at a settlement with France without consulting Britain. Although the cabinet felt that Germany would not fight over Morocco, it was concerned that the Kaiser might try to establish a naval base at Agadir. Some ministers favored sending a squadron to Moroccan waters to counter Germany's show of force; others, who prevailed, among them Grey, Asquith, and Lloyd George, preferred to watch and wait, being ready to take military action should Germany try to bully France into making concessions dangerous to British naval superiority in the western Mediterranean.

In 1912–13, Balkan nationalism flared up anew against Turkey. At the Congress of Berlin in 1878, Disraeli, who was anxious to guard British influence in the lands washed by the Aegean and eastern Mediterranean, had seen to it that the provinces of Macedonia and Thrace, which stretched from Salonica to Constantinople, remained a part of the Turkish Empire. This annoyed the Balkan Christians and remained a sore point for the next thirty-five years. In 1911, the Italians invaded the Turkish North African provinces of Tripoli and Cyrenaica, and forced Turkey to weaken its defenses in European Turkey by sending the bulk of its army to Africa. The next year, Serbia, Montenegro, Bulgaria, and Greece invaded Macedonia, in order, they said, to free Christian peoples from their Mohammedan overlords, but, of course, they had in mind the division of Macedonia among themselves. The Great Powers, realizing that the situation could easily involve Austria and Russia, intervened to bring the war to an end in May, 1913, through an international conference held at London. The treaty that was drawn up practically ousted Turkey from Europe, but within a year the victorious Serbs, Montenegrins, Bulgars, and Greeks quarreled over the spoils and a Second Balkan War was fought. The significance of that war is threefold: it marked the rise of Serbia as the most important power in the Balkans—a power that had territorial ambitions toward Bosnia-Herzegovina and bitterly hated the Austrians; the war had been fought in violation of a settlement arranged by the Great Powers, signifying that their influence in Balkan affairs had been seriously weakened; and, Turkey, having lost two wars without help from either Britain or France, its traditional protectors, and fearful of Russian aims in European Turkey, gravitated steadily toward closer economic and military relations with Germany.

The Balkan situation needed only a spark to ignite a massive explosion. A young Bosnian patriot provided that spark by assassinating Austrian Archduke Ferdinand and his wife during a state visit to Sarajevo, Bosnia, on June 28, 1914. This outrage, which the Austrians insisted had been plotted with the knowledge of the Serbian government, led Austria first to consult Germany, and then, having secured permission from its ally to act as it saw fit, send Serbia an ultimatum. It contained a demand that Serbia satisfy ten points including the suppression of agitation against Austria, the outlawing of secret societies, and Austrian participation in the prosecution within Serbia of conspirators. Deeming the Serbian reply unsatisfactory, Austria declared war on July 28. The worst fears of Europe were at once realized: it became apparent that the Austro-Serbian war could neither be localized, as Germany and Austria had expected, nor limited to the original belligerents. Russia was unwilling to see its rival crush Serbia and consequently completed mobilizing its forces on July 30. France and Germany did likewise on July 31–August 1 in accordance with the obligations contained in their treaties with Russia and Austria. Germany then declared war on Russia and France on August 1 and August 3, respectively.

The British cabinet, particularly Sir Edward Grey at the Foreign Office, had watched these events on the Continent with grave concern. Britain had had serious differences with Germany since 1905, but it had steadfastly avoided concluding any formal military commitment that would have provoked its rival. Yet, British efforts to assuage German apprehension, including an offer to curtail the naval build-up on condition that Germany should do the same, and statements that Britain no longer opposed the Berlin-Bagdad railway project or additional German imperialistic ventures in Africa, were met coldly in Berlin. In addition, Lord Haldane's mission to Berlin in February, 1912, aimed at softening hard feelings, collapsed when Germany refused to talk seriously unless Britain promised to remain neutral in the event of war.

Despite Grey's efforts, British relations with Germany steadily deteriorated. By way of precaution, on July 26 the cabinet ordered the British fleet, then on trial maneuvers, to remain on the alert, but at the same time proposed to Germany, France, and Italy that their ambassadors should confer in London on ways and means to avert war. Germany spurned the suggestion out of loyalty to its Austrian ally, and the Austro-Serbian war rapidly escalated into a world war. As all the major powers except Britain had entered the conflict by August 2, the cabinet had to decide what to do. Grey, Asquith, and Haldane believed that Britain had no choice but to fight, and the Conservatives and Irish Nationalists in Parliament supported this view. Yet it is doubtful that the country would actually have gone to war at this time had not Germany violated Belgian neutrality, which Britain, France, and Prussia had guaranteed in 1839. Germany refused to honor this obligation because, in accordance with the plan formulated by Count Schlieffen (German chief of staff, 1891–1905), Germany's offensive necessitated an attack through Belgium aimed at Paris in order to knock France out of the war before the Russians could launch an attack on the eastern front. On August 2 Germany demanded of Belgium the right to transport troops through its territory. Belgium refused, and, on the fourth, German troops invaded it.

That action resolved all differences of opinion among members of the cabinet and Parliament. On the third, Grey made a historic speech in Parliament in which he advised it for the first time of the military conversations conducted with France since 1905 and the matter of honor involved in going to the assistance of Belgium and France. A few hours before his speech, Grey had promised with the cabinet's approval not to allow the German fleet to enter the Channel or North Sea. On the fourth, the Germans left unanswered the British ultimatum that Germany should immediately withdraw its troops from Belgium. When it had not answered by the deadline of midnight, August 4–5, Britain was at war.

All the Dominions and territories of the Empire rallied to Britain's defense against the Central Powers. Before the awful slaughter of four years of war ended on November 11, 1918, more than 8,600,000 British and Empire troops had been enlisted, of whom more than 3,000,-000 were killed, wounded, or missing in action. While the United Kingdom organized itself magnificently—it had 5,704,000 men under arms—the Empire likewise contributed immensely to the war effort. India supplied 1,100,000 men; Australia, 417,000; New Zealand (granted Dominion status in 1907), 220,000; South Africa, 136,000; and the colonies, about 150,000. Canada, whose population was approximately one-thirteenth that of the United States, suffered as many casualties as its southern neighbor, incurred a war debt equal to about seven times its prewar debt of $385,000,000, and had approximately 8 per cent of its total population of about eight million in uniform.

Both groups of belligerents generally believed that the war would be of short duration, and entered the conflict with enthusiasm—an enthusiasm that the first three months on the western front soon dulled. In accordance with the Schlieffen plan, five German armies under the command of Helmuth von Moltke swept across the Belgian, Luxembourgian, and French frontiers in a campaign designed to outflank French defenses, capture Paris, and humble the enemy before the less efficient Russian forces could cause any difficulty in the east. The plan failed. Belgium was rapidly overcome, but the campaign took three times longer than anticipated. With ninety thousand British troops under Sir John French in the field by late August, the Anglo-French-Belgian army commanded by Marshal Joffre fought a retreating campaign that was as costly for the enemy as it was for them. Along a hundred-mile front on the Marne River, after five days of heavy fighting, the Allies broke the German offensive on September 10 and rolled it back to the Aisne. Paris had been saved and the German offensive foiled. The French and British also stopped the enemy's advance to the sea by preventing the capture of the ports of Dunkirk, Calais, and Boulogne, thereby protecting the Anglo-French communication lines. As winter closed in, the opposing forces dug a system of trenches extending from the Belgian coast to the Swiss frontier. Despite a number of major offensives by both sides, none of which was successful in breaking the enemy's lines until the collapse of the last German drive in May, 1918, no more than a few thousand yards of no man's land changed hands. It was drenched with the blood of hundreds of thousands of soldiers, torn by shells and tank tracks, crisscrossed with barbed wire and bunkers, infected with poison gas, and strewn with the human and material debris of war. These first three months of the war in the west set the pattern for the next three years. The months from August through October also shocked the sensibilities of politicians and public alike: they now realized that the short, little war everyone had envisaged had grown into a Gargantuan conflict. The casualty lists that reached hamlets and cities alike brought sorrow and anguish to the families of nearly 1,700,000 men who had been killed or wounded in that period.

On the eastern front the Germans fared somewhat better. Although the Russians surprised them and the Austrians by mustering a stronger offensive than expected, the Germans stopped it by inflicting a crushing defeat at Tannenberg (August 26–September 1, 1914). Meanwhile Serbia had been joined in the Balkan theater by Montenegro, but this slight advantage for the Allied Powers was more than offset by the entrance of Turkey into the war in November, 1914, on the side of Germany and Austria. Turkey's strategic position and human and economic resources were of great advantage to the Central Powers, and, for the rest of the war, British troops had to be deployed in large numbers to guard Egypt and India, Cyprus and Malta, and later, to fight costly campaigns in Palestine and Mesopotamia. Italy entered the war in 1915 on the side of Britain and France. Its role was limited to protracted and indecisive campaigns in the mountains of northern Venezia and in Albania, but it forced the Austro-Hungarians to tie up thousands of troops that were more desperately needed on the eastern front.

Despite repeated crises, the outbreak of war had caught the British unprepared. While the navy was, as usual, in readiness, the army was weak and small. It consisted of no more than 450,000 regulars and reservists, many of whom were stationed in the colonies, and less than 300,000 men in the home guard. But before the war was a week old, thousands of men rushed to enlist. Regulars in Britain were quickly assembled into an expeditionary force and hurried off to the Channel ports and Belgium, while other regulars stationed in the colonies rested aboard slow troopships en route to Europe. Enlistments were so heavy that conscription could be postponed until January, 1916, by which time the attrition of war required the calling up of many more than the three million men in uniform by the end of 1915. The economy was put on a war footing: horses were rounded up for the cavalry and artillery; trucks by the thousands were commandeered by the government; railroads came under the control of the War Railway Council; holidays and idleness were forgotten as both men and women manned the wheels of industry to produce weapons and supplies. Unemployment, a serious domestic problem before the war, was solved overnight. Shortages of vital materials, including food, caused prices to soar and brought hardship to the poor. A temporary financial crisis beginning a week before Britain declared war led to a run on the banks, hurried issues of paper money without backing in gold, closing of the stock market, and a sharp rise in bank interest rates. The home guard took up stations at transportation, communication, and other centers of strategic importance. Thousands of aliens were escorted to detention camps. A strictly enforced blackout enveloped the whole country. The Official Secrets Act (1911) was enforced: persons who made or communicated "any sketch, plan, model, article, or note" prejudicial to the state were classed as felons and made liable to imprisonment of from three to seven years. Other Acts, notably the Trading with the Enemy Act (1914), made it a misdemeanor punishable by a year's imprisonment or £500 fine, or both, for anyone to trade in designated goods with the enemy.

A month after the British and French forces had checked another German drive toward the Channel ports at the First Battle of Ypres (October–November, 1914) and settled into the lengthening miles of muddy trenches, the cabinet began to consider the feasibility of invading the Dardanelles. The plan had been suggested by Grand Duke Nicholas, commander-in-chief of the Russian forces, as a means by which to divert Turkish assaults in the Caucasus, and to open an avenue of supplies to the Russian forces in eastern Europe. Gallipoli, a heavily fortified narrow peninsula between the Dardanelles and the Aegean, garrisoned by 250,000 Turks assisted by German advisers, had to be captured before Constantinople, the ultimate goal, could be attacked. Turkish control of the Dardanelles had prevented the British fleet from penetrating to the Black Sea, allowing the Turks to launch an invasion (unsuccessful but costly to Russia) of the Caucasus. Moreover, so long as Turkey remained in the war, Serbia, Montenegro, and the neutral states of Bulgaria and Greece were trapped in an Austro-

Turkish vise. In addition, Turkey posed an ominous threat to Cyprus and the strategically important Suez Canal, and, farther east, to Persia, which lay on the road to India. For these reasons the British War Council of the cabinet, confident that its forces could hold their own on the western front now that the fighting had settled down to trench warfare, agreed to undertake the invasion of Gallipoli. Winston Churchill, First Lord of the Admiralty, who believed that war on several fronts would more quickly break the enemy's strength and lessen attrition on the western front, heavily influenced the cabinet's decision.

The invasion was a total failure. The British initially hoped to employ Greek forces supported by the Mediterranean fleet, but King Constantine preferred neutrality and the Russians vetoed the proposal that they send troops. Hence imperial troops, mostly Australians and New Zealanders (part of the Anzac Corps), took up the task with the assistance of British and French units. The campaign opened in February and March, 1915, when an Anglo-French fleet bombarded the Gallipoli bastions in a vain effort to force the heavily fortified and mined narrows of the Dardanelles opposite Chanak. The bombardment was terrific, but the Turkish cannons had the better of the Allied fleet, which suffered the loss or disablement of several capital ships and withdrew. In April nearly 300,000 men (and more subsequently) under the command of Sir Ian Hamilton landed at several points on the Aegean coast. The Turks, who had had time to make thorough preparations, put up a stiff resistance. Other bombardments and landings in the summer were equally futile in breaking the enemy's defenses. Long communication lines, poor planning, the autumn rains, weak leadership in the field, and growing dissatisfaction in London with the lack of progress in the campaign combined to frustrate the heroic efforts of men who fought with their backs to the sea and were unable to advance into the highlands. By early December the authorities decided to evacuate the troops, and the costly Dardanelles campaign ended ingloriously on the night of December 18–19, 1915, with the withdrawal of men and supplies.

Gallipoli had several serious consequences. What had begun optimistically as an opportunity to drive Turkey from the war ended with the scales tipped in the Balkans in favor of the Central Powers. Bulgaria, formerly a neutral, joined them and overran Serbia despite everything the Allies, who landed troops in Salonika in violation of Greek neutrality, could do to prevent it. In 1917, however, the neutralist government of King Constantine was overthrown by the revolutionary regime of Eleutherios Venizelos, and Greece declared war on the Central Powers. Rumania had joined in the war against the Central Powers a year earlier, but it was quickly overwhelmed by the Germans.

On the western front in 1915 neither the Allied nor the Central Powers could make significant gains notwithstanding the massive operations each undertook to break the other's lines. On March 10 the British, preceded by a devastating artillery barrage, attempted to dislodge the Germans at Neuve-Chapelle, gained only a mile or two, and fell back with enormous casualties. The Germans did likewise in late April at the Second Battle of Ypres, in which they used poison gas for the first time despite its prohibition as an illegal weapon (along with dumdum bullets and submarines) at the Hague Convention of 1899. Periodically during the rest of the spring and summer both sides mustered major offensives without altering the situation at all.

The British had suffered heavy casualties, some said, because of a critical shortage of high-explosive shells, and accusing fingers were pointed at Kitchener at the War Office and Sir John French in the field. Lloyd George responded by urging munitions workers, some of whom he denounced as slackers and drunkards, to produce more, and by rejecting out of hand Opposition charges of government culpability in ammunition shortages that reputedly caused military failures at the front. This lengthy dispute, lasting through December, 1915, resulted in French's replacement on the western front by Sir Douglas Haig and in the resignation of Admiral Sir John Fisher as first sea lord because of constant friction with Churchill.

In the autumn a huge offensive was launched against the German lines in northern France. Joffre was certain that the operation would force a German retreat beyond the Meuse, but the British did not share his optimism that this might end the war in the west. Neither Foch's advance between Rheims and Verdun nor the Anglo-French assault toward Loos and Lens succeeded despite the overwhelming superiority (in some sectors 5 to 1) of the Allied forces. No more than five miles was taken in any sector, and the commanders in the field, seeing that casualties were mounting in a hopeless venture, halted the drive in contradiction of Joffre's orders. The French lost 190,000 men in four days; the British, 60,000; the Germans, about 213,000. The war in the west at the end of 1915 ended as it had begun. In the east, the Russians had retreated in the spring and summer in the face of a major Austro-German offensive, but only after putting up a stiff resistance despite cold weather, insufficient weapons and ammunition, and inadequately trained troops.

While the Russians retreated and the war in the west dragged on without change the British enjoyed some success in Mesopotamia against the Turks. Concerned lest Turkey capture the vitally important Persian oil fields and threaten the route to India, General Townshend advanced up the Tigris to Amara and Nasiriya, while a second Indo-British army moved almost two hundred miles farther inland to Kut-el-Amara. These successes emboldened Townshend to attack the main Turkish forces at Ctesiphon, where he suffered heavy casualties and withdrew. The Turks counterattacked, recapturing Kut in April, 1916. The Mesopotamian campaign cost forty thousand Indo-British casualties, but it, as well as the Russian and Anglo-French operations in Turkish Armenia and Gallipoli, had weakened Turkish resistance. Consequently the British managed to reoccupy Kut in February, 1917, thereby saving the oil fields and protecting the land route to India.

These campaigns in the Middle East were accompanied by two important diplomatic arrangements. The first, the Sykes-Picot agreement of 1916 (which formalized and more carefully defined the McMahon pledge of 1915) with the Arabs of the Hejaz, promised them an independent Arabia or a confederation of Arab states at the conclusion of the war on condition that they attacked the Turks, that Palestine should be accorded a special status, and that the British and French spheres of economic influence should be left intact. The second was a promise by Lord Balfour (November, 1917) that the Jews might anticipate a home in Palestine at war's end. These partially contradictory arrangements proved troublesome later, but for the time being they greatly assisted the Allied cause: the Arabs defected from the Turkish Empire and helped in the Palestine campaign of 1917, and world Jewry contributed vast sums of money in support of the war effort.

The first two years of the war also witnessed the capture of most of the German colonies in Africa and the Far East. In November, 1914, the British deposed the Khedive of Egypt and ended Turkish sovereignty there by making it a British protectorate. German Togoland fell easily to units from the Gold Coast Colony in August, 1914. The operations in the Cameroons proved to be far more taxing because of its size and the nature of the terrain, but it, too, capitulated in January, 1916, when the Germans retreated into Spanish territory. The South Africans, led by Louis Botha and Jan Smuts, captured German South-

West Africa by July, 1915, and took German East Africa in the early winter of 1917. The actions against the German colonies in the Far East were modest and less troublesome. Japan, which had joined the Allies on August 23, 1914, seized the Chinese port of Tsingtao in the German protectorate of Kiaochow in mid-November. Meanwhile small detachments of Australian and New Zealand troops occupied the Mariana, Caroline, and Marshall Islands, German New Guinea, the Bismarck Archipelago, the Solomons, and Samoa. These victories helped to silence German wireless operations directed against Allied shipping and to wrest control of Pacific waters from Admiral Graf von Spee's marauding cruisers.

The contribution of the Royal Navy in World War I was less dramatic than in earlier wars, primarily because, with the exception of a few battles such as Jutland and the Falkland Islands, the war at sea was fought out in engagements between individual or small groups of ships. The navy nevertheless played a crucial role: it patrolled the Channel; it convoyed merchantmen and troopships; and it helped to lessen the peril from submarines. Both British and Germans had expended vast sums on their fleets prior to the war. Unlike the Germans, however, who had concentrated on battleships and heavy cruisers, the British had not neglected to build lighter and swifter craft. The navy was large enough to patrol the North Sea and Channel, blockade German ports, pursue German raiders like the *Scharnhorst, Gneisenau,* and *Emden* over half the world, and guard the Mediterranean sea lanes with help from French and Italian squadrons. Despite the German submarines (which numbered more than three hundred by 1917), for instance, Allied escort ships safely convoyed more than 16,500 merchantmen across the North Atlantic with losses of only 1 per cent during the last nineteen months of the war.

The Germans knew that Britain's war effort would have to be crippled at sea. For that reason, German naval yards mass-produced submarines, which were deployed early in 1915 primarily in a ring around the British Isles. Germany announced that it would sink all vessels, neutral as well as enemy, in this blockade zone. The most significant incident that resulted was the sinking on May 7, 1915, of the British liner *Lusitania* off the Irish coast. The nearly 1200 casualties included 128 Americans who sailed despite a warning from German diplomats in Washington that Allied ships sailing from American ports might be sunk. The catastrophe provoked riots in England against alien shopkeepers and stimulated war talk in the United States. Rather than risk

American entry into the war, the Germans stopped submarine warfare against neutrals until early in 1917.

The most important naval action of the war, though not decisive for either side, was the Battle of Jutland. The Germans had previously been careful not to risk the loss of their fleet in a major engagement on the high seas. But, in May, 1916, they stationed part of it off the southwestern coast of Norway to lure the British into a trap. Once the British ships appeared, the decoy squadron was to sail hurriedly for a rendezvous with the main body of the German fleet, the object being then to annihilate the British North Sea fleet. The latter sighted the decoy on May 31 and gave chase in a running battle for fifty miles before Admiral Sir David Beatty realized that he had encountered the enemy's principal capital ships. His command of 145 ships engaged the enemy's 110 ships and attempted to encircle them. During the night of May 31–June 1, however, the Germans slipped through the British cordon and returned to Heligoland. The British lost fourteen ships to the Germans' eleven and suffered considerably more casualties. Whether the British or the Germans won this battle is unimportant, but the British have considered it a victory, for, with the exception of a few sallies in 1916 and 1918, the German fleet at Kiel refused to leave port, thereby tacitly acknowledging British control of the seas.

The British public had been slow to gear itself for the struggle ahead, but the country gradually assumed a posture of constant readiness. The domestic history of Britain during these war years is overshadowed by the military campaigns; yet no nation can survive in modern warfare without the regulation of its national life and great personal devotion on the home front. The public generally took the early months of the war in its stride and did not actually comprehend fully the nature of the conflict or the burdens it would bring. By late December all had changed. War news became more important than the latest football and cricket scores. The government doubled the income tax and drastically increased excise taxes on goods such as tobacco and whiskey. A war loan of more than £3,000,000 was fully subscribed in a few weeks. Work in offices, schools, and factories became a national obligation instead of merely a means of livelihood or an education. Industry retooled and mass-produced weapons and ammunition. Women's dresses were shortened to save cloth, and short haircuts for men, like those of the soldiers, became the vogue. Yarmouth and King's Lynn, Tyneside and Lowestoft, endured the first Zeppelin raids early in 1915. The raids multiplied against London, the Midlands, and the Scottish lowlands during the remainder of the year.

Hundreds of thousands of casualties decimated the British and imperial regiments which, during the first two years of the war, were refilled by eager volunteers. While enlistments continued high, there was no need for conscription, but as casualties mounted enlistments dropped significantly. Parliament therefore passed a Military Service Act in 1915 that conscripted all unmarried men between the ages of eighteen and forty-one, and later fifty. Several Dominion governments also introduced conscription, in the case of Canada over the strong objection of the French-speaking population of Quebec, who felt no obligation to help the Anglo-Saxon element, who they believed had discriminated against them since 1760, or to aid France, with whom they felt no bond.

Public criticism of the alleged lack of ammunition stirred the government into creating a Ministry of Munitions (June, 1915) headed by Lloyd George. It coordinated the several regulative agencies in charge of war production into one centralized agency at the cabinet level, and provided regulative procedures to superintend labor, settle its disputes with management, and to limit corporate profits. Despite government efforts to control the economy, prices for most commodities rose sharply from a base of 100 in 1914 to nearly 180 by the end of the war. Food shortages at home, caused primarily by decreased trade, the sinking of merchantmen carrying foodstuffs, and the needs of troops abroad, encouraged an increase in acreage under cultivation by about 25 per cent. Lawns, parks, football fields, and private gardens were spaded up and converted into "victory gardens" tended by the young and the old, who were given an additional hour to finish their chores by the passage of the Daylight Savings Act in May, 1916. The government also had to consider financial aid to the dependents of servicemen. Early in the war qualified dependents were paid a small separation allowance from a fund raised by deductions of a few pennies from soldiers' pay and a substantially larger allotment of public funds. Late in 1915 Parliament passed a War Pensions Act to provide assistance to the widows and children of soldiers who were killed or seriously disabled.

The women of Britain joined service organizations and assumed some of the tasks in business and industry formerly done by their husbands and fathers. However, the contribution that women could make to the war effort was not fully exploited until early in 1916, when they took their places in much larger numbers in the communications and transportation services, in the factories, and even at the plows in order to release men for duty in the armed services. Families grew accustomed to a new routine of life in which mothers and daughters were hurried off in time for the afternoon shift in factories, to tend the wounded in military hospitals, to help brighten the lives of servicemen at camps and airfields, and to scan the skies for enemy aircraft. The suffragettes (discussed below) temporarily forgot the urge to agitate for women's rights because the war provided them with ample opportunity to be men's peers in society and industry if not yet at the ballot box. The war also tended to minimize class distinctions. Casualties sorrowed rich as well as poor and the specter of death shrouded the lives of peers as well as dustmen. Days were so busy that the wealthy found it difficult to preserve the genteel customs of the prewar period. Higher taxes, rationing, and government regulations on trade and travel, for instance, put a damper on frivolous spending, the enjoyment of luxury products, and lazy days at the track or seaside. Battlefield commissions were bestowed on men who had been neither to university nor to Sandhurst, and this tended to weaken the elite status that the officer class had formerly enjoyed.

The political scene had undergone some modification since the outbreak of war when Asquith's Liberal government, which had been in power since 1908, was still at the helm. For the first few months the exigencies of the crisis quieted party squabbles: the Liberals, Conservatives, Irish Nationalists, and Labourites cooperated in molding a solid front. But this happy situation did not obtain for long. Early in 1915 the Conservatives, led by Andrew Bonar Law with help principally from Lord Lansdowne and Austen Chamberlain, voiced serious qualms about one-party government in wartime. The war had not gone well on any front where British troops fought, which gave rise to Opposition criticism of Liberal leadership. Charges of government inefficiency were legion. Mounting casualties inevitably brought denunciation of the party in power. The use of poison gas at the Second Battle of Ypres and unrestricted submarine warfare shocked the country's sensibilities and raised doubts about the prospects of victory. It was also suspected, with good reason, that the cabinet had quarreled over the wisdom of undertaking the Gallipoli campaign, over the shortage of high-explosive shells, and over the difficulties at the Admiralty between Churchill and Fisher. When Fisher resigned in mid-May, 1915, the dissension in the cabinet became painfully apparent.

Primarily for these reasons, as well as because much of the criticism of the government was directed at him personally, Asquith agreed to form a coalition cabinet consisting of twelve Liberals, eight Conservatives, and one Labourite. The principal Conservative members were Bonar Law (Colonial Office), Balfour (Admiralty), Chamberlain (India Office), Lord Curzon (Lord Privy Seal), and Lansdowne (England's first minister without portfolio). Arthur Henderson, a Labourite, became president of the Board of Education. Among the Liberals, Lloyd George undoubtedly wielded the greatest influence and authority as minister of munitions, a post to which he brought verve and efficiency.

At the time of these cabinet changes the country generally felt that Lloyd George could have given the government better leadership, and consequently greater success in the war, than Asquith, but the latter held on until December, 1916. Members of his party as well as the Opposition found him wanting on at least two counts. He seemed too placid and contemplative to cope with the national crisis, but this criticism failed to take into account the obvious virtue of having a prime minister who, although not frantically active, did a thorough and conscientious job. He was also unwilling to exercise authority in the war council (created in November, 1914), preferring to rely on decisions reached by the full cabinet, which was too large and deliberative a body to make the rapid judgments necessary in wartime. Continued criticism forced Asquith to appoint a new war council in November, 1915, consisting of himself, Lloyd George, Bonar Law, Kitchener, and Balfour. Although it was more effective than its predecessor, there was so much bickering between the heads of departments and Asquith that several of them, including Churchill and Lloyd George, resigned. This left Asquith no alternative but to resign himself. King George V, following normal procedure, asked the Opposition leader, Bonar Law, to form a new government. Since the Liberals controlled Parliament and Asquith refused to serve in a Conservative cabinet, Bonar Law declined. Lloyd George consequently became prime minister on December 6, 1916.

The energetic prime minister immediately remodeled the cabinet. He created a war cabinet, a kind of private directory consisting of five members—himself, Bonar Law, Lord Curzon, Henderson, and Lord Milner. They assumed complete authority in decision-making, a task to which they could bring their full attention because, with the exception of Bonar Law (Chancellor of the Exchequer), none of them headed government departments. Lloyd George increased the number of ministers, but they were not cabinet members. Therefore, until the end of the war, the customary structure of the cabinet ceased to exist. The foreign secretary, the first sea lord, and the chief of the general staff usually attended cabinet meetings, but the other ministers attended only when it discussed policies relating to their departments. Lloyd George also instituted the practice, since followed, of keeping minutes of cabinet proceedings, which eased the conduct of business and forever recorded decisions that had formerly been only a matter of memory. In addition, he created the imperial war cabinet, consisting of the British war cabinet, the secretaries of state for foreign affairs, colonies, and India, the prime ministers of the Dominions, and a few representatives from Newfoundland and India. It met only three times in 1917–18, but its work was immensely important in coordinating the war effort within the Empire. Its meetings helped to enhance the status of the Dominions vis-à-vis Great Britain, and it has been postulated that they gained a greater measure of independence in the conduct of their foreign affairs, although it was not until the passage of the Statute of Westminster in 1931 that the Empire-Commonwealth underwent a substantial constitutional revision that made the Dominions equal partners with Britain.

On Easter Sunday, April 24, 1916, a rebellion in Dublin aimed at winning an independent Irish republic confronted Asquith's government with the most serious domestic crisis of the war years. Although the roots of this rebellion lie deep in the troubled history of Anglo-Irish relations, its proximate causes date from 1912. Despite the peace that had characterized Ireland since the death of Parnell in 1891, and a temporary split among the Irish Nationalists until the party was reunited under the leadership of John Redmond, the desire for home rule had not died. The Liberals, traditionally the party that sponsored home rule legislation, needed the help of the Irish Nationalists and Labourites after 1910 to stave off repeated Conservative efforts to dislodge them. The Nationalists supported the Liberal administration in the belief that Asquith would propose a new home rule bill, the fourth since the 1880s. Its provisions, put up for debate in 1912, were little different from an earlier bill of 1893, but, in addition to the usual problem of obtaining enough support in Parliament to pass it, there was the further problem of opposition by the Protestant Ulsterites, who believed that a domestically independent Ireland controlled by the Roman Catholics would subjugate them to an alien way of life. The Ulsterites argued that they were ethnically Anglo-Scottish, that they were essentially an urban and industrial people, that they were Protestants, and that they should consequently remain part of Great Britain.

The Commons passed the Home Rule Bill in three successive sessions over a period of two years so that, even though the Lords rejected it each time, it became law under the terms of the Parliament Act of 1911. But, since the war had begun by the time of the Bill's effective date, its implementation was suspended for the duration. Meanwhile trouble arose in Northern Ireland. About 220,000 Ulsterites signed a covenant against home rule in 1912 and secretly collected arms, many of which the government seized in June, 1913. They also created a paper provisional government, organized a militia (the Ulster Volunteer Force), and drilled openly in defiance of the law, confident that they could do so because of Bonar Law's reassuring remarks in Parliament that the Unionist Conservatives supported their position. Occasional riots and an exchange of gunfire between the Catholics, who had also armed, and the government troops threatened to escalate friction between Catholics and Ulsterites into civil war. Britain's entry into war in August temporarily quieted the unrest, but the opposing elements in Ireland refused to forget their animosity even though many of them joined English regiments on the western front.

The war was only a few months old when the radical republican Sinn Fein society ("Ourselves Alone"), unwilling to accept the compromise of home rule, entered into treasonous correspondence with Germany and laid plans for rebellion against England. As early as March 4, 1916, the London *Times* noted with alarm the growing activity of the Sinn Feiners and urged the government to take appropriate action before it was too late. On the night of April 20 a German merchantman disguised as a neutral vessel attempted to land arms and ammunition near Tralee, but it was intercepted by a British warship and was scuttled. Among those captured and later executed was Sir Roger Casement, who had once tried to induce Irish prisoners of war in Germany to defect to the enemy. On April 24 a rebellion broke the serenity of Easter Sunday in Dublin and the surrounding countryside. The rebels seized the general post office, the city hall, the law courts, and many houses, and tried unsuccessfully to assault government headquarters at Dublin Castle. Troops from the Curragh were the victims of rebel snipers and reinforcements rushed from Belfast suffered heavy casualties. Fighting was heaviest in the shadow of the Nelson

Monument on O'Connell Street. By the evening of April 28 the troops had cornered the rebels in a few buildings in and around the post office. More than 700 rebels surrendered on May 1, others having been killed or wounded in the gunfire that riddled several public buildings. Once the government had broken resistance in Dublin the rebels in the outlying regions surrendered. According to the estimate in the *Annual Register,* 5000 rebels had fought in the uprising; approximately 180 buildings valued at £2,000,000 had been damaged or destroyed; and 800 civilians and nearly 500 soldiers had been killed or wounded. Many of the 3000 rebels who were arrested were tried and imprisoned in England, but only fifteen were executed. An army of occupation kept the peace in Ireland until the end of the war.

The Irish rebellion added to the government's burden at a time when British and French troops on the western front were meeting the greatest German offensive since the war's inception. The temporary collapse of the Russians late in 1915 permitted the Germans to concentrate their forces in the west. They believed it essential to take Verdun, which was only a few miles from their railroad terminals, feeling that its capture might well break French morale and end the war. The Battle of Verdun began on February 21. The Germans had expected to capture it in four days; the French still held it three months later. Casualties on both sides numbered more than 600,000.

The Allies counterattacked on July 1 along the Somme salient. Half a million soldiers, including sixteen British regiments under Haig, moved laboriously through no man's land. More than 200,000 fell in less than a week. Nowhere did they gain more than ten miles. The snows of early November brought to a close the carnage of the battles of Verdun and the Somme, which had killed or wounded 1,800,000 Allied and German soldiers since February. As winter closed in, the opposing forces once more took to their trenches. Meanwhile, in June, 1916, the Russians launched a surprisingly powerful offensive along a front extending from the Austro-Polish to the Rumanian frontier. Pushing the front westward in some sectors as many as sixty miles, they not only scored a significant advance but also helped to ease the pressure on the Anglo-French forces by forcing the Germans to transfer troops to the eastern front. The Italians likewise assisted their Allies by staging a counteroffensive against the Austrians in northern Italy.

The Central Powers, victorious only in the Balkans in 1916, contemplated the possibility of a truce, and cautiously broached the subject to the Allies without specifying what terms they would accept. The Allies, primarily because of urging by President Woodrow Wilson of the United States, also considered making peace in 1915–16, but, because as a precondition they demanded territorial and monetary compensations that the Germans were unwilling to concede, the overtures came to naught.

On the German failure to break through in western Europe, Hindenburg and General Erich Ludendorff advised the Kaiser to resume unrestricted submarine warfare, which they had suspended in May, 1915, after the destruction of the *Lusitania*. They realized that the policy might bring America into the war, but they believed that the Allies could be beaten before the arrival of enough American troops to make any difference. On January 31, 1917, the Germans announced that their submarines would sink the ships of both neutrals and belligerents that entered the waters of a war zone surrounding the British Isles and along the French and Italian coasts. When submarines sank several American ships, causing the Americans to forget their President's admonition that they should remain neutral in thought as well as in action, and it was learned that German Foreign Secretary Arthur Zimmermann was negotiating with the Mexican government (then supporting Pancho Villa's raids on the Texas frontier) for an invasion of the United States should it enter the war, Congress declared war on April 6, 1917. The first American troops reached France in June, but did not play a significant role until the last great German offensive in 1918. But America's entry into the war did bolster British and French resistance and morale, coming as it did shortly after the first Russian revolution of March, 1917, which seriously undercut what was left of Russia's war effort.

The spring of 1917 witnessed another Allied offensive north and south of the Somme River. Haig and General Robert Nivelle, Joffre's successor, felt that this time they had a good chance of breaking through the Ypres salient and driving the Germans from Flanders. France was wallowing in defeatism bred by enormous losses, financial exhaustion, and war weariness, and Britain, although greatly aided by the Empire, was being pressed to the wall to meet its responsibilities. But the Germans were worse off. The poor harvest of 1916 coupled with the effective Allied blockade of the German coast made the winter of 1916–17 a nightmare in which grave food shortages and disease took the lives of thousands of persons while heavy casualties in the army were rapidly depleting their reserves. Thus weakened, the

Germans made an orderly retreat behind the so-called Hindenburg line stretching from Arras to Noyon. They surrendered a thousand square miles, but they left nothing of use to the enemy because they systematically ravaged the countryside. The Allied offensives against the Hindenburg line in 1917 were unsuccessful. The Battle of Arras (April to June), spearheaded by the Canadians who took Vimy Ridge, raged while the French pressed the Battle of Aisne (April to November). The British offensive (July to December) centered in Flanders took Passchendaele Ridge and pushed the Germans back a few miles in the Battle of Cambrai.

Other British troops fought a different kind of war in 1917 in Palestine. Here an invasion led by Sir Archibald Murray followed groundwork laid by the Anglo-French Arab Bureau, in which the legendary T. E. Lawrence played a key role in organizing the Arabs under the titular leadership of King Hussein's son, Feisal, into an aggressive if often contentious guerrilla army. The Arabs captured sections of the coast from the Turks early in 1917 and were reinforced and later replaced by General Edmund Allenby's army, composed principally of Australians, New Zealanders, and Indians. His forces took Jerusalem in December while Lawrence's Arab cavalry raided across the Jordan. The war in Palestine lingered on indecisively until October, 1918, when Allenby carried out perhaps the most daring and imaginative offensive of the war in outflanking two Turkish armies to take Damascus. This victory, plus the success of the Arabs, who had gained control of Transjordan and Syria, won the war in the Near Eastern theater. On October 30, 1918, Turkey capitulated on all fronts.

A succession of German drives in the west between March and July, 1918, tested both attackers and defenders to the limit of their strength. The Russian collapse and Austrian victories in Italy enabled the Central Powers to concentrate their divisions in northern France. Their spring offensive began on March 21 near Saint-Quentin, where 600,000 men pressed against a short sector of the Anglo-French line. The old battlefield of the Somme, already twice scarred, soaked up the blood of thousands more until, before Amiens, millions of men under the new Allied supreme commander, Marshal Foch, halted the German assault. The Germans struck again on April 9, this time primarily against the British near Lille, and a third German drive commencing on May 26 carried the battle to the Marne, where, at Château-Thierry, only forty miles from Paris, it was stopped. It is paradoxical that at this point the opposing armies held roughly the same positions they had held in October, 1914. In 1918, however, the Germans had spent their strength to such an extent that two subsequent attacks were repulsed in June and July. The Austrians also lunged against the Italians along the Piave River in this period in a desperate effort to help their ally, but the Italians held on and later punished the exhausted enemy.

The war had at last turned in favor of the Allies. Hundreds of thousands of fresh American troops rushed in to assist the Anglo-French counteroffensive in the so-called Second Battle of the Marne beginning on August 8. The Germans could not stem the advance. Hopelessly outnumbered and lacking adequate artillery and ammunition, they retreated. By early October the Allied armies had practically expelled them from French soil and were marching toward Germany. Meanwhile the British propaganda war, waged by means of millions of leaflets dropped on the German lines and cities, contributed to the demoralization of a people who had already endured great hardships in the belief that victory would ultimately be theirs. The shock of the military reverses in 1918 undermined confidence in the government. German generals, confronted with a popular revolution aimed at overthrowing the empire, and a mutiny in the navy, forced Kaiser William II to abdicate on November 9. The next day he fled to neutral Holland for political asylum to escape the vengeance of the victors, who heaped all the blame for the war on him. Meanwhile Bulgaria had been successfully invaded and surrendered on September 30, Turkey surrendered a month later, and Austria signed an armistice on November 4.

World War I ended officially at 11 A.M. on November 11, 1918, when the cease-fire that the Allies and Germans had agreed upon six hours earlier in Foch's railway car in the forest of Compiègne took effect. Grateful soldiers everywhere laid down their weapons, embraced each other, and wept. Londoners poured into the streets and rejoiced. Crowds cheered King George and Queen Mary as they drove in triumphal procession through the city. Church bells in every village tolled in jubilation. Then the quiet that follows deep emotion descended on the British people as it did upon the other peoples of the world, victor as well as vanquished.

At that moment probably few contemplated or cared what the war had cost Britain, yet it had deeply altered national and private life. Social and economic changes had been adopted that came to fruition in the locust years of the 1920s. The war had brought regimentation to a people who had always counted the maximum of personal freedom a cardinal virtue. Despite the growth of trade-unions in numbers and power, the government had regulated wages and intervened in strikes, and labor had been under public pressure to accede to the exigencies of the times. New boards and agencies had been created. Free trade, the economic creed since the mid-nineteenth century, gave place to a measure of protectionism that was increased in the early 1930s and has not yet been abandoned. Britain's expenditures in the war totaled nearly £10,000,000,000 which greatly increased a national debt that could not be substantially reduced in the postwar period because of serious depressions. Industry, geared to war production, found it difficult to adjust to the manufacture of capital and consumer goods, and suffered from grossly reduced markets caused by the collapse of world trade, particularly in war-torn Europe. Millions of veterans were thrust on a labor market that could not absorb them. The cost of living had risen from a base of 100 in 1914 to 225 in 1918, and 260 in 1919. In the same period wages rose from an index of 100 to 260. The working classes had fared better in this inflated economy than had the upper classes, whose wealth was eroded by inflation as well as by high taxes and decreased opportunities for profitable investment. In effect, therefore, the war had narrowed the gulf between the rich and the poor.

The war had naturally preoccupied the government to such an extent that it could give little thought to domestic legislation. Parliament passed only two significant bills of that nature in 1918, one of which was the Representation of the People Act. It extended the vote to all male adults who could prove residence in a constituency for six months, or occupied business premises rated annually at ten pounds or more. Beneficiaries of poor relief were no longer disfranchised. Plural voting was restricted to the extent that no one could vote in more than two of the constituencies in which he qualified as an elector. The Act also recognized the redistribution and growth of the population since the last reapportionment of seats in Parliament in 1884. In 1918 each member of Parliament represented some 70,000 persons in English, Scottish, and Welsh constituencies, and each Irish member of Parliament 43,000 persons. The redistribution of some constituencies enlarged the size of the Commons from 670 members to 707.

In addition, the Act enfranchised approximately six million women thirty years of age and older who lived—or whose husbands lived— in a residence having an annual value of five pounds. This section of the Act recognized the contribution that women had made to the war effort and partly satisfied the strenuous prewar efforts of the militant suffragettes, proponents of equal rights for women, who had been responsible for the passage of the Act of 1907 enabling women to be elected to county and borough councils. The enfranchisement of women in national elections had often been discussed, but proposals to effect it had been overwhelmingly defeated. Late in the nineteenth century a group of women led by Dr. Garrett Anderson and Mrs. Fawcett had induced members of Parliament to introduce women suffrage bills, but all were defeated. The militant era of the women's rights movement dates from 1903, when Mrs. Emmeline Pankhurst, a Manchester widow and socialist, founded the Women's Social and Political Union. Its members, often unmindful of their appearance and the limits of propriety, heckled politicians, demonstrated outside Buckingham Palace, the Home Office, and other public buildings, and held mass rallies in Trafalgar Square and Hyde Park. They chained themselves to the grille in the Women's Gallery in the Commons, kicked and scratched the guards who removed them as public nuisances, refused to pay fines when convicted in court, and went on hunger strikes when imprisoned. Such antics frustrated the police and the Home Office, which Parliament authorized in the so-called "Cat and Mouse Act" to release suffragettes in danger of illness or death because of hunger strikes until they regained their strength, at which point they were again incarcerated. The war provided women with ample opportunity to serve the country, and, in consequence, most of the flag-waving, demonstrations, and obstructionism ceased, although some suffragettes continued to rail against female discrimination. The Sex Disqualification Act (1919) allowed women to take university degrees, follow professions, and serve in public life. In 1928, Stanley Baldwin's government reduced the age limit for women entitled to vote to twenty-one.

In January, 1918, mostly through the efforts of H. A. L. Fisher, the eminent Oxford historian and president of the Board of Trade, Parliament passed an Education Act, which benefited principally the working classes. It required that every child between the age of five and fourteen attend school full-time, provided publicly supported nursery schools and schools for mentally defective children, forbade the employment of children under twelve, and restricted work by children from twelve to fourteen years of age. It also raised teachers' salaries, created a pension fund for them, and provided more extensive and free medical care for all pupils. An indication of the government's concern for education was the increase of the budget of the Board of Education for fiscal year 1918–19 by £4,000,000.

The Parliament elected in 1910 still sat in November, 1918. The law required that a general election be held at least every five years, but in 1916 all parties agreed not to hold one for the duration of the war. The coalition government in existence since May, 1915, had satisfied the interests of all parties except the pacifist wing of the Labour party, which had refused to cooperate with Asquith and Lloyd George. The first order of business at war's end, therefore, was to hold an election. This "Khaki Election" of 1918 was unusual in that the Liberals and Conservatives asked the electorate to return the coalition to power in order that those most familiar with the problems created by the war might be given the opportunity to solve them. But, while the Liberals and Conservatives preached national unity, the Labourites and a dissident faction of the Liberal party headed by Asquith refused to support a continuation of the coalition. Even so, it won an overwhelming victory, securing nearly 500 seats. Asquith's followers made a very poor showing, and the Labourites gained only 61 seats. The coalition headed by Lloyd George remained in office until autumn, 1922.

In January, 1919, delegates from twenty-seven Allied Powers convened in Paris to write treaties that they imposed on the defeated countries. The task of preparing an agenda and directing the conference's work fell to the Council of Ten, consisting of two delegates each from Great Britain, France, the United States, Italy, and Japan. This council was divided into two committees: the Council of Four, including Lloyd George, Wilson, Vittorio Orlando of Italy, and Georges Clemenceau of France; and the Council of Five, composed of the foreign ministers of the principal Allies. The Council of Four ultimately made all the important decisions, relying primarily on the advice of specialists. As Orlando left the conference before it had concluded its work, angry over his colleagues' failure to honor promises made in the Treaty of London that had induced Italy to side with the Allies, Lloyd George, Wilson, and Clemenceau were the architects of the treaties of Versailles (Germany), St. Germain (Austria), Trianon (Hungary), Neuilly (Bulgaria) and Sèvres (Turkey).

The motives of these statesmen are difficult to categorize without qualification. Like the other heads of delegations, they were torn between passion and reason, and greatly concerned about the effect of their decisions on the attitudes of voters at home. Clemenceau, an old socialist and strenuous anti-Teuton whose memory extended back to the Franco-Prussian War (1870–71), bared his teeth unashamedly: Germany must be severely punished so that it would never again threaten France or disrupt peace in Europe. Wilson believed that the ills of Europe had grown from secret treaties, the flouting of international law, and the frustrations of subject peoples within the German and Austro-Hungarian empires. He consequently became the apostle of national self-determination and international arbitration of national disputes. The League of Nations, founded on the principles of the Covenant and embodied in the Treaty of Versailles, was his brain child—an altruistic, and, as events later proved, ineffective organization designed to implement the treaties and to settle peaceably issues that would otherwise be hammered out on the battlefield. Lloyd George, although also something of an idealist, and, like Wilson, somewhat inexperienced in the ways of diplomacy, tried wherever possible to steer a middle course. On the one hand he did his best to secure a lasting peace; on the other he sought, even to the point of demanding unrealistic reparations, to please the British electorate and ensure them a brighter future. In the end he accomplished neither.

Britain must share responsibility with the others for the punitive terms of the treaties, which cannot be treated in detail here. Moreover, as a sometimes reluctant member of the League of Nations, Britain became a guarantor and instrument of peace, and consequently also shares the praise and blame for the minor triumphs and more numerous failures that characterized the League's operations in regulating international affairs in the succeeding twenty years.

Britain and the Dominions made territorial gains through the treaties, by acquiring German colonies in Africa and the Far East under mandate (that is, being responsible to the League for establishing and operating stable governments in them). Britain acquired parts of Togoland and the Cameroons, German East Africa (Tanganyika), Iraq, Palestine, and Transjordan. New Zealand gained German Samoa; Australia, German New Guinea and the Solomon Islands; the Union of South Africa, German South-West Africa. Britain's acquisitions generally gave it trouble, particularly in the Near East where, because of the Sykes-Picot agreement with the Arabs and the Balfour Declaration promising the Jews "a national home," Arabs and Jews clashed frequently. In 1919, Britain also had powerful military and economic interests in Persia and Afghanistan. Largely because of Persian Anglophobia and Russian intrigue, Britain was forced to withdraw its troops from Persia in 1921, although it retained economic advantages. An Anglo-Afghan war in 1919–20 compelled Britain to surrender the control of Afghan foreign affairs which it had exercised since 1880.

Many of the other provisions of the treaties were concerned with the redistribution of territory in Europe and the setting-up of new countries, in the attempt to give nationality groups their own governments—a principle impossible to apply to everyone's satisfaction in the ethnically mixed areas of eastern Europe. The other main problem was the question of reparations. Months before the armistice had been signed the French and Belgians began to clamor for reparations from Germany. Motivated entirely by passion, and completely unrealistic about Germany's ability to pay, the Allies talked in astronomical figures. Only Wilson appeared to realize the impossibility of imposing, much less of collecting, a debt of billions of dollars in gold from Germany to pay for the total cost of the Allied war effort, including damage to property and pensions, which the French, British, and Belgians insisted upon. Britain's insistence stemmed both from its huge debt to the United States and from a campaign promise in 1918 that, if elected, the government would press for reparations. Endless debates at the conference and at numerous reparations commissions afterward failed to resolve the problem. Immediately after the war the Allies also confiscated foreign investments and property owned by Germans, as well as thousands of freight cars and locomotives, carloads of livestock, telephone poles, and tens of thousands of tons of coal. Only a small fraction of the £6,600,000,000 in reparations proposed by a commission in 1921 was ever collected.

The peace settlement of 1919–20 had serious weaknesses that contributed to the instability of Europe in the succeeding twenty years. Until very recently, historians generally agreed that these weaknesses, particularly the severe punishment inflicted on Germany, the exclusion of Russia from the treaties, and the economic problems created by the destruction of the economic system in central Europe, contributed to the rise of dictators who brought on World War II. Although this thesis has been challenged, there is no question that the peace settlement did have major flaws. Wilson's doctrine of national self-determination, which led to the creation of the states of Czechoslovakia, Poland, and Yugoslavia, and in the process reduced Austria to a third-rate power, surrounded Germany with extremely weak states. Unlike that made at the Congress of Vienna, the 1919–20 settlement provided for no buffer states to contain German aggression. On all sides, except for

France, itself greatly weakened by the war, Germany was bordered by insignificant states. Moreover, as suggested above, the treaties had grossly violated the principle of nationality. Greeks ruled Turks; Albanians ruled Greeks; Czechs ruled Germans, Hungarians, Ruthenians, Poles, and Slovaks; Poles ruled Germans and Russians, and so forth. In addition, just as the French had magnified their loss of Alsace-Lorraine in 1871, so too did the Germans magnify their hatred of the French after 1920. Further, because the treaties stripped Germany of virtually all its alien peoples, they helped to foster German racialism. They had also slighted the Italians. There is little doubt that the rise to power of Mussolini's Fascists was immensely eased by the Italian people's distrust of their former Allies and the inability of their government to secure more at Paris. And not least, the Allies' refusal to have anything to do with the Bolsheviks, whom they excluded from all international conferences until 1923 and admitted only occasionally afterward, did much to discourage Russian cooperation in foreign affairs. The war not only altered the face of Europe and the prewar balance of power; it also created economic problems that brought on two serious depressions.

Lloyd George's coalition ministry faced three problems in 1919–22: the decline of British exports, severe unemployment, and rebellion in Ireland, the first two of which were obviously closely related. Although the armistice was followed by heavy buying in Britain by European states to meet current needs, which temporarily maintained high industrial production, exports, and employment, by early 1920 orders had fallen off sharply. Famine haunted European cities, but they had no money to purchase British commodities at the then inflated prices. Consequently each nation tried its best to be self-sufficient. Moreover, the total collapse of the German mark by 1923, and the disruption of the economic balance in central Europe following the dismemberment of the Austro-Hungarian Empire, deprived Britain of a considerable volume of world trade, upon which it depended. The United States, formerly one of Britain's best customers, adopted high tariffs that effectively excluded most British goods. As a consequence, British prosperity faded rapidly. While inflation eroded the real value of wages, taxes were kept at their wartime highs in order to help erase a deficit of about £326,000,000 in the fiscal year 1919–20 and a national debt of nearly £8,000,000,000.

An example of the effect of declining world trade may be seen in the British coal industry. Over 98,000,000 tons of coal had been exported in 1913, but only 44,000,000 in 1920. Inflating prices led to miners' demands for higher wages and shorter hours. The owners, faced with declining markets such as in Italy, which was rapidly developing hydroelectric power, refused to meet the demands. A royal commission headed by Lord Sankey found in 1919 that the coal industry was both wasteful and inefficient, and, accordingly, recommended nationalization of the mines, a seven-hour day, and higher wages. The government accepted the report, but continued unrest among miners and minority reports by members of the commission and the mine owners' representatives undercut efforts to implement it. The coal commission report was soon forgotten while unemployment figures rose. A long strike in 1921 failed to accomplish anything for the miners, and, by 1924, nearly 7 per cent of Britain's miners were out of work. The situation in the coal industry steadily deteriorated until it led to the general strike of 1926 (discussed below).

Although the coal industry was hardest hit by the postwar depression, others also suffered. The textile industry, centered in Lancashire, had reached the peak of production in 1914, and since gradually declined. In 1921, when the mill owners tried to reduce wages by 30 per cent, the workers struck for six months. The engineering industries, enlarged by the demands of war, fell off sharply and likewise suffered from strikes and lockouts in 1921–22. The only industries that prospered after the war were those of chemicals, auto manufacture, and aircraft, but this group was a small segment of the total economy and there was little foreign demand for their products.

Unemployment naturally resulted from a depressed economy, as well as from the presence of the 25,000 men mustered out of the armed forces each month. Thousands clamored at the labor exchanges for work, only to be asked to sign discouragingly long waiting lists. Between August and December, 1920, the ranks of the unemployed grew from 300,000 to 800,000. In the summer of 1921 the figure stood at 1,000,000; by the following spring it had risen to 2,000,000—about 15 per cent of the labor force. In 1918–24 the Exchequer doled out more than £100,000,000 to families impoverished by the slump. In the same period the government paid nearly £155,000,000 in unemployment insurance under the 1911 Act and a similar Act passed in December, 1919, that slightly raised the weekly allowance for 12,000,000 workers. Additional millions were expended in state charity and poor relief. Although the economy recovered somewhat in 1924–29 because of increased world trade, American pump-priming of European industry, and Germany's partial industrial recovery and financial stabilization, the Great Depression beginning in 1929 again prostrated Britain. It became customary to regard 1,000,000 or more unemployed as the *normal* figure until the onset of World War II.

Rebellion in Ireland worried the cabinet no less than did the state of the economy. Bitter hatred divided Ulsterites and Nationalists. The Sinn Feiners continued their acts of violence and obstructionism despite the presence of an army of occupation and frequent impositions of martial law. Although most Irishmen on both sides of the Boyne took no part in rebellion, they could not help but be drawn into the ideological, political, religious, and ethnic controversies that rent their homeland. During the war, various Irish factions had advanced three possible solutions to the dilemma: home rule for the whole island; an Irish Free State under a republican system of government and no connection with Britain; or a divided Ireland, Ulster remaining a part of the United Kingdom. Most Nationalist Irish would have been content with home rule and the Ulsterites with a divided Ireland, but the Sinn Feiners pressed for a completely independent Irish Free State outside the Empire. In order to resolve these differences, Lloyd George had invited delegates from all factions to convene in London. They had met intermittently from July to March, 1917–18, but their conversations came to nothing because of basic disagreement between the Nationalists and Ulsterites and the intransigence of the Sinn Feiners who, realizing that Britain meant to keep Ireland within the Empire, boycotted the meetings. The failure of the conference had raised the rebels' stock as had the imposition of conscription in Ireland in April, 1918. It had been strenuously opposed by the Nationalist members, who walked out of Parliament in protest, and by the Catholic hierarchy, who circulated a widely subscribed anticonscription oath among the laity. The government had consequently been unable to enforce conscription, and in the general election of 1918 seventy-three Sinn Feiners were elected to Parliament. All refused to attend in order to dramatize their demand for independence.

Meanwhile the Sinn Feiners organized a secret Irish Republican Army, and, in January, 1919, at the Mansion House in Dublin, twenty-six members of Parliament (the others were in British jails) constituted themselves the independent assembly of an Irish republic under the presidency of Eamon de Valera. When the I.R.A. began a reign of terror against the British authorities, blasting bridges, cars, and roads, ambushing and murdering police, raiding jails and the like, the government countered by establishing a special police force composed of army veterans called the "Black and Tans" because of their khaki uniforms and black caps, which reinforced the Royal Irish Constabulary. Both "armies" carried on vicious guerrilla warfare, in which the barbarous acts of the one were matched by those of the other. This unbridled terrorism shocked the British public, which demanded a better solution. But Lloyd George could think of nothing except home rule or some variant thereof, and accordingly, late in 1920, a new Home Rule Bill, which created separate governments and separate Parliaments for North and South Ireland, became law. But this compromise failed to satisfy the I.R.A. or lessen terrorism. When systematic reprisals by the Black and Tans in the spring of 1921 failed to weaken I.R.A. resistance, and Asquith's independent Liberals made Lloyd George's visits to the Commons an increasingly embarrassing experience, he received help from George V who, speaking before the Ulster Parliament in June, 1921, pleaded with the Irish to put an end to bloodshed. Meanwhile General Smuts of South Africa, a quiet man who understood the temper of rebels because he had been one himself, convinced de Valera to meet with the prime minister in London. Their talks failed to produce a compromise, but further meetings the following October between a committee of the cabinet and two less refractory Sinn Feiners, Arthur Griffith and Michael Collins, resulted in an agreement, signed on December 6, 1921. It provided for the partition of Ireland and the creation of the Irish Free State with dominion status within the British Commonwealth of Nations. In January, 1922, the Parliament of southern Ireland endorsed the agreement by a narrow margin. De Valera's followers dissented and continued their acts of violence until July, 1923, when they laid down their arms but pledged to pursue by peaceful political means their crusade for a united Irish republic free from any connection with the crown. The Irish Free State (Eire) remained a Dominion in the Commonwealth until Easter Day, 1949, when it became a republic. Thus ended a drama that had preoccupied kings and chief ministers since the twelfth century.

Lloyd George's resolution of the Irish question, with Eire still in the Commonwealth and Northern Ireland a part of the United Kingdom, added fresh leaves to the laurels he had earned since 1916. Within a few months of the formal institution of the Irish Free State, however, his coalition government fell from power. Although powerful Conservative leaders like Austen Chamberlain and Arthur Balfour were willing to continue the coalition, a majority of the Conservative members of Parliament, led by Bonar Law and Stanley Baldwin (1867–1947), a rising politician who had been president of the Board of Trade since May, 1921, opposed it. Moreover, the old Liberal party's association with the coalition had contributed to the rapid decline of the party as a vibrant national organization since 1916, when Asquith and his followers had left it. The same period witnessed an equally rapid growth of the Labour party, which received two million votes and elected fifty-seven members of Parliament in 1918.

The Conservatives' decision to desert the coalition resulted partly from the conviction that continued association with it would hurt the party's organization and independent voice in politics. They were also dissatisfied with the manner in which Lloyd George had handled the Chanak crisis with Turkey in 1922, the immediate cause of his fall from power. The Treaty of Sèvres (1920) had created a neutral zone on both sides of the Straits, which was occupied under League auspices by British, French, and Italian troops. The treaty also granted the Greeks mandatory rights over Smyrna and surrounding territory in Asia Minor, which they sought to enlarge permanently at Turkey's expense. When the Greeks asked the League for permission to occupy Istanbul, a request that was denied, the forces of Mustafa Kemal's revolutionary nationalist opposition to the sultan repudiated the treaty and opened an offensive that routed the Greeks and resulted in Turkish occupation of the neutral zone. The Conservatives sympathized with the Turks, who they believed were stabilizing the Near East despite the rapacity of the Greek government headed by the restored King Constantine. On the other hand, Lloyd George resented the Turks' violation of the treaty and feared their intentions. He consequently encouraged the Greeks to destroy the Kemalist rebels. When they endangered the British garrison at Chanak on the Dardanelles, he asked help from France and Italy and alerted the Dominion prime ministers that their assistance might be needed in the event of war. The Italians and French withdrew from the neutral zone and the Dominion prime ministers responded vaguely on the amount of help they might render, telling Lloyd George that such a decision rested with their Parliaments. Britain consequently stood alone against the Turks. Fortunately the patience of Kemal and the commander at Chanak averted a war, but Lloyd George's support of the Greeks and his failure to win the confidence of Britain's allies and Dominions irreparably weakened his position as prime minister. He therefore resigned on October 19, 1922.

Bonar Law replaced him at the head of a Conservative government and called for a general election. The country returned the Conservatives to power with a substantial majority. The popular vote was principally divided between the Conservatives (347 seats) and Labourites (142 seats); the Asquith Liberals gained 60 seats, Lloyd George's Liberals only 57. Illness forced Bonar Law to resign in May, 1923, and Baldwin succeeded him. He held office until 1929 except for a few months in 1924, when J. Ramsay MacDonald (1866–1937), a serious and soft-spoken Scotsman who had been with the party from its earliest days, became prime minister of Britain's first Labour government. Baldwin's first ministry fell because of labor troubles, failure to improve the economy, heavy unemployment, and an attempt to inaugurate a high-tariff policy coupled with preferential trade treaties within the Commonwealth. Not only the Liberals and Labourites, but a majority of the Conservatives as well feared that protectionism would inflate prices at home and weaken the balance of trade abroad. They challenged Baldwin's program and forced him to appeal to the electorate. The results, which returned 256 Conservatives, 192 Labourites, and 158 Liberals, clearly repudiated protectionism and left Baldwin no alternative but resignation.

In January, 1924, MacDonald became prime minister. A few Liberals accepted places in the cabinet, as did two strong socialists, but the other ministers were cautious moderates. MacDonald disappointed trade-unionists and militant socialists by refusing to sponsor socialist reforms, but he could hardly have been expected to do otherwise considering the Conservatives' strength in the Commons, the *rapprochement* between the Asquith and Lloyd George Liberals on the issue of free trade, and his lack of a parliamentary majority. Apart from a popular reduction in taxes, the first since the war, efforts to settle the now common strikes, and a Housing Act (August, 1924), which raised government subsidies to build low-rent dwellings for working-class families, the Labour government merely marked time in domestic matters.

It accomplished considerably more in the field of foreign affairs, of which MacDonald himself took charge. At a conference of financial experts in London he played a significant role in launching the Dawes plan, named after Charles G. Dawes, head of the American delegation. It called for a reduction of Germany's reparations payments, foreign loans to bolster its monetary system, and French withdrawal from the Ruhr Valley. On the other hand, MacDonald failed to consummate permanent relations with Communist Russia, which Britain had broken off in 1918. The Labour party, having an oblique philosophical connection with Bolshevik socialism, whose revolutionary methods it decried, recognized the new regime in February and sent an ambassador to Moscow. The two governments negotiated two treaties calling for commercial exchanges and a British loan. This broad-minded attempt to improve Anglo-Russian relations with an eye toward increasing British foreign trade met strong opposition from the Conservatives, particularly when the Labourites appeared to sympathize with Communism by dropping charges against J. R. Campbell, a British Communist journalist for the *Daily Worker* who had been indicted for attempting to incite workers and soldiers to disloyalty. Strong criticism from both Conservatives and Liberals led MacDonald to ask the king to dissolve Parliament. The subsequent election was fought primarily over the issue of Labour's relations with the Communists. The results were greatly affected by the publication of a letter, whose authenticity has been questioned, written by the Russian Bolshevik Zinoviev to the Russian chargé d'affaires in London, advising how the latter could organize the small British Communist party for revolution by using the Labour party. MacDonald quite honestly disclaimed any prior knowledge of the note and the Foreign Office protested to the Russians, who denied having sent it, but the incident unquestionably ruined Labour's chances at the polls. Labour won 151 seats while the Conservatives picked up a commanding majority with 415, which enabled them to repudiate the two treaties with Russia and sever diplomatic relations. The most startling result of the 1924 election, however, was the remarkably poor showing of the Liberal party which, though united, won only forty-two seats and 18 per cent of the popular vote. The party had quite clearly lost public confidence and lacked both leadership and an appealing legislative program of the sort that had made it so popular before 1914. The growth of trade-unionism and the increasing reputation of the Labour party as the party of social and economic reform robbed the Liberals of many supporters during and after the war. Other Liberals now joined the Conservative party. Moreover, the best minds in politics wore Conservative and Labourite colors, for the Liberals had done little to attract able young men or to adopt fresh ideas. Winston Churchill, a defector from Conservative ranks in 1903, now deserted the Liberal party to accept the Chancellorship of the Exchequer in Baldwin's second ministry. The party of Grey, Gladstone, and Lloyd George had fallen on evil days and declined steadily in national politics, to the point of insignificance by 1945.

Since Baldwin had been in office for too short a time in 1923–24 to have shown whether he was capable of dealing with Britain's domestic problems, the country waited anxiously for the hat trick that the Conservatives were expected to play by way of solving them. But Baldwin was no magician and his government merely did what it could by rather conventional means to cope with labor unrest and the deflated economy until the life of Parliament expired in 1929. A stocky, athletic-looking man who appeared considerably younger than his fifty-seven years, Baldwin nonetheless inspired loyalty from all ranks of his party, which he had unified to a surprising degree. He was neither priggish nor overbearing; in fact, many thought him too comfortable and easygoing to head the government, and yet he had the knack of appealing to the ordinary citizen, whose aspirations and problems he genuinely took to heart. "Tranquillity" characterized his ministry, just as moderation typified the government's attitude toward solutions to the troubles of the times. But if he lacked Lloyd George's driving energy and devotion to work, he at least kept calm under very trying circumstances and thereby helped to live up to the watchword of his administration. Above all he was honest and trustworthy, and he never tried to deceive the electorate by promising panaceas impossible of attainment.

Baldwin scored some successes in domestic affairs and kept Parliament busy enacting remedial legislation. Churchill's first budget wisely restored the duties on luxury items that Reginald McKenna's budget of 1915 had instituted as a wartime expedient, but that the MacDonald government had cut. The Conservatives thereby proved that they had not been lulled into overconfidence by the first signs of economic improvement that swept over Europe and America in 1924–25. At the same time Churchill returned Britain to the gold standard and restored the value of the pound to its prewar level of $4.86. These measures ultimately helped to stimulate industrial growth and to lower unemployment slightly. But the return to the prewar parity with gold tended to hurt British sales abroad because the increased value of the pound on foreign exchanges by about 10 per cent, as well as the high wages and high production costs of British manufacturing, discouraged a significant rise in foreign trade profits. Consequently, while the volume of exports rose in 1925–29, the value of exports actually declined.

As we have seen, the coal industry had suffered most in the postwar slump, and the efforts of three successive governments to improve the situation had failed. By 1925 the coal miners were in an ugly mood and the mine owners were looking for ways to reduce costs. Moreover, the Trades Union Congress, angry over the return to the gold standard, which it blamed for continued high unemployment, and greatly disappointed by Labour's defeat at the polls, was anxious for a showdown with the government. The opportunity came with the coal operators' announcement in June, 1925, that they would soon be forced to cut wages or increase working hours from seven to eight for the same wages. Their announcement was prompted by Baldwin's decision to terminate government subsidies to the coal industry that had enabled the owners to sustain the level of wages paid to miners since 1921. When the miners threatened to strike, and the T.U.C. brought pressure on the government for immediate action, it agreed to extend the subsidy for another nine months pending the report of another royal commission.

The commission, composed of bankers, economists, and industrialists, headed by the Liberal diplomat, Sir Herbert Samuel, recommended (March, 1926) that the government subsidy should cease, that a wage reduction was preferable to an eight-hour day, and that reforms in working conditions and mine operation should be adopted as soon as possible. When the subsidy ended, on May 1, 1926, and the mine owners posted the reduced wages, the general council of the T.U.C., announcing its refusal to accept the Samuel report, informed the government that a general strike would begin at midnight, May 3. The printers, railway and transport workers, and those in the iron, steel, and building trades walked off their jobs at that hour or refused to report for work the next morning. Practically everything ground to a halt: no streetcars, buses, or trains ran; the morning papers were stinted editions prepared hurriedly before the strike deadline; business was interrupted; the streets were strangely silent. The situation might have caused the public grave hardship but for the immediate action of the government, which had expected the strike and made provision to maintain transportation facilities and the flow of food supplies. Thousands of volunteers enrolled by the government replaced strikers. They transported food, operated trains and buses, manned the underground, and, in the case of special constables, helped the police to keep order. Car pools got businessmen and clerks to and from offices and stores. Far from coercing the government into accepting labor's demands or weaning public sympathy to the side of the working class, Britain's first general strike aroused the antipathy of the middle and upper classes and hurt most of the three million workers affected. The strike ended on May 11 for most workers, although the railwaymen stayed out until the fourteenth and the disappointed miners spent an idle summer and autumn until empty pockets compelled them to return to the pits. At that time they accepted terms less favorable than those they had rejected in March—an eight-hour day with no pay increase and greater unemployment that followed the passage of the Mining Industry Act (1926), which effected economies by easing the amalgamation of smaller collieries with larger firms. Labor had indeed given a remarkable demonstration of solidarity, but the strike had impoverished the miners and humiliated the trade-unions. And not least important was Baldwin's emergence from the crisis as something of a national hero.

Parliament's first impulse was to punish the Trades Union Congress, which it did in two statutes passed in 1927. The Trades Disputes Act declared a general strike illegal and forbade unions to use members' dues to support the Labour party without their specific permission. The Unemployment Insurance Act reduced the benefits as well as the contributions paid by workers, and, in the face of mounting deficits in the insurance fund, stopped the payment of extended benefits beyond the minimal period. But Baldwin realized that the workingman needed help, not a spanking. Accordingly, Parliament passed important social and economic legislation proposed principally by Neville Chamberlain and Winston Churchill. The program had begun in 1925 with the passage of the Widows, Orphans and Old Age Pensions Act that raised the benefits under the national health insurance system and provided new pensions for widows and orphans. The shortage of low-rent housing, partly ameliorated by Labour's housing bill in 1924, was further alleviated by continuing heavy government subsidization of local authorities, a practice introduced in 1923. The Local Government Act (1929) transferred the administration of poor relief, now called public assistance, from the rural district councils to the county councils. Apart from improving the mechanics of the system, the most important aspect of this measure was that it helped to erase the shame or stigma formerly attached to public charity by recognizing that unemployment and poverty necessitating relief were social problems beyond the control of their victims. The Act also centralized certain other functions of local government, such as road construction and maintenance. In 1926, Parliament nationalized radio by creating the British Broadcasting Corporation (BBC), and instituted a Central Electricity

Board under the supervision of the Ministry of Transport in order to lower the cost of electricity for private consumers.

The Conservatives showed little leadership in foreign affairs. Indeed, they took a step backward by refusing to ratify the Geneva Protocol (1924)—which required members of the League of Nations to submit international disputes for arbitration either by the League Council or the International Court of Justice or else be branded an aggressor—thereby weakening both the League and the World Court. Although the world war was still fresh in everyone's mind, most nations by the mid-1920s were again making the bilateral treaties that had characterized diplomacy before the war. The Russo-German Treaty of Rapallo (1922), though it involved only amity and trade relations, disquieted both France and the weak new states of eastern Europe. Moreover, without good reason, France felt insecure about Britain's friendship. For these reasons most European states, with the notable exception of Russia, negotiated bilateral treaties collectively called the Locarno Pact (October, 1925). Its purpose was to ensure security against aggression, which the League of Nations, having no military arm, could not provide. France signed treaties with Poland and Czechoslovakia promising to assist them, and vice versa, in the event of a German attack. Germany signed arbitration treaties with Czechoslovakia and Poland but refused to accept the finality of its eastern frontiers. Germany also signed similar treaties with France and Belgium. Britain and Italy promised in another treaty to assist any of the three signatories should any of them commit aggression against the others. Despite the fact that these treaties were directed primarily against a resurgence of German militarism, the League admitted Germany to membership in September, 1926.

In 1928, Britain joined fourteen other states, including the five Dominions and India, in signing the Paris Peace Pact (an extension of the Kellogg-Briand Pact of 1927), which denounced war as an instrument of national policy and obliged the signatories to settle disputes at the conference table. These and other treaties of the 1920s patently revealed Europe's fear of war and lack of confidence in the League. On the other hand, although eager for peace, the British government refused to be bound by any treaty in restraint of war should its territorial integrity or the Empire's be threatened, and was particularly sensitive to naval disarmament or limitation. Lloyd George had willingly signed the treaty concluded at the Washington Naval Conference (1921–22), which sustained Britain's naval strength in capital ships (10,000 tons) by fixing a ratio of 5 (525,000 tons) for Britain and the United States, 3 (315,000 tons) for Japan, and 1.67 (175,000 tons) for Italy and France. However, at the Geneva Naval Conference of 1927, which considered limiting the construction of cruisers between eight thousand and ten thousand tons, many of which Britain had built or had under construction, Baldwin refused to agree to a limitation or to accept a parity with any other nation in total cruiser tonnage. At the London Conference of 1930, arranged by MacDonald, Britain, the United States, and Japan agreed to extend the restriction on capital ship construction and to limit the total tonnage of their cruiser fleets. Yet, at Britain's insistence, the agreement included a clause that permitted the signatories to disregard the treaty if the limitations jeopardized their national security. On the one hand, therefore, the world powers went through the motions of partial disarmament and arrangements for preserving peace, and on the other proceeded to prepare for war.

The Baldwin ministry had been unable to do much about the lagging economy or to improve Britain's international position. Under the circumstances it was surprising that the Conservatives held office for nearly the full term of Parliament. Since an election had to be held in 1929, Baldwin set it for May 30, hoping to get the votes of the millions of women enfranchised in the Fourth Reform Act, which became operative on May 1. The election stirred great interest, not only because of the issues but also because all three parties campaigned on the radio for the first time. Baldwin ran on his record, pointing out in his party's slogan of "Safety First" that he had protected the country against socialism and Communism, and that there was an improvement in foreign trade and in employment. He simply asked the electorate to allow the Conservatives to finish the job they had started, not bothering to specify what they had begun or hoped to finish. The Liberals and Labourites took more positive positions. Lloyd George, again the Liberal leader since Asquith's retirement in 1926, made capital of the Conservatives' failure to improve the economy. In the popular pamphlet *We Can Conquer Unemployment*, and others written by economic experts like John Maynard Keynes, the Liberals promised to solve economic problems by promoting agricultural improvements, arranging business consolidations, and starting a public works program. For the impoverished miners they saw larger welfare benefits and more jobs. MacDonald also made promises: he would enhance trade-unionism, nationalize the coal and transportation industries, reduce the cost of public utilities, and arrange larger benefits for the unemployed.

The election results were indecisive: Labour won 287 seats; the Conservatives, 260; and the Liberals, 59. Eighty per cent of the 28,500,000 eligible voters cast ballots. The Conservatives obtained about 8,665,000 votes; the Labourites, 8,262,000; the Liberals, 5,301,000. But the 7,000,000 voters enfranchised since the 1924 election (mostly women) cast their ballots roughly in a ratio of 2 to 2 to 1, respectively, for the Liberals, Labourites, and Conservatives. Britain's youth was obviously dissatisfied with the Conservative administration and Baldwin had misjudged his appeal to the ladies. The Liberals gained seventeen seats and received approximately 6 per cent more votes than in 1924. Lest one jump to the conclusion that their popularity was on the rise, however, their gains should be viewed in relationship to the Labourites' impressive gain of 136 seats and the anemic campaign waged by the Conservatives. The public still had little confidence in Lloyd George, notwithstanding his brilliant campaign. Political analysts regarded the results as simply a swing of the pendulum to the side of the only other party capable of winning it. Next time, they mused, Baldwin would have another turn at the wicket.

17

Depression and War, 1929–1945

The nagging problems of finance, unemployment, and foreign trade consumed the attention of the Labour government elected in 1929. Philip Snowden made ready the budget while J. H. Thomas, Lord Privy Seal, sought ways to lower unemployment. They had scarcely gotten under way when the British people in common with most of the world felt the initial shock of the collapse of the American stock market on "Black Friday" in late October that heralded the onset of the Great Depression. American businessmen, deceived by the first flush of economic normalcy following World War I, had grossly overspeculated, taking the lead in international trade and finance, and, in 1929, paid the price. The steady clicking of ticker tapes on Wall Street that chronicled the ruin of investors and business firms virtually overnight had repercussions throughout the world. Germany, whose economy had been bolstered by the Dawes plan and was looking forward to better times because of the new Young plan that promised loans for fifty-nine years to help meet its reparations payments, was among the first to suffer. Britain withstood the worst effects of the depression longer than most industrial countries, but its economy likewise deteriorated seriously in 1931 when Germany suspended reparations payments, world trade fell off sharply, and unemployment increased rapidly.

The economic dislocations in America and Europe, where Britain had invested heavily and had its best customers, erased the gains arduously won by British business and agriculture since 1924. Unemployment tells the tale: it rose from 1,400,000 in November, 1929, to 2,500,000 in December, 1930. In 1933, 3,000,000 persons, nearly 25 per cent of the labor force, were without work. Between 1929 and

1931 the state's unemployment insurance fund went into debt by £115,000,000. In the same period exports dropped about 30 per cent, and in 1929–33 wholesale prices of British goods fell 25 per cent. The unemployed survived on the government dole, which, by the summer of 1931, had cost the Exchequer several millions. Predicting a budgetary deficit for the fiscal year 1931–32 of £120,000,000, Snowden, contrary to every instinct of the Labour party, raised taxes on personal income, death duties, beer, gasoline, and other items to meet rising expenditures.

In the first two years of the depression MacDonald's government managed to maintain the value of the pound, and London consequently became one of the last refuges for foreign investors who deposited funds on short term in British banks. But the government was thereafter unable to save the pound in the face of mounting deficits that forced the cabinet to consider drastic economies. Snowden appointed a committee, headed by Sir George May, to study ways of cutting expenses. On July 31, 1931, it recommended that the budget be cut by £96,000,000 and that new taxes be imposed to raise an additional £24,000,000. It further recommended a reduction in the pay of civil servants and servicemen, and a cut of one-fifth in weekly unemployment benefits. The May report had immediate and unexpected results: it undermined the confidence of foreign investors, who withdrew their money from banks, which in turn drained the country of gold reserves, and it split the cabinet. The cabinet committee charged with evaluating the report had initially advised the government to reduce the budget by £78,000,000. When some members of the cabinet and the Trades Union Congress opposed the cuts because they would hurt those most in need of help and impair Labour's chances in a future election, the cabinet whittled the reductions to only £22,000,000. In the end it could not agree on any figure, and its disagreement hamstrung the Bank of England, which had been trying to negotiate foreign loans totaling £80,000,000, but was told by the international bankers that no loans would be made unless the cabinet resolved its differences.

With the cabinet in a quandary, MacDonald resigned on August 24. King George V at once summoned the leaders of all three parties to Buckingham Palace, where they agreed to serve in a coalition (Nationalist) government headed by MacDonald. Four Conservatives, two Liberals, and four Labourites joined the new cabinet. But some Labourites and executives of the Trades Union Congress repudiated MacDonald's decision to cooperate with the other parties, formed the

Parliamentary Labour party, elected Arthur Henderson its leader, and expelled the prime minister and his supporters from its ranks. But Mac-Donald's followers, plus the Liberals and Conservatives in the Commons, ensured the coalition government a comfortable majority. The Bank of England secured its foreign loans and the cabinet approved a budgetary reduction of £70,000,000. These remedies failed, however, to curtail the drain on gold, and forced Parliament to abandon the gold standard on September 21. The value of the pound fell from $4.86 to $3.49. (In 1933, it had again risen to about $5.00.)

Parliament had expected that the abandonment of the gold standard would lower the prices of British goods on the world market, and therefore improve the economy by increasing trade. It had no such effect, however, primarily because competing nations were also leaving the gold standard. The United States did so in 1933 and France in 1936. Norway, Sweden, Denmark, Portugal, and most of the Empire-Commonwealth joined Britain in the so-called "sterling area." Japan devaluated its currency. Germany prohibited the export of capital and granted favorable exchange premiums to foreign customers. Practically all the states on gold were eventually forced to devaluate their currencies or impose monetary restrictions. Consequently, the temporary advantage which Britain had gained by abandoning gold was virtually erased by 1935, but its decision to do so nevertheless helped it through one of the worst financial crises in modern times and relieved pressure on its banks, not one of which failed in the depression.

The volume of exports did rise gradually in 1932–37—at the end of which time the worst of the slump had passed and the economy stood roughly on a par with that of 1929—but not because of the abandonment of the gold standard. Two other developments helped trade: the adoption of protective tariffs in 1932 and the arrangement of preferential trade treaties within the Commonwealth. The Nationalist government (1931–35) registered an overwhelming victory in the general election of October, 1931. It won 502 seats; the Parliamentary Labourites, only 52. The electorate had given MacDonald the permission for which he had asked during the campaign—a "doctor's mandate" to take whatever steps were necessary to heal the sick economy. Parliament at once imposed an ad valorem duty of 10 per cent on all imports except certain raw materials, foodstuffs, and goods from Commonwealth nations. Meanwhile the prime minister appointed an import duties advisory committee, chaired by Sir George May, to consider whether to impose still higher duties. Parliament accepted its recommendation to raise them on most manufactured goods to from 20 to 33 per cent. The committee sat intermittently until 1939, making tariff revisions here, and granting exemptions there, particularly to those foreign customers whose countries admitted British goods at favorable rates. Since most of the world's industrial states also raised their tariff schedules in the early 1930s, something like a tariff war began. High tariffs helped domestic business in most cases, but they created havoc in international commerce. In the face of mounting tariff walls and heavy competition, Britain revived the idea of imperial federation which dated from the 1880s, and which Joseph Chamberlain had been unable to implement within the Empire at the turn of the century, when Britain was on the short end of trade rivalry with Germany. At that time Britain had been unwilling to concede much commercial advantage to the Dominions, but in the 1930s it could not afford to be high-handed. In 1932, at the Ottawa Imperial Economic Conference, Britain signed mutually advantageous bilateral trade treaties with the Dominions. As a result, in 1932–38, the proportion of Britain's total imports purchased from Commonwealth countries rose by approximately 13 per cent.

The Nationalist government hailed this agreement as the dawn of a new era within the Commonwealth, but that era had already begun in 1931 with the passage of the Statute of Westminster. Only a detailed history of the Commonwealth could provide a just description of the actions and policies by which the Dominions acquired practical autonomy in the conduct of foreign affairs and weakened the other cords that fettered them politically and judicially to the mother country in the decade or so following World War I. The example of Canada will perhaps show the way in which imperial relationships were changing.

Canada emerged from the war with a new prestige earned by its citizens on the battlefield. Although organized as a separate corps, the Canadian army was under the ultimate command of the British military, a situation that irked the Canadians and created misunderstanding. This is partly why, for instance, Prime Minister Robert Borden complained to Lloyd George in 1916 about Britain's not keeping him informed as to military policy. As a result, Lloyd George created the imperial war cabinet in 1917 in which Borden and the other Dominion prime ministers helped to coordinate the war effort. They attended the peace conference of 1919–20 as representatives of separate powers, helped to write the treaties, and signed them individually. The Dominions and India became charter members of the League of Nations and had representatives on international committees conducting League business. The new spirit that gripped Canadians after the war was likewise reflected in 1922, when Prime Minister Mackenzie King notified Lloyd George that Britain should not count on Canada's automatic support in the Chanak crisis. In 1923, without having the constitutional right to do so, the Canadian government alone negotiated the Halibut Treaty with the United States, and, four years later, sent a minister to Washington. Canada and South Africa took the lead at the imperial conference of 1923 in convincing Britain that each Dominion ought to negotiate its own treaties, and that none was *ipso facto* bound by the precepts of British foreign policy. The Dominions did not join Britain as guarantors of the Franco-German frontier at Locarno in 1925, but they chose to sign the Paris Peace Pact of 1928. At the 1926 imperial conference, Britain agreed in principle that members of the Commonwealth were not collectively obligated by the commitments of any member unless the individual Parliaments gave their consent. At the same conference the delegates attempted to define the nature of the emerging Commonwealth. The resulting Balfour Declaration described the Dominions as "autonomous communities within the British Empire, equal in status, in no way subordinate one to another in any respect of their domestic or external affairs, though members of the British Commonwealth of Nations."

This declaration, plus the discussions held during the 1930 imperial conference, laid the basis for the famous Statute of Westminster. It formalized the existence of the Commonwealth (comprised initially of the United Kingdom, Canada, Australia, New Zealand, the Union of South Africa, Newfoundland, and the Irish Free State), united them under the symbolical bond of the British crown, and granted them full sovereignty in foreign affairs. The Act also denied the imperial Parliament at Westminster the right to rescind any law passed by a Dominion Parliament or to pass Acts binding in the Dominions. In addition, although the authority and functions of the governors general in the several Dominions were not defined in the Statute of Westminster, the nature of the Act itself as well as the imperial conferences held since 1926 made it clear that henceforth the governors were merely symbolical links between the crown and the Dominion governments, without whose approval no particular governor could be appointed.

The Statute of Westminster did not end all imperial authority in the Dominions. Only the imperial Parliament, for example, could finally amend the Constitutional Acts of Canada (1867), Australia (1900), and New Zealand (1907). The judicial committee of the privy council remained for several Commonwealth nations the highest court of appeal—a kind of imperial supreme court. At the same time, however, the give and take between Britain and the Dominions since 1931 has tended to minimize the latter's dependence on the mother country, and they have often made important decisions on the basis of self-interest. As the Dominions assumed more importance in world affairs, they began to resent the hint of subservience implicit in the word "Dominion," and have ceased to use it. Moreover, the word "British" has been abandoned when referring to the Commonwealth of Nations. Other Dominions, such as Eire (1937) and the Union of South Africa (1961) have left the Commonwealth, while India chose to become a republic when it gained independence in 1947. The exact nature of the Commonwealth has always defied definition, and its bonds have been alternately strengthened and weakened by the vicissitudes of world politics and its members' domestic problems. Yet it continues to exert the image, if not the reality, of moral, commercial, and military unity in an age of particularism. Constitutional historians have naturally tended to emphasize the importance of the Statute of Westminster to the Dominions, and have neglected to point out its advantages to Britain. All else aside, the Dominions repaid Britain's concessions a thousandfold in World War II.

Gradually, the Western democracies had lost confidence in the League of Nations, which, between 1920 and 1935, proved by trial and error that it could settle problems between small states, minor differences between powerful states, but not serious disputes between great states. After 1935 the great powers by and large pursued their goals of foreign policy individually so that the concept of collective security died, disarmament was abandoned, and bilateral treaties of mutual defense were concluded. While their determination to maintain peace, evidenced at the peace conference of 1920 and in the succeeding few years, faded in the face of rising nationalism, the growth of dictatorships in Germany, Italy, and Japan was encouraged by the discontent and frustration of their peoples in the post-Versailles period. The dictators committed aggression in Manchuria, China, Ethiopia, and Austria. The failure of the Western democracies to support the League in stopping aggression spelled its doom. Another disturbing fact in the 1930s was the unwillingness of the great powers to risk the use of military force to stop aggression. Britain was not alone in nursing a deep fear of war born of its sacrifices and suffering in World War I. Statesmen knew full well from the record of history that what counted in the pragmatic, amoral world of Hitler, Mussolini, and Tojo was firm diplomacy backed by the threat of force. Yet they were afraid of the consequences of force and tried to appease the Nazis and Fascists by making concessions to them.

In 1966, an Indian politician remarked that next to the rise of Communist China as a world power the most important event in Far Eastern history during this century was Japan's victory over Russia in 1905. Japan emerged from that war an industrial and military giant towering over the decaying Chinese Empire. China consequently became the victim of Japanese demands for economic and territorial concessions in the First World War, concessions which were confirmed at the peace conference and enlarged in the uneasy peace that followed. Japan ranked third in the world's pyramid of naval power at the 1921 Washington Conference, and signed the Four-Power and Nine-Power Treaties (both in 1922), promising to keep the peace in Asia and to respect China's territorial integrity. But, by 1927, Japan had already formulated plans for military aggression in China and the South Seas.

In September, 1931, shortly after a military junta had gained control of the government behind the figurehead of the emperor, the Japanese army invaded Manchuria. China appealed to the League of Nations. The United States, though not a member of the League, joined Britain in seeking collective action, but most member states were uninterested in what appeared to be a minor problem in an unimportant region. In 1932, the League sent to Manchuria an investigatory commission headed by Britain's Lord Lytton. It declared Japan guilty of aggression, but recognized its "special interests" there. Neither the League nor any nation independently took punitive steps against Japan. Britain seemed anxious to help China, but it realized that unilateral action risking war would be foolhardy in view of apathy within the international community. Japan withdrew from the League in 1933, and, in 1937, embarked on the conquest of China. This Sino-Japanese war merged with World War II in 1939.

The indifference of the Western democracies and their more immediate concern over Germany and Italy doomed Nationalist China. Of course, Britain and France had good reason to fear the dictators. Mussolini's Fascist government, in power since 1922, had improved Italy's lagging economy by expanding foreign markets and by drastic agricultural and industrial reforms, and in the early 1930s he sought Italy's restoration to the status of a great power at the expense of weaker neighbors. Accordingly, in 1934, Italian troops clashed with Ethiopians at Walwal on the border of Somaliland. The League sent a committee that included an Englishman to investigate the incident. While it studied the facts, Mussolini planned the invasion of the ancient Empire of Haile Selassie, whose ancestors had humiliated an Italian force at Adowa in 1896. The invasion of Ethiopia in October, 1935, shocked the League Assembly and inspired impassioned speeches, including one by British Foreign Secretary Sir Samuel Hoare. But action was another matter. Britain reacted equivocally to the crisis. On the one hand the bulk of the British people favored strong punitive measures against Italy; on the other, Baldwin's Nationalist government, which had won the election of October, 1935, by a comfortable margin on a platform of peace, refused to do more than support economic sanctions. The League Assembly imposed them between November, 1935, and July, 1936, but they had little effect, principally because the embargo did not include oil, and because businessmen convinced their governments that sanctions in a depression were bad for trade. Italy consequently kept its conquests and flouted the League.

British diplomats had not been idle during the Ethiopian crisis, but it cannot be said that they helped the situation. Hoare and Premier Pierre Laval of France tried to convince Mussolini and Selassie to accept a settlement whereby Ethiopia would surrender enough territory to placate Italy. They refused. The publication of the plan after the fact stirred the ire of Britons and backfired on Baldwin, who made Hoare the scapegoat. Earlier, in March, 1935, Britain became a signatory with France and Italy of the abortive Stresa agreement designed to protect them against German attack. The British public disliked an alliance with the Italian dictator, but the diplomats and the cabinet followed the advice of the military in trying to avoid a possible war with both Italy and Germany, the latter of which was judged the greater threat to peace. Hitler had replaced Hindenburg as German president early in 1933 and quickly transformed his status to Führer with dictatorial powers. Germany promptly repudiated the Versailles Treaty and demanded the restoration of its prewar frontiers. Britain embarked on a program of rearmament early in 1935, trying, meanwhile, to stay on cordial terms with Germany. The two powers signed a naval agreement in the same year that allowed Germany to rebuild its fleet up to a strength of 35 per cent of the British tonnage. Having done that, Britain could not very well oppose Hitler's reoccupation and remilitarization of the Rhineland in March, 1936. The British government likewise pursued a policy of neutrality during the Spanish civil war beginning in 1936, in which Italy and Germany made no effort to conceal military help sent to the Rightist rebels led by General Franco. Under international law the Spanish Loyalist government was entitled to buy war matériel in neutral countries, but widespread fear of Communism and Russia's avowed friendship for the Loyalists caused Baldwin's government to refuse to allow the shipment of matériel to them, and hence doomed the Spanish republic.

Britain was saddened on January 20, 1936, by the death of King George V, a quiet man whose gentle manner and singular powers of persuasion had solved several government crises since 1910. Edward VIII, the eldest of four sons, succeeded to the throne. His concern for the public welfare, particularly the poor, ensured his popularity, but he wore the crown unenthusiastically, his thoughts turning toward Mrs. Wallis Simpson, an American, divorced, and twice married. Her second divorce from an Englishman in October, 1936, worried Baldwin, who knew of Edward's intention to marry her. When hints to both Edward and Mrs. Simpson failed to weaken their resolution, Baldwin bluntly told the king that such a marriage would cause scandal to the country and irreparably damage the crown's prestige. Except for a few outspoken apologists for Edward like Churchill, most of the press, the Anglican hierarchy, and the Commonwealth opposed the marriage. Deeply troubled but determined to go through with it, Edward suggested a morganatic marriage, that is to say, one that would exclude Mrs. Simpson and her progeny from the throne. Baldwin rejected this compromise and left Edward the choice of forsaking either the marriage or the crown. On December 10 he announced his decision to renounce the throne in a message addressed to the House of Commons. The passage of the Declaration of Abdication Act ended his reign and brought his brother, George VI (1936–52), to a throne he had not expected to inherit. Shy and reserved, he was temperamentally unsuited to wear the crown, yet he served his country well.

He and Queen Elizabeth were crowned at Westminster Abbey on May 12, 1937. A month later, advanced age and illness forced Baldwin to resign. Neville Chamberlain (1869–1940), who had had a long career as a Conservative backbencher and, since 1931, a cabinet member, succeeded him as prime minister. His cabinet included Hoare (Home Office), Simon (Exchequer), and Anthony Eden, a brilliant young diplomat with a star-crossed future whom Lord Halifax replaced at the Foreign Office early in 1938. Chamberlain needed all the help he could get, for war clouds were rapidly gathering on the horizon, but he unwisely chose to pursue his own instincts in matters of foreign policy. Baldwin's attitude toward Hitler and Mussolini had been conciliatory, but Chamberlain carried appeasement even further. He had no faith in collective security or in the League, which was dead but as yet unburied. He felt that the world could live with Hitler, and that direct conversations with him could settle whatever issues might threaten peace.

Chamberlain did not have to wait long to test these principles. In 1936, Hitler and Mussolini formed the Rome-Berlin Axis aimed at drawing Austria into its orbit. In March, 1938, after careful preparations by the Nazi fifth column, the German army invaded and annexed Austria. No nation objected. Britain and France suspected that Czechoslovakia would be Hitler's next objective, but, unlike France, which had signed a mutual defense pact with Czechoslovakia in 1925, Britain was not obliged to defend the Sudetenland (part of Czechoslovakia) against German aggression. Yet Chamberlain realized full well that a Franco-German war must eventually involve Britain, and therefore sought to prevent it. He sent Lord Runciman to Prague in the summer of 1938 to appraise the situation and to find a way, if possible, to circumvent the military annexation of the Sudetenland, whose predominantly German population had been clamoring for reunion with Germany. Then Chamberlain went himself to Berchtesgaden in Bavaria for talks with Hitler, who succeeded in convincing the prime minister that Germany's goals were still negotiable. Chamberlain was duped, for actually the Führer was simply buying a little time to build Germany's strength against Britain, which he believed to be the Reich's foremost enemy next to Russia. Chamberlain, worried by the Berchtesgaden talks, returned to England convinced that, while he must continue to negotiate, he must also prepare more rapidly for war. The government put men to work digging trenches, erecting coastal defenses, planning for the evacuation of children from London and heavily industrialized areas, and preparing for air attacks. Throughout this period Chamberlain kept hoping that reason and justice would prevail in Europe despite Hitler's increasingly hostile remarks.

At first Hitler had been satisfied to await a plebiscite in the Sudetenland, but then he demanded immediate annexation or he would take it by force. British and French diplomats gasped. Chamberlain looked for the worst. Perhaps another heart-to-heart talk with Hitler, he conjectured, would ease the tension. Thus, while the Foreign Office warned Hitler that Britain could not stand idle should a Franco-German war erupt over Czechoslovakia, Chamberlain asked the dictator for another meeting. The European situation looked black and the government went about preparing for war as though hope was spent. But on September 28, Hitler invited Chamberlain, French Premier Edouard Daladier, and Mussolini to a conference at Munich. Without consulting the Czechs or Russians, they agreed to the immediate cession of the Sudetenland to Germany and guaranteed the territorial integrity of the rest of the country. The world rejoiced at the news Chamberlain brought back to London—"peace in our time." No British statesman for years had received such a thunderous welcome from his countrymen.

But peace was fickle and the ebullient public who hailed the Peacemaker in September labelled him the Appeaser in March. The Labourites, led by Clement Attlee and Aneurin Bevan, denounced Chamberlain's folly, and powerful Conservative spokesmen like Churchill, Eden, and Harold Macmillan joined in the chorus. But Chamberlain did not waver in his convictions until March 15, 1939, when Hitler flagrantly violated the Munich settlement by invading Bohemia and Moravia. Then all changed in Britain. Rearmament was quickened. The Royal Air Force stockpiled planes, and the army was brought to full strength and then enlarged by conscription in April. The home guard took their places on the rooftops, at communication and transportation centers, and in the bunkers along the southeastern coast. Plans were formulated for civil defense against German air raids. Chamberlain assured France of Britain's loyalty in the event of war. Poland, Rumania, and Greece were told the same. Britain also concluded an understanding with Turkey for the defense of the eastern Mediterranean. In the following summer, while Europe awaited Hitler's next move, Britain learned of the Russo-German nonaggression treaty which freed Hitler from fear of a two-front war and doomed Poland to invasion from both east and west. Frantic diplomatic maneuvering to muster a "Stop Hitler Front" failed. On August 24 Germany seized Danzig, a city of nearly 400,000, mostly Germans, located at the head of the Polish Corridor. The news brought instant mobilization in Britain. Despite last minute pleas for peace from several quarters, including the pope and President Roosevelt, on September 1 Germany invaded Poland. Britain demanded the withdrawal of German troops and received no reply. On the 3rd,

Chamberlain issued a two-hour ultimatum expiring at 11 A.M.—withdrawal or war. Hitler ignored it. At 11:15 Chamberlain's terse speech over the radio and the wail of sirens in London signaled the beginning of another world war. France declared war at the same hour.

The German war machine moved so rapidly against Poland that neither Britain nor France had time to help. Bombers decimated rail centers and airfields, rendering Anglo-French assistance via air transport impossible. On September 17, the Russians invaded from the east. Ten days later Warsaw surrendered, and Hitler and Stalin partitioned Poland. The Russians later annexed the Baltic states of Latvia, Lithuania, and Estonia, and demanded that Finland surrender the Karelian Isthmus bordering Leningrad, and Petsamo in the arctic region. When the Finns refused, the Russians invaded and forced them to agree to a peace that ensured their independence but ceded the Karelian Isthmus and the Hangö Peninsula to Russia. Thus the Russians created a buffer zone between themselves and Germany and acquired a great deal of territory. The false peace between these two traditional antagonists lasted until 1941.

Meanwhile the western front was strangely quiet. British, French, Dutch, and Belgian troops stood watch along the Maginot line and the Belgian and Dutch frontiers; the Germans along the Siegfried line. While the soldiers endured maddening suspense the diplomats of the free world worked to strengthen the Allied position, and the nations and territories of the Commonwealth-Empire declared war and prepared for it. In the early stages of the Battle of the Atlantic the British navy tried to clear the seas of German merchantmen and fought submarines and surface raiders. It also blockaded the German coast in order to strangle Hitler's overseas trade in essential war material and foodstuffs.

The Allies expected a massive German assault against the Maginot line, but on April 9, 1940, Hitler instead moved against Norway and Denmark. Denmark collapsed in a few days, Norway in a month, and Sweden declared its neutrality but thereafter sold strategic materials to Germany. Through these easy conquests Hitler had acquired rich agricultural resources, naval and air bases on the North Sea, and some control of the sea lanes between England and Russia.

These Allied reverses shook Britain's confidence in the Nationalist government. Chamberlain had not been a firm or inspiring leader, and his indecisiveness made the country—including many Conservatives—uneasy. Liberals and Labourites had refused to join his nine-member war cabinet, which included Churchill at the Admiralty. But, as the war required the cooperation of the opposition parties, it had been agreed to postpone a national election for the duration and not to contest by-elections. Parliament instituted regulations on food, trade, shipping, employment, the manufacture of munitions, and the like as it had in World War I, and the country prepared for German air attacks. Hundreds of thousands of aged folk, young mothers, and school-children grudgingly left London for the greater safety of the west country and Wales, where their less sophisticated countrymen put them up with as little enthusiasm. But the bombers did not come and the autumn and winter of 1939–40—a period Churchill aptly described as "the twilight war"—tensed nerves and made men eager to exchange boredom for battle. When the Germans invaded Norway and the six-teen-thousand-man Anglo-French commando force at Narvik had to be evacuated, Chamberlain tried to explain away the loss by praising the success of the evacuation! But Parliament and the public were not satisfied, and on May 10 he resigned. Churchill (1874–1965), whose career as newspaper correspondent, soldier, parliamentarian, author, and cabinet member had already spanned four decades, became prime minister at the age of sixty-five. He at once appointed a war cabinet representative of all three parties. It consisted of himself as minister of defense; Clement Attlee, Labour party leader, as government spokes-man in the Commons; Ernest Bevin, formerly general secretary of the Transport Workers Union, minister of labour and national service; the Labourite Herbert Morrison, minister of supply; and the press mag-nate Lord Beaverbrook, minister of aircraft production. The war cabi-net concentrated on policy decisions and left minor problems to several administrative committees headed by government ministers.

On the day of Churchill's appointment the Germans smashed across the Dutch, Belgian, and Luxembourg frontiers while the *Luftwaffe* rained destruction on Amsterdam, Rotterdam, Brussels, and other cities. Thirty-two Belgian and Dutch divisions had no chance against the armored might of ninety German divisions. The Dutch surrendered in five days; the Belgians in three weeks. The French and British armies, the latter consisting of only nine divisions, rushed up the Meuse Valley to help, but they arrived too late and were caught in a sweep-ing German pincer movement that crushed the main French line at Sedan and progressed almost uninterruptedly up the Somme River to the Channel. French, Belgian, and British soldiers caught north of that line were trapped and pushed back to the sea. Nearly 340,000 men (about 225,000 of them British) were forced to await rescue on the beach at Dunkirk while German planes decimated their ranks. In this crisis thousands of volunteers in every sort of craft helped the Royal Navy to rescue them. The vast majority arrived safely in England thanks to the courage of their countrymen and the R.A.F., which provided a modicum of air cover while the operation ran its grim course between May 29 and June 3. Hundreds of guns, several thousand tons of ammunition, and a mountain of supplies had to be left behind.

The weary smiles of the survivors belied the catastrophe that had befallen the Allies. The remnants of the French army could not hold the Germans and Paris was occupied in mid-June. The terms of surrender ceded to Germany nearly half of France—the north and the entire Atlantic coastline. Italy, which had declared war on France on June 10, acquired some territory in the southeast. The remainder of France was not occupied, but the government of Marshal Philippe Pétain, the hero of Verdun in World War I who had replaced Premier Paul Reynaud on June 16, promised to surrender the French fleet to Germany and to guarantee cooperation in the unoccupied section. He established a totalitarian regime at Vichy that was recognized by Britain and the other Western powers for the sake of convenience, but was generally held in contempt for its collaboration. Many Frenchmen refused to accept Pétain's policy. Foremost among them was General Charles de Gaulle, who escaped with other leaders to England to fight again under the banner of the Free French army. Others stayed behind to wage underground war against the Germans and the Vichy regime. Reynaud had secured the British government's consent to the surrender, but he had been asked to turn over the French Atlantic fleet to Britain lest it fall into enemy hands. When its admiral refused to agree, a British squadron sank or disabled the ships in the Algerian port of Oran.

Churchill realized the gravity of Britain's position and did not try to deceive his countrymen. In a speech to the Commons on May 13, 1940, he said: "we are in the preliminary stage of one of the greatest battles in history," and told them that "many, many long months of struggle and of suffering" lay ahead, and that "without victory, there is no survival . . . for the British Empire. . . ." He asked Britons for their help; as for himself, he said, "I have nothing to offer but blood, toil, tears and sweat." When the fall of France in June, 1940, left Britain alone in Europe to face the Nazis, he went on the air again to say: "What General Weygand called the 'Battle of France' is over. I expect that the battle of Britain is about to begin. Upon this battle depends the survival of Christian civilization." Should Germany prevail, he warned, a "new dark age" would descend upon mankind. "Let us therefore brace ourselves to our duty," he pleaded, "and so bear ourselves that if the British Commonwealth and Empire lasts for a thousand years men will say, 'This was their finest hour.' "

Churchill was right. The Battle of Britain began in earnest in August, 1940, when thousands of bombers began to pound defense installations, industrial complexes, and ordinary people's homes, first to destroy resistance for an invasion planned for September, and later to destroy morale. While the Germans prepared for invasion on the French and Belgian coasts, the British endured one of the most terrifying bombardments in history. Hundreds of bombers came nightly until May, 1941, and every night weary civilians manned the rooftops, fought fires, cared for the dead and wounded, filed down into the underground stations for an uncomfortable sleep, or huddled under staircases or in garden bomb shelters. Giant spotlights lit the balloons and skies over London, Portsmouth, Hull, Sheffield, Liverpool, and most other large cities while fighter pilots steered their Spitfires and Hurricanes toward the enemy formations. Much of old London and Southwark was destroyed or damaged. On November 12, 1940, the 250,000 inhabitants of Coventry saw their city and its magnificent fifteenth-century cathedral crumble in ruins. Nearly 61,000 civilians died because of air raids by the end of the war. The figure might have been much higher but for efficient civil defense and the inaccuracy of German bombers. Throughout this period Churchill and the war cabinet worked and slept in a blockhouse in central London, and on many early mornings the prime minister walked through the streets to survey the previous night's damage. His determination and strength of character were communicated to those near him and his radio messages sustained the spirit of Britons everywhere. Far from destroying British morale, the Battle of Britain steeled the country for arduous tasks ahead.

The North African campaign commenced during the height of the Battle of Britain. Italian armies numbering 250,000 men moved out of Libya and Eritrea to expel 80,000 British soldiers scattered in Palestine, Kenya, Egypt, and British Somaliland. In late August, 1940, the British evacuated Somaliland and, under General Sir Archibald Wavell's command, made ready to defend Egypt against the forces of

Marshal Graziani, who forced Wavell to fall back almost to Alexandria, where he made a stand. Meanwhile the British Mediterranean squadron under the brilliant tactician Admiral Sir Andrew Cunningham disrupted Italian supply lines and in November damaged part of the Italian fleet at Taranto. In December, Wavell counterattacked, and the raid turned into a major drive in which British, Anzac, and Indian troops rolled nearly five hundred miles westward to Benghazi, routing ten Italian divisions. In January, 1941, other British units occupied Eritrea and Somaliland, and in April liberated Ethiopia.

Meanwhile two developments imperiled the Allied position in the eastern Mediterranean theater. The first was Graziani's replacement by the German General Erwin Rommel, the Desert Fox, whose Afrika Korps smashed the British in April, 1941, and drove them back into Egypt. The second was the reverse suffered by Anglo-Greek forces in Greece in a campaign lasting from October to May, 1940–41, which necessitated the transference of nearly 60,000 men from Wavell's command. When Athens fell to the Germans in April, the entire British force was evacuated, some 20,000 of them to Crete, which German paratroopers and bombers at once attacked. When the loss of thousands of British lives proved the island indefensible, it was abandoned. The favorable position the Allies had enjoyed at the beginning of winter, 1940, had steadily deteriorated as one defeat followed another in the Balkans and North Africa. It was small comfort that an Anglo-Free French force captured Syria and Iraq in June and July, 1941, and that the British and Russians (to whom Britain, like the United States, was soon sending millions of dollars in military and economic aid) saved Iran from the clutches of the enemy.

Britain was, however, receiving some aid from the United States. Since 1936 Roosevelt had been watching events in Europe and Asia with increasing concern while the largely isolationist American Congress maintained a smug aloofness behind the pseudo-protection of three thousand miles of ocean and four Neutrality Acts passed between 1935 and 1939 that were aimed at preventing the sort of involvement with belligerents that had brought the United States into World War I. At Roosevelt's insistence, in September, 1939, Congress had amended the Acts to the extent that the embargo on munitions was ended on condition that belligerent nations purchase and transport them on a strictly cash-and-carry basis. In this way the United States was able to lend some help to Britain and France. America moved a step closer to war during the period of limited belligerency from the fall of France in 1940 to Pearl Harbor in 1941. American businessmen sold huge quantities of munitions and supplies to the Allies. In September, 1940, the United States gave Britain fifty destroyers in exchange for ninety-nine-year leases for naval and air bases in Bermuda and Newfoundland. The following February Congress inaugurated the lend-lease policy under which the United States gave outright or on consignment millions of dollars in munitions and supplies to the Allies, including Russia after June, 1941. Meanwhile American armed forces went to Greenland and protected the shipping lanes in the western Atlantic. In August, 1941, Churchill and Roosevelt met off the coast of Newfoundland to draft the Atlantic Charter, which laid the basis for the United Nations. The meeting also brought the Allies greater American support short of actual war, particularly after German submarines attacked American destroyers in September and October. In September, Congress repealed the Neutrality Acts and authorized arming of American merchantmen.

War in Europe had provided the Japanese with the opportunity to press their conquest of China and, threatening to create a "New Order" in Asia, to cast greedy eyes on the South Pacific and Indo-China, where Britain, France, and Holland held lands rich in oil, rubber, and foodstuffs. Throughout 1939 and 1940 the Japanese government brought pressure on Britain to evacuate its concession at Tientsin on the Chinese mainland, and at one point tightly blockaded it. The situation improved as a result of the Craigie-Arita agreement whereby Britain continued to hold Tientsin but promised that its officials and subjects would do nothing in China prejudicial to Japanese interests. In June, 1940, despite this understanding, the Japanese stood poised on the borders of Hong Kong, bringing enormous pressure on that British colony whose position had already been jeopardized in the spring of 1939 by Japan's seizure of the island of Hainan in the South China Sea. Britain and America became alarmed as Japan, capitalizing on the collapse of France in 1940, obtained the right to establish garrisoned air bases in Indo-China, only a few hundred miles from Burma, Malaya, and the Philippines. Japan also took advantage of a territorial dispute in Indo-China between Thailand and Vichy France, and in the spring of 1941, annexed both Thailand and Indo-China. These bold thrusts, as well as the military alliance that Japan had signed with Germany and Italy in September, 1940, led Britain, the United States, Holland, and China to conclude, in October, 1941, joint defense plans against further Japanese encroachments.

Cordell Hull, American secretary of state, engaged in protracted negotiations attempting to stabilize the situation, but the talks collapsed in November, 1941, in the face of Japan's refusal to limit its plans for the fulfillment of the "New Order." On December 7, the Japanese attack on Pearl Harbor plunged America into the war. Britain, honoring its pledge to assist the United States, at once declared war on Japan and the Dominion governments followed suit. Churchill hurried to Washington just before Christmas to coordinate the war effort, while Eden conferred with Stalin in Moscow. These talks resulted in an agreement that was eventually signed by twenty-six united nations, which promised to commit all their resources to defeat the enemy, never to conclude a separate peace, and to abide by the articles of the Atlantic Charter. Thus was born in wartime an international organization dedicated to the maintenance of peace.

The Japanese had greater military strength than many had imagined. In the first months after Pearl Harbor, they overran most of the Far East. The twelve thousand British, Canadian, and Indian troops at Hong Kong surrendered on Christmas Day, and the great naval base of Singapore capitulated on February 15. The battle for the Philippines opened with the Japanese invasion on December 8, 1941. The American-Filipino army led by General Douglas MacArthur abandoned Manila on December 22 and the province of Bataan with its fortress at Corregidor on April 9. The Japanese overran in rapid succession Sumatra, Java, Borneo, New Guinea, the Celebes, and a host of smaller islands, acquiring rich oil, rubber, and tin deposits that the Dutch had refused to sell or lease to them. In spring, 1942, practically the entire South Pacific flew the flag of the Rising Sun. Slowly the Allies recovered from these shocks and retaliated. The American Pacific fleet bombarded Japanese strongholds on the Gilberts, Marshalls, Wake Island, and New Guinea, and won victories off the Solomons, in the Coral Sea, and in the Bismarck Sea in 1942 and 1943. India, frustrated by Britain's refusal to grant it self-government, at first joined the Allied cause reluctantly, but came alive in 1944 when the Japanese invaded. Indo-British troops fought in drenching rain, insect-infested jungles, and terrible heat in northeastern India for seven months before the Japanese retreated into Burma. By that time the Americans, Australians, and New Zealanders had recovered the Gilberts, the Marshalls, and the Marianas, and the Canadians and Americans had occupied several Aleutian islands evacuated by the Japanese.

Meanwhile in 1942, in North Africa, the Allies had not yet cracked

Rommel's superb Afrika Korps. Under General Sir Claude Auchinleck, Wavell's successor, the British erased Axis gains and drove the Germans beyond Benghazi, but there Rommel stayed the advance and counterattacked, recovering the ground he had lost and more. By June, 1942, he had overwhelmed twenty-five thousand men at Tobruk and threatened the Suez Canal and the Middle East, where he hoped to merge ultimately with a German army pushing down through the Ukraine and the Caucasus. To avert this catastrophe, the British concentrated every available man and machine at El Alamein, seventy miles west of Alexandria, and held off Rommel's repeated attacks in July and August. Denied support from Europe, the Germans had spent their strength while the British, refreshed by reinforcements, prepared under General Sir Bernard Montgomery to drive the Afrika Korps from Egypt and Libya once and for all. The definitive offensive of the North African theater commenced in late October, 1942. Driving west, the British Eighth Army entered Tripoli on January 23. The previous November an Anglo-American army commanded by General Dwight Eisenhower had invaded French North Africa, and the converging Allied armies trapped the Germans in northern Tunisia; in May, a quarter million enemy soldiers surrendered.

The liberation of North Africa raised among the Allied political leaders the question where to strike next. The lessons of World War I convinced Churchill that the Allies should invade through the Balkans in order to prevent the Russians from acquiring territory in eastern Europe. His motives appear to have been mainly political, and, as events later proved, not without wisdom. But military leaders pointed out the difficulties of a Balkan invasion as compared to an Italian invasion, and Churchill had to accede to the requirements of logistics. Unquestionably, however, a second front had to be established somewhere in Europe to relieve pressure on the Russians, then fighting a desperate defensive operation. Accordingly, Churchill and Roosevelt, meeting at Casablanca and Washington in January and May, 1943, decided to invade Sicily. After repeated air attacks 150,000 British, Canadian, and American troops seized the island's southern and eastern beaches. They met only token resistance, marched to Palermo, and in mid-August captured Messina, gateway to the Italian mainland. The relative ease with which Sicily had been taken as well as air raids on Naples and Rome demoralized the Italian people, and when Mussolini failed to convince Hitler that Italy desperately needed massive German support, the Fascist Grand Council arrested Il Duce, although he later escaped behind the German lines. The new government of Marshal Pietro Badoglio renounced Fascism, and, in September, negotiated a secret armistice with Eisenhower.

The Italian surrender strained the resources of Germany and forced a larger concentration of its troops in the Italian theater. An Anglo-American army commanded by General Mark Clark landed at Salerno near Naples on September 8 and fought a desperate campaign with their backs to the sea, holding on for several weeks while a British army that had crossed the Strait of Messina hurried north to relieve them. The two armies merged and captured Naples, and at that point the Allies made public the secret armistice with the Badoglio government, which declared war on Germany on October 13. Hitler, realizing that repeated reverses in Italy would eventually imperil the Reich itself, ordered his troops to stand ground along a wide front north of Naples. The Fifth Army shattered this line in May, 1944, with the help of another army that had landed at Anzio, to the north, outflanking the Germans. The Allies entered Rome on June 4. While Canadian, British, Polish, Greek, and American units advanced slowly up both coastlines during the succeeding autumn and winter, Marshal Tito's guerrilla army cleared Yugoslavia of Germans, and Greek patriots, supplied by Britain, also expelled the enemy.

Some months before the occupation of Rome the Allies had been making plans for the liberation of the Low Countries and France and the conquest of Germany, whose cities and industries had been the targets of heavy air raids. A meeting of the foreign ministers of Britain, Russia, and the United States in November, 1943, at which it was decided to punish war criminals and provide for the political and economic rehabilitation of central Europe at the conclusion of the war, was followed by talks among Churchill, Roosevelt, and Chiang Kai-shek at Cairo about the defeat of Japan, and by further talks at Teheran among Churchill, Roosevelt, and Stalin respecting Europe and the peace terms that Germany would have to accept.

The invasion of Normandy, a masterpiece of engineering skill and military coordination, came on June 6, 1944. Five Allied divisions commanded by Eisenhower crossed the Channel in four thousand ships under cover of eleven thousand aircraft and established beachheads at several points. The troops suffered heavy casualties, but in less than a month, a million Allied soldiers were advancing through northwestern France for a rendezvous with paratroopers dropped behind the German lines. While Anglo-Canadian troops protected the left flank at Caen in one of the bloodiest battles of the war, the Americans hurried across the Breton peninsula and isolated Cherbourg, which surrendered on June 26. Two weeks later the American First Army under General Omar Bradley captured strategic Saint-Lô, pierced the enemy's defenses at Coutances, and held the ground while General George Patton's armored division pushed up the Loire Valley. As these armies advanced toward the Seine and Paris in August, an Anglo-French-American army invaded the French Mediterranean coast between Toulon and Cannes. This maneuver forced the Germans to divert troops to the south, eased the Allied advance on Paris, and liberated southern France with the help of the French underground.

Allied victories followed in swift succession in France and the Low Countries in the summer and autumn of 1944. Again with the aid of the underground, Paris was liberated on August 25; Brussels and Antwerp were taken on September 3 and 4. By the middle of the month the Allies stood poised on the German frontier, and the first troops crossed into Germany as early as September 12, although it was two months before they could make much of a dent in the Siegfried line. Aachen, Metz, and Strasbourg fell by late November, but, beginning on December 16, the Germans launched a grinding counteroffensive lasting ten days (the Battle of the Bulge) along an eighty-mile front in the Ardennes, and nearly succeeded in splitting the Allied armies and capturing Antwerp before the Americans stopped them at Bastogne. Early in January the Allies resumed their march on Germany without any more significant setbacks. While British forces captured Bremen and Hamburg and penetrated Schleswig into Denmark, French and American armies occupied central and southern Germany as far as the Elbe River and western Czechoslovakia.

The Russians also launched a great offensive, involving three million men, in September, 1944, and drove the Germans from Finland, the Baltic republics, eastern Poland, and the Ukraine, and later from Hungary, Rumania, and Bulgaria, all of which they occupied, as Churchill had feared. British forces invaded Albania, and by the spring of 1945 the Balkans had been cleared of Germans except for a small sector of Croatia and Bosnia that later surrendered. What remained of the once mighty *Wehrmacht* fell back on all sides toward Berlin. V-E Day came on May 7 with the unconditional surrender of Germany in a schoolroom in the cathedral city of Rheims. Churchill announced the victory over the BBC, the country rejoiced, and the House of Commons offered prayers of thanksgiving in St. Margaret's Church. On June 5, an Allied

Control Council assumed the government of Germany and divided it into four occupation zones.

The war in the Far East ended about twelve weeks after V-E Day. Allied naval victories in 1943 had cleared the way for an invasion of the Philippines, while Admiral Lord Louis Mountbatten invaded Burma with British, Indian, African, Chinese, and American troops composing the British Fourteenth Army. By May, 1945, it had recaptured Rangoon, reopened the Burma Road to China, and penetrated Thailand and Malaya. In the early months of 1945, also, American marines captured Iwo Jima and Okinawa, and the Japanese homeland and Japanese positions in China and Korea were bombed. This air offensive, accompanied by British and American naval bombardment of the Japanese coast, continued with increasing intensity from May to early August. When the Japanese government rejected two demands of unconditional surrender made by the United States, Britain, and China, President Harry Truman, mindful of the heavy casualties that must result from an invasion of the Japanese home islands, ordered the dropping of the first atomic bomb on Hiroshima on August 6, and another on Nagasaki on the ninth. On the fifteenth, the Japanese surrendered.

18

Britain since 1945

The staggering cost of the Second World War to Britain has deeply affected the course of its postwar history. More than 5,000,000 persons had served in the regular armed forces and the home guard. Practically every able-bodied person between the ages of fourteen and sixty-four worked in some phase of the war effort, including 7,000,000 women, 80,000 of whom did hard agricultural labor. Close to 300,000 servicemen, 61,000 civilians, and 35,000 merchant mariners had been killed, and another 700,000 Britons were wounded or lost in action. Approximately half the merchant fleet had been sunk, and a third of that not rebuilt despite a construction program that accounted for much of the total wartime expenditures of £25,000,000,000. The volume of exports had declined by 70 per cent since 1939 while imports of foodstuffs and matériel created one of the most serious imbalances of trade in the nation's history. Britain had customarily paid for its imports by exchanging industrial products for them, but while the economy was busy making war matériel the system had been practically abandoned. Britain consequently had to sell many foreign investments, and, despite America's generosity in the lend-lease program, to borrow huge sums abroad. Approximately 4,500,000 houses, nearly 35 per cent of the total, had been destroyed or heavily damaged by bombs. A 50 per cent reduction in food imports in 1939–45 (mostly because of shipping losses) necessitated a substantial increase in the acreage under cultivation. National spirit remained high, however, despite necessary government controls, shortages, bombings, and extremely heavy taxes, especially on tobacco, liquor, and amusements. Britons responded magnificently to the demands of war, partly because, to a surprising degree under the circumstances, the government respected their individual rights. With the exception of a few brief strikes, generally among miners, workers exhibited far greater concern for the public interest than had been the case in World War I.

These facts must be considered in relationship to the events of the two decades after 1945. Financial and economic problems, resulting chiefly from the war, have forced every British government to impose controls that have tended to weaken public confidence in the welfare state, strained the patience of Britons anxious to return to normalcy, induced tens of thousands to emigrate, and taxed the resourcefulness of industry. These domestic problems have in turn greatly affected Britain's stature and involvement in international affairs. World War II so weakened the nation that it could no longer carry the burden of world leadership. Although Britain did well to fulfill its obligations during the late 1940s and early 1950s in the defense of western Europe and parts of Asia, economic problems have forced it to shrink from too great involvement in the cold war and to withdraw most of its armed forces from centers of strategic importance. Moreover, since 1939, the British Empire has steadily declined in territory and influence in the face of nationalism, particularly in Africa and Asia. Although some former colonies have joined the Commonwealth (which in 1966 was composed of twenty-three members), in many cases they have drifted from close allegiance to Britain and no longer consider its problems their own.

World War II and its aftermath likewise contributed to a social revolution in Britain. Genealogical titles, class distinctions, and marked differences in personal wealth have ceased to be of much significance. The nationalization of certain basic industries, the institution of a national health program, high taxes, broader educational opportunities, and a wider application of social justice for all Britons have contributed to the demise of a privileged society and made the welfare state a costly reality.

Long before V-E Day the Churchill government laid plans for Britain's postwar reconstruction and the expansion of social welfare programs. In December, 1942, Sir William Beveridge, formerly director of the London School of Economics and a distinguished authority on social problems, published his famous report, which at once captured world-wide attention as the most imaginative document of its kind. Conceived on the principle that all persons, regardless of station or income, were entitled to a minimum standard of living, it proposed the creation of a new Ministry of Social Security to administer welfare programs formerly controlled by twelve separate government departments. It further recommended the institution of a national health system embracing all workers and their families, a substantial increase in old-age pensions, children's allowances, and maternity and death benefits to cover extraordinary personal expenses. Beveridge suggested that this far-reaching program should be financed by a compulsory, flat rate of contributions by workers, employers, and the government, which should bear the greater part of a financial burden estimated at roughly £3,350,000,000 in the first year. The report envisaged financial security for all Britons against unemployment, sickness, and heavy familial expenses "from the cradle to the grave." Other government committees sought solutions to different problems as a basis for postwar legislation. One led by Justice Uthwatt in 1941 was concerned with better urban land use and town planning, a task that was eased considerably by German bombers and rockets. Another headed by Justice Scott in 1942 studied questions of rural land development and the rejuvenation of decaying towns through industrial growth. A third issued a white paper, written in 1944 by John Maynard Keynes, economic adviser to the Treasury, who proposed a policy to ensure full employment. A fourth committee recommended sweeping educational reforms. Finally, in 1943 and 1945, the coalition government and the Labour party, respectively, formulated four- and five-year plans that incorporated many of the suggestions made by the investigatory committees.

Two reforms, a Town and Country Planning Act and an Education Act, both passed in 1944, anticipated the sort of social welfare legislation that characterized the first three postwar years. The Town and Country Planning Act (amended in 1947) created a new ministry to supervise the work of the local planning authorities without whose approval no property could be developed. It also encouraged these authorities to clear slums and rebuild housing with heavy government subsidization. Approximately 200,000 new houses were to be built annually for the succeeding ten years, more if building materials became more plentiful. Despite the construction of several million new dwellings since 1945, however, many British cities, including London, Birmingham, and Sheffield, have faced critical housing shortages. Consequently tens of thousands of families have had to live in flats without running water or proper sanitary facilities, or in dilapidated prefabricated houses that were meant to be temporary. The Education Act replaced the Board of Education with a Ministry of Education, to which each local education authority was responsible in seeing that provision was made for adequate elementary, secondary, and adult educational facilities. It raised the so-called school-leaving age from fourteen to fifteen years (effective in 1947), required the provision of free milk and lunches for all school children, increased the number of teacher-training and vocational schools, and enlarged opportunities for continuing education by establishing county colleges and university scholarships. This Act not only added great numbers of pupils to the rolls and necessitated the training of many new teachers; it also encouraged more students to enter university with full or partial government support. Notwithstanding the opportunities for higher education thus created, the Act put a major crimp in the educational system by instituting the "eleven plus" examination taken by pupils at the age of eleven or twelve, by which it is determined whether they enter high-grade grammar schools or the less respected secondary modern schools that have increasingly adopted American educational methods and curriculums. Many graduates of secondary modern schools have gone on to universities, but many others who failed the much-feared "eleven plus" have not, often because the "system" discouraged them at too early an age to judge their academic potential. The Education Act has remained the basic rubric for English education. Similar Acts were passed for Scotland (1946) and Northern Ireland (1947). ·

The coalition government called for a general election on July 5, 1945—the first since November, 1935. Churchill asked the Labourites and Liberals to stand with the coalition in seeking a governmental continuum until the end of the war with Japan, but they declined and resigned from the cabinet in May, leaving the prime minister in charge of a caretaker government. The Labourites, skeptical about their chances at the polls in view of Churchill's great popularity, campaigned vigorously. Clement Attlee, Aneurin Bevan, Ernest Bevin, and Herbert Morrison, leaders of the party, refrained from criticizing Churchill, but accused the Conservatives of profit-taking and of failure to cope adequately with social and economic problems. In *Let Us Face the Future*, they published a five-year plan that has been variously interpreted as a sincere program for social justice or a catchall to win public support. The election was influenced to some extent—how much is hard to say—by a remark made by Harold Laski, a left-wing Labourite and lecturer at London University, that the party, if elected, would not be bound by decisions reached by Churchill at the Potsdam Conference, where Churchill, Attlee, Truman, and Stalin discussed a

German peace treaty and Germany's eastern frontier. Churchill exploited the statement, Attlee repudiated it, and the electorate took it under advisement.

The election results, announced on July 26 after the compilation of the service vote, went overwhelmingly against the Conservatives. Labour won 393 seats; the Conservatives, 189; the Liberals, 12; and others, 46. The popular vote was equally decisive, Labour gaining nearly as many votes as the other parties combined. Such a landslide had been entirely unexpected. The electorate had apparently ignored Labour's charges of Conservative corruption in the war, and it had no less respect for Churchill, but the Conservatives had been unable to banish the ghost of Neville Chamberlain and the policy of appeasement. Moreover, Labour's program of postwar reconstruction appealed to Britons eager to get on with the job of rebuilding and anxious about the Conservatives' reluctance to promise sweeping social and economic reforms. Churchill, bitterly disappointed by what seemed to him a repudiation by an ungrateful nation, resigned on July 26.

Clement R. Attlee (1883–1967) became prime minister, only the second Labourite to do so in the party's fifty-year history. He had served a long political apprenticeship since his election to Parliament in 1924 as member for Limehouse, but he had risen rapidly in the party's administrative hierarchy, first as under-secretary for war in the 1924 Labour government, then deputy party leader in 1929–35, and finally leader for ten years before becoming prime minister. Thin, balding, and stoop-shouldered, he looked more like a tired civil servant than a chief of state, and his restrained, almost apologetic, smile typified the quiet, shrewd, self-effacing leader that he was. If as an orator he lacked color, precision, and imagination, he had a deep devotion to the party, tenacity of purpose, and unimpeachable integrity. Such qualities made him a strong leader but not an engaging personality, although his cabinet appointees, for the most part seasoned veterans of politics and trade-unionism, compensated for the color and verve he lacked. Aneurin Bevan (Health) had earned a reputation for radical socialist ideas and a nasty temper, but he was a superb orator. Ernest Bevin (Foreign Office), orphaned at the age of eight, had risen from wretched poverty to become an executive of the Dockers' Union and chairman of the Trades Union Congress. Herbert Morrison (Commons leader and foreign secretary briefly in 1951) had overcome poverty, and an education that ended with elementary school, to forge a brilliant career that earned him the trust of Conservatives and Labourites alike. Sir

Stafford Cripps (Board of Trade), son of Lord Parmoor and a distinguished lawyer, had been a member of Churchill's war cabinet and a skilled negotiator in India. Chuter Ede (Home Office) was able and energetic, but little known outside Labour circles. Hugh Dalton (Exchequer), lecturer at the London School of Economics, under-secretary for foreign affairs in the 1930s, and an outspoken critic of appeasement, rounded out the principal appointments. Lesser ministries were filled by promising young men destined for greater things in the 1950s and 1960s, among them Hugh Gaitskell (Fuel and Power, and later Exchequer) and Harold Wilson (Works and Buildings).

The Labourites had campaigned on a platform calling for the rehabilitation of the economy and the adoption of a welfare system patterned on the recommendations of the Beveridge report. Consequently recovery of the economy became the primary goal of the Attlee administration. The volume of exports in 1945 had fallen to about one-third of the 1938 figure. In order to pay for food and war supplies, Britain had had to sell over £1,000,000,000 in overseas investments. It had lost its "invisible" income from banking and insurance, and had also contracted foreign debts of £3,000,000,000. Britain's main postwar objective, therefore, was to increase the volume of its exports so as to raise overseas credits high enough to pay for essential imports, and to so arrange its domestic economy that it could support social welfare programs at home and defense obligations abroad. In 1945, the Board of Trade estimated that exports had to be increased by 75 per cent to rectify the international balance-of-payments situation.

To this end the Attlee administration imposed greater controls on the production, distribution, and consumption of goods. Labour's overwhelming victory at the polls accorded it a popular mandate to cure the ailing economy in part by nationalizing certain basic industries and services, and to provide every person with a modicum of protection against sickness, unemployment, and poverty. Accordingly, in 1945–51, the government assumed ownership and operation of the Bank of England, the coal industry, and the gas, electricity, and transport and communication services, which included airlines, railways, buses, long-haul trucking, docks, harbors, telephones, and both domestic and overseas telegraph and wireless operations. The government also instituted a national health service, registered substantial gains in housing construction, carried town planning forward, took steps to increase agricultural production, encouraged industrial growth, and did its best under very trying circumstances to balance the budget and rectify the imbalance of foreign trade. By 1951, therefore, when the Conservatives were returned to power, Britain had recovered from the most serious effects of the war and could afford to relax some of the controls to which its citizens had grudgingly grown accustomed since 1939. Other problems, however, baffled Labourites and Conservatives alike. In general, these were related to fluctuations in the world economy, incidents in the cold war, trade blocs that affected foreign trade, and dissension within the Commonwealth, over all of which Britain had little control.

A full discussion of the nationalization statutes, which differed in accordance with the peculiarities of each industry or service, obviously cannot be entertained here, but brief mention of a few should convey an impression of the state's increased role in the nation's economy. The Bank of England, but none of Britain's other banks, became a public institution subject to some degree to government regulation of credit, a position that made it roughly analogous to the Federal Reserve Bank in the United States. Apart from the exchange of government stock for Bank stock, nationalization did not greatly change its character and operations. As before, the Bank continued to advise the Treasury, finance its loans, and mint and circulate money. The only appreciable change was that it enjoyed greater authority over certain policies of the private banks. The Nationalization of Coal Industry Act (1946) created a nine-member Coal Board subject to the minister of fuel and power. The Coal Board operated eight hundred companies with nearly 770,000 employees, developed the industry, manufactured and marketed by-products, set prices, trained miners, and encouraged research. Civil aviation came under public administration in 1946 through the nationalization of two corporations—British Overseas Airways Corporation, founded in 1939, and British European Airways, created in 1946. The existence of the Central Electricity Board (founded in 1926) greatly eased government assumption of the electricity industry in 1947; the association of the domestic telegraph system with the post office department, which dated from 1870, likewise smoothed the government's path. Overseas cables and wireless operations were nationalized in 1947 by the Cable and Wireless Act of 1946. The Transport Act of 1947 created the British Transport Commission, which was empowered to operate the six divisions of the British Railways complex, the London transport system, canals, steamships, and long-haul trucking. Early in 1949, the Central Gas Council assumed the management of approximately one thousand gas companies, a third of which had been formerly owned by municipalities. In each case the government compensated the former owners of nationalized companies or exchanged government stock for company stock.

Nationalization brought millions of workers, billions in property, and 20 per cent of the nation's industry under government control. In some cases it led to bitter criticism, but on the whole there was comparatively little objection, for to the average Briton nationalization made little immediate difference. Strikes were as frequent, inconveniences caused, for instance, by railway inefficiency as exasperating, credit as hard to get, utility rates as high, and shortages of services and commodities as common. The public viewed the patriarchal society spawned by the Labour government as merely the substitution of one master for another. But, all things considered, matters did not get worse, which is another way of saying that the government did a reasonably good job as the nation's proprietor.

The Labourites also hoped for the early nationalization of the steel industry, but there they encountered substantial opposition as well as a sticky constitutional problem that resulted in reform of Parliament. In 1946 the Commons expressed an interest in nationalizing steel, and subsequently appointed a Steel Control Board to oversee steel production and distribution, and to regulate prices. But the Conservatives in Parliament, mill owners and operators, and even some labor leaders in the steel industry questioned the wisdom of socializing the industry, which, unlike the industries that had been nationalized, could not be construed as a public utility. Moreover, the steel industry enjoyed exemplary labor-management relations and showed handsome profits without disadvantage to the consumer. As Attlee had expected, the Nationalization of the Steel Industry Bill of 1948 passed the Commons easily. But he knew that the House of Lords, a Conservative party stronghold, would exercise its suspensive veto to delay its enactment for two years—to 1950, an election year that might return the Conservatives to power. Attlee therefore agreed to postpone action on the bill until after the election. When it gave the Labourites a slight edge in Parliament, the steel bill was passed in 1951.

The Lords had been the butt of heavy criticism since the 1911 Act stripped it of meaningful legislative authority. Its detractors railed against the undemocratic anachronism of a hereditary upper House and suggested that it be "reformed." A few even proposed that it be abolished altogether. Consequently, in 1947, the Commons passed a bill to reduce the Lords' suspensive veto from two years to one, but the Act did not become effective until 1949. In retaining the traditional structure and composition of the Lords, the Labourites, though mildly troubled by its hostility to sweeping reforms, recognized its usefulness to the modern democratic state, which it aids by considering legislative measures dispassionately—that is to say, without having to worry about the effect of its deliberations on election results. It likewise renders healthy criticism of the administration, serves to delay hasty or ill-advised legislation, and provides a haven for distinguished politicians and other public servants whose experience and wisdom might otherwise be lost. In short, despite its constitutional limitations, the House of Lords performs valuable services in the legislative process.

The Labourites also reformed the House of Commons in 1948 in the Representation of the People Act, which abolished parliamentary representation of Oxford and Cambridge Universities and put an end to plural voting. Henceforth qualified electors might vote in either the constituency in which they resided or that in which they had business premises, but not both. Another Act (1949) redistributed parliamentary seats and reduced the size of the Commons from 640 members to 625. It also rectified the numerical disparity among Welsh, Scottish, Northern Irish, and English constituencies by making each member of Parliament representative of approximately fifty-six thousand persons. Minor alterations in the size of constituencies have been made since 1949 as the growth of the population dictated.

With respect to industries in private hands, such as textiles, pottery, and clothing, teams of experts representing the government, industry, and trade-unions surveyed current practices with an eye to augmenting production through technological innovations. To discourage the outflow of gold and currency, the government forbade the importation of most luxury goods as well as popular staples like tobacco and liquor. It also at first limited the amount of British currency travelers could take abroad, and, in 1947, altogether banned its use for tourist travel. Rationing of meat, dairy products, sugar, and fats, begun during the war, was continued in order to reduce costly food imports. Rationing of bread began in March, 1946. Other types of food—fresh tropical fruit, rice, cooking oil, and raisins, for example—became so scarce that they might as well have been rationed. Gasoline (prohibited for passenger cars in 1947), liquor, beer, and tobacco were heavily taxed. As a result of surtaxes and luxury taxes, clothing, furniture, cosmetics, jewelry, and shoes, among other items, cost double and triple the prices of 1938. In the bitter winter of 1946–47, a severe shortage of coal closed down factories, drastically reduced the supply of electricity and gas, and caused heavy unemployment. Inflation, as usual, robbed consumers of purchasing power. The cost-of-living index (1938 = 100) rose to 174 in 1948. Wages, on the other hand, also rose in the same period to 172, largely because of full employment. In an effort to increase the production of goods intended for export, the Ministry of Production appealed to workers to labor assiduously, and Sir Stafford Cripps, at the Exchequer after September, 1947, admonished Britons to accept austerity in a spirit of patriotism and as a necessity for economic survival.

Agriculture likewise demanded the government's careful attention. As part of a four-year plan for national economic growth, £450,000,-000 was earmarked for agriculture and farm machinery in 1948–52. The government set annual goals for agricultural production, guaranteed farm prices and markets, increased acreage under cultivation, paid farmers subsidies to raise more livestock, made loans to encourage farm improvements, and distributed the latest information on agricultural research. As a result, production rose on an average of 20 per cent for the years 1945–51. The only poor agricultural year was 1947–48, owing to widespread flooding from the heavy snows of the previous winter.

Britain made a remarkable economic recovery in 1945–51. Despite decreased markets for coal, for example, Britons mined 214,000,000 tons in 1950 as against 227,000,000 tons in 1938. Crude steel production rose in the same period from 10,398,000 to 16,000,000 tons. Total industrial production climbed about 35 per cent in 1947–50. This significant improvement allowed the government to discontinue rationing of bread, jam, and potatoes in 1948; clothing and shoes in 1949; and milk and soap in 1950. Sugar and tea, however, were rationed until 1952, and butter, fats, and meat to 1954. Heavy foreign purchases in the first year or so after the war advanced British exports by 11 per cent. In addition, Britain benefited by $4,400,000 in American loans and gifts from August, 1945, to August, 1947, as well as from $2,700,-000,000 in American aid in 1948–51 under the European Recovery Program (Marshall Plan). But notwithstanding the significant gains in industry and agriculture and America's generosity, the British economy remained sensitive to comparatively minor fluctuations in world trade. Inflationary prices in the United States in 1946–47, for instance, hurt Britain's balance of payments and forced the Attlee administration to impose the austerity measures already described. Another drop in sales on the American market, this time because of a recession in 1949, depressed British exports and forced Parliament that September to devalue the pound sterling from $4.03 to $2.80. Except for Pakistan, all members of the sterling bloc followed suit. But this expedient did little to encourage foreign trade or improve the balance of payments, even though, as expected, devaluation forced down prices of British goods on the world market. The financial crisis passed in the wake of the Korean war, beginning in 1950, which stimulated heavy American purchases in Britain. In view of the seriousness of these fiscal problems, the Labour government did well to balance the budget. It registered substantial surpluses each year after 1946–47, primarily because of reductions in imports, larger profits from foreign trade, American aid, and high taxes, which both increased revenue and helped to fight inflation. The economy had recovered sufficiently by 1951 that Britain voluntarily relinquished American aid.

The social welfare legislation of the Attlee government has had a far-reaching impact on the British people. The National Insurance Act (1946), based on the Beveridge report and other investigations made since 1942, consolidated previous legislation on that subject and abolished the system of state-approved insurance societies. The insurance fund, raised by contributions of workers, employers, and the state, financed benefit payments for the unemployed. Claims arising from industrial accidents and occupational diseases that had frequently led to litigation were processed more easily because the Industrial Injuries Act (1946) made the state, not the employer, responsible for paying compensation. Victims of abject poverty, regardless of the circumstances involved, received weekly subsistence benefits for food and shelter as a result of the National Assistance Act of 1948. The 1946 and 1949 Housing Acts carried forward plans made during the war to finance house construction with government subsidies. The Town and Country Planning Act of 1947 placed primary responsibility for urban renewal and development upon the borough and county councils. Within three years, they were to survey existing housing, industrial, shopping, and recreational facilities in their communities and make recommendations for the future to the minister of town and country planning. Because of congestion in some of the large towns, the ministry projected the creation of twenty new towns averaging thirty thousand to sixty thousand inhabitants. Government funds would pay for essential public utilities, civic buildings, and some housing in these model communities, but private concerns were expected to underwrite the bulk of the construction. Sixteen such towns had been built by 1964, half within easy commuting distance of London, the rest in Scotland and Wales. The drain of population from the inner city to the suburbs has forced the government to revise upward its limitations on the size of these towns.

No other postwar social welfare legislation aroused as much attention and debate as did the National Health Services Act of 1946, effective in July, 1948. The service is based on the principle that all persons, regardless of ability to pay, are entitled to complete and free medical care. Although the Act introduced novel features such as free dental and optical care, nationalization of hospitals, and free medicine, drugs, and orthopedic appliances, it was essentially a modification and extension of the public health system in which the state had been involved on a limited scale for more than a generation. The service is entirely voluntary, on the part of both doctors and patients. Its organization is complex, but it operates quite simply. Upon registration at any post office, the patient chooses a physician from a list of those who have agreed to serve in the system. Doctors may elect to accept or refuse registrants. The state pays general practitioners a basic annual salary, plus capitation fees scaled in accordance with the number of patients on their rosters, which originally could not exceed 3500. (In 1959, practitioners averaged 2200 patients.) Specialists and consultants are paid proportionately more, and all doctors may also take private patients at regular fees. Hospital rooms are available free of charge, although private rooms may be had at a slight charge. Dentists, pharmacists, optometrists and certain other practitioners may elect to register with the service, but their patients or customers need not register. In addition, the public is entitled to various free supplementary services, including midwifery, maternity and child welfare, home nursing, vaccination, blood transfusions, and ambulance and laboratory services. The Act also called for the establishment of regional medical and dental centers, but these have not yet been set up on a wide scale.

The health service inspired both praise and condemnation for approximately two years after its inception. By 1950, however, both the public and the medical profession generally recognized its benefits for all concerned. A comparatively small section of the British Medical Association (600 of 49,000 doctors in 1959) and only 3 or 4 per cent of the population has refused to join, arguing that "socialized medicine" impairs the intimate relationship between doctor and patient, that doctors' offices are overcrowded, and that the service has lowered the quality of medical care. While there is little question that the system is open to criticism in certain details, on the whole it has functioned remarkably well.

Austerity measures and fiscal crises naturally brought Conservative attacks on the Labour government. Certain aspects of the nationalization program (especially plans to socialize the iron and steel industries), controls, and fuel and food shortages led to Conservative charges of economic mismanagement and fiscal irresponsibility. The general election of February, 1950, was fought primarily over these issues. The Conservatives promised to reduce taxes, build more houses, and remove excessive state regulation. The Labourites pointed to the improvement in foreign trade, their success in handling financial problems, and full employment in basic industries. The election results proved indecisive: Labour won 315 seats; the Conservatives, 296; the Liberals, 9; and others, 3. Labour's majority slipped to only seven seats, too few to feel confident that its bills could weather the probable crossing of party lines on particular issues.

Even so, Labour went ahead in 1951 with the nationalization of the iron and steel industries. The government also evinced confidence in proposing a budget for 1951–52 calling for a substantial increase in expenditures and tax increases on personal income and capital gains, even though the rash of buying induced by the needs of the Korean war had by that time worn off, and Britain again faced a nasty deficit-of-payments situation. The public grumbled more audibly about high taxes and seemed unimpressed by the discontinuation of rationing on certain items. These signs of public discontent were matched by budget disputes in the cabinet that forced Attlee to call another general election for October, 1951. The results dashed his hopes for a larger Parliamentary majority and a popular vindication of his audacious fiscal policy. The Conservatives won 321 seats while the Labourites captured 294 and the Liberals and others took only 9. The popular vote had changed little, however, as only slightly more than 1 per cent of the electorate voted for the Conservatives as compared to 1950.

Attlee at once resigned. In December, 1955, he exchanged leadership of the party for an earldom. Hugh Gaitskell, former university lecturer in economics, a moderate socialist, Chancellor of the Exchequer in 1951, and not yet fifty years of age, became Labour leader until his untimely death in January, 1963, brought Harold Wilson to the forefront. The party suffered after 1951 from more than the usual disputes within its ranks. Attlee had generally had the support of the Trades Union Congress, but he and his successors often quarreled with left-wingers like Aneurin Bevan. Gaitskell was frequently at odds with trade-unionists, with whom he had little in common. He abjured radical socialism and preached moderation, and in doing so widened the split between his followers and the party's radical wing. The quarrel ranged over the full spectrum of politics and economics, but it centered on the questions of nuclear disarmament, neutrality in the cold war, and further nationalization of industry. Factionalism diminished following the deaths of Bevan and Gaitskell in 1960 and 1963, respectively, but it did not disappear. Labour conferences since 1955 have bristled with severe criticism of party leadership, and Harold Wilson has come in for his share of it. In 1966, for example, Frank Cousins, general secretary of the Transport Workers Union and sometime cabinet member, resigned from the cabinet in protest over Wilson's imposition of wage and price controls to combat inflation and improve the precarious balance of payments. But the bulk of the Labour party and Trades Union Congress supports the prime minister, who gives every indication of being a strong leader eager to promote economic recovery and to pursue a pro-American foreign policy.

The Conservatives dominated British politics from 1951 to 1964. The government of Winston Churchill (1951–55), who served as both prime minister and defense minister, included Anthony Eden (Foreign Office), Richard A. Butler (Exchequer), and Lord Salisbury (Privy Seal). A fresh crisis over the balance of payments, inherited from the Labourites, plagued the country in 1951–52, during which time the Conservatives could only hold on and hope for the best. The crisis passed when exports rose and large numbers of American tourists narrowed the dollar gap. Iron and steel, chemicals, automobiles, and engineering tools found many foreign customers, and helped to raise gold and dollar reserves, stimulated employment, and encouraged industrial growth. The Conservatives overturned some of the pre-1951 socialist legislation by denationalizing the iron and steel industry in gradual steps beginning in 1953, but they were careful not to remove all government controls. Churchill let the other nationalized industries alone, for the still fragile economy probably could not have withstood another massive jolt. The last rationing ended in 1954. In addition, the Town and Country Planning Act of 1954, empowering local authorities to develop land for urban housing and to encourage construction through private enterprise, resulted in a substantial increase in house-building. The Conservatives thereby honored an election promise to construct at least 300,000 houses annually. They also amended the

National Insurance Act by raising both old-age pensions and sickness and unemployment benefits by a fourth and a fifth, respectively. Steadily rising health service costs forced the government to charge nominal fees for drug prescriptions and to ask the public to pay half the cost of spectacles and dentures. Except for some strikes in 1953 and 1954, which led to higher wages and encouraged inflation, by 1955 the economy had been stabilized for the first time since the war.

Meanwhile the death of George VI on February 6, 1952, had saddened the nation. He died as he had lived, quietly and unobtrusively, and was succeeded by his daughter, Elizabeth II, the demure wife of Prince Philip Mountbatten, whom she had married in 1947. In 1953 a mild stroke incapacitated Churchill. He made a remarkable recovery, but could no longer bear the full burden of office. Eden, whom he had nominated as his successor as early as World War II, carried on behind the scenes until 1955, when Churchill resigned. He had been knighted in 1953, but he later declined an earldom—the consolation prize awarded to most former prime ministers—because he valued the privilege to sit and speak on occasion in the Commons. He counseled the Conservative party until his death in January, 1965, at the age of ninety.

Leadership of the nation and the Conservative party came to Eden (b. 1897), a dashing, dutiful, and dauntless veteran of diplomacy and politics, at a most propitious moment. The economy, although still sensitive to fluctuations in world trade, had leveled off on the side of prosperity. Exports were rising and unemployment was low. Steady increases in the cost of living seemed not to trouble families, who hastened to buy commodities that were no longer scarce or rationed. If taxes were high, so too were wages. To take advantage of the public's even temper, Eden called for a general election on May 26.

The campaign stirred little popular enthusiasm, for there was no crucial question demanding an immediate answer. Chronic economic problems, nuclear disarmament, and the cold war, important though they were, could not distract a people enjoying life to the fullest for the first time since the war. Under these circumstances, it is not surprising that neither major political party made a concerted effort in the campaign. The Conservatives, confident of victory, merely stood on their record of having terminated rationing and other controls; of success in the housing program; and of the reduction of personal income tax by 5 per cent in 1953–55, a reduction that benefited principally the working class, 2,400,000 of whom now paid no income taxes at all. The Labourites made a somewhat stronger appeal, despite the running quarrel between the left-wing and moderate elements of the party, which undermined efforts to settle on a firm platform, although Labour probably erred in dragging up such questions as nationalization, price controls, and higher taxes on corporate profits. Modest proposals for totally free pharmaceutical and dental services and higher sickness and old-age benefits had a somewhat wider appeal, although the prosperity of 1955 made such promises less inviting than they might have been, say, in 1951.

As expected, the election strengthened the Conservatives in Parliament. They won 344 seats to the Labourites' 277 and the others' 8. Only 77 per cent of the electorate voted, a drop from the record high of 84 per cent in 1950, and 82 per cent in 1951. Party allegiance among the electorate, however, had changed little: less than 2 per cent more voters supported the Conservatives in 1955 than in the previous general election.

The government of Anthony Eden, essentially a carbon copy of Churchill's, lasted only from April, 1955, to January, 1957. Every government since World War II had had its share of fiscal and trade problems, and Eden's was no exception. Early in 1956, inflation, a fall in exports, and an overextension of public credit in a loose money market combined to raise retail prices, encourage importation, weaken domestic output, and increase unemployment. Harold Macmillan, Butler's successor at the Exchequer, at once cut imports from dollar markets and tightened controls on installment purchases. By late 1956, gold reserves had risen and the dollar gap had been narrowed. The lackluster Eden administration will probably be remembered best for the invasion of Egypt by British and French troops in November, 1956 (discussed below), an invasion that said much about Britain's position in the postwar international scene.

Britain had emerged from the Second World War with enormous prestige. By virtue of that position and the fact that it was the only European nation that had not been overrun by invading armies (excluding neutrals, of course), it had the opportunity to take leadership in Europe. But its statesmen chose not to accept that responsibility. While it is true that Britain fulfilled its obligations in Europe in connection with German occupation, and joined in several defensive alliances, including the Brussels Treaty Organization, the North Atlantic Treaty Organization, and the Southeast Asia Treaty Organization, in general it shrank from too great an involvement in world affairs, chiefly because of serious domestic problems. As a result, British influence in world affairs has steadily declined since World War II, and especially since 1956.

Britain's major contribution in the Allied victory in World War II ensured it a prominent role in the postwar reconstruction of Europe. In wartime conferences off Newfoundland and at Washington, Quebec, and Casablanca, Churchill and Roosevelt had planned war strategy and laid a basis for their nations' cooperation after the restoration of peace. But the military alliance between Britain and Russia did not result in a similar understanding. This became apparent at Yalta (February, 1945), where Churchill, Roosevelt, and Stalin agreed to partition Germany into four zones of military occupation, but where, as Churchill had repeatedly warned, Stalin made a bid to occupy Poland, moving toward his goal of making it a Soviet satellite. Since Russian cooperation on the eastern front was a vital factor in the Allied war effort, Churchill reluctantly consented rather than risk antagonizing Stalin by insisting on a free Poland. But Churchill's permissiveness regarding Poland encouraged, at least tacitly, the postwar consolidation of Russian authority throughout eastern Europe. On the other hand, Churchill was adamant at Yalta about postponing a decision on German reparations payments to Russia until war's end, when a commission could consider the problem more dispassionately. It was also to Britain's and America's advantage to permit Russian reannexation of territory ceded to Japan in 1905 as a *quid pro quo* for Russian military support against Japan in the final stages of the war.

The surrender of Germany led to the Potsdam Conference (July-August, 1945), where Attlee, Truman, and Stalin considered its disposition. British, like American, policy in this regard was to work toward German political and economic unity while destroying the vestiges of Nazism. Accordingly, Britain supported German disarmament, punishment of war criminals, decartelization of German industry, and the restoration of democratic political and judicial institutions. Attlee and Truman realized that the speedy conclusion of a German peace treaty was vital to the realization of those goals, but they were unable to weaken Stalin's determination to postpone a treaty, to keep Russian troops in occupation of eastern Germany and Poland, and to seek unreasonable reparations payments. On the other hand, the Russians willingly joined Britain and the United States as charter members of the United Nations Organization even though they subsequently abused their veto power to confound the work of the Security Council.

Soviet maneuvers to gain control of former Nazi satellites in eastern Europe and the Balkans set the pattern for the cold war in the immediate postwar years. Like the United States, Britain hoped to prevent the absorption of those areas by Russia, but British concessions in 1944 had actually encouraged Soviet encroachments. In talks with Stalin at Moscow, Churchill had conceded Russia's predominant interests in Hungary, Bulgaria, and Rumania in exchange for Russia's recognition of British interests in Greece and Turkey and throughout the eastern Mediterranean area, where Britain had vital economic investments and territories to protect. Consequently, once the Russians had either occupied eastern European and Balkan countries or managed to create Communist regimes in them, there was nothing that Britain could do. At meetings of the Council of Foreign Ministers at Paris and London in 1946 and 1947 she was faced with the *fait accompli* of Russian satellites behind the Iron Curtain. At the Paris meeting, however, Britain was able to block Russian efforts to gain control of the Turkish straits through military occupation with Turkish consent. Had not Britain strongly resisted that Russian design, Turkey might have fallen within the Soviet orbit just as Greece might have succumbed to Communist guerrilla forces in 1946–49 but for British and American financial and military aid to Prime Minister Constantine Tsaldaris' government. By 1948, Britain concluded that further efforts at collective action with the Russians were futile, and afterward gravitated steadily toward closer economic and military ties with western Europe in harmony with the policy of the United States, as the succeeding pages will show.

In June, 1950, the center of international tension shifted from Europe to Korea. Nearly twenty thousand British servicemen fought and six hundred died in the Korean War, which began with the invasion of South Korea by North Korean Communist forces and ended in a troublesome armistice in 1953. The war forced both the Attlee and Churchill administrations to rearm and to re-examine Britain's relations with the Chinese People's Republic (C.P.R.). As the British had accorded Mao Tse-tung's regime *de facto* recognition in 1950, the year after his victory over the Nationalists of Chiang Kai-shek, Chinese intervention in the war posed a difficult problem for Britain, particularly because the Labour government feared that General MacArthur might fulfill his threat to bomb and invade China. Attlee therefore went to Washington to secure Truman's assurance that the United States would not provoke a Chinese war—an assurance that hung in the balance until

Truman relieved MacArthur of command the following April. British concern stemmed partly from the precarious position of Hong Kong, and partly from a desire to maintain the heavy Anglo-Chinese trade in nonmilitary goods. Moreover, the British government genuinely believed that the C.P.R. should have official recognition and supported its admission to the United Nations.

The menacing gestures of the Soviet Union and the C.P.R. in the years following World War II demonstrated the urgency of creating opposing power blocs to counterbalance the military strength of the Communist world. Accordingly, the West determined to resist Communist imperialism through economic and military aid to countries endangered by it. At the same time, western European states made treaties for the defense of free Europe. The Brussels Treaty of March, 1948, bound Britain, France, Belgium, the Netherlands, and Luxembourg in a defensive alliance by which all would come to the military aid of any member attacked by Russia. It soon became apparent that this organization should be expanded to include other nations on both sides of the Atlantic. Discussions among foreign ministers resulted in the creation of the North Atlantic Treaty Organization (NATO) in April, 1949, comprised initially of the United States, Britain, France, the Netherlands, Belgium, Luxembourg, Italy, Portugal, Denmark, Norway, Iceland, and Canada. The signatories agreed to lend immediate and corporate military support to any member attacked by Russia, and also to confer and to take appropriate collective action should the independence or territorial integrity of any of them be threatened by Communist countries.

Britain's identification with the destiny of the Continent put an end to its century-long policy of making only short-term, bilateral treaties. In addition, membership in NATO obliged Britain to spend billions on defense, which it could ill afford, and to maintain an air force and several divisions in western Europe. At the same time, however, Britain was careful not to surrender its right of independent action. Hence, while it had joined the NATO alliance, it refused to support the idea of a fully integrated supranational western European army, a plan that had been suggested by members of the Brussels Treaty Organization, who also proposed to integrate armies from the Federal Republic of Germany (West Germany) and Italy. Early in 1952, West Germany, Italy, France, Belgium, the Netherlands, and Luxembourg signed a treaty creating the European Defense Community. It was aborted in 1954 when the French assembly, fearful of resurgent militarism in

Germany, refused to ratify the treaty. Britain and the United States, however, believed that West Germany must sooner or later be entirely freed from Allied control and permitted to share in the defense of western Europe as a fully independent and equal partner. To this end, Anthony Eden, while foreign secretary, invited members of the Brussels Treaty Organization, Canada, and the United States to meet in London in September, 1954. A major obstacle was overcome when France agreed to admit West Germany and Italy into the Brussels Treaty Organization, which was thereby expanded into the Western European Union. In 1955, because of British and American assurances that they would never default on their military obligations in Europe, the French assembly likewise approved the entry of West Germany into the NATO alliance as a full and equal partner entitled to raise an army of 500,000 men. The Soviet Union at once retaliated by organizing the Warsaw Pact among its satellites. Later in 1955, Khrushchev conferred with Eisenhower and Eden at Geneva. They failed to find a solution to the German question because Khrushchev insisted that a German peace treaty leading to unification could result only from direct negotiations with the East German regime, which the western powers refused to recognize.

The spread of Communism in Asia worried Britain and its allies no less. China overran Tibet in 1950; Communists threatened the Philippines until 1953; British Malaya fought them until it gained independence in 1957; the French dominions in Indo-China had been attacked by the Communist Vietminh, resulting in the partition of Vietnam into two nations along the seventeenth parallel. In order to forestall further aggression, in September, 1954, Britain, the United States, France, Australia, New Zealand, Thailand, Pakistan, and the Philippines signed the Treaty of Manila leading to the Southeast Asia Treaty Organization (SEATO), which obliged consultation on defense in the event of a crisis, without the obligation to fight.

Near Eastern developments perforce involved Britain inasmuch as it had long been the controlling power there. Accordingly, Britain fell heir to civil strife in Cyprus, Palestine, and Egypt by virtue of its occupation of these lands. Cyprus, a British protectorate since 1878, with a population of divided Greek Christian and Turkish Moslem ancestry, became a crown colony in 1925. This displeased the Greek Cypriots who, seeking political reunion with Greece, rioted and rebelled against the British authorities during the 1930s. Nor did the Turkish Cypriots rest easily in the face of the threats and terrorism of the more numerous Greeks. In 1947, Britain offered the Cypriots a partially elected assembly. The Greeks reacted violently, first in nationalistic outbursts in behalf of reunion with the homeland, and later in organized resistance under Archbishop Makarios. This further convinced the Turks that their position would be dangerous under a Greek-dominated legislature, and led the British to postpone plans for Cypriot self-government. In the 1950s, the Greeks resumed acts of terrorism against the British and fought a bloody civil war with the Turks on the island. Neither Britain, the U.N., nor the pressure of world opinion for a settlement could stay the zeal of Makarios for reunion with Greece. He was consequently arrested and deported. Finally, in 1959, Britain offered Cyprus independence on condition that it should never join Greece and that the British garrison be allowed to remain on the island. Makarios, returned from exile, agreed to these terms, organized a republic, became its first president, and brought Cyprus into the Commonwealth in 1961. It soon became apparent, however, that independence had not weakened the hatred between Greek and Turkish Cypriots, who resumed terrorist tactics against each other. In 1963, the U.N. sent a small peace-keeping force to the island to restore order, but the threat of war still hangs over it. How different had been the political evolution of tiny Malta, a British colony since 1815 which gratefully accepted responsible government in 1947 and independence in 1964.

As in Cyprus, so also in Palestine, nationalist and religious rivalries harassed the British authorities because both Moslem Arabs and Zionist Jews had expected to control the country after World War I. The situation was complicated by Britain's promises to both sides, to the Arabs the establishment of an Arab state or confederation of states, and to the Jews a "national home" in Palestine that would not jeopardize Arab interests. When the peacemakers denied the Arabs independence in 1919 and Britain threw open the doors of Palestine to Jewish immigrants from Europe, the Arabs became exercised about the possibility of being eventually outnumbered. The expected heavy Jewish immigration did not materialize in the 1920s, however, but the Arabs nevertheless suspected that Britain meant to rob them of political and property rights. Although Britain gave repeated assurances that Jewish settlement would be limited to one section of Palestine, anti-Jewish riots in Tel Aviv and Jerusalem in 1921 and 1929 aggravated the situation. The Colonial Office had hoped to establish a legislative assembly in Palestine in order to give its peoples political experience against the day when they would become independent. The Arabs insisted that such an assembly be elected on the basis of popular representation, which, of course, meant subjugating the Jews to a hostile, Arab-dominated government in contradiction of the 1917 Balfour Declaration. Apart from these problems, the British government had to contend with heavy pressure from millions of Moslems in the Empire, who threatened to rebel unless the demands of the Palestinian Arabs were met, as well as from the powerful leaders of the international Zionist movement. To have granted concessions in Palestine to the one would have automatically alienated the other. The problem grew more serious in the later 1930s because of a marked increase in Jewish immigration encouraged by Nazi anti-Semitism, and the stated intention of the Colonial Office to partition Palestine into separate Arab and Jewish states. In 1938 an Arab rebellion was suppressed with the greatest difficulty. This led in turn to a British promise in 1939 to grant Palestine independence within ten years, during which time Jewish immigration would be restricted to seventy-five thousand persons.

After World War II, hundreds of thousands of homeless European Jews sought to enter Palestine, which the Zionists, supported by a strong underground movement, meant to transform into the state of Israel. When the British adamantly kept most of the refugees out, the Colonial Office again came under pressure from Zionists as well as from the Arab world, which, in 1944, had formed an Arab League composed of Egypt, Syria, Lebanon, Transjordan, Iraq, Saudi Arabia, and Yemen. As Britain dared not alienate either Jews or Arabs, and altering its policy of restricting Jewish immigration would surely have provoked a civil war or even an invasion of Palestine by the Arab League, it decided to surrender its mandate (held since 1922) and dump the problem in the lap of the United Nations. In November, 1947, the U.N. Assembly agreed to partition Palestine into two states, and six months later the British withdrew. The Jews at once declared Israel independent. Egyptian, Transjordanian, Syrian, and Lebanese forces then invaded Israel on three sides while the Palestinian Arabs fought the Israelis in half a dozen ancient cities. In 1949, the U.N. effected a cease-fire and an armistice between Israel and the four Arab states. Although the Israeli war for independence had ended, the last chapter of the story had yet to be written, and Egypt meant to be the author.

Developments in Egypt following World War II must be viewed in the broad perspective of Anglo-Egyptian relations dating from 1882, when Gladstone sent troops to protect the strategically important Suez

Canal. From that time to 1956, when President Gamal Nasser seized the Canal, the control of Egyptian and Sudanese affairs was an axiom of British foreign policy. British military and civil authority grew steadily in the years preceding World War I. When Turkey joined the Central Powers, Britain made Egypt its protectorate, a *fait accompli* confirmed in both the Sèvres and Lausanne treaties. Anti-British nationalists frequently rioted against the authorities and committed innumerable acts of terrorism to induce them to grant Egypt independence. In 1922, Britain terminated the protectorate but kept troops, advisers, and civil servants in the country pending the conclusion of a treaty protecting British interests.

Notwithstanding this concession and the establishment of a Parliamentary system of government headed by King Fuad, so much popular opposition arose to a treaty favorable to Britain that it was not negotiated until 1936. Meanwhile factional, religious, and nationalistic rivalries rent the country, which, though technically self-governing, was still controlled militarily and economically by Britain. King Farouk, who succeeded his father, Fuad, in 1936, restored public order and firm government, conditions favorable to the conclusion of an Anglo-Egyptian treaty, the need for which was becoming more urgent because of the threat posed to northeastern Africa by Mussolini's conquest of Ethiopia. The treaty of 1936 confirmed the independence of Egypt, created a defensive alliance that permitted British troops to garrison the Canal zone and the Sudan for an initial term of twenty years, allowed the Royal Navy to use Alexandria as a naval depot, and guaranteed British use of Egyptian transportation and communication facilities in the event of war.

Conditions in Egypt remained unchanged until 1951, when the Egyptian government unilaterally abrogated the treaty in accordance with the goals of Arab nationalism, then sweeping North Africa and the Near East, and demanded that Britain evacuate the Canal zone as well as the Sudan, which Egypt hoped to annex. In 1952 a cadre of Egyptian army officers rebelled against Farouk's corrupt government, forced his abdication, instituted a republic, and made General Naguib president. Colonel Nasser overthrew Naguib in February, 1954. The Western powers supported his regime diplomatically and economically. Britain, conscious of Arab hostility to its military position in Egypt, consented to withdraw its forces by June, 1956, on condition that it continue to control the Canal, that it have the express right to defend the Canal against foreign attack, and that the question of a political union

of Egypt and the Sudan be determined by a plebiscite in the latter
territory. The Sudanese rejected union with Egypt and remained temporarily under British control.

Events soon showed that the Western powers had misjudged Nasser.
While on the one hand he accepted American aid for the construction
of a dam at Aswan, on the other he purchased arms from Communist
countries, gravitated toward closer relations with the Communist bloc,
and hurled repeated threats at Israel. He also supplied weapons to the
Arab rebels fighting for independence against France in Algeria. Thereupon Britain joined Turkey, Iran, Iraq, Pakistan, and the United
States in the Central Treaty Organization (CENTO) in order to protect the Near and Middle East against Communist encroachments.
When the United States abruptly terminated aid to Egypt in July,
1956, Nasser retaliated by seizing control of the Suez Canal Company,
nationalized the Canal, and restricted entry to it, in violation of treaties
guaranteeing its use an an international waterway and the rights of
Britain defined in the 1954 treaty. Prime Minister Eden, fearing that
the nationalization of the Canal was but the first of several steps to
overthrow Western authority and interests in the Near East, which
might then become a sphere of Communist influence, joined France in
urging the United States to take the lead in some form of collective
action to restore the *status quo* in Egypt. The American government
responded equivocally, but it did say that under no circumstances would
it support the use of force. As Russian veto power made U.N.
action impossible, Britain and France alone continued to oppose Nasser's revolutionary and illegal actions. When Nasser refused to permit
Israeli ships to enter the Canal and laid plans for an invasion of the
Jewish republic by an army of Egyptians, Syrians, and Jordanians, the
Israelis at once attacked Egypt through the Sinai Peninsula. On Nasser's refusal to agree to an Anglo-French ultimatum that they be permitted to land troops to protect the Canal, on November 5, 1956, British
planes bombed Egyptian installations and a British and French army
attacked Port Said.

The invasion caused an international crisis as well as a governmental crisis in Britain. The Labourites, supported by a few Conservatives, condemned the action as immoral. A Labour party rally in
Trafalgar Square, highlighted by Anuerin Bevan's impassioned speech,
very nearly turned into a riot when hundreds of demonstrators hurried
down Whitehall to Downing Street to denounce the prime minister.
The American government reproached Eden, requesting the with-

drawal of the British and French troops, and several Commonwealth governments, including Canada, supported the American position. Egypt, of course, demanded that Britain and France be branded aggressors for having violated the U.N. Charter. American and Russian resolutions in the Security Council calling for restraint in the use of force by Britain and France were vetoed by those two powers. On the initiative of Canada, the General Assembly arranged a cease-fire, Israeli and Egyptian forces withdrew from the line of battle, and British and French troops evacuated the Canal zone. A small U.N. contingent, composed chiefly of Canadians, arrived in Egypt to keep the peace in the neutralized Gaza Strip on the Egyptian-Israeli frontier. Although the situation had been stabilized by April, 1957, the Suez crisis had culminated in events that had practically driven British interests from the Arab world. Mohammed Mossadegh of Iran had nationalized the British oil refineries and promoted closer ties with the Soviet Union; Jordan had expelled British advisers; and Arab revolutionaries supported by Nasser had murdered King Faisal II of Iraq. In 1958, Nasser formed the United Arab Republic, consisting of Egypt, Syria, and Yemen, a tiny state that hoped to annex the British territory of Aden. It was clear, therefore, that Britain had lost much of its former influence in an area where it had once been paramount.

It was indicative of the changing character of the Commonwealth that Eden had not solicited the opinion of its members or sought their assistance before invading Egypt. Such lack of consultation before World War II would have been unusual. To be sure, representatives of the Commonwealth had conferred frequently, often two and three times annually, since the war, and members had joined in regional trade and defense arrangements, but they were drifting apart. So many new nations have risen from the ashes of the old Empire that the Commonwealth has ceased to be an association of English-speaking peoples —British if you will—or even a community of states bound by traditional loyalties. These young states, mostly African and Asian, have joined the Commonwealth for reasons of trade, defense, and the like, not because they feel any real identity with Britain. Everywhere in the Empire the forces of nationalism, anti-imperialism, and anticolonialism have been working to destroy in a few years what it had taken Britain over a century to build. These forces created new states, often after long and tedious negotiations conducted in an environment of tension and distrust of British intentions.

It is beyond the scope of this history to discuss the post-1945 independence movements in the colonies and mandated territories of Britain except where these movements touch directly on British domestic affairs and foreign policy. The question must be raised, however, as to what role Britain has played in preparing emerging nations for independence. It would be jejune and brazen to comment generally on the different factors that have helped colonies in winning independence—factors that appropriately should be explained in national histories or a careful study of imperial relations—but it is necessary to consider the over-all results of these relations.

The question of independence for dependent peoples, one which must properly be viewed in the broad perspective of British colonial policy in the last hundred years, has provoked extensive disagreement. Some scholars have argued cogently that Britain has sometimes surrendered sovereignty too quickly to largely illiterate peoples fraught with tribal, religious, and social problems and both politically and economically incapable of sustaining a viable independence. It cannot be denied that serious deficiencies and chronic problems have weakened and still hinder the advancement of young states such as Ghana (1957), Malaysia (1957), Nigeria (1960), Tanzania (1961), and Kenya (1963). But compared with states developing from French and Belgian dependencies, the former British colonies have been by and large successful in ordering their political, social, and economic affairs. This is hardly an accident of history. The bulk of the Asian and African states that acquired independence after many decades under British rule have profited, more than they willingly admit, from the experience in government given them by British colonial administrators. Native statesmen, teachers, professionals, and civil servants, though admittedly too few in number, have been trained for the most part in British universities or colonial institutions patterned on the British system. They have been taught not only how to operate a government properly, but also how to regulate society in a way most beneficial to the public welfare. The British have also taught colonials to cope with problems in ways particularly suited to local conditions. Can the British be faulted when colonials whom they judged ready for independence have not lived up to expectations for reasons largely unrelated to their experiences under British rule? Independence is a heady brew that has turned some men mad—too mad, in fact, to appreciate that it can work for the general good only through restraint and compromise. Factionalism, opportunism, and imprudence have sometimes destroyed the political, social, and economic stability that obtained at the time independence was acquired. On the whole, one must admire Britain's willingness to gamble on the success of young nations, and its reluctance, frequently at great sacrifice to its own interests, to allow colonials to become independent until such time as they were thought ready to assume that responsibility.

The resignation of Anthony Eden as prime minister in January, 1957, as much because of chronic ill health as because of the repercussions of the Suez crisis, was something of a watershed in British politics. On the one hand, it brought to an end what might be called the age of Churchill, whose political views and foreign policy had lived on during the administration of his protégé; on the other hand, it provided the Conservatives with the opportunity to rebuild their party under Harold Macmillan, Eden's successor. Macmillan, at sixty-two, member of Parliament since 1924, and a cabinet member since 1951, outdistanced both R. A. Butler and Selwyn Lloyd, foreign minister since April, 1955, who seemed at one point to have the inside tracks in the race for party leadership. Butler's success at the Treasury and Lloyd's firm grasp of international problems commended them strongly, but a word from Churchill carried more weight with party members and the queen, who chose Macmillan as prime minister. That is not to say that he stood, like Eden, in Churchill's shadow. Unlike the latter, who never admitted Britain's limitations, Macmillan willingly accepted the painful fact that Britain was no longer able to hold or financially support a position of world leadership. He felt that every effort should be made to restore cordial relations with the United States, for he realized that, like it or not, Britain's destiny lay with the American giant, not with France or the Commonwealth.

Despite occasional setbacks, the British economy had gradually improved in the 1950s under Conservative governments, a situation for which Macmillan, as minister of housing and Chancellor of the Exchequer under Churchill and Eden, was partly responsible. Prosperity had come at last, and Macmillan meant to nurture it. The postwar economic growth of Britain had lagged behind the remarkable recovery of France and West Germany, but still it was substantial. While prices had remained comparatively stable since 1954, domestic production and exports had increased. Wages had also risen from an average of about £9 or £10 a week in 1950 to about £14 (about $39) in 1959. Prosperity may be viewed in another way: television sets, vacuum cleaners, washing machines, and automobiles were beyond the financial capacity of most working-class families in the late 1940s; they were common possessions by 1959. Domestic demand plus larger sales abroad increased the value of the gross national product by about 30 per cent in the 1950s. Industrial goods accounted for 40 per cent of the GNP in 1958 as compared with only 5 per cent each for agriculture, mining, construction, and fishing. Britain remained primarily a nation of manufacturers, but the character of industrial output had changed. Textiles, shipbuilding, and mining, once the mainstays of the economy, had steadily declined in the face of heavy competition in the world market. Moreover Britain's loss of oil fields in the Near East and the resulting increase in the price of petroleum and petroleum by-products encouraged the development of nuclear power for peaceful purposes. Britain has consistently set the pace in this field since the completion in May, 1956, of the world's first nuclear power station generating electricity for commercial use at Calder Hall, Cumberland. Other nuclear reactors have been built at Harwell (Berkshire), Chapelcross (Dunfriesshire), and Dounreay (Caithness). Still others are under construction at half a dozen places throughout the United Kingdom.

It was greatly to the advantage of Macmillan and the Conservatives that prosperity, the barometer of political success for every administration since the Great Depression, was high in 1959, an election year. In shaping that prosperity, the government had lowered the bank rate and taxes to encourage trade and industry. "Supermac," the affectionate nickname tagged on Macmillan, who looks like a soft-spoken and bookish Edwardian, had indeed worked wonders. When he took office in 1957, the country verged on serious inflation, unemployment was again rising, and Britain's international stature was at an unprecedented low as a result of the Suez debacle. By 1959 all this had changed for the better.

In the campaign the Conservatives, proud of their accomplishments, made no effort to conceal them. The Labourites, led by Gaitskell, were still suffering from internal disputes over such questions as nuclear disarmament, support of American foreign policy, and further nationalization of industry. They denounced class and privilege as though the Conservatives were still guilty of upholding such trappings of a bygone generation, and accused them of apathy bred by longevity in office. Charges of this sort had previously worked to the advantage of the Opposition, but they were ineffective in 1959, when Conservative successes and economic prosperity left the Labourites without an attractive program. The results of the general election surprised even the

Conservatives, who had expected victory but nothing like the landslide that swept them back into office for the third time since 1951. They won 365 seats, a gain of twenty over 1955, while the Labourites captured 258 seats and the Liberals only 6.

The results were ultimately less important to the Conservatives than to the Labourites, who had learned that promises of socialist reforms and a vigorous campaign alone could not overcome party strife. Gaitskell did his best after the election to heal the rift with the left-wingers, a task that was eased by the death of Bevan in 1960. When Gaitskell himself died in 1963, without surrendering an inch to those who would have pulled Britain out of NATO, scrapped nuclear weapons, and driven American nuclear submarines and air bases from British soil, Harold Wilson took up the task of restoring unity and public trust in the party. Although Wilson, like Gaitskell, had been a brilliant student and university lecturer, he had more success as Labour party leader, probably because he could mingle with less discomfort among die-hard socialists and ordinary workingmen. Both the rank and file and the Trades Union Congress have accorded him wider support than they gave Gaitskell, although he has come in for more than his share of biting criticism at the annual party conferences.

National prosperity had been the determining factor in the Conservative victory in 1959. To all appearances the country had attained all the appurtenances of affluence. But appearances were deceiving. The Conservatives had successfully halted a trend toward higher unemployment, curbed the rising cost of living, and rectified some of the imbalance of trade. But their solutions to these problems were merely temporary expedients that had a way of evaporating at the slightest hint of a fiscal crisis. Try as they might, the Conservatives had been unable, primarily because of heavy competition from the United States, France, and West Germany, to increase Britain's share of world trade, which had remained since World War II at about 17 or 18 per cent. As we have seen, the economy was supersensitive to even minor fluctuations in the world market, primarily in relationship to American business. Later, in the late 1950s and early 1960s, inflation became the businessman's principal concern, for, while prices remained high, which discouraged foreign sales, the consumer developed a taste for foreign products. This not only discouraged domestic growth but also increased the deficit in foreign trade, which, in 1960, hovered dangerously at nearly £350,000,000.

Meanwhile prices soared, with the inevitable concurrent demands by industrial and government employees for commensurate pay increases. This price-wage spiral, typical of an inflationary economy, persisted in the early 1960s despite government efforts to halt it by means of raising the bank rate from 5 to 7 per cent (the highest rate in forty years), requesting that pay raises not exceed 2½ per cent a year, and increasing excise taxes by 10 per cent to discourage spending.

A succession of Chancellors of the Exchequer in 1958–62 had been unable to find a way out of the miasma of inflation and its adverse effect on the balance of payments. As the cost of living increased, so too did public criticism of the government. Dissatisfaction with the Macmillan administration first became apparent in Conservative defeats in by-elections in 1960 and 1961. Rising unemployment, particularly in the already depressed mining, shipbuilding, and textile centers of southern Scotland, Northern Ireland, Wales, and northwestern England, provoked heavy criticism in the press. During the bitter winter of 1962–63, the worst in half a century, when heavy snow, sub-zero temperatures, and the "killer" smog caused fuel shortages and extensive property damage, factory closings and snarled transportation, and the death of hundreds of persons from bronchial ailments, unemployment rose by 30 per cent over the previous summer. While the government could hardly be blamed for the weather, its critics did fault it for the shortage of fuel, for inefficient railway operation, and for narrow, uncleared highways more suited to the horse and buggy than to the modern automobile. Sensitive to such criticism, Macmillan appointed councils and commissions to study ways of controlling the price-wage spiral, to encourage exports, and to recommend new techniques and economies in both private and government-controlled industry. The most celebrated of these investigatory bodies were the National Incomes Commission, the National Economic Development Council, the Committee on the Gas Industry, and the commission headed by Dr. Richard Beeching, who cut railway schedules and closed down local stations in what proved to be a largely ineffective and highly unpopular effort to increase efficiency and lessen deficits in the archaic British Railways system.

Macmillan himself came in for a great deal of invective. In 1959, he had been hailed as "Supermac"; by 1963 even members of his own party were repeating in whispers Butler's apt characterization of him as "the best Prime Minister we have." Macmillan went into retreat early in July, 1962. On the twelfth and thirteenth a succession of cabinet members and heads of departments paraded in and out of 10 Downing

Street. Late on the thirteenth the press announced the resignations of seven cabinet members and nine other ministers in one of the most sweeping cabinet shake-ups in recent times. Macmillan wielded a heavy ax, all at once, and with only a few hours' notice to those involved. The public generally applauded the new appointments, but both the press and the Labourites accused the prime minister of doing others in for the sake of his own image. The most important change came at the Exchequer. Selwyn Lloyd, a faithful party servant who a few years earlier had been in contention for party leadership, gave place to Reginald Maudling, formerly colonial secretary and president of the Board of Trade. Butler surrendered the Home Office to Henry Brooke and took up a post at the Foreign Office, where he was to oversee negotiations relating to the possible entry of Britain into the Common Market (discussed later). Another party stalwart, Maxwell-Fyfe, now Lord Kilmuir, an important Conservative after World War II, was "sent out to pasture" while less aged and more ambitious hopefuls like Edward Heath, Duncan Sandys, and Peter Thorneycroft moved up a notch in the administrative hierarchy.

Whatever the motives of the prime minister, the cabinet changes helped to prolong the life of his administration by dissociating from it those whom the public had identified with economic problems since 1959. Whether or not the gradual improvement in the economy in the succeeding year is attributable to Maudling, who made promises of fiscal and trade reform without having sufficient time to implement them, is hard to say, but it did improve—not significantly, but enough to inspire greater confidence in an upward trend.

Serious illness requiring hospitalization and surgery overtook Macmillan in October, 1963. This, plus discouragement over public criticism of Conservative policy, and the damage done to the party by the Profumo affair of June, 1963, which implicated the secretary of state for war in a sex scandal that raised questions of public trust and national security, all weighed as factors in the prime minister's decision to resign as Conservative leader. The announcement of his resignation in mid-October at the annual party conference set off an intense struggle for party leadership, to which Butler, Maudling, and Lord Hailsham, minister for science and technology, were the principal aspirants. When none secured sufficient party support, Macmillan recommended to Queen Elizabeth the appointment of Lord Home as prime minister. In order to sit in the Commons, a prerequisite of his new office, he renounced his peerage (made possible by the Peerage

Act of July, 1963) and was elected to Parliament in a Scottish constituency as Sir Alec Douglas-Home. Sixty years of age, thin, an indifferent speaker, and formerly foreign minister under Macmillan, he at once took up the difficult task of forming a cabinet representative of the party's divergent elements. Ian Macleod and Enoch Powell, both of whom had opposed Douglas-Home's candidacy, lost their posts in the cabinet as Commons leader and minister of health, respectively, to Selwyn Lloyd and Anthony Barber. Other major appointments included Butler (Foreign Office), Heath (Board of Trade), Sandys (Commonwealth and Colonial Affairs), Thorneycroft (Defense), Ernest Marples (Transport), Henry Brooke (Home Office), and Sir Edward Boyle (Education). Macmillan was offered a ministry, but retired early in 1964 from public life to take a position in the famous publishing house bearing his name.

The government of Douglas-Home lasted just four days short of one year—until the general election of October, 1964. It may fairly be said that both the prime minister and his brief administration lacked luster. Inordinately sensitive to criticism, he spent a great deal of time making speeches in an effort to bolster the rapidly slipping Conservative party image. The economy naturally demanded his attention. While inflationary prices gradually eroded foreign sales, imports rose steadily in the spring and summer of 1964. The deficit of payments again verged on the critical, notwithstanding Maudling's assurances, which were borne out, that the economy would achieve a growth rate of 4 per cent before year's end. In the face of growing public dissatisfaction with the state of the economy, apprehensive Conservative spokesmen promised more housing, better educational facilities, higher welfare benefits, and curbs on inflation.

The shadow of defeat hung over Douglas-Home from the first. As the statutory term of Parliament would expire in October, 1964, politicians prepared for the upcoming election. National polls indicated that the Labourites were rapidly gaining ground. The Conservatives could do no more, except at the risk of calling their stewardship into question, than to repeat what they insisted had been their substantial achievements. The Labourites, led by dynamic Harold Wilson, strove to convince the electorate that only they could achieve significant economic growth and fiscal stability. Hence all issues, domestic as well as foreign, were aired repeatedly at political meetings throughout the country. When Parliament was dissolved in September and Douglas-Home, unable to postpone the inevitable any longer, called for an election on October 15, there was little else to be said in the formal campaign. Under these circumstances the results were something of a surprise. Had the election come in the previous spring or summer, Labour probably would have won by a substantial margin. But by October, for reasons not yet clear, the Conservative position had improved markedly, and the results proved far closer than expected. The Labourites won 317 seats; the Conservatives, 304; the Liberals, 9. The difference in the popular vote between Labour and Conservative was less than 1 per cent of the total ballots cast. Labour's over-all majority of only four seats was cut to three following a by-election early in 1965.

The Labour government, the first since 1951, could not have been blamed had it marked time until another election might increase its margin in the Commons. It was to Wilson's credit that, despite gloomy predictions of failure because of a stalemate in Parliament, he laid bold plans to improve housing and transportation, modernize industry, and strengthen the pound sterling. Within a few months of the election, Parliament had renationalized most of the large steel companies, raised the bank and tariff rates to fight inflation and discourage unessential imports, and imposed a capital gains tax. Wilson had clearly gambled with the uncertain future of his Labour government, but the stakes were well worth the risk. A huge signboard in Piccadilly Circus told the tale of Britain's critical economic plight: either exports go up or we go down! Unless defeated on a major issue, the Labourites could have held on until 1969, but with their narrow margin constantly a deterrent to a firm policy and with public opinion polls indicative of strong popular support of his administration, Wilson called for another general election in March, 1966. It increased the Labour majority by more than one hundred seats, which Wilson regarded as a popular mandate to cure Britain's economic ills by radical measures, to proceed as he had in peaceful negotiations over the rebellious actions of Rhodesia's Prime Minister Ian Smith, and to continue to support American action in Vietnam. Shortly after the election Wilson imposed a wage-and-price freeze aimed at strengthening the pound sterling as an international currency and staved off efforts by the party's left wing to depose him as Labour leader.

The balance-of-trade question plagued the Wilson administration, as it had troubled every government since the Second World War. After twenty years of alternating periods of financial stability and crisis, the economic situation had not changed appreciably. Britain traditionally had been one of the strongest and most independent states, but World

War II had cost so much that serious question arose whether it could sustain a viable economy and a decent standard of living on the basis of trade with the United States and the members of the Commonwealth in the face of increasingly heavy competition from the states of western Europe. Strong federalist forces had been at work to make free Europe into a single military and economic community. The Organization for European Economic Cooperation (OEEC) had been formed in April, 1948, to administer Marshall Plan aid and to lay long-range plans for economic growth. The Brussels Treaty Organization (1948) and the North Atlantic Treaty Organization (1949), in addition to creating defensive alliances against the U.S.S.R., envisaged economic, social, and cultural collaboration. In 1952, largely through the efforts of French economist Jean Monnet and French Foreign Minister Robert Schuman, the Netherlands, Belgium, Luxembourg, France, West Germany, and Italy formed the European Coal and Steel Community (ECSC), a truly supranational economic union whose common assembly set prices, eased the flow of raw materials and finished products, and regulated tariffs among the member states. In March, 1957, the ECSC moved a step closer to full economic integration by establishing the European Economic Community (EEC) or Common Market. Its members pledged to rescind all tariff barriers, to set a uniform tariff on imports from outside the Common Market, and, eventually, to allow the uninterrupted flow of capital, goods, and labor anywhere within the Community. They also formed the European Atomic Energy Community (Euratom) to promote the common development of atomic energy for peaceful purposes.

Britain had willingly joined the BTO, OEEC, and NATO, but it rejected membership in the ECSC, Euratom, and EEC. Edward Heath, Eden's spokesman at the meetings leading to the establishment of the Common Market, had carefully explored the wisdom of British membership. The protracted negotiations in 1956–58 aroused intense discussion among British politicians and the public. In general, Liberals favored immediate entry; Conservatives were cautiously interested; and Labourites opposed it. Entry into the Common Market involved a difficult decision. Many feared that membership would induce a fall in wages and prices as a result of the inevitable influx of Continental goods and raw materials, which were considerably cheaper than British goods. Everyone realized that membership would require alterations of trade treaties between Britain, the United States, and the Commonwealth nations, some of whom, notably Australia, New Zealand, Canada, Ceylon, India, and most of the African states, depended on the British market to absorb anywhere from 30 to 70 per cent of their exports. A sudden collapse of inter-Commonwealth trade would endanger the economic welfare of several member states and might possibly destroy the Commonwealth. Furthermore, would not membership in the Common Market alienate the United States, long Britain's friend, ally, and steady customer? Would Britain enjoy any greater economic security within the Common Market than it had had within the Commonwealth? Finally, what effect would membership have vis-à-vis the precious right of national self-determination, not only economically, but in matters of foreign policy and defense as well? The British knew that some European statesmen viewed economic integration as a first step toward eventual political unification of free Europe. While the Conservatives pondered these questions, General de Gaulle came to power in France in 1958 and at once made it clear that France meant to dominate western European affairs. He vetoed British membership in the Common Market over the objections of the other members, thereby openly acknowledging his Anglophobia and distrust of British intentions.

Because the Common Market effectively stifled British trade in Europe, in 1959 Britain joined Denmark, Sweden, Norway, Portugal, Austria, and Switzerland in the European Free Trade Association (EFTA), commonly called the "Outer Seven," in order to bring pressure on the "Inner Six" of the Common Market. The EFTA failed to break down the tariff barriers of the Common Market, which, unlike EFTA, was a highly integrated and natural economic unit capable of overriding national economic patterns. Before long it became apparent that the EFTA could not survive without trade with the Common Market on the latter's terms. For this reason, as well as because several Commonwealth nations put up high tariffs against certain British imports, Britain in 1961 again opened negotiations for entry into the Common Market provided that the interests of the Commonwealth and the EFTA could be accommodated. The Liberals once more supported Macmillan's efforts while the Labourites, in common with most Commonwealth governments, opposed them. It was of cardinal significance, and indicative of the political implications of economic integration, that, while the Board of Trade had managed negotiations leading to the creation of the free trade area, the Foreign Office controlled the bulk of the negotiations in 1961. Macmillan thereby as much as admitted that Britain's entry into the Common Market might in time lead to the loss of its right of self-determination if not of sovereignty itself. It came as no surprise, therefore, that the negotiations aroused much discussion and adverse criticism.

As before, it was not Britain that made the excruciating decision, for General de Gaulle again blocked the British application for membership. Since 1964, the Labourites have struggled within the context of traditional trade relationships and conventional policies in the hope of finding a solution to Britain's economic problems for which there appears to be no remedy outside the Common Market. By the spring of 1967, because of rising imports that again worsened the balance of payments situation, Wilson's administration decided to apply once more for entry into the Common Market. Whether or not her application will be successful cannot now be determined, but General de Gaulle will probably have the last word.

What lies ahead for the gallant, productive, and imaginative people of Great Britain is not for the historian to say. It is his business faithfully to portray the past, not to forecast the future. But man in his unfathomable ingenuity can be expected to rise to the occasion in the future as he has done in the past. If that be true, and if the British people have managed through the two millenniums and more covered in this book to cope with crises no less serious than that faced by the present generation, there is every reason to expect that the last chapter of British history lies well in the unforeseeable future.

Tables

Rulers of England

Alfred, 871–899
Edward, 899–924
Ethelstan, 924–939
Edmund, 939–946
Edred, 946–955
Edwig, 955–959
Edgar, 959–975
Edward, 975–978
Ethelred, 978–1016
Edmund, 1016
Canute, 1017–1035
Harold, 1035–1040
Harthacanute, 1040–1042
Edward, 1042–1066
Harold, 1066
William I, 1066–1087
William II, 1087–1100
Henry I, 1100–1135
Stephen, 1135–1154
Henry II, 1154–1189
Richard I, 1189–1199
John, 1199–1216
Henry III, 1216–1272
Edward I, 1272–1307
Edward II, 1307–1327
Edward III, 1327–1377
Richard II, 1377–1399
Henry IV, 1399–1413
Henry V, 1413–1422

Henry VI, 1422–1461
Edward IV, 1461–1483
Edward V, 1483
Richard III, 1483–1485
Henry VII, 1485–1509
Henry VIII, 1509–1547
Edward VI, 1547–1553
Mary I, 1553–1558
Elizabeth I, 1558–1603
James I, 1603–1625
Charles I, 1625–1649
Interregnum, 1649–1660
Charles II, 1660–1685
James II, 1685–1688
William III and Mary II, 1689–1702
Anne, 1702–1714
George I, 1714–1727
George II, 1727–1760
George III, 1760–1820
George IV, 1820–1830
William IV, 1830–1837
Victoria, 1837–1901
Edward VII, 1901–1910
George V, 1910–1936
Edward VIII, 1936
George VI, 1936–1952
Elizabeth II, 1952–

Chief Ministers

Sir Robert Walpole, 1721–1742
Lord Wilmington and John Carteret, 1742–1744
Henry Pelham, 1744–1754
Duke of Newcastle, 1754–1756
William Pitt, 1756–1757
William Pitt and the Duke of Newcastle, 1757–1761
Duke of Newcastle and Lord Bute, 1761–1762
Lord Bute, 1762–1763
George Grenville, 1763–1765
Lord Rockingham, 1765–1766
William Pitt, Lord Chatham, 1766–1768
Duke of Grafton, 1768–1770
Lord North, 1770–1782
Lord Rockingham, 1782
Lord Shelburne, 1782–1783
Duke of Portland, Lord North, and Charles J. Fox, 1783
William Pitt, the Younger, 1783–1801
Henry Addington, 1801–1804
William Pitt, the Younger, 1804–1806
Lord Grenville and Charles J. Fox, 1806–1807
Duke of Portland, 1807–1809
Spencer Perceval, 1809–1812
Lord Liverpool, 1812–1827
George Canning, 1827
Lord Goderich, 1827
Duke of Wellington, 1828–1830
Earl Grey, 1830–1834
Lord Melbourne, 1834
Sir Robert Peel, 1834–1835
Lord Melbourne, 1835–1841
Sir Robert Peel, 1841–1846
Lord John Russell, 1846–1852
Lord Derby and Benjamin Disraeli, 1852
Lord Aberdeen, 1852–1855
Lord Palmerston, 1855–1858
Lord Derby and Benjamin Disraeli, 1858–1859

Lord Palmerston, 1859–1865
Lord John Russell, 1865–1866
Lord Derby and Benjamin Disraeli, 1866–1868
William E. Gladstone, 1868–1874
Benjamin Disraeli, 1874–1880
William E. Gladstone, 1880–1885
Lord Salisbury, 1885–1886
William E. Gladstone, 1886
Lord Salisbury, 1886–1892
William E. Gladstone, 1892–1894
Lord Rosebery, 1894–1895
Lord Salisbury, 1895–1902
Arthur James Balfour, 1902–1905
Henry Campbell-Bannerman, 1905–1908
Herbert Henry Asquith, 1908–1916
David Lloyd George, 1916–1922
Andrew Bonar Law, 1922–1923
Stanley Baldwin, 1923–1924
James Ramsay MacDonald, 1924
Stanley Baldwin, 1924–1929
James Ramsay MacDonald, 1929–1931 (Labour); 1931–1935
    (National)
Stanley Baldwin, 1935–1937
Neville Chamberlain, 1937–1940
Winston Churchill, 1940–1945
Clement Attlee, 1945–1951
Sir Winston Churchill, 1951–1955
Sir Anthony Eden, 1955–1957
Harold Macmillan, 1957–1963
Lord Home (Sir A. Douglas-Home), 1963–1964
Harold Wilson, 1964–

Bibliography

This selective bibliography is designed for students who may wish information for further study. As it is obviously impossible to include all the important works in a book of this kind, many excellent ones have been omitted because their detailed treatment make them more useful to advanced students and scholars than to the undergraduates for whom this book has been written. Several more comprehensive bibliographical guides are available in most college and public libraries.

Works that deal either generally with English history or with specific facets of it, such as economic, constitutional, imperial, and social history, are numerous and only a few need be mentioned here. Some of these are: Adams, G. B. (rev. by Schuyler, R. L.), *Constitutional History of England* (New York: Holt, Rinehart & Winston, 1962). Barnard, M., *History of Australia* (Sydney: Angus & Robertson, 1963). Brooke, C., and Smith, D. M., eds., *History of England*, 8 vols. (Edinburgh: Nelson, 1961–). Brown, P. H., *History of Scotland*, 3 vols. (Cambridge: Cambridge Univ. Press, 1902–9). Carrington, C. E., *The British Overseas* (Cambridge: Cambridge Univ. Press, 1950). Clark, G. N., ed., *Oxford History of England*, 15 vols. (Oxford: Clarendon Press, 1934–65). Creighton, D. G., *Dominion of the North* [Canada] (Boston: Houghton Mifflin, 1944). Cunningham, W., *Growth of English Industry & Commerce*, 3 vols. (Cambridge: Cambridge Univ. Press, 1910–12). Curtis, E. A., *History of Ireland*, 3rd ed. (London: Methuen, 1937). DeKiewiet, C. W., *History of South Africa* (Oxford: Clarendon Press, 1941). Dietz, F. C., *Economic History of England* (New York: Holt, 1942). Grierson, H. J. C., *Background of English Literature* (New York: Barnes & Noble, 1961). Hunt, W., and Poole, R. L., eds., *Political History of England*, 12 vols.

(London: Longmans, 1905-10). Jenks, E., *Short History of English Law*, 2nd ed. (Boston: Little, Brown, 1922). Jennings, I., *The British Constitution* (Cambridge: Cambridge Univ. Press, 1942). Lipson, E., *Economic History of England*, 3 vols. (New York: Macmillan, 1929-31). Lloyd, J. E., *History of Wales* (London: Benn, 1935). Mullett, C. F., *The British Empire* (New York: Holt, 1938). Mullinger, J. B., *History of the University of Cambridge* (London: Longmans, 1888). Naidis, M., *India: A Short Introductory History* (New York: Macmillan, 1966). Roberts, P. E., *History of British India* (London: Oxford Univ. Press, 1952). Rowse, A. L., *Spirit of English History* (London: Macmillan, 1944). Scott, E., *Short History of Australia* (New York: Scribner's, 1955). Sorley, W. R., *History of English Philosophy* (New York: Putnam, 1921). Traill, H. D., and Mann, J. S., eds., *Social England*, 6 vols. (London: Cassell, 1901-4). Wakeman, H. O., *Introduction to the History of the Church of England* (London: Rivingston, 1908).

In the following suggested readings, which are arranged by chapter, many of the books listed for one chapter will be useful for the preceding and succeeding chapters as well. To economize on space, most subtitles have been eliminated and abbreviations have been used. An increasing number of paperbacks on English history are available to students. The more important paperback series covering broad periods of English history are: the Pelican series, eight vols.; the Mentor series, five vols., beginning with 1485; and the excellent three-volume history by G. M. Trevelyan in the Doubleday Anchor series. More specialized topics are covered in paperbacks included under chapter headings and are identified by publisher according to the following key:

AA = Ann Arbor; ANV = Anvil; BA = Bantam; BAL = Ballantine; B&N = Barnes & Noble; CAP = Capricorn; COL = Colliers; COP = Cornell; CN = Harper's Colophon; CUP = Cambridge; DA = Doubleday Anchor; DU = Dutton Everyman; GAL = Galway; HM = Houghton Mifflin; HT = Harper's Torchbooks; JHP = Johns Hopkins; LB = Little, Brown; MAC = Macmillan; MER = Meridian; NO = Norton; OX = Oxford; PEN = Penguin; PH = Phoenix; SC = Scribner's; SEN = Sentry; SIG = Signet; VIN = Vintage; W = Wiley.

Chapter 1

Arbman, H., *The Vikings* (New York: Praeger, 1961). Birely, A., *Life in Roman Britain* (London: Batsford, 1964). Charlesworth, M. P., *et al.*, *Heritage of Early Britain* (London: Bell, 1952). Clapham, A. W., *English Architecture before the Norman Conquest* (Oxford: Clarendon Press, 1930). Cottrell, L., *The Great Invasion* (London: Evans, 1958). Duckett, E. S., *Alfred the Great* (PH); *Saint Dunstan of Canterbury* (New York: Norton, 1955); *Anglo-Saxon Saints and Scholars* (New York: Macmillan, 1947). Godfrey, J., *The Church in Anglo-Saxon England* (Cambridge: Cambridge Univ. Press, 1962). Haskins, C. H., *Normans in European History* (NO). Knowles, D., *The Monastic Order in England, 943–1216* (Cambridge: Cambridge Univ. Press, 1940). Larson, L. M., *Canute the Great* (New York: Putnam, 1912). Leach, A. F., *Schools of Medieval England* (London: Methuen, 1915). Leeds, E. T., *Early Anglo-Saxon Art and Archeology* (Oxford: Clarendon Press, 1936). Lyon, B., *Constitutional and Legal History of Medieval England* (New York: Harpers, 1960). Lyon, H. R., *Anglo-Saxon England and the Norman Conquest* (London: Longmans, 1962). Plucknett, T. F. T., *Concise History of the Common Law* (London: Butterworth, 1948). Plummer, C., *Life and Times of Alfred the Great* (Oxford: Clarendon Press, 1902). Quennell, M. and C. H. B., *Everyday Life in Anglo-Saxon, Viking, and Norman Times* (London: Putnam, 1927). Stephenson, C., *Borough and Town* (Cambridge: Medieval Academy of America, 1933). Thomas, P. G., *English Literature before Chaucer* (London: Arnold, 1924).

Chapter 2

Appleby, J. T., *John, King of England* (New York: Knopf, 1959). Archer, T. A., and Kingsford, C. L., *The Crusades* (New York: Putnam, 1904). Ballard, A., *The English Borough in the Twelfth Century* (Cambridge: Cambridge Univ. Press, 1914). Barber, R., *Henry Plantagenet* (London: Pall Mall, 1965). Barlow, F., *The Feudal Kingdom of England, 1042–1216* (New York: Longmans, 1955). Barrow, G. W. S., *Feudal Britain (1066–1314)* (London: Arnold, 1956). Bennett, H. S., *Life on the Medieval Manor* (CUP). Douglas, D. C., *William the Conqueror and the Norman Impact upon England* (Berkeley: Univ. of California Press, 1964). Galbraith, V. H., *Making of Domesday Book* (Oxford: Clarendon Press, 1961). Green, J. R., *Henry*

II (London: Macmillan, 1898). Haskins, C. H., *Renaissance of the Twelfth Century* (MER). Holt, J. C., *Magna Carta* (Cambridge: Harvard Univ. Press, 1965). Hoyt, R. S., *The Royal Demesne in English Constitutional History, 1066–1272* (Ithaca: Cornell Univ. Press, 1950). Lennard, R. V., *Rural England, 1086–1135* (Oxford: Clarendon Press, 1959). Muntz, H., *The Golden Warrior* (SC). Norgate, K., *Richard the Lion Heart* (London: Macmillan, 1924). Painter, S., *Reign of King John* (JHP). Richardson, H. G., *English Jewry under Angevin Kings* (London: Methuen, 1960). Slocombe, G. E., *Sons of the Conqueror* (London: Hutchinson, 1960). Stephens, W. R. W., *English Church from the Norman Conquest to the Accession of Edward I* (London: Macmillan, 1901). Thrupp, S. L., *Merchant Class of Medieval London* (AA). Walker, C. H., *Eleanor of Aquitaine* (Chapel Hill: Univ. of North Carolina Press, 1950). Warren, W. L., *King John* (New York: Norton, 1961).

Chapter 3

Bryant, A., *The Age of Chivalry* (New York: Doubleday, 1963). Clarke, M. V., *Medieval Representation and Consent* (London: Longmans, 1936). Coulton, G. G., *Chaucer and His England* (B&N). Crossley, F. H., *The English Abbey* (BA). Dunn-Pattison, R. P., *The Black Prince* (New York: Dutton, 1910). Gasquet, F. A., *Henry the Third and the Church* (London: Bell, 1905). Haskins, C. H., *Rise of Universities* (COP). Hilton, R. H., and Fagan, H., *The English Rising of 1381* (London: Lawrence & Wishart, 1950). Hutton, E., *Franciscans in England, 1224–1538* (London: Constable, 1926). Kramer, S., *English Craft Guilds and the Government* (New York: Columbia Univ. Press, 1905). Moore, C. H., *Medieval Church Architecture of England* (New York: Macmillan, 1912). Perroy, E., *The Hundred Years' War*, trans. by W. B. Wells (CAP). Plucknett, T. F., *Legislation of Edward I* (Oxford: Clarendon Press, 1949). Powicke, M., *Military Obligation in Medieval England* (Oxford: Clarendon Press, 1962). Rait, R. S., *Life in the Medieval University* (Cambridge: Cambridge Univ. Press, 1912). Salzman, L. F., *English Trade in the Middle Ages* (Oxford: Clarendon Press, 1931); *English Industries of the Middle Ages* (rev. ed.) (Oxford: Clarendon Press, 1923). Schofield, W. H., *English Literature from the Norman Conquest to Chaucer* (New York: Macmillan, 1906). Steel, A., *Richard II* (Cambridge: Cambridge Univ. Press, 1941).

Chapter 4

Abram, A., *Social England in the Fifteenth Century* (London: Routledge, 1909). Bennett, H. S., *The Pastons and Their England* (Cambridge: Cambridge Univ. Press, 1922). Cam, H., *England Before Elizabeth* (HT). Chrimes, S. B., *English Constitutional Ideas in the Fifteenth Century* (Cambridge: Cambridge Univ. Press, 1936). Davies, J. D. G., *King Henry IV* (London: Barker, 1935). Evans, J., *English Art, 1307–1461* (Oxford: Clarendon Press, 1949). Gairdner, J., ed., *The Paston Letters, 1422–1509*, 4 vols. (Westminster: Constable, 1900–1); *History of the Life and Reign of Richard the Third* (Cambridge: Cambridge Univ. Press, 1898). Hibbert, C., *Agincourt* (London: Batsford, 1964). Hunt, P., *Fifteenth Century England* (Pittsburgh: Univ. of Pittsburgh Press, 1962). Jacob, E. F., *Henry V and the Invasion of France* (New York: Macmillan, 1950). Kendall, P. M., *Warwick the King Maker* (New York: Norton, 1957); *The Yorkist Age* (DA); *Richard the Third* (DA). Kingsford, C. L., *Prejudice and Promise in Fifteenth-Century England* (Oxford: Clarendon Press, 1925); *Henry V* (New York: Putnam, 1903). Mowat, R. B., *Henry V* (Boston: Houghton Mifflin, 1919); *The Wars of the Roses* (London: Lockwood, 1914). Schofield, C. L., *Life and Reign of Edward IV*, 2 vols. (London: Longmans, 1923). Trevelyan, G. M., *England in the Age of Wycliffe, 1368–1520* (HT).

Chapter 5

Bagwell, R., *Ireland under the Tudors*, 3 vols. (London: Longmans, 1885–90). Baskerville, G., *English Monks and the Suppression of the Monasteries* (London: Cape, 1937). Bowden, P. J., *The Wool Trade in Tudor and Stuart England* (London: Macmillan, 1962). Bowle, J., *Henry VIII* (Boston: Little, Brown, 1964). Campbell, W. E., *Erasmus, Tyndale and More* (Milwaukee: Bruce, 1950). Chapman, H. W., *Lady Jane Grey* (Boston: Little, Brown, 1963); *The Last Tudor King, Edward VI* (London: Cape, 1958). Chrimes, S. B., *Lancastrians, Yorkists, & Henry VII* (New York: St. Martin's Press, 1964). Dickens, A. G., *The English Reformation* (New York: Schocken, 1964). Elton, G. R., *Tudor Revolution in Government* (CUP). Emmison, F. G., *Tudor Secretary: Sir William Petre* (Cambridge: Harvard Univ. Press, 1961). Farrow, J., *The Story of Thomas More* (New York: Sheed &

Ward, 1954). Ferguson, C. W., *Naked to Mine Enemies* [Cardinal Wolsey] (LB). Gaspari, F., *Humanism and the Social Order in Tudor England* (Chicago: Univ. of Chicago Press, 1954). Hughes, P., *The Reformation in England*, 3 vols. (New York: Macmillan, 1951–54). Hutchinson, F. T., *Cranmer and the English Reformation* (COL). Lehmberg, S. E., *Sir Thomas Elyot, Tudor Humanist* (Austin: Univ. of Texas Press, 1960). Lockyer, R., *Tudor and Stuart Britain* (New York: St. Martin's Press, 1964). Lupton, J. H., *Life of John Colet* (Hamden, Conn.: Shoe String Press, 1961). Mattingly, G., *Catherine of Aragon* (VIN). Maynard, T., *The Crown and the Cross* [Thomas Cromwell] (New York: McGraw-Hill, 1950). Morpurgo, J. E., ed., *Life Under the Tudors* (London: Falcon, 1950). Morris, C., *The Tudors* (London: Batsford, 1955). Morrison, N. B., *Mary Queen of Scots* (New York: Vanguard Press, 1960). Pickthorn, K., *Early Tudor Government, Henry VII* (Cambridge: Cambridge Univ. Press, 1934). Pollard, A. F., *Henry VIII* (HT). Powicke, F. M., *The Reformation in England* (OX). Prescott, H. F. M., *Mary Tudor* (MAC). Ramsey, P., *Tudor Economic Problems* (London: Gollancz, 1963). Read, C., *The Tudors* (New York: Holt, 1936). Richardson, W. C., *Tudor Chamber Administration, 1485–1547* (Baton Rouge: Louisiana State Univ. Press, 1952). Ridley, J., *Thomas Cranmer* (OX). Salzman, L. F., *England in Tudor Times* (London: Batsford, 1926). Smith, L. B., *Tudor Prelates and Politics, 1536–1558* (Princeton: Princeton Univ. Press, 1953); *A Tudor Tragedy; Life of Catherine Howard* (London: Cape, 1961). Tawney, R. H., *The Agrarian Problem in the Sixteenth Century* (London: Longmans, 1912). Temperley, G., *Henry VII* (Boston: Houghton Mifflin, 1914). Zeeveld, W. G., *Foundations of Tudor Policy* (Cambridge: Harvard Univ. Press, 1948).

Chapter 6

Beckinsale, B. W., *Elizabeth I* (London: Batsford, 1963). Bradford, E., *The Wind Command Me: A Life of Sir Francis Drake* (New York: Harcourt, Brace, 1965). Campbell, M. C., *English Yeoman Under Elizabeth and the Early Stuarts* (London: Merlin, 1960). Curtis, M. H., *Oxford and Cambridge in Transition, 1552–1642* (Oxford: Clarendon Press, 1959). Donaldson, G., *The Scottish Reformation* (Cambridge: Cambridge Univ. Press, 1960). Haller, W., *Rise of Puritanism* (HT). Harrison, G. B., ed., *The Elizabethan Journals*, 2 vols. (DA). Hurstfield, J., *The Queen's Wards: Wardship and Marriage under*

Elizabeth I (Cambridge: Harvard Univ. Press, 1958); *Elizabeth I and the Unity of England* (New York: Macmillan, 1960). Jenkins, E., *Elizabeth and Leicester* (New York: Coward-McCann, 1962). Jordan, W. K., *Philanthropy in England, 1480–1660* (New York: Russell Sage Foundation, 1959). Knappen, M. M., *Tudor Puritanism* (Chicago: Univ. of Chicago Press, 1939). Leonard, E. M., *Early History of English Poor Relief* (Cambridge: Cambridge Univ. Press, 1900). Macgregor, G., *The Thundering Scot* [John Knox] (Philadelphia: Westminster Press, 1957). Magnus, P., *Sir Walter Raleigh* (London: Collins, 1956). Mattingly, G., *The Armada* (SEN). Mercer, E., *English Art, 1553–1625* (Oxford: Clarendon Press, 1962). Neale, J. E., *Elizabeth I and Her Parliaments*, 2 vols. (NO); *Queen Elizabeth* (DA). Oakeshott, W., *Founded upon the Seas: Some English Maritime and Overseas Enterprises* (Cambridge: Cambridge Univ. Press, 1942). Read, C., *Lord Burghley and Queen Elizabeth* (New York: Knopf, 1960). Rowse, A. L., *Sir Walter Raleigh* (New York: Harper's, 1962); *England of Elizabeth* (MAC); *Elizabethans and America* (CN). Ryan, L. V., *Roger Ascham* (Stanford: Stanford Univ. Press, 1963). Simpson, A., *The Wealth of the Gentry, 1540–1640* (Chicago: Univ. of Chicago Press, 1961). Strachey, L., *Elizabeth and Essex* (New York: Harcourt, Brace, 1928). Trimble, W. R., *The Catholic Laity in Elizabethan England* (Cambridge: Harvard Univ. Press, 1964). Waldman, M., *Queen Elizabeth* (COL). Williamson, J. A., *Maritime Enterprise, 1485–1558* (Oxford: Clarendon Press, 1913); *Sir Francis Drake* (COL).

Chapter 7

Ashley, M., *The Greatness of Oliver Cromwell* (COL); *Cromwell's Generals* (New York: St. Martin's Press, 1955). Barker, A. E., *Milton and the Puritan Dilemma, 1641–1660* (Toronto: Univ. of Toronto Press, 1942). Beer, G. L., *Origins of the British Colonial System, 1578–1660* (New York: Macmillan, 1908). Blitzer, C., *Commonwealth of England, 1641–1660* (CAP). Bowen, C. D., *Francis Bacon* (LB); *The Lion and the Throne* [Sir Edward Coke] (LB). Brailsford, H. N., *The Levellers and the English Revolution* (Stanford: Stanford Univ. Press, 1961). Braithwaite, W. C., *The Beginnings of Quakerism*, 2nd ed., rev. and ed. by H. J. Cadbury (Cambridge: Cambridge Univ. Press, 1955). Buchan, J., *Oliver Cromwell* (Boston: Houghton Mifflin, 1934). Burne, A. H., and Young, P., *The Great Civil War* (1642–

1646) (London: Eyre & Spottiswoode, 1959). Cole, R., *Human History: The Seventeenth Century and the Stuart Family*, 2 vols. (Freeport, Me.: Bond Wheelwright, 1959). Coltman, I., *Private Men and Public Causes* (London: Faber & Faber, 1962). Cranston, M. W., *John Locke* (London: Longmans, 1957). Eusden, J. D., *Puritans, Lawyers, and Politics in Early Seventeenth Century England* (New Haven: Yale Univ. Press, 1958). Firth, C. H., *Oliver Cromwell and the Rule of the Puritans*, 3rd ed. (New York: Putnam, 1933). French, A., *Charles I and the Puritan Upheaval* (London: Allen & Unwin, 1955). Gardiner, S. R., *Oliver Cromwell* (COL). Gooch, G. P., *English Democratic Ideas in the Seventeenth Century* (HT). Gregg, P., *Free-Born* (John Lilburne) (London: Harrap, 1961). Hall, A. R., *The Scientific Revolution, 1500–1800*, 2nd ed. (New York: Longmans, 1962). Hardacre, P. H., *The Royalists During the Puritan Revolution* (The Hague: Nijhoff, 1956). Havran, M. J., *Catholics in Caroline England* (Stanford: Stanford Univ. Press, 1962). Hexter, J. H., *The Reign of King Pym* (Cambridge: Harvard Univ. Press, 1941). Hill, C., *Intellectual Origins of the English Revolution* (Oxford: Clarendon Press, 1965); *Society & Puritanism in Pre-Revolutionary England* (New York: Schocken, 1964); *The Century of Revolution, 1603–1714* (Edinburgh: Nelson, 1961). Hole, C., *A Mirror of Witchcraft* (London: Chatto & Windus, 1957). Hulme, H., *Sir John Eliot, 1592–1632* (New York: New York Univ. Press, 1957). Jones, I. D., *The English Revolution* (London: Heinemann, 1948). Kenyon, J. P., *The Stuarts* (London: Batsford, 1958). McElwee, W. L., *The Wisest Fool in Christendom, James I and VI* (New York: Harcourt, Brace, 1958). Mitchell, W. M., *Rise of the Revolutionary Party in the English House of Commons* (New York: Columbia Univ. Press, 1957). Mosse, G. L., *The Struggle for Sovereignty in England, 1558–1628* (East Lansing: Michigan State Univ. Press, 1950). New, J. F. H., *Anglican and Puritan: The Basis of Their Opposition, 1558–1640* (Stanford: Stanford Univ. Press, 1964). Notestein, W., *English People on the Eve of Colonization* (HT). Peters, R. S., *Hobbes* (Harmondsworth, Middlesex: Penguin, 1956). Petersson, R. T., *Sir Kenelm Digby* (London: Cape, 1956). Powell, J. R., *The Navy in the English Civil War* (Hamden, Conn.: Archon, 1962). Ramsay, R. W., *Henry Ireton* (London: Longmans, 1949). Solt, L., *Saints in Arms* (Stanford: Stanford Univ. Press, 1959). Trevelyan, G. M., *England Under the Stuarts*, 15th ed. (New York: Putnam, 1930). Trevor-Roper, H.,

Archbishop Laud, 1573–1645 (Hamden, Conn.: Archon, 1962). Turberville, A. S., *Commonwealth and Restoration* (London: Nelson, 1936). Underdown, D., *Royalist Conspiracy in England, 1640–1660* (New Haven: Yale Univ. Press, 1960). Wedgwood, C., *A Coffin for King Charles* (New York: Macmillan, 1964); *The King's Peace, 1637–1641* (New York: Macmillan, 1955); *The King's War, 1641–1647* (New York: Macmillan, 1959); *Thomas Wentworth, First Earl of Strafford* (New York: Macmillan, 1962); *Life of Cromwell* (COL). Westfall, R. S., *Science and Religion in Seventeenth Century England* (New Haven: Yale Univ. Press, 1958). Ross Williamson, H., *The Gunpowder Plot* (New York: Macmillan, 1952). Willson, D. H., *King James VI and I* (New York: Holt, 1956). Wilson, C. H., *England's Apprenticeship, 1603–1763* (New York: St. Martin's Press, 1965). Wingfield-Stratford, E., *Charles, King of England, 1600–1637; King Charles and King Pym, 1637–1643; King Charles the Martyr, 1643–1649* (London: Hollis & Carter, 1949–50). Yule, G. S., *The Independents in the English Civil War* (Cambridge: Cambridge Univ. Press, 1958).

Chapter 8

Bahlman, D., *The Moral Revolution of 1688* (New Haven: Yale Univ. Press, 1957). Beer, G. L., *The Old Colonial System, 1660–1754,* 2 vols. (New York: Macmillan, 1912). Bell, W. G., *The Great Plague in London in 1665* (London: Bodley Head, 1951). Bolton, G., *Sir Christopher Wren* (London: Hutchinson, 1956). Bryant, A., *King Charles II* (New York: Longmans, 1931). Chapman, H. W., *Mary II, Queen of England* (London: Cape, 1953). Cherry, G. L., *Early English Liberalism, 1660–1702* (New York: Bookman, 1962). Churchill, W., *Marlborough, His Life and Times,* 6 vols. (New York: Scribner's, 1933–38). Coleman, D. C., *Sir John Banks* (Oxford: Clarendon Press, 1963). Davies, G., *The Restoration of Charles II, 1658–1660* (San Marino, Calif.: Huntington Library, 1955). De Beer, E. S., ed., *John Evelyn Diary,* 6 vols. (Oxford: Clarendon Press, 1955). Emden, C. S., *Pepys Himself* (London: Oxford Univ. Press, 1963). Ewald, W. B., *Rogues, Royalty, and Reporters* (Boston: Houghton Mifflin, 1956). Feiling, K., *History of the Tory Party, 1640–1714* (Oxford: Clarendon Press, 1924). Ferguson, O. W., *Jonathan Swift and Ireland* (Urbana: Univ. of Illinois Press, 1962). Jones, J. R., *The First Whigs, Politics of the Exclusion Crisis, 1678–1683* (London: Oxford Univ.

Press, 1961). Keeton, G. W., *Lord Chancellor Jeffreys and the Stuart Cause* (London: Macdonald, 1965). Kenyon, J. P., *Robert Spencer, Earl of Sunderland, 1641–1702* (London: Longmans, 1958); *Pepys Diary* (MAC). Kronenberger, L., *Marlborough's Duchess* (New York: Knopf, 1958). Macaulay, T. B., *History of England from the Accession of James II*, Firth ed., 6 vols. (London: Macmillan, 1913–15). Mathieson, W. L., *Scotland and the Union, 1695–1747* (Glasgow: Maclehose, 1905). Morrah, P., *1660: The Year of Restoration* (London: Chatto & Windus, 1960). Morshead, O. F., ed., *Diary of Samuel Pepys* (HT). Ogg, D., *England in the Reigns of James II and William III* (Oxford: Clarendon Press, 1957); *England in the Reign of Charles II* (OX). Overton, J., *Life in the English Church, 1660–1714* (London: Longmans, 1885). Owen, J. H., *War at Sea Under Queen Anne, 1702–1708* (Cambridge: Cambridge Univ. Press, 1938). Pearson, H., *Merry Monarch; Life of Charles II* (New York: Harper's, 1960). Pinkham, L., *William III and the Respectable Revolution* (Cambridge: Harvard Univ. Press, 1954). Plum, H. G., *Restoration Puritanism* (Chapel Hill: Univ. of North Carolina Press, 1943). Simms, J. G., *The Williamite Confiscation in Ireland, 1692–1703* (London: Faber & Faber, 1956). Smout, T. C., *Scottish Trade on the Eve of Union, 1660–1707* (Edinburgh: Oliver & Boyd, 1963). Trevelyan, G. M., *England Under Queen Anne*, 3 vols. (London: Longmans, 1930–34). Turner, F. C., *James II* (New York: Macmillan, 1948). Walcott, R., *English Politics in the Early Eighteenth Century* (Cambridge: Harvard Univ. Press, 1956). Weld, C. R., *History of the Royal Society* (London: Parker, 1848). Wilson, C. H., *Profit and Power, England and the Dutch Wars* (New York: Longmans, 1957). Wilson, J. H., *Nell Gwyn, Royal Mistress* (New York: Pellegrini & Cudahy, 1952); *All the King's Ladies, Actresses of the Restoration* (Chicago: Univ. of Chicago Press, 1958).

Chapter 9

Becker, C. L., *The Heavenly City of the Eighteenth Century Philosophers* (New Haven: Yale Univ. Press, 1932). Bird, H., *Battle for a Continent: The French and Indian War, 1754–1763* (New York: Oxford Univ. Press, 1965). Boswell, J., *Life of Johnson* (OX). Carpenter, S. C., *Eighteenth Century Church and People* (London: Murray, 1959). Carswell, J., *The South Sea Bubble* (Stanford: Stanford Univ. Press, 1960). Cole, G. D. H., and Postgate, R., *The British Common*

People, 1746–1946 (New York: Knopf, 1947). Cragg, G. R., *Reason and Authority in the Eighteenth Century* (Cambridge: Cambridge Univ. Press, 1964). Green, V. H. H., *Young Mr. Wesley* (London: Arnold, 1961). Grinnell-Milne, D., *Mad Is He?* [James Wolfe] (London: Bodley Head, 1963). Humphreys, A. R., *The Augustan World* (HT). Ketton-Cremer, R. W., *Horace Walpole* (New York: Longmans, 1940). Laprade, W. T., *Public Opinion and Politics in Eighteenth Century England to the Fall of Walpole* (New York: Macmillan, 1936). Lecky, W. E. H., *England in the Eighteenth Century*, 8 vols. (London: Longmans, 1878–90). Lewis, M., *History of the British Navy* (PEN). Mingay, G. E., *English Landed Society in the Eighteenth Century* (London: Routledge & Kegan Paul, 1963). Namier, L. B., *Crossroads of Power* (London: Hamilton, 1962). Osgood, H. L., *American Colonies in the Eighteenth Century*, 4 vols. (New York: Columbia Univ. Press, 1924). Owen, J. B., *Rise of the Pelhams* (London: Methuen, 1957). Petrie, C., *The Jacobite Movement*, 3rd ed. (London: Eyre & Spottiswoode, 1959). Plumb, J. H., *Sir Robert Walpole*, 2 vols. (London: Cresset, 1956, 1960); *Men and Places* (London: Cresset, 1963). Riley, P., *English Ministers and Scotland, 1707–1727* (London: Athlone, 1964). Stephen, L., *English Literature and Society in the Eighteenth Century* (London: Duckworth, 1904). Sykes, N., *Church and State in the XVIII Century* (Cambridge: Cambridge Univ. Press, 1934). Taylor, G. R. S., *Robert Walpole and His Age* (London: Cape, 1931). Thompson, E., and Garratt, G. T., *Rise and Fulfillment of British Rule in India* (London: Macmillan, 1934). Tunstall, B., *William Pitt, Earl of Chatham* (London: Hodder & Stoughton, 1938). Turberville, A. S., *House of Lords in the Eighteenth Century* (Oxford: Clarendon Press, 1927). Wilkes, J. W., *A Whig in Power* [Henry Pelham] (Evanston, Ill.: Northwestern Univ. Press, 1964). Williams, E. N., *Life in Georgian England* (New York: Putnam, 1962). Williams, G., *The British Search for the Northwest Passage in the Eighteenth Century* (London: Longmans, 1963). Winstanley, D. A., *Lord Chatham and the Whig Opposition* (Cambridge: Cambridge Univ. Press, 1912).

Chapter 10

Alden, J. R., *General Gage in America* (Baton Rouge: Louisiana State Univ. Press, 1948); *American Revolution, 1763–1783* (HT). Andrews, C. M., *The Colonial Background of the American Revolution*

(New Haven: Yale Univ. Press, 1924). Barnes, D. G., *George III and William Pitt* (Stanford: Stanford Univ. Press, 1939). Black, E. C., *The Association: British Extraparliamentary Political Organization, 1769–1793* (Cambridge: Harvard Univ. Press, 1963). Butterfield, H., *George III and the People, 1779–1780* (London: Bell, 1949); *George III and the Historians* (NO). Christie, I., *Wilkes, Wyvil, and Reform* (New York: St. Martin's Press, 1962). Derry, J., *The Younger Pitt* (London: Batsford, 1962). Dickerson, O. M., *The Navigation Acts and the American Revolution* (Philadelphia: Univ. of Pennsylvania Press, 1951). Donoughue, B., *British Politics and the American Revolution* (New York: St. Martin's Press, 1964). Drinkwater, J., *Charles James Fox* (London: Benn, 1928). Feiling, K., *Warren Hastings* (New York: St. Martin's Press, 1954). Furber, H., *John Company at Work: European Expansion in India in the Late Eighteenth Century* (Cambridge: Harvard Univ. Press, 1948). Gipson, L. H., *The British Empire before the American Revolution*, 13 vols. (New York: Knopf, 1958–). Gutteridge, G. H., *English Whiggism and the American Revolution* (Berkeley: Univ. of California Press, 1942). Harris, R. W., *Political Ideas, 1760–1792* (London: Gollancz, 1963). Hobhouse, C., *Fox* (Boston: Houghton Mifflin, 1935). Lewis, W. S., *Horace Walpole* (New York: Pantheon, 1960). Mackenzie, A. M., *Scotland in Modern Times, 1720–1939* (London: Chambers, 1941). Mackesy, P., *War for America, 1775–1783* (Cambridge: Harvard Univ. Press, 1964). Magnus, P., *Edmund Burke* (London: Murray, 1939). Marcus, G. J., *Quiberon Bay* (London: Hollis & Carter, 1960). Namier, L. B., *England in the Age of the American Revolution*, 2nd ed. (New York: St. Martin's Press, 1961); *The Structure of British Politics at the Accession of George III*, 2nd ed. (New York: St. Martin's Press, 1957). Namier, L. B., and Brooke, J., *Charles Townshend* (New York: St. Martin's Press, 1964). Norris, J., *Shelburne and Reform* (New York: St. Martin's Press, 1963). Pares, R., *War and Trade in the West Indies, 1739–1763* (Oxford: Clarendon Press, 1936); *King George and the Politicians* (Oxford: Clarendon Press, 1953). Philips, C. H., *The East India Company, 1784–1834* (New York: Barnes & Noble, 1961). Rea, R. R., *English Press in Politics, 1760–1774* (Lincoln: Univ. of Nebraska Press, 1963). Rudé, G., *Wilkes and Liberty* (Oxford: Clarendon Press, 1962). Schuyler, R. L., *Fall of the Old Colonial System* (New York: Oxford Univ. Press, 1945). Shy, J., *Toward Lexington: Role of the British Army in the Coming of the American Revolution*

(Princeton: Princeton Univ. Press, 1965). Sosin, J., *Agents and Merchants, British Colonial Policy and the Origins of the American Revolution* (Lincoln: Univ. of Nebraska Press, 1965). Tarling, N., *Anglo-Dutch Rivalry in the Malay World, 1780–1824* (London: Cambridge Univ. Press, 1962). Trevelyan, G. O., *Early History of Charles James Fox* (New York: Harper's, 1880). Valentine, A., *Lord George Germain* (Oxford: Clarendon Press, 1962). Willcox, W. B., *Portrait of a General; Sir Henry Clinton in the War of Independence* (New York: Knopf, 1964).

Chapter 11

Ashton, T. S., *The Industrial Revolution, 1760–1830* (GAL); *Iron and Steel in the Industrial Revolution* (London: Longmans, 1924). Ashton, T. S., and Sykes, J., *The Coal Industry of the Eighteenth Century* (Manchester: Univ. of Manchester Press, 1929). Bowden, W., *Industrial Society in England towards the End of the Eighteenth Century* (New York: Macmillan, 1925). Checkland, S. G., *Rise of Industrial Society in England, 1815–1885* (New York: St. Martin's Press, 1965). Court, W. H. B., *Rise of the Midland Industries, 1600–1838* (London: Oxford Univ. Press, 1938). Dumville, J., and Kershaw, S., *The Worsted Industry* (London: Pitman, 1924). Fay, C. R., *Great Britain from Adam Smith to the Present Day*, 3rd ed. (London: Longmans, 1932). Fitton, R. S., and Wadsworth, A. P., *The Strutts and the Arkwrights, 1758–1830; A Study of the Early Factory System* (Manchester: Univ. of Manchester Press, 1958). George, D., *England in Transition: Life and Work in the Eighteenth Century* (PEN). Hammond, J. L. and Barbara, *Rise of Modern Industry* (New York: Harcourt, Brace, 1926); *The Village Labourer, 1760–1832* (London: Longmans, 1911); *The Town Labourer, 1760–1832* (London: Longmans, 1917); *The Skilled Labourer, 1760–1832* (London: Longmans, 1919). Harris, J. H., *The Copper King: Thomas Williams of Llanidan* (Liverpool: Univ. of Liverpool Press, 1964). Honey, W. B., *English Pottery and Porcelain*, 3rd ed. (London: A. & C. Black, 1947). Lipson, E., *History of the Woolen and Worsted Industries* (London: A. & C. Black, 1921). Mantoux, P., *The Industrial Revolution of the Eighteenth Century* (HT). Marshall, T. H., *James Watt, 1736–1819* (Boston: Small, Maynard, 1925). Moffit, L. W., *England on the Eve of the Industrial Revolution* (London: King & Son, 1925). Pinchbeck, I., *Women Workers and the Industrial Revolution, 1750–1850* (London: Routledge, 1930).

Pressnell, L. S., *Country Banking in the Industrial Revolution* (Oxford: Clarendon Press, 1956). Prothero, R. E., *English Farming, Past and Present*, 5th ed. (London: Longmans, 1936). Redford, A., *Economic History of England, 1760–1860* (London: Longmans, 1931); *Labour Migration in England, 1800–1850* (London: Longmans, 1926). Ruggles-Brise, E. J., *English Prison System* (London: Macmillan, 1921). Schmidt, M., *John Wesley*, trans. by N. R. Goldhawk (New York: Abingdon, 1963). Steegman, J., *Sir Joshua Reynolds* (New York: Macmillan, 1933). Turberville, A. S., *English Men and Manners in the 18th Century* (OX). Usher, A. P., *History of Mechanical Inventions*, rev. ed. (Cambridge: Harvard Univ. Press, 1954). Warner, W. J., *The Wesleyan Movement in the Industrial Revolution* (London: Longmans, 1930). Wearmouth, R. F., *Methodism and the Working Class Movements of England, 1800–1850* (London: Epworth, 1947). Webb, S. and B., *History of Trade Unionism*, 2nd ed. (London: Longmans, 1896). Wedgwood, J., *Personal Life of Josiah Wedgwood the Potter*, rev. and ed. by C. H. Herford (London: Macmillan, 1915).

Chapter 12

Adamson, J. W., *English Education, 1789–1902* (Cambridge: Cambridge Univ. Press, 1964). Aspinall, A., *Lord Brougham and the Whig Party* (Manchester: Univ. of Manchester Press, 1927). Bartlett, C. J., *Great Britain and Sea Power, 1815–1853* (Oxford: Clarendon Press, 1963). Bearce, G. G., *British Attitudes towards India, 1784–1858* (New York: Oxford Univ. Press, 1961). Brock, W. R., *Lord Liverpool and Liberal Toryism, 1820–1827* (Cambridge: Cambridge Univ. Press, 1941). Brown, F. K., *Fathers of the Victorians: Age of Wilberforce* (Cambridge: Cambridge Univ. Press, 1961). Brown, P. A., *French Revolution in English History* (New York: Dutton, 1924). Bryant, A., *Years of Endurance, 1793–1802; Years of Victory, 1802–1812; Age of Elegance, 1812–1822* (New York: Harper's, 1942–50). Clapham, J. H., *Economic History of Modern Britain, 1820–1929*, 3 vols. (Cambridge: Cambridge Univ. Press, 1950–52). Cooper, L., *Age of Wellington* (New York: Dodd, Mead, 1963). Cowherd, R. G., *Politics of Dissent, 1815–1848* (New York: New York Univ. Press, 1956). Dicey, A. V., *Law and Opinion in England during the Nineteenth Century* (London: Macmillan, 1914). Fay, C. R., *Huskisson and His Age* (New York: Longmans, 1951). Fulford, R., *George the Fourth* (CAP). Gash, N., *Mr. Secretary Peel: Life of Peel to 1830* (Cambridge: Harvard

Univ. Press, 1961). Gosden, P. H., *The Friendly Societies in England, 1815–1875* (Manchester: Univ. of Manchester Press, 1961). Gray, D., *Spencer Perceval* (New York: Barnes & Noble, 1963). Halévy, E., *History of the English People,* 5 vols. (B&N). Hall, W. P., *British Radicalism, 1791–1797* (New York: Columbia Univ. Press, 1912). Klingberg, F. J., *Anti-Slavery Movement in England* (New Haven: Yale Univ. Press, 1926). Knapland, P., *James Stephen and the British Colonial System, 1813–1847* (Madison: Univ. of Wisconsin Press, 1953). Luvaas, J., *The Education of an Army; British Military Thought, 1815–1940* (Chicago: Univ. of Chicago Press, 1964). McDowell, R. B., *Public Opinion and Government Policy in Ireland, 1801–1846* (London: Faber & Faber, 1952). Machin, G., *The Catholic Question in English Politics, 1820–1830* (Oxford: Clarendon Press, 1964). Mahan, A. T., *Influence of Sea Power upon the French Revolution and Empire, 1793–1812* (Boston: Little, Brown, 1894). Mathieson, W. L., *England in Transition, 1789–1832* (London: Longmans, 1920). Mill, J. S., *On Bentham and Coleridge* (HT). Naylor, J., *Waterloo* (New York: Macmillan, 1960). New, C. W., *Life of Henry Brougham to 1830* (Oxford: Clarendon Press, 1961). Newman, C., *Evolution of Medical Education in the Nineteenth Century* (New York: Oxford Univ. Press, 1957). Perkins, B., *Castlereagh and Adams: England and the United States, 1812–1823* (Berkeley: Univ. of California Press, 1964). Pollard, H. M., *Pioneers of Popular Education, 1760–1850* (London: Murray, 1956). Porritt, E. and A., *The Unreformed House of Commons: Parliamentary Representation before 1832* (Cambridge: Cambridge Univ. Press, 1903). Read, D., *Peterloo: The "Massacre" and Its Background* (Manchester: Univ. of Manchester Press, 1958). Rolo, P., *George Canning* (New York: St. Martin's Press, 1965). Stanhope, J., *The Cato Street Conspiracy* (London: Cape, 1962). Temperley, H., *Foreign Policy of Canning, 1822–1827* (London: Bell, 1925). Thompson, F. M. L., *English Landed Society in the Nineteenth Century* (London: Routledge & Kegan Paul, 1963). Turberville, A., *House of Lords in the Age of Reform, 1784–1837* (London: Faber & Faber, 1958). Ward, S., *Wellington* (New York: Arco, 1964). Warner, O., *William Wilberforce and His Times* (London: Batsford, 1962). Webster, C. K., *Foreign Policy of Castlereagh, 1815–1822* (London: Bell, 1925). Weller, J., *Wellington in the Peninsula, 1808–1814* (New York: Barnes & Noble, 1963). White, R., *Life in Regency England* (London: Batsford, 1963). Wood, A., *Nineteenth Century Britain,*

1815–1914 (London: Longmans, 1960). Young, D. M., *Colonial Office in the Early Nineteenth Century* (London: Longmans, 1961).

Chapter 13

Althoz, J., *Liberal Catholic Movement in England, 1848–1864* (London: Burns & Oates, 1962). Ausubel, H., *John Bright* (W). Battiscombe, G., *John Keble* (London: Constable, 1963). Bell, H., *Lord Palmerston*, 2 vols. (London: Longmans, 1936). Benson, E., *Queen Victoria* (London: Longmans, 1935). Best, G., *Shaftesbury* (New York: Arco, 1965). Briggs, A., *Chartist Studies* (New York: St. Martin's Press, 1959). Brinton, C., *English Political Thought in the Nineteenth Century* (HT). Brose, O., *Church and Parliament, 1828–1860* (Stanford: Stanford Univ. Press, 1959). Byrne, L. G., *The Great Ambassador* [Stratford Canning] (Columbus: Ohio State Univ. Press, 1964). Cecil, D., *Melbourne* (Indianapolis: Bobbs-Merrill, 1954). Chapman, J. K., *Career of Arthur Hamilton Gordon, First Lord Stanmore, 1829–1912* (Toronto: Univ. of Toronto Press, 1964). Christie, O. F., *Transition from Aristocracy, 1832–1867* (London: Putnam, 1928). Clark, G. K., *Peel and the Conservative Party* (London: Bell, 1929). Cockshut, A., *The Unbelievers: English Agnostic Thought, 1840–1890* (London: Collins, 1964). Collier, R., *Great Indian Mutiny* (BAL). Collins, H., and Abramsky, C., *Karl Marx and the British Labour Movement* (New York: St. Martin's Press, 1965). Costin, W. C., *Great Britain and China, 1833–1860* (Oxford: Clarendon Press, 1937). Cowling, M., *Mill and Liberalism* (Cambridge: Cambridge Univ. Press, 1963). Davis, H. W. C., *Age of Grey and Peel* (Oxford: Clarendon Press, 1929). Decker, C. R., *The Victorian Conscience* (New York: Twayne, 1952). Erickson, A. B., *Public Career of Sir James Graham* (Oxford: Blackwell, 1952); *Edward Cardwell: Peelite* (Philadelphia: American Philosophical Society, 1959). Fairweather, E. R., *The Oxford Movement* (New York: Oxford Univ. Press, 1964). Gash, N., *Politics in the Age of Peel* (New York: Longmans, 1953). Gibbs, P., *Crimean Blunder* (New York: Holt, Rinehart, 1960). Guedalla, P., *Palmerston, 1784–1865* (London: Putnam, 1927). Harrold, C. F., *John Henry Newman* (London: Longmans, 1945). Heasman, K., *Evangelicals in Action* (London: Bles, 1962). Houghton, W. E., *Victorian Frame of Mind, 1830–1870* (New Haven: Yale Univ. Press, 1957). Inglis, K. S., *Churches and the Working Classes in Victorian England* (Toronto: Univ. of Toronto Press, 1963). Jones,

W. D., *Lord Derby and Victorian Conservatism* (Athens: Univ. of Georgia Press, 1956). Knaplund, P., *The British Empire, 1815–1939* (New York: Harper's, 1941). McCallum, R. B., *The Liberal Party from Earl Grey to Asquith* (London: Gollancz, 1963). Maccoby, S., *English Radicalism, 1832–1852; English Radicalism, 1853-1886* (London: Allen & Unwin, 1935, 1939). McCord, N., *The Anti-Corn Law League, 1838–1846* (London: Allen & Unwin, 1958). McDowell, R. B., *British Conservatism, 1832–1914* (London: Faber & Faber, 1959). Maclagan, M., *Clemency Canning* (Oxford: Blackwell, 1963). Metcalf, T. R., *Aftermath of Revolt: India, 1857–1870* (Princeton: Princeton Univ. Press, 1964). Neff, W. F., *Victorian Working Women* (New York: Columbia Univ. Press, 1929). Norman, E. R., *Catholic Church and Ireland in the Age of Rebellion, 1859–1873* (New York: Cornell Univ. Press, 1965). Packenham (Longford), E., *Queen Victoria* (New York: Harper's, 1964). Pelling, H. M., *History of British Trade Unionism* (London: Macmillan, 1963). Rolt, L., *George and Robert Stephenson: The Railway Revolution* (London: Longmans, 1960). Schuyler, R. L., and Weston, C., *British Constitutional History Since 1832* (ANV). Shepperson, W., *British Migration to America* (Minneapolis: Univ. of Minnesota Press, 1957). Somervell, D. C., *Disraeli and Gladstone* (New York: Doran, 1926). Southgate, D., *Passing of the Whigs, 1832–1886* (New York: St. Martin's Press, 1962). Thane, E., *Young Mr. Disraeli* (New York: Harcourt, Brace, 1936). Thompson, E. P., *Making of the English Working Class* (VIN). Ward, J. T., *The Factory Movement, 1830–1855*. New York: St. Martin's Press, 1962). Webster, C. K., *Foreign Policy of Palmerston, 1830–1841*, 2 vols. (London: Bell, 1951). Woodham-Smith, C., *The Great Hunger* [Ireland] (SIG).

Chapters 14 and 15

Anstey, R., *Britain and the Congo in the Nineteenth Century* (New York: Oxford Univ. Press, 1962). Ashworth, W., *Economic History of England, 1870–1939* (New York: Barnes & Noble, 1960). Asquith, H. H., *Fifty Years of British Parliament* (Boston: Little, Brown, 1926). Ausubel, H., *In Hard Times: Reformers among the Late Victorians* (New York: Columbia Univ. Press, 1960). Birrell, F., *Gladstone* (COL). Cole, M., *Story of Fabian Socialism* (Stanford: Stanford Univ. Press, 1961). Cross, C., *Liberals in Power, 1905–1914* (London: Barrie & Rockliff, 1963). Cruikshank, M., *Church and State in Eng-*

lish *Education, 1870 to the Present* (New York: St. Martin's Press, 1963). Garvin, J. L., and Amery, J., *Joseph Chamberlain*, 4 vols. (New York: St. Martin's Press, 1932–51). Gollin, A. M., *Pro-Consul in Politics: Lord Milner, 1905–1925* (London: Blond, 1964). Green, F. E., *History of the English Agricultural Labourer, 1870–1920* (London: King, 1920). Grenville, J. A. S., *Lord Salisbury and Foreign Policy* (London: Athlone, 1964). Hall, P. G., *Industries of London since 1861* (New York: Hillary House, 1962). Hancock, W. K., *Smuts: The Sanguine Years, 1870–1919* (Cambridge: Cambridge Univ. Press, 1962). James, R. R., *Rosebery* (New York: Macmillan, 1963). Kruger, R., *Goodbye Dolly Grey* [Boer War] (Philadelphia: Lippincott, 1960). Lockhart, J. G., and Woodhouse, C. M., *Cecil Rhodes* (New York: Macmillan, 1963). McBriar, A. M., *Fabian Socialism and English Politics, 1884–1918* (Cambridge: Cambridge Univ. Press, 1962). McCaffrey, L., *Irish Federalism in the 1870's* (Philadelphia: American Philosophical Society, 1962). Maccoby, S., *English Radicalism, 1886–1914* (London: Allen & Unwin, 1953). Magnus, P., *King Edward the Seventh* (New York: Dutton, 1964); *Gladstone* (DU). Marder, A. J., *Anatomy of British Sea Power: Pre-Dreadnought Era, 1880–1905* (New York: Knopf, 1940). Mendelssohn, P., *The Age of Churchill, 1874–1911* (New York: Knopf, 1961). Minney, R., *The Edwardian Age* (Boston: Little, Brown, 1965). Monger, G., *End of Isolation: British Foreign Policy, 1900–1907* (London: Nelson, 1963). Nowell-Smith, S., *Edwardian England, 1901–1914* (New York: Oxford Univ. Press, 1964). O'Leary, C., *Elimination of Corrupt Practices in British Elections, 1868–1911* (Oxford: Clarendon Press, 1961). Robb, J. H., *The Primrose League, 1883–1906* (New York: Columbia Univ. Press, 1942). Watson, B., *A Hundred Years War: The Salvation Army, 1865–1965* (London: Hodder & Stoughton, 1965).

Chapter 16

Aitkin, A., *Gallipoli to the Somme* (London: Oxford Univ. Press, 1963). Aitkin, W. M., *Decline and Fall of Lloyd George* (London: Collins, 1963). Anderson, H., *Farewell to Old England* (London: Angus & Robertson, 1964). Caulfield, M. F., *The Easter Rebellion* (New York: Holt, Rinehart & Winston, 1963). Crosby, G. R., *Disarmament and Peace in British Politics, 1914–1919* (Cambridge: Harvard Univ. Press, 1957). Fitzsimons, M. A., *Empire by Treaty: Britain and the Middle East in the Twentieth Century* (South Bend, Ind.:

Univ. of Notre Dame Press, 1964). Grey of Fallodon, Viscount, *Twenty-Five Years, 1892–1916* (New York: Stokes, 1925). Lyman, R. W., *The First Labour Government* (Chester Springs, Pa.: Dufour, 1957). Maccoby, S., *English Radicalism: The End?* (London: Allen & Unwin, 1961). McElwee, W., *Britain's Locust Years, 1918–1940* (London: Faber & Faber, 1962). Magnus, P., *Kitchener* (London: Murray, 1958). Marder, A. J., *From the Dreadnought to Scapa Flow*, 2 vols. (New York: Oxford Univ. Press, 1961–65). Moorehead, A., *Gallipoli* (New York: Harper's, 1956). Nicolson, H., *King George V* (London: Constable, 1952); *Lord Curzon: Last Phase, 1919–1925* (Boston: Houghton Mifflin, 1934). Pope-Hennesey, J., *Queen Mary, 1867–1953* (New York: Knopf, 1960). Webb, B., *Our Partnership* (New York: Longmans, 1948).

Chapter 17

Bailey, S., *British Parliamentary Democracy* (HM). Bloomfield, P., *Uncommon People: Study of England's Elite* (London: Hamilton, 1955). Blythe, R., *Age of Illusion: England in the Twenties and Thirties* (London: Hamilton, 1963). Broad, C. L., *Winston Churchill*, 2 vols. (New York: Hawthorn, 1958–63). Bryant, A., *Turn of the Tide, 1939–1943* (London: Collins, 1957). Butler, D. E., *Electoral System in Britain, 1918–1951* (New York: Oxford Univ. Press, 1953). Churchill, R. S., *Rise and Fall of Anthony Eden* (New York: Putnam, 1959). Churchill, W. S., *The Second World War*, 6 vols. (BA). Cross, C., *Fascists in Britain* (London: Barrie & Rockliff, 1961). Daalder, H., *Cabinet Reform in Britain, 1914–1963* (Stanford: Stanford Univ. Press, 1963). Dalton, H., *Fateful Years, 1931–1945* (London: Muller, 1957). Eden, A., *Facing the Dictators* (Boston: Houghton Mifflin, 1962). Edwardes, M., *Last Years of British India* (London: Cassell, 1963). Fulford, R., *Votes for Women* (London: Faber & Faber, 1957). Hall, W. P., *Empire to Commonwealth* (New York: Holt, 1928). Hatch, A., *The Mountbattens* (New York: Random House, 1965). Hoffman, J. D., *Conservative Party in Opposition* (London: MacGibbon & Kee, 1964). Macleod, I., *Neville Chamberlain* (London: Muller, 1961). Nanda, B. R., *Mahatma Gandhi* (Boston: Beacon Press, 1958). Roskill, S. W., *White Ensign: British Navy at War, 1939–1945* (Annapolis, Md.: U. S. Naval Institute, 1960). Slim, W. S., *Defeat into Victory* (New York: McKay, 1961). Taylor, A. J. P., *Politics in War Time* (New York: Atheneum, 1965). Wheare, K. C., *Constitutional Struc-*

ture of the Commonwealth (New York: Oxford Univ. Press, 1960).
Wheeler-Bennett, J. W., *King George VI* (New York: St. Martin's
Press, 1958). Wood, D., and Dempster, D. D., *Narrow Margin: The
Battle of Britain* (London: Hutchinson, 1961).

Chapter 18

Bullock, A., *Life and Times of Ernest Bevin* (London: Heinemann,
1960). Camps, M., *Britain and the European Community, 1955–1963*
(Princeton: Princeton Univ. Press, 1964). Carter, G. M., *Politics of
Inequality: South Africa since 1948* (New York: Praeger, 1958).
Childers, E. B., *Road to Suez* (London: MacGibbon & Kee, 1962).
Dancy, J., *Public Schools and the Future* (London: Faber & Faber,
1963). Dow, J. C. R., *Management of the British Economy, 1945–1960*
Cambridge: Cambridge Univ. Press, 1964). Driberg, T., *Beaverbrook*
(London: Weidenfeld & Nicolson, 1956). Epstein, L. D., *British Poli-
tics in the Suez Crisis* (Urbana: Univ. of Illinois Press, 1964). Foot,
M., *Aneurin Bevan, 1895–1945* (London: MacGibbon & Kee, 1962).
Glubb, J. B., *War in the Desert* (New York: Norton, 1962). Hughes,
E., *Macmillan* (London: Allen & Unwin, 1962). Lindsey, A., *Social-
ized Medicine in England and Wales* (Chapel Hill: Univ. of North
Carolina Press, 1962). Mansergh, N., *Survey of British Common-
wealth Affairs* (London: Oxford Univ. Press, 1952). Pelling, H., *The
British Communist Party* (New York: Macmillan, 1958). Pinder, J.,
Britain and the Common Market (London: Cressett, 1961). Rodgers,
W. T., ed., *Hugh Gaitskell, 1906–1963* (London: Thames & Hudson,
1964). Shinwell, E., *The Labour Story* (London: Macdonald, 1963).
Sinkin, M. and T., *Britain and India: Requiem for Empire* (Balti-
more: Johns Hopkins Univ. Press, 1964). Smith, D., *Harold Wilson*
(London: Hale, 1964). Willey, F. T., *Education Today and Tomorrow*
(London: Joseph, 1964). Williams, F., *Twilight of Empire: Memoirs
of Clement Attlee* (New York: Barnes, 1962). Woodhouse, C. M.,
British Foreign Policy since the Second World War (New York:
Praeger, 1962).

General Index

Abbot, George (Archbishop of Canterbury), 192
Abercromby, Gen. Sir Ralph, 361, 363
Aberdeen, 4th Earl of (George Gordon), 405, 428, 429, 434, 435, 437
Adams, John, 306
Adams, Samuel, 300, 306
Addington, Henry (1st Viscount Sidmouth), 367–68
Adelaide of Saxe-Meiningen, Queen of William IV of England, 396
Adrian IV, Pope, 49, 53–54
Adrian VI, Pope, 130
Agilbert, Bishop, 17
Agricola, Gracus, 6
Aidan, Saint, 16
Aislabie, John, 269–70
Alaric (Gothic king), 10
Alban, Saint, 8
Albert of Saxe-Coburg-Gotha, Prince, 407, 419, 446
Alexander III, Pope, 50
Alexander I, Czar of Russia, 369, 374, 381, 382
Alexander II, Czar of Russia, 437
Alexander III, Czar of Russia, 494
Alexander II, King of Scotland, 77
Alexander III, King of Scotland, 77
Alfred the Great, King of England, 15, 16, 18, 20–22, 48
Allen, Ethan, 311
Allen, William Cardinal, 156

Allenby, Gen. Edmund (1st Viscount Allenby), 531
Althorp, John Charles (3rd Earl of Althorp), 398
Alva, Duke of (Fernando Alvarez de Toledo), 156
American Revolution, 305–15
Amherst, Gen. Jeffrey (Baron Amherst), 287
Ampère, André Marie, 453
Anderson, Elizabeth Garrett, 534
Angus, 6th Earl of (Archibald Douglas), 153
Anjou, Duke of (later Henry III of France), 161, 164
Anne, Queen of England, 217, 230, 232, 234, 240, 262, 265, 291
reign of, 242–49
Anne Boleyn, 2nd Queen of Henry VIII of England, 132, 134, 135, 137
Anne of Cleves, 4th Queen of Henry VIII of England, 137–38
Anne of Denmark, Queen of James I of England, 184
Anselm, Archbishop of Canterbury, 43–44, 49
Archibald Tineman (4th Earl of Douglas and 1st Duke of Touraine), 96
Argyle, 3rd Duke of (Archibald Campbell), 249
Argyle, 5th Earl of (Archibald Campbell), 153

Disraeli, Benjamin (*cont'd*)
428–30, 434, 442, 445, 447, 461–62, 464, 465, 482, 485, 492, 494
prime ministry of, 468–69, 477–79, 481
Doherty, John, 409, 410
Dorchester, Marquis of (Evelyn Pierrepont, 2nd Duke of Kingston), 378
Douglas, 4th Earl of (Archibald Tineman, 1st Duke of Touraine), 96
Douglas, Lady Margaret (niece of Henry VIII of England), 153
Douglas-Home, Sir Alexander (Lord Home), 603–5
Drake, Adm. Sir Francis, 163–66
Drummond, Thomas, 407
Dudley, Edmund, 142
Dudley, Guildford, 143
Dudley, Lady Jane. *See* Grey, Lady Jane
Dudley, John (Earl of Warwick and Duke of Northumberland), 139–40, 142, 143–44, 149, 158
Duncan, Adm. Adam (1st Viscount Duncan of Camperdown), 360
Dundas, Henry (1st Viscount Melville and Baron Dunira), 361
Dunstand, Saint, 21, 22, 24, 39
Dupleix, Marquis Joseph François, 281–82
Durham, 1st Earl of (John George Lambton), 402, 413, 441, 466

Ecgfrith, King of Northumbria, 18
Ede, Chuter, 578
Eden, Sir Anthony (Earl of Avon), 559–61, 568, 586–88, 596–97, 599
Edgar, King of England, 31
reign of, 21, 22, 24, 25
Edmund (Crouchback), Earl of Lancaster, 66
Edmund I, King of England, 21
Edmund II (Ironside), King of England, 24, 27
Edward, King of Angles and Saxons, 21

Edward, Prince (son of Henry VI of England), 107–10, 117–18
Edward, Prince of Wales (Black Prince), 86, 88–89
Edward I (Longshanks), King of England, 64, 68, 194
reign of, 74–82
constitutional reform, 80–81
Parliaments, 75, 80–81
Scotland, 77–79
Wales, 76–77
Edward II, King of England, 76, 82–85
Edward III, King of England, 95, 98, 104, 112
reign of, 85–93
Black Death, 87–88
the Church, 92–93
Hundred Years' War, 85–89
reliance on Parliament, 90
Edward IV, King of England (earlier Earl of March), 118, 119, 123
reign of, 108–14
Edward V, King of England, 111
Edward VI, King of England, 137, 139, 150, 155, 157, 168, 169
reign of, 142–43, 147
Edward VII, King of England, 501–7
Edward VIII, King of England (after abdication, Duke of Windsor), 559
Edward Augustus, Duke of Kent, 407
Edward the Confessor, King of England, 22, 25–27, 29, 32, 46, 69
William I and, 35–37, 49–51
Edward the Etheling, 27
Edwig, King of England, 21
Edwin, King of Mercia, 31
Edwin, King of Northumbria, 16
Effingham, 1st Earl of (Kenneth Alexander Howard), 165
Egbert, King of the West Saxons, 18, 19
Einstein, Albert, 261
Eisenhower, Dwight D., 569, 570
Eldon, 1st Earl of (John Scott), 387
Eleanor (daughter of Henry II of England), 55

GAVILAN COLLEGE
LIBRARY

LIBRARY

ue

D.A
30
E7

21904

1000